PHILIPP HALFMANN'S

Advanced Concepts of Strength & Conditioning for Tennis

First Edition (1.2)

PHILIPP HALFMANN, M.S.
Director

Department of Exercise & Sports Science

IAAPH
Berlin, Germany

PHILIPP HALFMANN

Philipp was born and raised in Germany. He is the son of Hubert J. Halfmann and Waltraud Halfmann, who are both pharmacists. He grew up near Dortmund, city of national soccer champion Borussia Dortmund, where his father and mother still live today.

He started playing tennis at age four (4) and as a teenager became one of the top juniors in the state, competing at national and international junior tournaments. Upon graduating from Freiherr-vom-Stein Gymnasium (high school) in Luenen, Philipp entered the German Armed Forces, where he learned about discipline, teamwork and sports science. After training members of his fellow company which then received an award for being the fastest company during a 10 mile NATO cross-country race, Philipp chose coaching as his life-long career.

In 2001, after being honorably discharged from the military, Philipp moved to New York City to study at Bernard Baruch College and play tennis for the Bearcats, with whom he won the CUNYAC Tournament Championships twice, served as the assistant tennis coach, and graduated in 2005 with a Bachelor of Science degree. He went on to work as the head tennis professional at the Turnberry Isle Resort & Country Club in Miami, Florida, where he coached under the guidance of Australian tennis legend Fred Stolle, winner of 18 Grand Slam Championships. In 2006, Philipp attended Florida International University (FIU), where he earned his Master's degree in exercise & sports science. During his time at FIU, Philipp became graduate assistant to 13 year NBA Head Strength & Conditioning coach Mick Smith and worked as assistant strength & conditioning coach with various NCAA Div I teams and professional athletes, such as NBA champion Antoine Walker. Starting in 2010 Philipp worked as a tennis touring coach for Swiss national Alexander Ritschard, who won the Swiss National Junior Championships 2010 & 2011 (singles & doubles), improved his world junior ranking by 600 spots within 12 month, and earned an ATP ranking at age 16 (1 of 5 juniors to do so worldwide in 2010). In 2012 Philipp founded the International Association for Athletic Performance & Health (IAAPH), located in Berlin, Germany. He now also serves as an expert for the German Performance & Sports Nutrition magazine LOOX.

Philipp lives with his wife, Sophia, in Berlin, Germany, and in Miami, Florida. Outside of sports, Phil enjoys a wide range of music, reading, and spending time with his family.

"Thank you for your interest in my new book. I'm looking forward to your feedback."

Philipp Halfmann

PREFACE

Congratulations and thank you for purchasing the first edition of Advanced Concepts of Strength & Conditioning for Tennis. This edition provides a developmental approach to the various aspects of tennis strength and conditioning based on new concepts that have been fueled by scientific research and hands-on field experience. Over 1000 athletes have used the information and procedures provided in this first edition to enhance their development. These techniques and the accompanying information are supported by a selected pool of peer-reviewed references. Any quality textbook shouldn't merely provide an explanation of underlying scientific principles but should also illustrate how the information provided can be effectively applied in order to yield a superior outcome.

The main reason for writing this book was the unsatisfactory outcome of my own career as a tennis player, which was greatly impacted by the incompetency of the high-performance coaches I experienced along the way. To that must be added the difficulties I encountered during the process of becoming a well-rounded, competent tennis coach. From a coach's or educational standpoint, a cohesive, quality, tennis-specific resource was sorely lacking, one that could provide coaches and players with a solid educational foundation for the effective development of various athletic performance parameters. For that reason the first edition of this book provides the reader with a comprehensive and cohesive body of knowledge as well as applications that can be utilized to develop all aspects of athletic conditioning for all skill levels, from recreational players to college athletes to professional players, in a safe and professional environment. The reader will gain insight into how to evaluate and enhance all aspects of tennis conditioning in a developmental fashion, which is essential for improving the overall level of play on the tennis court and for minimizing the risk of injury.

BACKGROUND

Strength & conditioning can be defined as the study of athletic performance optimization through various forms of training. **Advanced Concepts of Strength & Conditioning for Tennis** relates to all forms of tennis related training and is intended to provide a strength & conditioning foundation, which strives to optimize force production capabilities of the human body during unstable, dynamic situations like, for instance, those experienced during a tennis match.

Although the subject of strength & conditioning has been presented from many different angles, I have focused on refining the interaction between the musculoskeletal system and the nervous system for optimal sports performance. I hope this textbook provides a valuable educational resource for a wide range of tennis players and coaches, both recreational and professional.

APPROACH

It has been my goal to write a textbook that illustrates a developmental approach to athletic conditioning that can be easily understood and utilized by tennis players and coaches of all skill levels. The content is organized in sensible, constructive order where each chapter first provides an explanation of underlying scientific principles and then presents practical solutions in form of applications or exercises, which have been selected and grouped based on purpose, training emphasis, and skill level.

This textbook represents the distillation of nearly 10 years of experience as a professional coach working with collegiate and professional athletes. This experience comes from a combination of research, study, playing, coaching, and teaching activities that have laid the foundation for a better understanding of the different areas of expertise necessary for a coach to be successful. During my time at Florida International University and my time on tour, I developed an integrated strength & conditioning approach consisting of eight distinct training phases. This integrated approach is based on a library of research material, applications and exercises aimed at developing and maximizing the athletes' athletic potential while minimizing the risk of injury and making it possible for them to raise their game to the next level. Over time, this library of research material, applications, and exercises evolved into the blueprint for this 1st edition of **Advanced Concepts of Strength & Conditioning for Tennis**.

ORGANIZATION

The organization of the textbook is informed by the logic of the sensible steps used during the developmental approach to athletic conditioning. The textbook contains eight chapters, divided into two sections. Section I, consisting of chapters 1 - 3, deals with the essential topics of career development, kinesiology and exercise physiology, including an introduction to the four pillars of success, to terminology and basic concepts and to the basic structure and function of the musculoskeletal system. Section II, chapters 4 through 8, focuses on the various aspects of athletic conditioning in a sensible order. Chapter 4, Fitness Assessment, lays the initial foundation for optimal training by addressing methods of performance measurement because fitness assessments must be carried out before a comprehensive training program can be developed and implemented. Chapter 5 provides various static, dynamic and ballistic stretching techniques, which can be used to correct possible deficiencies found during the fitness assessment process. Chapter 6 introduces a formidable arsenal of resistance training exercises that can be utilized during all phases of training while chapter 7 provides exercises for speed, agility and quickness (SAQ) development through a wide range of medicine ball, speed ladder, cone and various other body weight drills. The final chapter addresses current research, hot topics and practices concerning proper sports nutrition such as nutrient timing and ingestion.

The textbook is specifically designed for the purpose of **teaching** and **applying**. Thus scientific exercise concepts are introduced at the beginning of the chapter followed by corresponding practical applications or exercises, whereby the reader can expand his/her competency while also being presented with a resource for immediate practical solutions as well as training recommendations. The practical applications presented include: body composition tests, flexibility & performance tests, dynamic, static and ballistic stretching exercises as well as auxiliary, compound, integrated strength & power, stability, functional, ballistic and plyometric exercises. Multiple practical applications are presented throughout each chapter providing detailed descriptions in conjunction with pictures, diagrams and videos. This information serves as the underlying basis for understanding many of the tests and exercises used in strength & conditioning for amateur and professional tennis players.

HOW TO USE THIS BOOK

In order to optimize the performance benefits provided by the book it is important to understand how the applications are setup and how to use the information provided by each section. Therefore, an application overview and brief description of the various components is provided next.

Each application has a title ❶ and ID number ❷ so that each application can easily be identified. The summary ❸ section is an "executive summary" that provides a brief application overview while "Purpose" ❹ states why the application is being utilized. Following is the "Description"❺, which explains in a step by step process how to perform the application in proper form. The "Degree of Difficulty" ❻ indicates what level of expertise is required to perform the application (e.g. advanced athletes) and the "Required Equipment" ❼ section shows what equipment is necessary to perform the application. "Relevance" ❽ explains why the application is important or how it can enhance the athlete's performance potential.

With respect to proper exercise execution "Key Factors" ❾ provide important factors that the coach/athlete needs to pay attention to, whereas "Common Errors" ❿ lists characteristics that need to be avoided during the execution of the application. The "Recommended Exercises"⓫ component presents other applications that can be utilized to improve a specific performance parameter and "Breathing" ⓬ refers to the timing of breathing during the application.

The sections "Targeted Muscles", "Action", and "Plane of Motion" ⓭ belong together: "Targeted Muscles" lists the musculature the applications aims to improve, "Action" describes the movement characteristics of the respective musculature and "Plane of Motion" shows in which direction the movement of the application occurs. "Picture/Diagram" ⓮ provides a visual aide for proper execution and the internet & DVD symbol ⓯ indicates that additional information is available online or on DVD respectively.

ID: 618

In order to access **supplemental exercise content** (e.g. video clips) simply visit our website and enter the respective exercise ID number, found at the bottom of the page between the **internet & DVD symbol** (e.g. 618), 15 into the provided search box on our website.

The **video clips** can be used to support your understanding of proper exercise execution and implementation.

For more information regarding the DVD or website membership, **free downloads**, templates, or **training plans** visit our website.

http://www.tennis-conditioning-book.com

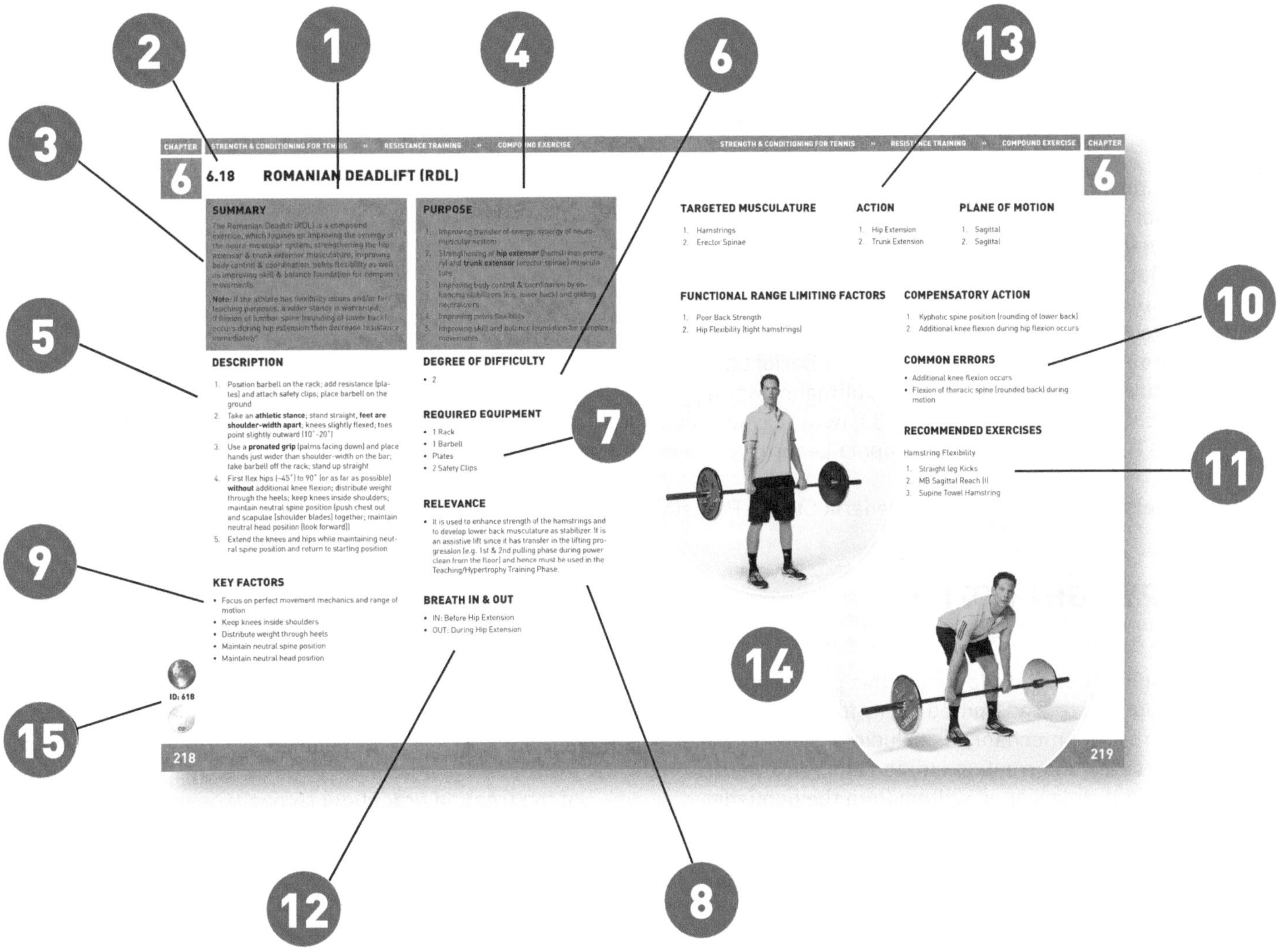

2 1 4 6 13

3

CHAPTER | STRENGTH & CONDITIONING FOR TENNIS » RESISTANCE TRAINING » COMPOUND EXERCISE

6 **6.18 ROMANIAN DEADLIFT (RDL)**

SUMMARY

The Romanian Deadlift (RDL) is a compound exercise, which focuses on improving the synergy of the neuro-muscular system, strengthening the hip extensor & trunk extensor musculature, improving body control & coordination, pelvis flexibility as well as improving skill & balance foundation for complex movements.

Note: If the athlete has flexibility issues and/or for teaching purposes, a wider stance is warranted. If flexion of lumbar spine (rounding of lower back) occurs during hip extension then decrease resistance immediately!

PURPOSE

1. Improving transfer of energy; synergy of neuro-muscular system
2. Strengthening of **hip extensor** (hamstrings primary) and **trunk extensor** (erector spinae) musculature
3. Improving body control & coordination by enhancing stabilizers (e.g. lower back) and gliding neutralizers
4. Improving pelvis flexibility
5. Improving skill and balance foundation for complex movements

5

DESCRIPTION

1. Position barbell on the rack; add resistance (plates) and attach safety clips; place barbell on the ground
2. Take an **athletic stance**; stand straight, **feet are shoulder-width apart**; knees slightly flexed; toes point slightly outward (10°-20°)
3. Use a **pronated grip** (palms facing down) and place hands just wider than shoulder-width on the bar; take barbell off the rack; stand up straight
4. First flex hips (~45°) to 90° (or as far as possible) **without** additional knee flexion; distribute weight through the heels; keep knees inside shoulders; maintain neutral spine position (push chest out and scapulae (shoulder blades) together; maintain neutral head position (look forward))
5. Extend the knees and hips while maintaining neutral spine position and return to starting position

DEGREE OF DIFFICULTY

- 2

7

REQUIRED EQUIPMENT

- 1 Rack
- 1 Barbell
- Plates
- 2 Safety Clips

RELEVANCE

- It is used to enhance strength of the hamstrings and to develop lower back musculature as stabilizer. It is an assistive lift since it has transfer in the lifting progression (e.g. 1st & 2nd pulling phase during power clean from the floor) and hence must be used in the Teaching/Hypertrophy Training Phase.

9

KEY FACTORS

- Focus on perfect movement mechanics and range of motion
- Keep knees inside shoulders
- Distribute weight through heels
- Maintain neutral spine position
- Maintain neutral head position

BREATH IN & OUT

- IN: Before Hip Extension
- OUT: During Hip Extension

15 ID: 618

218

STRENGTH & CONDITIONING FOR TENNIS » RESISTANCE TRAINING » COMPOUND EXERCISE | CHAPTER 6

TARGETED MUSCULATURE

1. Hamstrings
2. Erector Spinae

ACTION

1. Hip Extension
2. Trunk Extension

PLANE OF MOTION

1. Sagittal
2. Sagittal

FUNCTIONAL RANGE LIMITING FACTORS

1. Poor Back Strength
2. Hip Flexibility (tight hamstrings)

COMPENSATORY ACTION

1. Kyphotic spine position (rounding of lower back)
2. Additional knee flexion during hip flexion occurs

10

COMMON ERRORS

- Additional knee flexion occurs
- Flexion of thoracic spine (rounded back) during motion

RECOMMENDED EXERCISES

Hamstring Flexibility

1. Straight leg Kicks
2. MB Sagittal Reach (I)
3. Supine Towel Hamstring

11

14

219

12 8

IAAPH GMBH

Rungestrasse 22-24
10179 Berlin
DE - Germany

Phone: +49 30 5770 3634 0
Fax: +49 30 5770 3634 9
E-mail: books@iaaph.org

ADVANCED CONCEPTS OF STRENGTH & CONDITIONING FOR TENNIS ISBN: 978-3-9815392-0-2

CREDITS

President & Publisher: Philipp Halfmann
Senior Editor: Philipp Halfmann
Copyeditor: Barry Fay
Production Company: 300plus GmbH, Berlin (www.300pl.us)
Layout & Design: Christian Kloewer
Photo Editing: Christian Kloewer
Photography: Tobias Semmelmann , Darioj Laganà (www.norte.it)
Illustratons: Vicegold, Laurids Düllmann, Marius Land , Christian Kloewer
Icons: Oxygen Icons CC BY-SA 3.0 (www.oxygen-icons.org)
Lead Hair & Makeup Artist: Sophia Lenore (www.sophia-lenore.com)

Models: Caroline Dittmann, Frederik Storm, Pamela Burbank, Philipp Halfmann

COPYRIGHT NOTICE

LIABILITY NOTICE

Neither the publisher nor the author(s) assumes any responsibility for any loss or injury and/or damage to persons or property arising out of or related to any use of the material contained in this book. It is the responsibility of the treating practitioner/coach, relying on independent expertise and knowledge of the athlete, to determine the best treatment and method of application for the athlete.

TABLE OF CONTENT

A

A

CHAPTER 1: INTRO

"Tennis Training & Conditioning - An Introduction To A Successful Career"

Being a professional tennis player can be a very rewarding experience and career choice but it can also be grueling and one of the toughest jobs in professional sports. Since tennis is not just a domestic sport but played all over the world, competition is tough and being on the road a lot is a necessity.

Because travelling outside the country is a requirement for improving one´s ranking, a significant financial commitment (~$100,000 annually on ITF/ATP/WTA Tour) is required.

Also, unlike team sports, success in tennis is based on what you accomplish on your own and you also have to be able to deal with disappointment.

Many variables play a role, some that you can control and some that you can´t.

Throughout this text we will explore in more detail the ones that you actually can control.

THE FOUR PILLARS OF SUCCESS

Like anything in life, making something of value takes time to develop and becoming a successful tennis player is no different. It is important for you to understand that you will need to have a great support team but most decisive is your desire to achieve success and the willingness and determination to work hard for it. It is important for any player to understand that parents and coaches cannot create a successful player; only you, the player, have the ability to make that happen!

Just to bring matters into perspective let's use an analogy. Becoming a successful tennis player is like giving birth. The doctor (e.g. parents, coaches) can help with the delivery of the baby but he cannot deliver it for you. After that, we will explore the pillars of success in more detail.

When it comes to training, the notion of "more is better" simply is wrong and actually causes a decrease in performance! The body is an organism just like plants. Take the relationship of plants and water as an example: Plants need water in order to grow and blossom but that doesn't mean that you continuously water them for six hours a day. Doing it kills your plant in the same way that pushing your child harder and harder kills his/her tennis career! The right mix of hard work, rest, and positive encouragement & support is the answer.

Career management is the parents' responsibility from the start and picking the best support team (tennis coaches, conditioning coach, athletic trainer, registered nutritionist, sports psychologist) early on is one of the most important decisions they have to make.

PARENTS

Parents play a vital role; they are an important member of your (the player's) support team. Parents have to take the time to bring you to tournaments and practices and they have to be able to afford the expenses (tennis lessons, tournament & hotel fees, gas & air fare, massages, etc.). In other words, without your parents' commitment, a career in tennis is most likely not going to happen.
On the other hand, it is important for parents to understand that they can't be too controlling just because they provide time and money but on the other hand they need make sure that members of the support team are doing their job.

COACHES

There are many coaches out there and almost every one of them claims to have worked with professional players. Most of the time, it's more wishful thinking than reality, which leads us to the first rule: "Don't listen to what people say; look at how they do their job".

LEVEL OF EDUCATION

For instance, what is their completed level of education? What kind of degree did they earn - do they have a "Bachelor" or "Master´s" degree? What was their major? Was it related or unrelated to coaching/sports? If someone has a Masters degree doesn't necessarily mean that they are smarter but it means that they had the determination to get through 5+ years of university classes.

It means that they set out to achieve something and they started and finished the job.

Is the coach certified by a tennis teaching organization (e.g. USPTA or USPTR)? What level of proficiency did they accomplish? Again, it doesn't mean that certified coaches are "better" than someone without a license but it is an indication that they take teaching and educating themselves seriously.

How many certifications does the potential coach have? If someone possess more than one license, it indicates that he/she is open to different ways/methods to accomplish something. They are open-minded to different approaches. Believe it or not, there are many ways to become successful – Nick Bollettieri has one way of teaching, while Ion Tiriac/Gunther Bosch (Boris Becker's former manager & coach respectively) had another way.

What is the physical appearance of the potential coach? Many coaches suffer from the fat-and-happy syndrome meaning they are not in good physical shape themselves. Why is that important? Because for one, it's a matter of self-discipline. A coach cannot expect his student(s) to work out hard, eat right, etc. when he can't do it himself. A coach is also a role model for his athletes and should himself be able to do what he preaches, otherwise he will lose credibility. Does Nick Bollettieri, Tony Roche, or Dean Goldfine look overweight? The answer is NO.

Keep in mind that being on the court during the day and then sitting in class in the evening to obtain a quality education costs a lot of time, money, determination and requires effort and discipline. For some coaches lying is easier and they will get paid regardless because most people are blinded by a big name and/or they don't know any better. Keep in mind that just being able to hit a tennis ball is not going to help you become a successful professional tennis player. Again, just because someone has a Master's degree doesn't mean that he/she is a genius but it is an indication that they have the determination and resilience to achieve a goal.

PROFESSIONAL WORK ETHIC

If you have a chance to watch the coach conduct a training session, watch for the following:

- Is the coach on time?
- Do they have a plan for what they try to accomplish or do they just do the same routine/drills all the time?
- Are they really involved in their teaching – do you feel the coach cares if the student learns something?

Being on time is a matter of respect and discipline. The coach having a plan shows that he/she took the time to sit down, think about what they want to accomplish and has found ways to implement strategies to reach a desired outcome. If they are really involved it indicates that they want you to get better, and are not just interested in getting paid.

These are some of the things you can use to evaluate a potential coach. Apart from the aforementioned, it is essential to be on the same page on a personal level – coach and player should trust each other and get along personally in order to have success.

RESULTS

This is the most important factor – did the coach train any successful player(s) and when was that? Successful is defined as top 100 ITF Junior ranking or Top 100 ATP/WTA Tour ranking. Who cares if someone is coaching for 30 years but never developed a successful tennis player? Who cares if the tennis program is top 10 in the nation if none of the players made it on the tour?

People say that if someone is successful they must be doing something right. There are many tennis academies that are run by a former tour player or coach who had one top player i.e. 25 years ago. Unfortunately their training methods are not based on current scientific evidence. Instead, they still practice nowadays like they practiced 25 years ago. The problem is that tennis, like anything else, evolves over the years, and their way of training has become outdated. For example, if you watch a match of the great Bjorn Borg from the 1970's you will think the play is in slow-motion as compared to the tennis of the 21st century. The racquets were heavy and made out of wood, the head sizes were smaller and the rallies lasted forever. Therefore, the physical demands back then were different than what they are today. Back then players needed endurance and quickness to be able to play long rallies for 5 hours in a row but today players need to be powerful as well as fast. Wouldn't you think that the training demands for a long-distance runner are different than for an American football player? So why send your child somewhere, pay a lot of money, and practice with inefficient training methods? There is no excuse for charging a lot of money and not being able to deliver satisfactory results!

PHYSICAL CONDITIONING

Physical conditioning is a major component for a successful tennis career because it enables you to perform at your best by making you stronger and less prone to injury. Getting you physically well prepared is the focus of this book. It doesn't matter if you have the best forehand in the world, if you can't get to the ball in time or can't play due to injury, does it? Or how can you be successful if you can only play your best tennis for one set instead of performing well for the entire duration of the match?

INJURY PREVENTION

Injury prevention is the most important factor! How many former top players had their careers cut short due to overuse injuries (e.g. shoulder problems, lower back pain, knees, etc.) that could have been prevented with a well-planned and executed strength & conditioning program along with regular physiotherapy? Unfortunately, there have been a lot of them (e.g. Goran Ivanisevic, Patrick Rafter, Tommy Haas). Reason being is that most tennis coaches are not well educated in the fields of kinesiology, physiology, and conditioning and not every junior player has the money available to pay for a good conditioning coach and physiotherapist.

EDUCATION REQUIREMENTS

A solid knowledge of anatomy, kinesiology, and exercise physiology principles is necessary to develop a conditioning program that makes sense and is actually helpful to you. As previously mentioned, the notion that "more is better" when it comes to training is simply wrong! Any conditioning coach following this approach has no clue about scientific exercise principles and working with such a coach must be avoided because "more is better" will lead to injuries and a decline in your performance due to over-training. It can also be that the coach will reinforce wrong technique, misplaced intensities, the wrong rest intervals...just to name a few possibilities. How does reinforcing the wrong things over and over again make you a better tennis player? For example, adequate rest intervals are vital, otherwise an organism (e.g. the human body) will die instead of getting stronger.

Ideally, your strength & conditioning coach should minimally have the following qualifications:

1. Bachelor's degree in Exercise & Sports Science (or related – e.g. sports medicine, athletic training) from an accredited university; Master's degree is preferred
2. Tennis background – should have competed in national tournaments so the coach understands and has experienced the physical demands of professional tennis
3. 1+ years working with NCAA Division I or II level athletes or professional athletes

A coach who just has a "Personal Trainer" certificate is under-qualified and inadequately educated to design a quality training program since most certifications can be attained during a weekend seminar and the demands of the general population don't translate to professional athletes. Another factor is that most personal training "certifications" are not accredited – anybody can conduct a weekend workshop and hand out "Personal Trainer" certifications at the end.

CERTIFICATIONS

You should make sure that any certification is accredited because otherwise it is meaningless. You can conduct an „Elite Tennis Conditioning Seminar" over the weekend and give everyone a certificate...then some coach can use that to represent himself as an expert in the field.

That's like you making a license to become a dentist over the weekend and then presenting yourself to clients as a specialist.

A list of accredited programs can be found at www.NOCA.org.

SPORTS NUTRITION

Physical conditioning must be supported by optimal sports nutrition in order to be effective and show results. Just working out hard without supplying the body with the proper nutrients (building blocks) will not produce any positive results. In fact, it could actually lead to a decrease in performance due to overtraining. Sports nutrition focuses on:

- providing fuel for your physical activities
- repairing and rebuilding muscle tissue after competition/training
- optimizing athletic performance during competition/training
- promoting overall health and wellness

DEVELOPING MENTAL TOUGHNESS

Being mentally strong (tough) is a necessity for a successful tennis career because the athlete will experience pressure and disappointments and will need to learn how to deal with them. Oftentimes, mental training and development is neglected because it doesn't seem that important at first and it is also more difficult to quantify any progress. Despite this, working on mental toughness is as important as working on stroke production or physical fitness. It is important to find a mental health professional or coach that the athlete can trust because the athlete needs to open up; they need to be able to talk about how they feel in pressure situations without feeling embarrassed about it. People's personalities are different, which means that a one-fits-all approach will not work; various approaches must be tried by a mental health professional and finding the right one can be costly and challenging.

In most cases a lot of pressure comes from the parents and coaches because they want to see results for all the resources (time & money) they invest. In turn, the players know how much their support team does for them and hence don't want to disappoint, which takes away from their ability to "relax" on the court and just play the game. The players have their own goals and aspirations; they want to win themselves. When too much emphasis is placed on winning, skill development during competition is inhibited because during pressure situations in a match the player will revert to whatever style of play he is comfortable with and hence will not find the courage to use newly developed skills that might be more beneficial. If the athlete has been working on improving different aspects of his game (e.g. tactics, strokes) then he/she must get the chance to try them during competition but they cannot do it if winning is the predominant goal set of their support team. What is the point of working during practice to improve if the athlete cannot use his/her new "skill set" during a match? If skill development, be it mental, technical, or physical, is desired then losing is a natural part of the player's growth process.

If the athlete needs to develop his mental abilities then the athlete needs to have some freedom to decide on what he/she wants to do instead of allowing coaches/parents to impose their will on him/her because it will have a positive effect on the athlete's (self) confidence since he/she will have accomplished something on their own, which in turn will serve as a self-motivating force to work hard. The support team members need to support the player via positive encouragement/feedback and empathy, even if it is difficult, instead of focusing on the negative or criticizing him/her, or even comparing him/her with other people who do a better job. Praising the tennis or the physical skill development of the athlete is much more important to the athlete's mental development and love for the game than focusing on performance (winning). This can be accomplished by motivating the athlete to do his/her best while refraining from publically displaying disappointment or immoderate involvement in a match because the athletes perceive this as embarrassing in front of their peers. Another factor is that the athlete needs to learn how to positively self-talk, especially during practice, so that he/she practices the positive self-reinforcement that will be required during pressure situations on the court – this, instead of verbally abusing oneself when committing an error.

PLAYER DEVELOPMENT: HAVING A STRATEGY

It is helpful to devise a strategy to reach an overall long-term goal (e.g. top 100 ATP/WTA ranking by age 20) early on. Parents and athletes must understand that one doesn't become a good tennis player overnight. In fact most athletes will stop pursuing a career in professional tennis before the age of 20. But it is more important to define what "success" means with regards to short-term goals. Success shouldn't always be defined as winning or be related to a particular ranking. Instead, success should be defined in terms of developmental achievements (e.g. improvements in physical fitness or stroke production) because it has a positive effect on motivational factors and if the athlete achieves all the short-term goals then he/she will also reach the long-term goal! At the same time, rankings can be used as an indicator of the athlete's capabilities but they are not always absolute as a measure of performance. For example, if an athlete can only travel to a limited number of tournaments to earn points due to time (e.g. school) or monetary constraints, the ranking will not be representative of his/her true ability. In conclusion, one should not focus exclusively on ranking. The athlete's development with respect to stroke production, physical fitness, mental toughness, and improvement at regular competitions (tournaments) should be emphasized instead.

When parents and athletes focus too much on rankings, they can lose sight of the continuous development needed to achieve the overall long-term goal. This holds true especially on the junior circuit (ITF). Parents and athletes travel the globe to go to tournaments in the pursuit of valuable ranking points. Let's assume that the athlete constantly improves his ranking and makes it into the top 10 junior ITF rankings, which is without a doubt a great accomplishment. However, this will oftentimes not mean anything with regard to the overall goal of reaching the top 100 ATP/WTA.

Even though the athlete is a "star" on the junior circuit, he/she is a nobody in the "real" world: the ATP/WTA Tour. By the time the athlete reaches the top 10 in the ITF rankings, he/she is most likely 17/18 years old and will then begin competing at the lower level ATP/WTA tour events (e.g. Futures).

If they don't receive a wildcard for the main draw they have to play the qualification rounds, where they will be competing against adults. Instead of winning most of the time like in the juniors, they will again become familiar with losing during the early rounds of those qualies and will fail to get any points.

After this happens for a few months in a row, self-confidence cannot help but decline and, consequently, performance as well - and it might already be too late to stem this tide. Skill development is more important to focus on than ranking because such development will lead "naturally" to the high ranking being sought.

CHAPTER 2:

"Introduction to Kinesiology Principles"

Kinesiology is the study of muscles, bones, and joints (also called arthrosis) as they relate to movement. The human body consists of more than 600 muscles and approximately 206 bones. The good news is that this chapter will only be dealing with the larger muscles that are involved in joint movements, which cuts down the number of muscles to less than 100. Coaches should have an adequate knowledge of these larger muscle groups and their respective movement characteristics because proper muscular maintenance and strengthening will affect athletic performance as well as aid in injury prevention

ANATOMICAL POSITION & DIRECTIONAL TERMS

In order to properly use the exercises presented in later chapters, understanding planes of motion, joint movement and anatomical terminology is important.

During the anatomical position a person is standing upright, feet are close together, arms remain close to the body, and palms are facing forward.

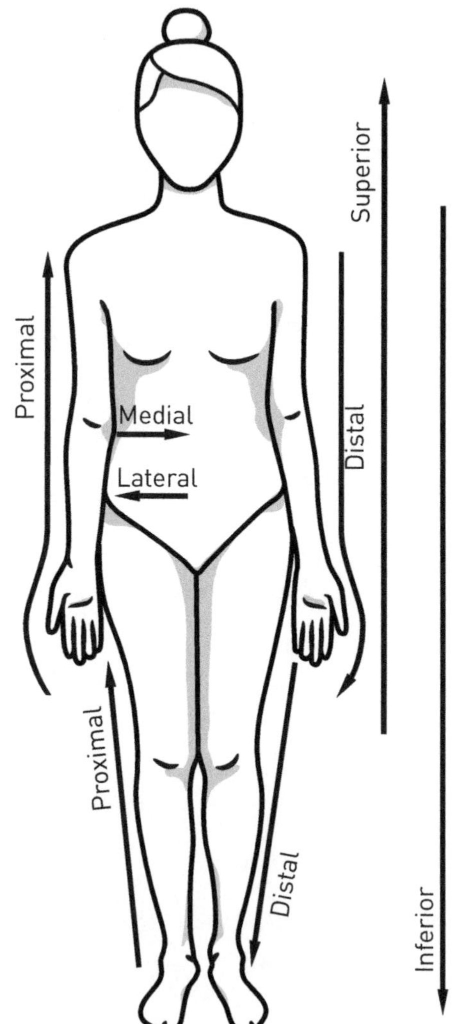

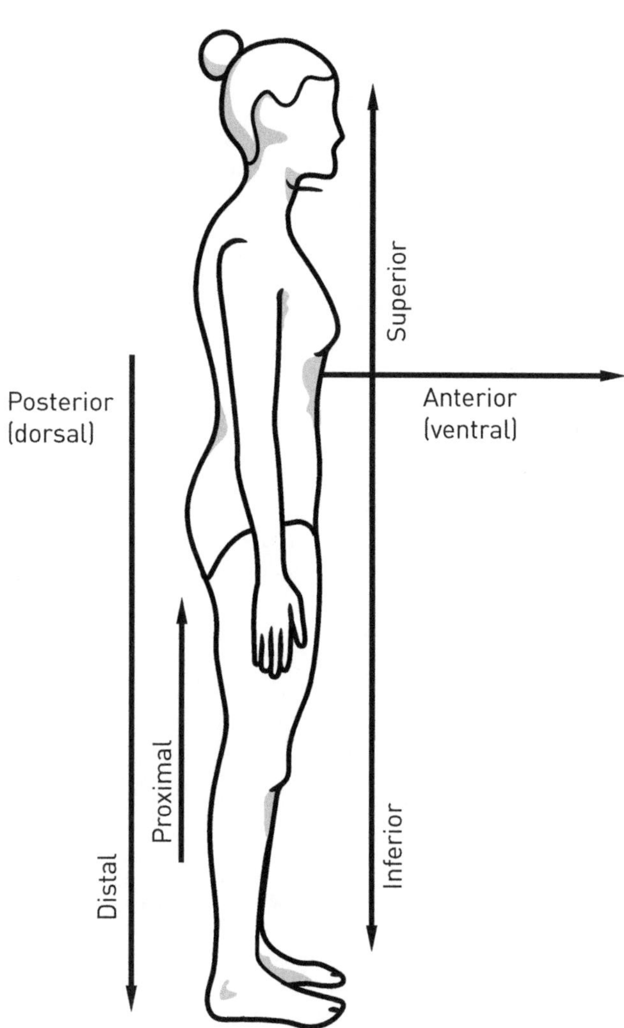

Picture of Anatomical Position including Anatomical Terminology

ANATOMICAL DIRECTIONAL TERMS IN ALPHABETICAL ORDER

Anatomical Terminology	Explanation
Anterior	In front or frontal part
Anteroinferior	In front and below
Anterolateral	In front and to the outside
Anteromedial	In front and to the inner side
Anteroposterior	Front & rear
Anterosuperior	In front and above
Bilateral	Both sides (right & left)
Contralateral	Opposite side
Deep	Below the surface
Distal	Away from the center or point of origin
Dorsal	Relating to the back; posterior
Inferior	Below
Inferolateral	Below and to the outside
Inferomedial	Below and to the inside
Ipsilateral	On the same side
Lateral	Towards the outside
Medial	Towards the inside/center
Palmar	Palm of the hand
Plantar	Relating to the sole of the foot
Posterior	Behind/rear/backside
Posteroinferior	Behind and below
Posterolateral	Behind and toward the outside
Posteromedial	Behind and towards the inside
Posterosuperior	Behind and above
Prone	Face down
Proximal	Towards point of origin
Superficial	Near the surface
Superior	Above
Superolateral	Above and towards the outside
Superomedial	Above and toward the inside
Supine	Face up
Ventral	Relating to the belly; anterior part
Volar	Relating to the palm of the hand

PLANES OF MOTION

A **plane of motion** is a two-dimensional imaginary "mirror", which dissects the body into two equal parts and describes the direction a body segment is moving. There are 3 major planes of motion:

1. Sagittal plane: dissects the body into a left & right side → flexion/extension (anterior/posterior direction)
2. Frontal plane: dissects the body into a front & rear side → abduction/adduction (lateral/medial direction)
3. Transverse plane: dissects the body into an upper & lower half → rotation

Generally, flexion/extension movements occur in the sagittal plane, abduction/adduction movements occur in the frontal plane, and rotation movements occur in the transverse (horizontal) plane.

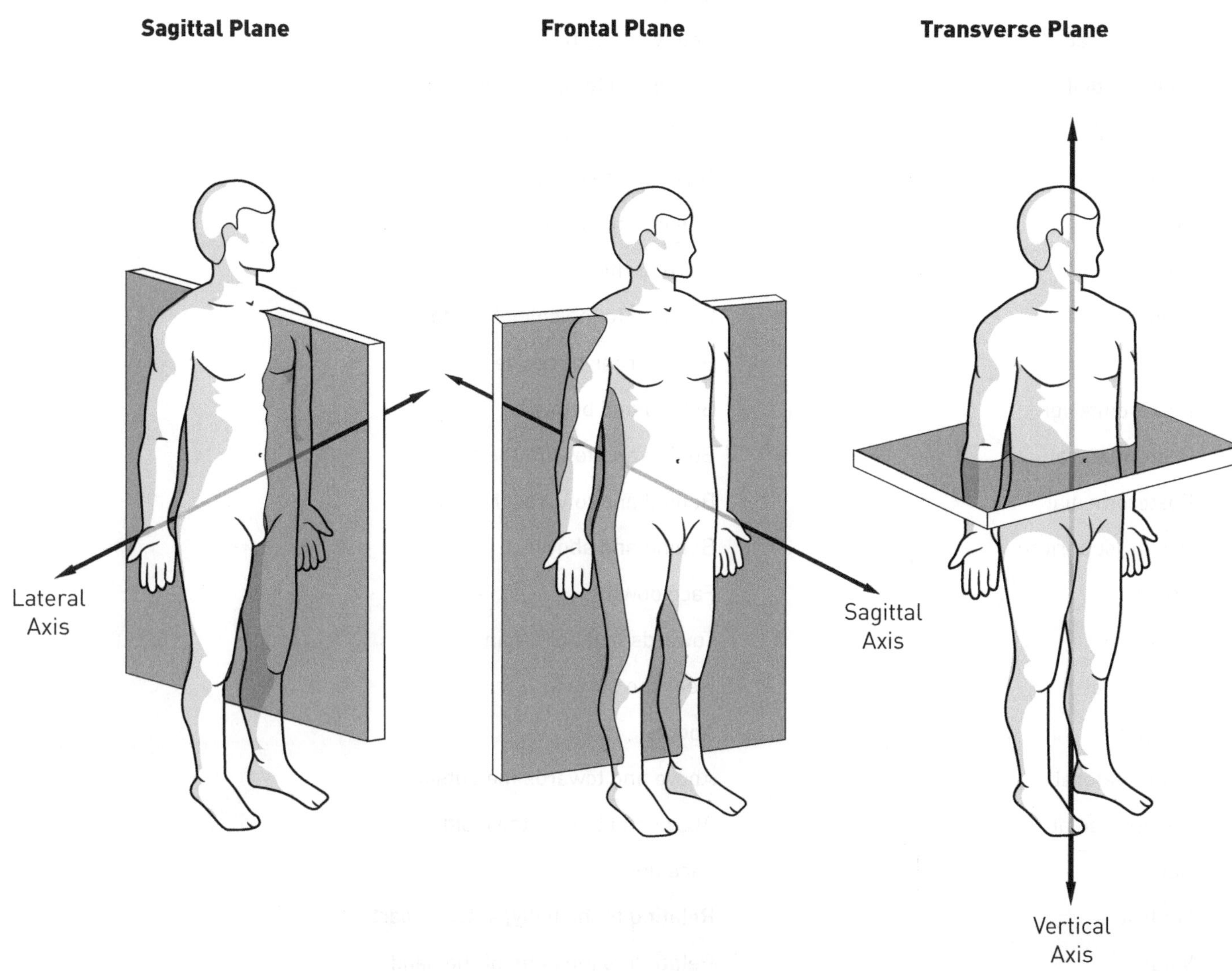

JOINT CLASSIFICATIONS

The articulation of 2 or more bones is called a **joint** or athrosis. Joints can be classified by their structure or by the degree of movement they allow.

Joints that are classified by structure are fibrous joints, cartilaginous joints, and synovial joints; joints classified by movement (function) are synarthrodial joints, amphiarthrodial joints, and diarthrodial joints.

There are exceptions but in general fibrous joints correspond to synarthrodial joints, cartilaginous joints to amphiarthrodial joints, and synovial joints to diarthrodial joints.

With respect to movement characteristics, fibrous/synarthrodial joints are immovable, cartilaginous/amphiarthrodial joints are slightly movable, and synovial/diarthrodial joints are freely movable.

		Structural Classification		
		Fibrous	Cartilaginous	Synovial
Functional Characteristic	Synarthrodial	x		
	Amphiarthrodial		x	
	Diarthrodial			x

With reference to exercise, synovial/diarthrodial joints require attention and hence are the focus in this book. There are six (6) sub-categories of diarthrodial/synovial joints:

1. Ball & Socket Joint (called Enarthrodial; e.g. shoulder)
2. Hinge Joint (called Ginglymus; e.g. knee)
3. Saddle Joint (called Sellar; e.g. thumb)
4. Pivot Joint (called Trochoidal; e.g. radioulnar below elbow)
5. Gliding Joint (called Arthrodial; e.g. wrist)
6. Ellipsoid Joint (called Condyloidal; e.g. fingers)

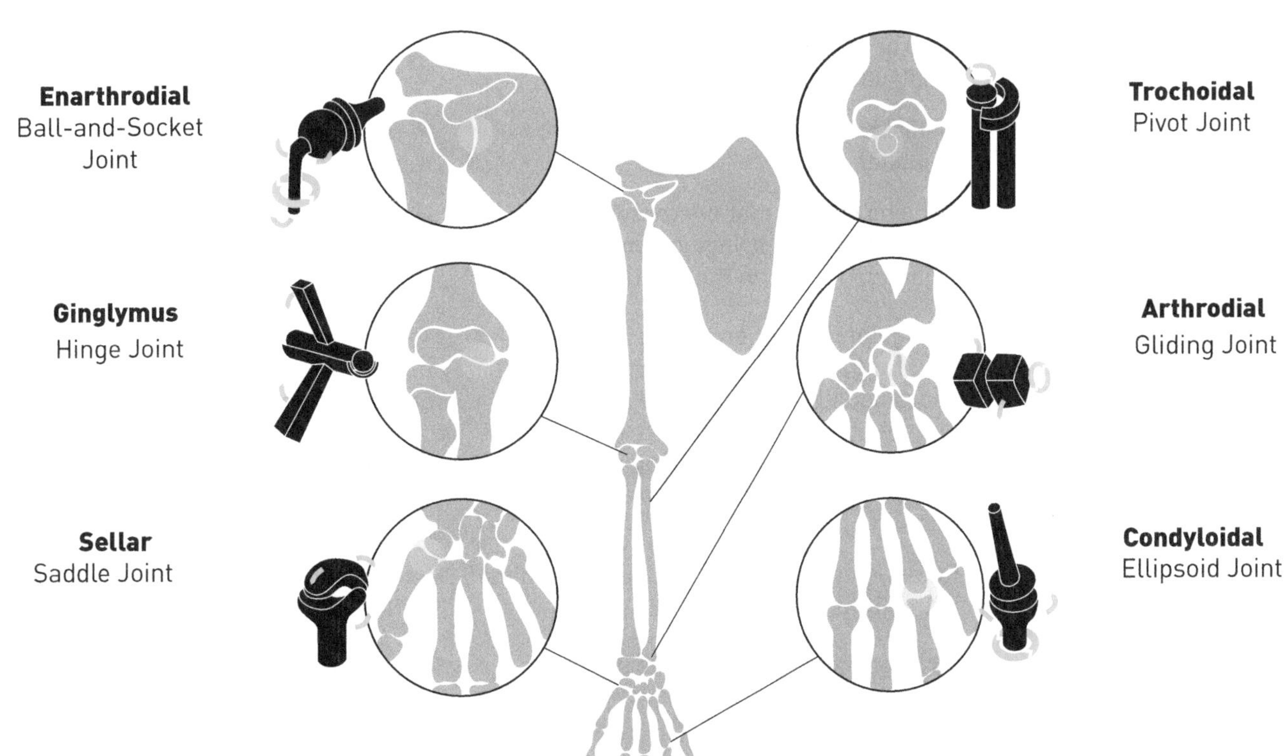

JOINT MOVEMENTS

How much movement can occur at a particular joint depends on its **range of motion** (ROM), which can be measured using a goniometer; the **goniometer** is placed at the joint's axis of rotation to measure the ROM. A person's ROM at a particular joint depends upon the flexibility properties of tendons acting upon that joint. Joint movement terminology is based upon ROM changes or joint angle changes, which means that the relative position of two or more bones (a joint) changes. For example, when a person "flexes the elbow", such as during a bicep curl, then the radius/ulnar move closer together towards the humerus (hand moves towards the shoulder).

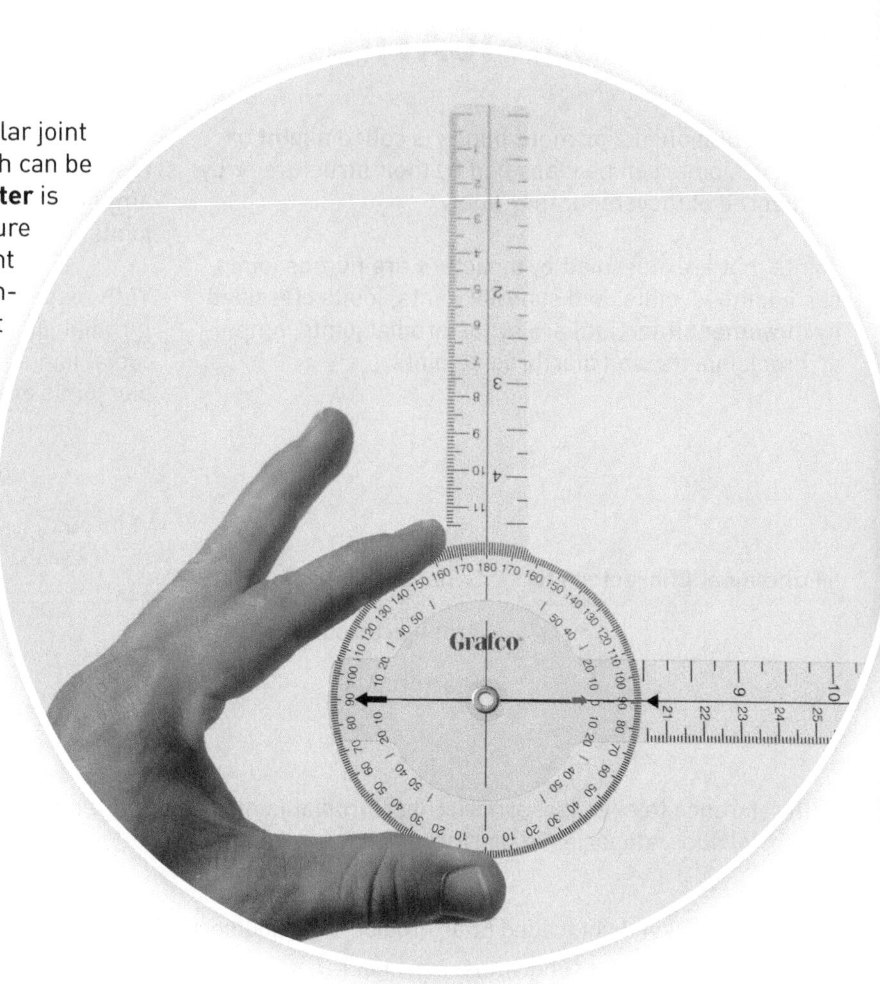

Following are some relevant joint movement terms that are grouped in corresponding pairs (it is not a comprehensive list as some terms do not apply in this book):

General Movement Terminology	Description	Example
Abduction	Lateral movement away from the center (midline) in the frontal plane	Lateral Arm Raises
Adduction	Medial movement towards the center (midline)	Returning the arm from lateral arm raises back towards the thigh
Flexion	Bending motion that decreases the joint range of motion; bringing bones closer together, usually, in the sagittal plane	Bicep Curl where hand moves towards the shoulder; bending of elbow
Extension	Straightening motion that increases the joint range of motion; moving bones farther apart, usually, in the sagittal plane	Tricep extension where the hand moves away from the shoulder; straightening of the elbow
External Rotation	Rotary motion away from the center (midline) in the transverse plane; outward rotation	External Shoulder Rotation; Rotator Cuff Circuit
Internal Rotation	Rotary motion towards the center (midline) in the transverse plane	Internal Shoulder Rotation; Rotator Cuff Circuit
Circumduction	Circular motion of a limb clockwise or counterclockwise	Arm swings in the sagittal plane

Ankle/Foot Movement Terminology	Description	Example
Eversion	Turning sole of the foot outwards (lateral) in the frontal plane	Standing on inner edge of the foot
Inversion	Turning sole of the foot inward (medial) in the frontal plane	Standing on outer edge of the foot
Dorsal Flexion (dorsiflexion)	Flexion motion of the ankle in the sagittal plane	Moving the toes towards the shin
Plantar Flexion	Extension motion of the ankle in the sagit-tal plane	Standing on the ball of the foot (toes); e.g. Calf Raises

Forearm (radioulnar) Movement Terminology	Description	Example
Pronation	Internal rotation of the radius where it crosses the ulnar in the transverse plane; "palms down" position	Extending the arm forward with the palm facing towards the ground
Supination	External rotation of the radius where it is parallel to the ulnar in the transverse plane; "palms up" position	Extending the arm forward with the palm facing up

Shoulder Girdle (scapulae) Movement Terminology	Description	Example
Depression	Downward motion of the shoulder girdle in the frontal plane; usually from a previously elevated position	Downward phase during shoulder shrugging
Elevation	Upward motion of the shoulder girdle in the frontal plane	Upward phase during shoulder shrugging whereby shoulders are closer to the ears
Protraction (abduction)	Shoulder girdle moves forward; scapulae abducts in the transverse plane	Any pressing action in front of the body, e.g. bench press
Retraction (adduction)	Shoulder girdle moves backward; scapulae adducts in the transverse plane	Occurs during pulling action when shoulders are horizontally abducted; e.g. seated row
Upward Rotation	Scapulae rotates upward were the inferior angle of the scapulae moves laterally and upward in the frontal plane	Occurs during overhead activities, e.g. Military Press
Downward Rotation	The scapulae rotates back towards the spi-ne where the inferior angle of the scapulae moves medially and downward	Occurs when returning arms from an overhead activity

Shoulder Joint (radioulnar) Movement Terminology	**Description**	**Example**
Horizontal Abduction	The humerus (arm) moves away from the body in the transverse plane	Occurs when lowering the barbell towards the chest during the bench press or when performing Bend-Over Row
Horizontal Adduction	The humerus (arm) moves towards the midline of the body in the transverse plane	Occurs when pushing the barbell away from the chest upward during the bench press

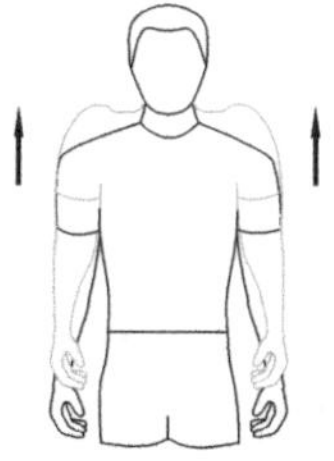
Scapula elevation

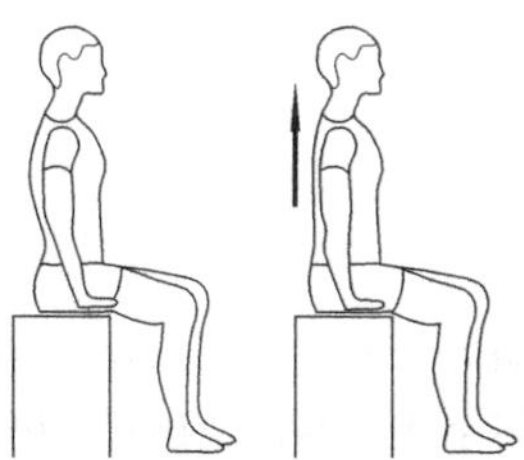
Scapula depression

Scapula abduction

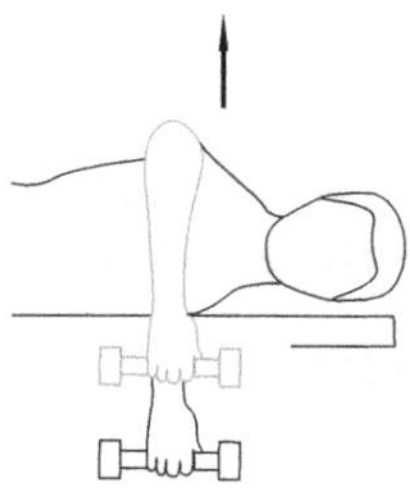
Scapula adduction

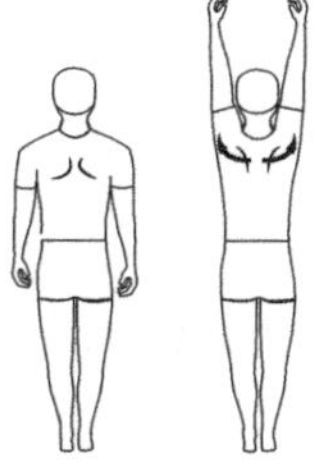
Scapula upward rotatior

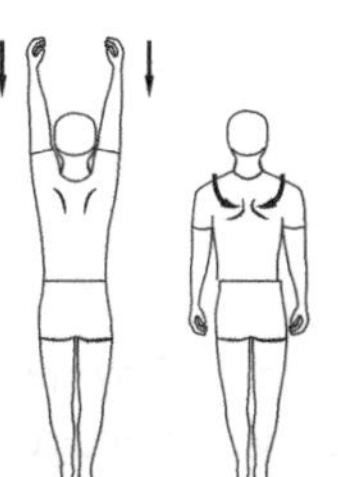
Scapula downward rotat

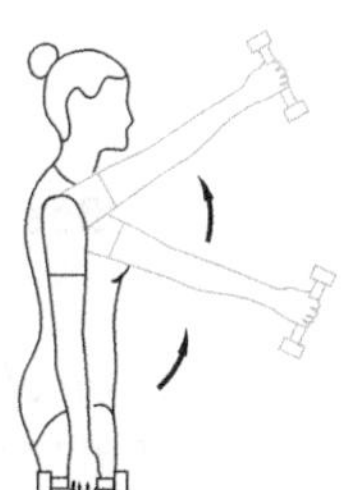
Shoulder flexion

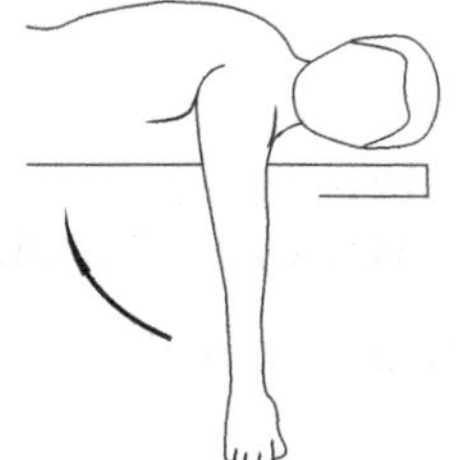
Shoulder extension

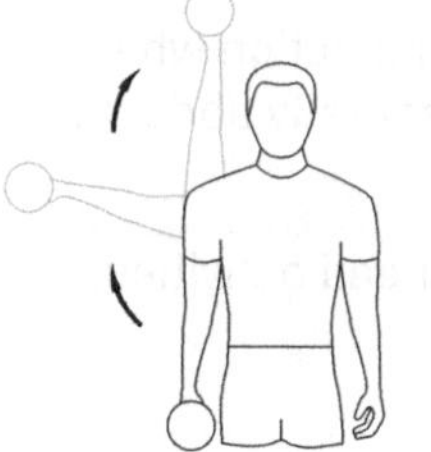
Shoulder abduction

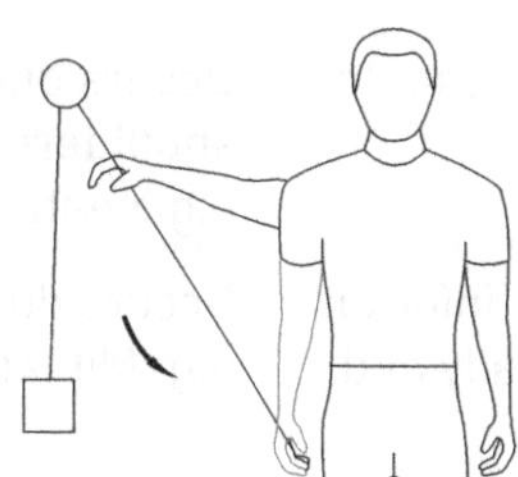
Shoulder adduction

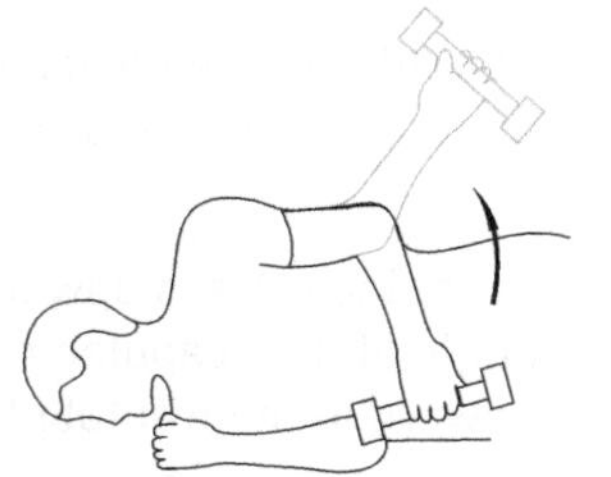
Shoulder external rotation

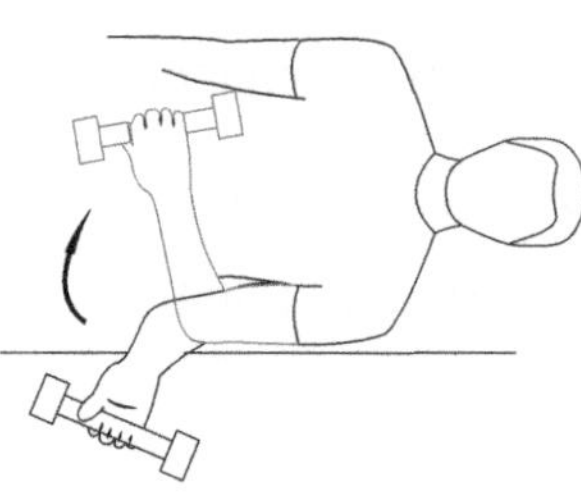
Shoulder internal rotation

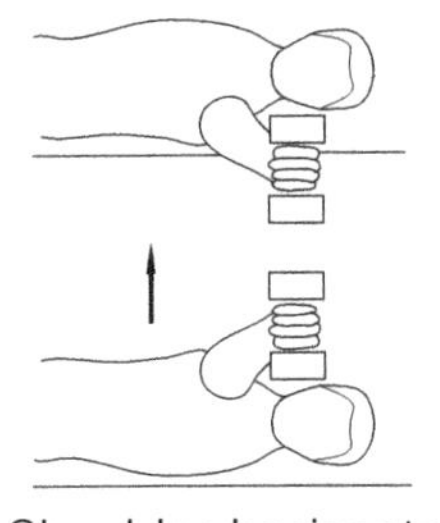
Shoulder horizontal abduction

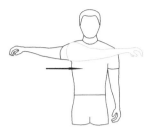

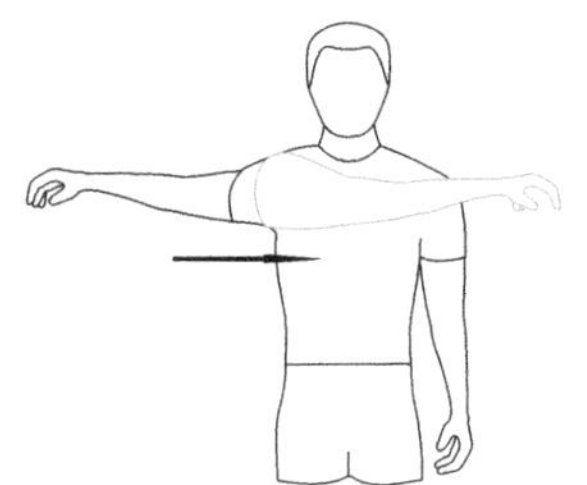
Shoulder horizontal adduction

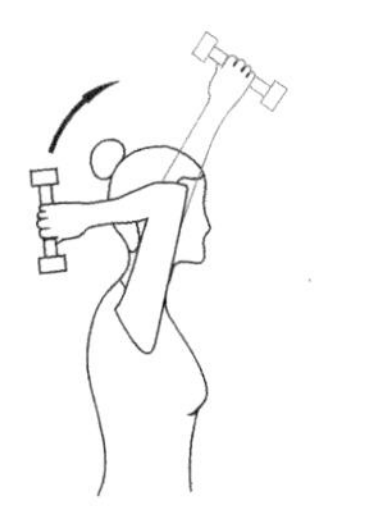
Elbow extension

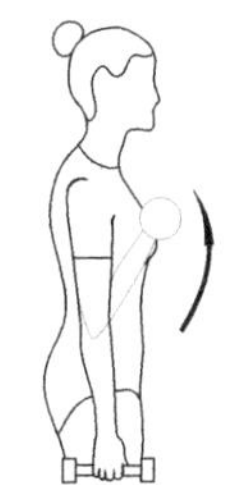
Elbow flexion

Radioulnar pronation

Radioulnar supination

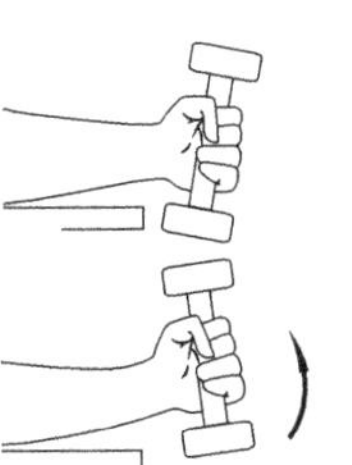
Wrist abduction

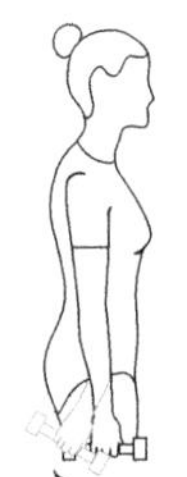
Wrist adduction

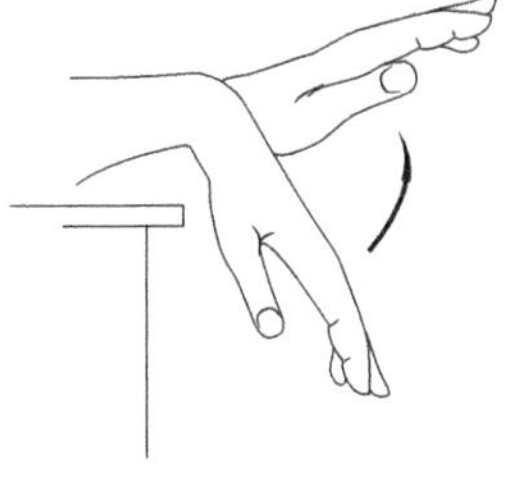
Wrist extension

Wrist flexion

Hip flexion

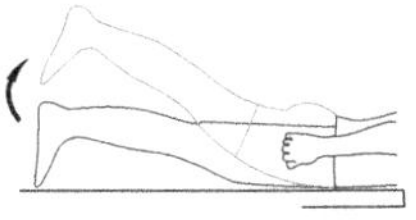
Hip extension

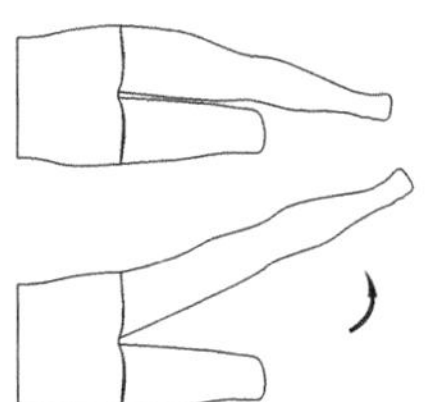
Hip abduction

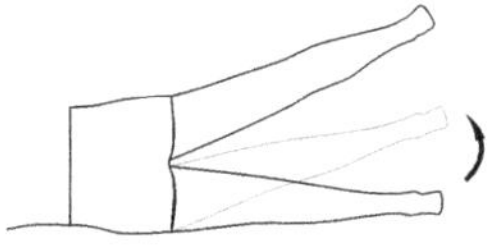
Hip adduction

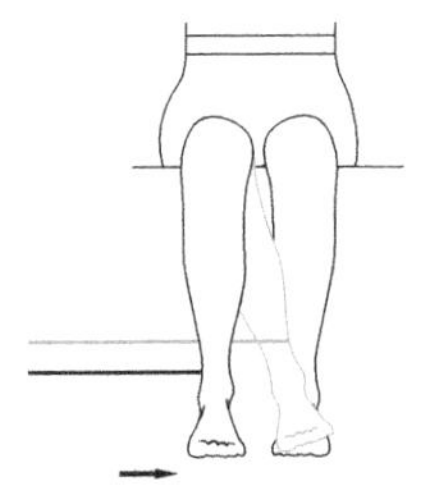
Hip external rotation

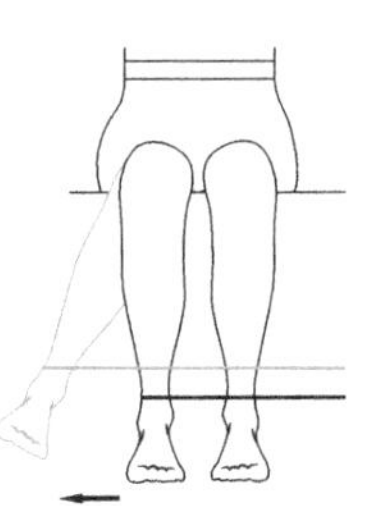
Hip internal rotation

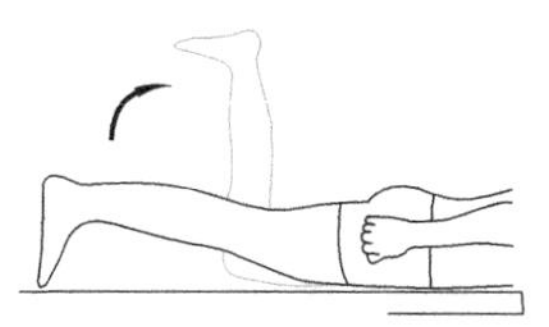
Knee flexion

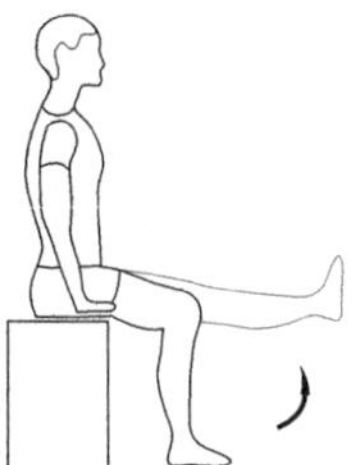
Knee extension

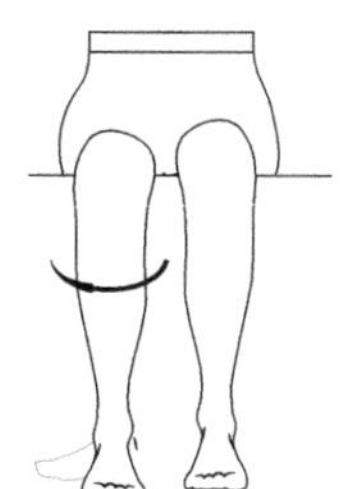
Knee external rotation

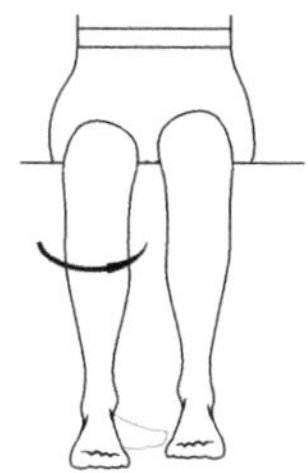
Knee internal rotation

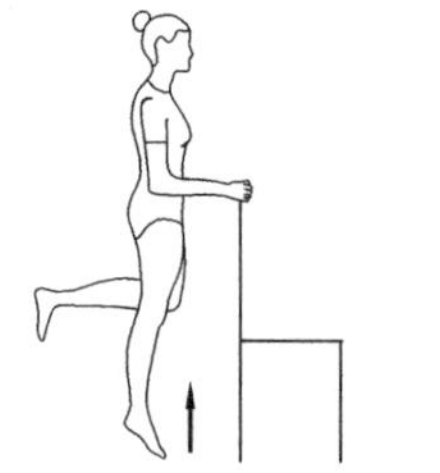
Ankle plantar flexion

Ankle dorsal flexion

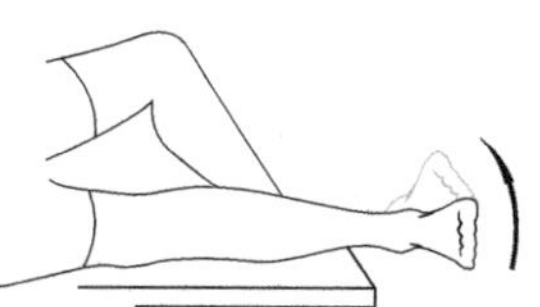
Transverse tarsal & subtalar inversion

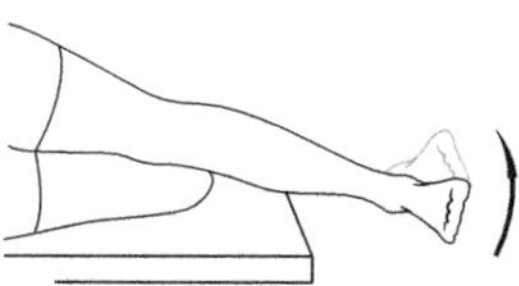
Transverse tarsal & subtalar eversion

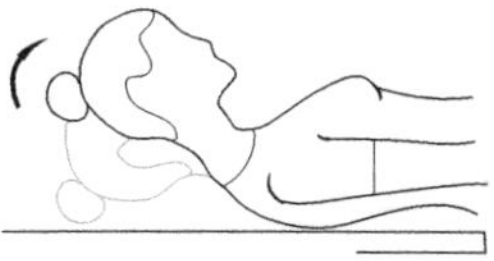
Cervical flexion

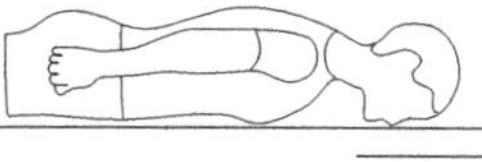
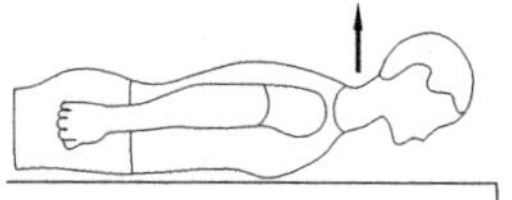
Cervical extension

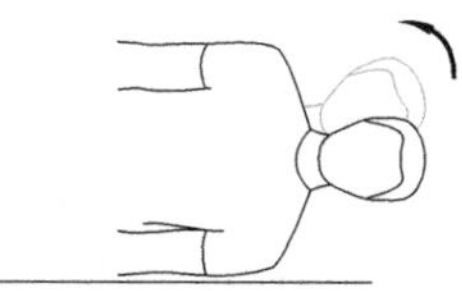
Cervical lateral flexion

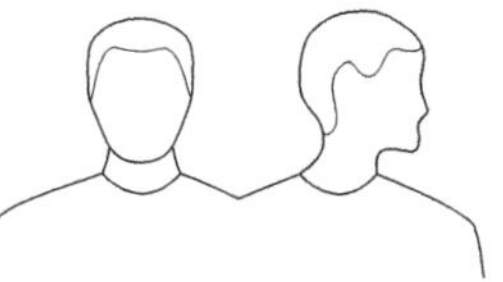
Cervical rotation

JOINT MOVEMENT & KINETIC CHAIN EFFICIENCY

Body motions or body segment motions can either be described as translation or rotation. **Translation** is a linear motion, either in a straight line or a curve, where all parts of the body or an entire body segment (e.g. humerus) move in the same direction and hence a change in position occurs. On the other hand, during **rotation** a body or body segment moves around a pivot point where all parts of the body or the body segment move in the same direction, either clockwise or counterclockwise, but no change in position occurs (pivot point or axis of rotation remains unchanged). Essentially, movement of the human body can be considered translation of the person's center of mass but movement of the center of mass only occurs when muscles provide energy to rotate bones around their axis of rotation.

Kinetics, as it relates to the musculoskeletal system, refers to the mechanics that describe the motion of a body or body segment that is due to forces acting upon a joint (body segment). According to Newton's 2nd law of motion, which describes the relationship between a force acting upon a body (object) and the motion that body (object) experiences due to that force, a **force** (F) can be expressed as mass (m) of an object times its acceleration (a) or F = m * a. With regards to exercise, a force can be thought of as a muscular pushing or pulling action that controls movement, causes movement, or inhibits movement of the entire body or a body segment. In order to exert force, muscles require energy and efficient transfer of energy is required in order to transfer the maximum amount of force. Since **power** can be expressed as force x distance over time (power=force x distance/time), efficient force transfer, and hence energy transfer, will have a positive effect on maximum power output. Therefore, optimizing energy transfer is crucial for optimizing overall performance on the court.

In reality, an athlete needs to push off the ground to transfer forces through the various joints in order to move a body or body segment; hence ground reaction forces are at 100% at the surface. In other words, a chain of events needs to occur in order to move an object (e.g. hit a tennis ball). For example, during the service motion the athlete pushes off the ground, transferring forces/energy through the ankles, knees, hips, trunk, shoulders, elbows, and wrists before the racquet acts upon the ball over the head. This chain of events is also referred to as the **kinetic chain**, which can be thought of as a linkage of various body segments (joints) so that an action can occur via kinetic energy transfer. A kinetic chain can either be "closed" or "open", depending on the connection of the distal ends of the extremities (hands or feet) with the ground or an immovable object (e.g. weight machine).

If either hands or feet are directly connected with the ground/immovable object, the kinetic chain is said to be "closed". On the other hand, if the hands or feet are not directly connected with the ground/immovable object, the kinetic chain is considered "open". Following these definitions, the Back Squat would be considered a closed chain exercise, whereas the Single Leg Squat would be considered an open chain exercise.

With respect to the flow of energy, an exercise can also be considered to have an "open" or a "closed" circuit. For example, the Overhead Squat is an example of a closed chain, closed circuit exercise because both feet are on the ground and both hands connect with the barbell, thereby closing the circuit. A Single Arm Dumbbell Overhead Squat on the other hand would be considered a closed chain, open circuit exercise since both feet are connected with the ground but the hands do not close the circuit. Closed chain, closed circuit exercises are used to achieve strength gains and improve overall power output, whereas closed chain, open circuit exercises will lead to improvements with respect to energy transfer since stability requirements at the joints are elevated. Because of the fact that all synovial joints have some translation due to natural laxity at the joint capsule, strengthening the musculature surrounding the joint capsule will enhance energy transfer since joint laxity will decrease, which will diminish the "leakage" of energy due to translation (undesirable movement at the joint).

MUSCLE & JOINT INTERACTION

The force a muscle produces can either be utilized to rotate or stabilize a joint, depending on the moment arm (lever) characteristics of the muscle producing a torque (rotation) across a joint and the overall amount of torque that is ultimately being produced. A torque (T) is the product of an applied force (F) and the length of the moment arm distance (d); T = F * d. In order to produce a torque, a force generated by muscle contraction must fulfill two characteristics:

1. The force must be applied in a plane that is perpendicular (90°) to the joint's axis of rotation
2. The force must have a moment arm (leverage)

How a force can be converted into a torque can be illustrated using a simple analogy: a muscle's pulling force can produce a torque, thereby rotating a joint, the same way that a pulling force is required to open a door.

A door is mounted on a doorframe using hinges, which are equivalent to the axis of rotation of a given joint, which in this case is in a vertical plane (V). Since the axis of rotation is vertical, a force (F) must be applied in the horizontal plane (H) in order to cause rotation of the hinges to open the door. Now, in order for the door to swing open the force (F) must have a moment arm distance (d), which means that the force cannot go directly through the axis of rotation since the moment arm distance (d) would be 0 and hence no torque could be produced (T = F * d). Forces F1, F2, and F3 are horizontal to the vertical axis of rotation (V) but only forces F1 & F2 provide for a moment arm distance. Therefore, force F3 cannot produce a torque and the door doesn't move whereas forces F1 & F2 produce a torque and the door swings open.

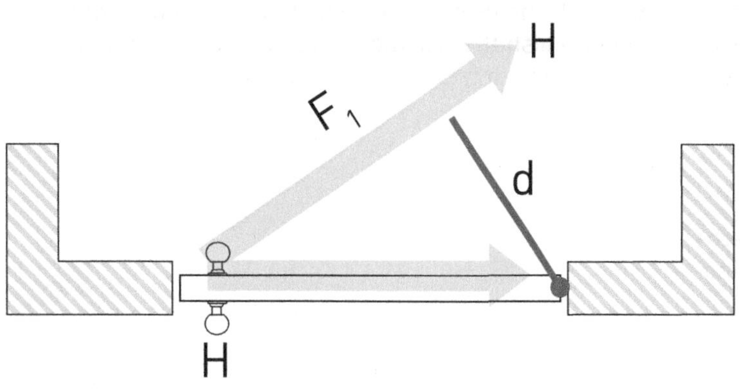

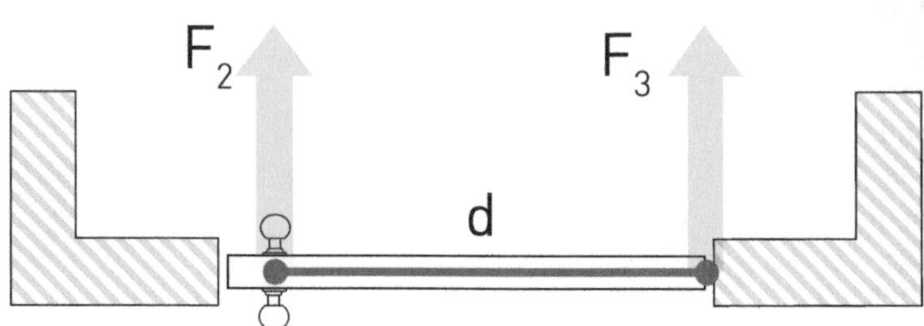

Top view

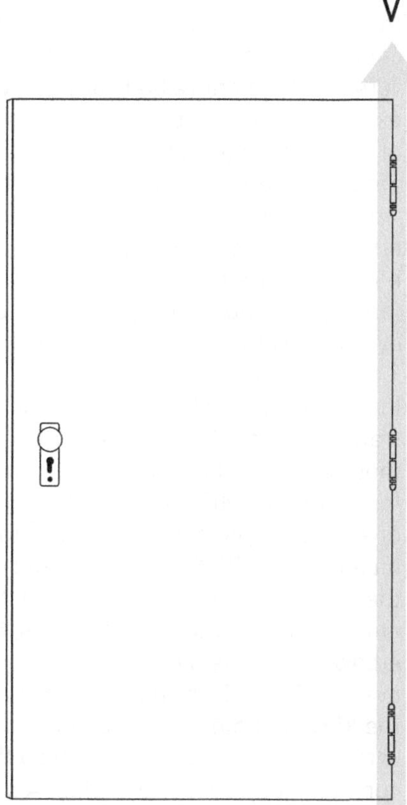

Side view

TYPES OF MUSCLE ACTIVATION

When the nervous system sends out a signal towards the muscle, tension develops inside the muscle tissue and a contraction occurs. The term muscle contraction can be confusing at times because the word "contraction" suggests the shortening of the muscle tissue, which is not always the case. Therefore, the term muscle activation is commonly used for various types of muscle contractions since the nervous system "activates" a muscle before a contraction can occur.

In general, a muscle can produce a force when it contracts and, as previously mentioned, that force can either inhibit movement, cause movement, or control movement at a joint. More specifically, muscle contractions can either be isometric or isotonic.

Isometric literally means "equal measure of length", which refers to the length of the muscle fibers. As a result, a force is being produced by the muscles without changing the length of the muscle fibers, which inhibits joint movement because the internal torque (force) equals the external torque (force); (C, see picture below).

Isotonic literally means "of equal tension". With regards to muscle contractions it refers to the fact that the tension created during a muscle contraction remains relatively constant but the muscle tissue alters its length; it either lengthens or shortens. The shortening of an isotonic contraction is called **concentric contraction** and the lengthening of an isotonic contraction is referred to as an **eccentric contraction**.

The term **concentric** literally means "coming towards the center" and refers to the direction the muscle fibers are moving during the contraction. Therefore, when the muscle produces a pushing or pulling force, the muscle fibers shorten (come towards the center) and cause the joint to rotate in the direction of the force because the internal torque exceeds the external torque. For example, during a Bicep Curl using a cable machine, the athlete pulls on the handle thereby moving the forearm towards the shoulder (elbow flexion) (A, see picture below), and the internal torque produced by the muscle exceeds the external torque provided by the resistance attached to the cable (external resistance + gravity).

In contrast, the term **eccentric** literally means "away from the center", which also refers to the direction the muscle fibers are moving during the muscle activation. As a result, the muscle fibers elongate (move away from the center) and the muscle tension, and hence force production, constantly decreases to control the movement. In other words, the muscle fibers are being elongated by an external force (external resistance + gravity) that exceeds the internal force produced by the muscle. Using the previous example again, during the Bicep Curl when employing a cable machine, the athlete returns to starting position, lowering the forearm towards the thigh (elbow extension) (B, see picture below), and the external torque provided by the resistance (gravity) attached to the cable exceeds the internal torque provided by the bicep.

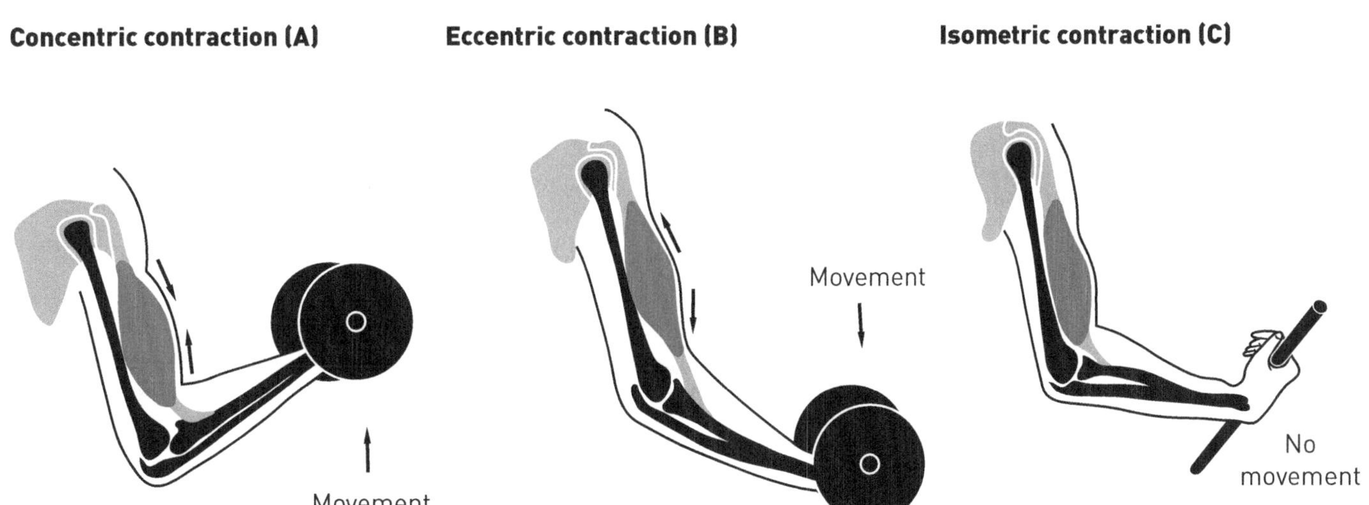

ROLE OF MUSCLES DURING CONTRACTION

Muscles can take on various responsibilities during a muscle contraction. These can be placed into five (5) categories:

1. Agonist
2. Antagonist
3. Stabilizer
4. Synergist
5. Gliding Neutralizers

Agonists are muscles that are mainly responsible for causing a particular movement via concentric contraction. They are also known as prime movers or primary muscles. For example, the biceps is considered an agonist during a Bicep Curl (elbow flexion).

Antagonists allow the agonists to perform a certain movement by relaxing. They are generally located on the opposite side of the joint and perform the opposite joint movement when contracting concentrically. Using the previous example, the triceps is considered the antagonist of the biceps. The biceps is responsible for elbow flexion and the triceps is responsible for elbow extension.

Stabilizers, as the name implies, allow the agonist to perform a joint movement by contracting and stabilizing the action to allow for a firm base of support. Continuing the previous example, the brachioradialis acts as a stabilizer of the biceps during elbow flexion (and extension).

Synergists, also known as guiding muscles, assist in refining the action of the agonist and inhibit undesirable actions of other muscles. Apart from being a stabilizer, the brachioradialis also acts as a synergist during elbow flexion (Bicep Curl).

Neutralizers contract to neutralize (counteract) actions of other muscles thereby preventing their involvement in undesirable movements.

Bodybuilding focuses on isolating the agonist musculature by using machines that will take on the stabilization requirements so that all the energy can be used to increase the resistance and prolong the time under tension a resistance can be moved. Since the athlete needs to stabilize body actions on the court, purely focusing on agonist development (bodybuilding) would be counterproductive in terms of athletic development since the athlete's strength, and thereby power capabilities, depends on how long the stabilizers can function properly. If stabilizers fatigue rapidly, movements can no longer be performed by the agonists and overall performance suffers. Therefore, later chapters in this textbook introduce exercises that develop agonists as well as antagonists, stabilizers, synergists, and gliding neutralizers to maximize the athletic performance potential in an integrated fashion.

CHAPTER 3:

"Introduction to Exercise Physiology Principles"

HOMEOSTASIS: CONTROL OF THE INTERNAL ENVIRONMENT

Exercise physiology can be defined as the scientific study of what is happening inside the body due to exercise (physical activity). More specifically, exercise physiology is the study of cued-responses to exercise and the adaptations that occur with training; a short-term change is called a **response** and a long-term change causing a relatively permanent change in structure or function is referred to as an **adaptation**. Exercise can be defined as a single session of physical activity that is at least of moderate intensity. Therefore, leisure walking is not an exercise; it's a physical activity! Training is the systematic grouping of exercises (e.g. jogging 4x/week; not once a week).

An exercise response occurs when there is:

1. an increase in heart rate
2. increase in heart's contractility
3. increase in depth & breathing
4. increase in sweating
5. a redistribution of blood flow
6. mobilization of fuel supply

Exercise responses permit the athlete to work out and they are designed to reverse the direction of the homeostatic disturbances (explained shortly).

A training adaptation (relatively permanent) occurs when

1. the blood volume increases
2. an increase in the size of a cell (hypertrophy) occurs

The magnitude of an exercise response/adaptation varies depending on the intensity, duration, and nature of the exercise. Exercise responses and training adaptation exhibit a negative feedback pattern (explained shortly), where the body attempts to reverse the direction of the homeostatic disturbance.

In exercise physiology emphasis is be given to "how" an adaptation occurs rather than "why". By understanding how an adaptation occurs one can better predict, control, and improve the adaptation; often times the objective of studying exercise physiology is improving performance!

HOMEOSTASIS VS. STEADY-STATE

When the body's biological control systems maintain physiological variables at manageable constant values at rest, it is called **homeostasis**. More specifically, the term homeostasis describes the maintenance of an unchanging/constant "normal" internal environment by a biological control system, where a physiological variable (e.g. body temperature) remains within a normal range when the body is not under any stress (e.g. at rest). On the other hand, the term **steady state** describes the maintenance of an internal environment by a biological control system, where a physiological variable (e.g. body temperature) remains relatively constant yet deviates from its normal value, which occurs when the body is experiencing stress (e.g. exercise). Due to the external stress the body cannot maintain a normal constant internal environment and has to make adjustments in order to retain a constant environment under stress, where the body's response to the external stress is equal to its magnitude. In other words, the term homeostasis is being used to describe the body's maintenance during resting conditions whereas the term steady state refers to the body's maintenance during exercise; exercise is a stressor which disrupts homeostasis, also called **homeostatic disturbance** (e.g. an increase in temperature). More specifically, homeostatic disturbances occur at the cellular level causing a temporary decrease in $O2$ levels, whereas the $CO2$ levels go up, which causes acidity levels to increase.

The body's metabolic changes are regulated by **biological control systems** in the same manner an air conditioning unit responds to changes in outside temperature to maintain indoor temperature at a certain constant level.

BIOLOGICAL CONTROL SYSTEMS

In order to track metabolic changes the body has numerous biological control systems that monitor the body's internal environment; the biological control systems' task is to maintain a physiological variable (e.g. blood pressure or body temperature) at a manageable constant value. How exactly these control systems operate remains under investigation but each biological control system consists of a(n):

1. Receptor
2. Control center
3. Effector

When a homeostatic disturbance in the internal environment occurs a signal arises, called **stimulus**. The stimulus excites the receptors, which send a message to the control center. The control center assesses the strength of the stimulus (message, situation) and sends out an appropriate response to the effector to correct the disturbance, thereby returning the internal environment back to" normal" (manageable constant values), hence removing the stimulus.

NEGATIVE FEEDBACK LOOP

The response procedure of the control system to a stimulus is called **negative feedback (loop)** because the response of the control system decreases the initial stimulus, which initially caused the control system to respond, in order to return the internal environment back to normal. In other words, the control system's response is opposite to the stimulus. If the stimulus increases a variable then the control system will respond by decreasing the variable back to normal values and vice versa. For example, a homeostatic disturbance such as an increase in the cell's acidity provokes an integrative system response designed to restore (decrease) acidity/alkalinity values (normal blood pH level of 7.4) back to normal, thus the nature of the response is in an opposite direction to the homeostatic disturbance. The precision and capability by which the control systems operate is called the **gain of the control system**; the higher the gain, the higher the capabilities of the control system.

Summary of control system operation:

1. Homeostatic disturbance occurs causing a stimulus
2. Stimulus excited receptors
3. Receptors forward message to control center
4. Control center assesses situation
5. Control center sends message to effector (messenger; e.g. hormones)
6. Effector corrects disturbance and removes stimulus

EXAMPLE OF CONTROL SYSTEM OPERATIONS: REGULATION OF BLOOD GLUCOSE

Blood glucose levels are being regulated by a control system, called the **endocrine system**. The endocrine system consists of eight (8) major glands (hypothalamus, pineal gland, pituitary gland, thyroid gland, parathyroid gland, adrenal gland, pancreas, testes [male]& ovaries[female]) throughout the body that can make (synthesize) and release chemical substances, called **hormones** (messengers), into the blood stream. Then the hormones are being transported via the blood stream (circulatory system) to an effector, signaling the effector to cause a certain metabolic response.

Let's assume you eat a high-carbohydrate (glucose) meal. Once the food is digested blood glucose levels rise above normal. The rise in blood glucose levels causes a disturbance, which stimulate receptors in the pancreas. The receptors send a message to the control center in the pancreas, which analyses the situation and orders the synthesis of a hormone, called **insulin**, which is then being released into the blood stream and transports glucose to cells throughout the body. Insulin then signals the cells to absorb glucose from the blood stream into the cells, which causes blood glucose levels to return to "normal".

Failure of the blood glucose control system causes a disturbance in homeostasis, which results in disease, called **diabetes mellitus** (type I & II). Both types of diabetes are caused by high blood glucose concentrations, called **hyperglycemia**. In type I diabetes, the beta cells in the pancreas that synthesize the hormone insulin are damaged, which means that the body cannot produce any more insulin to decrease blood glucose levels. This example shows a failure of the effector component.

In type II diabetes, insulin is being produced but the cells have become resistant to insulin, which means that the cell receptors don't respond to absorb glucose from the blood stream.

EXERCISE CHALLENGES HOMEOSTATIC CONTROL SYSTEMS

A competitive tennis match or working out hard in the gym can pose a challenge to various of the body's control systems since exercise increases metabolic demands (e.g. lactic acid build up) thereby challenging homeostasis. Therefore, if one understands how things are being processed inside the body then one can understand what needs to be adjusted to make the athlete stronger or to prevent the ill effects and maximize the positive effects.

METABOLISM

Metabolism consists of chemical pathways that either combine molecules (molecule **synthesis**) with each other or separate them from each other (breakdown of molecules). The synthesis of molecules refers to an **anabolic reaction**, whereas the break-up of molecules is termed **catabolic reaction**.

All cells require biological energy to fuel metabolic activity. For muscle cells the immediate source of energy is **ATP** (adenosine triphosphate; ATP = ADP + Pi = adenosine diphosphate + inorganic phosphate), which consists of three parts:

1. adenine
2. ribose
3. three linked phosphates

The body derives the required biological energy by converting foods into energy (ATP) via chemical processes on the cellular level; this metabolic (chemical) process of turning foods into biological energy is referred to as **bioenergetics**.

During a tennis match or practice the body continuously needs to be able to derive energy from foods (nutrients) so that muscle contractions can occur, which allows the athlete to perform. The body's inability to convert energy from foods into ATP is a performance limiting factor since muscle contraction is inhibited, which means that the body cannot perform any more work. Therefore, in order to have a successful career as a professional athlete one needs to have a thorough understanding of bioenergetics as it relates to exercise and nutrition (food choices).

Since metabolism occurs on the cellular level one needs to know cell structure and understand how cells operate.

UNDER THE MICROSCOPE

- The body mainly consists of four elements:
- 1. Oxygen (65%)
- 2. Carbon (18%)
- 3. Hydrogen (10%)
- 4. Nitrogen (3%)
- 5. Other elements (4%; calcium, magnesium, chloride, potassium, iron, zinc, sodium)
- These other elements use chemical bonds to form compounds (molecules). Any compound that contains carbon is called organic (alive) and any compound lacking carbon is called inorganic.

CELL STRUCTURE & FUNCTION

Conceptually, a cell can be thought of as a factory that can produce (synthesize) various compounds to ensure that the body operates properly. A single cell can be divided into three parts:

1. cell (or plasma) membrane
2. nucleus
3. cytoplasm

CELL MEMBRANE

The cell membrane is **semipermeable**, which means that certain substances can enter the cell but others cannot. Its main responsibility is to (1) safe-guard the inner components of the cell, (2) control the movement of substances that can enter and leave the cell, and (3) provide receptors for specific molecules arriving from outside the cell. There are 3 mechanisms by which substances can pass through the cell membrane:

1. **Diffusion** → small, lipophilic (fat-soluble) molecules (e.g. oxygen) freely pass through the membrane like a VIP at a concert (e.g. water/small fats)
2. **Facilitated Diffusion** (specific transport mechanisms) → hydrophilic (water-soluble substances) and/or small charged molecules (glucose, amino acids, ions) cannot simply pass through the membrane into the cell by diffusion; they have to wait for the transport mechanisms to carry them over or to open channels for them to pass through
3. **Active Transport** (Vesicular (Bulk) Transporter) → they move large macromolecules (e.g. glucose) via two processes, called **endocytosis** (into the cell) and **exocytosis** (out of the cell). There are three ways for a large molecule to enter the cell (endocytosis):

   a. **Phagocytosis** → "Cell Eating"; bacteria and/or waste are engulfed by **phagosomes** and then fuse with lysosomes, which carry enzymes that destroy the content of the phagosomes.
   b. **Pinocytosis** → small vesicles carry fluids inside the cell; means "cell drinking" and is being used by most cells to sample the surrounding extracellular fluid.
   c. **Receptor-Mediated Endocytosis** → is a key-and-lock mechanism, where a substance (e.g. hormones, low-density lipoproteins carrying cholesterol) binds to a specific receptor on the membrane and is shipped into the cell by vesicles;

   You can think if these as a guest-list-only event at a club: the bouncers at a club who only allow people come in that are on the list, everyone else has to wait outside. Lysosomes bind to the vesicle inside the cell and release its content into the cytoplasm.

The cell membrane (**plasmalemma**; **sarcolemma** in muscle tissue; "lemma" means sheath) is double-layered; it is made of (phospho) lipids & protein. When a nutrient has crossed the cell membrane then it either enters the **blood system** or the **lymphatic system**, depending on if the nutrient is water-soluble or fat-soluble; nutrients that enter the blood system are water-soluble and nutrients entering the lymphatic system are fat-soluble!

NUCLEUS

The nucleus is located in the center of the cell and it contains the genetic code (genes) – **DNA (deoxyribonucleic acids)**. Genes regulate protein synthesis (determines cell composition) and cellular activity.

CYTOPLASM

Cytoplasm (= **sarcoplasm** in muscle cells; means "cell-forming material") is the cell fluid, which consists of (1) **organelles** ("little organs") and (2) enzymes. Most of the cellular activity occurs in the cytoplasm. The cytoplasm holds 8 important organelles:

Organelle	Function
1. **Mitochondria**	Power generating unit; provides the energy (adenosine triphosphate [ATP] production) for cellular function via oxidation
	Site of aerobic energy production (oxidative phosphorylation)
2. **Ribosomes**	They synthesize proteins for intracellular & extracellular purposes
	Free floating ribosomes make proteins for intracellular purposes
	Ribosomes attached to the rough endoplasmic reticulum make proteins for the cell membrane & extracellular purposes
3. **Lysosomes**	Is the security crew; store digestive enzymes that digests unwanted substances
4. **Peroxisomes**	Waste removal crew; contain variety of enzymes (e.g. oxidase & catalase)
	Oxidase converts aggressive reactive molecules [called **free radicals**] into hydrogen peroxide, which is further converted by catalase into water & oxygen
	Break down long-chain fatty acids in lipid metabolism
5. **Rough Endoplasmic Reticulum (ER)**	Is the network within the cytoplasm
	Stores calcium ions
	Is the site of protein synthesis
	Makes the digestive enzymes for lysosomes
6. **Smooth Endoplasmic Reticulum (ER)**	Is the network within the cytoplasm
	Stores calcium ions
	Aids in lipid metabolism
7. **Golgi Apparatus**	Is the packaging & shipping unit (like FedEx); it sorts, processes, and packages the products coming from the ER
8. **Cytoskeleton**	Is the cells' skeleton supporting cell structure and movement

THE ROLES OF ENZYMES IN CHEMICAL REACTIONS

Enzymes have two functions, (1) they control the speed of cellular chemical reactions and (2) they control the metabolic pathways in cells. Enzymes do not cause a reaction but they control/regulate the speed at which the reactions occur.

Enzymes (which are proteins) regulate the speed of a chemical reaction by lowering the **energy of activation**, which is the initial energy required so that a reaction can actually occur; by lowering the initial energy of activation enzymes increase the rate of product formation. When enzymes increase the speed of a chemical reaction in cells, then they are called **catalysts**. For an enzyme to work as a catalyst, the enzyme molecule must first bind to a reactant molecule, called **substrate**. The enzyme (catalyst) molecule acts on the reactant molecule (substrate) to generate a **product** molecule, which is subsequently being released. Theoretically, one enzyme molecule could generate multiple product molecules. In reality, enzymes act on two or more different substrates and generate more than one product. Only if a substrate molecule closely fits and binds to a particular site on the enzyme molecule, called the **active site**, can the enzyme act on the substrate and catalyze (accelerate) the reaction (Lock-and-Key model).

COENZYMES

Although enzymes are proteins, many enzymes possess other non-protein components called **cofactors**, which are necessary for the enzymes to function properly. Other enzymes contain vitamins and this vitamin-derived cofactors function as **coenzymes**, which act as transport molecules to carry chemical components from one reaction to another so that enzymes can fulfill their functions.

There are three coenzymes that are important in energy metabolism:

1. **Flavin Adenine Dinucleotide (FAD)**
2. **Nicotinamide Adenine Dinucleotide (NAD)**
3. **Coenzyme A (CoA)**

FAD and NAD participate as hydrogen (electron) carriers in certain oxidation-reduction reactions and they transport electrons from one place to another inside cells. FAD acquires electrons by picking up pairs of hydrogen atoms (have 1 electron each), which then are brought and released to electron acceptors.

NAD picks up one electron in a hydrogen atom and the other electron comes as a free electron, which is "stolen" from another hydrogen atom. Only the free electron of a hydrogen atom is "stolen" and the rest remains as is (leaving a hydrogen ion solution). Coenzyme A picks up chemical groups, called acetyl groups, in certain metabolic reactions and brings them to another reaction.

FACTORS ALTERING ENZYME ACTIVITY

Factors that alter enzyme activity are equivalent with the rate by which the enzymes' substrate is converted into products. There are two factors that influence enzyme activity:

1. the temperature of the enzyme solution (products)
2. pH (acidity level) level of the enzyme solution

Enzyme activity is best at body temperature (37°C) or slightly above it. ATP production then increases during exercise because the speed at which reactions occur also increases due to enhanced enzyme activity.

Each enzyme has its own optimal pH level at which enzyme activity is most efficient. During heavy exercise, skeletal muscles produce large quantities of lactic acid. Lactic acid is a strong acid which leads to a decrease in body pH levels (increase in acidity). This decrease in body pH levels ultimately leads to a strong decrease in ATP production, which results in the cessation of work.

FUEL FOR EXERCISE

The body uses nutrients to grow, restore body tissue, and provide energy to perform work. The body requires some **nutrients** in large quantities, called **macronutrients**, and other nutrients in smaller quantities, called **micronutrients**. Macronutrients provide energy, whereas micronutrients do not yield any energy directly but they assist in the transfer of energy (e.g. B-vitamins).

MICRO NUTRIENTS: NON-ENERGY YIELDING

- Water (2nd simplest form; made of hydrogen & oxygen)
- Minerals (simplest form; each is a chemical element)
- Vitamins (made of hydrogen, oxygen, and carbon -> organic): vitamin B & C are water-soluble, vitamin A & D & E & K are fat-soluble

MACRO NUTRIENTS: ENERGY YIELDING

The primary energy yielding nutrients used during exercise are:

- Carbohydrates (CHO) (made of hydrogen, oxygen, and carbon -> organic): yield 4kcal/g
- Lipids (made of hydrogen, oxygen, and carbon -> organic): yield 9kcal/g
- Protein (made of hydrogen, oxygen, and carbon -> organic): yield 4kcal/g; only minor contribution (2-5%) during exercise

Nutrients containing carbon are called **organic** (=alive)! Which nutrient predominantly provides the energy during exercise depends on:

- exercise intensity (low intensity = fat; high intensity = carbs)
- exercise duration (long duration=fat; short duration=carbs)

Carbohydrates predominantly provide energy for high intensity/short duration activities, whereas lipids (fat) provide the energy for moderate intensity/long duration activities.

EXERCISE INTENSITY

When exercise intensity increases, the body will use more carbohydrates and less fat. The **cross-over point**, where more carbohydrates are being used than fat, occurs when exercise intensity increases steadily. At – and beyond the cross-over point, carbohydrates become the dominant source of fuel.

There are two factors, with respect to high exercise intensity, that cause the shift from fat to carbohydrates (fat -> carbs):

1. recruitment of fast-twitch fibers
2. an increase in blood epinephrine levels

More and more fast-twitch fibers are being recruited when exercise intensity is high. Fast-twitch fibers are better equipped to metabolize carbohydrates than fat! Therefore, the more fast-twitch fibers an athlete has, the more carbohydrates are being used compared to fat.

With high intensity exercise, blood levels of epinephrine increase and this increase in epinephrine levels is responsible for higher glycogen breakdown, carbohydrate metabolism, and higher lactate production. Lactate production is a byproduct of anaerobic metabolism, which increases with exercise intensity. High levels of lactate inhibits fat metabolism, which means less fat is being used during high-intensity exercise. Therefore, the more lactate is being produced, the less fat is metabolized, which leads to an increased usage of carbohydrates during high-intensity exercise.

EXERCISE DURATION

Factors that control the rate of fat metabolism during prolonged exercise are the enzymes that control lipolysis (lipases). The lipases activity is stimulated by the hormones **epinephrine**, **norepinephrine**, and **glucagon**. During prolonged low-to-medium intensity exercise, epinephrine levels in the blood rise, which leads to better lipase activity, which in turn promotes lipolysis and lipolysis promotes fat metabolism.

CARBOHYDRATES

Carbohydrates are the ideal form of energy during **anaerobic metabolism** (short duration/high intensity activities; e.g. 100m sprint). Carbohydrates provide 4kcal/g. At the molecular level a carbohydrate atom consists of 6 carbon (C) molecules, 12 hydrogen (H) molecules, and 6 oxygen (O) molecules; also referred to as CHO. There are three forms of carbohydrates (mono – and disaccharides are known as simple sugars; polysaccharides are complex carbohydrates), which are dependent upon the length of the carbohydrate molecule:

1. **Monosaccharides** (simple sugars: glucose & fructose)
   a. Glucose (= blood sugar)
   b. Fructose (the sweetest form; occurs naturally in honey)
   c. Galactose

2. **Disaccharides** (2 monosaccharides)
   a. Maltose (= glucose + glucose): maltose is produced during starch (energy storage form in plants) breakdown (e.g. carbohydrate digestion)
   b. Sucrose (= glucose + fructose): regular table sugar
   c. Lactose (= glucose + galactose): lactose is the principle carbohydrate of milk; "milk sugar"

3. **Polysaccharides** (also called complex carbohydrates)
   a. Glycogen: energy reserves in the body, composed of glucose
   b. Starches: energy reserves in plants, composed of glucose
   c. Fibers: provide little or no energy because their bonds can't be broken by human enzymes, which means that they don't contribute any energy to the body because they can't be broken down into monosaccharides (glucose) but they can lower glucose levels (blood sugar)

The catabolic chemical reaction that breaks down carbohydrates into smaller compounds is called **hydrolysis**. On the other hand, the anabolic chemical reaction where carbohydrates are put together to form a larger molecule is called **condensation**.

- Hydrolysis (broken apart by water; a water molecule splits into H and OH)
- Condensation (synthesis of 2 monosaccharides)

GLUCOSE

Glucose (also known as blood sugar), which is a monosaccharide that can be found in foods but not eaten directly, provides almost all the energy in the human brain and it is the body's preferential source of energy during exercise. The body takes carbohydrates, breaks them down, derives glucose, and converts it via **glycolysis** to ATP (adenosine triphosphate), which is the immediate source of energy for muscle cells. The body uses ATP for immediate energy needs or stores it in the form of glycogen to be used at later time.

When the blood glucose level falls below normal ranges (70 – 110 mg/dL) then glucose can be made in the liver from carbohydrates and protein but not from fat; no body fat can be converted into glucose but glucose can be converted into fat in the liver! The conversion of protein to glucose is called **gluconeogenesis** and it happens in the liver, where proteins from the lean body mass (muscles) are converted into glucose.

LACTOSE INTOLERANCE

Lactose intolerance occurs when the intestinal cells do not produce enough of the enzyme lactase to ensure that the disaccharide lactose is being digested and absorbed efficiently. Lactase production declines with age. Only about 30% of the world's population will retain an adequate amount of lactase production throughout their lifetime.

The symptoms of lactose intolerance are:

- bloating
- abdominal discomfort
- diarrhea

Total elimination of milk products is not necessary, since the body can take in about 6g of lactose (1/2 cup milk) without any symptoms. A strategy to deal with lactose intolerance is to:

- gradually increase the amount of milk products that are being consumed
- take milk products with other foods
- spread their intake over the day

This will change the bacteria in the GI tract so that the change in bacteria will help digest & absorb more lactose; there is no reappearance of the missing enzyme lactase!

STARCH

Starch, a polysaccharide found in plants, is broken down into monosaccharides, which can either supply energy immediately or they can be stored.

GLYCOGEN

The storage form of glucose in the body is **glycogen**, which is a complex carbohydrate (polysaccharide) stored in animal tissue. Glycogen is being stored in the liver and in muscle tissue. During exercise, muscle cells break down glycogen stores into glucose, called **glycogenolysis**, which occurs not only in muscle cells but also in the liver. During glycogenolysis the liver releases glucose into the blood stream so that cells then can absorb the glucose and thus have the energy to do work.

The liver stores about 1/3 of the body's total glycogen capacity and releases glucose into the bloodstream as needed. After a meal, when the blood glucose level rises, the liver synthesizes glycogen by attaching short glucose molecules into longer, branching glucose chains (glycogen) via condensation reactions. When the blood glucose level falls below normal ranges (70 – 110 mg/dL) then the liver breaks down glycogen (glycogenolysis) into single glucose molecules by means of hydrolysis. Liver glycogen stores are being depleted within 90-180 minutes of work, not days!

Muscle cells have 2/3 of total body glycogen storage capacity but they can't break down the glycogen and transport it to another location (only the liver can do it); muscle cells have to use their glycogen stores for themselves during exercise! Also, glycogen holds water and thus is rather bulky, which is one of the reasons why low carbohydrate diets show quick drops in weight, but it's water weight because less glycogen is being stored; it's not fat that's being lost.

Excess glucose that couldn't be stored in the form of glycogen will be broken into smaller compounds in the liver. The liver breaks down glucose in smaller molecules and puts them together in the form of fat. Then the fat is being transported from the liver and stored in fatty tissues in the body.

LIPIDS

Fat belongs to the group of nutrients called **lipids**. Stored body fat is an ideal fuel source for **aerobic metabolism** (long duration/low-to-medium intensity exercise) since fat has the highest energy density (9kcal/g). There are three forms of lipids:

- **Triglycerides** (fats and oils): in foods, 95% of fats are triglycerides; in the body, 99% of fats are stored as triglycerides!
  - Triglycerides are composed of 3 fatty acids (OH) attached to 1 glycerol ("ol" = alcohol) molecule; fatty acids are the primary type of fat used by muscle cells during aerobic metabolism
  - Fatty acids are stored in the body as triglycerides and triglycerides are mainly stored in fat cells and to a lesser degree in skeletal muscle cells. If need be, triglycerides can be broken down into fatty acids and glycerol as a source of energy. This process is called **lipolysis** (triglycerides → 3 fatty acids + 1 glycerol). The enzymes that control lipolysis are called lipases. The glycerol portion of lipolysis is not a direct form of energy but the liver uses the glycerol to synthesize glucose, which of course yields energy.
- **Phospholipids**: Phospholipids are not a source of energy used by the body during exercise. Instead, phospholipids provide an insulating layer around nerve cells! **Lecithin** is an **emulsifier** (substance that allows mixing of water and oil); it's present in cell membranes and helps fat moving in and out of the cells because phospholipids are water – and fat-soluble. Phospholipids allow fat-soluble substances, like hormones and vitamins, to pass easily in and out of cells.
- **Sterols**: Sterols do not provide any energy during exercise. The most famous steroid is cholesterol. Foods derived from both plants and animals contain steroids but only those steroids derived from animals contain **cholesterol**! "Good" cholesterol does not refer to a type of cholesterol found in foods. "Good" cholesterol refers to how the body transports cholesterol in the blood! Cholesterol is not some bad ingredient of food but a compound made by the body (the liver) and used by the body. Cholesterol that is made in the body is called **endogenous** ("endo" = within; "gen" = arising). Cholesterol that comes from outside the body is called **exogenous** ("exo" = outside the body). The liver produces its own cholesterol (800 – 1500mg/day) and the daily value of cholesterol that should be consumed is 300mg/day. So, the liver actually produces most of the daily cholesterol needs itself! Excessive amounts of cholesterol in the blood can clock the arteries, a disease called **atherosclerosis** (athero = "porridge or soft"; scleros = "hard"; osis = "condition") that causes heart attacks and strokes!

PROTEIN

Most people associate protein with strength and meat with protein. So is eating tons of meat efficient in order to gain muscle mass? Not really. Meat is one good source of protein but so are eggs, milk, and grains & vegetables.

AMINO ACIDS

Amino means "nitrogen containing". **Amino acids** are the building blocks of proteins. There are a total of 20 amino acids; 9 are **essential** (body can't synthesize them) amino acids and the remaining 11 amino acids are **non-essential** (body can synthesize them).

Essential Amino Acids	Non-Essential Amino Acids
Histidine	Alanine
Isoleucine	Arginine
Leucine	Asparagine
Lysine	Aspartic Acid
Methionine	Cysteine
Phenylalanine	Glutamic Acid
Threonine	Glutamine
Tryptophan	Glycine
Valine	Proline
	Serine
	Tyrosine

Amino acids are connected to each other via **condensation reactions**, forming **peptide bonds**. When numerous amino acids join together then they form a **polypeptide**, which essentially are called **proteins**.

STEPS IN PROTEIN SYNTHESIS

Protein synthesis occurs at the cellular level by **ribosomes**, which actually make proteins for intracellular and extracellular purposes. Proteins for intracellular purposes are synthesized by free-floating ribosomes in the cytoplasm, whereas proteins for extracellular purposes are synthesized inside the rough endoplasmic reticulum.

1. DNA in nucleus contains information necessary for protein synthesis
2. The transcription of the DNA information results in a message (called mRNA), which contains the "blueprint" for protein synthesis
3. mRNA exists the nucleus and moves to ribosomes, where protein synthesis occurs based on the information from the mRNA
4. Transfer RNA (tRNA) transport amino acids, which are building blocks for proteins, to the ribosomes
5. The message contained in the mRNA is being translated (translation) and amino acids are linked together to form proteins

DIGESTION & ABSORPTION OF PROTEIN

When one eats foods that contain protein then the body doesn't store that food protein directly but breaks it down to amino acids from which the body then can make its own protein.

Proteins are partially broken down in the stomach via the enzyme **pepsin** before they move into the small intestine, where they are further broken down and digested. The amino acids can be used to provide energy or to make other needed compounds. All amino acids that are not immediately being used are transported to the liver via capillaries.

PROTEIN QUALITY

The quality of protein is based on two factors:

1. Digestibility
2. Amino Acid Composition

In order to provide the amino acids for protein synthesis, the body breaks down the protein from food sources into amino acids. The protein's food sources influences its digestibility and hence rate of availability. In general, animal proteins (90 – 99%) have a higher digestibility than plant proteins (70 – 90%), soy protein (>90%) being the exception.

In order to synthesize protein, the body needs to have all the amino acids that are needed available at once. The liver can produce any non-essential amino acids but the diet has to supply any essential amino acids, otherwise the body breaks down its own protein (e.g. muscle protein) to obtain them. In other words, the more essential amino acids the protein provides, the higher its quality.

Apart from soy protein, plant protein from vegetables, nuts, seeds, grains, and legumes are lower in quality because they lack one or more essential amino acids. Consuming a combination of the aforementioned vegetable proteins enhances the quality of proteins but it is not very convenient.

FOOD SOURCES FOR HIGH-QUALITY PROTEIN

- Meat
- Fish
- Poultry
- Soy Products
- Cheese
- Eggs
- Yogurt
- Milk

BIOENERGETICS: BIOLOGICAL ENERGY TRANSFORMATION

The **1st law of thermodynamics** states that energy is not produced or created but just transferred around. In other words, the body doesn't produce any energy but simply transfers the energy derived from foods inside the body to an external environment.

According to Lord Kelvin, the **2nd law of thermodynamics** can be expressed as: "No process is possible in which the sole result is the absorption of heat from a reservoir and its complete conversion into work." Meaning when energy is being converted a 100% conversion is not possible because some energy will be "lost" as heat. With regards to exercise, the rate and the magnitude of the energy loss depends upon intensity and the environment one is affected by. For example, with respect to changes in the environment, when one steps into an ice cold bath then the body's core temperature drops and the body burns a ton of calories because it tries to maintain/ increase core body temperature. On the other hand, during weight lifting exercise intensity is high and the magnitude of the energy loss is going to be significant and fatigue sets in.

ENERGY TRANSFER VIA COUPLED REACTION

A chemical reaction that "adds" energy to a **reactant** (an ingredient of the initial reaction) before another reaction can occur is called **endergonic reactions** (e.g. condensation; anabolic reaction; potential energy). In other words, during an anabolic reaction (e.g. condensation) the energy is being transformed into potential energy (explained shortly). On the other hand, a chemical reaction that "releases" energy due to a chemical reaction is termed **exergonic reactions** (e.g. hydrolysis; catabolic reaction; kinetic energy). In other words, during a catabolic reaction (e.g. hydrolysis) the energy is being transformed into kinetic energy (explained shortly).

As previously mentioned, the body derives the required biological energy by converting foods into energy (ATP) via chemical processes on the cellular level. More specifically, during energy metabolism, cells use exergonic (energy releasing) reactions to break down food to form ATP via an endergonic (energy adding) reaction, which then can be used to do the work. This is called a **coupled reaction** (e.g. Reduction-Oxidation Reaction or RedOx reaction), where energy is released in reaction A so that reaction B can occur. Therefore, a coupled reaction (RedOx reaction) provides ATP, which then can be used to do the work.

REDUCTION-OXIDATION REACTION

Reduction-Oxidation reaction, also called **Red-Ox reaction**, is just a combination of oxidation and reduction reaction. It is a "partnership" just like hydrolysis and condensation is a partnership.

Oxidation simply means that an electron is removed from an atom or molecule during the reaction; it does not mean that oxygen is used in the reaction. Instead, the term originated because of the fact that oxygen generally tends to accept electrons and hence acts as an **oxidizing agent** (something that helps in getting it done).

The oxidizing agent is the atom that accepts the electron during the reduction process. This important property of oxygen (accepting electrons) is used by cells during aerobic energy metabolism to produce usable energy (e.g. Electron Transport Chain) in the mitochondria.

Reduction means that an electron is added to the atom or molecule. The reducing agent is the donor atom that gives away the electron during a reduction.

During Red-Ox reactions, the atom that lost an electron is looking to gain an electron again and the atom that gained an electron is looking to donate it again. It's important to point out that reduction-oxidation reactions involve the transfer of hydrogen atoms (which have just 1 electron) instead of free electrons! There are two coenzymes that are important for hydrogen transfer/transport:

- **Nicotinamide Adenine Dinucleotide (NAD):** is derived from vitamin B3 (niacin)
- **Flavin Adenine Dinucleotide (FAD):** is derived from vitamin B2 (riboflavin)

KINETIC ENERGY VS. POTENTIAL ENERGY

All the energy inside the body is in either one of two energy states:

- **Kinetic Energy** (F = m x a; m = mass of the object, a = acceleration/speed; Newton's 2nd law of motion) → form of energy during catabolic reactions, where energy is being released
- **Potential Energy** (Potential Energy: PE = m x g x h; where, PE = Potential Energy, m = Mass of object, g = Acceleration of Gravity = 9.8 m/s2, h = Height of object) → form of energy during anabolic reactions, where energy is being stored; it can also be energy through position.

For example, when glycogen is formed then it's in a potential energy state but when it is being processed for release then it's in the kinetic energy state. One of the other things that can be confusing with respect to potential energy is that it's not only some sort of energy storage but it also can be energy by position due to gravitational pull. For example, if you roll a rock on top of a hill and release it then the amount of energy that will develop by the time it's at the bottom of the hill is significant due to gravitational pull; all that occurs is conversion of potential energy into kinetic energy (you take the center of mass and multiply it by the speed/velocity/acceleration it moves down the hill and you can measure how much energy was transferred).

During the transfer or conversion from potential energy to kinetic energy, or vice versa, some energy cannot be converted and is "lost" to the environment in the form of heat. Also, potential energy continues to decline the longer the potential state exists. For example, the coliseum in Rome at one point in time it was a solid structure and it had potential energy but it's not the same structure today because the stones and minerals are broken down due to environmental oxidation (hydrogen and oxygen broke the structure down). Or if you have a battery in your car but you don't drive it a long time to recharge the battery, then the battery doesn't have enough energy left to start the car due to energy leakage over time.

The transfer of kinetic energy can actually increase or decrease the size of molecules and hence alter the molecule's **potential for energy**. For example, one can have an exergonic reaction (e.g. hydrolysis, catabolic), where energy is being released (e.g. when ATP energy bonds split then that provides for a lot of energy for the size of the molecule) and hence the size of the molecule decreases. On the other hand, during an endergonic reaction (e.g. condensation, anabolic), the size of the energy molecules increases because energy was transferred to it ("added"). Therefore, via a coupled reaction the molecule's potential for energy has grown. So, it was a kinetic activity that caused the potential energy to increase.

For example, ADP + P (adenosine diphosphate + phosphate) cannot rephosphorylate (regenerate) ATP, an endergonic reaction, without an exergonic reaction, the splitting of creatine phosphate (CP), providing energy. Therefore, an endergonic reaction cannot occur without an exergonic reaction providing energy, which is basically an example of the constant recycling of energy inside the body. Once the body can no longer recycle or transfer potential energy into kinetic energy, fatigue sets in, and performance will suffer.

Also, some of the energy is "lost" via heat to the external environment. Here is another example where some energy is "lost" during a coupled reaction but the overall gain of energy is greater:

The synthesis of glycogen, H2O + glucose, is an endergonic reaction. During that process 268kcal/mol are being "lost" because of the reaction but the outcome of energy is 688 kcal/mol. Therefore, some energy is "lost" but a greater gain in total energy occurs.

BIOLOGICAL ENERGY METABOLISM: ATP PRODUCTION

As previously mentioned ATP (adenosine triphosphate) is the immediate source of energy for muscle cells. ATP consists of three parts:

1. adenine
2. ribose
3. three linked phosphates

During **ATP synthesis**, an anabolic reaction, the enzyme **ATP synthase** facilitates the assembly of this high-energy bond, energy is stored, and can be used to perform work when needed.

ADP + Pi ---------> ATP + H2O
ATP synthase
adenosine diphosphate + inorganic phosphate = ATP

During **ATP breakdown**, a catabolic reaction, the enzyme **ATPase** facilitates the break-down of this high-energy bond, energy is released and can be used to do the work.

ATP --------------> ADP + Pi + Energy
ATPase

Since muscle cells need ATP constantly and ATP storage in muscle cells is limited, muscle cells need to reproduce ATP, which can be accomplished via three metabolic pathways (energy systems):

1. **ATP-CP System** (stored ATP usage & creatine phosphate breakdown): anaerobic pathway (no oxygen involved)
2. **Glycolysis** (breakdown of glucose/glycogen): anaerobic pathway (no oxygen is directly involved)
3. **Oxidative Rephosphorylation** (aerobic breakdown of glucose, fat, protein): aerobic pathway

ATP-CP ENERGY SYSTEM

The ATP-CP energy system consists of two energy storage reservoirs, ATP & creatine phosphate (CP). The enzyme **creatine kinase** catalysis the breakdown of creatine phosphate in order to provide ATP, which occurs in the sarcoplasm of muscle cells. ATP-CP is the energy system that predominantly provides energy at the beginning of exercise & for short-term high-intensity activities lasting up to 15 seconds.

The ATP-CP system consists of two energy storage reservoirs:

1. ATP
2. Creatine phosphate (CP)

The primary energy reservoir is **ATP**. ATP storage capacity in the body is 80g-100g and provides energy for maximal output for 1-3 seconds, depending on exercise intensity and the individual's body size (bigger people store more energy and can produce more force; mass moves mass principle). The body doesn't like to keep a lot of ATP stored because it's such a heavy molecule. Instead, the body prefers to have a small amount of ATP stored, use it, and reformulate it, use it, and reformulate it, so there is a constant cycle of keeping just enough ATP in the system. Otherwise if one had to store enough ATP to last for an entire day, body weight would increase dramatically. It takes about 90 seconds to replenish ATP.

The secondary energy reservoir is **creatine phosphate**. The body stores 320g-600g of creatine phosphate and provides energy for maximal output for up to 10 seconds, depending on exercise intensity and the individual's CP stores.

The recycling of ATP with the help of creatine phosphate is the simplest and hence quickest way since it only requires one enzyme, creatine kinase, to facilitate the reaction. Basically, creatine phosphate is hydrolyzed (H2O) with the help of the enzyme creatine kinase and thereby provides the energy to form ADP and inorganic phosphate. In other words, the energy derived from the breakdown of creatine and the phosphate molecule will drive the inorganic phosphate into the sarcoplasmic solution, where it attaches to ADP with the help of the enzyme ATP synthase, thereby forming ATP. So, the exergonic reaction, hydrolysis of creatine phosphate, provides the energy so that the endergonic reaction, the synthesis of ATP, can occur and the enzyme ATP synthase facilitates that ATP formation process. Now, once energy is required to perform work, ATP will be broken down via hydrolysis (H2O) with the help of the enzyme ATPase, and ADP remains left over in the sarcoplasm and the rephosphorylation process (breaking down creatine phosphate) repeats itself.

ATP PRODUCTION CYCLE VIA CREATINE PHOSPHATE

CP + H2O ---- creatine kinase---> ADP + inorganic phosphate + energy ------ATP synthase----> ATP + H2O ----ATPase---->ADP + Pi + energy

1. Hydrolysis of CP via creatine kinase, which provides energy for condensation of ATP and a phosphate molecule
2. Condensation of ADP & phosphate forms ATP; ADP picks up the phosphate molecule and synthesizes ATP via ATP synthase
3. Hydrolysis of ATP occurs to release energy for muscle contraction
4. ADP is left over and needs another phosphate molecule, which it gets from the hydrolysis of CP, to reform ATP

Creatine phosphate reproduction, called **rephosphorylation**, requires ATP and only occurs during recovery. Even though ATP replenishment only takes 90 seconds, CP takes 2-5 minutes to replenish because one has 4-6 times the amount of creatine phosphate (CP) stored than ATP. Because creatine phosphate is used to form ATP, it is helpful to take large amounts of creatine supplements to increase creatine phosphate stores, thereby improving short-term high-intensity exercises. The ATP-CP system provides energy for muscular contraction at the beginning of exercise & for short-term high-intensity bouts up to 15 seconds.

GLYCOLYSIS

Glycolysis, the "splitting of glucose", is the breakdown of glucose or glycogen into pyruvic acid in order to provide ATP, which occurs in the liver and in the sarcoplasm of muscle cells. Glycolysis is the energy system that predominantly provides energy for higher-intensity activities lasting 15-90 seconds and it provides a net gain of 2-3 molecules of ATP and lactate. The most important rate-limiting enzyme during glycolysis is **phosphofructokinase (PFK)**.

The initial steps of glycolysis are the additions of two phosphates to the glucose molecule at the expense of two molecules of ATP. The result is a 6 carbon sugar-diphosphate molecule and two low-energy ADP molecules. This 6 carbon sugar-diphosphate molecule is being split into two 3-carbon sugar-phosphate molecules. Each one of the 3-carbon sugar-phosphate molecules is converted through a series of reactions to **pyruvate** and **hydrogen**. So glycolysis produces ATP but also two byproducts: **pyruvic acid** and hydrogen ions, which basically is **lactate**.

Although hydrogen provides potential energy, the hydrogen build up becomes a problem because it causes an increase in the cell's acidity (pH levels), which prevents the cell from converting potential energy to kinetic energy and hence leads to a halt in energy conversion. Therefore, the two hydrogen transport molecules, coenzymes NAD & FAD, are important for glycolysis to continue because hydrogen ion removal must occur so that cells can continue to provide energy; NAD accepts and transports 1 hydrogen atom (H) so that glycolysis can proceed (NAD → NADH). In turn, NADH has to donate its hydrogen portion to reform NAD so that hydrogen transport/removal can continue. The reformation from NADH/FADH to NAD or FAD respectively can occur aerobically with the help of oxygen (Aerobic ATP Production) or anaerobically (Anaerobic Glycolysis) with the help of lactic acid.

In other words, the reason lactic acid formation occurs is the "recycling" or conversion of NADH to NAD anaerobically. Whether the hydrogen ions are being removed/transferred aerobically or anaerobically is exercise intensity specific. During higher intensities oxygen is not available (anaerobic glycolysis) to transport hydrogen so pyruvic acid accepts them instead thereby forming lactic acid, but during lower intensities oxygen is available (aerobic glycolysis) for hydrogen transport.

ANAEROBIC GLYCOLYSIS

During higher intensities, when oxygen is not available to accept and transport the hydrogen ions, pyruvic acid accepts the hydrogen ions to form lactic acid, which rapidly dissociates to form lactate and hydrogen, thereby reforming NADH/FADH to **NAD** or **FAD** respectively. Then lactate can either be used during anaerobic metabolism by the liver to produce glucose via gluconeogenesis, where new glucose is being synthesized, released into the blood stream, transported to muscle tissue, and used by muscle cells as energy or lactate can be used by slow skeletal muscle cells or the heart during aerobic metabolism to form ATP, where lactate is being removed from the blood and converted into pyruvate, which is transformed into acetyl CoA, which can enter the Krebs cycle.

In other words, NAD/FAD reformation and hence hydrogen removal/transport can occur anaerobically or aerobically depending on whether pyruvic acid accepts hydrogen to form lactic acid/lactate, thereby providing energy anaerobically, or whether pyruvic acid is broken down to form acetyl CoA, which enters the Krebs cycle to provide energy aerobically. Lactate can be used to provide immediate energy for muscle cells during aerobic metabolism by transforming lactate to pyruvate to acetyl Co A, which can enter the Krebs cycle, or lactate can be used during anaerobic metabolism to synthesize glucose/glycogen in the liver, which then can be used again my muscle cells for energy. The process by which lactate is being transported to the liver and converted into glucose/glycogen is called the **Cori Cycle**.

AEROBIC ATP PRODUCTION

Aerobic ATP production, which occurs predominantly during prolonged low-moderate intensity exercise, is the oxidation (breakdown) of glucose/glycogen (called glycolysis), lipids (triglycerides; called lipolysis), and proteins (amino acids; called proteolysis) into acetyl CoA, which enters the **Krebs Cycle**, where hydrogen removal occurs and the **electron transport chain** inside the mitochondria of the muscle cell provides the energy for aerobic ATP production. Aerobic ATP production predominantly provides energy for low-medium intensity activities lasting 120 seconds +; it provides a net gain of 32 molecules of ATP and water.

AEROBIC GLYCOLYSIS

For example, during **aerobic glycolysis** (carbohydrate breakdown), when oxygen is available to accept and transport hydrogen ions, pyruvic acid in the sarcoplasm is broken down to acetyl CoA, which enters the Krebs Cycle, and the formation of NAD & FAD occurs. **The Krebs cycle** is called after Sir Hans Adolf Krebs, a German-born British physician and biochemist; its primary purpose is the oxidation (removal of hydrogen) of carbohydrates, lipids, and proteins using coenzymes NAD & FAD as hydrogen (potential energy) carriers. In the Krebs cycle NAD & FAD accept the hydrogen and transport hydrogen in its reduced form (NADH & FADH) to the electron transport chain in the mitochondria of the cell, where NADH & FADH donate the hydrogen (which reforms NADH/FADH to NAD/FAD) thereby providing energy through the breakdown of the hydrogen bonds (oxidation) to combine ADP + Pi to form ATP, before the hydrogen is then picked up by oxygen to form water - (H2O).

This process of aerobic ATP production via the Krebs cycle and electron transport chain is called oxidative phosphorylation.

LIPOLYSIS

During lipolysis triglycerides are broken down into fatty acids and glycerol. The fatty acids can be further converted into acetyl CoA via a series of reactions, called **beta oxidation**, and acetyl CoA can enter the Krebs cycle. The glycerol portion of lipolysis is not a direct form of energy because glycerol cannot effectively be converted by skeletal muscle cells but the liver uses the glycerol to synthesize glucose, which of course yields energy. During beta oxidation in the mitochondria fatty acids are oxidized (broken down) thereby forming acetyl CoA, which can enter the Krebs Cycle. The enzymes that control lipolysis are called **lipases**.

PROTEOLYSIS

During proteolysis, proteins are broken down into amino acids. What happens after that depends on the particular amino acid; it can be converted into glucose, pyruvic acid, acetyl CoA, or other Krebs cycle intermediaries.

EFFICIENCY OF OXIDATIVE PHOSPHORYLATION

The aerobic energy system only has a 34% efficiency rate in converting energy from foods into biologically usable energy; 66% are wasted in the form of heat. This can be calculated by comparing how much potential energy 1 mole (1g of molecular weight) of glucose yields during aerobic metabolism (respiration) with how much potential energy 1 mole of glucose yields when properly oxidized.

Now, during aerobic metabolism one glucose molecule yields a net gain of 32 ATP molecules and one ATP molecule contains 7.3kcal of potential energy. Therefore, the total potential energy of 1 mole of glucose converted during aerobic metabolism (respiration) is 233.6kcal (32 ATP x 7.3kcal/ATP = 233.6kcal). On the other hand, when 1 mole of glucose is properly oxidized it yields 688kcal of potential energy (see calculation below).

Glucose Oxidation:	**When a glucose molecule ($C_6H_{12}O_6$) is broken down through proper oxidative means then it will yield 6 CO_2, 6 H_2O, and -688kcal/mol.**	
Simplified reaction:	$C_6H_{12}O_6$ (aq) + 6 O_2 (g) → 6 CO_2 (g) + 6 H_2O (l)	
	ΔG = - 2880 kJ per mole of $C_6H_{12}O_6$	/ 4.184 to get kcal
	ΔG = - 688 kcal per mole of $C_6H_{12}O_6$	

Therefore, the efficiency ratio of aerobic metabolism (respiration) can be calculated by taking the total of 233.6kcal of potential energy from oxidative phosphorylation (aerobic metabolism) and divide that by 688kcal of potential energy from proper glucose oxidation.

This means that only ~34% of the potential energy from proper glucose oxidation can be transferred into biologically usable energy via oxidative rephosphorylation (aerobic metabolism), which means the aerobic energy system can provide a maximum of 32 ATP (688kcal / 7.3kcal/ATP = 94 ATP; 94 ATP x 0.34 = 31.96 ATP) which then can be used for mechanical activity (66% is lost as heat). This describes the loss of energy due to the energy transferring process, which refers to the 2nd law of thermodynamics.

Efficiency Ratio of Aerobic Metabolism	=	(Potential Energy from Aerobic Metabolism / Potential Energy of Glucose) x 100
	=	(233.6kcal/mole of glucose / 688kcal/mole of glucose) x 100
	=	0.339 x 100
	=	33.9%

WHY JOGGING IS A WASTE OF TIME FOR TENNIS CONDITIONING

Many tennis coaches require their players to include jogging into their regular training program in order to maintain or enhance endurance capabilities but from a conditioning standpoint continuous steady-state jogging is inefficient and hence a waste of time. There are more effective training components, such as interval training, that allow the athlete to improve additional performance parameters besides improving aerobic energy system efficiency (endurance capabilities).

More specifically, instead of (for example) 60 minutes steady state jogging, tennis players should engage in interval training of approximately 45 minutes, where each interval consists of 7 – 8 minutes of interval work, where the athlete sprints 10 sec & lightly jogs 25 – 30 sec. Once the interval work is accomplished, the athlete gets a 90 second break.

ENERGY SYSTEM CONTRIBUTION DURING COMPETITION

With regards to energy system dynamics, a tennis player requires contributions from all three energy systems (ATP-CP, Anaerobic Glycolysis, Oxidative Rephosphorylation) during a match but the anaerobic energy systems (ATP-CP, Anaerobic Glycolysis) predominate and hence improving their capabilities should be emphasized during training.

Jogging is inefficient because it requires a lot of time and targets the "wrong" energy system; it mainly enhances the aerobic energy system (Oxidative Rephosphorylation) and slow twitch muscle fiber recruitment but neglects the anaerobic energy systems and fast twitch muscle fiber recruitment. So, why would one send the athletes jogging for hours each week if that time could be used much more beneficial?

INTERVAL TRAINING

Interval training, which is characterized by alternating low – and high exercise intensities over a prolonged period of time enhances the efficiency of bioenergetic processes (energy transfer) for aerobic and anaerobic energy pathways; it mirrors and optimizes the metabolic demands (energy system dynamics) experienced during a tennis match and hence is a much more sport-specific form of training.

Now, depending on age, gender, level of play, and court surface, work-to-rest ratios during a tennis match vary. According to the ITF rule book, during professional play there are rest intervals of 20 seconds between points, 90 seconds during change-overs, and 120 seconds between sets.

WORK-TO-REST RATIOS

Let's assume that, on average, a point lasts 10-15 seconds and 7 points are being played per game. That means that a game lasts (7x20sec = 140 sec rest; 7x10sec = 70sec of work // 7x15sec = 105sec of work => 140sec + 70sec = 210sec // 140sec + 105sec = 245sec => 210sec to 245sec = 3min 20sec — 4min 5sec) approximately 3 ½ – 4 minutes, of which 1 – 1 ½ min are of high intensity work and 2 ½ minutes of low intensity (rest) activity. Therefore, on average, the work-to-rest intervals during a tennis match are 1:2 ½ to 1:3, which means 10 seconds of high intensity activity follow 25 – 30 seconds of lower intensity activity, which means that during interval training the athlete sprints for 10 seconds and lightly jogs for 25 – 30 seconds.

Now, each game lasts approximately 3 ½ – 4 minutes and 2 games are played before there is another 90 second rest interval due to change-over. Therefore, we have 7 – 8 minutes of interval work before the athlete gets a 90 second break, which means that the athlete alternates 10 sec sprinting & 25 – 30 sec light jogging for 7 – 8 minutes before getting 90 seconds to recover. Therefore, if each interval includes the duration of 2 games and 10 games are played per set, then 5 intervals will represent a set, which means that an interval training session of 5 intervals will last 41 – 46 minutes (7 min x 5 = 35 min; 8 min x 5 = 40 min // 4×90 sec = 360 sec = 6 min of recovery).

CHAPTER 4:

"Performance Testing for Athletes: Fitness Assessment"

Many tennis players do not understand the advantages of stretching before and after training or competition and therefore regard it as nuisance - but flexibility has a direct and significant impact on tennis performance. However, before an athlete begins to engage in flexibility enhancement training, it would be prudent to understand the athlete's specific needs and limitations. First, the importance of assessing overall fitness with regards to improving performance will be addressed. After that, various body composition analysis techniques will be introduced. Thirdly, tests will be introduced that can be used to identify common flexibility deficiencies seen among tennis players. Note that Chapter 5 ("Performance Preparation") will present exercises that practitioners can use to correct inhibiting flexibility factors. Finally, tests applicable to specific variables affecting performance on the court such as power, speed, endurance, dynamic stability, and overall agility will be examined.

THE IMPORTANCE OF FITNESS ASSESSMENT

Identifying flexibility deficiencies is one of the key components of a fitness assessment because it can affect multiple parameters of performance. A coach should always work on issues that cause limitation during different activities. For example, stride length impacts running economy (how efficiently the athlete moves on the court) hence affecting the amount of energy needed to move on the court. This becomes more evident during endurance events such as marathons. According to specific research, marathon runners were able to improve their times by 8% just by changing movement mechanics (they are not wasting energy for work that is undesirable). Let's say the athlete requires 4 hours (240 minutes) to finish a marathon. By improving movement mechanics (i.e. flexibility, and hence running economy) one could improve running time by almost 20 minutes (240 min x 0.08 = 19.2 min)!

Assessment of athletic performance should be a significant consideration because it can help a coach develop a "Needs Analysis", which will dictate training priorities. As a dedicated tennis player, optimal time management becomes essential as one must practice on court, train in the gym, perform agility drills, do sprint work, work on improving endurance, get physical therapy (e.g. massage), and have enough time to eat and sleep to produce superior results during competitive matches (not to mention other primary aspects of a balanced life). Therefore, assessment of athletic performance helps to train and prepare efficiently and effectively.

For example, if the athlete has great power capabilities but lacks endurance, the focus should be on improving endurance while maintaining power capabilities. Maintaining capabilities doesn't require as much time as improving them; maintenance can be attained with lower weekly volume but higher training intensities.

Tests for flexibility, body composition and performance create the **baseline data** that is necessary for tracking and determining realistic goals and determining training variables. As a basic example, if a coach implements the **Shoulder Mobility Test** it may turn out that the shoulder responsible for the service motion has poor flexibility. Poor shoulder flexibility, among other factors, negatively impacts service speed and increases the risk of injury. If one of the athlete's goals is to have a more powerful serve, the coach could implement the recommended exercises **(see Shoulder Mobility on page 82)** regularly after each practice/match to improve flexibility. Reassessment every 4-6 weeks will allow the coach to determine how much shoulder flexibility has improved from the protocol.

Body composition analysis allows the coach and player to track changes in body tissue that can result in weight gain and loss. Tracking changes in body composition has implications with regards to overall training volume and intensity as well as nutrition. For example, losing body weight during training or competition must be avoided as it is associated with injuries due to overtraining, nutrient deficiencies and an ultimate decline in performance. The optimal time to lose weight (if necessary) is during the offseason.

TESTING CONSIDERATIONS

Before one can start with performance testing, one must make sure to perform the exercise correctly, which means previous practice of the exercise is warranted before implementing the test. In other words, it does not make sense to test if the tester isn't competent or the athlete is not proficient in the exercise utilized.

In order for a test to provide valid or even reliable results the coach must strictly adhere to test protocol **(see Test Logistics & Sequence on page 65)**. There are a number of things the coach can do to improve the validity/reliability of test results - being well prepared is most of the challenge. Since all athletes need to be familiar with all test exercises, it is prudent to have a practice session or 'test run' prior to the real test day. This also helps the coach (and other testers) to get used to the format and testing dynamics (e.g. time management).

If the test is not conducted properly and in an orderly fashion and/or the results are not recorded accurately, the test is invalid.

For example, if during the implementation of the Push-Up Test **(see Push Up Test on page 98)** the incorrect technique is used (e.g. athlete fails to go through a full range of motion with each repetition), the test data is invalid. Without strict adherence to protocol a coach cannot truly compare the athlete's performance to normative data (which is developed from specific implementation).

It is also important that the coaches and participants are psychologically and physiologically prepared. **Psychological preparedness** refers to the motivation of the person to be tested. If the test participant is not motivated to perform the test, it will be nearly impossible to optimize test outcomes. Providing for a competitive environment, pitting athletes of relative capabilities against one another, and informing the athletes about the benefits of the tests can enhance motivation. **Physiological preparation** is best achieved for most assessments by implementing a specific dynamic warm-up which serves to prepare the nervous system for high-intensity efforts, enhance test-specific muscle fiber recruitment and improve transient flexibility of the muscle tissue to be used so there is less resistance to each movement pattern employed. In other words, the coach must implement a warm-up program that will potentially maximize performance. Performing static stretches before engaging in a power or strength test is not recommended as static stretches have been shown to produce transient relaxation within the muscle tissue, which decreases its ability to produce maximal force and generate power.

With respect to body composition analysis, it is important to note that psychological factors must also be considered, especially with deconditioned or young female athletes.

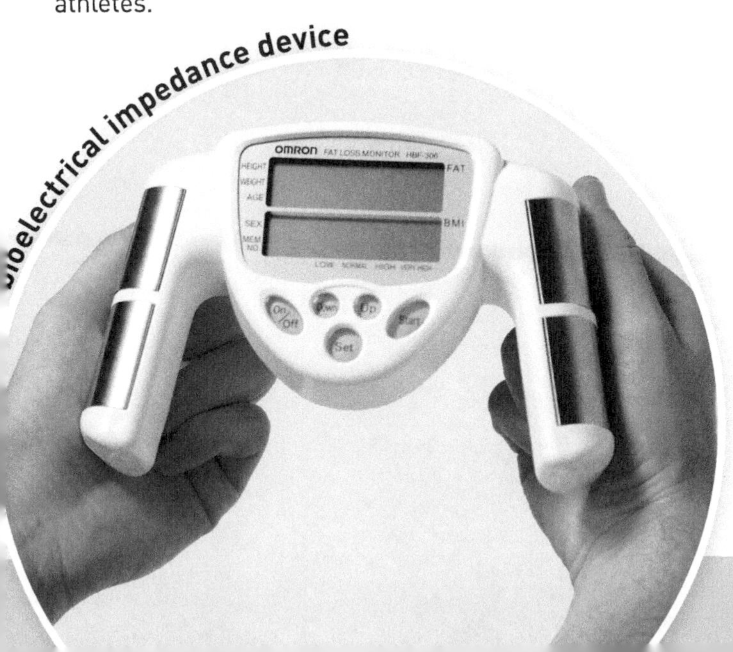

UNDER THE MICROSCOPE

TESTING CONSIDERATIONS

- Perform body composition analysis first; do flexibility before performance tests
- Ensure Proficiency: Practice the performance test exercises before you test
- Control physiological test variables
  - Illness
  - Hydration
  - Fatigue
  - Dynamic Warm-Up
- Optimize psychological test variables
  - Motivation
- Replicate test every time
- Consistency of environmental factors
  - Court surface
  - Temperature/humidity
  - Safe environment (e.g. enough room)
  - Use precise distance & time measurements
- Follow same test sequence
- Perform 2-3 tests per session
- Re-Test every 2-3 month

Many people are self-conscious about their body image and are not comfortable showing skin, which is a necessity during girth/circumference and skinfold measurements. If the athlete is out of shape and/or uneasy about using any of the aforementioned measurement techniques, a **bioelectrical impedance** device can be used instead. It would be prudent to attempt to educate the athlete about the reason for the assessment and how it relates to his/her overall health and performance – and assure them that their values are confidential and will only be used for their benefit. Developing rapport and educating the athlete can oftentimes go a long way.

For a detailed summary of testing considerations take a look at "Under the Microscope: Testing Considerations".

BODY COMPOSITION ANALYSIS

Body composition assessment is better gauge than simply measuring someone's body weight. Body composition tests (BCT) are subjective, whereas body weight measurements are objective. "Subjective" means that BCTs are athlete-specific, which means that they give a detailed evaluation of whether the athlete is in shape or not, whereas simply looking at body weight does not (very fit person vs. unfit individual). Furthermore, circumference measurements, which are part of the BCT, will reveal specifically where the body stores fat.

In other words, BCTs can show the individual's specific location of lean mass and fat mass; body weight does not. More specifically, the data collected by BCTs can be used to evaluate overall and regional body fat and this will affect training priorities and dietary recommendations. For example, if the athlete is determined to be overweight, the training focus could be shifted towards endurance and the dietary program adjusted accordingly.

Gender can also play a role in setting training priorities. For example, in the case of female athletes, who generally store fat below hip level, storing fat at the thighs may not necessarily be a bad thing with respect to balance properties because the center of mass/gravity is lower; they are "bottom-heavy".

If one looks at male athletes, they might be rather "top-heavy" since they tend to store body fat above hip level. Therefore, if one trains an overweight male athlete, training priorities might shift to losing weight first to enhance balance properties, whereas training priorities for a female athlete might be different.

There are numerous methods, clinical assessments and field tests that have been developed to evaluate body fat percentage. Clinical assessments are conducted in a lab setting, where test variables can be controlled and high-precision instruments are used. Clinical assessments include hydrostatic weighing ({under}water displacement method), air displacement plethysmography (air displacement method), and dual X-ray absorptiometry. Hydrostatic weighing sets the standard for calculating body fat percentage due to its accuracy, cost, time, and the technical expertise needed. During hydrostatic weighing the difference between the weight of the individual on land and the eventual underwater weight is used to calculate body volume.

On the other hand, field tests are more practical because they are easier to implement, use less expensive equipment and also yield accurate results. Field tests include girth/circumference measurements, waist-to-hip ratios, skinfold measurements, bioelectrical impedance, and near infrared light interactance. Because of its reliability, practicality and convenience we will introduce girth/circumference measurements, skinfold measurements, and bioelectrical impedance body fat assessment methods in more detail later on.

FLEXIBILITY TESTING

All of the flexibility tests can be performed either on the tennis court or in the gym, whichever is most convenient for the coach. There are two reasons why testing flexibility is essential. First, poor flexibility can be a major limiting factor upon performance as it can have a negative effect on all aspects of training such as speed, power, agility, and balance (more detailed information about flexibility is provided in chapter 5 – Performance Preparation **(see Chapter 5: Performance Preparation on page 111)**. Secondly, and most importantly, poor flexibility can be the cause of injuries. Identifying areas of poor flexibility can prevent downtime due to recurring injuries during an athlete's career and it can affect the quality of life later on. For more information take a look at "**Under the Microscope: Osteoarthritis**".

UNDER THE MICROSCOPE

OSTEOARTHRITIS

Many former professional athletes suffer from osteoarthritis, which is the degeneration of hyaline cartilage (e.g. knee joint); more specifically, the breakage and loss of cartilage, which causes severe joint pain. Since joint health is related to compression within the joint as well as proper biomechanics, the use of weight-bearing activities that improve joint alignment while properly modulating the pull of muscle and connective tissues on a given joint is essential. If alignment is compromised, any repetitive motions seen in the sport of tennis can cause friction and erosion of the cartilage will occur, which can cause pain and negatively affects mobility and function. If the joint is balanced and loaded properly, integrity of the joint capsule itself will be enhanced along with all associated musculature and connective structures.

In conclusion, flexibility testing is essential as it can help identify specific musculoskeletal limitations, which can then be targeted via stretching techniques to improve joint alignment and overall joint health.

Specific flexibility tests are provided in this chapter. Each test provides recommended exercises that can be used to address limitations in the various joints being tested. As is usual during testing, preparation is crucial to achieving optimal results and saving time. The use of **still photography** is recommended because it helps to compare progress in joint flexibility over time.

PERFORMANCE TESTING

All performance tests are performed on the tennis court. To ensure test reliability it is imperative to maintain the same test environment each and every time the tests are performed. If one initially tests on a red clay court, testing should continue on that surface, preferably on that same court. Re-testing at the same or similar temperature and humidity also improves the ability to clearly see progressions during re-tests. This can be challenging when the athlete is traveling to tournaments in different countries or lives on different continents during the year.

UNDER THE MICROSCOPE

PRE-PERFORMANCE TESTING CHECKLIST

- No illness
- Do proper warm-up
- Be well hydrated
- Ensure optimal glycogen stores
- Get 8-10 hours of sleep the night before
- Have equipment tested & ready to use
- Create safe testing environment

PRE-TESTING

Prior to performance testing make sure that the athlete is physiologically prepared. This means that the athlete is healthy (no illness or severe fatigue, jetlag), has engaged in a proper warm-up, is well hydrated, adheres to proper nutrition 2-3 hours before testing and gets enough sleep (8-10 hours) the night before. Also, ensure that all the equipment is calibrated (e.g. scale), tested (batteries ok?) and accounted for. Conducting the test in a safe environment is also crucial. Make sure there are no tennis balls lying around, there is adequate visibility, and there is enough space to decelerate.

During test setup, precisely measure and use the exact distances needed for the test and record performance immediately; have pre-formatted documentation sheets ready for each test. Everything needs to be implemented in the same manner each time the athlete is tested and the same pre-test factors should be considered (e.g. same pre-test warm up routine).

TEST LOGISTICS & SEQUENCE

Ideally one wants to have a one-on-one situation during testing; meaning one athlete is being tested by one tester/coach. When there is a group of athletes being tested, some of the more experienced athletes can assist in managing test protocols during the test. Line administration is recommended, which will involve the use of test stations. Make sure to clearly define the scoring system for each test to all testers so that they are on the same page and group the athletes by capabilities or competitiveness.

Due to time constraints (e.g. test setup, rest intervals) it is recommended that three (3) tests per day be performed unless the coach desires to designate an entire "test day". In that case one can use the combine format, where you perform five (5) tests in the morning and five (5) tests in the afternoon.

If one chooses to test one day at a time, the testing order is as follows:

Day 1
• MB Serve Throw • H-Drill • Bilateral Lunge
Day 2
• MB Twist Throw • 25 Yard Sprint • Step Up
Day 3
• Ball-Drop & React • T-Drill • Push-Up • Stability Pad Squat

If one uses the combine format on a designated test day, the test order is:

Morning
• Ball-Drop & React • H-Drill • Step-Up • MB Twist Throw • Bilateral Lunge
Afternoon
• 25 Yard Sprint • Push-Up • MB Serve Throw • Stability Pad Squat • T-Drill

USE OF TEST DATA & RE-TESTING

Once the coach has implemented all the desired flexibility and performance tests, useful baseline data has been attained. Depending on the athlete's deficiencies in the flexibility tests, the coach may want to incorporate the recommended exercises (see test protocols) into the **dynamic and static stretch routines**, which are performed regularly before (dynamic) and after (static) each training, match, or workout.

These same principles hold true for the performance test results as well. The athlete should incorporate all performance drills into the **conditioning program** and regularly perform the recommended exercises to improve respective performance deficiencies.

After a short training cycle retesting is warranted to establish whether the designed program led to performance improvements. It is recommended to assess key components at least every 3-4 weeks of training.

BODY COMPOSITION ANALYSIS

Body composition analysis is part of the physical fitness assessment; it estimates how much fat tissue and non-fat (lean muscle) tissue the body contains. In other words, body composition is the relationship between fat-free mass and fat mass. This relationship is more significant than merely measuring total body weight. For example, if two individuals are the same age and each is 6'3 tall and weighs 250lbs but one of them, person A, never did any activity and the other, person B, is a professional football player (playing wide receiver), person A will be out of shape and person B will be extremely fit despite both weighing 250lbs. When both participate in the body composition analysis they find out that person A has 23% body fat and person B just 8%. In other words, person A carries 57.5 lb (250 lb x 0.23 = 57.5 lb) of fat around but person B only 20 lb (250 lb x 0.08 = 20 lb) fat! As it relates to sport performance one must realize that fat mass is essentially "dead weight". It cannot produce force so extra fat mass has the potential to diminish all endeavors that demand translocation of the body such as running or jumping.

The minimum amount of body fat needed to maintain bodily functions, called essential body fat levels, is 3%-5.9% for males and 11%–14.9% for females. Generally, if essential body fat falls below these minimums levels, important physiological activities (metabolism) will be compromised, which will negatively affect performance. Some athletes may be able to function on low essential body fat levels due to a genetic predisposition.

Athletes usually have body fat levels of 6%-11.9% for male athletes and 15%-21.9% for female athletes. One must realize however that an "athletic" body fat percentage is a value that reflects a quantity that is optimal for a given sport. "Athletic" body fat may vary among different athletes (shot putter vs sprinter).

Normal body fat levels for males are 12%-20.9% and 22%-30.9% for females. To be considered over-weight, body fat levels must be 21%-24.9% for males and 31%-37.9% for females; ≥25% more for males and ≥38% more for females is considered obese! Therefore, looking back at the previous example, person A would be considered over-weight (23%), whereas person B would be considered an "athlete". Most male tennis players, on average, will have 14%-17% body fat whereas females will have 21%-25%. For specific percent body fat ranges applicable for adults and children (age 6 – 17) take a closer look at the following tables.

Category	**% Body Fat**	
Adults	Male	Female
Essential	3 – 5.9	11 - 14.9
Pro Athlete	6 - 11.9	15 – 19.9
Fit	12 - 15.9	20 - 23.9
Normal	16 - 20.9	24 - 30.9
Over-weight	21 - 24.9	31 - 37.9
Obese	≥25	≥38

Category	**% Body Fat**	
Children (6-17)	Boys	Girls
Essential	3 - 6	11 - 14.9
Very Lean	6.1 - 10	15 – 19.9
Optimal	10.1 - 15.9	20 - 24.9
Normal	16 - 23.9	25 - 29.9
Over-weight	24 - 30.9	30 - 34.9
Obese	≥31	≥35

BODY COMPOSITION: FIELD TESTS

As previously mentioned, there are numerous tests that estimate body composition. Due to practicality, convenience, cost and reliability, using circumference (girth) measurement, the skinfold method and the bioelectrical impedance method is recommended. Be advised that the standard method used in research settings is hydrostatic weighing due to its accuracy on the one hand and the cost, time and technical expertise needed on the other. The **standard error of the estimate** (SEE) reveals the amount the respective field test results deviate from the hydrostatic weighing method.

CIRCUMFERENCE MEASUREMENTS

Circumference measurements are the easiest to administer since no equipment is needed except for a simple measuring tape. The measurements aim is to estimate body fat at particular body sites; this means that they can also be used as a motivational tool especially during attempted weight loss. As the athletes work hard during training you can track their body fat changes and reveal their "positive" results and this serve to increase their motivation as well. It should be noted that the error of estimation may increase with very muscular individuals as additional lean mass can be mis-interpreted as being fat.

SKINFOLD MEASUREMENTS

Skinfold measurement is the most popular method to estimate body fat (or body density). The skinfold method uses a **caliper** to estimate the fat layer between skin and muscle, called **subcutaneous fat** (fat below the skin). Generally, these calipers range from $20 - $300 and choosing a caliper usually depends on personal preference and budget; it is recommended that the LANGE & HARPENDEN calipers be used because of their precision and reliability. When using the skinfold method several things need to be done correctly:

1. Locating skinfold site and mark with a pen
2. Pinching the skinfold away from underlying tissue
3. Measuring with the caliper
4. Choosing the proper equation

Caliper

4.01 CIRCUMFERENCE MEASUREMENT

SUMMARY

Circumference measurements are a quick and easy way to calculate the body fat at particular sites because the measurements are a good indication of the amount of body fat a person has.

PURPOSE

Estimation of body proportions as they relate to fat distribution

STANDARD ERROR OF THE ESTIMATE

± 2.5% - 4%

The "gold" standard in measuring body density (body fat) is hydrostatic weighing (clinical setting) and the standard error of the estimate reveals the amount the test results deviate from the hydrostatic weighing method.

EQUIPMENT

Tape Measure

RELEVANCE

- Estimation of body composition is **area specific**; provides information about regional fat storage
- Can have positive affect on athlete's motivation when they see quantifiable differences between tests even if body weight is unchanged
- Excess body fat limits athletic performance on the court (e.g. agility)
- Limited body fat increases likelihood of injuries due to inadequate shock-absorbing capabilities, inefficient thermoregulation, and impaired metabolism

DESCRIPTION

The athlete to be tested:

1. Stands erect, with feet together, and remains relaxed
2. Exhales

Tester takes respective measurements before athlete inhales.

Test Score Table: Circumference Measurements

Testing Site	Adults		Children	
	Men	Women	Boys	Girls
1. Waist				
2. Abdomen				
3. Hips				
4. Thigh				
5. Neck				

ID: 401

CIRCUMFERENCE MEASUREMENT

Testing Sites	Description
Neck	Measure maximum circumference directly below the **larynx** (or Adam's apple), or midpoint of the neck
Waist	Measure circumference at the narrowest part of the torso between the **ziphoid process** (nipple level) and the **umbilicus** (belly button)
Abdomen	Measure circumference at the level of the **umbilicus** (belly button)
Hips	Measure maximum circumference of the **buttocks** above the **gluteal fold**
Thigh	Measure maximum circumference of the **right thigh** below the **gluteal fold**

Waist

Abdomen

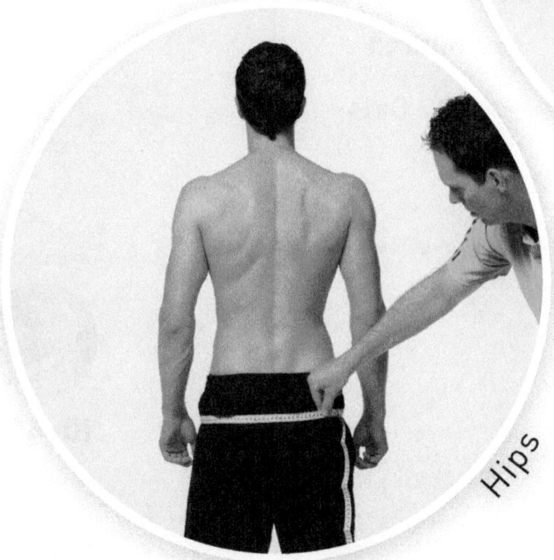

Hips

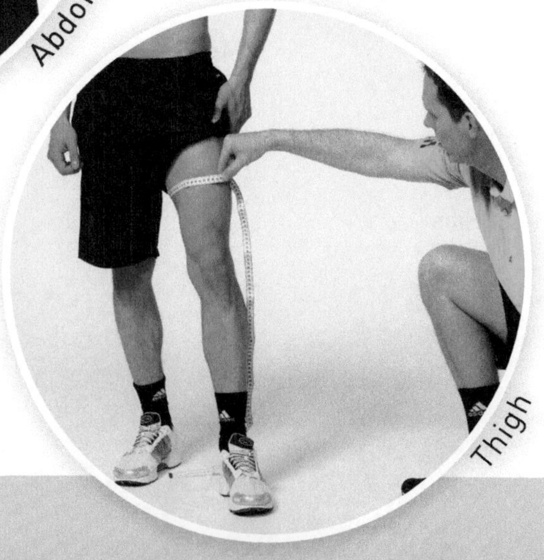

Thigh

4.02 SKINFOLD MEASUREMENTS

SUMMARY

Skinfold measurements calculate total body fat storage based on subcutaneous (fat layer between skin and muscle) body fat at particular sites throughout the body.

PURPOSE

Estimation of subcutaneous fat mass

STANDARD ERROR OF THE ESTIMATE

Approximately ± 3.5%

An error in estimation usually occurs due to testing errors by the tester. Testing errors can occur because of:

a. Inexperience of tester
b. Variations in tissue composition/skin compression
c. Erroneous site identification
d. Too much fat mass at a particular site

The "gold" standard in measuring body density (body fat) is hydrostatic weighing (clinical setting) and the standard error of the estimate shows by how much the test results deviate from the hydrostatic weighing method.

EQUIPMENT

Pen, Caliper

RELEVANCE

- Estimation of body composition is **age**, **gender**, **area specific**; provides information about regional fat storage
- Can have positive effects on athlete's motivation when they see quantifiable differences between tests even if body weight is unchanged
- Excess body fat limits athletic performance on the court (e.g. agility)
- Limited body fat increases likelihood of injuries due to inadequate shock-absorbing capabilities, inefficient thermoregulation, and impaired metabolism

DESCRIPTION

The athlete to be tested:

1. Stands erect, with feet together, and remains relaxed
2. Exhales

Tester takes respective measurements before athlete inhales.

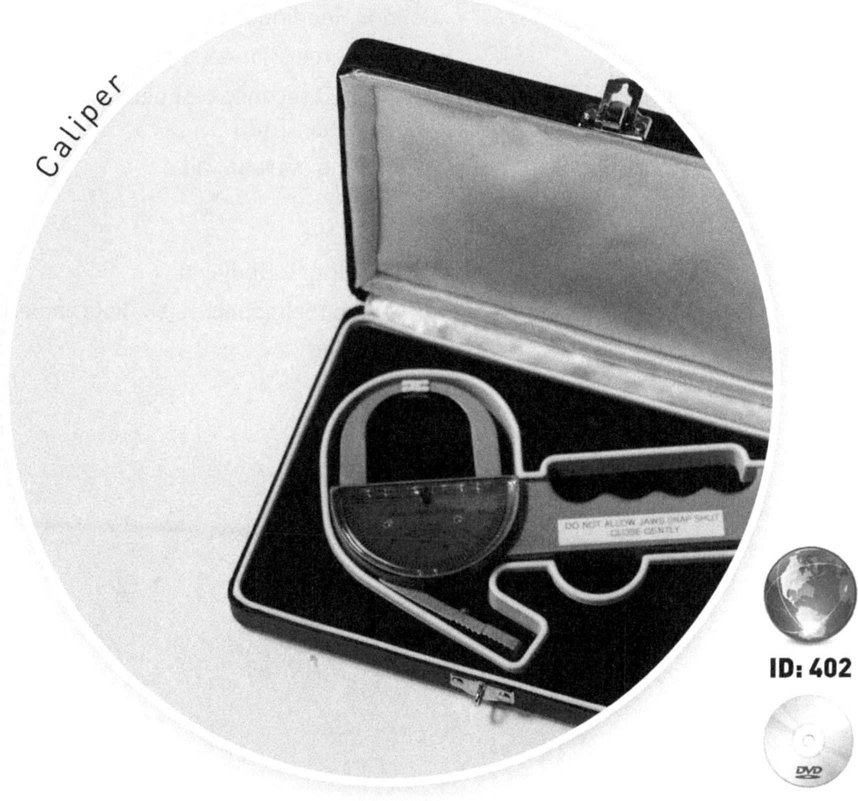
Caliper

ID: 402

Skinfold Guideline	
Pre-Test Checklist:	• Ensure testee has dry skin; slippery skin causes test errors • Calibrate caliper to 10g/mm² • Have a pen ready for marking test sites; ensures proper test results for subsequent measures • Testee cannot exercise prior to testing; skinfold measurement immediately following exercise can lead to inaccurate results due to fluid volume shifts
Test Checklist:	• Take measurements from the right side of the testee • Identify population and gender-specific sites • Use pen and mark appropriate fold locations for reliable subsequent measurements
	Hand Placement • Tester holds skinfold caliper in the right hand; index finger is on the trigger. Tester slightly turns caliper to ease reading of values • Tester uses thumb and index finger of left hand (thumb point towards the ground) to push into fat mass until underlying muscle can be felt • Firmly grasps skinfold and pull away from muscle tissue; skinfold should have parallel sites • Pull caliper trigger, place caliper arms perpendicular (90°) to the fold about ½ inch below the fingers in the center of the fold and release • Maintain pressure on the skinfold, release caliper trigger, and assess measurement within 2 seconds; maintain pressure of the hold until measurement has been assessed • Record the value
	Caliper Readings • Take three (3) measurements per site • Allow 20 seconds rest between measurements; subsequent values must not deviate by more than 2mm • Take the average value
	Calculating % Body Fat • Add up the respective skinfold values and apply them to the gender and population specific formula

Skinfold Measurement Sites: Adults (Recreational Players)			
Men (Age 18-61)	**Women (Age 18-55)**	**Fold Orientation**	**Fold Location**
1. Triceps	1.Triceps	Vertical	Take distance between acromion process (shoulder) and olecranon process (elbow); site is on rear midline of upper arm (triceps)
2. Chest	2.Chest	Diagonal	Measure distance between nipple and anterior axillary (arm pit); site is in the center
3. Subscapular	3.Subscapular	Diagonal	Below the inferior angle of the scapulae; taken at a 45° angle away from the spine

Midaxillary

Suprailiac

Abdomen

Thigh

Skinfold Measurement Sites: Adults (Recreational Players)			
Men (Age 18-61)	**Women (Age 18-55)**	**Fold Orientation**	**Fold Location**
4. Midaxillary	4. Midaxillary	Vertical	Find midaxillary line (vertical) and xiphoid process (horizontal) of sternum (just below nipple level); site is at intersection
5. Abdomen	5. Abdomen	Vertical	2 cm (3/4 inch) to the right of umbilicus (belly button)
6. Suprailiac	6. Suprailiac	Diagonal	Site is in line with the natural angle of the iliac crest at the anterior axillary line, superior to the iliac crest
7. Thigh	7. Thigh	Vertical	Site is in the midline of the quadriceps between inguinal crest (hip) and the superior aspect of the patella (kneecap).

7 Site Skinfold Calculation: Adults (Recreational Players)		
Formula:	(1st Value + 2nd Value + 3rd Value)/3= Average Value (mm)	
1. Triceps	(____ mm + ____ mm + ____ mm) = ____ mm / 3	= ________ mm
2. Chest	(____ mm + ____ mm + ____ mm) = ____ mm / 3	= ________ mm
3. Subscapular	(____ mm + ____ mm + ____ mm) = ____ mm / 3	= ________ mm
4. Midaxillary	(____ mm + ____ mm + ____ mm) = ____ mm / 3	= ________ mm
5. Abdomen	(____ mm + ____ mm + ____ mm) = ____ mm / 3	= ________ mm
6. Suprailiac	(____ mm + ____ mm + ____ mm) = ____ mm / 3	= ________ mm
7. Thigh	(____ mm + ____ mm + ____ mm) = ____ mm / 3	= ________ mm
	Sum of Skinfold Measurements (Σ SKF):	= ________ mm
	Age of the Athlete (in years):	= ________ yrs
Body Density (Db) Formula MEN (g/cc) =	1.1120 – 0.00043499 x (Σ SKF) + 0.00000055 x (Σ SKF)² - 0.00028826 x (Age)	
Reference: Jackson & Pollock =	1.1120 – 0.00043499 x (_____) + 0.00000055 x (_____)² - 0.00028826 x (_____)	
=	__________	g/cc
Body Density (Db) Formula WOMEN (g/cc): =	1.0970 – 0.00046971 x (Σ SKF) + 0.00000056 x (Σ SKF)² - 0.00012828 x (Age)	
Reference: Jackson =	1.0970 – 0.00046971 x (_____) + 0.00000056 x (_____)² - 0.00012828 x (_____)	
=	__________	g/cc

Calculating Percent Body Fat (%BF) for Various Populations					
Population	**Gender**		**% BF Formula**		**Results**
White	%BF for Men	=	(495/Db) - 450	=	(495/____) - 450 = ______%
	%BF for Women	=	(501/Db) - 457	=	(501/____) - 457 = ______%
Black	%BF for Men	=	(437/Db) - 393	=	(437/____) - 393 = ______%
	%BF for Women	=	(485/Db) - 439	=	(485/____) - 439 = ______%
Hispanic					
	%BF for Women	=	(487/Db) - 441	=	(487/____) - 441 = ______%

3 Site Skinfold Measurement Sites: Adults (Recreational Players)			
Men (Age 18-61)	**Women (Age 18-55)**	**Fold Orientation**	**Fold Location**
	1. Triceps	Vertical	Take distance between acromion process (shoulder) olecranon process (elbow); site is on rear midline of upper arm (triceps)
1. Chest		Diagonal	Measure distance between nipple and anterior axillary (arm pit); site is in the center
2. Abdomen		Vertical	2 cm (3/4 inch) to the right of umbilicus (belly button)
	2. Suprailiac	Diagonal	Site is in line with the natural angle of the iliac crest at the anterior axillary line, superior to the iliac crest
3. Thigh	3. Thigh	Vertical	Site is in the midline of the quadriceps between inguinal crest (hip) and the superior aspect of the patella (kneecap).

3 Site Skinfold Calculation: Adults (Recreational Players)		
Formula:	(1st Value + 2nd Value + 3rd Value)/3= Average Value (mm)	
Men		
1. Chest	(____ mm + ____ mm + ____ mm) = ____ mm / 3	= ________ mm
2. Abdomen	(____ mm + ____ mm + ____ mm) = ____ mm / 3	= ________ mm
3. Thigh	(____ mm + ____ mm + ____ mm) = ____ mm / 3	= ________ mm
	Sum of Skinfold Measurements (Σ SKF):	= ________ mm
	Age of the Athlete (in years):	= ________ yrs
Women		
1. Triceps	(____ mm + ____ mm + ____ mm) = ____ mm / 3	= ________ mm
2. Suprailiac	(____ mm + ____ mm + ____ mm) = ____ mm / 3	= ________ mm
3. Thigh	(____ mm + ____ mm + ____ mm) = ____ mm / 3	= ________ mm
	Sum of Skinfold Measurements (Σ SKF):	= ________ mm
	Age of the Athlete (in years):	= ________ yrs

Body Density (Db) Formula MEN (g/cc) =	1.109380 – 0.0008267 x (Σ SKF) + 0.00000055 x (Σ SKF)² - 0.00028826 x (Age)	
Reference: Jackson & Pollock =	1.109380 – 0.0008267 x (____) + 0.00000055 x (____)² - 0.00028826 x (____)	
=	__________	g/cc
Body Density (Db) Formula WOMEN (g/cc): =	1.0994921 – 0.0009929 x (Σ SKF) + 0.00000023 x (Σ SKF)² - 0.0001392 x (Age)	
Reference: Jackson et al. =	1.0994921 – 0.0009929 x (____) + 0.00000023 x (____)² - 0.0001392 x (____)	
=	__________	g/cc

2 Site Skinfold Measurement Sites: Athletes (Age 15 – 29)

Men	Women	Fold Orientation	Fold Location
 Triceps	1. Triceps	Vertical	Take distance between acromion process (shoulder) and olecranon process (elbow); site is on rear midline of upper arm (triceps)
1. Subscapular	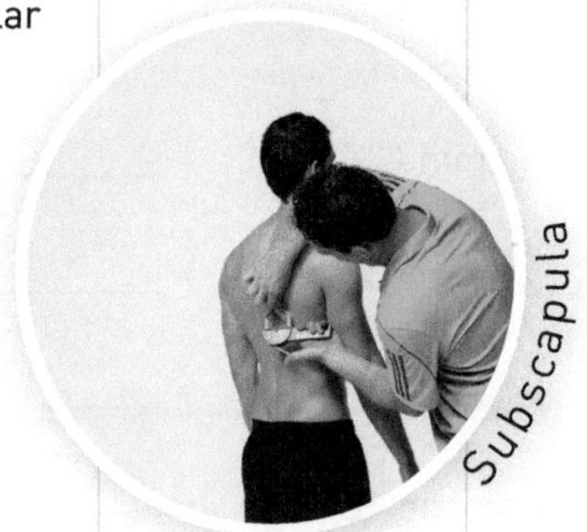 Subscapula	Diagonal	Below the inferior angle of the scapulae; taken at a 45° angle away from the spine
 Suprailiac	2. Suprailiac	Diagonal	Site is in line with the natural angle of the iliac crest at the anterior axillary line, superior to the iliac crest
2. Thigh	 Thigh	Vertical	Site is in the midline of the quadriceps between inguinal crest (hip) and the superior aspect of the patella (kneecap).

2 Site Skinfold Calculation: Athletes		
Formula:	(1st Value + 2nd Value + 3rd Value)/3= Average Value (mm)	
Men		
1. Subscapular	(____ mm + ____ mm + ____ mm) = ____ mm / 3	= ________ mm
2. Thigh	(____ mm + ____ mm + ____ mm) = ____ mm / 3	= ________ mm
	Sum of Skinfold Measurements (Σ SKF):	= ________ mm
	Age of the Athlete (in years):	= ________ yrs
Women		
1. Triceps	(____ mm + ____ mm + ____ mm) = ____ mm / 3	= ________ mm
2. Suprailiac	(____ mm + ____ mm + ____ mm) = ____ mm / 3	= ________ mm
	Sum of Skinfold Measurements (Σ SKF):	= ________ mm
	Age of the Athlete (in years):	= ________ yrs

Body Density (Db) Formula MEN (g/cc) =		1.1043 – (0.00133 x Thigh) – (0.00131 x Subscapular)	
Reference: Sloan & Weir et al. =		1.1043 – (0.00133 x _____) – (0.00131 x _____)	
	=	__________	g/cc
Body Density (Db) Formula WOMEN (g/cc): =		1.0764 – (0.00081 x Suprailiac) – (0.00088 x Triceps)	
Reference: Sloan & Weir et al. =		1.0764 – (0.00081 x _____) – (0.00088 x _____)	
	=	__________	g/cc

Calculating Percent Body Fat (%BF) for Athletes					
Population	Gender		% BF Formula		Result
Athletes	%BF for Male & Female	=	(457/Db) – 414.2	=	(457/_____) – 414.2 = _____%

Skinfold Measurement Sites: Kids (Age 6 – 17)			
Boys (6 – 17 yr)	Girls (6 – 17 yr)	Fold Orientation	Fold Location
1. Tricep	1. Tricep	Vertical	Take distance between acromion process (shoulder) and olecranon process (elbow); site is on rear midline of upper arm (triceps)
2. Medial Calf	2. Medial Calf	Diagonal	

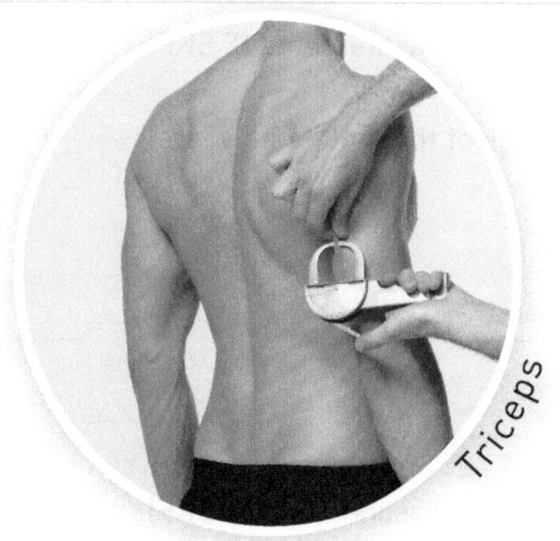
Triceps

Medial Calff

2 Site Skinfold Calculation: Kids (6 – 17 yr)		
Formula:	(1st Value + 2nd Value + 3rd Value)/3= Average Value (mm)	
Boys		
1. Triceps	(____ mm + ____ mm + ____ mm) = ____ mm / 3	= ________ mm
2. Medial Calf	(____ mm + ____ mm + ____ mm) = ____ mm / 3	= ________ mm
	Sum of Skinfold Measurements (Σ SKF):	= ________ mm
	Age of the Athlete (in years):	= ________ yrs
Girls		
1. Triceps	(____ mm + ____ mm + ____ mm) = ____ mm / 3	= ________ mm
2. Medial Calf	(____ mm + ____ mm + ____ mm) = ____ mm / 3	= ________ mm
	Sum of Skinfold Measurements (Σ SKF):	= ________ mm
	Age of the Athlete (in years):	= ________ yrs

Calculating Percent Body Fat (%BF) for Kids					
Population	Gender		% BF Formula		Results
Athletes	%BF for Boys	=	73.5 x (Σ SKF) + 100	=	73.5 x ____ + 100 = ______%
	%BF for Girls	=	61 x (Σ SKF) + 510	=	61 x ____ + 510 = ______%

EQUIPMENT CONSIDERATION

Following is a comprehensive equipment list for the respective fitness assessment tests to facilitate overall fitness testing. It is prudent to ensure that all of the equipment is in proper working condition and testing population specific.

For example, if one usually conducts college-level fitness testing (adults) but now wants to engage in fitness testing for high school kids then the equipment needs to be adjusted accordingly (e.g. adjustable step box) since limb length differs between adults and children.

Fitness Assessment - Equipment List	
Item	Quantity
Adjustable Step Box	1
Agility Rings	6
Chair	1
Cones	6
Flat Bench/Table	1
Floor Mat	1
Goniometer	1
Heart Rate Monitor	1
Medicine Ball	1
Physio Ball	1
Scale	1
Stability Pad	2
Stopwatch	1
Tape Measure	1
Tennis Ball	4
Tennis Court	1

4.03 SHOULDER MOBILITY TEST

SUMMARY

The Shoulder Mobility test assesses the flexibility of the musculature that acts on the shoulder joint as well as associated connective tissues of the rotator cuff.

PURPOSE

Assessment of shoulder and rotator cuff flexibility and proper scapulothoracic function

DESCRIPTION

The athlete to be tested:

1. Take right hand and place it behind the head; reach down the spine as far as possible
2. Maintain neutral head position – look straight forward
3. Take left hand and try to connect behind the back with the right hand
4. Tester checks if individual can touch and connect both hands
5. Tester records based on the superior arm (here right arm); use the middle finger
6. If the individual is able to touch hands with 2+ fingers then tester writes down "right shoulder test ok – reach to touch successful"
7. Now, individual switches hands; left hand is placed behind the head, right hand tries to touch it
8. In case the individual can't connect the hands, the tester uses tape measure and records how far individual could reach based on how far the hands are apart

Note: Upper arm – assesses external rotators, lat, triceps (externally rotated, abducted with elbow flexion) Lower arm – internal rotator, pec major and minor (internally rotated, adducted, elbow flexion)

EQUIPMENT

- Tape Measure

RELEVANCE

- It determines range of motion (ROM) capability and likelihood of shoulder injury occurrence
- ROM impacts force and hence power production of the serve and groundstrokes
- Limited ROM increases likelihood of injuries
- Can point out detrimental muscular imbalances or postural compensations (e.g. shortening of the latissimus dorsi or pectoralis minor that causes the shoulder joint to migrate forward)

TESTED MUSCULATURE

- Rotator cuff musculature and connective tissue
- Teres major
- Triceps
- Pectoralis major & minor
- Latissimus dorsi
- Internal & external shoulder rotators

RECOMMENDED EXERCISES TO IMPROVE ROM

1. Bar Rotator Cuff Stretch
2. Towel Shoulder Stretch
3. Arm Circles

ID: 403

TEST SCORE TABLE

- Good: 2+ Fingers connect
- Fair: Middle finger connects
- Poor: No fingers touch

Fair

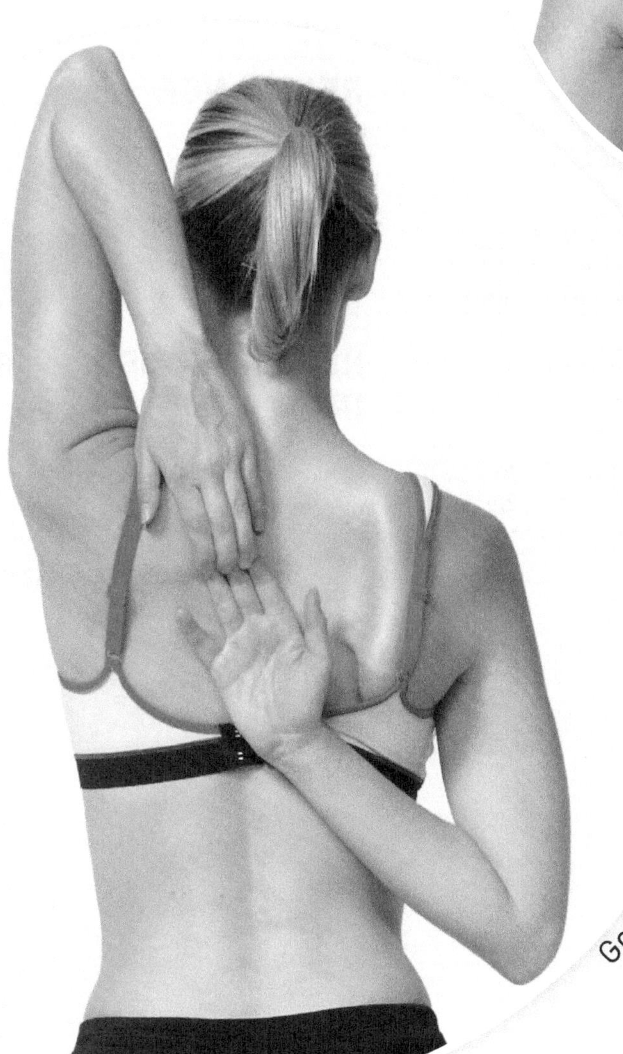

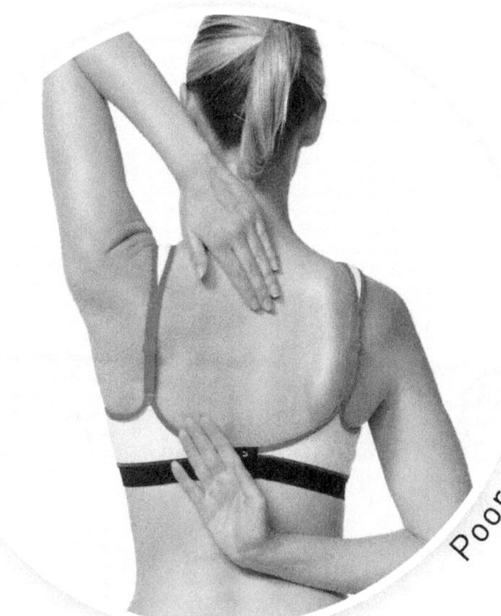

4.04 HIP FLEXION TEST

SUMMARY

The Hip Flexion Test assesses flexibility of the hip extensors (primary gluteus maximus).

DESCRIPTION

1. Place floor mat on the ground
2. Lie down in supine (face up) position
3. Move both knees towards the chest while pulling on the hamstring with both hands
4. Maintain neutral head position – look up
5. **Release one leg** towards the floor so that **hamstring touches ground**
6. Utilizing a goniometer, the tester measures the degree of hip flexion attainable (in the leg maintained toward the chest) while keeping the hip in contact with the floor
7. Tester should assess both hips unilaterally, and then perform a bilateral assessment

Note: A bilateral assessment will usually provide reduced ROM results compared to unilateral assessment, due to an enhanced pull from the thoracolumbar fascia.

TEST SCORE TABLE

- Good: 120° hip flexion or greater
- Fair: 100° - 119° hip flexion
- Poor: Below 100° hip flexion

PURPOSE

Assessment of hip extensor flexibility

EQUIPMENT

- Goniometer
- Floor mat

RELEVANCE

- It determines range of motion (ROM) capability of hip extensors and overall running economy
- Hip extensor ROM impacts maximum running speed
- Limited ROM increases likelihood of injuries and limits training potential (e.g. squats)

RECOMMENDED EXERCISES TO IMPROVE ROM

1. High Knee Pulls
2. Supine Knee to Chest

TESTED MUSCULATURE

- Glutes

Start

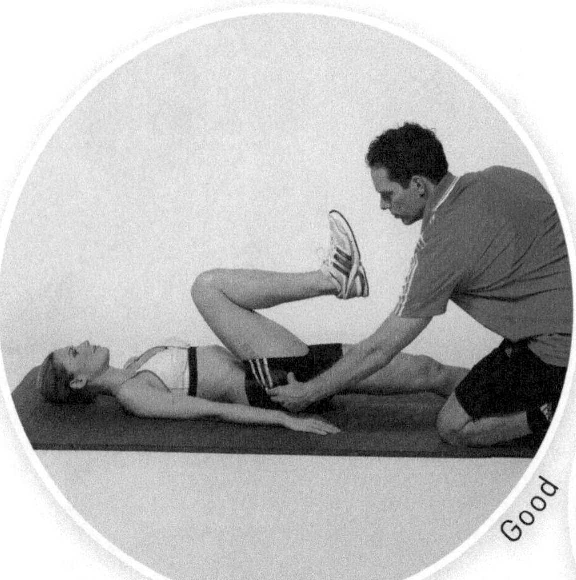
Good

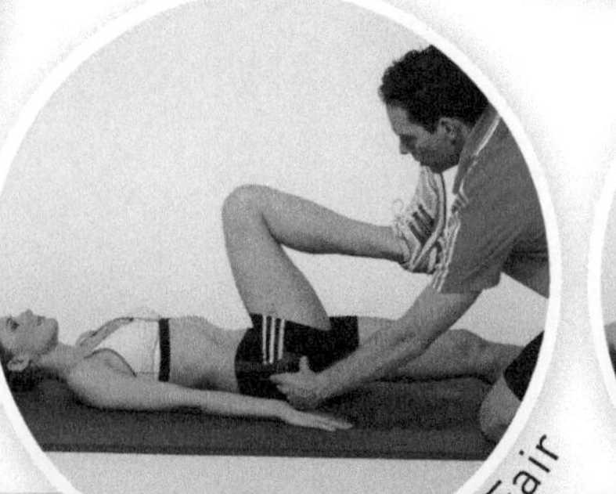
Fair

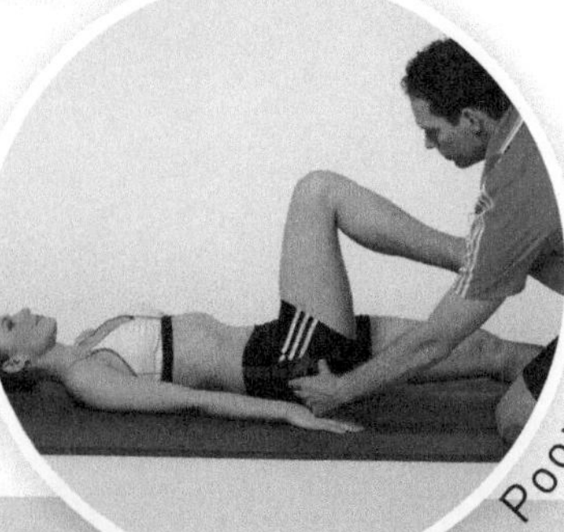
Poor

ID: 404

4.05 TRUNK EXTENSION TEST

SUMMARY

The Trunk Extension Test assesses hip flexor and trunk flexor musculature flexibility. **If athlete has a history of lower-back pain (LBP), do not perform this test!**

PURPOSE

Assessment of hip flexor and abdominal flexibility

DESCRIPTION

1. Place floor mat on the ground
2. Lie down in prone (face down) position
3. Place your hands directly underneath the shoulder joints
4. Maintain neutral head position – look straight forward
5. Fully extend the elbows while attempting to maintaining ground contact with the hips
6. The **anterior superior iliac spines** (ASISs) of the hip joint should maintain ground contact when full elbow extension is attained for a good score

Note: If athlete has a history of lower-back pain (LBP), do not perform this test!

RELEVANCE

- It determines range of motion (ROM) during synchronized elongation of the hip flexors and abdominals
- Hip flexors ROM impacts overall running economy as well as maximum running speed and jumping during service motion and overheads
- Limited ROM of abdominals can cause lower back pain (LBP)

RECOMMENDED EXERCISES TO IMPROVE ROM

1. Lunge & Overhead Reach
2. Scorpion Stretch

TEST SCORE TABLE

- Good: The hips maintain full contact with the floor
- Fair: The hips come off the floor up to 1 inch below the ASISs
- Poor: The hips come off the floor to a greater degree than 1 inch below the ASISs

TESTED MUSCULATURE

- Iliopsoas (iliacus and psoas major)
- Abdominals (rectus abdominis)

EQUIPMENT

- Floot mat

ID: 405

4.06 TRUNK ROTATION TEST

SUMMARY

The Trunk Rotation test is an assessment of trunk rotator mobility.

PURPOSE

Assessment of external and internal oblique flexibility

DESCRIPTION

1. Face the net on a tennis court while standing in the center of the baseline at the intersection of the "T"
2. Ensure that the lower-body does not move during the test; feet are perpendicular to baseline and no rotation is allowed in the hips
3. **Rotate** the upper-body as far as possible to the first side to be assessed until rotation is initiated in the lower body – this is the end range of motion
4. Use a goniometer or simple protractor to record the attainable range of rotation (Baseline T to max rotation point)
5. Repeat the process rotating in the other direction – note that tennis athletes commonly have an imbalance in the trunk musculature and this issue should be addressed in the exercise prescription

TEST SCORE TABLE

- Good: 46-70° from midline
- Fair: 30-45° from midline
- Poor: Less than 30° from midline

RECOMMENDED EXERCISES TO IMPROVE ROM

1. Lunge & Twist
2. Supine Cross-Over
3. Scorpion

EQUIPMENT

- Goniometer

RELEVANCE

- It determines range of motion (ROM) capability of trunk rotators
- Trunk rotator ROM impacts power in all strokes involving rotation
- Low ROM of trunk rotators can limit power transfer from the hips to the upper extremity, thus reducing transfer of force to the racquet

TESTED MUSCULATURE

- Internal obliques
- External obliques

ID: 406

4.07 TRUNK FLEXION TEST

SUMMARY

The Trunk Flexion Test is an assessment of lower back flexibility.

PURPOSE

Assessment of erector spinae flexibility

DESCRIPTION

1. Sit upright on a bench or chair while maintaining the hips and knees flexed at 90° (thighs parallel to ground) and legs abducted to 45° (V-stance)
2. While flexing the trunk, reach down and backwards between your legs as far as possible
3. No bouncing should be allowed during the reach, but rounding of the back is acceptable
4. Examine the relationship between the shoulder and hip joints

TEST SCORE TABLE

- Good: Shoulder and hip joints are in line during full trunk flexion
- Fair: Midpoint of shoulder joint is 1-2 inches above the hip joint at full trunk flexion
- Poor: Midpoint of shoulder joint is greater than 1-2 inches above the hip joint at full trunk flexion

RECOMMENDED EXERCISES TO IMPROVE ROM

1. Supine Erector Spinae
2. Squat to Overhead Reach
3. Duck Walk

TESTED MUSCULATURE

- Erector spinae
- Thoracolumbar fascia

EQUIPMENT

- Bench or chair

RELEVANCE

- It determines functional trunk flexion capability
- A tight lower back and/or posterior kinetic chain can lead to lower back pain (LBP)
- Tightness in any area of the hips or trunk can compromise optimal spinal and pelvic alignment – which can lead to a variety of injuries and limitations

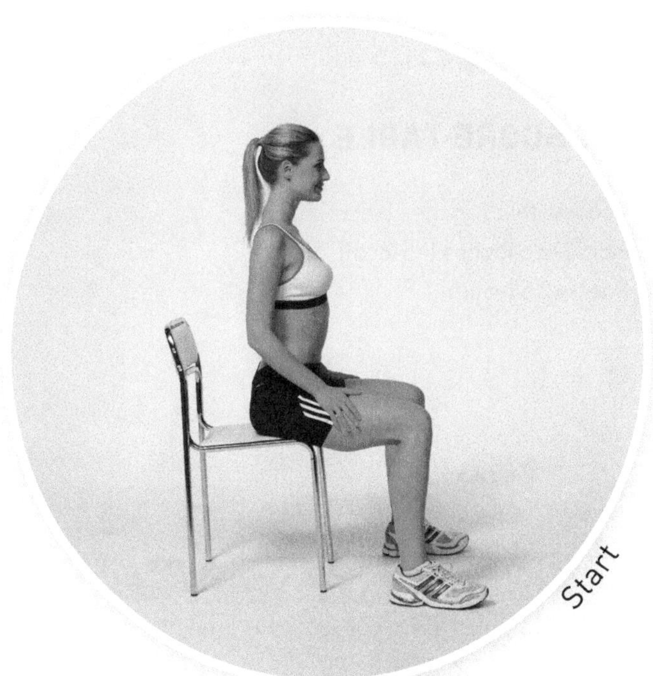

ID: 407

4.08 UNILATERAL KNEE FLEXION

SUMMARY

The Unilateral Knee Flexion Test is an assessment of quadriceps flexibility.

PURPOSE

Assessment of quadriceps flexibility

DESCRIPTION

1. Place floor mat on the ground
2. Lie on the floor mat in prone position (face down) with the legs close together
3. Bend one knee and bring the heel towards the gluteal
4. With ipsilateral (same side) hand, grasp the ankle and pull heel as close to gluteal as possible
5. Ensure that the athlete does not rotate or abduct the hip to compensate for a low ROM
6. Use tape measure to determine distance between heel and buttocks
7. Repeat with other leg

TEST SCORE TABLE

- Good: within 2 inches (~5cm)
- Fair: 2-2.5 inches (~5-6cm)
- Poor: >2.5 (~6cm)

EQUIPMENT

- Floor Mat
- Tape Measure

RELEVANCE

- It determines the ROM of the knee extensors
- Knee extensor ROM can impact maximum running speed and jumping movements such as serve motions or overheads
- Limited ROM of quadriceps can cause knee pain (patella tendinitis)

TESTED MUSCULATURE

- Quadriceps

RECOMMENDED EXERCISES TO IMPROVE ROM

1. Butt Kicks
2. Single Leg RDL & Quad Stretch
3. Side-Lying Quad Stretch

Poor

ID: 408

4.09 UNILATERAL KNEE EXTENSION

SUMMARY

The Unilateral Knee Extension test is an assessment of hamstring flexibility

PURPOSE

Assessment of hamstring flexibility

DESCRIPTION

1. Lie on a floor mat in a supine position (face up) with the legs close together
2. Bend **one knee** and bring it as close to the chest as possible
3. **Fully extend the knee** of the assessed leg while the other leg remains in contact with the floor mat
4. The athlete should be able to fully extend the leg at 90° of hip flexion
5. Repeat with the other leg

EQUIPMENT

- Floor Mat
- Goniometer

TEST SCORE TABLE

- Good: knee is fully extended with hip flexed at 90°
- Fair: knee is fully extended with hip flexed at 80° - 89°
- Poor: knee is fully extended with hip flexed < 80°

Good

RELEVANCE

- It determines ROM of the knee flexors and overall running economy
- Knee flexor ROM impacts maximum running speed and jumping movements such as service motion and overheads
- Limited ROM of hamstrings can cause injury (hamstring strain)

TESTED MUSCULATURE

- Hamstrings

RECOMMENDED EXERCISES TO IMPROVE ROM

1. Straight Leg Kicks
2. Supine Towel Hamstring Stretch

Fair

Poor

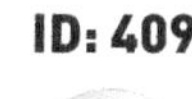

ID: 409

4.10 THOMAS TEST

SUMMARY

The Thomas Test can be used as an assessment of hip flexor ROM.

PURPOSE

Assessment of iliopsoas flexibility

DESCRIPTION

1. Have the athlete lie in a supine position on a bench
2. Have the athlete draw both knees to the chest.
3. Have the athlete release the leg to be assessed off of the edge of the bench.
4. The leg is examined to see if there is contact of the hamstring with the bench without forcing the leg downward.
5. The process is repeated with the opposite leg.

EQUIPMENT

- Flat Bench

Good

RELEVANCE

- Hip flexor tightness can cause a non-optimal pelvic tilt that can lead to lower back pain and injury
- Hip flexor tightness can alter running mechanics and rapid lunging ability for returning a well placed shot

TESTED MUSCULATURE

- Iliopsoas (hip flexors)

RECOMMENDED EXERCISES TO IMPROVE ROM

1. 3-Way Heel Reaches (II): Single Leg Reach
2. Lunge Hip Flexor Stretch

TEST SCORE TABLE

- Good: The hamstring completely contacts the bench when the hip is extended from the position where the knees are driven to the chest
- Fair: The hamstring levitates up to 1 inch above the bench when the hip is fully extended in a passive fashion
- Poor: The hamstring levitates more than 1 inch above the bench

ID: 410

Poor

FLEXIBILITY TESTING CALCULATIONS

Name: **Date:**

Test Time: **Tester:**

Location: **Other:**

Test		**Score**		**Value**
Shoulder Mobility				
Right Shoulder	☐ Good	☐ Fair	☐ Poor	_____cm
Left Shoulder	☐ Good	☐ Fair	☐ Poor	_____cm
Hip Flexion				
Right Hip	☐ 120°	☐ 100° - 119°	☐ < 100°	_____°
Left Hip	☐ 120°	☐ 100° - 119°	☐ < 100°	_____°
Trunk Extension	☐ Good	☐ Fair	☐ Poor	
Trunk Rotation				
Right Side	☐ 46° - 70°	☐ 30° - 45°	☐ < 30°	_____°
Left Side	☐ 46° - 70°	☐ 30° - 45°	☐ < 30°	_____°
Trunk Flexion	☐ Good	☐ Fair	☐ Poor	_____°
Bilateral Knee Flexion				
Right Leg	☐ Good	☐ Fair	☐ Poor	_____cm
Left Leg	☐ Good	☐ Fair	☐ Poor	_____cm
Bilateral Knee Extension				
Right Leg	☐ Good	☐ Fair	☐ Poor	_____°
Left Leg	☐ Good	☐ Fair	☐ Poor	_____°
Thomas Test				
Right Leg	☐ Good	☐ Fair	☐ Poor	_____°
Left Leg	☐ Good	☐ Fair	☐ Poor	_____°

4.11 MB SERVE THROW TEST

SUMMARY

The Medicine Ball Serve Throw Test focuses on upper-body power generating capability utilizing a 6 lb medicine ball (MB). Perform 3 practice throws before testing.

PURPOSE

Assessment of total-body power-coordination generating capability

DESCRIPTION

1. Stand behind the baseline in ready-to-serve position
2. Feet are shoulder-width apart
3. Anterior (front) foot points to the net post; posterior (back) foot is parallel to baseline and in line with net post and front foot
4. Body position is perpendicular to the baseline so that shoulder faces towards the net
5. Take MB in both hands behind your head
6. Forcefully jump diagonally (high towards the net) and throw the MB towards the appropriate service box as far as possible
7. Record time (in seconds) from release of MB to ground contact
8. Use tape measure and record distance from baseline to point of ground contact (distance) in METERS (m)

EQUIPMENT

- 6 lb (2.72 kg) medicine ball
- Tape measure
- Stopwatch

ENERGY SYSTEM

- Immediate Energy System: ATP-CP

RELEVANCE

- Indicates how much power the athlete can generate through coordinated muscle activation seen during the service motion.

CALCULATING POWER

- Speed (m/s) = Distance (m) / Time (s)
- Force (in Joule) = MB (kg) x Speed
- Work (in Newton) = Force x Distance
- Power (in W; kinetic energy in J) = Work (N)/Time (s)

RECORVERY TIME

- 90 seconds is optimal

PRE-TEST WARM UP

1. 2 Racquets Serves
2. Lateral Skips w. Arm Swings

ID: 411

4.12 KNEEL & JUMP TEST

SUMMARY

The Kneel & Jump Test focuses on assessing hip flexor speed.

PURPOSE

Assessment of hip flexor speed

DESCRIPTION

1. Kneel on the ground with knees shoulder-width apart
2. Use arm swing to create momentum
3. Elevate yourself off the ground
4. Jump: Flex hips rapidly
5. Land on your feet in a squat position with legs shoulder-width apart

RECORVERY TIME

- 90 seconds is optimal

ENERGY SYSTEM

- Immediate Energy System: ATP-CP

RELEVANCE

- Hip flexion is a factor in running speed and jumping; if hip flexors are weak power production during the serve – and running speed during groundstrokes will be limited
- If Thomas Test results show hip flexor ROM deficiency, implement this exercise into your Resistance Training warm-up routine

TEST OUTCOME

- Can perform exercise = hip flexor speed ok
- Cannot perform exercise = hip flexor speed insufficient

PRE-TEST WARM UP

1. Lunge & Overhead Reach
2. Scorpion

ID: 412

4.13 MB TWIST THROW TEST

SUMMARY

The Medicine Ball Twist Throw Test focuses on upper-body power generating capability utilizing a 6 lb medicine ball (MB).

PURPOSE

Assessment of upper-body power generating capability

DESCRIPTION

1. Feet are shoulder-width apart
2. Body position is perpendicular to the baseline so that shoulder faces towards the net
3. Knees are slightly bent
4. Arms are straight and medicine ball is in both hands
5. Turn the trunk away from the net as far as possible
6. Forcefully rotate the trunk back towards the net and throw the MB for maximum distance towards the net
7. Take the time (s) from release of ball until contact with the ground
8. Use tape measure and record distance from baseline to point of ground contact (distance) in METERS (m)

EQUIPMENT

- 6 lb (2.72 kg) medicine ball
- Tape measure
- Stopwatch

RECORVERY TIME

- 90 seconds is optimal

ENERGY SYSTEM

- Immediate Energy System: ATP-CP

RELEVANCE

- It is an indicator of how much power the athlete can generate for groundstrokes.

CALCULATING POWER OUTPUT

- Speed (m/s) = Distance (m) / Time (s)
- Force (in Joule) = MB (kg) x Speed
- Work (in Newton) = Force x Distance
- Power (in W; kinetic energy in J) = Work (N)/Time (s)

PRE-TEST WARM UP

1. Forward Lunge and Ankle Reach
2. MB Diagonal Chops

ID: 413

4.14 H-DRILL TEST

SUMMARY

The H-Drill Test focuses on all-court agility capability.

PURPOSE

Assessment of all-court agility capability

DESCRIPTION

1. Split-Step to initiate the drill
2. Face the net and move via side-step along the baseline towards the deuce court ring
3. Stick the landing with the right foot and push off towards the ad-court ring
4. Move via side-step along the baseline towards the ad-court ring
5. Stick the landing with the left foot and push off towards the center of baseline
6. Split-step at center of baseline
7. Sprint towards the rings in the center of service-box
8. Split-Step into the rings
9. Sprint towards the rings at right sideline
10. Place left foot into the ring
11. Push off and sprint towards the ring on left sideline
12. Place right foot into the ring
13. Push off and sprint towards rings at service center-line
14. Backpedal past the baseline

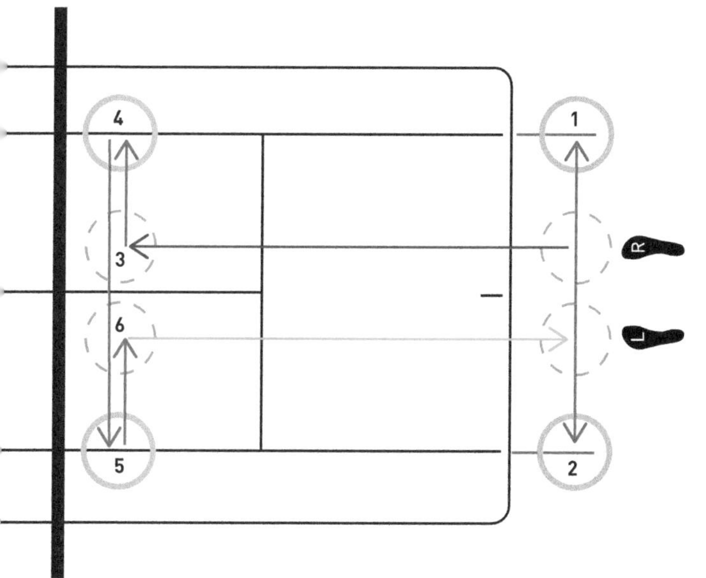

RELEVANCE

- Indicates how quickly the athlete can move on the court and change direction with regard to transition game from baseline to the net.

ENERGY SYSTEM

- Immediate Energy System: ATP-CP

RECORVERY TIME

- 120 seconds is optimal

CALCULATING FORCE OUTPUT

Total Running Distance ~ 46 m

Body weight (lb)/2.2 = kg

Force = (body weight [kg] x total running distance m) / time s

PRE-TEST WARM UP

1. High Knee Pulls with Dorsi Flexion
2. Butt Kickers
3. Straight leg Kicks
4. Single Leg RDL & Quad Stretch
5. Bilateral Lunge

NOTE

The athlete is to get to each cone in the quickest manner possible without neglecting to keep the eyes on the opponent's side of the court.

EQUIPMENT

- 6 Rubber Agility Rings, Stopwatch

ID: 414

4.15 26 YARD SPRINT TEST

SUMMARY

The 26 Yard Sprint Test is an assessment of linear speed.

PURPOSE

Assessment of speed

DESCRIPTION

1. Place 2 Rubber Rings ~2m lateral to the baseline
2. Split-step into rubber rings to initiate the test
3. Sprint to the opposite baseline
4. Record time

PRE-TEST WARM UP

1. High Knee Pulls with Dorsi Flexion
2. Butt Kickers
3. Straight leg Kicks
4. Single Leg RDL & Quad Stretch
5. Bilateral Lunge

ENERGY SYSTEM

- Immediate Energy System: ATP-CP

RELEVANCE

- It is an indicator of how quickly the athlete can accelerate and reach top speed

EQUIPMENT

- 2 Rubber Agility Rings
- Stopwatch

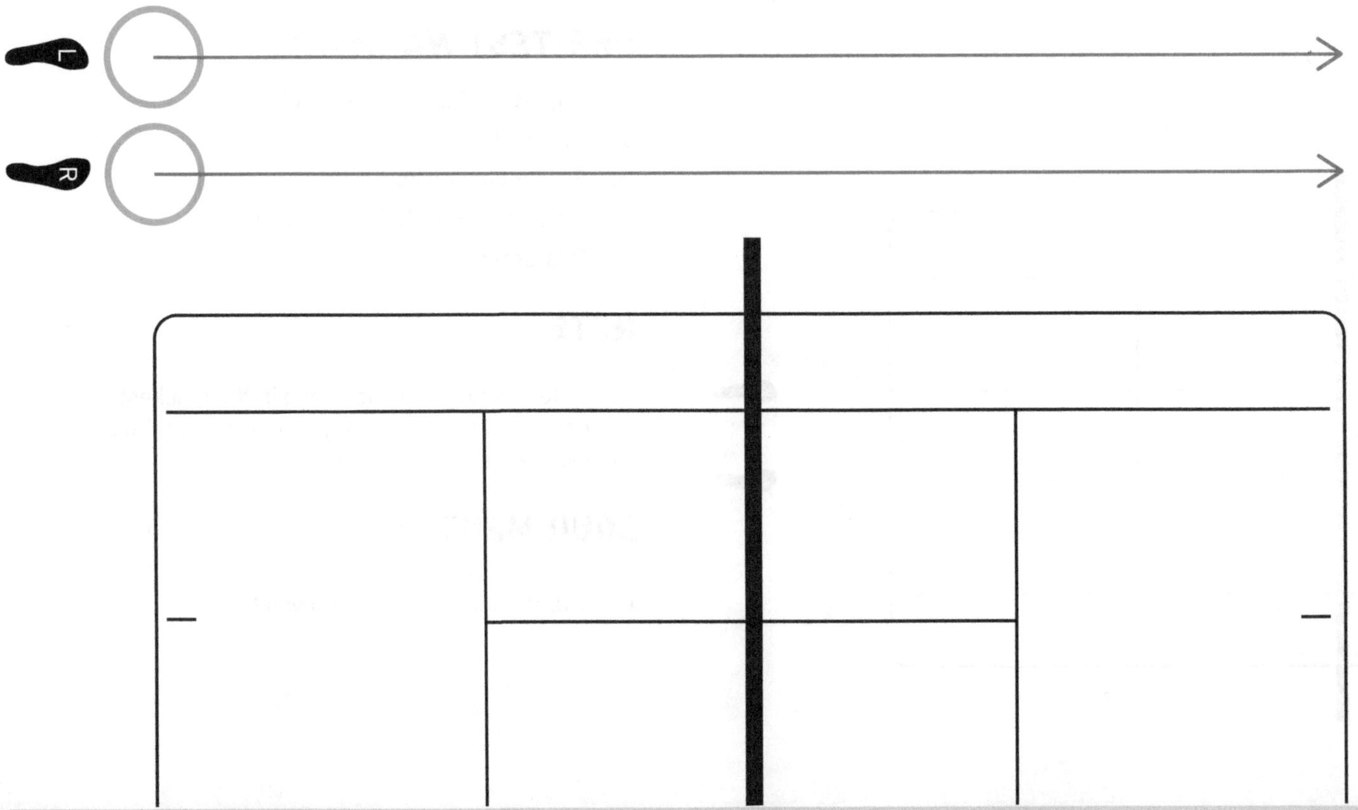

ID: 415

4.16 BILATERAL LUNGE TEST

SUMMARY

The Bilateral Lunge Test is a performance test, which focuses on local lateral endurance capability.

PURPOSE

Assessment of local lateral endurance capability

DESCRIPTION

1. Determine body weight (kg = lb/2.2)
2. Wear a HR monitor, stand erect and perform 1 lateral lunge (one leg remains straight while the other has knee-flexion at 90°) to either side; toes should point slightly outwards
3. Place 1 rubber agility ring at point of ground contact on each side and record distance (m) from center of the ring to ring
4. Perform as many lateral lunges into the rings as possible
5. Record time to exhaustion, # of repetitions, HR at time of exhaustion, HR after 1 minute, HR after 2 minutes, HR after 3 minutes

EQUIPMENT

- 2 Rubber Agility Rings
- Scale
- Tape Measure
- Heart Rate (HR) Monitor
- Stopwatch

ENERGY SYSTEM

- Aerobic Energy System

RELEVANCE

- It is an indicator of how well the athlete can maintain lateral movement (endurance) as well as energy system efficiency in terms of energy production and recovery.

PRE-TEST WARM UP

1. Bilateral Lunge
2. Duck Walk

CALCULATING FORCE OUTPUT

- Force = (Mass {kg} x Distance {m}) / Time {s}
- Force = (Body Weight {kg} x (# of Reps/2 x distance {m}) / Time {s}

ID: 416

4.17 PUSH UP TEST

SUMMARY

The Push Up Test is a performance test, which focuses on local upper-body anaerobic endurance capability.

PURPOSE

Assessment of local upper-body anaerobic endurance

DESCRIPTION

1. Determine body weight of the athlete (lbs / 2.2 = kg) using a scale
2. Place 2 rubber rings on the ground, shoulder-width apart
3. Place a tennis ball on ground in line with sternum (chest)
4. Place hands inside rings and go into ready position
5. Measure distance (inches x 0.0254 = distance in m) between the chest and tennis ball with extended arms
6. Perform push up; lower your body until your chest touches the tennis ball and come up again until arms are fully extended
7. Repeat as many push ups as possible within 60 seconds
8. Count & record # of repetitions

EQUIPMENT

- Scale
- 2 Rubber Agility Ring
- Tennis ball
- Stopwatch

ENERGY SYSTEM

- Anaerobic Energy System

RELEVANCE

- Indicates how long the upper body musculature can perform work before detrimental fatigue sets in. Upper-body force production capabilities should be in line with lower-body force production. Imbalances of upper-body & lower-body force production capabilities should be avoided to ensure effective energy transfer (kinetic chain efficiency).

CALCULATING FORCE OUTPUT

- Force = (Mass {kg} x Distance {m}) / Time {s}
- inches x 0.0254 = distance in m
- Total Distance = # of reps x distance x 2
- Force = (Body Weight {kg} x (total distance {m}) / Time {s}

PRE-TEST WARM UP

1. Push-Up to Single Limb Raise I

ID: 417

4.18 STEP UP TEST

SUMMARY

The Step Up Test focuses on local lower-body anaerobic endurance capability utilizing an adjustable box, a scale, and a stop watch.

PURPOSE

Assessment of local lower-body anaerobic capacity

DESCRIPTION

1. Determine body weight of the athlete (lbs / 2.2 = kg) using a scale
2. Adjust the box so that the knee is at 90° and record box height (inches x 0.0254 = distance in m) using a tape measure
3. One leg is on top of the box, the other on the ground
4. Place rubber ring where foot contacts ground
5. Extend the leg on top of the box and land inside the rubber ring
6. Repeat as many step ups as possible within 60 seconds
7. Count & record # of repetitions
8. Perform test on both legs

EQUIPMENT

- Adjustable Box
- Scale
- Tape Measure
- 1 Rubber Agility Ring
- Stopwatch

PRE-TEST WARM UP

1. High Knee Pulls
2. Straight Leg Kicks
3. Single Leg RDL & Quad

ENERGY SYSTEM

- Anaerobic Energy System

RELEVANCE

- Indicates how long the athlete can last before performance-limiting fatigue sets in. Both legs should have equal endurance capabilities. If one leg is stronger than the other, imbalance needs to be corrected.

CALCULATING FORCE OUTPUT

- Force = (Mass {kg} x Distance {m}) / Time {s}
- inches x 0.0254 = distance in m
- Total Distance = # of reps x box height x 2
- Force = (Body Weight {kg} x (# of Reps x Box Height {m} x 2) / Time {s}
- Force (Right Leg) =
- Force (Left Leg) =

ID: 418

4.19 BALL-DROP & REACT TEST

SUMMARY

The Ball-Drop & React Test is an assessment of reaction time and linear speed.

PURPOSE

Assessment of overall reaction capability

DESCRIPTION

1. Determine body weight of the athlete (lbs / 2.2 = kg) using a scale
2. Athlete stand on the center of baseline (not behind)
3. Athlete moves side-to-side via sidestep so that hips face forward and stay over the baseline
4. Coach stands at service T
5. Use tape measure and set height at 1.6 m (5"3') – between shoulder and top of the head
6. Coach takes 1 tennis ball in one hand and a stop-watch in the other hand
7. Extend the ball-holding arm sideways at 1,6 m (5"3') height (e.g. shoulder level)
8. While athletes moves sideways on the baseline, coach randomly drops one ball and simultaneously starts the stop-watch
9. Athlete should catch the ball before it bounces the 2nd time
10. Record time when athlete catches the ball

EQUIPMENT

- Scale
- Stopwatch
- Tape Measure
- 1 Tennis Ball

ENERGY SYSTEM

- Immediate Energy System: ATP-CP

RELEVANCE

- It is an indicator of how quickly the athlete can recognize a short ball, react and transition from baseline to service line.

CALCULATING FORCE OUTPUT

- Force = (Mass {kg} x Distance {m}) / Time {s}
- Force = (Body Weight {kg} x 5.43 m) / Time {s}
- Force Output =

PRE-TEST WARM UP

1. High Knee Pulls w. Dorsi Flexion
2. Straight Leg Kicks
3. Single Leg RDL & Quad Stretch

ID: 419

4.20 T-ENDURANCE DRILL TEST

SUMMARY

The T-Endurance Drill Test focuses on all-court endurance capability utilizing 4 Rubber Rings and a stopwatch. The drill should always be performed on the same surface (e.g. clay court) and during similar weather conditions (e.g. temperature).

PURPOSE

Assessment of all-court endurance capability

DESCRIPTION

1. Athlete needs to complete drill 58 times (2 km)
2. Step on the scale to determine body weight (lbs/2.2 = kg)
3. Split-Step to initiate the drill
4. Face the net and move via side-step along the baseline towards the deuce court ring (sideline extension)
5. Stick the landing inside the ring with the right foot and push off towards the ad-court ring
6. Move via side-step along the baseline towards the ad-court ring (sideline extension)
7. Stick the landing inside the ring with the left foot and push off towards the center of baseline
8. Split-step at center of baseline
9. Sprint towards the rings at net
10. Split-Step into the rings
11. Backpedal past the baseline
12. Split-step and repeat
13. Record the time to completion in seconds

ENERGY SYSTEM

- Aerobic Energy System

RELEVANCE

- Indicates how well the athlete can maintain rallies during the match before fatigue sets in causing an error.

CALCULATING FORCE OUTPUT

- Sideline-to-Sideline= 8.90 m
- Ready Position-to-Net Rings= 12.8 m
- Total Running Distance = 34.5 m
  = 0.0345 km
- Force = (body weight [kg] x 2,000 m) / time s

EQUIPMENT

4 Rubber Agility Rings, Scale, Stopwatch

PRE-TEST WARM UP

1. High Knee Pulls with Dorsi Flexion
2. Butt Kickers
3. Straight leg Kicks
4. Single Leg RDL & Quad Stretch
5. Bilateral Lunge

NOTE

- The athlete is to get to each cone in the quickest manner possible without neglecting to keep the eyes on the opponent's side of the court.

ID: 420

4.21 STABILITY PAD SQUAT TEST

SUMMARY

The Stability-Pad Squat Test focuses on dynamic lower-extremity stability capability.

PURPOSE

Assessment of dynamic stability for lower extremities

DESCRIPTION

1. Setup 2 stability pads shoulder-width apart
2. Stand on both pads; toes pointing forward
3. Distribute weight evenly through your feet and squat (bend your knees until they reach 90°)
4. Extend your knees until you stand erect
5. Perform as many perfect repetitions within 60 seconds as possible
6. Record the # of perfect repetitions to completion

EQUIPMENT

- 2 Stability Pads
- Stopwatch

NOTE

If a squat cannot be performed with legs at "shoulder-width" apart, increase distance between pads until squat can be performed correctly.

ENERGY SYSTEM

- Anaerobic Energy System

RELEVANCE

- Indicates how well the athlete can maintain balance during an unstable movement.

CALCULATE DYNAMIC STABILITY PROFICIENCY

- DS = Reps / 60 (s)

PRE-TEST WARM UP

1. High Knee Pulls with Dorsi Flexion
2. SL RDL & Quad Stretch
3. Duck Walk

ID: 421

4.22 EXTERNAL ROTATOR FUNCTION TEST

SUMMARY

The External Rotator Function Test is an assessment of the strength and function of the musculature that allows for external rotation in the shoulder joint.

PURPOSE

To examine lack of function or strength in a component of the shoulder that is at high risk of injury in tennis.

DESCRIPTION

1. Have the athlete sit on a bench and position his/her shoulder in 90° of abduction and external rotation if possible.
2. The athlete's fingers should be facing the ceiling and the coach should stabilize the arm in this position at the elbow.
3. The coach now applies resistance to the forearm in an attempt to drive the shoulder through internal rotation while the athlete resists this action.
4. Performance of the test is then assessed based on pain and capability.

EQUIPMENT

- Chair or bench

ENERGY SYSTEM

- None

RELEVANCE

- Indicates if there is an issue in the rotational capacity of the shoulder joint. In tennis, the internal rotators are prone to becoming tight and the external rotators are prone to becoming weak or pulled out of optimal position by the dominant internal rotators.

TEST OUTCOME

- Good: The athlete can maintain the initial position without pain against maximal resistance.
- Fair: The athlete can maintain moderate resistance but compensatory movements are made to keep the position.
- Poor: Inability to resist any force in the rotated position, or encounters pain while resisting the action performed by the coach.

RECOMMENDED EXERCISES

1. Rotator Cuff Circuit

4

4.23 SINGLE LEG STABILITY TEST

SUMMARY

The Single Leg Stability Test is an assessment of the ability to control the lower body over a planted leg.

PURPOSE

To assess asymmetrical balance

DESCRIPTION

1. Have the athlete perform 10 repetitions of a single leg squat to a depth of 45° while keeping the arms to the sides
2. Note any movement compensations or deficiencies that may occur at the beginning of the set or as fatigue sets in

Note: If athlete fails the test, implement the "Recommended Exercises" into the training program according to the observed movement abnormalities!

RELEVANCE

- Indicates if the athlete has adequate strength and control of the lower extremities that can translate into a lower risk of injury (e.g. low back) and explosive starts and stops.

TEST OUTCOME

Pass: The knee does not drive in front of the toes, the torso remains erect, the hips and knees remain neutral.
Fail: Movement abnormalities to look for:

1. Knee bows inward (weak hip abductors)
2. Opposite hip drops (pelvic instability; weak hip abductors)
3. Excessive forward lean of the torso (pelvis/spine relationship dysfunction; tight hamstrings)
4. Knees drive in front of the toes (tight gluteus, squat form)

RECOMMENDED EXERCISES

1. Sidelying Straight Leg Hip Abduction
2. Sidelying Straight Leg Hip Abduction
3. Romanian Deadlift
4. Supine Knee to Chest

ID: 423

PERFORMANCE TESTING CALCULATIONS

Name:	**Date:**
Test Time:	**Tester:**
Location:	**Other:**

PERFORMANCE TESTS

Test	**Score**		
Medicine Ball Serve Throw	Total Power:		Watts
Kneel & Jump		❑ Pass	❑ Fail
Medicine Ball Twist Throw	Total Power:		Watts
H-Drill	Total Force:		Joule
25 Yard Sprint	Time:		Seconds
Bilateral Lunge	Total Force:		Joule
Push Up	Total Force:		Joule
Step Up	Total Force:		Joule
Ball Drop & React	Total Force:		Joule
T-Drill	Total Force:		Joule
Stability Pad Squat	Dynamic Stability:		Reps/min
External Rotation Function	❑ Good	❑ Fair	❑ Poor

Name: **Date:**

Test Time: **Tester:**

Location: **Other:**

MEDICINE BALL SERVE THROW

Variables					**Calculations**			
Convert inches to meter	->	________	inches	x	0.0254	=		m
Convert lb to kg	->	________	lb	/	2.2	=	________	kg
Speed	=	Distance (m) / Time (s)						
	=	________	m/s		=		________	m/s
Force	=	MB Weight (kg) x Speed (m/s)						
	=	________ kg	x	________	m/s	=	________	Joule
Work	=	Force (J) x Distance (m)						
	=	________ J	x	________	m	=	________	Newton
Power	=	Work (N) / Time (s)						
	=	________ N	x	________	s	=	________	Watts

MEDICINE BALL TWIST THROW

Variables		Calculations						
Convert inches to meter	->	________	inches	x	0.0254	=		m
Convert lb to kg	->	________	lb	/	2.2	=	________	kg
Speed	=	Distance (m) / Time (s)						
	=	________	m/s		=		________	m/s
								s
Force	=	MB Weight (kg) x Speed (m/s)						
	=	________ kg	x	________	m/s	=	________	Joule
Work	=	Force (J) x Distance (m)						
	=	________ J	x	________	m	=	________	Newton
Power	=	Work (N) / Time (s)						
	=	________N	x	________	s	=	________	Watts

H-DRILL

Variables		Calculations						
Convert inches to meter	->	________	inches	x	0.0254	=		m
Convert lb to kg	->	________	lb	/	2.2	=	________	kg
Speed	=	Distance (m) / Time (s)						
	=	________	m/s		=		________	m/s
								s
Force	=	MB Weight (kg) x Speed (m/s)						
	=	________ kg	x	________	m/s	=	________	Joule

BILATERAL LUNGE

Variables								
				Calculations				
Convert inches to meter	->	______	inches	x	0.0254	=	______	m
Convert lb to kg	->	______	lb	/	2.2	=	______	kg
Time (to Exhaustion)	=	______	seconds					
# of Repetitions	=	______	/	2	=		______	
Distance	=	______	m					
Total Distance	=	(# of Reps/2) x distance				=	______	m
Force	=	(Body Weight {kg} x Total Distance {m}) / Time (s)						
	=	______	kg	x	______	m	/ sec	
	=	______	Joule					

PUSH UP

Variables								
				Calculations				
Convert inches to meter	->	______	inches	x	0.0254	=	______	m
Convert lb to kg	->	______	lb	/	2.2	=	______	kg
Time	=	60	seconds					
# of Repetitions	=	______	/	2	=		______	
Distance	=	______	m					
Total Distance	=	(# of Reps/2) x distance				=	______	m
Force	=	(Body Weight {kg} x Total Distance {m}) / Time (s)						
	=	______	kg	x	______	m	/ 60 sec	
	=	______	Joule					

STEP UP

Variables								Calculations		
Convert inches to meter	->	________	inches	x	0.0254	=	________	m		
Convert lb to kg	->	________	lb	/	2.2	=	________	kg		
Time	=	60	seconds							
# of Repetitions	=	________	/	2	=		________			
Box Height	=	________	m							
Total Distance	=	(# of Reps/2) x box height				=	________	m		
Force	=	(Body Weight {kg} x Total Distance {m}) / Time (s)								
	=	________	kg	x	________	m	/	60 sec		
	=	________	Joule							

CHAPTER 5:

"Performance Preparation for Athletes: Warm Up & Stretching"

Generally, one performs a warm-up prior to exercise to decrease the risk of injury but the question is does warming up really accomplish that? There is no scientific evidence that a warm-up decreases the risk of injury but by warming up one changes the dynamics of the muscle tissue; the musculature becomes more tolerant to stress, which suggests that the risk of injury is reduced. More specifically, if the muscle tissue is less taut, particularly at the joint capsule, there are greater elastic properties and there is greater neural transmission efficiency and an improvement in proprioception, which means there is better coordination for the subsequent movements. Therefore, there is less risk of overextending oneself to the point of muscle strain due to lack of pliability and the proprioceptors will be more dynamically enhanced, which means greater stability will be achieved. Therefore, one can assume that higher stability and higher range of motion will reduce the risk of injury but this has not actually been proven because no documentation has been assembled to verify the contention. Proof would require researchers to isolate all the variables, a difficult task to say the least.

Warm-ups do provide up to 20% enhancement in the athlete's performance outcomes. This is accomplished because warm-ups enhance neural signal transmission via an increase in cellular respiration, raise the body temperature which in turn lays the groundwork for enzymatic activity and hence overall metabolism.

So, warm-ups potentially decrease the risk of injury and increase the performance potential by up to 20%, two reasons why warm-ups are a great idea!

Before the athlete starts with any stretching exercises a general warm-up should be undertaken. Warm-ups increase muscle temperature, thereby reducing viscosity and lowering resistance in the tissue. There are a number of different stretching techniques that can be used to improve flexibility and other performance parameters (e.g. power):

1. Ballistic Stretching
2. Dynamic Stretching
3. Static Stretching
4. Proprioceptive Neuromuscular Facilitation (PNF)

Ballistic stretching is generally undertaken before one engages in any resistance training in the gym but can also be done before any speed, agility, and quickness drills on court. It involves the use of a resistance (e.g. body weight) that is accelerated to elongate the muscle tendons. There are two (2) forms of ballistic stretching:

1. Ballistic Unlimited Stretching
2. Ballistic Limited Stretching

The main difference is that Ballistic Limited Stretching uses a **learned range of motion**, whereas Ballistic Unlimited Stretching does not.

During ballistic unlimited stretching one takes a limb, accelerates it using momentum forces, and allows the tissues to decelerate using the momentum itself. One might even use an object to increase the rotation inertia so that it stretches the tissue even farther. But, there are consequences with this uncontrolled (unlimited) stretching: the likelihood of an injury increases. For instance, if the athlete takes an object in both hands, swings it over the head and just lets the arms go into full flexion, there will be a proprioceptive (defensive) response that causes a rapid muscle contraction to help defend against that movement; when too much tension is created an injury can occur.

During ballistic limited stretching one uses velocity-specific movements to increase range of motion but because there already is a terminal end-point associated with the exercise (nervous system adaptations "learned" by motor cortex), the possibility of creating too much tension does not represent a problem. For example, if the athlete has previously learned how to perform a "Hang Snatch", he/she will be familiar with a terminal position (he/she knows the end point by virtue of the neuromuscular development produced by the original learning of the exercise). The resistance will then move slightly past the end point but it will suppress the proprioceptive activity that would normally come into play so as to cause an increase in deceleration. Therefore, it is a learned range of motion but with unlimited (uncontrolled) ballistics, there are no learned properties and this can lead to overstretch and injury. On the other hand, controlled ballistics use momentum forces greater than "control forces" so there is some proprioceptive activity but it's limited because there is inhibition by the nervous system (motor cortex and the spinal cord). In other words, with ballistic limited stretching there is not going to be a point where injury occurs because the athlete has learned the activity and its associated range of motion.

Before attempting ballistic stretching exercises, the athlete must be healthy and should warm-up the musculature enough so that injury will be avoided. Injury occurs when excessive force is applied to the tissue. If the tissue is already compromised (unhealthy), less force will be capable of causing injury. Force (in J) is defined as mass (kg) x speed (m/s). Because an accelerated resistance is used, the control of the stretch is limited due to the velocity and force applied. Imagine, if you will, bungee jumping. During the jump, the body weight (kg) is the resistance that stretches the bungee cord (muscle tissue; tendons) and gravity provides the speed (m/s) that accelerates one towards the ground. If the force created is too much, the bungee extends too far and snaps. Analogously, if one used a resistance that creates too much force, causing over-stretch, it can then cause muscle tissue tears, leading to injury. **Ballistic Limited Stretching exercises** are provided later on in this chapter.

Dynamic stretching is an optimal pre-competition and/or pre-workout activity because it is most effective in enhancing the power-generating capabilities of the muscle tissue. During dynamic stretching one uses exercises in motion that provide stretching for the respective muscle group(s). When performing the various dynamic stretches make sure to do them in a controlled fashion and gradually built up to the fullest range of motion.

Static stretching on the other hand is most beneficial post-competition/-training/-workout because it minimizes the **delayed onset of muscle soreness** (DOMS) and maximizes progress in flexibility. For example, one day in the gym the athlete works out the legs really hard and doesn't stretch out afterwards because there are other things to do. The athlete doesn't feel any soreness during the day and goes to bed. The next morning he/she wakes up, gets out of bed, but the legs feel completely sore so that the athlete can barely walk, which impairs the training planned for that day. If the athlete would have stretched out completely the previous day, soreness would have been reduced noticeably and the athlete could practice today without any problems. To enhance flexibility you should hold each stretch for ~45 seconds (rule of thumb: hold stretch and exhale 15x) or for 2 minutes for each muscle group. Therefore, the post-match/practice static stretch routine will last 10-20 minutes depending on the number of exercises performed.

Proprioceptive Neuromuscular Facilitation (PNF) Stretching

During PNF stretching the athlete holds a static stretching position for a short period of time (5-10 seconds) before contracting the targeted muscle (agonist) or opposite muscle (antagonist) against a resistance but the muscle fibers do not change in length (isometric contraction); the Sumo Squat **(see Sumo Squat" on page 155)** is an example of PNF stretching. PNF stretching is often used during rehabilitation and often requires an experienced health professional to minimize the risk of injury.

In the previous chapter information was provided on how to evaluate flexibility and performance factors. Based on the findings, deficiencies or limitations, particular exercises need to be performed before and after each match, training, or workout. Before pre – and post-match/training exercises are introduced the importance of improving flexibility will be explained in more detail.

THE IMPORTANCE OF FLEXIBILITY

The most underrated – and underemphasized - component of most training programs is flexibility. The reason for this is that the tangible outcomes are tough to quantify. For instance, when one does flexibility training, is there a direct gain in size or speed? No, but flexibility affects all the training components such as speed and power indirectly because flexibility is one of the factors limiting the athlete's ability to develop power. For example, stride length impacts running and jumping economy (how efficiently one moves on the court), thereby affecting the amount of energy needed to move on the court. Therefore, flexibility does affect speed and power, but indirectly.

Many tennis players have **muscular imbalances**, especially at the shoulder joint where the force producing shoulder (right shoulder for right-handers) is more muscular and flexible than the less dominant shoulder. This becomes evident when taking a closer look at the shoulder blades (scapulae), which are "uneven", causing postural imbalance. Also, muscular imbalance of the trunk and hip musculature can cause severe problems because, for instance, the athlete can have tightness on one side due to agitation (contracture) which can cause ¼ inch limb length discrepancy, which matters with respects to the kinetic chain (transfer of energy), where unevenness can lead to back pain or knee pain.

Good flexibility **reduces tension, produces muscle relaxation** and **aids in recovery**. More specifically, myofascial deformation occurs when the fascia's tension capabilities are corrupted.

When that happens the fascia doesn't have the elastic properties and the tissue shortens. When one regularly uses the stretching exercises provided here in the training program, the muscles will become more pliable and the athlete will not experience shortening of the muscle in certain areas.

Since muscles (**tendons**) connect bones with each other, poor flexibility causes problems. If the muscles are short, the bones will consequently be closer together but if the bones are closer together movement at the joint will be limited (e.g. feet will turn inward during squats – foot position will be influenced due to instability and/or muscle tightness [in abductors pulling on femur]). Flexibility is also a component of recovery. If you static stretch well after a long match or tough practice, muscle soreness will be reduced to a large extent and this will allow the athlete to play/practice the next day instead of resting.

As previously mentioned, warming up and stretching the muscle tissue reduces the risk of injury and increases performance potential. Subsequently, good flexibility positively affects **movement range** of the respective joints as well as overall dynamic **energy transfer** efficiency. The movement range of the joints impacts one's speed developing capabilities because flexibility can limit the ability of the athlete to lengthen his/her stride. Most athletes' stride length is compromised by loss of dynamic stability due to locomotion (the loss and regain of stability). The goal is to maintain dynamic equilibrium, which can only be accomplished when the center of gravity remains within the base of support. Therefore, if stride length shortens, the base of support will decrease, which makes it more difficult to maintain the center of mass over the base of support, making it more difficult to maintain dynamic stability. Stride length is affected, amongst other things, by the flexibility of the hamstrings. When the athlete has tightness in the hamstrings, the legs cannot extend out all the way, which decreases the distance one covers with each step and this will limit overall speed. Also, if the athlete experiences tightness or imbalance in the gluteals (buttocks) and hip flexors, he/she can't change the pelvic position as it relates to the spine and he/she will experience dynamic instability and inefficiency in energy transfer.

In addition to the aforementioned, flexibility also plays an important role in overall joint health because it influences the integrity of the joints. For more information take a look at "Under the Microscope: Osteoarthritis" **(see Under the Microscope: Osteoarthritis" on page 64)**. Next we provide you with a general warm-up and various stretching exercises that you can use pre-resistance training, pre-competition/training, and post-competition/training.

THE WARM-UP & COOL-DOWN

Many tennis players, especially recreational players, regard the warm-up & cool-down as a nuisance and hence shorten up their routine or don't warm-up/cool-down at all. Any competitive athlete, who does not warm-up/cool-down properly is irresponsible and puts his/her career at risk. Even stretching without prior warm-up can be a cause of injury. The purpose of the warm-up, as the name implies, is to warm-up the musculature, thereby increasing muscle temperature through increased blood flow to the muscles. This will decrease the risk of injury (e.g. muscle sprains & strains) because the elastic properties of a "warm" muscle are better than those of a "cold" muscle. Also, the warm-up noticeably increases performance potential through improved range of motion (ROM) and increased speed of muscle contraction (and relaxation) due to elevated enzyme activity (accelerates energy production). Additionally, the warm-up is also a mental preparation phase for competition, which contributes to improved performance. Therefore, you must warm-up, focusing on the muscles in the legs, trunk, and shoulders to prepare for optimal performance during a match or practice session.

If no warm-up is performed before a match or practice session, the risk of injury increases and performance potential will decrease noticeably because "cold" muscles are less able to exert force. This, then, decreases the potential power output, which diminishes the athlete's ability to move effectively (e.g. accelerate).

The duration of the warm-up/cool-down period should be 10 – 20 minutes, respectively. The warm-up includes general warm-up exercises and ballistic stretching or dynamic stretching exercises; the cool-down has a jog-out phase and incorporates static stretching exercises or PNF exercises.

5.01 RECTANGLE RUN – LOWER BODY

SUMMARY

The Rectangle Run – Lower Body is a general warm-up routine, which focuses on warming up the musculature of the lower & upper extremities utilizing no equipment.

PURPOSE

Warming up musculature of lower extremities (legs)

DESCRIPTION

1. Face the net at all times
2. Remain outside the court lines
3. Start at the net post to your left
4. Start with backpedalling towards the ad-court corner past the baseline
5. Side-step towards the deuce-court corner past the side-line
6. Forward-jog towards the right net post
7. Side-step alongside the net towards the left net post

TARGETED MUSCULATURE

1. Hip Adductors
2. Hip Abductors
3. Glutes
4. Hamstrings
5. Quadriceps
6. Calves

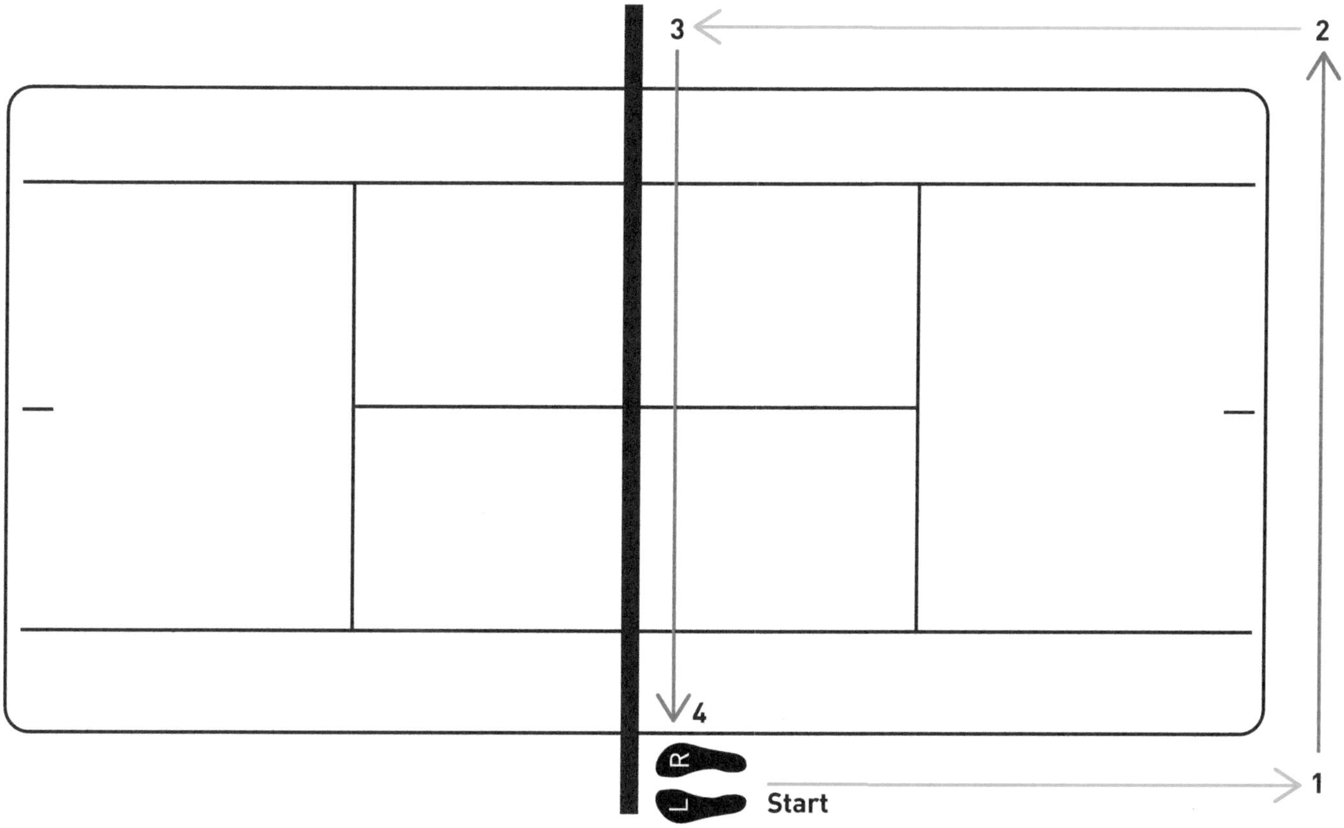

3
2
4
R
L
Start
1

ID: 501

5.02 RECTANGLE RUN – TOTAL BODY

SUMMARY

The Rectangle Run – Total Body is a general warm-up routine, which focuses on warming up the musculature of the lower & upper extremities utilizing no equipment.

PURPOSE

Warming up musculature of lower & upper extremities (arm & legs).

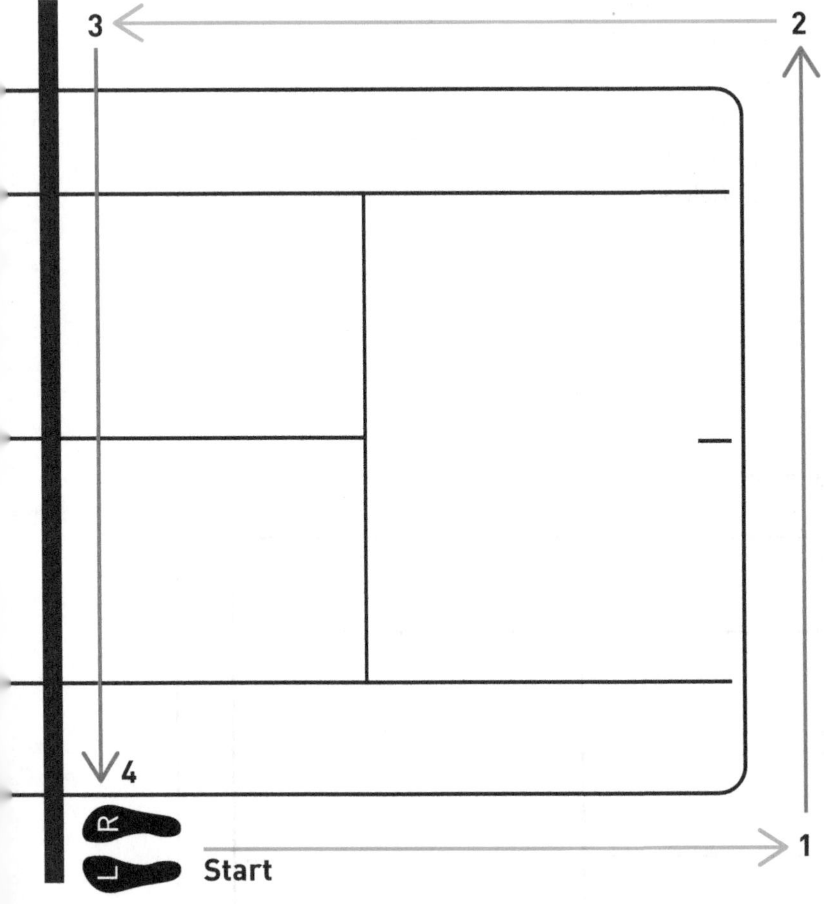

DESCRIPTION

1. Face the net at all times
2. Remain outside the court lines
3. Start at the net post to your left
4. Start with backpedalling towards the ad-court corner past the baseline while forward rotating the arms
5. Side-step towards the deuce-court corner past the side-line while scissor-swinging the arms
6. Forward-jog towards the right net post while backward rotating the arms
7. Side-step alongside the net towards the left net post while rotating trunk with arm swings

TARGETED MUSCULATURE

1. Hip Adductors
2. Hip Abductors
3. Glutes
4. Hamstrings
5. Quadriceps
6. Calves
7. Shoulders

ID: 502

5.03 CLAP PUSH-UP

SUMMARY

The Clap Push-Up is a limited ballistic stretching exercise for the upper-body, which focuses on reducing the risk of injury, optimizing power-production capabilities, and improving flexibility utilizing no equipment.

PURPOSE

1. Reducing the risk of injury
2. Optimizing power-production capabilities of musculature
3. Improving flexibility

RECOMMENDED RESISTANCE TRAINING EXERCISES

1. DB Bench Press
2. DB Bench Flyes

RELEVANCE

- Warms-up musculature of upper extremities used during stroke production activities
- If "Shoulder Mobility Test" shows deficiency, implement this exercise into the Resistance Training warm-up routine

DESCRIPTION

1. Only hands and toes touch the ground
2. Place hands slightly outside shoulders and extends arms fully
3. Keep body straight during movement (no hip flexion or extension)
4. Bend arms and release chest towards the ground
5. Extend arms explosively, elevating upper-body off the ground as far as possible
6. Clap hands
7. Return hands to starting position and decelerate upper-body towards the ground

TARGETED MUSCULATURE

1. Chest (Pectoralis Major & Minor)
2. Shoulder (Deltoids)
3. Triceps

ID: 503

5.04 WEIGHTED ROLL-UP

SUMMARY

The Weighted Roll-Up is a limited ballistic stretching exercise for the wrist flexor/extensor musculature, which focuses on reducing the risk of injury, optimizing power-production capabilities, and improving flexibility utilizing no equipment.

PURPOSE

1. Reducing the risk of injury
2. Optimizing power-production capabilities of musculature
3. Improving flexibility

DESCRIPTION

1. Hold short bar in both hands, palms down
2. Raise arms to shoulder-level in front of you and extend arms fully
3. Quickly roll-up the weight towards you
4. Quickly roll-down weight towards the ground

RECOMMENDED RESISTANCE TRAINING EXERCISES

1. DB Wrist Extension/Flexion
2. Hand Squeezers

REQUIRED EQUIPMENT

- Short bar
- Rope
- Weight

RELEVANCE

- Warms-up musculature of wrist flexor/extensor musculature used during stroke production activities

TARGETED MUSCULATURE

1. Wrist Flexors
2. Wrist Extensors

ID: 504

5.05 2 RACQUET SERVES

SUMMARY

The 2-Racquet Serves is a limited ballistic stretching exercise for the shoulder complex musculature, which focuses on reducing the risk of injury, optimizing power-production capabilities, and improving flexibility utilizing 2 racquets.

PURPOSE

1. Reducing the risk of injury
2. Optimizing power-production capabilities of musculature
3. Improving flexibility

RECOMMENDED RESISTANCE TRAINING EXERCISES

1. MB Overhead Throws
2. MB Serves

DESCRIPTION

1. Hold 2 racquets in your hands
2. Go through the full service motion including follow-through

KEY FACTORS

1. Maintain stability during follow-through
2. Keep looking forward during follow-through

EQUIPMENT

- 2 Racquets

RELEVANCE

- Warms-up musculature of shoulder musculature used during serving
- If "Shoulder Mobility Test" shows deficiency, implement this exercise into the Resistance Training warm-up routine

TARGETED MUSCULATURE

1. Rotator Cuff
2. Deltoids
3. Trapezius
4. Latissimus Dorsi
5. Triceps
6. Pectoralis Major & Minor

ID: 505

5.06 MB TOSS-UPS

SUMMARY

The Medicine Ball Toss-Ups is a limited ballistic stretching exercise for the triceps, which focuses on reducing the risk of injury, optimizing power-production capabilities, and improving flexibility utilizing a 6 lb medicine ball.

PURPOSE

1. Reducing the risk of injury
2. Optimizing power-production capabilities of musculature
3. Improving flexibility

RECOMMENDED RESISTANCE TRAINING EXERCISES

1. Overhead DB Triceps Extensions

DESCRIPTION

1. Hold medicine ball in both hands and behind your head
2. Toss medicine ball straight in the air
3. Catch medicine ball with extended arms
4. Repeat

EQUIPMENT

- 6 lb Medicine Ball (MB)

RELEVANCE

- Warms-up tricep musculature used during serving
- If "Shoulder Mobility Test" shows deficiency, implement this exercise into the Resistance Training warm-up routine

TARGETED MUSCULATURE

1. Triceps

ID: 506

5.07 MB TRUNK ROTATIONS

SUMMARY

The MB Trunk Rotations is a limited ballistic stretching exercise for the trunk rotators, which focuses on reducing the risk of injury, optimizing power-production capabilities, and improving flexibility utilizing a 4 lb medicine ball.

PURPOSE

1. Reducing the risk of injury
2. Optimizing power-production capabilities of musculature
3. Improving flexibility

RECOMMENDED RESISTANCE TRAINING EXERCISES

1. MB Trunk Rotation Throws

DESCRIPTION

1. Take an athletic stance; stand straight, feet are shoulder-width apart; knees slightly flexed
2. Hold medicine ball in both hands; push chest forward
3. Raise arms to chest level and straighten the elbows (keep slight bend)
4. Rotate upper-body from left side to right side and right side to left; control speed of trunk rotation

KEY FACTORS

1. Feet maintain ground contact during rotation
2. Head remains in neutral position during rotation
3. Arms remain straight and on chest level; rotation occurs at the trunk

EQUIPMENT

- 4-10 lb Medicine Ball (MB)

RELEVANCE

- Warms-up musculature used during groundstrokes
- If "Trunk Rotation Test" shows deficiency, implement this exercise into the Resistance Training warm-up routine

TARGETED MUSCULATURE

1. Obliques
2. Trunk Rotators

ID: 507

5.08 SEATED MB TRUNK TWIST

SUMMARY

The Seated MB Trunk Twist is a limited ballistic stretching exercise for the trunk rotators, which focuses on reducing the risk of injury, optimizing power-production capabilities, and improving flexibility utilizing a 4 lb medicine ball.

PURPOSE

1. Reducing the risk of injury
2. Optimizing power-production capabilities of musculature
3. Improving flexibility

DESCRIPTION

1. Sit on the ground so that buttocks and feet touch the floor
2. Flex knees at 90°
3. Hold medicine ball in both hands
4. Raise arms to shoulder-level and straighten the elbows
5. Rotate upper-body from left side to right side and right side to left

TARGETED MUSCULATURE

1. Obliques
2. Trunk Rotators

RELEVANCE

- Warms-up musculature used during groundstrokes
- If "Trunk Rotation Test" shows deficiency, implement this exercise into the Resistance Training warm-up routine

KEY FACTORS

1. Maintain neutral hips and a flat back

RECOMMENDED RESISTANCE TRAINING EXERCISES

1. MB Trunk Rotation Throws
2. Russian Twists

EQUIPMENT

- 4-10 lb Medicine Ball (MB)

ID: 508

5.09 JUMP SQUAT

SUMMARY

The Jump Squat is a limited ballistic stretching exercise for the glutes, which focuses on reducing the risk of injury, optimizing power-production capabilities, and improving flexibility utilizing no equipment.

PURPOSE

1. Reducing the risk of injury
2. Optimizing power-production capabilities of musculature
3. Improving flexibility

DESCRIPTION

1. Stand up straight
2. Feet are shoulder-width apart, toes point slightly outwards
3. Lean back with your buttocks and bend knees to 90°
4. Keep the weight on your heels
5. Explosively jump up vertically
6. Land on your heels and absorb the landing into the squat position

TARGETED MUSCULATURE

1. Glutes
2. Groin

RELEVANCE

- Warms-up musculature used during groundstrokes and serving
- Improves performance of hip extensors
- If "Hip Flexion Test" shows deficiency, implement this exercise into the Resistance Training warm-up routine

KEY FACTORS

1. Land heels first

RECOMMENDED RESISTANCE TRAINING EXERCISES

1. Squat
2. Lateral Squat
3. Lunge

ID: 509

5.10 KNEEL & JUMP

SUMMARY

The Kneel & Jump is a limited ballistic stretching exercise for the glutes, which focuses on reducing the risk of injury, optimizing power-production capabilities, improving flexibility and stability utilizing no equipment.

PURPOSE

1. Reducing the risk of injury
2. Optimizing power-production capabilities of musculature
3. Improving flexibility
4. Improving stability

RECOMMENDED RESISTANCE TRAINING EXERCISES

1. Squat
2. Lateral Squat
3. Lunge

DESCRIPTION

1. Kneel on the ground shoulder-width apart
2. Use arm swing to create momentum
3. Elevate yourself off the ground
4. Flex hips rapidly
5. Land on your feet in a squat position shoulder-width apart

RELEVANCE

- Warms-up musculature used during groundstrokes and serving
- Improves performance of hip flexors
- If "Hip Flexion Test" shows deficiency, implement this exercise into the Resistance Training warm-up routine

TARGETED MUSCULATURE

1. Glutes
2. Groin

KEY FACTORS

1. Land heels first

ID: 510

5.11 LATERAL JUMP LUNGES

SUMMARY

The Lateral Jump Lunge is a limited ballistic stretching exercise for the piriformis & glutes, which focuses on reducing the risk of injury, optimizing power-production capabilities, and improving flexibility utilizing no equipment.

PURPOSE

1. Reducing the risk of injury
2. Optimizing power-production capabilities of musculature
3. Improving flexibility

RECOMMENDED RESISTANCE TRAINING EXERCISES

1. Lateral Squat
2. Lateral Lunge

DESCRIPTION

1. Stand straight and place feet close together
2. Left foot maintains ground contact, right foot moves towards the right and touches the ground: toes point outwards slightly
3. During the landing of the right foot keep the weight on the heels
4. Absorb upper-body until right knee is flexed at 90°; left leg is straight
5. Forcefully extend the right leg and jump back to starting position
6. Side-step
7. Right foot maintains ground contact, left foot moves towards the left and touches the ground: toes point outwards slightly
8. During the landing of the left foot keep the weight on the heels
9. Absorb upper-body until left knee is flexed at 90°; right leg is straight
10. Forcefully extend the right leg and jump back to starting position
11. Side-Step and repeat

RELEVANCE

- Warms-up musculature used during groundstrokes and serving
- Improves performance of lateral hip flexors
- If "Hip Flexion Test" shows deficiency, implement this exercise into the Resistance Training warm-up routine

TARGETED MUSCULATURE

1. Piriformis
2. Glutes
3. Groin

KEY FACTORS

1. Knees may not protrude past the toes

ID: 511

5.12 HIGH KNEE PULL

SUMMARY

The High Knee Pull is a dynamic stretching exercise for the lower-body, which focuses on reducing the risk of injury, optimizing power-production capabilities, improving flexibility utilizing no equipment.

PURPOSE

1. Reducing the risk of injury
2. Optimizing power-production capabilities of musculature
3. Improving flexibility

RECOMMENDED RESISTANCE TRAINING EXERCISES

1. Squat
2. Front Squat
3. Deadlift

RELEVANCE

- Warms-up musculature of lower extremities used during running & jumping activities
- If "Thomas Test" shows deficiency, implement this exercise into the warm-up routine
- If "Thomas Test" shows deficiency, implement the "Recommended Resistance Training Exercises" into the gym workout routine

DESCRIPTION

1. Take a step and raise the left knee towards the chest
2. Grab your leg with both hands just below the knee
3. Pull knee as close to your chest as possible
4. Hold the knee for 1 second
5. Release the left knee
6. Take a step and raise the right knee and repeat

TARGETED MUSCULATURE

1. Glutes
2. Hip Flexors (iliopsoas)
3. Hip Adductors

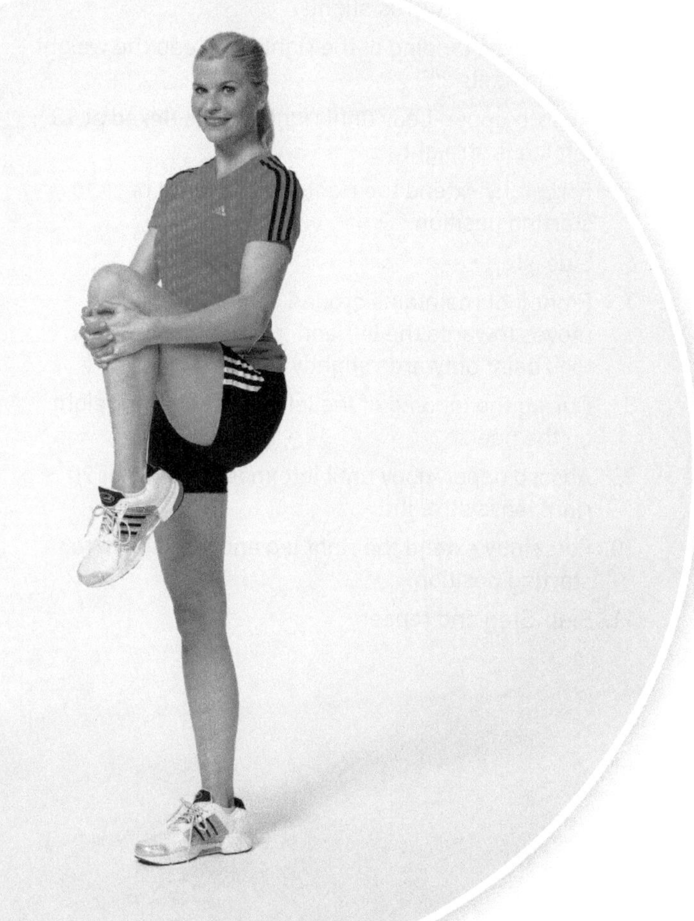

ID: 512

5.13 HIGH KNEE PULLS W. DORSI FLEXION

SUMMARY

The High Knee Pull with Dorsi Flexion is a dynamic stretching exercise, which focuses on reducing the risk of injury, optimizing power-production capabilities, improving flexibility and stability utilizing no equipment.

PURPOSE

1. Reducing the risk of injury
2. Optimizing power-production capabilities of musculature
3. Improving flexibility
4. Improving stability

DESCRIPTION

1. Take a step and raise the left knee towards the chest
2. Grab your leg with both hands just below the knee
3. Pull knee as close to your chest as possible
4. During the knee pull flex your feet and stand on your toes
5. Hold the knee for 1 second
6. Release the left knee
7. Take a step and raise the right knee and repeat

RECOMMENDED RESISTANCE TRAINING EXERCISES

1. Squat
2. Front Squat
3. SL Calve Raises
4. Deadlift

RELEVANCE

- Warms-up musculature of lower extremities used during running & jumping activities
- If "Stability Squad Test" shows deficiency, implement this exercise into the warm-up routine
- If "Hip Flexion" shows deficiency, implement this exercise into the warm-up routine
- If "Hip Flexion" shows deficiency, implement the "Recommended Resistance Training Exercises" into the gym workout routine

TARGETED MUSCULATURE

1. Buttocks (Glutes)
2. Calves (Gastrocnemius)
3. Calves (Soleus)
4. Hip Flexors (Iliopsoas)
5. Hip Adductors

ID: 513

5.14 BUTTOCKS KICKS

SUMMARY

The Buttocks Kicks is a dynamic stretching exercise, which focuses on reducing the risk of injury, optimizing power-production capabilities, and improving flexibility utilizing no equipment.

PURPOSE

1. Reducing the risk of injury
2. Optimizing power-production capabilities of musculature
3. Improving flexibility

DESCRIPTION

1. Face forward
2. Keep knees & feet inside the shoulders
3. Kick yourself in the buttocks with the heels of your feet
4. Knees point towards the ground

RECOMMENDED RESISTANCE TRAINING EXERCISES

1. Leg Extensions
2. Forward & Reverse Lunge

RELEVANCE

- Warms-up musculature of lower extremities used during running & jumping activities
- If "Bilateral Knee Flexion Test" shows deficiency, implement this exercise into the warm-up routine
- If "Bilateral Knee Flexion Test" shows deficiency, implement the "Recommended Resistance Training Exercises" into the gym workout routine

TARGETED MUSCULATURE

1. Quadriceps

ID: 514

5.15 STRAIGHT LEG KICKS

SUMMARY

The Straight Leg Kicks is a dynamic stretching exercise, which focuses on reducing the risk of injury, optimizing power-production capabilities, and improving flexibility utilizing no equipment.

PURPOSE

1. Reducing the risk of injury
2. Optimizing power-production capabilities of musculature
3. Improving flexibility

RECOMMENDED RESISTANCE TRAINING EXERCISES

1. Good Mornings
2. Romanian Deadlift (RDL)
3. Single Leg RDL

DESCRIPTION

1. Face forward
2. Keep leg straight and raise it as far in front of you as possible
3. The ipsilateral (opposite) hand touches the toes of the raised leg
4. Release the leg back to the ground
5. Repeat with other leg

TARGETED MUSCULATURE

1. Hamstrings

RELEVANCE

- Warms-up musculature of lower extremities used during running & jumping activities
- If "Bilateral Knee Extension Test" shows deficiency, implement this exercise into the warm-up routine
- If "Bilateral Knee Extension Test" shows deficiency, implement the "Recommended Resistance Training Exercises" into the gym workout routine

ID: 515

5.16 SINGLE LEG RDL

SUMMARY

The Single Leg (SL) Romanian Deadlift (RDL) is a dynamic stretching exercise, which focuses on reducing the risk of injury, optimizing power-production capabilities, improving flexibility and stability utilizing no equipment.

PURPOSE

1. Reducing the risk of injury
2. Optimizing power-production capabilities of musculature
3. Improving flexibility
4. Improving stabilityv

RELEVANCE

- Warms-up musculature of lower extremities used during running & jumping activities
- Improves stability of lower extremities
- If "Stability Squad Test" shows deficiency, implement this exercise into the warm-up routine
- If "Bilateral Knee Extension Test" shows deficiency, implement this exercise into the warm-up routine
- If "Bilateral Knee Extension Test" shows deficiency, implement the "Recommended Exercises" into the gym workout routine

RECOMMENDED EXERCISES

1. RDL
2. Good Morning
3. Single Leg RDL
4. Stability Pad Squats

DESCRIPTION

1. Stand on the left leg
2. Lower the upper-body as far towards the ground as possible while the right leg goes up as far as possible behind you
3. Maintain stability and hold stretch for a second
4. Return with upper-body and right leg to normal position
5. Stand on the right leg and repeat with left foot

TARGETED MUSCULATURE

1. Hamstrings

ID: 516

5.17 SL RDL & QUAD STRETCH

SUMMARY

The Single Leg (SL) Romanian Deadlift (RDL) with Quad Stretch is a dynamic stretching exercise, which focuses on reducing the risk of injury, optimizing power-production capabilities, improving flexibility and stability utilizing no equipment.

PURPOSE

1. Reducing the risk of injury
2. Optimizing power-production capabilities of musculature
3. Improving flexibility
4. Improving stability

DESCRIPTION

1. Stand on the left leg
2. Right hand grabs the toes of the right foot
3. Pull the right foot towards the buttocks while lowering the upper-body as far towards the ground as possible
4. Maintain stability and hold stretch for a second
5. Return upper-body to normal position and release the right hand
6. Stand on the right leg and repeat with left hand/foot

RECOMMENDED RESISTANCE TRAINING EXERCISES

1. Squat
2. Front Squat
3. Deadlift
4. SL RDL
5. Stability Pad Squats

RELEVANCE

- Warms-up musculature of lower extremities used during running & jumping activities
- Improves stability of lower extremities
- If "Stability Squad Test" shows deficiency, implement this exercise into the warm-up routine
- If "Bilateral Knee Flexion and/or Extension Test" shows deficiency, implement this exercise into the warm-up routine
- If "Bilateral Knee Flexion and/or Extension Test" shows deficiency, implement the "Recommended Resistance Training Exercises" into the gym workout routine

TARGETED MUSCULATURE

1. Hamstrings
2. Quadriceps

ID: 517

5.18 PIRIFORMIS STRETCH

SUMMARY

The Piriformis Stretch is a dynamic stretching exercise, which focuses on reducing the risk of injury, optimizing power-production capabilities, and improving flexibility utilizing no equipment.

PURPOSE

1. Reducing the risk of injury
2. Optimizing power-production capabilities of musculature
3. Improving flexibility

RECOMMENDED RESISTANCE TRAINING EXERCISES

1. Lateral Lunge
2. Lateral Squat

DESCRIPTION

1. Face forward
2. Stand on the left leg
3. Move the right leg and bend the knee so that the toes point inside and the knee outside
4. Grab the right chin with both hands
5. Pull lower right leg up towards your hips
6. Hold stretch for 1 second
7. Release right leg, take a step, and repeat with left leg

RELEVANCE

- Warms-up musculature of lower extremities used during lateral movement/change of direction
- If "Stability Pad Squad Test" shows deficiency, implement this exercise into the warm-up routine
- If "Bilateral Lunge Test" shows deficiency, implement the "Recommended Resistance Training Exercises" into the gym workout routine

TARGETED MUSCULATURE

1. Piriformis

ID: 518

5.19 DUCK WALK

SUMMARY

The Duck Walk is a dynamic stretching exercise, which focuses on reducing the risk of injury, optimizing power-production capabilities, and improving flexibility utilizing no equipment.

PURPOSE

1. Reducing the risk of injury
2. Optimizing power-production capabilities of musculature
3. Improving flexibility

DESCRIPTION

1. Feet shoulder width apart
2. Drop into the lowest squat attainable
3. Look up towards the sky
4. Back remains straight
5. Weight remains on the heels
6. Place hands behind your head so that elbows point sideways (shoulder is at 90°)
7. Walk forward using small steps

RECOMMENDED RESISTANCE TRAINING EXERCISES

1. Front Squat
2. Squat
3. Lunge (forward/reverse/lateral)

RELEVANCE

- Warms-up musculature of lower extremities used during groundstrokes and lateral movement/change of direction
- If "Thomas Test" shows deficiency, implement this exercise into the warm-up routine
- If "Bilateral Knee Flexion" shows deficiency, implement the "Recommended Resistance Training Exercises" into the gym workout routine

TARGETED MUSCULATURE

1. Glutes
2. Quadriceps
3. Hip Adductors
4. Dorsi Flexors

ID: 519

5.20 SQUAT

SUMMARY

The Squat is a dynamic stretching exercise, which focuses on reducing the risk of injury, optimizing power-production capabilities, improving flexibility and stability, utilizing no equipment.

PURPOSE

1. Reducing the risk of injury
2. Optimizing power-production capabilities of musculature
3. Improving flexibility
4. Improving stability

RECOMMENDED RESISTANCE TRAINING EXERCISES

1. Squat
2. Front Squat
3. Overhead Squat

DESCRIPTION

1. Stand in neutral stance (feet are shoulder-width apart; knees are slightly bent)
2. Flex hips until knees are at 90°; keep weight on the heels of the feet and arms out in front of you
3. Extend hips until you are standing
4. Repeat

DEGREE OF DIFFICULTY

- 1

RELEVANCE

- Warms-up musculature of lower extremities used during groundstrokes and jumping
- This is a pre-requisite exercise for Overhead Squat, Squat, and Front Squat
- If "Hip Flexion Test" shows deficiency, implement this exercise into the warm-up routine
- If "Stability Pad Squat Test" shows deficiency, implement the "Recommended Resistance Training Exercises" into the gym workout routine

TARGETED MUSCULATURE

1. Glutes
2. Hip Adductors
3. Hip Abductors
4. Piriformis

ID: 520

5.21 BILATERAL SQUAT

SUMMARY

The Bilateral Squat is a dynamic stretching exercise, which focuses on reducing the risk of injury, optimizing power-production capabilities, improving flexibility and stability, utilizing no equipment.

PURPOSE

1. Reducing the risk of injury
2. Optimizing power-production capabilities of musculature
3. Improving flexibility
4. Improving stabily

DESCRIPTION

1. Stand straight with feet close together
2. Step sideways with the left foot until both feet are shoulder-width apart
3. Flex hips and drop down in the center between the legs; bend both knees until they are at 90°; knee must not move beyond toes; toes point slightly outward (10°-20°)
4. Extend knees and hips and step out of the squat to the left; move feet close together
5. Side-step to the right
6. Step sideways with the right foot until both feet are shoulder-width apart
7. Flex hips and drop down in the center between the legs; bend both knees until they are at 90°; knee must not move beyond toes; toes point slightly outward (10°-20°)
8. Extend knees and hips and step out of the squat to the right; move feet close together
9. Repeat

DEGREE OF DIFFICULTY

- 1

RELEVANCE

- Warms-up musculature of lower extremities used during groundstrokes and lateral change of direction (agility)
- This is a pre-requisite exercise for Bilateral Squat w. Trunk Rotation, Squat with Bar Rotation, and Bilateral Squat w. Bar Rotation
- If "Thomas Test" shows deficiency, implement this exercise into the warm-up routine
- If "Stability Pad Squat Test" shows deficiency, implement the "Recommended Resistance Training Exercises" into the gym workout routine

TARGETED MUSCULATURE

1. Hip Abductors
2. Hip Adductors
3. Piriformis
4. Glutes

RECOMMENDED RESISTANCE TRAINING EXERCISES

1. Bar Bilateral Squat
2. Bilateral Squat w. Bar Rotation

ID: 521

5.22 BILATERAL LUNGE

SUMMARY

The Bilateral Lunge is a dynamic stretching exercise, which focuses on reducing the risk of injury, optimizing power-production capabilities, improving flexibility and stability, utilizing no equipment.

PURPOSE

1. Reducing the risk of injury
2. Optimizing power-production capabilities of musculature
3. Improving flexibility
4. Improving stability

DESCRIPTION

1. Take an athletic stance; stand straight, feet are shoulder-width apart; knees slightly flexed; toes point slightly outward (10°-20°)
2. Step sideways with the left foot and bend the left knee until left knee is at 90° and right leg is straight; knee must not move beyond toes; toes point slightly outward (10°-20°)
3. Push-off with the left foot, return to athletic stance, and lunge to the right side until right knee is at 90°; knee must not move beyond toes; toes point slightly outward (10°-20°)

RELEVANCE

- Warms-up musculature of lower extremities used during groundstrokes and lateral change of direction (agility)
- This is a pre-requisite exercise for Bilateral Lunge w. Trunk Rotation, Bar Bilateral Lunge, and Bilateral Lunge w. Bar Rotation
- If "Thomas Test" shows deficiency, implement this exercise into the warm-up routine
- If "Bilateral Lunge Test" shows deficiency, implement the "Recommended Resistance Training Exercises" into the gym workout routine

RECOMMENDED RESISTANCE TRAINING EXERCISES

1. Bar Bilateral Lunge
2. Bilateral Lunge w. Bar Rotation

TARGETED MUSCULATURE

1. Hip Abductors
2. Hip Adductors
3. Glutes

DEGREE OF DIFFICULTY

- 1

ID: 522

5.23 FORWARD & REVERSE LUNGE

SUMMARY

The Forward & Reverse Lunge is a dynamic stretching exercise, which focuses on reducing the risk of injury, optimizing power-production capabilities, and improving flexibility utilizing no equipment.

RECOMMENDED RESISTANCE TRAINING EXERCISES

1. Front Squat
2. Squat
3. Lunge (forward/reverse/lateral)

RELEVANCE

- Warms-up musculature of lower extremities used during groundstrokes
- If "Thomas Test" shows deficiency, implement this exercise into your warm-up routine

TARGETED MUSCULATURE

1. Glutes
2. Quadriceps
3. Hamstrings

DEGREE OF DIFFICULTY

- 1

PURPOSE

1. Reducing the risk of injury
2. Optimizing power-production capabilities of musculature
3. Improving flexibility

DESCRIPTION

1. Stand straight with feet close together
2. Step into a forward lunge with the left foot until left knee is at 90°; knee must not move beyond toes
3. Push-off with the left foot and step into reverse lunge without moving the right foot; right knee is at 90°
4. Step into forward lunge again
5. Repeat & Switch
6. Repeat

ID: 523

5.24 CROSS-OVER LUNGE

SUMMARY

The Cross-Over Lunge is a dynamic stretching exercise, which focuses on reducing the risk of injury, optimizing power-production capabilities, improving flexibility and stability utilizing no equipment.

PURPOSE

1. Reducing the risk of injury
2. Optimizing power-production capabilities of musculature
3. Improving flexibility
4. Improving stability

DESCRIPTION

1. Stand up straight; feet are shoulder width apart
2. Perform a cross-over move; right leg crosses over behind the left foot, stepping into a lunge; keep weight on the heel of front foot (left foot)
3. Move trailing foot (right foot) in line (parallel) with left foot; feet are shoulder-width apart
4. Cross-over with left foot behind the right foot, stepping into a lunge; keep weight on the heel of front foot (right foot)
5. Move trailing foot (left foot) in line (parallel) with right foot; feet are shoulder-width apart

RECOMMENDED RESISTANCE TRAINING EXERCISES

1. Split Jerk
2. Forward Lunge to Overhead Press
3. Lunge (forward/reverse/lateral

RELEVANCE

- Warms-up musculature of lower extremities used during groundstrokes
- Serves as pre-requisite exercise for "Cross-Over Lunge with Heel Reach", "Lunge with Bar Rotation" and "Cross-Over Lunge w. Bar Rotation"

TARGETED MUSCULATURE

1. Glutes
2. Quadriceps
3. Hamstrings
4. Abductors
5. Adductors

DEGREE OF DIFFICULTY

- 1

ID: 524

5.25 QUICK CARIOCA

SUMMARY

The Quick Carioca is a dynamic stretching exercise, which focuses on reducing the risk of injury, optimizing power-production capabilities, and improving flexibility, utilizing no equipment.

PURPOSE

1. Reducing the risk of injury
2. Optimizing power-production capabilities of musculature
3. Improving flexibility of hip abductors & adductors

DESCRIPTION

1. Stand in athletic stance
2. Perform anterior- and posterior cross overs in alternating fashion
3. Hips remain neutral throughout the movement; no hip rotation

DEGREE OF DIFFICULTY

- 1

RELEVANCE

- Warms-up musculature of lower extremities used in lateral movement during groundstrokes
- If the athlete is trying to improve lateral foot speed and movement implement this exercise into the warm-up routine

RECOMMENDED RESISTANCE TRAINING EXERCISES

1. Abductor Box Jumps
2. Adductor Box Jumps
3. Lateral Squats
4. Lateral Lunges

TARGETED MUSCULATURE

1. Hip Adductors
2. Hip Abductors

ID: 525

5.26 SQUAT & OVERHEAD REACH

SUMMARY

The Squat & Overhead Reach is a dynamic stretching exercise, which focuses on reducing the risk of injury, optimizing power-production capabilities, improving flexibility and stability, utilizing no equipment.

PURPOSE

1. Reducing the risk of injury
2. Optimizing power-production capabilities of musculature
3. Improving flexibility
4. Improving stability

DESCRIPTION

1. Stand in athletic stance (feet are shoulder-width apart; knees are slightly bent), keep hands close to the body in front of you
2. Flex hips until knees are at 90° and raise arms over your head; keep weight on the heels of the feet and arms wide over your head
3. Extend hips until you are standing and lower arms to starting position
4. Repeat

RECOMMENDED RESISTANCE TRAINING EXERCISES

1. Squat
2. Front Squat
3. Overhead Squat

PRE-REQUISITE EXERCISES

- Squat

DEGREE OF DIFFICULTY

- 2

RELEVANCE

- Warms-up musculature of lower – and upper extremities used during groundstrokes and jumping
- This is a pre-requisite exercise for Overhead Squat, Squat, and Front Squat
- If "Hip Flexion Test" shows deficiency, implement this exercise into the warm-up routine
- If "Stability Pad Squat Test" shows deficiency, implement the "Recommended Resistance Training Exercises" into the gym workout routine

TARGETED MUSCULATURE

1. Hip Extensors
2. Hip Adductors
3. Hip Abductors
4. Piriformis
5. Glutes
6. Deltoids
7. Latissimus Dorsi

ID: 526

5.27 BILATERAL SQUAT W. TRUNK ROTATION

SUMMARY

The Bilateral Squat with Trunk Rotation is a dynamic stretching exercise, which focuses on reducing the risk of injury, optimizing power-production capabilities, improving flexibility and stability, utilizing no equipment.

PURPOSE

1. Reducing the risk of injury
2. Optimizing power-production capabilities of musculature
3. Improving flexibility
4. Improving stability

RECOMMENDED RESISTANCE TRAINING EXERCISES

1. Bar Bilateral Squat
2. Bilateral Squat w. Bar Rotation

DESCRIPTION

1. Stand straight with feet close together
2. Step sideways with the left foot until both feet are shoulder-width apart
3. Bend both knees until they are at 90°; knee must not move beyond toes
4. Rotate trunk to the left and to the right
5. Extend knees and move feet close together
6. Side-Step
7. Step sideways with the right foot until both feet are shoulder-width apart
8. Bend both knees until they are at 90°; knee must not move beyond toes
9. Rotate trunk to the left and to the right

PRE-REQUISITE EXERCISES

- Bilateral Squat

TARGETED MUSCULATURE

1. Hip Adductors
2. Hip Abductors
3. Piriformis
4. Glutes
5. Obliques

DEGREE OF DIFFICULTY

- 2

RELEVANCE

- Warms-up musculature of lower extremities used during groundstrokes and lateral change of direction (agility)
- This is a pre-requisite exercise for Squat with Bar Rotation and Bilateral Squat w. Bar Rotation
- If "Thomas Test" shows deficiency, implement this exercise into the warm-up routine
- If "Stability Pad Squat Test" shows deficiency, implement the "Recommended Resistance Training Exercises" into the gym workout routine

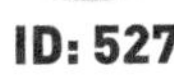

5.28 BILATERAL LUNGE WITH TRUNK ROTATION

SUMMARY

The Bilateral Lunge with Trunk Rotation is a dynamic stretching exercise, which focuses on reducing the risk of injury, optimizing power-production capabilities, improving flexibility and stability, utilizing no equipment.

PURPOSE

1. Reducing the risk of injury
2. Optimizing power-production capabilities of musculature
3. Improving flexibility
4. Improving stability

DESCRIPTION

1. Stand straight with feet close together
2. Step sideways with the left foot and bend the left knee until left knee is at 90° and right leg is straight; knee must not move beyond toes
3. Rotate trunk to the left, then to the right
4. Push-off with the left foot and lunge to the right side until right knee is at 90° and left leg is straight; knee must not move beyond toes
5. Rotate trunk to the left, then to the right
6. Bend both knees until they are at 90°; knee must not move beyond toes
7. Rotate trunk to the left and to the right

RECOMMENDED RESISTANCE TRAINING EXERCISES

1. Bar Bilateral Lunge
2. Bilateral Lunge w. Bar Rotation

PRE-REQUISITE EXERCISES

- Bilateral Lunge

DEGREE OF DIFFICULTY

- 2

RELEVANCE

- Warms-up musculature of lower extremities used during groundstrokes and lateral change of direction (agility)
- This is a pre-requisite exercise for Bar Bilateral Lunge, and Bilateral Lunge w. Bar Rotation
- If "Thomas Test" & "Trunk Rotation Test" shows deficiency, implement this exercise into the warm-up routine
- If "Bilateral Lunge Test" shows deficiency, implement the "Recommended Resistance Training Exercises" into the gym workout routine

TARGETED MUSCULATURE

1. Hip Adductors
2. Hip Abductors
3. Glutes
4. Obliques

ID: 528

5.29 LUNGE & TWIST

SUMMARY

The Lunge & Twist is a dynamic stretching exercise, which focuses on reducing the risk of injury, optimizing power-production capabilities, improving flexibility and stability utilizing no equipment.

PURPOSE

1. Reducing the risk of injury
2. Optimizing power-production capabilities of musculature
3. Improving flexibility
4. Improving Stability

DESCRIPTION

1. Take a large step out with the leading leg
2. Drop trailing knee towards the ground in a controlled fashion until both knees are at 90°
3. Rotate the torso all the way from right to left
4. Keep weight on forward heel
5. Stand up and progress into next lunge

RECOMMENDED RESISTANCE TRAINING EXERCISES

1. Russian Twist
2. MB Trunk Rotation Throws
3. Lunge (forward/reverse/lateral)

TARGETED MUSCULATURE

1. Glutes
2. Quadriceps
3. Hamstrings
4. Hip Flexors
5. Obliques

PRE-REQUISITE EXERCISES

- Forward & Reverse Lunge

DEGREE OF DIFFICULTY

- 2

RELEVANCE

- Warms-up musculature of lower extremities and trunk used during groundstrokes
- If "Trunk Rotator Test" shows deficiency, implement this exercise into the warm-up routine
- If "Hip Flexor/Trunk Extension" shows deficiency, implement the "Recommended Resistance Training Exercises" into the gym workout routine

ID: 529

5.30 LUNGE & OVERHEAD REACH

SUMMARY

The Lunge & Overhead Reach is a dynamic stretching exercise, which focuses on reducing the risk of injury, optimizing power-production capabilities, improving flexibility and stability utilizing no equipment.

PURPOSE

1. Reducing the risk of injury
2. Optimizing power-production capabilities of musculature
3. Improving flexibility
4. Improving Stability

DESCRIPTION

1. Look forward at all times
2. Take a large step out with the leading leg
3. Drop trailing knee towards the ground in a controlled fashion until both knees are at 90°
4. Extend the arms and rotate them over your head as far as possible behind your head (full shoulder flexion)
5. Keep weight on forward heel
6. Stand up and progress into next lunge

RECOMMENDED RESISTANCE TRAINING EXERCISES

1. PB MB Pull Ups
2. Overhead Squat
3. Lunge (forward/reverse/lateral)

DEGREE OF DIFFICULTY

- 2

RELEVANCE

- Warms-up musculature of lower extremities and trunk used during groundstrokes
- If "Shoulder Mobility Test" & "Hip Flexor/Trunk Extension" shows deficiency, implement this exercise into the warm-up routine
- If "Hip Flexor/Trunk Extension" shows deficiency, implement the "Recommended Resistance Training Exercises" into the gym workout routine

TARGETED MUSCULATURE

1. Glutes
2. Quadriceps
3. Hamstrings
4. Hip Flexors
5. Deltoids
6. Latissimus Dorsi
7. Lower Back

PRE-REQUISITE EXERCISES

- Forward/Reverse Lunge

ID: 530

5.31 FORWARD LUNGE & ANKLE REACH

SUMMARY

The Forward Lunge & Ankle Reach is a dynamic stretching exercise, which focuses on reducing the risk of injury, optimizing power-production capabilities, improving flexibility and stability utilizing no equipment.

PURPOSE

1. Reducing the risk of injury
2. Optimizing power-production capabilities of musculature
3. Improving flexibility
4. Improving Stability

DESCRIPTION

1. Look forward at all times
2. Take a large step out with the left leg
3. Drop right knee towards the ground in a controlled fashion until both knees are at 90°
4. Rotate the torso all the way to the right and touch/reach the ankle of the right foot
5. Keep weight on forward heel
6. Stand up and progress into next lunge now rotating and touching towards the left side

RECOMMENDED RESISTANCE TRAINING EXERCISES

1. Russian Twist
2. MB Trunk Rotation Throws
3. Lunge (forward/reverse/lateral)

PRE-REQUISITE EXERCISES

- Forward/Reverse Lunge
- Lunge & Twist

RECOMMENDED RESISTANCE TRAINING EXERCISES

- Russian Twist
- MB Trunk Rotation Throws
- Lunge (forward/reverse/lateral)

DEGREE OF DIFFICULTY

- 3

RELEVANCE

- Warms-up musculature of lower extremities and trunk used during groundstrokes
- If "Trunk Rotator Test" shows deficiency, implement this exercise into the warm-up routine
- If "Hip Flexor/Trunk Extension" shows deficiency, implement the "Recommended Resistance Training Exercises" into the gym workout routine

TARGETED MUSCULATURE

1. Glutes
2. Quadriceps
3. Hamstrings
4. Hip Flexors
5. Obliques

5.32 CROSS-OVER LUNGES W. HEEL REACHES

SUMMARY

The Cross-Over Lunge w. Heel Reaches is a dynamic stretching exercise, which focuses on reducing the risk of injury, optimizing power-production capabilities, improving flexibility and stability utilizing no equipment.

PURPOSE

1. Reducing the risk of injury
2. Optimizing power-production capabilities of musculature
3. Improving flexibility
4. Improving stability

DESCRIPTION

1. Stand up straight with feet shoulder-width apart
2. Perform a cross-over move; right leg crosses over behind the left foot, stepping into a lunge while arms are straight, trunk rotates to the left, and left hand reaches toward the heel of the right foot
3. Keep weight on the heel of front foot (left foot)
4. Move trailing foot (right foot) in line (parallel) with left foot; feet are shoulder-width apart
5. Cross-over with left foot behind the right foot, stepping into a lunge while arms are straight, trunk rotates to the right, and right hand reaches toward the heel of the right foot
6. Keep weight on the heel of front foot (right foot)
7. Move trailing foot (left foot) in line (parallel) with right foot; feet are shoulder-width apart
8. Perform a cross-over move; right leg crosses over behind the left foot, stepping into a lunge while arms are straight, trunk rotates to the left, and left hand reaches toward the heel of the right foot

RECOMMENDED RESISTANCE TRAINING EXERCISES

1. Cross-Over Lunge Bar Rotations
2. Split Jerk
3. Forward Lunge to Overhead Press
4. Lunge (forward/reverse/lateral)

RECOMMENDED RESISTANCE TRAINING EXERCISES

- Cross-Over Lunge Bar Rotations
- Split Jerk
- Forward Lunge to Overhead Press
- Lunge (forward/reverse/lateral)

ID: 532

DEGREE OF DIFFICULTY

- 2

RELEVANCE

- Warms-up musculature of lower & upper extremities used during groundstrokes
- Serves as pre-requisite exercise for "Lunge with Bar Rotation" and "Cross-Over Lunge w. Bar Rotation"

TARGETED MUSCULATURE

1. Glutes
2. Quadriceps
3. Hamstrings
4. Abductors
5. Adductors
6. Obliques

PRE-REQUISITE EXERCISES

- Cross-Over Lunges

5.33 LATERAL SKIPS WITH ARM SWINGS

SUMMARY

The Lateral Skips w. Arm Swings is a dynamic stretching exercise, which focuses on reducing the risk of injury, optimizing power-production capabilities, and improving flexibility utilizing no equipment.

PURPOSE

1. Reducing the risk of injury
2. Optimizing power-production capabilities of musculature
3. Improving flexibility (lateral shoulder abduction)

DESCRIPTION

1. Stand up straight with feet together and arms raised sideways to shoulder level (180° Lateral Shoulder Abduction)
2. Perform skips to your right side while swinging arms across the chest
3. Alternate arms across the chest over and under during swings
4. Perform skips to your left side with arm swings

RECOMMENDED RESISTANCE TRAINING EXERCISES

1. Lateral Squats
2. DB Flys

RELEVANCE

- Warms-up musculature of lower & upper extremities used during groundstrokes
- If "Shoulder Mobility Test" shows deficiency, implement this exercise into the warm-up routine

TARGETED MUSCULATURE

1. Hip Adductors
2. Hip Abductors
3. Pectoralis Major
4. Anterior Deltoid
5. Posterior Deltoid

ID: 533

5.34 SUPINE ERECTOR SPINAE

SUMMARY

The Supine Erector Spinae stretch is a static stretching exercise, which focuses on improving flexibility of the lower back, reducing the risk of injury and aids in the muscle recovery process.

PURPOSE

1. Improving flexibility of the lower back
2. Reducing the risk of injury
3. Aiding muscle recovery process

DESCRIPTION

1. Place floor mat on the ground
2. Lay down in supine position (face up); head remains ground contact
3. Flex hips and knees to 90°; knees are shoulder-width apart
4. Grab the lower hamstring with both hands and pull knees towards chest/shoulders
5. Maintain neutral spine position (head ground contact); hips can come off the ground

RECOMMENDED RESISTANCE TRAINING EXERCISES

1. Romanian Deadlift

COMMON ERRORS

- Compromised pelvic position during stretch
- Flexion of cervical spine (head flexion) during stretch

REQUIRED EQUIPMENT

- 1 Floor Mat

RELEVANCE

- Reduces delayed onset of muscle soreness of lower back musculature

KEY FACTORS

- Maintain neutral pelvic and spine position
- Hold stretch for 45 seconds

TARGETED MUSCULATURE

1. Erector Spinae

ID: 534

5.35 SUPINE OBLIQUE

SUMMARY

The Supine Oblique is a static stretching exercise, which focuses on improving flexibility of trunk rotator musculature (obliques), reducing the risk of injury and aids in the muscle recovery process.

PURPOSE

1. Improving flexibility of trunk rotator (obliques)
2. Reducing the risk of injury
3. Aiding muscle recovery process

DESCRIPTION

1. Place floor mat on the ground
2. Lay down in supine position (face up); knees are shoulder-width apart
3. Flex knees to 90°
4. Place hands behind the head (90° of shoulder abduction)
5. Externally rotate trunk, thereby bringing knees towards the ground, while maintaining ground contact with both scapulae (shoulder blades); upper leg rests on top of lower leg.
6. Hold stretch and perform to the other side

RECOMMENDED RESISTANCE TRAINING EXERCISES

1. Forward Lunge & Ankle Reach
2. Physio Ball Trunk Rotation III

COMMON ERRORS

- Shoulders come off the ground
- Hip flexion occurs during rotation
- Flexion of cervical spine (head flexion) during stretch

REQUIRED EQUIPMENT

- 1 Floor Mat

RELEVANCE

- Reduces delayed onset of muscle soreness of trunk rotator, glutes and lower back musculature
- If "Trunk Rotation Test" and/or "Hip Flexion Test" show deficiencies, implement this exercise into post-exercise stretching routine

KEY FACTORS

- Maintain ground contact with scapulae
- Maintain neutral head position
- Hold stretch for 45 seconds

TARGETED MUSCULATURE

1. Obliques

ID: 535

5.36 SUPINE CROSS-OVER

SUMMARY

The Supine Cross-Over is a static stretching exercise, which focuses on improving flexibility of hip abductor - and trunk rotator musculature (obliques), reducing the risk of injury and aids in the muscle recovery process.

PURPOSE

1. Improving flexibility of trunk rotator (obliques), gluteus medius & minimus (hip abductors), and lower back musculature
2. Reducing the risk of injury
3. Aiding muscle recovery process

DESCRIPTION

1. Place floor mat on the ground
2. Lay down in supine position (face up); knees are extended shoulder-width apart
3. Extend arms and raise them to 90° of shoulder abduction
4. Flex one hip to 90°; knee is extended
5. Internally rotate trunk, hereby bringing foot towards the ground, while maintaining ground contact with both scapulae (shoulder blades)
6. Hold stretch and perform to the other side

RECOMMENDED RESISTANCE TRAINING EXERCISES

1. Forward Lunge & Ankle Reach
2. Physio Ball Trunk Rotation III

REQUIRED EQUIPMENT

- 1 Floor Mat

RELEVANCE

- Reduces delayed onset of muscle soreness of trunk rotator, glutes and lower back musculature
- If "Trunk Rotation Test" and/or "Hip Flexion Test" show deficiencies, implement this exercise into post-exercise stretching routine

KEY FACTORS

- Maintain ground contact with scapulae
- Maintain neutral head position
- Hold stretch for 45 seconds

TARGETED MUSCULATURE

1. Hip Abductors (gluteus medius & minimus)
2. Obliques

COMMON ERRORS

- Shoulders come off the ground
- Hip flexion occurs during rotation
- Flexion of cervical spine (head flexion) during stretch

ID: 536

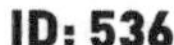

5.37 SEATED V-STANCE

SUMMARY

The Seated V-Stance is a static stretching exercise, which focuses on improving flexibility of knee flexor and trunk extensor musculature, reducing the risk of injury and aids in the muscle recovery process.

PURPOSE

1. Improving flexibility of knee flexor and trunk extensor musculature (and plantar flexors if applicable)
2. Reducing the risk of injury
3. Aiding muscle recovery process

RECOMMENDED RESISTANCE TRAINING EXERCISES

1. Straight Leg Kicks
2. Standing Physio Ball Hip Flexion to Extension

DESCRIPTION

1. Place floor mat on the ground
2. Sit down and abduct hips to a "V" with knees extended
3. Lean forward with upper body and reach for each foot and down the middle of the "V" with both hands
4. Grab toes if possible for an additional calve stretch

COMMON ERRORS

- Failing to achieve full range of motion, particularly down the middle

REQUIRED EQUIPMENT

- 1 Floor Mat

RELEVANCE

- Reduces delayed onset of muscle soreness of knee flexor and trunk extensor musculature
- Stretching (ankle) plantar flexors aids in the prevention of "shin splints"

KEY FACTORS

- Hold stretch for 45 seconds

TARGETED MUSCULATURE

1. Hamstrings (knee flexors)
2. Gastrocnemius (plantar flexor)
3. Soleus (plantar flexor)

ID: 537

5.38 SUPINE KNEE TO CHEST

SUMMARY

The Supine Knee to Chest is a static stretching exercise, which focuses on improving flexibility, reducing the risk of injury and aids in the muscle recovery process.

PURPOSE

1. Improving flexibility of the glutes
2. Reducing the risk of injury
3. Aiding muscle recovery process

DESCRIPTION

1. Place floor mat on the ground
2. Lay down in supine position (face up) and keep legs close together with toes pointing straight upwards
3. Flex one hip to 90°, hold leg with both hands below the knee, and pull it towards the chest

RECOMMENDED RESISTANCE TRAINING EXERCISES

1. High Knee Pulls
2. Back Squat

COMMON ERRORS

- Compromised pelvic position during stretch
- Flexion of cervical spine (head flexion) during stretch

REQUIRED EQUIPMENT

- 1 Floor Mat

RELEVANCE

- Reduces delayed onset of muscle soreness of hip extensor musculature
- If "Hip Flexion Test" shows deficiencies, implement this exercise into post-exercise stretching routine

KEY FACTORS

- Maintain neutral pelvic position: point toes of non-flexed leg straight up
- Maintain neutral spine and head position
- Hold stretch for 45 seconds

TARGETED MUSCULATURE

1. Glutes (gluteus maximus)

ID: 538

5.39 SIDE-LYING QUAD

SUMMARY

The Side-Lying Quad is a static stretching exercise, which focuses on improving flexibility of knee extensors (and hip flexors if applicable), reducing the risk of injury and aids in the muscle recovery process.

PURPOSE

1. Improving flexibility of knee extensors (hip flexors if applicable)
2. Reducing the risk of injury
3. Aiding muscle recovery process

DESCRIPTION

1. Place floor mat on the ground
2. Lay flat on the side with legs close together; the to-be-flexed leg rests on top of the other; extend bottom arm; look forward
3. Grasp the toes of the to-be-flexed leg and pull the heel towards the gluteus (buttocks); lower leg remains straight; maintain neutral pelvic position
4. If applicable, extend hip behind the torso for an additional **hip flexor stretch;** maintain posterior pelvic position

RECOMMENDED RESISTANCE TRAINING EXERCISES

1. Butt Kicks
2. Front Squat

COMMON ERRORS

- Compromised pelvic position during stretch by focusing on hip flexors rather than quadriceps; pulling knee behind torso rather than bringing heel to buttocks
- Flexion of cervical spine (head flexion) during stretch

REQUIRED EQUIPMENT

- 1 Floor Mat

RELEVANCE

- Reduces delayed onset of muscle soreness of knee extensor (and hip flexor) musculature
- If "Knee Flexion Test" shows deficiencies, implement this exercise into post-exercise stretching routine

KEY FACTORS

- Maintain neutral pelvic position
- Maintain neutral spine and head position
- Hold stretch for 45 seconds

TARGETED MUSCULATURE

1. Quadriceps
2. Hip Flexors (iliopsoas, rectus femoris, sartorius, gluteus minimus) if applicable

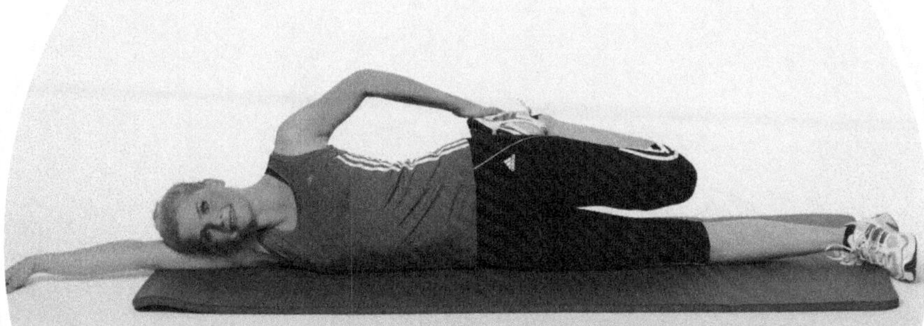

ID: 539

5.40 SUPINE TOWEL HAMSTRING

SUMMARY

The Supine Towel Hamstring is a static stretching exercise, which focuses on improving flexibility, reducing the risk of injury and aids in the muscle recovery process.

PURPOSE

1. Improving flexibility of knee flexors (hamstring) and ankle plantar flexors (gastrocnemius; calve)
2. Reducing the risk of injury
3. Aiding muscle recovery process

RECOMMENDED RESISTANCE TRAINING EXERCISES

1. Straight Leg Kicks
2. Romanian Deadlift

DESCRIPTION

1. Place floor mat on the ground
2. Lay down flat in supine position (face up) with legs close together and toes pointing straight up
3. Flex the hip and lift one leg off the ground; maintain head ground contact (neutral head position)
4. Hold towel in both hands and wrap it around the toes
5. Keep knee extended and slowly pull leg into ~90° of hip flexion (towards the head) or as far as possible
6. Maintain hip ground contact of the non-stretched leg and point toes straight up (neutral pelvic position)

COMMON ERRORS

- Compromised pelvic position during stretch
- Flexion of cervical spine (head flexion) during stretch

REQUIRED EQUIPMENT

- 1 Floor Mat
- Towel

RELEVANCE

- Reduces delayed onset of muscle soreness of knee flexor musculature
- Stretching (ankle) plantar flexors aids in the prevention of "shin splints"
- If "Knee Extension Test" shows deficiencies, implement this exercise into post-exercise stretching routine

KEY FACTORS

- Maintain neutral pelvic position: point toes of non-flexed leg straight up
- Maintain neutral spine and head position
- Hold stretch for 45 seconds

TARGETED MUSCULATURE

1. Hamstrings
2. Gastrocnemius & Soleus (Plantar Flexors)

ID: 540

5.41 SUMO SQUAT

SUMMARY

The Sumo Squat is a static stretching exercise, which focuses on improving flexibility, reducing the risk of injury and aids in the muscle recovery process.

PURPOSE

1. Improving flexibility of glutes, hip adductors, and groin musculature
2. Reducing the risk of injury
3. Aiding muscle recovery process

DESCRIPTION

1. Move feet wider than shoulder-width
2. Drop down into a (deep) squat, place elbows at the medial aspect of the knees (inside knees), and move palms of hands together; abduct feet slightly (toes point outward); maintain neutral spine position; look forward
3. Hold stretch for 10 seconds before pushing knees together

RECOMMENDED RESISTANCE TRAINING EXERCISES

1. Duck Walk
2. Power Clean Receive

COMMON ERRORS

- Flexion of cervical spine (head flexion) and thoracic spine during stretch

RELEVANCE

- Reduces delayed onset of muscle soreness of hip extensors & hip adductor musculature
- If "Hip Flexion Test" shows deficiencies, implement this exercise into post-exercise stretching routine

KEY FACTORS

- Maintain neutral spine and head position
- Hold stretch for 45 seconds

TARGETED MUSCULATURE

1. Glutes
2. Hip Adductors (adductor brevis, longus, magnus)

ID: 541

5

5.42 SEATED PIRIFORMIS

SUMMARY

The Seated Piriformis is a static stretching exercise, which focuses on improving flexibility of external hip rotators, reducing the risk of injury and aids in the muscle recovery process.

PURPOSE

1. Improving flexibility of external hip rotator
2. Reducing the risk of injury
3. Aiding muscle recovery process

DESCRIPTION

1. Place floor mat on the ground
2. Lay down in supine position (face up) and flex the knees
3. Flex the right hip thereby bringing the right knee closer to the body; position the right ankle just below the flexed left knee
4. Move the upper body off the ground and towards the knees until stretch can be felt in the buttocks; place arms behind the body on the ground to hold position
5. Switch legs

RECOMMENDED RESISTANCE TRAINING EXERCISES

1. Piriformis Stretch

RELEVANCE

- Reduces delayed onset of muscle soreness of external hip rotator musculature

KEY FACTORS

- Maintain neutral thoracic spine and head position
- Hold stretch for 45 seconds

TARGETED MUSCULATURE

1. Piriformis

COMMON ERRORS

- Compromised pelvic position during stretch
- Flexion of cervical and thoracic spine during stretch

ID: 542

5.43 BUTTERFLY

SUMMARY

The Butterfly is a static stretching exercise, which focuses on improving flexibility of hip adductor musculature, reducing the risk of injury and aids in the muscle recovery process.

PURPOSE

1. Improving flexibility of hip adductor musculature
2. Reducing the risk of injury
3. Aiding muscle recovery process

DESCRIPTION

1. Place floor mat on the ground
2. Sit down, abduct hips, flex knees, and move feet together
3. Place hands on top of the knees and slowly push knees towards the ground

RECOMMENDED RESISTANCE TRAINING EXERCISES

1. Duck Walk
2. Lateral Lunge

COMMON ERRORS

- Compromised pelvic position during stretch
- Flexion of cervical spine (head flexion) during stretch

REQUIRED EQUIPMENT

- 1 Floor Mat

RELEVANCE

- Reduces delayed onset of muscle soreness of hip adductor musculature

KEY FACTORS

- Hold stretch for 45 seconds

TARGETED MUSCULATURE

1. Hip Adductors (adductor brevis, longus, magnus)

ID: 543

5.44 LUNGE HIP FLEXOR

SUMMARY

The Lunge Hip Flexor is a static stretching exercise, which focuses on improving flexibility of hip flexor musculature, reducing the risk of injury and aids in the muscle recovery process.

PURPOSE

1. Improving flexibility of hip flexor musculature
2. Reducing the risk of injury
3. Aiding muscle recovery process

DESCRIPTION

1. Place floor mat on the ground
2. Step into a forward lunge position; the knee of the rear foot has ground contact; knee of the front foot is flexed at 90° and doesn't protrude past toes
3. Reposition the front foot forward until rear leg/ hip is hyper-extended; maintain neutral spine and head position (straight back; look forward)

Note:

4. If contralateral (opposite) elbow touches the lateral aspect of the forward knee, **obliques** will also be stretched

COMMON ERRORS

- Leaning forward with upper body and pushing knee past the toes
- Flexion of cervical spine (head flexion) during stretch

REQUIRED EQUIPMENT

- 1 Floor Mat

RELEVANCE

- Reduces delayed onset of muscle soreness of hip flexor musculature

KEY FACTORS

- Knee doesn't protrude past the toes
- Maintain neutral spine and head position
- Hold stretch for 45 seconds

TARGETED MUSCULATURE

1. Hip Flexors (iliopsoas, rectus femoris, sartorius, gluteus minimus)
2. Obliques (if applicable)

ID: 544

5.45 STANDING CALVE

SUMMARY

The Standing Calve is a static stretching exercise, which focuses on improving flexibility of the calve musculature, reducing the risk of injury and aids in the muscle recovery process.

PURPOSE

1. Improving flexibility of calve musculature (plantar flexors)
2. Reducing the risk of injury
3. Aiding muscle recovery process

DESCRIPTION

1. Stand up straight, take a step, and position one leg in front of the other; place arms against a wall/ fence
2. Maintain ground contact with the heel of the rear foot, lean forward, and transition body weight to the front foot

RELEVANCE

- Reduces delayed onset of muscle soreness of plantar flexor (calve) musculature
- Stretching (ankle) plantar flexors aids in the prevention of "shin splints"

KEY FACTORS

- Maintain heel of rear foot on the ground; toes point forward
- Hold stretch for 45 seconds

TARGETED MUSCULATURE

1. Gastrocnemius
2. Soleus

ID: 545

5.46 KNEELING SHIN

SUMMARY

The Kneeling Shin is a static stretching exercise, which focuses on improving flexibility, reducing the risk of injury and aids in the muscle recovery process.

DESCRIPTION

1. Place floor mat on the ground
2. Kneel down, keep legs close together, flex knees at 90°, and plantar flex the ankle; knees, shins, and toes have ground contact
3. Flex knees, lean back and touch heels with buttocks

COMMON ERRORS

- Leaning torso forward
- Flexion of cervical spine (head flexion) and thoracic spine (rounded back) during stretch

PURPOSE

1. Improving flexibility of dorsi flexor musculature (tibialis anterior)
2. Reducing the risk of injury
3. Aiding muscle recovery process

REQUIRED EQUIPMENT

- 1 Floor Mat

RELEVANCE

- Reduces delayed onset of muscle soreness of dorsi flexor (ankle) musculature
- Stretching (ankle) dorsi flexors aids in the prevention of "shin splints"

KEY FACTORS

- Maintain neutral spine and head position
- Hold stretch for 45 seconds

TARGETED MUSCULATURE

1. Tibialis Anterior

ID: 546

5.47 ANTERIOR DELTOID

SUMMARY

The Anterior Deltoid is a static stretching exercise, which focuses on improving flexibility of the anterior shoulder musculature, reducing the risk of injury and aids in the muscle recovery process.

PURPOSE

1. Improving flexibility of the anterior shoulder musculature
2. Reducing the risk of injury
3. Aiding muscle recovery process

DESCRIPTION

1. Stand perpendicular to a wall/object; shoulder faces wall/object
2. Horizontally abduct shoulder to 90°, extend elbow and supinate hand position; raise arm behind the torso until hand is in line with shoulder; palm of the hand touches the wall/object
3. Maintain neutral pelvic and spine position; push chest out; look forward

COMMON ERRORS

- Elbow flexion occurs

RECOMMENDED EXERCISES

- 2 Racquet Serve
- Dumbbell Bench Press

REQUIRED EQUIPMENT

- Wall/Fence/Object

RELEVANCE

- Reduces delayed onset of muscle soreness of anterior shoulder musculature
- Stretching the anterior deltoid (internal rotators/horizontal adductors) aids in the prevention of shoulder soreness due to excessive stroke production, especially serving

KEY FACTORS

- Maintain hand on shoulder level (90° horizontal shoulder abduction)
- Maintain neutral spine and head position
- Hold stretch for 45 seconds

TARGETED MUSCULATURE

1. Anterior Deltoid

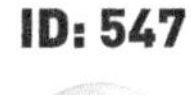

5.48 TOWEL SHOULDER

SUMMARY

The Towel Shoulder Stretch is a static stretching exercise, which focuses on improving flexibility of internal shoulder rotators, reducing the risk of injury and aids in the muscle recovery process.

PURPOSE

1. Improving flexibility of internal shoulder rotators (pectoralis major, subscapularis, latissimus dorsi, teres major)
2. Reducing the risk of injury
3. Aiding muscle recovery process

DESCRIPTION

1. Take towel in the right hand and place it behind the head; reach down the spine as far as possible
2. Maintain neutral head position – look straight forward
3. Take left hand and grab the towel behind the back
4. Pull towel over the right shoulder and slowly apply the stretch to the right shoulder
5. Now, individual switches hands; left hand holds the towel and is placed behind the head, right hand grabs the towel
6. Pull towel over the right shoulder and slowly apply the stretch to the left shoulder

RECOMMENDED EXERCISES

- 2 Racquet Serve

KEY FACTORS

- Maintain neutral pelvic position
- Maintain neutral spine and head position
- Hold stretch for 45 seconds

REQUIRED EQUIPMENT

- 1 Towel

RELEVANCE

- Reduces delayed onset of muscle soreness of internal shoulder rotators musculature
- If "Shoulder Mobility Test" shows deficiencies, implement this exercise into post-exercise stretching routine
- Stretching the anterior deltoid (internal rotators/horizontal adductors) aids in the prevention of shoulder soreness due to excessive stroke production, especially serving

ID: 548

COMMON ERRORS

- Compromised pelvic position during stretch
- Flexion of cervical spine (head flexion) and/or thoracic spine (rounded back) during stretch

TARGETED MUSCULATURE

1. Pectoralis Major
2. Subscapularis
3. Latissimus Dorsi
4. Teres Major

5.49 POSTERIOR DELTOID

SUMMARY

The Posterior Deltoid is a static stretching exercise, which focuses on improving flexibility of the posterior shoulder musculature, reducing the risk of injury and aids in the muscle recovery process.

PURPOSE

1. Improving flexibility of posterior shoulder musculature
2. Reducing the risk of injury
3. Aiding muscle recovery process

DESCRIPTION

1. Horizontally adduct the shoulder at 90°
2. Move other arm underneath and flex the elbow to hold position of the horizontally adducted arm
3. Maintain neutral pelvic and spine position; push chest out; look forward

COMMON ERRORS

- Compromised pelvic position during stretch
- Flexion of cervical and thoracic spine during stretch

RELEVANCE

- Reduces delayed onset of muscle soreness of posterior shoulder musculature

KEY FACTORS

- Maintain neutral spine and pelvic position
- Hold stretch for 45 seconds

TARGETED MUSCULATURE

1. Posterior Deltoid

RECOMMENDED EXERCISES

- Lateral Skips with Arm Swings

ID: 549

5.50 SINGLE ARM PECTORALIS

SUMMARY

The Single Arm Pectoralis is a static stretching exercise, which focuses on improving flexibility of the chest musculature, reducing the risk of injury and aids in the muscle recovery process.

DESCRIPTION

1. Stand in front of an object (e.g. pole)
2. At 90° shoulder flexion horizontally abduct the shoulder, externally rotate and flex the elbow; elbow and palm of the hand touch the pole
3. Step forward with the contralateral foot and lean forward with the upper body
4. Maintain neutral pelvic and spine position; push chest out; look forward

COMMON ERRORS

- Compromised pelvic position during stretch
- Flexion of cervical spine (head flexion) during stretch

RECOMMENDED EXERCISES

- Dumbbell Bench Press

PURPOSE

1. Improving flexibility of the chest musculature
2. Reducing the risk of injury
3. Aiding muscle recovery process

REQUIRED EQUIPMENT

- Door/Tree/Pole/Object

RELEVANCE

- Reduces delayed onset of muscle soreness of chest musculature
- Stretching the anterior deltoid (internal rotators/horizontal adductors) aids in the prevention of shoulder soreness due to excessive stroke production, especially serving

KEY FACTORS

- Maintain neutral spine and head position
- Hold stretch for 45 seconds

TARGETED MUSCULATURE

1. Pectoralis Major

ID: 550

5.51 BAR ROTATOR CUFF

SUMMARY

The Bar Rotator Cuff is a static stretching exercise, which focuses on improving flexibility of rotator cuff and shoulder, reducing the risk of injury and aids in the muscle recovery process.

PURPOSE

1. Improving flexibility of rotator cuff and shoulder
2. Reducing the risk of injury
3. Aiding muscle recovery process

DESCRIPTION

1. Extend the left arm behind the torso, internally rotate, and flex the elbow to ~90°
2. Grab the straight bar with the right hand, take it over the shoulder, and connect with the left hand
3. Pull bar upward and then apply downward pressure on the bar; maintain neutral pelvic and spine position; look forward

REQUIRED EQUIPMENT

- 1 Straight Bar

RELEVANCE

- Reduces delayed onset of muscle soreness of rotator cuff and external; rotator musculature
- If "Knee Flexion Test" shows deficiencies, implement this exercise into post-exercise stretching routine

COMMON ERRORS

- Flexion of cervical spine (head flexion) during stretch

RECOMMENDED EXERCISES

- 2 Racquet Serves

KEY FACTORS

- Maintain neutral pelvic, spine and head position
- Hold stretch for 45 seconds

TARGETED MUSCULATURE

- Subscapularis
- Pectoralis Major
- Latissimus Dorsi

ID: 551

5.52 WRIST FLEXOR

SUMMARY

The Wrist Flexor is a static stretching exercise, which focuses on improving flexibility of the wrist flexor musculature, reducing the risk of injury and aids in the muscle recovery process.

PURPOSE

1. Improving flexibility of wrist flexor musculature
2. Reducing the risk of injury
3. Aiding muscle recovery process

DESCRIPTION

1. Flex shoulder to 90°, extend the elbow, externally rotate the arm, and extend the wrist; fingers point outward
2. Grab fingers with the other hand and pull towards the shoulder

COMMON ERRORS

- Pulling on the palm of the hand

RECOMMENDED EXERCISES

- Hang Clean

RELEVANCE

- Reduces delayed onset of muscle soreness of wrist flexor musculature

KEY FACTORS

- Pull on the fingers
- Hold stretch for 45 seconds

TARGETED MUSCULATURE

- Flexor Carpi Radialis
- Flexor Carpi Ulnaris
- Flexor Digitorum Superficialis & Profundus
- Flexor Pollicis Longus

ID: 552

5.53 WRIST EXTENSOR

SUMMARY

The Wrist Extensor is a static stretching exercise, which focuses on improving flexibility of wrist extensor musculature, reducing the risk of injury and aids in the muscle recovery process.

PURPOSE

1. Improving flexibility of wrist extensor musculature
2. Reducing the risk of injury
3. Aiding muscle recovery process

DESCRIPTION

1. Flex shoulder to 90°, extend the elbow, externally rotate the arm, and flex the wrist; fingers point inward
2. Grab knuckles with the other hand and pull towards the chest

COMMON ERRORS

- Pulling on fingers

RECOMMENDED EXERCISES

- 2 Racquet Serve

RELEVANCE

- Reduces delayed onset of muscle soreness of wrist extensor musculature

KEY FACTORS

- Pull on knuckles
- Hold stretch for 45 seconds

TARGETED MUSCULATURE

- Extensor Carpi Ulnaris
- Extensor Carpi Radialis Brevis
- Extensor Carpi Radialis Longus
- Extensor Digitorum
- Extensor Pollicis Longus

ID: 553

5.54 OVERHEAD TRICEP

SUMMARY

The Overhead Triceps is a static stretching exercise, which focuses on improving flexibility of the elbow extensor musculature, reducing the risk of injury and aids in the muscle recovery process.

PURPOSE

1. Improving flexibility of elbow extensor musculature
2. Reducing the risk of injury
3. Aiding muscle recovery process

DESCRIPTION

1. Flex the shoulder, flex the elbow and move hand on top of the spine between the scapulae
2. Take opposite hand and pull at the elbow towards spine and midline of the body
3. Maintain neutral pelvic and spine (head) position; look forward

COMMON ERRORS

- Compromised pelvic position during stretch
- Flexion of cervical spine (head flexion) during stretch

RECOMMENDED EXERCISES

- MB Toss-Up
- Bicep Curl

TARGETED MUSCULATURE

- Tricep

RELEVANCE

- Reduces delayed onset of muscle soreness of elbow extensor musculature
- If "Shoulder Mobility Test" shows deficiencies, implement this exercise into post-exercise stretching routine

KEY FACTORS

- Maintain neutral pelvic, spine and head position
- Hold stretch for 45 seconds

ID: 554

5

5.55 OVERHEAD LATISSIMUS DORSI

SUMMARY

The Overhead Latissimus Dorsi is a static stretching exercise, which focuses on improving flexibility of posterior shoulder musculature, reducing the risk of injury and aids in the muscle recovery process.

PURPOSE

1. Improving flexibility of posterior shoulder musculature
2. Reducing the risk of injury
3. Aiding muscle recovery process

DESCRIPTION

1. Fully abduct shoulders until arms are overhead
2. Flex the elbows and grasp the elbows with both hands; remain neutral head position; look forward
3. Lean trunk to the left (left lumbar lateral flexion), use the left hand and pull the right elbow towards the head
4. Also perform stretch to the other side

COMMON ERRORS

- Flexion of cervical spine (head flexion) during stretch

RECOMMENDED EXERCISES

- Overhead Squat

RELEVANCE

- Reduces delayed onset of muscle soreness of shoulder adductor, extensor, internal rotator and horizontal abductor musculature
- If "Shoulder Mobility Test" shows deficiencies, implement this exercise into post-exercise stretching routine

KEY FACTORS

- Maintain neutral head position
- Hold stretch for 45 seconds

TARGETED MUSCULATURE

- Latissimus Dorsi

ID: 555

CHAPTER 6:

“Strength & Conditioning for Tennis: Resistance Training”

Everything in sports is ground driven including the action on the tennis court. When one looks at tennis, the athletes initial energy output mostly begins at the feet (most sports start at the feet; bottom-up energy transfer). As the athlete starts the motion (e.g. tennis player hits a serve) and releases the ball, the energy at the release point becomes less than 100%; it's a bottom-up transfer of energy. How much energy can be conserved/applied at the point of action depends on how effectively the energy can be transferred through the body (the joints that make up the movement chain) and then applied to the object (ball). The trunk (the core) area is very important in energy transfer because most connecting points in the movement chain are found there and hence core development takes on real importance. In other words, the velocity of the tennis ball and the energy at the serve location is going to be determined by how much force can be generated from the athlete's feet, how much gets transferred through the core (body) and then how much of that energy gets applied to the ball.

So, if there is a player that is very efficient, he/she might achieve an energy transfer of (e.g.) 85% of that initial energy (feet) at the point of contact, which means higher velocities.

But if there is a player that is rather inefficient transferring energy through the body, he/she might only be able to apply (e.g.) 50% of the initial energy, which means lower velocities. So, the potential in the player's body is 50% greater than what he/she is producing and that's why there are some players that start out at 120 mph for their first serve but once their form improves and they are conditioned properly then they increase to 130 – 140 mph serves. Those potentials exist; the athletes simply need to realize them.

In order to enhance transfer of energy, "core training" comes into play because the core has many connection points in the movement chain that need to be strong and efficient in order to transfer energy effectively. Some energy gets absorbed ("lost") via the muscles (heat) but most of the energy gets "lost" due to ineffectiveness of transfer energy at the joints. The athlete can feel the exertion from producing force without being efficient at it. The goal is to enhance the transfer of energy process with exercises and training programs presented here; controlling of force (direction) is much more important for athletes then simply being able to apply force in a single direction.

STRENGTH & CONDITIONING

Conceptually, **strength** applies to force production whereas **conditioning** applies to the application of movement (e.g. through speed, agility and quickness). In other words, **strength** is the application of high force against a **heavy resistance** whereas **conditioning** is the repeated application of force against a **lighter resistance** (the primary resistance in conditioning is body weight; sometimes there is use of medicine balls (MB) but the resistance needs to be low because the resistance should not cause deviation to the form of the movement. For instance, when sprinting a person wouldn't use weight vests heavier than 20lbs because it would slow the athlete down too much. Also, velocity-based (plyometric) medicine ball (MB) throws do not exceed 8-10 lb; during strength applications with a MB the weight can be as much as 25 lb. So, during conditioning, emphasis is on higher movement speed with light resistance, thereby challenging the metabolic energy systems. With respect to strength resistance training though, the focus is on generating high force output using heavy resistance. This chapter introduces the weight lifting component, **conditioning for strength** (high force/heavy resistance), to supplement conditioning for speed thereby achieving superior athletic conditioning by becoming a more powerful athlete.

If the athlete wants to improve overall **conditioning for speed** (speed, agility, and quickness; SAQ), he/she needs to incorporate high velocity, light resistance exercises into the integrated periodization model. How to integrate SAQ exercises into the training program to improve athletic conditioning and endurance is the focus of „SAQ Training: Developing Speed, Agility, and Quickness" **(see SAQ Training: Developing Speed, Agility, and Quickness" on page 379)**

PROGRAM CONSIDERATIONS

There are a few factor that will determine how successful any athletic training is going to be. Following these steps will maximize training program outcomes:

1. Determine the main long-term goal of the program
2. Determine how much time is available for goal attainment
3. Determine the short-term goals; the training emphasis for each section
4. Use the integrated periodization model (IPM) to address several different issues over time
5. For exercise selection purposes determine how improvements in athletic performance affects overall performance on the court
6. Focus on perfect technique because it affects movement economy and hence performance
7. Determine if the selected exercises are population appropriate

The coach or athlete needs to determine the main long-term goal, which, for instance, could be improving endurance, power, agility, or overall conditioning and how much time is available to reach that goal. Then the integrated periodization model (IPM) can be used to define the short-term goals (objectives) and respective training phases. The IPM addresses several different objectives while allowing the athlete to focus on the various components of strength and power via velocity-based applications. For example, if the main goal for the athlete is to improve speed, he/she has to decide how speed can be improved by choosing the most appropriate exercise and whether the benefit is going to be short-term or long-term? If a component gives the athlete short-term benefits, that component should only be used short-term. For example, the bench press can be used to enhance upper body force production (Basic Strength Phase) but then the bench press will eventually be converted into rapid medicine ball chest throws (Integrated Power Phase).

The presented exercises will maximize athletic performance, not weightlifting ability! The athlete needs to concentrate on perfect form when doing the movements, not the amount of weight being used. Select exercises based on their degree of difficulty (1= beginner; 2 = intermediate; 3 = advanced; 4 = professional) because it is important that the athlete can actually perform all of the selected exercises well. At a maximum, the physiological improvement rate an athlete can achieve is no more than 2.5% per week. So, theoretically, after 10 weeks the athlete could show 20-25% improvement. This can be accomplished by improving the athlete's performance potential via excellent nervous system development (neural pathway efficiency), which can be achieved by means of movement economy improvements. Neural pathway efficiency makes the athlete better by enhancing communication between nervous system and muscles.

If the fastest type of muscle fibers can be preferentially recruited, this will lead to an increase in the firing rate and synchronicity, which allows for more force production without any muscle tissue changes.

TRAINING FACTORS: CONDITIONING FOR STRENGTH

Most of the factors for conditioning for strength complement speed or velocity as well. At first, the ability to sustain power output is the focus because the athlete needs to be able to perform on the court over a period of time; there is repeatability of the action. If the athlete can do something well only once, overall performance will suffer because the athlete has to repeat the actions for success. During a tennis match power needs to be sustained for (approximately) 15 second durations, with at least 60 minutes of repeatability. Therefore, the applied force depends on ATP-CP system efficiency whereas the conditioning force relies more on glycolytic pathways. That's the difference between applied force and the conditioning force and the reason for maximizing energy system efficiency and thresholds.

Developing neural pathway efficiency is very important and velocity specific. An athlete can become better by enhancing communication between the nervous system and muscular system. Velocity of the movements is important for fast twitch muscle fiber recruitment; fast twitch muscle fiber recruitment can increase the firing rate and synchronicity of muscle fibers, which allows for more force creation without any muscle tissue changes.

Muscle balance is important with regards to stability and injury prevention. The main goal is the prevention of injury because only a healthy athlete can be the best athlete.

The economy of total body movement mechanics is vital because it directly affects performance. The later phases of the integrated periodization model are sport-specific, during which the athlete performs exercises in perfect form because it enhances the movement economy. This cannot be done under heavy load because that changes the economy of the movement. For example, if one adds a lot of weight to a tennis racquet and has the athlete swing that, it could very well negatively impact the mechanics of the swing. Instead the body will only become more proficient in swinging a heavy racquet.

INTEGRATED PERIODIZATION MODEL (IPM)

The integrated periodization model (IPM) makes sense during strength resistance training because it addresses several training objectives and allows for progressive overload by minimizing the risk of overtraining. In this approach, strength resistance training (applied force dominant; weight lifting component) complements speed, agility, and quickness (SAQ) training (conditioning force dominant), to optimize training effectiveness. For example, when the athlete engages in transition strength/power exercises (resistance goes down, complexity increases) during strength resistance training, the athlete should complement those activities (in the gym) with appropriate SAQ training activities (on the court) that will improve overall conditioning.

Depending on the experience of the athlete with respect to resistance training, the programs vary. Athletes new to exercise need to emphasize perfect form first. Otherwise movement economy is going to suffer, which has a negative effect on transfer of energy, which leads to suboptimal performance on the court. Therefore, inexperienced athletes will have to spend a considerable amount of time learning how to perform the various exercises (e.g. back squat) correctly before they can focus on becoming stronger, faster, or more powerful. If one carefully teaches an athlete and continuously monitors his technique, his performance will reflect the input. Focusing on technique is actually the athletic component and hence requires attention. For example, Olympic weightlifting is extremely athletic since during the Power Clean the body has to stabilize and control everything. More specifically, the body has to transfer energy through the heels, via the trunk, and manage the energy at the top. Also, rapid hip flexion to extension transfers into faster speed, which is the rational for powerful athletic development. Athletes, on the other hand, who are proficient in the exercises can neglect the early training phases and start with more advanced exercises in earlier training phases. With this in mind it is obvious that each athlete must have his/her personal training goal, which is going to be reflective of the overall program.

Therefore, having the same goal for each athlete and hence the same program must be avoided. There can be a general goal towards which everyone strives (e.g. 225 lb for Power Clean) but the training programs have to be specific to the athlete's needs.

In general, the program uses an integrated approach, which is divided into eight (8) phases, based on training emphasis:

1. Skill Acquisition Phase
2. Hypertrophy Phase
3. Basic Strength Phase
4. Integrated Strength Phase
5. Strength-Power Phase
6. Integrated Power Phase
7. Power Phase
8. Power Performance Phase

It is important to understand that the respective phases are not exclusive. For example, it's called basic strength phase because that is the emphasis; it doesn't mean that all exercises have to be basic strength exercises! The same applies to the exercise category percentages (1 Repetition Maximum; 1RM) for each training phase; the values are not absolute but are indicatory.

SKILL ACQUISITION PHASE

During the skill acquisition phase the athlete will become familiar with the movement patterns of the different exercises. The athlete must learn various basic exercises (e.g. Back Squat, Lateral Lunge, Push-Press, which will be included in more complex movement patterns in later training phases; oftentimes light/moderate resistance will be used.

The volume is high (3 – 6 sets) and the intensity is low 50% - 75% of 1RM; the repetition range is 10-20 per set.

HYPERTROPHY PHASE

The hypertrophy phase is complementary to the Skill Acquisition phase but now the resistance increases. So, the athlete learns perfect technique by using previously learned exercises and then the perfect technique is being loaded. Emphasis is on improving muscle balance, hypertrophy (increasing muscle mass), and the glycolytic energy system efficiency. Therefore, at the end of this phase the athlete should have perfect technique, while being able to apply some force in an efficient manner.

Generally, the program consists of two assistive power lifts that are ballistic in nature (e.g. Jump Shrug or Clean Pull from the floor), one strength/power combination lift (e.g. 60 lb DB Jump Shrug), four compound exercises, and two auxiliary exercises (e.g. Leg Curls). Keep in mind that the preparation/hypertrophy phases have a little bit of power preparation and are often molded together; they are completely separated for athletes that are new to weight lifting.

The volume is high (3 – 5 sets) and the intensity is moderate (70% - 80% of 1RM); the repetition range is 8-12 per set.

BASIC STRENGTH PHASE

In the basic strength phase previously learned exercises are combined (combining two exercises into one), loaded, and the velocity of the movement increased; the focus is on maximizing force production and improving phosphagen (ATP-CP) and glycolytic energy systems. For example, the squat might be an exercise the athlete performs in the hypertrophy phase but during the basic strength phase the athlete performs a squat into a press. It's still very strength-based but the athlete is also trying to improve energy transfer between the body segments; it is the combination of resistance-type training methods in order to improve transfer of energy.

There are two components to the Basic Strength phase: strength exercises and power/auxiliary exercises. Generally, the program consists mainly of strength exercises with some power and auxiliary exercises. The strength/power/auxiliary exercise ratio is 50/30/20 (50% strength exercises/30% power exercises/20% auxiliary exercises).

Keep in mind that the general training phase recommendations do not fit every athlete because each athlete is unique and will have different issues that need to be addressed during training but the Basic Strength Phase generally consists of:

- 2 power exercises
- 1 strength/power combination exercise
- 3-4 compound exercises
- 2-3 auxiliary exercises

If total volume needs to be increased, add auxiliary exercises to the program.

For power exercises the volume is moderate (2 – 4 sets) and the intensity is very high (82.5% – 92% of 1 RM); repetition range is 4-7 per set and recovery between sets is 120 seconds.

For strength exercises the volume is moderate (2 – 4 sets) and the intensity is high (75% – 87.5% of 1 RM); repetition range is 5-10 per set and recovery between sets is 90-120 seconds.

HERE IS A SAMPLE WORKOUT:

1. **Push-Jerk** → power exercise, 3 x 4-5 reps at 85% of 1 RM, 120 seconds rest
2. **Hang Clean to High Receive** → power exercise, 3 x 5 reps at 85% of 1 RM, 90 seconds rest
3. **Push-Press** → a combination strength/power exercise, 3 x 6 reps at 85% of 1RM, 90 seconds rest
4. **Bench Press** → a compound exercise, pyramid set 8,6,5 reps, 90 seconds rest
5. **Standing Dumbbell Military Press** → a compound exercise, 3 x 6 reps at 80% of 1 RM, 90 seconds rest
6. **Weighted Dips** → a compound exercise, 3 x 6 reps at 80% of 1 RM, 90 seconds rest
7. **Modified Upright Row Super-Set Standing Calve Raises** → a combination of compound exercise and auxiliary exercise, 3 x 6-8 (rows) and 3 x 10-15 (Raises), 90 seconds rest

Basic Strength Phase					
Exercise	Sets	Reps	Rest	Work	Intensity
Push-Jerk	3	4-5	120	45 sec	85%
Hang Clean w. High Receive	3	5	120	45 sec	85%
Push-Press	3	6	120	54 sec	85%
Bench Press	3	8, 6, 5	90	65 sec	85%
Standing DB Military Press	3	6	90	54 sec	75%
Weighted Dips	3	6	90	54 sec	75%
Modified Upright Row	3	7	90	65 sec	75%
Total:	21	126	36 min	17.35 min	

INTEGRATED STRENGTH PHASE

In the integrated strength phase, previously learned exercises are combined and made more challenging by increasing stability requirements and velocity while total resistance decreases significantly; the focus is on challenging the nervous system, not the muscular system! The intensity of the lifts will still be challenging but the total amount of resistance will be reduced. So, the total volume will go down even if the sets and repetitions will be consistent because the 3rd factor, the total amount of weight lifted, decreases (Volume = sets x reps x total amount of weight lifted). After the strength phase, the body is going to be fatigued if the athlete did the exercises with the recommended intensities and rest intervals. More specifically, cell components, such as the sarcoplasmic reticulum, as well as neural transmission and tissue integrity (tissue trauma) will be compromised. Basically the muscle tissue goes through trauma due to the exhaustion caused by the Basic Strength Phase. Therefore, exercises during the Integrated Strength Phase are not loaded heavily (muscle system emphasis) but they are going to be more challenging for the nervous system. In other words, we want cell components to recover and maintain the integrity of neural transmission without causing additional fatigue to it. Therefore, neural transmission fatigue is going to occur in the muscle tissue that has been used during the Basic Strength Phase.

For example, during the Basic Strength Phase the athlete had done Push-Jerks, which now can be modified by using less resistance; this will produce less stress on the muscle tissue but it would be more neurologically stimulating to do Single Arm Split-Jerks instead. It's kind of the same exercise but different, if you will. It's not the weight that makes the exercise more challenging but the asymmetrical loading and the increased speed of the movement. For example, the athlete would do 215 lb Push-Jerks in the Basic Strength Phase but would do "only" 80 lb Single Arm Dumbbell Push-Jerks during the Integrated Strength Phase, which is still challenging but not as taxing on the body as the 215 lb barbell Push-Presses.

The program consists predominantly of strength and power exercises with some auxiliary exercises. The strength/power/auxiliary exercise ratio is 40/40/20 (40% strength exercises/40% power exercises/20% auxiliary exercises).

The volume is moderate (2 – 4 sets) and the intensity is low (30% - 50% of 1RM); the repetition range is 10 - 15 per set.

As previously mentioned, athletes don't engage in brand new exercises. Instead they use exercises that have been used during previous training phases and make them more challenging. So, let's take exercises from the Basic Strength Phase and adapt them. Exercises presented here are the more challenging versions of the Basic Strength Phase exercise presented earlier:

1. **Push Jerk** → (asymmetrical) Single Arm Push-Jerk; here "asymmetrical" means the athlete is using one arm (one side) action. The challenge here is trunk and shoulder stabilization hence the volume is moderate so that the body is able to handle (e.g. 6-8 reps) the stress. Remember, the hips and the trunk have to engage six times but the shoulder stabilizers get a break after three reps. Start with the non-dominant site first because by the 3rd set stabilizers are going to be fatigued; there is less stabilizer fatigue that way.
2. **Hang Clean with High Receive** → Hang Snatch with High Receive, which is a similar action but much more challenging because the athlete has to learn the high receive and the resistance needs to be stabilized over the head, hence the athlete needs to learn the snatch during the preparation/hypertrophy phase. For athletes that are not good at the hip flexion component, Plate Snatches or Plate Jacks can be used instead; it still forces the athlete to flex his/her hips rapidly
3. **Push-Press** → Single Arm Front Squat to Press; the low volume is enough because the exercise is tough since the legs and trunk have to do 8 repetitions. The deceleration component is a heavy contributor to fatigue.
4. **Bench Press** → Alternating Dumbbell Press superset (SS) MB Chest Passes (as fast as possible) {3 per side x 6 – 10 reps}; the 6 reps are used by people who are more proficient in lifting, which warrants higher weight; the alternating movement causes the body to be split so the stability component is enhanced
5. **Standing Dumbbell Military Press** → Forward Lunge to Press; since the athlete was doing DB Military Presses before, he/she should have pretty good shoulder stabilization. The Forward Lunge to Press is more complex because the athlete is moving in two planes of motion with center of mass change; the athlete lowers his/her center of mass (sagittal plane) but elevates the center of mass of the resistance (frontal plane) simultaneously. The Forward Lunge to Press is also a very good teaching model for the Split-Jerk. It also increases the ROM of the glutes and the latissimus dorsi.
6. **Weighted Dips** → Weighted Dips; there is no change here except for speed of the action and resistance increase; dips are a foundation exercise because it is a body-weight exercise and closed-chain (because the contact surface doesn't move; in a machine the contact surface could be moving depending on the machine); the body has to do complete stabilization and control.
7. **Modified Upright Row with Calve Raises** → Kneeling Ballistic MB Throw; this exercise is postural so the kneeling athlete needs to maintain the integrity of the hips so when the MB is dropped, the athlete is able to decelerate and throw it back immediately.

Integrated Strength Phase

Exercise	Sets	Reps	Rest	Work	Intensity
Single-Arm Push-Jerk	3	3/side	120	54 sec	85%
Hang Snatch w. High Receive	3	5	120	45 sec	85%
Single-Arm Front Squat to Push-Press	2	4/side	120	48 sec	85%
Alternating DB Bench Press	3	7	90	65 sec	85%
Forward Lunge to Press	2	6/side	90	48 sec	75%
Weighted Power Dips	2	Amap*	90	~90 sec	75%
MB Ballistic Shoulder Flexion	3	12	90	108 sec	75%
Total:	18	~148	33 min	19.8 min	

*As many as possible

STRENGTH-POWER PHASE

During the strength-power phase, strength and power exercises are combined, which is very taxing on the body because resistance (intensity) and the speed of the action are high.

The program consists predominantly of strength/power compound exercises with some auxiliary exercises. The strength/power & auxiliary exercise ratio is 60/40 (60% strength/power exercises and 40% auxiliary exercises).

For strength/power exercises the volume is low (1 – 3 sets) and the intensity is higher (82.5% - 90% of 1RM); the repetition range is 3 - 5 per set.

For auxiliary exercises the volume is low (1 – 3 sets) and the intensity is moderate (70% - 80% of 1RM); the repetition range is 3 - 5 per set.

INTEGRATED POWER PHASE

In the integrated power phase, previously learned exercises are combined and made more challenging by increasing stability requirements and velocity while total resistance decreases significantly; the focus is on challenging the nervous system, not the muscular system. The muscles will be sore, though, because they have to deal with unfamiliar movements, which cause recruitment of muscle fibers that usually wouldn't be recruited because they were previously needed to stabilize actions. In other words, the athlete learns how to use the ground reaction force and utilize it in a fashion that allows the athlete to accelerate using different body segments synergistically.

The program consists predominantly of strength/power exercises with some auxiliary exercises. The strength/power & auxiliary exercise ratio is 60/40 (60% strength/power exercises and 40% auxiliary exercises).

For strength/power exercises the volume is moderate (2 – 4 sets) and the intensity is low (75% - 90% of 1RM); the repetition range is 3 – 7 per set.

For auxiliary exercises the volume is low (1 – 3 sets) and the intensity is moderate (70% - 80% of 1RM); the repetition range is 3 - 7 per set.

Most of the power exercises include the Snatch, the Clean, and the Push-Jerk.

All of these exercises have one thing in common: the body moves in the sagittal plane whereas the resistance (bar) moves in the frontal plane. A common error is that athletes have not learned during the preparation phase how to transfer energy in multi-planar fashion but almost all actions in tennis occur multi-planar, using flexion in the transverse plane or extension. Essentially, the athlete takes vertical power and transfers it into horizontal power, which occurs through the loss and regain of stability in a rapid fashion. Also, rapid hip flexion and extension is necessary for explosive movement on the court. When the athlete runs and hits a ball, hip flexion evolves into plantar flexion and into knee flexion (running component) before the athlete has to integrate transverse velocity with vertical velocity, which together affects horizontal velocity. During tennis all the reaction forces are transferred via the trunk through the arms into the racquet to apply force to the ball. The athlete needs to use the ground reaction forces, transfer them through the legs, and transfer the energy into the trunk where rotational power is generated by the obliques in the transverse plane. Even during the serve, the athlete rotates the trunk and hips and then extends to generate power.

None of the previously listed power exercises have a rotational component, which is where the integrated power exercises come into play, whereby previously strengthened movements are combined with exercises that have a rotational component and use asymmetrical loading.

Exercises are presented and modified for power training while giving the body a little bit of a break but nonetheless preparing it for tennis. As was the case with the Integrated Strength phase, during the Integrated Power phase some strength exercises will continue to be used while some power exercises are integrated into the program because the athlete still needs to move some resistance but that total resistance will decrease because of all the dynamic changes. The resistance is going to vary rather significantly because the athlete needs to maintain an ATP-CP focus but a glycolytic component is also involved, namely, the ballistics and plyometrics exercises; they are the conditioning factor. The plyometrics and ballistic conditioning exercises will be integrated into **contrast training** (heavy resistance and slower movements supersetted with light resistance and fast movement) during this phase. Modified contrast training is also an option, whereby the athlete engages in true power exercises in which one exercise is a high resistance power exercise and the other exercise is a low resistance power exercise. For example, a ballistic medicine ball (MB) exercise, which involves a heavy ball, segues into a plyometric medicine ball exercise (light MB). Both exercises have a power emphasis but there is a difference with respect to resistance and velocity of the action.

It changes the neural patterns; the high resistance power exercise is ATP-CP dominant and the low resistance power exercise attends to glycolytic pathways.

Also, **functional training** is used to optimize the synchronicity of the neuromuscular system in order to improve movement patterns and sport-specific activities. Therefore, functional training exercises are an option because the athlete needs to be able to rotate and accelerate while losing stability because the tennis player transfers the energy onto 1 foot during stroke production, then generates force through trunk rotation, and accelerates through the shot; the athlete is switching movement planes throughout stroke production. So, if the athlete cannot balance on one foot and transfer all the energy through the hands and racquet to hit the ball, he/she will be ineffective.

Sample: 1-Day Full Body Workout

1. **Power Clean from the Floor**; this is a complex exercise; the athlete needs to be explosive and conduct the exercise in perfect form for efficient energy transfer
2. **Single Arm Snatch from the Floor**; this is a truly integrated type of action with heavy resistance; the athlete needs to be familiar with weight management because the athlete needs to bring the DB down again, he/she cannot just let them drop like rubber plates
3. **Single Arm Split Jerk**; use 75% of 1RM for this exercise (not total weight with both hands) because the stability component is high; it is a strength/power exercise that is a bit easier but the athlete has to be very proficient at Split-Jerks before doing this exercise; the athlete needs significant trunk and shoulder stability
4. **Front Squat to Alternating Dumbbell Push-Press**; use 75% of 1RM for this exercise (not total weight with both hands); use 2 DB; the center of gravity is low initially but then the athlete needs to move one part of the resistance upwards, which causes an unnatural balance of mass because the 2nd DB is not a component of the body's mass. So the body needs to figure out how to deal with an asymmetrical mass and accelerate into a higher center of mass. For example, if the athlete uses a 80 lb DB for Push-Presses then use a 60 lb DB (=75%).
5. **Lateral Box Jumps**; it's a very good exercise for hip flexion speed; for guys no more than 16-18 inches of box height, girls will use 10-14 inches (they don't have the same vertical jumping ability because they fatigue more quickly. If they don't need to jump as high, they don't need to decelerate as much, which makes the action quicker but the amount of hip flexion required is also a factor; the fatigue rate is determined more by the deceleration component than by the velocity of the movement
6. **Jump Pull-Ups**; the exercise combines hip power with pulling power with trunk control
7. **Lateral Lunge with Rotation** (don't load the exercise and use Medicine Ball or Barbell); it's a very velocity driven exercise integrated with rotation; it is asymmetrically loaded; the athlete generates force in the frontal plane and then needs to transition the force into a single foot and then rotate, stabilize, and return. It teaches the body segments how to work together. During the rebound, the center of mass shifts forward, causing instability, which means the athlete has to regain stability and then apply force to return
8. **Single Leg Romanian Deadlift to Clean Receive**
9. **Clap Push-Ups**

POWER PHASE

In the power phase, previously learned exercises are made more challenging by increasing the resistance; the focus is on maximizing power output using the phosphagen (ATP-CP) energy system and the glycolytic pathways for conditioning.

Oftentimes during the Power Phase, the tendency will be to over-emphasize the ATP-CP energy system (high resistance power exercises) while underutilizing the glycolytic energy system using low resistance power exercises (e.g. ballistics, plyometrics and agility exercises). Therefore, when the athlete is doing power training, 60% of the exercises will be ATP-CP driven and 40% of the exercises will use the glycolytic energy pathways. The volume of high resistance power exercises is moderate while the low resistance power exercises volume is high because the emphasis is on enhancing the athlete's movement capabilities on the court.

For high resistance power exercises the volume is moderate (2 – 4 sets) and the intensity is very high (87.5% - 95% of 1RM); the repetition range is 2 - 5 per set.

For low resistance power exercises the volume is high (3-5 sets) and the intensity is moderate because the speed of the action needs to be high; the repetition range is 6 - 15 per set.

Integrated Power Phase					
Exercise	Sets	Reps	Rest	Work	Intensity
Power Clean (floor)	3	4	120	54 sec	87.5%
Single Arm Snatch (floor)	3	2	120	24 sec	87.5%
Single Arm Split-Jerk	3	3/side	120	54 sec	75%
Front Squat to Alternating DB Push-Press	3	3/side	90	72 sec	75%
Lateral Box Jumps	2	20	90	40 sec	Body
Jump Pull-Ups	3	8	90	72 sec	Body
Lateral Lunge with Rotation	2	6/side	90	72 sec	Bar
Single Leg RDL to Clean Receive	2	5/side	90	60 sec	70%
Clap Push-Ups	2	8	90	32 sec	Body
Total:	23	76	39 min	20.6 min	

SAMPLE: 1-DAY POWER WORKOUT

The first 5 exercises are ATP-CP driven, the last 4 exercises are geared towards the glycolytic pathways.

1. **Clean & Jerk** (clean and split jerk); 90 – 120 seconds rest for sub-maximal load; 120 – 180 seconds for maximum loads; during the Clean & Jerk the athlete doesn't switch legs in this case because the focus is to maximize power output; the athlete lifts as much as possible as quickly as possible with perfect form for a few repetitions; the intensity depends on the weight for the heaviest Split-Jerk.
2. **Snatch** (hang); 3 x 4 reps; 90 – 120 seconds rest for sub-maximal load; 120 – 180 seconds for maximum loads; after these two exercises the shoulder stabilizers are going to be fatigued due to the overhead receives.
3. **Box Jumps**; 3 x 5 – 6 reps; near maximal jumps (use two boxes to step down); this is a maximum ballistic exercise, concentric hip action
4. **High Pull** (floor); 3 x 5 – 6 reps; here you have no deceleration component because you don't catch the bar; concentric hip action
5. **Single Arm DB Push-Press;** 2 x 3 reps; here we have a rapid hip flexion component
6. **Plate Blocks**; high speed is better than more weight! if the athlete cannot get his/her arms fully extended and form suffers, stop early; if the athlete has a lot of upper body strength and power, 10 reps are no problem
7. **Physio Ball/Medicine Ball Press Pass**; 3 x 12 – 15 reps, 45 seconds rest
8. **MB Trunk Twist Throws**; 2 x 6 – 12 reps per side

POWER PERFORMANCE PHASE

During the power performance phase the resistance goes down significantly because the focus is on the economy and velocities of tennis-specific actions, which means that low resistance or body-weight type activities are being utilized at high velocities. If the exercises were to be performed under heavy load, the movement economy would undergo changes. For instance, if one adds a lot of weight to a tennis racquet and has the athlete swing it, the perfect mechanics of the swing could be altered, which means that the body only becomes more proficient in swinging a heavy racquet. Essentially, one uses the provided resistance training exercises (Integrated Strength & Integrated Power Phase exercises) with the glycolytic energy pathways – this will ensure that the athlete is still maintaining the foundations of high resistance power training.

Power Strength Phase					
Exercise	Sets	Reps	Rest	Work	Intensity
Clean & Jerk (floor)	3	3	180	54 sec	95%
Hang Snatch	3	4	180	24 sec	92.5%
Box Jumps	3	5	120	54 sec	High Box
High Pull (floor)	3	5	90	72 sec	75%
Single Arm Push-Press	2	3	90	40 sec	Body weight
Plate Blocks	3	8	45	72 sec	Low Weight
MB Chest Pass	3	12	45	72 sec	
MB Trunk Twist Pass	3	12	45	72 sec	
Total:	23	76	38.25 min	22.3 min	

CALCULATE APPROPRIATE TRAINING PHASE INTENSITY

THE 1 REPETITION MAXIMUM

Each training phase has corresponding exercise intensity percentages, which are deviations from the maximum resistance that can be lifted once. This is called the 1 repetition maximum (1RM).

The athlete needs to know the 1RM for certain lifts so that the exercise program using the integrated periodization model can be designed most effectively. The 3% formula accurately predicts the 1RM for free-weight lifts of up to 10 repetitions; it is not valid for machine-based exercises.

For more information on machine-based vs. free-weights training, take a closer look at "Under the Microscope: Machine-Based Training vs. Free-Weights Training" **(see Machine-Based Training vs. Free-Weights Training on page 183)**.

The 3% formula: 1RM = ([0.03 x # of repetitions] + 1) x weight used

The athlete performs a compound lift to establish (predict) the 1RM because a free-weight compound exercise identifies the stabilizer and prime mover relationship; athletes are only as strong as their weakest link. For example, if an athlete bench presses 250 lb using a smith machine (2 rods that only allow the bar to move upward or downward), the 250 lb will not reflect his bench pressing capability because the stabilizers will fatigue and the force needed to lift the resistance off the chest cannot be transferred effectively. In other words, athletes often will not have the required stabilizer strength, which is the disconnection between prime mover strength and energy transfer in force application. So there might be an athlete that can do heavy squat or bench presses but he/she doesn't perform as well on the court as the athlete that can do the high jumpers or power cleans very well. Therefore, total force production (how strong the athlete is) is less important with respect to performance than how well the athlete can manage his/her body weight.

Example Calculation of 1 Repetition Maximum

We have an athlete that can lift 175 lb for 6 repetitions during the back squat. What is the athlete's 1RM?

1RM = ([0.03 x # of repetitions] + 1) x weight used

= ([0.03 x 6] + 1) x 175 lb

= 1.18 x 175 lb

= 206.5 lb

The athlete would be using 205 lb for the 1RM because there is no 206.5 lb in weight lifting (how are you going to put 161.5 lb on the bar?).

How to Calculate Maximum Weight for X Repetitions

Since the athlete's 1RM for the back squat is 205 lb, the weight for 10 repetitions can be calculated by using the corresponding percentage of the 1RM found in the tables below. So, if the 1RM is 205 lb and 75% corresponds to 10 repetitions, the predicteded weight will be 154 lb (205 lb x 0.75 = 153.75 lb). It is important to understand that when the athlete uses 154 lb for 10 repetitions the intensity will add up to 100% of the athlete's capacity. If the program constantly has the athlete performing at 100% of exertion, overtraining will result because the stress on the athlete will be too high.

The tables presented next show repetition ranges and their corresponding 1RM percentages. The percentages can vary a bit depending on the athlete's stabilizer strength.

Percentage of 1 Repetition Maximum (1RM)			
		Regular Athletes	**Advanced Athletes**
Repetitions	Predominant Energy System	% of 1RM	% of 1RM
1	ATP	100 – 97.5	100
2	ATP-CP	95	97.5
3	ATP-CP	92.5	95
4	ATP-CP	90	92.5
5	Glycolytic	87.5	90
6	Glycolytic	85	87.5
7	Glycolytic	82.5	85
8	Glycolytic	80	82.5
9	Glycolytic	77.5	80
10	Glycolytic	75	77.5
11	Glycolytic	72.5	75
12	Glycolytic	70	72.5

UNDER THE MICROSCOPE

MACHINE-BASED TRAINING VS. FREE-WEIGHTS TRAINING

Oftentimes, during strength & conditioning training the athlete doesn't exceed 10 repetitions unless the athlete is in the preparation or hypertrophy phase. Another scenario can occur during plyometrics/ballistics training, where challenging the glycolytic energy pathways is the focus. For example, the athlete uses a 5 lb medicine ball and throws it against a wall for 30 repetitions as fast as possible to encourage neural turnover since the resistance is low. This would be an example of low resistance power. High resistance power on the other hand uses more weight, which ultimately slows down the movement. In general for power training everything is high velocity but the rate of movement is faster for low resistance power exercises (e.g. 5 lb medicine ball throws) than for high resistance power (e.g. 225 lb power clean) exercises. The exercise percentages are generally being used for high resistance strength and power exercise.

Also, leverage is the key in lifting resistance and effective energy transfer. During tennis the athlete generally has a tennis racquet that will improve the leverage of the movement or the generation of force. During bodybuilding, machines like the Leg Press machine help the athlete move a lot of resistance. There are athletes that can leg press 1,400 lb but they cannot Back Squat that amount of weight; they cannot even squat 700 lb. During athletic training, the body provides its own leverage system because it is the only leverage system the athlete can take advantage of during the sport. It is acceptable to isolate different muscle groups during the initial training phases (preparation phase, hypertrophy phase), during which machines can be used, so exercises can be selected that target muscle groups that are difficult to engage by simply using free-weights. Therefore, machines such as the Leg Curl or Leg Press machine are used because it is very difficult to attain lower hamstring strength training without a machine.

Repetition Ranges & Energy Systems

It is important to note that the 1RM %-values are not exact; they depend on the strength of the athlete's stabilizers. Also, with regards to energy system conversions, all energy systems work together to supply energy but one energy system will predominate during a given time and exercise intensity.

1 RM – 4 RM: ATP-CP ENERGY SYSTEM

This is the first section. If the athlete can do 1 repetition (1 RM), the 1RM is done at 100% intensity. ATP stored in muscle tissue supplies the energy directly without any conversion (ATP energy system).

At 2 RM the athlete should be able to do 97.5% intensity but stabilizer weakness already becomes a factor due to muscle fatigue. Stabilizer fatigue occurs quickly because stabilizers have to contract all the time (stabilizers don't get a break), which makes energy transfer inefficient (e.g. stabilizers keep head of humerus in the socket so that the application of force can be directed properly). For example, when an athlete has muscular imbalances when they engage in Power Cleans, their pulls (1st & 2nd pulling phase) occur in an incorrect body position, which then causes the stabilizers to correct it.

At 3 RM, muscle stores of ATP are almost drained, which means that the body needs to re-phosphorylate to make ATP available again but there is no re-phosphorylation under stress and a slowdown of the energy conversion process occurs. Instead, the body uses CP (creatine phosphate), splits it, and drives the CP into an ADP molecule and then produces energy that way but the whole process slows down during the 2 cycles of energy production.

At 4 RM the athlete is at 92.5% intensity, which also means the end of available CP. There is a noticeable difference when you are getting to 5 RM. Adaptations from 1RM – 4RM are considered to be neural because they are maximizing neural pathway capabilities via quicker firing rates, synchronicity and recruitment of preferential fast twitch muscle fibers; all these factors have to be in sync. If the athlete was just doing the program within these high intensity percentages, he/she would get stronger without adding muscle mass. Therefore, it is not a matter of the athlete's muscularity but rather force production potential of the muscle tissue.

Athletes have the fastest nervous systems, which allow them to process information the quickest. Athletes can be "neurologically challenged", which is similar to being "cerebrally challenged"; neurologically challenged refers to nervous system capabilities. The athletes' nervous systems have rapid attainment of neural pathways. So, even though they haven't experienced certain exercises, they can pick them up much more quickly because the nervous system is an extension of the brain and it figures out the neural patterns. Some athlete's nervous systems are not as coordinated and they need a lot of continuous motor patterning. Some athletes have to practice harder to become better athletes, whereas others don't even have to go to practice and they still are the best, which is due to the genetic predisposition.

5 RM – 7 RM: ANAEROBIC GLYCOLYTIC ENERGY SYSTEM

5 RM – 7 RM are in the secondary section; focus is on challenging anaerobic glycolytic pathways. 5 RM is going to be approximately at 90% intensity, 6 RM provide 87.5% intensity, and 7RM is about 85% intensity. The intensity percentages are determined by the athlete's stabilizer strength.

8 RM – 12 RM: EFFICIENT MUSCLE FIBER RECRUITMENT

8 RM – 12 RM is the 3rd section; here the focus is on taxing the muscle fibers. When the athlete gets to 8RM, the intensity will be around 80-82.5%, at 9RM the intensity gets to 77.5%-80%, 10 RM corresponds to 75%-77.5%, 11 RM yields 72.5%-75%, and 12 RM is 70%-72.5% of maximum intensity. The percentage ranges decrease as the number of repetitions increase. As body builders know, time under tension causes muscle fiber recruitment to offset the fatigue of the rapidly recruited fast twitch fibers through the neural enhancement that occurs in 1RM-4RM. In other words, because the nervous system is so efficient in the 1RM-4RM realm, athletes will try to recruit the fastest fatiguing muscle fibers. If the athlete gets to 8RM, those fast twitch muscle fibers will already be fatigued and hence recruitment of slow twitch muscle fibers will occur.

HOW TO DETERMINE THE 1 RM

The 3% formula is being used to predict the athlete's 1RM but predictions can be inaccurate at times. Therefore, the 1 RM can be determined using the following procedure:

1. Chose an exercise
2. Do a dynamic warm up going through full range of motion
3. Do a warm-up set at 50% of the predicted 1RM for 6-7 repetitions
4. Rest 2 min
5. Do a 2nd set with 5-6 repetitions, increasing the weight noticeably
6. Rest for 2 min
7. Do a 3rd set with 2-3 repetitions, increasing the weight again
8. Rest for 3 min
9. Go for maximum weight and 1-2 repetitions

Example

An athlete having a predicted 400 lb 1 RM for the bench press:

- 1st set: 200 lb for 6-7 reps
- Rest 2 min
- 2nd set: 245 lb for 5 reps
- Rest 2 min
- 3rd set: 320 lb for 2-3 reps
- Rest 3 min
- Max set: 400 lb for 1 rep

The various exercises presented in this chapter are divided into categories based on their purpose (categories; e.g. power exercises), degree of difficulty and corresponding goals:

1. Beginner: Enhancing neural preparation
2. Intermediate: Improving energy pathways
3. Advanced: Efficient muscle fiber recruitment
4. Professional: Improving coordination

At first, the goal is to enhance neural preparation for more complex movements, which means that the athlete needs to master the movement mechanics. More specifically, the speed of the movement is slow and the volume of the selected exercises is high; using the athlete's body weight or light resistance is recommended. Generally, this corresponds to level 1 degree of difficulty exercises.

Once the athlete becomes more proficient, resistance is added to load the action, which leads to improving energy pathways. Generally, this corresponds to level 2 degree of difficulty exercises.

The next step is to enhance the efficiency of muscle fiber recruitment. This can be accomplished by challenging the action. Generally, this corresponds to level 3 degree of difficulty exercises.

Then coordination of the movements becomes the emphasis, which means that the speed of the action increases before one can load the action again at maximum speed. Generally, this corresponds to level 4 degree of difficulty exercises.

Exercises have been categorized according to the various training phases used during the integrated periodization model. The exercises are not necessarily exclusive to their respective training phase. Depending on overall training emphasis and lifting experience of the athlete, exercises can also be used during other training phases. For example, the Push-Press is part of the Strength/Power phase but can also be used during the strength phase. For athletic training **compound exercises** are essential because the athlete learns how to transfer energy effectively across several body segments. Compound exercises are defined as movements that are using multiple joints (more than 1 joint). Bodybuilding also includes multi-joint exercises but those don't enhance transfer of energy capabilities.

Goal	Concept	Difficulty
Neural preparation	Master it	1
Improved energy pathways	Load it	2
Recruitment efficiency	Challenge it	3
Coordinated movement	Speed it up	4
Speed of action	Load it again	4
Sport specific implementing	Really speed it up	4

For example, let's compare the Leg-Press exercise and the Back Squat; both exercises are closed-chain compound exercises.

The Back Squat is used during athletic training and the Leg-Press is commonly used during bodybuilding because the Back Squat mimics real life energy transfer in that the energy is driven upwards; ground reaction force transfers through the multiple joints. The leg press, on the other hand, is not selected very often as an exercise in athletic strength & conditioning programs because the athlete never extends the hips during the pressing action. In other words, during sports the athlete never applies force through the heels while the hips remain flexed. Let's take another knee flexion exercise, e.g. prone knee flexions, and the **Romanian Deadlift (RDL)**. Even though both exercises target the hamstring, the prone leg flexion is not a compound movement because it only involves one joint, i.e. the knee; it is an isolated movement for the lower belly of the hamstring. The RDL, on the other hand, is more for the upper belly/origin of the hamstring. So, there are two different actions for the hamstring, one is during knee flexion and the other one is during hip extension. Instead of using a machine for the prone knee curls (flexions) the athlete could rather do Russian Leans (buddy hamstrings) or supine leg curls on a physio ball.

The **Russian Lean** is a decelerated action with a heavy knee flexion component. It is very difficult to manage the full range of motion compared to exercises on a knee flexion machine because the athlete is mechanically disadvantaged from the start of the exercise and then has to fight gravity when leaning forward. Therefore, the hips need to maintain neutral position to transfer energy efficiently; many athletes will flex their hips during the movement because they are mechanically disadvantaged. During the Russian Lean the athlete goes down slowly into eccentrically loaded hip flexion. Then the athlete drops down to the floor, pushes off, and pulls back upward. No one is strong enough to lie on the ground while someone holds the ankles and come up because the position is so mechanically disadvantaged.

The Russian Lean is also a single joint exercise but it requires a lot of dynamic stability. Sometimes the athlete will use a machine for knee flexion and sometimes he/she will do the Russian lean because the exercises center differently.

6.01 RUSSIAN TWIST

SUMMARY

The Russian Twist is an auxiliary exercise, which focuses on improving the synergy of the neuro-muscular system, strengthening the trunk lateral flexor and trunk rotator musculature, improving body control & coordination and flexibility as well as improving skill & balance foundation for complex movements.

DESCRIPTION

1. Place floor mat on the ground
2. Sit down on the buttocks, push chest forward, flex knees, and keep feet off the ground
3. Hold resistance (plate/MB) in both hands, rotate trunk to the left side, touch resistance placed next to the left hip to the ground, rotate trunk to the right side and touch resistance placed next to the right hip to the ground

RECOMMENDED EXERCISES

1. Forward Lunge & Ankle Reach
2. Lunge with Bar Rotation
3. Supine Oblique Stretch

BREATH IN & OUT

- IN: Before Trunk Rotation
- OUT: During Trunk Rotation

PURPOSE

1. Improving transfer of energy; synergy of neuro-muscular system
2. Strengthening of **trunk (lumbar) lateral flexor and rotator** (obliques & quadratus lumborum) muscu-lature
3. Improving body control & coordination by enhan-cing stabilizers and gliding neutralizers
4. Improving flexibility
5. Improving skill and balance foundation for complex movements

DEGREE OF DIFFICULTY

- 1

RELEVANCE

- Strengthening the trunk (core) aids in more efficient energy transfer, which has a positive effect on stroke production (power) on the court
- Enhances strength of the obliques and quadratus lumborum and developes trunk musculature as stabilizer.
- Prevention of lower back pain due to pelvic instability

KEY FACTORS

- Focus on perfect movement mechanics and range of motion
- Keep feet off the ground
- Maintain neutral head position

COMMON ERRORS

- Feet touch the ground during motion
- Resistance does not touch the ground
- Excessive flexion of thoracic spine (rounded back) during motion
- Athlete loses balance

ID: 601

TARGETED MUSCULATURE	ACTION	PLANE OF MOTION
1. Obliques	1. Lumbar (trunk) Rotation & Lumbar Lateral Flexion	1. Transverse & Frontal
2. Quadratus Lumborum	2. Lateral Pelvic Rotation & Lateral Lumbar Flexion	2. Frontal

6.02 SUPINE HIP LIFT

SUMMARY

The Supine Hip Lift is an auxiliary exercise, which focuses on improving the synergy of the neuromuscular system, strengthening the trunk flexor musculature, and improving body control & coordination and flexibility.

PURPOSE

1. Improving transfer of energy; synergy of neuromuscular system
2. Strengthening of **trunk (lumbar) flexor** musculature
3. Improving body control & coordination by enhancing stabilizers and gliding neutralizers
4. Improving flexibility

DESCRIPTION

1. Place floor mat on the ground
2. Lie down in supine (face up) position, horizontally abduct shoulders (make a T) to 90°, keep knees extended (straight), and flex hips until feet point towards the ceiling (90° hip flexion)
3. In a controlled fashion, push feet straight upward farther towards the ceiling thereby flexing the lumbar spine and lifting buttocks off the floor
4. Slowly extend lumbar spine and return buttocks towards the ground without allowing the legs to swing

RECOMMENDED EXERCISES

Rectus Abdominis Flexibility

1. Forward Lunge & Overhead Reach

Oblique Flexibility

1. Forward Lunge & Ankle Reach
2. Lunge with Bar Rotation
3. Supine Oblique Stretch

BREATH IN & OUT

- IN: Before Hip Lift
- OUT: During Hip Lift

DEGREE OF DIFFICULTY

- 1

REQUIRED EQUIPMENT

- 1 Floor Mat

RELEVANCE

- Strengthening the trunk (core) aids in more efficient energy transfer, which has a positive effect on stroke production on the court
- Enhances strength of the obliques and quadratus lumborum and developes trunk musculature as stabilizer.
- Prevention of lower back pain due to pelvic instability

KEY FACTORS

- Focus on perfect movement mechanics and range of motion
- Keep hips flexed at 90°
- Maintain neutral head position

COMMON ERRORS

- Feet swing when returning buttocks towards the ground
- Jerking motion

ID: 602

TARGETED MUSCULATURE

1. Rectus Abdominis (distal end)
2. Obliques

ACTION

1. Lumbar Flexion
2. Lumbar Flexion

PLANE OF MOTION

1. Sagittal
2. Sagittal

6.03 TOE TOUCHES

SUMMARY

The Toe Touches is an auxiliary exercise, which focuses on improving the synergy of the neuro-muscular system, strengthening the trunk flexor musculature, and improving body control & coordination and flexibility.

DESCRIPTION

1. Place floor mat on the ground
2. Lie down in supine (face up) position, keep knees extended (straight), and flex hips until feet point towards the ceiling (90° hip flexion)
3. In a controlled fashion, touch the feet with both hands thereby flexing the lumbar spine and lifting the upper body off the floor
4. Slowly extend lumbar spine and return upper body towards the ground without allowing the legs to swing

RECOMMENDED RESISTANCE TRAINING EXERCISES

Rectus Abdominis Flexibility

1. Forward Lunge & Overhead Reach

Oblique Flexibility

2. Forward Lunge & Ankle Reach
3. Lunge with Bar Rotation
4. Supine Oblique Stretch

BREATH IN & OUT

- IN: Before Toe touch
- OUT: During Toe touch

PURPOSE

1. Improving transfer of energy; synergy of neuro-muscular system
2. Strengthening of trunk (lumbar) flexor musculature
3. Improving body control & coordination by enhancing stabilizers and gliding neutralizers
4. Improving flexibility

DEGREE OF DIFFICULTY

- 1

RELEVANCE

- Strengthening the trunk (core) aids in more efficient energy transfer, which has a positive effect on more powerful stroke production on the court
- Enhances strength of the rectus abdominis and develops trunk musculature (obliques) as stabilizer.
- Prevention of lower back pain due to pelvic instability

KEY FACTORS

- Focus on perfect movement mechanics and range of motion
- Keep hips flexed at 90°
- Maintain neutral head position

COMMON ERRORS

- Feet swing when returning upper body towards the ground
- Excessive flexion of thoracic spine (rounded back) during motion
- Jerking motion

TARGETED MUSCULATURE	ACTION	PLANE OF MOTION
1. Rectus Abdominis (proximal end)	1. Lumbar Flexion	1. Sagittal
2. Obliques	2. Lumbar Flexion	2. Sagittal

REQUIRED EQUIPMENT

- 1 Floor Mat

ID: 603

6.04 PHYSIO BALL PRONE KNEE CURL

SUMMARY

The Physio Ball Prone Knee Curl is an auxiliary exercise, which focuses on improving the synergy of the neuro-muscular system, strengthening the trunk flexor musculature, and improving body control & coordination and flexibility as well as improving skill & balance foundation for complex movements.

PURPOSE

1. Improving transfer of energy; synergy of neuro-muscular system
2. Strengthening of **trunk (lumbar) flexor** musculature
3. Improving body control & coordination by enhancing stabilizers and gliding neutralizers
4. Improving flexibility
5. Improving skill and balance foundation for complex movements

DESCRIPTION

1. Place feet on top of the physio ball, keep legs straight and hands on the ground so that palms are underneath shoulders
2. Push chest out, shoulder blades together, and maintain neutral head and pelvic position
3. In a controlled fashion, flex the lumbar spine: flex knees and bring them towards the chest
4. Slowly extend lumbar spine: extend knee and return to starting position

RECOMMENDED EXERCISES

Rectus Abdominis Flexibility

1. Forward Lunge & Overhead Reach

Oblique Flexibility

1. Forward Lunge & Ankle Reach
2. Lunge with Bar Rotation
3. Supine Oblique Stretch

BREATH IN & OUT

- IN: Before Knee Flexion
- OUT: During Knee Flexion

DEGREE OF DIFFICULTY

- 2

REQUIRED EQUIPMENT

- 1 Physio Ball

RELEVANCE

- Strengthening the trunk (core) aids in more efficient energy transfer, which has a positive effect on stroke production on the court
- Enhances strength of the rectus abdominis and develops trunk musculature (obliques) as stabilizer.
- Prevention of lower back pain due to pelvic instability

KEY FACTORS

- Focus on perfect movement mechanics and range of motion
- Maintain neutral pelvic position
- Maintain neutral head position

COMMON ERRORS

- Compromised neutral pelvic position

TARGETED MUSCULATURE

1. Rectus Abdominis (proximal end)
2. Obliques

ACTION

1. Lumbar Flexion
2. Lumbar Flexion

PLANE OF MOTION

1. Sagittal
2. Sagittal

ID: 604

6.05 EXTERNAL SHOULDER ROTATION

SUMMARY

The External Shoulder Rotation is an auxiliary exercise, which focuses on improving the synergy of the neuro-muscular system, strengthening the external shoulder rotator musculature and improving muscular endurance.

PURPOSE

1. Improving transfer of energy; synergy of neuro-muscular system
2. Strengthening of **external shoulder rotator** musculature (infraspinatus & teres minor) to maintain integrity of shoulder joint capsule
3. Improving muscular endurance

DESCRIPTION

1. Fasten elastic band (to a pole) at hip level
2. Stand up in athletic position; feet underneath shoulders, knees are slightly flexed
3. Hold the elastic band with the hand farthest away from the pole, flex the elbow, and keep it close to the hip/trunk; hand is in front of the umbilicus (belly button)
4. Rotate at the elbow pulling the elastic band at hip level away from the body, thereby moving the hand away from the body, without moving the elbow away from the trunk/hip

RECOMMENDED EXERCISES

Infraspinatus & Teres Minor Flexibility

1. 2 Racquet Serve
2. Posterior Deltoid

BREATH IN & OUT

- IN: Before External Shoulder Rotation
- OUT: During External Shoulder Rotation

DEGREE OF DIFFICULTY

- 1

REQUIRED EQUIPMENT

- 1 Elastic Band

RELEVANCE

- Strengthening the external shoulder rotators aids in more efficient energy transfer, which has a positive effect on stroke production on the court (e.g. serve
- Enhances strength of the infraspinatus & teres minor.
- Prevention of shoulder pain due to tendinitis and rotator cuff impingement within subacromial space

KEY FACTORS

- Focus on perfect movement mechanics and range of motion
- Maintain neutral pelvic position
- Maintain neutral head position

COMMON ERRORS

- Elbow moves away from the hip/trunk during pulling phase

ID: 605

TARGETED MUSCULATURE

1. Infraspinatus
2. Teres Minor

ACTION

1. External Shoulder Rotation
2. External Shoulder Rotation

PLANE OF MOTION

1. Transverse
2. Transverse

6.06 INTERNAL SHOULDER ROTATION

SUMMARY

The Internal Shoulder Rotation is an auxiliary exercise, which focuses on improving the synergy of the neuro-muscular system, strengthening the internal shoulder rotator musculature, improving muscular endurance as well as the dynamic stabilization of rotator cuff musculature.

PURPOSE

1. Improving transfer of energy; synergy of neuro-muscular system
2. Strengthening of **internal shoulder rotator** musculature (subscapularis) to maintain integrity of shoulder joint capsule
3. Improving muscular endurance
4. Improving dynamic stabilizer musculature acting on the humeral head (rotator cuff)

DESCRIPTION

1. Fasten elastic band (to a pole) at hip level
2. Stand up in athletic position; feet underneath shoulders, knees are slightly flexed
3. Hold the elastic band with the hand closest to the pole, flex the elbow, and keep it close to the hip/trunk; hand is facing away from the umbilicus (belly button)
4. Rotate at the elbow by pulling the elastic band at hip level towards the body, thereby moving the hand towards the umbilicus, without moving the elbow away from the trunk/hip

RECOMMENDED EXERCISES

Subscapularis Flexibility

1. Towel Shoulder
2. Bar Rotator Cuff

COMMON ERRORS

- Elbow moves away from the hip/trunk during pulling phase

DEGREE OF DIFFICULTY

- 1

REQUIRED EQUIPMENT

- 1 Elastic Band

RELEVANCE

- Strengthening the internal shoulder rotators aids in more efficient energy transfer, which has a positive effect on stroke production on the court (e.g. serve
- Enhances strength of the infraspinatus & teres minor and developes shoulder stabilizer.
- Prevention of shoulder pain due to tendinitis and rotator cuff impingement within subacromial space

KEY FACTORS

- Focus on perfect movement mechanics and range of motion
- Maintain neutral pelvic position
- Maintain neutral head position

BREATH IN & OUT

- IN: Before External Shoulder Rotation
- OUT: During External Shoulder Rotation

ID: 606

TARGETED MUSCULATURE

1. Subscapularis

ACTION

1. Internal Shoulder Rotation

PLANE OF MOTION

1. Transverse

6.07 HORIZ. ABD. EXTERNAL SHOULDER ROTATION

SUMMARY

The Horizontal Abducted External Shoulder Rotation is an auxiliary exercise, which focuses on improving the synergy of the neuro-muscular system, strengthening the external shoulder rotator musculature, improving muscular endurance and dynamic stabilization of rotator cuff musculature.

DESCRIPTION

1. Fasten elastic band (at a pole) on chest level
2. Stand up in athletic position; feet underneath shoulders, knees are slightly flexed
3. Abduct shoulders to 90°, flex the elbows, and hold elastic band in both hands; hands point **forward**
4. Rotate at the elbows until hands point **upwards**, thereby pulling the elastic band

RECOMMENDED EXERCISES

Infraspinatus & Teres Minor Flexibility

1. 2 Racquet Serve
2. Posterior Deltoid

COMMON ERRORS

- Elbow moves away from the hip/trunk during pulling phase

BREATH IN & OUT

- IN: Before External Shoulder Rotation
- OUT: During External Shoulder Rotation

PURPOSE

1. Improving transfer of energy; synergy of neuro-muscular system
2. Strengthening of **external shoulder rotator** musculature (infraspinatus & teres minor) to maintain integrity of shoulder joint capsule
3. Improves muscular endurance
4. Improves dynamic stabilizer musculature acting on the humeral head (rotator cuff)

DEGREE OF DIFFICULTY

- 2

REQUIRED EQUIPMENT

- 1 Elastic Band

RELEVANCE

- Strengthening the external shoulder rotators aids in more efficient energy transfer, which has a positive effect on more powerful stroke production on the court (e.g. serve)
- Enhances strength of the infraspinatus & teres minor and developes shoulder stabilizer.
- Prevention of shoulder pain due to tendinitis and rotator cuff impingement within subacromial space

KEY FACTORS

- Focus on perfect movement mechanics and range of motion
- Maintain neutral pelvic position
- Maintain neutral head position

ID: 607

TARGETED MUSCULATURE	ACTION	PLANE OF MOTION
1. Infraspinatus	1. External Shoulder Rotation	1. Transverse
2. Teres Minon	2. External Shoulder Rotation	2. Transverse

6.08 HORIZ. ABD. INTERNAL SHOULDER ROTATION

SUMMARY

The Horizontal Abducted Internal Shoulder Rotation is an auxiliary exercise, which focuses on improving the synergy of the neuro-muscular system, strengthening of internal shoulder rotator musculature, improving muscular endurance and dynamic stabilization of rotator cuff musculature.

PURPOSE

1. Improving transfer of energy; synergy of neuro-muscular system
2. Strengthening of **internal shoulder rotator** musculature (subscapularis) to maintain integrity of shoulder joint capsule
3. Improving muscular endurance
4. Improving dynamic stabilizer musculature acting on the humeral head (rotator cuff)

DESCRIPTION

1. Fasten elastic band (at a pole) on chest level
2. Stand up in athletic position; feet underneath shoulders, knees are slightly flexed
3. Abduct shoulders to 90°, flex the elbows, and hold elastic band in both hands; hands point **upward**
4. Rotate at the elbows until hands point **forward**, thereby pulling the elastic band

DEGREE OF DIFFICULTY

- 2

REQUIRED EQUIPMENT

- 1 Elastic Band

RECOMMENDED EXERCISES

Subscapularis Flexibility

1. Towel Shoulder
2. Bar Rotator Cuff

RELEVANCE

- Strengthening the internal shoulder rotators aids in more efficient energy transfer, which has a positive effect on more powerful stroke production on the court (e.g. serve)
- Enhances strength of the infraspinatus & teres minor and developes shoulder stabilizer.
- Prevention of shoulder pain due to tendinitis and rotator cuff impingement within subacromial space

COMMON ERRORS

- Elbow moves away from the hip/trunk during pulling phase

KEY FACTORS

- Focus on perfect movement mechanics and range of motion
- Maintain neutral pelvic position
- Maintain neutral head position

BREATH IN & OUT

- IN: Before Internal Shoulder Rotation
- OUT: During Internal Shoulder Rotation

ID: 608

TARGETED MUSCULATURE

1. Subscapularis

ACTION

1. Internal Shoulder Rotation

PLANE OF MOTION

1. Transverse

6.09 LATERAL RAISE WITH ROTATION

SUMMARY

The Lateral Raise with Rotation is an auxiliary exercise, which focuses on improving the synergy of the neuro-muscular system, strengthening of shoulder abductor musculature, improving muscular endurance and dynamic stabilization of rotator cuff musculature.

PURPOSE

1. Improving transfer of energy; synergy of neuro-muscular system
2. Strengthening of **shoulder abductor** musculature (supraspinatus) to maintain integrity of shoulder joint capsule
3. Improving muscular endurance
4. Improving dynamic stabilizer musculature acting on the humeral head (rotator cuff)

DESCRIPTION

1. Fasten elastic band under one foot and hold it in the hand on the ipsilateral (same) side
2. Stand up in athletic position with arms close to the body and the **thumb** pointing inward; feet underneath shoulders, knees are slightly flexed
3. Abduct shoulders to 90° and slightly rotate the arm so that **thumb** points forward
4. Slowly return to starting position

RECOMMENDED RESISTANCE TRAINING EXERCISES

Supraspinatus Flexibility

1. Towel Shoulder
2. Bar Rotator Cuff

COMMON ERRORS

- No rotation of the arm occurs (no change in thumb position)
- Shoulder is abducted past 90°

BREATH IN & OUT

- IN: Before Shoulder Abduction
- OUT: During Shoulder Abduction

DEGREE OF DIFFICULTY

- 1

REQUIRED EQUIPMENT

- 1 Elastic Band

RELEVANCE

- Strengthening the shoulder abductors aids in more efficient energy transfer, which has a positive effect on more powerful stroke production on the court (e.g. serve
- Enhances strength of the supraspinatus and developes shoulder stabilizer.
- Prevention of shoulder pain due to tendinitis and rotator cuff impingement within subacromial space

KEY FACTORS

- Focus on perfect movement mechanics and range of motion
- Maintain neutral pelvic position
- Maintain neutral head position

ID: 609

TARGETED MUSCULATURE	ACTION	PLANE OF MOTION
1. Supraspinatus	1. Shoulder Abduction	1. Frontal

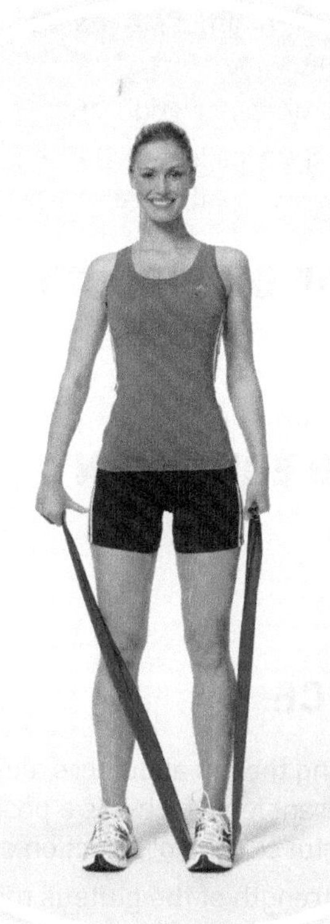

6.10 SIDELYING STRAIGHT LEG HIP ABDUCTION

SUMMARY

The Sidelying Straight Leg Hip Abducion is an auxiliary exercise, which focuses on improving the synergy of the neuro-muscular system, strengthening of hip abductor musculature, improving muscular endurance and dynamic stabilization of hip musculature.

PURPOSE

1. Improving transfer of energy; synergy of neuro-muscular system
2. Strengthening of **hip abductor** musculature (gluteus medius & minimus) to maintain integrity of hip joint capsule
3. Improving muscular endurance
4. Improving dynamic stabilizer musculature acting on the femural head (greater trochanter)

DESCRIPTION

1. Position floor mat on the ground
2. Lie on the side and maintain neutral pelvic – and head position
3. Lift the superior leg upwards thereby abducting the superior hip
4. Slowly return to starting position

DEGREE OF DIFFICULTY

- 1

REQUIRED EQUIPMENT

- 1 Floor Mat

RECOMMENDED EXERCISES

Glute Flexibility

1. Supine Cross-Over

RELEVANCE

- Strengthening the hip abductors aids in more efficient energy transfer, which has a positive effect on more powerful change of direction capabilities
- Enhances strength of the gluteus medius & minimus and developes hip stabilizer.

COMMON ERRORS

- Spinal alignment is altered
- Jerking motion

KEY FACTORS

- Focus on perfect movement mechanics and range of motion
- Maintain neutral pelvic position
- Maintain neutral head position

BREATH IN & OUT

- IN: Before Hip Abduction
- OUT: During Hip Abduction

ID: 610

TARGETED MUSCULATURE

1. Gluteus Medius
2. Gluteus Minimus

ACTION

1. Hip Abduction
2. Hip Abduction

PLANE OF MOTION

1. Frontal
2. Frontal

6.11 RUSSIAN LEAN

SUMMARY

The Russian Lean is an auxiliary exercise, which focuses on improving the synergy of the neuro-muscular system, strengthening of knee flexor musculature, and improving body control & coordination.

PURPOSE

1. Improving transfer of energy; synergy of neuro-muscular system
2. Strengthening of **knee flexors** (upper hamstring) musculature
3. Improving body control & coordination by enhancing stabilizers and gliding neutralizer

DESCRIPTION

1. Place floor mat on the ground
2. Kneel on the mat with knees underneath the shoulder and maintain neutral spine - and pelvic position; the other person maintains feet and lower legs on the ground at all times
3. Slowly lean forward, while maintaining neutral spine – and pelvic position, until lean can no longer be maintained and upper body falls towards the ground. Athlete absorbs the fall with the hands
4. Push off the ground and flex the knees to return to starting position

DEGREE OF DIFFICULTY

- 2

REQUIRED EQUIPMENT

- 1 Floor Mat
- 1 Person

RELEVANCE

- Strengthening the knee flexors aids in more efficient energy transfer, which has a positive effect on more powerful running ability on the court
- Enhances strength of the hamstrings and developes trunk musculature as stabilizer.

RECOMMENDED EXERCISES

Hamstring Flexibility

1. Straight Leg Kicks
2. Romanian Deadlift
3. Supine Towel Hamstring

KEY FACTORS

- Focus on perfect movement mechanics and range of motion
- Maintain neutral pelvic position
- Maintain neutral head position

COMMON ERRORS

- Hip flexion occurs during motion
- No controlled forward lean
- Excessive push off with limited knee flexion

BREATH IN & OUT

- IN: Before Knee Extension
- OUT: During Knee Flexion

TARGETED MUSCULATURE

1. Hamstrings (bicep femoris, semitendinosus, semimembranosus)

ACTION

1. Knee Flexion

PLANE OF MOTION

1. Sagittal

ID: 611

6.12 BACK SQUAT

SUMMARY

The Back Squat is a compound exercise, which focuses on improving the synergy of the neuro-muscular system, strengthening of hip extensor & knee extensor musculature, body control & coordination, flexibility as well as improving skill & balance foundation for complex movements.

Note: If the athlete has flexibility issues and/ or for teaching purposes, a stance wider than shoulder-width is warranted.

PURPOSE

1. Improving transfer of energy; synergy of neuro-muscular system
2. Strengthening of **hip extensor** (glutes primary; hamstrings secondary) & **knee extensor** (secondary) musculature
3. Improving body control & coordination by enhancing stabilizers and gliding neutralizers
4. Improving flexibility
5. Improving skill and balance foundation for complex movements

DESCRIPTION

1. Position barbell chest level on the rack; add resistance (plates) and attach safety clips
2. Take an athletic stance; stand straight, **feet are just wider than shoulder-width apart**; knees slightly flexed; toes point slightly outward (10°-20°)
3. Use a pronated grip (palms facing down) and place hands slightly wider than shoulder-width apart on the bar
4. Move head underneath the barbell and position barbell superior to the spine of the scapulae (on the top shelf created by the trapezius); do not place barbell on top of the cervical spine!
5. First flex hips (~45°) and then knees until knees are flexed to 90° (or as far as possible); maintain neutral pelvic position; keep knees inside shoulders; distribute weight through the heels; maintain neutral spine position (push chest out and scapulae [shoulder blades] together; maintain neutral head position (look forward)
6. Extend the knees and hips and return to starting position

DEGREE OF DIFFICULTY

- 1

REQUIRED EQUIPMENT

- 1 Rack
- 1 Barbell
- Plates
- 2 Safety Clips

RELEVANCE

- Results in faster running speed and more powerful stroke production on the court due to more efficient energy transfer
- It is used to enhance strength of the glutes and to develop lower back musculature as stabilizer. It is very limited as an assistive lift since it doesn't transfer in the lifting progression and hence is only used up to Basic Strength Training Phase.

KEY FACTORS

- Focus on perfect movement mechanics and range of motion
- Keep knees inside shoulders
- Distribute weight through heels
- Maintain neutral spine position
- Maintain neutral head position

ID: 612

RECOMMENDED RESISTANCE TRAINING EXERCISES

Hamstring Flexibility

1. Straight leg Kicks
2. Romanian Deadlift
3. Supine Towel Hamstring

Gluteal Flexibility

1. High Knee Pulls
2. Deadlift
3. Supine Knee to Chest

COMMON ERRORS

- Posterior pelvic tilt occurs; buttocks "tucks under"
- Bar is placed on top of cervical spine
- Flexion of thoracic spine (rounded back) during motion
- Athlete loses balance

BREATH IN & OUT

- IN: Before Hip Flexion
- OUT: During Hip Extension

FUNCTIONAL RANGE LIMITING FACTORS

1. Hip Flexibility (tight glutes & hamstrings)
2. Gluteus Maximus Flexibility
3. Upper Hamstring Flexibility
4. Weak Hip Extensors
5. Too Much Resistance

COMPENSATORY ACTION

1. Limited hip & knee flexion
2. Posterior Pelvic Tilt: buttocks tucks under during hip flexion
3. Posterior Pelvic Tilt: buttocks tucks under during hip flexion
4. Knees move medially (inwards)
5. Knees move laterally (outwards)

TARGETED MUSCULATURE

1. Gluteus Maximus
2. Upper Hamstring
3. Quadriceps

ACTION

1. Hip Extension
2. Hip Extension
3. Knee Extension

PLANE OF MOTION

1. Sagittal
2. Sagittal
3. Sagittal

6.13 FRONT SQUAT

SUMMARY

The Front Squat is a compound exercise, which focuses on improving the synergy of the neuro-muscular system, strengthening the knee extensor & hip extensor musculature, improving hip flexor speed, body control & coordination and flexibility as well as improving the skill & balance foundation for complex movements.

Note: If the athlete has flexibility issues and/ or for teaching purposes, a stance wider than shoulder-width is warranted.

PURPOSE

1. Improving transfer of energy; synergy of neuro-muscular system
2. Strengthening of **knee extensor** (quadriceps primary) & **hip extensor** (glutes/hamstrings secondary) musculature
3. Improving body control & coordination by enhancing stabilizers and gliding neutralizers
4. Improving flexibility for complex movements (e.g. triceps flexibility for high receive)
5. Improving skill (hip flexion/extension) and balance foundation for complex movements

DESCRIPTION

1. Position barbell chest level on the rack; add resistance (plates) and attach safety clips
2. Take an **athletic stance**; stand straight, **feet are shoulder-width apart**; knees slightly flexed; toes point slightly outward (10°-20°)
3. Use a pronated grip (palms facing down) and place hands slightly wider than shoulder-width apart on the bar
4. Move elbows underneath the barbell and position barbell on top of the chest and shoulders; shoulders are flexed at 90°; elbow are flexed and point forward
5. First flex hips (~45°) and then knees until knees are flexed to 90° (or as far as possible); maintain neutral pelvic position; keep knees inside shoulders; distribute weight through the heels; maintain neutral spine position (push chest out and scapulae [shoulder blades] together; maintain neutral head position (look forward)
6. Extend the knees and hips and return to starting position

REQUIRED EQUIPMENT

- 1 Rack
- 1 Barbell
- Plates
- 2 Safety Clips

RELEVANCE

- Results in faster running speed and more powerful stroke production on the court due to more efficient energy transfer
- It is used to enhance strength of the quadriceps/ hamstrings and to develop lower back musculature as a stabilizer. It is an assistive lift since it has transfer in the lifting progression (e.g. catching phase during power clean from the floor) and hence must be used in the Teaching/Hypertrophy Training Phase.
- For injury prevention purposes, the knee extensors (quadriceps) should be ~33% stronger than the knee flexors (hamstring) to maintain patellofemoral (knee) stability, especially during deceleration (e.g. change of direction) activities

FUNCTIONAL RANGE LIMITING FACTORS

1. Hip Flexibility (tight glutes & hamstrings)
2. Gluteus Maximus Flexibility
3. Upper Hamstring Flexibility
4. Weak Hip Extensors
5. Too Much Resistance

COMPENSATORY ACTION

1. Limited hip & knee flexion
2. Posterior Pelvic Tilt: buttocks tucks under during hip flexion
3. Posterior Pelvic Tilt: buttocks tucks under during hip flexion
4. Knees move medially (inwards)
5. Knees move laterally (outwards)

ID: 613

RECOMMENDED EXERCISES

Triceps Flexibility

1. Hang Clean
2. 2 Racquet Serves
3. Overhead Triceps

Quadriceps Flexibility

1. Buttocks Kicks
2. Knee Extension
3. Side-Lying Quad

Hamstring Flexibility

1. Straight leg Kicks
2. Romanian Deadlift
3. Supine Towel Hamstring

Gluteal Flexibility

1. High Knee Pulls
2. Deadlift
3. Supine Knee to Chest

DEGREE OF DIFFICULTY

- 2

COMMON ERRORS

- Posterior pelvic tilt occurs
- Elbows drop and bar is placed in front of the chest
- Flexion of thoracic spine (rounded back) during motion
- Weight distribution occurs through the toes

BREATH IN & OUT

- IN: Before Hip Flexion
- OUT: During Hip Flexion

KEY FACTORS

- Focus on perfect movement mechanics and range of motion
- Keep elbows up high; 90 °shoulder flexion
- Keep knees inside shoulders
- Distribute weight through heels
- Maintain neutral spine position
- Maintain neutral head position

TARGETED MUSCULATURE

1. Quadriceps
2. Hamstring
3. Glutes)

ACTION

1. Knee Extension
2. Hip Extension
3. Hip Extension

PLANE OF MOTION

1. Sagittal
2. Sagittal
3. Sagittal

6.14 OVERHEAD SQUAT

SUMMARY

The Overhead Squat is a compound exercise, which focuses on improving the synergy of the neuro-muscular system, trunk stability, hip extensor strength, hip flexor speed, body control & coordination, flexibility as well as improving skill & balance foundation for complex movements.

Note: If the athlete has flexibility issues and/ or for teaching purposes, a stance wider than shoulder-width is warranted.

DESCRIPTION

1. Position barbell chest level on the rack; add resistance (plates), if necessary, and attach safety clips
2. Take an **athletic stance**; stand straight, **feet are shoulder-width apart**; knees slightly flexed; toes point slightly outward (10°-20°)
3. Use a pronated grip (palms facing down) and place hands wide apart on the bar
4. Move head underneath the barbell and position barbell superior to the spine of the scapulae (on the top shelf created by the trapezius); do not place barbell on top of the cervical spine!
5. Use a hitch from the hips to move the bar and extend elbows over the head, extend the wrists; bar should be over or behind the head; arms are straight; wrists extended
6. First flex hips (~45°) and then knees until knees are flexed to 90° (or as far as possible); maintain neutral pelvic position; keep knees inside shoulders; distribute weight through the heels; maintain neutral spine position (push chest out and scapulae [shoulder blades] together; maintain neutral head position (look forward)
7. Extend the knees and hips and return to starting position

KEY FACTORS

- Focus on perfect movement mechanics and range of motion
- Keep knees inside shoulders
- Distribute weight through heels
- Maintain neutral spine position
- Maintain neutral head position

ID: 614

PURPOSE

1. Improving transfer of energy; synergy of neuro-muscular system
2. Improving skill and balance foundation for complex movements (e.g. snatch)
3. Improving flexibility for complex movements (e.g. latissimus dorsi & pectoralis flexibility for over-head snatch)
4. Strengthening of knee extensor & hip extensor musculature
5. Improving body control & coordination by enhancing stabilizers and gliding neutralizer.

DEGREE OF DIFFICULTY

- 3

REQUIRED EQUIPMENT

- 1 Rack
- 1 Barbell
- Plates
- 2 Safety Clips

RELEVANCE

- It is used to enhance flexibility of the shoulder girdle and to prepare for the overhead receive. It is an assistive lift since it has transfer in the lifting progression (e.g. catching phase during the snatch or push-jerk) and hence must be used in the Teaching/ Hypertrophy Training Phase.
- Results in faster running speed and more powerful stroke production on the court due to more efficient energy transfer
- For injury prevention purposes, the knee extensors (quadriceps) should be ~33% stronger than the knee flexors (hamstring) to maintain patellofemoral (knee) stability, especially during deceleration (e.g. change of direction) activities

RECOMMENDED EXERCISES

Shoulder Flexibility

1. Clap Push-Up
2. Dumbbell Bench Press
3. Single Arm Pectoralis

Latissimus Flexibility

1. Squat & Overhead Reach
2. Overhead Latissimus Dorsi

COMMON ERRORS

- Posterior pelvic tilt occurs
- Elbows flexion and shoulder flexion occur during squat movement
- Flexion of thoracic spine (rounded back) during motion
- Weight distribution occurs through the toes

BREATH IN & OUT

- IN: Before Hip Flexion
- OUT: During Hip Extension

FUNCTIONAL RANGE

LIMITING FACTORS

1. Hip Flexibility (tight glutes & hamstrings)
2. Gluteus Maximus Flexibility
3. Upper Hamstring Flexibility
4. Weak Hip Extensors
5. Too Much Resistance
6. Shoulder Flexibility (Pectoralis [anterior] & Latissimus dorsi [posterior] tightness)

COMPENSATORY ACTION

1. Limited hip & knee flexion
2. Posterior Pelvic Tilt: buttocks tucks under during hip flexion
3. Posterior Pelvic Tilt: buttocks tucks under during hip flexion
4. Knees move medially (inwards)
5. Knees move laterally (outwards)
6. Shoulders extend, elbows flex and bar moves in front of the head

TARGETED MUSCULATURE

1. Gluteus Maximus
2. Hamstrings
3. Quadriceps

ACTION

1. Hip Extension
2. Hip Extension
3. Knee Extension

PLANE OF MOTION

1. Sagittal
2. Sagittal
3. Sagittal

6.15 LATERAL SQUAT

SUMMARY

The Lateral Squat is a compound exercise, which focuses on improving the synergy of the neuro-muscular system, strengthening the hip abductors, hip extensor & knee extensor musculature, improving body control & coordination and flexibility as well as improving skill & balance foundation for complex movements.

Note: If the athlete has flexibility issues and/ or for teaching purposes, a stance wider than shoulder-width is warranted.

PURPOSE

1. Improving transfer of energy; synergy of neuro-muscular system
2. Strengthening of **hip abductor** (primary), hip extensor & knee extensor (secondary) musculature
3. Improving body control & coordination by enhancing trunk & hip stabilizers and gliding neutralizers
4. Improving flexibility
5. Improving skill and balance foundation for complex movements

DESCRIPTION

1. Position barbell chest level on the rack; add resistance (plates) and attach safety clips
2. Take an **athletic stance**; stand straight, **feet are just wider than shoulder-width apart**; knees slightly flexed; toes point slightly outward (10°-20°)
3. Use a pronated grip (palms facing down) and place hands slightly wider than shoulder-width apart on the bar
4. Move head underneath the barbell and position barbell superior to the spine of the scapulae (on the top shelf created by the trapezius); do not place barbell on top of the cervical spine!
5. In athletic stance step sideways to the right, and drop hips in the center into the squat; knees are **outside** shoulders; keep weight on heels
6. Step out of the squat position to the right back to athletic stance
7. Step back into the position to the left by dropping hips in the center into the squat; knees are **outside** shoulders
8. Step out of the squat position to the left back to athletic stance

COMMON ERRORS

- Posterior pelvic tilt occurs; buttocks "tucks under"
- Bar is placed on top of cervical spine
- Flexion of thoracic spine (rounded back) during motion
- Athlete loses balance

ID: 615

DEGREE OF DIFFICULTY

- 1

REQUIRED EQUIPMENT

- 1 Rack
- 1 Barbell
- Plates
- 2 Safety Clips

RELEVANCE

- Results in faster running speed and better agility (change of direction) on the court due to more efficient energy transfer
- Improved accuracy and power when athlete is out of position during groundstroke production

KEY FACTORS

- Focus on perfect movement mechanics and range of motion
- Keep knees outside shoulders
- Distribute weight through heels
- Maintain neutral spine position
- Maintain neutral head position

FUNCTIONAL RANGE LIMITING FACTORS

1. Hip Flexibility (tight glutes & hamstrings)
2. Gluteus Medius & Minimus Flexibility
3. Upper Hamstring Flexibility
4. Weak Hip Extensors
5. Too Much Resistance

COMPENSATORY ACTION

1. Limited hip & knee flexion
2. Posterior Pelvic Tilt: buttocks tucks under during hip flexion
3. Posterior Pelvic Tilt: buttocks tucks under during hip flexion
4. Knees move medially (inwards)
5. Knees move laterally (outwards)

TARGETED MUSCULATURE

1. Gluteus Medius & Minimus
2. Gluteus Maximus
3. Hamstrings
4. Quadriceps

ACTION

1. Hip Abduction
2. Hip Extension
3. Hip Extension
4. Knee Extension

PLANE OF MOTION

1. Frontal
2. Sagittal
3. Sagittal
4. Sagittal

RECOMMENDED EXERCISES

Hamstring Flexibility

1. Straight leg Kicks
2. Romanian Deadlift
3. Supine Towel Hamstring

Gluteal Flexibility

1. Bilateral Squat
2. Deadlift
3. Supine Cross-Over

BREATH IN & OUT

- IN: Before Hip Flexion
- OUT: During Hip Flexion

6.16 LATERAL LUNGE

SUMMARY

The Lateral Lunge is a compound exercise, which focuses on improving the synergy of the neuromuscular system, strengthening the hip abductors, hip extensor & knee extensor musculature, improving body control & coordination and flexibility and adductor dynamic range as well as improving skill & balance foundation for complex movements.

Note: If the athlete has flexibility issues and/ or for teaching purposes, a wider stance is warranted. Exercise can also be performed by using body weight only!

PURPOSE

1. Improving transfer of energy; synergy of neuromuscular system
2. Strengthening of **hip abductors** (primary), hip extensors & knee extensor (secondary) musculature
3. Improving body control & coordination by enhancing trunk & hip stabilizers and gliding neutralizers
4. Improving flexibility and adductor dynamic range
5. Improving skill and balance foundation for complex movements

DESCRIPTION

1. Position barbell chest level on the rack; add resistance (plates) and attach safety clips
2. Take an athletic stance; stand straight, **feet are just wider than shoulder-width apart**; knees slightly flexed; toes point slightly outward (10°-20°)
3. Use a pronated grip (palms facing down) and place hands slightly wider than shoulder-width apart on the bar
4. Move head underneath the barbell and position barbell superior to the spine of the scapulae (on the top shelf created by the trapezius); do not place barbell on top of the cervical spine!
5. Step sideways with the left foot and bend the left knee until left knee is at 90° and right leg is straight; keep weight on heels; knee must not move beyond toes; toes point slightly outward (10°-20°)
6. Push-off with the left foot, return to athletic stance, and lunge to the right side until right knee is at 90°; knee must not move beyond toes; toes point slightly outward (10°-20°)
7. Step out of the lunge position to the left back to athletic stance

DEGREE OF DIFFICULTY

- 1

REQUIRED EQUIPMENT

- 1 Rack
- 1 Barbell
- Plates (if necessary)
- 2 Safety Clips (if necessary)

RELEVANCE

- Results in faster running speed and better agility (change of direction) on the court due to more efficient energy transfer
- Improved accuracy and power when athlete is out of position during groundstroke production

KEY FACTORS

- Focus on perfect movement mechanics and range of motion
- Keep knees inside shoulders
- Distribute weight through heels
- Maintain neutral spine position
- Maintain neutral head position

ID: 616

RECOMMENDED EXERCISES

Hamstring Flexibility

1. Straight leg Kicks
2. Romanian Deadlift
3. Supine Towel Hamstring

Gluteal Flexibility

1. Bilateral Squat
2. Deadlift
3. Supine Cross-Over

COMMON ERRORS

- Posterior pelvic tilt occurs; buttocks "tucks under"
- Bar is placed on top of cervical spine
- Flexion of thoracic spine (rounded back) during motion
- Athlete loses balance

BREATH IN & OUT

- IN: Before Hip Flexion
- OUT: During Hip Extension

TARGETED MUSCULATURE

1. Gluteus Medius & Minimus
2. Gluteus Maximus
3. Hamstrings
4. Quadriceps

ACTION

1. Hip Abduction
2. Hip Extension
3. Hip Extension
4. Knee Extension

PLANE OF MOTION

1. Frontal
2. Sagittal
3. Sagittal
4. Sagittal

6.17 MODIFIED DEADLIFT (MDL)

SUMMARY

The Modified Deadlift (MDL) is a compound exercise, which focuses on improving the synergy of the neuro-muscular system, strengthening of hip extensor & knee extensor musculature, body control & coordination, pelvis flexibility as well as improving skill & balance foundation for complex movements.

DESCRIPTION

1. Position barbell on the rack; add resistance (plates) and attach safety clips; place barbell on the ground
2. Assume **modified athletic stance;** stand straight, **feet are wider than shoulder-width apart**; knees slightly flexed; toes point slightly outward (10°-20°)
3. First flex hips (~45°) and then knees until knees are flexed to 90° (or as far as possible); maintain neutral pelvic position; distribute weight through the heels; keep knees inside shoulders; maintain neutral spine position (push chest out and scapulae [shoulder blades] together; maintain neutral head position [look forward])
4. Use an **alternated grip** (one palm facing down, the other palm faces up) and place hands within shoulder-width on the bar
5. Extend the knees and hips while maintaining neutral spine position and return to starting position

KEY FACTORS

- Focus on perfect movement mechanics and range of motion
- Keep knees inside shoulders
- Distribute weight through heels
- Maintain neutral spine position
- Maintain neutral head position

PURPOSE

1. Improving transfer of energy; synergy of neuro-muscular system
2. Strengthening of **hip extensor** (glutes primary; hamstrings secondary) & **knee extensor** (secondary) musculature
3. Improving body control & coordination by enhancing stabilizers (e.g. lower back) and gliding neutralizers
4. Improving pelvis flexibility
5. Improving skill and balance foundation for complex movements

DEGREE OF DIFFICULTY

- 1

REQUIRED EQUIPMENT

- 1 Rack
- 1 Barbell
- Plates
- 2 Safety Clips

RELEVANCE

- It is used to enhance strength of the glutes and to develop lower back musculature as stabilizer. It is very limited as an assistive lift since it doesn't transfer in the lifting progression and hence is only used up to Basic Strength Training Phase.

ID: 617

RECOMMENDED EXERCISES

Hamstring Flexibility

1. Straight leg Kicks
2. Romanian Deadlift
3. Supine Towel Hamstring

Gluteal Flexibility

1. High Knee Pulls
2. Back Squat
3. Supine Knee to Chest

COMMON ERRORS

- Posterior pelvic tilt occurs; buttocks "tucks under"
- Flexion of thoracic spine (rounded back) during motion

BREATH IN & OUT

- IN: Before Hip Extension
- OUT: During Hip Extension

TARGETED MUSCULATURE

1. Glutes
2. Hamstring
3. Quadriceps

ACTION

1. Hip Extension
2. Hip Extension
3. Knee Extension

PLANE OF MOTION

1. Sagittal
2. Sagittal
3. Sagittal

6.18 TRADITIONAL DEADLIFT (TDL)

SUMMARY

The Traditional Deadlift (TDL) is a compound exercise, which focuses on improving the synergy of the neuro-muscular system, strengthening of hip extensor & knee extensor musculature, body control & coordination, pelvis flexibility as well as improving skill & balance foundation for complex movements.

Note: If the athlete has flexibility issues and/or for teaching purposes, a wider stance is warranted.
If flexion of lumbar spine (rounding of lower back) occurs during hip extension then decrease resistance immediately!

PURPOSE

1. Improving transfer of energy; synergy of neuro-muscular system
2. Strengthening of **hip extensor** (glutes primary; hamstrings) & **knee extensor** (quadriceps secondary) musculature
3. Improving body control & coordination by enhancing stabilizers (e.g. lower back) and gliding neutralizers
4. Improving pelvis flexibility
5. Improving skill and balance foundation for complex movements

DESCRIPTION

1. Position barbell on the rack; add resistance (plates) and attach safety clips; place barbell on the ground
2. Take an **athletic stance**; stand straight, **feet are shoulder-width apart**; knees slightly flexed; toes point slightly outward (10°-20°)
3. First flex hips (~45°) and then knees until knees are flexed to 90° (or as far as possible); maintain neutral pelvic position; distribute weight through the heels; keep knees inside shoulders; maintain neutral spine position (push chest out and scapulae [shoulder blades] together); maintain neutral head position [look forward])
4. Use a **pronated grip** (palms facing down) and place hands just wider than shoulder-width on the bar
5. Extend the knees and hips while maintaining neutral spine position and return to starting position

KEY FACTORS

- Focus on perfect movement mechanics and range of motion
- Keep knees inside shoulders
- Distribute weight through heels
- Maintain neutral spine position
- Maintain neutral head position

DEGREE OF DIFFICULTY

- 2

REQUIRED EQUIPMENT

- 1 Rack
- 1 Barbell
- Plates
- 2 Safety Clips

RELEVANCE

- It is used to enhance strength of the quadriceps/ hamstrings and to develop lower back musculature as stabilizer. It is an assistive lift since it has transfer in the lifting progression (e.g. 1st pulling phase during power clean from the floor) and hence must be used in the Teaching/Hypertrophy Training Phase.

ID: 618

RECOMMENDED EXERCISES

Hamstring Flexibility

1. Straight leg Kicks
2. Romanian Deadlift
3. Supine Towel Hamstring

Gluteal Flexibility

1. High Knee Pulls
2. Front Squat
3. Supine Knee to Chest

COMMON ERRORS

- Posterior pelvic tilt occurs; buttocks "tucks under"
- Flexion of thoracic spine (rounded back) during motion

BREATH IN & OUT

- IN: Before Hip Flexion
- OUT: During Hip Flexion

TARGETED MUSCULATURE	ACTION	PLANE OF MOTION
1. Gluteus Maximus	1. Hip Extension	1. Sagittal
2. Hamstrings	2. Hip Extension	2. Sagittal
3. Quadriceps	3. Knee Extension	3. Sagittal

FUNCTIONAL RANGE LIMITING FACTORS	COMPENSATORY ACTION
1. Poor Back Strength	1. Kyphotic spine position (rounding of lower back)
2. Hip Flexibility (tight glutes & hamstrings)	2. Limited hip & knee flexion
3. Gluteus Maximus Flexibility	3. Posterior Pelvic Tilt: buttocks tucks under during hip flexion
4. Upper Hamstring Flexibility	4. Posterior Pelvic Tilt: buttocks tucks under during hip flexion
5. Weak Hip Extensors	5. Knees move medially (inwards)
6. Too Much Resistance	6. Knees move lateral (outwards)

6.19 ROMANIAN DEADLIFT (RDL)

SUMMARY

The Romanian Deadlift (RDL) is a compound exercise, which focuses on improving the synergy of the neuro-muscular system, strengthening the hip extensor & trunk extensor musculature, improving body control & coordination, pelvis flexibility as well as improving skill & balance foundation for complex movements.

Note: If the athlete has flexibility issues and/or for teaching purposes, a wider stance is warranted. If flexion of lumbar spine (rounding of lower back) occurs during hip extension then decrease resistance immediately!

PURPOSE

1. Improving transfer of energy; synergy of neuro-muscular system
2. Strengthening of **hip extensor** (hamstrings primary) and **trunk extensor** (erector spinae) musculature
3. Improving body control & coordination by enhancing stabilizers (e.g. lower back) and gliding neutralizers
4. Improving pelvis flexibility
5. Improving skill and balance foundation for complex movements

DESCRIPTION

1. Position barbell on the rack; add resistance (plates) and attach safety clips; place barbell on the ground
2. Take an **athletic stance**; stand straight, **feet are shoulder-width apart**; knees slightly flexed; toes point slightly outward (10°-20°)
3. Use a **pronated grip** (palms facing down) and place hands just wider than shoulder-width on the bar; take barbell off the rack; stand up straight
4. First flex hips (~45°) to 90° (or as far as possible) **without** additional knee flexion; distribute weight through the heels; keep knees inside shoulders; maintain neutral spine position (push chest out and scapulae [shoulder blades] together; maintain neutral head position [look forward])
5. Extend the knees and hips while maintaining neutral spine position and return to starting position

KEY FACTORS

- Focus on perfect movement mechanics and range of motion
- Keep knees inside shoulders
- Distribute weight through heels
- Maintain neutral spine position
- Maintain neutral head position

DEGREE OF DIFFICULTY

- 2

REQUIRED EQUIPMENT

- 1 Rack
- 1 Barbell
- Plates
- 2 Safety Clips

RELEVANCE

- It is used to enhance strength of the hamstrings and to develop lower back musculature as stabilizer. It is an assistive lift since it has transfer in the lifting progression (e.g. 1st & 2nd pulling phase during power clean from the floor) and hence must be used in the Teaching/Hypertrophy Training Phase.

BREATH IN & OUT

- IN: Before Hip Extension
- OUT: During Hip Extension

ID: 619

TARGETED MUSCULATURE

1. Hamstrings
2. Erector Spinae

ACTION

1. Hip Extension
2. Trunk Extension

PLANE OF MOTION

1. Sagittal
2. Sagittal

FUNCTIONAL RANGE LIMITING FACTORS

1. Poor Back Strength
2. Hip Flexibility (tight hamstrings)

COMPENSATORY ACTION

1. Kyphotic spine position (rounding of lower back)
2. Additional knee flexion during hip flexion occurs

COMMON ERRORS

- Additional knee flexion occurs
- Flexion of thoracic spine (rounded back) during motion

RECOMMENDED EXERCISES

Hamstring Flexibility

1. Straight leg Kicks
2. MB Sagittal Reach (I)
3. Supine Towel Hamstring

6.20 FORWARD LUNGE

SUMMARY

The Forward Lunge is a compound exercise, which focuses on improving the synergy of the neuro-muscular system, strengthening the hip extensor & knee extensor musculature, improving body control & coordination, flexibility as well as improving skill & balance foundation for complex movements.

Note: If the athlete has flexibility issues drop body as low as possible. Exercise can also be performed by using body weight only!

PURPOSE

1. Improving transfer of energy; synergy of neuro-muscular system
2. Strengthening of **hip extensor** (glutes/hamstrings primary) & **knee extensor** (quadriceps secondary) musculature
3. Improving body control & coordination by enhancing stabilizers and gliding neutralizers
4. Improving flexibility for complex movements (e.g. gluteal flexibility for split-jerk)
5. Improving skill (hip flexion/extension) and balance foundation for complex movements

DESCRIPTION

1. Position barbell chest level on the rack; add resistance (plates) and attach safety clips
2. Take an **athletic stance**; stand straight, **feet are shoulder-width apart**; knees slightly flexed; toes point slightly outward (10°-20°)
3. Use a pronated grip (palms facing down) and place hands slightly wider than shoulder-width apart on the bar
4. Move head underneath the barbell and position barbell superior to the spine of the scapulae (on the top shelf created by the trapezius); do not place barbell on top of the cervical spine! Move away from the rack
5. From athletic stance, step forward with the left foot and flex the right knee until right knee is at 90° and left knee is at 90°; **hips drop down towards the ground in a straight line**; keep weight on heel of the front foot; knee must not move beyond toes; toes point forward
6. Push-off with the left foot, return to athletic stance, step forward with the right foot and flex the left knee until left knee is at 90° and right knee is at 90°; **hips drop down towards the ground in a straight line**; keep weight on heel of the front foot; knee must not move beyond toes; toes point forward
7. Step out of the lunge position with front foot and return to athletic stance

REQUIRED EQUIPMENT

- 1 Rack
- 1 Barbell
- Plates (if necessary)
- 2 Safety Clips (if necessary)

DEGREE OF DIFFICULTY

- 1

ID: 620

RECOMMENDED EXERCISES

Quadriceps Flexibility

1. Buttocks Kicks
2. Front Squat
3. Side-Lying Quad

Hamstring Flexibility

1. Straight leg Kicks
2. Romanian Deadlift
3. Supine Towel Hamstring

Gluteal Flexibility

1. High Knee Pulls
2. Back Squat
3. Supine Knee to Chest

RELEVANCE

- Results in faster running speed and more powerful stroke production on the court due to more efficient energy transfer
- It is used to enhance strength of the quadriceps/hamstrings/glutes and to develop trunk musculature as stabilizer. It is an assistive lift since it has transfer in the lifting progression (e.g. catching phase during split-jerk) and hence must be used in the Teaching/Hypertrophy Training Phase.

KEY FACTORS

- Focus on perfect movement mechanics and range of motion (90°/90° of knee flexion)
- Hips must drop down towards the ground in a straight line
- Distribute weight through heel of front foot
- Maintain neutral spine position
- Maintain neutral head position

COMMON ERRORS

- Front knee moves past toes due to initiating flexion of front knee
- Bar is placed on top of cervical spine
- Flexion of thoracic spine (rounded back) during motion
- Athlete loses balance

BREATH IN & OUT

- IN: Before Hip Flexion
- OUT: During Hip Extension

TARGETED MUSCULATURE

1. Glutes
2. Hamstrings
3. Quadriceps

ACTION

1. Hip Extension
2. Hip Extension
3. Knee Extension

PLANE OF MOTION

1. Sagittal
2. Sagittal
3. Sagittal

FUNCTIONAL RANGE LIMITING FACTORS

1. Hip Flexibility (tight glutes & hamstrings)
2. Gluteus Maximus Flexibility
3. Upper Hamstring Flexibility
4. Too Much Resistance

COMPENSATORY ACTION

1. Limited hip & knee flexion
2. Posterior Pelvic Tilt: leaning back of upper body to shorten glutes
3. Posterior Pelvic Tilt: no 90°/90° of knee flexion
4. Lumbar & thoracic spine flexion (rounded back)

6.21 STEP UP

SUMMARY

The Step Up is a compound exercise, which focuses on improving the synergy of the neuro-muscular system, strengthening of hip extensor & knee extensor musculature, improving body control & coordination, flexibility as well as improving skill & balance foundation for complex movements.

Note: Exercise can also be performed by using body weight only!

PURPOSE

1. Improving transfer of energy; synergy of neuro-muscular system
2. Strengthening of **hip extensor** (glutes primary) & **knee extensor** (quadriceps secondary) musculature
3. Improving body control & coordination by enhancing stabilizers and gliding neutralizers
4. Improving flexibility for complex movements (e.g. gluteal flexibility for split-jerk)
5. Improving skill (hip flexion/extension) and balance foundation for complex movements

DESCRIPTION

1. Position barbell chest level on the rack; add resistance (plates) and attach safety clips
2. Take an **athletic stance**; stand straight, **feet are shoulder-width apart**; knees slightly flexed; toes point slightly outward (10°-20°)
3. Use a pronated grip (palms facing down) and place hands slightly wider than shoulder-width apart on the bar
4. Move head underneath the barbell and position barbell superior to the spine of the scapulae (on the top shelf created by the trapezius); do not place barbell on top of the cervical spine! Move away from the rack towards the box
5. Face the box, place one foot in the center on top of the box; knee & hip are flexed at 90° (pre-adjust box height appropriately); upper body is straight (push chest out); look forward
6. Push through the heel of the front foot and extend the knee and hip; knee must not move beyond toes; toes point forward; upper body is straight (push chest out); look forward
7. Descend to starting position on same leg; upper body is straight (push chest out); look forward

COMMON ERRORS

- Front knee moves past toes due to pushing hips horizontal instead of vertical
- Bar is placed on top of cervical spine
- Flexion of thoracic spine (rounded back) during motion
- Athlete loses balance

ID: 621

DEGREE OF DIFFICULTY

- 1

REQUIRED EQUIPMENT

- 1 Box (height adjustable)
- 1 Rack
- 1 Barbell
- Plates
- 2 Safety Clips

RELEVANCE

- It is used to enhance strength of the glutes /quadriceps and to develop trunk musculature as stabilizer. It is very limited as an assistive lift since it doesn't transfer in the lifting progression. Generally, it is being used up to Basic Strength Training Phase but can also be used during Power Training Phase
- Results in faster running speed and more powerful stroke production on the court due to more efficient energy transfer
- It has limited application during the single leg landing phase of the serve where the athlete has to manage vertical & horizontal force couples; allows for better agility immediately after the serve

KEY FACTORS

- Focus on perfect movement mechanics and range of motion (90°/90° of knee/hip flexion)
- Hips must move vertically
- Distribute weight through heel of front foot
- Maintain neutral spine position
- Maintain neutral head position

BREATH IN & OUT

- IN: Before Hip Fleion
- OUT: During Hip Extension

RECOMMENDED EXERCISES

Quadriceps Flexibility

1. Buttocks Kicks
2. Front Squat
3. Side-Lying Quad

Gluteal Flexibility

1. High Knee Pulls
2. Back Squat
3. Supine Knee to Chest

TARGETED MUSCULATURE

1. Glutes
2. Quadriceps

ACTION

1. Hip Extension
2. Knee Extension

PLANE OF MOTION

1. Sagittal
2. Sagittal

6.22 LATERAL STEP UP

SUMMARY

The Lateral Step Up is a compound exercise, which focuses on improving the synergy of the neuro-muscular system, strengthening the hip abductors & extensors and knee extensor musculature, improving body control & coordination and flexibility as well as improving skill & balance foundation for complex movements.

Note: Exercise can also be performed by using body weight only!

PURPOSE

1. Improving transfer of energy; synergy of neuro-muscular system
2. Strengthening of **hip abductors** (gluteus medius & minimus) & **extensors** (gluteus maximus) & **knee extensor** (quadriceps secondary) musculature
3. Improving body control & coordination by enhancing stabilizers and gliding neutralizers
4. Improving flexibility
5. Improving skill (hip flexion/extension) and balance foundation for complex movements

DESCRIPTION

1. Position barbell chest level on the rack; add resistance (plates) and attach safety clips
2. Take an **athletic stance**; stand straight, **feet are shoulder-width apart**; knees slightly flexed; toes point slightly outward (10°-20°)
3. Use a pronated grip (palms facing down) and place hands slightly wider than shoulder-width apart on the bar
4. Move head underneath the barbell and position barbell superior to the spine of the scapulae (on the top shelf created by the trapezius); do not place barbell on top of the cervical spine! Move away from the rack towards the box
5. Shoulder faces the box, place one foot in the center on top of the box; toes point slightly outward (10°-20°); knee & hip are flexed at 90° (pre-adjust box height appropriately); upper body is straight (push chest out); look forward
6. Push through the heel of the front foot and extend the knee and hip; knee must not move beyond toes; toes point forward; upper body is straight (push chest out); look forward
7. Descend to starting position on same leg; upper body is straight (push chest out); look forward

COMMON ERRORS

- Front knee moves past toes due to pushing hips horizontally instead of vertically
- Bar is placed on top of cervical spine
- Flexion of thoracic spine (rounded back) during motion
- Athlete loses balance

ID: 622

DEGREE OF DIFFICULTY

- 1

REQUIRED EQUIPMENT

- 1 Box (height adjustable)
- 1 Rack
- 1 Barbell
- Plates
- 2 Safety Clips

RELEVANCE

- It is used to enhance strength of the glutes /quadriceps and to develop trunk musculature as stabilizer. It is very limited as an assistive lift since it doesn't transfer in the lifting progression. Generally, it is being used up to Basic Strength Training Phase but can also be used during Power Training Phase
- Results in faster running speed and better agility (change of direction) on the court due to more efficient energy transfer
- It has limited application during the single leg landing phase during groundstrokes where the athlete has to manage vertical & horizontal force couples; allows for better agility immediately after the groundstrokes

KEY FACTORS

- Focus on perfect movement mechanics and range of motion (90°/90° of knee/hip flexion)
- Hips must move vertically
- Distribute weight through heel of front foot
- Maintain neutral spine position
- Maintain neutral head position

BREATH IN & OUT

- IN: Before Hip Fleion
- OUT: During Hip Extensiont

RECOMMENDED EXERCISES

Quadriceps Flexibility

1. Buttocks Kicks
2. Front Squat
3. Side-Lying Quad

Gluteal Flexibility

1. Bilateral Squat
2. Lateral Lunge
3. Supine Cross-Over

TARGETED MUSCULATURE

1. Gluteus Medius & Minimus
2. Gluteus Maximus
3. Quadriceps

ACTION

1. Hip Abduction
2. Hip Extension
3. Knee Extension

PLANE OF MOTION

1. Frontal
2. Sagittal
3. Sagittal

6.23 STANDING MILITARY PRESS

SUMMARY

The Standing Military Press is a compound exercise, which focuses on improving the synergy of the neuro-muscular system, strengthening the shoulder girdle & shoulder joint and elbow extensor musculature, improving body control & coordination and flexibility as well as improving skill & balance foundation for complex movements.

Note: Exercise can also be performed with dumbbells!

PURPOSE

1. Improving transfer of energy; synergy of neuro-muscular system
2. Strengthening of **shoulder girdle** (trapezius) & **shoulder joint** (deltoid) & **elbow extensor** (triceps secondary) musculature
3. Improving body control & coordination by enhancing stabilizers and gliding neutralizers
4. Improving flexibility
5. Improving skill and balance foundation for complex movements

DESCRIPTION

1. Position barbell chest level on the rack; add resistance (plates) and attach safety clips
2. Take an **athletic stance**; stand straight, **feet are shoulder-width apart**; knees slightly flexed; toes point forward
3. Use a pronated grip (palms facing down) and place hands slightly wider than shoulder-width apart on the bar; wrists remain neutral and are in line with elbows; elbows remain close to the torso and point towards the ground; lift barbell off the rack and take a step back
4. Move head slightly backward, push barbell upward and extend the elbows; while barbell moves past the head, push head forward through the arms; look forward
5. Flex elbows, move head slightly back, and return barbell to starting position

KEY FACTORS

- Focus on perfect movement mechanics and range of motion
- Hands are just outside shoulders on the bar
- Wrists remain neutral and in line with elbows
- Maintain neutral spine position
- Move head out of the way

DEGREE OF DIFFICULTY

- 1

REQUIRED EQUIPMENT

- 1 Rack
- 1 Barbell
- Plates
- 2 Safety Clips

RELEVANCE

- It is used to enhance strength of the deltoids/trapezius/triceps and to develop trunk musculature as stabilizer. It is an assistive lift since it has transfer in the lifting progression (e.g. overhead phase during push-press) and hence must be used in the Teaching/Hypertrophy Training Phase.
- Results in more powerful stroke production due to more efficient energy transfer

ID: 623

RECOMMENDED EXERCISES

Deltoid Flexibility

1. 2 Racquet Serves
2. Dumbbell Bench Press
3. Anterior Deltoid

Triceps Flexibility

1. Front Squat
2. Overhead Triceps

COMMON ERRORS

- Wide grip is being used
- Wrist flexion occurs; elbows point forward
- Excessive extension (arching) of the spinal column
- Movement occurs behind the head

BREATH IN & OUT

- IN: Before Shoulder Flexion
- OUT: During Shoulder Flexion

TARGETED MUSCULATURE

1. Deltoids
2. Trapezius
3. Triceps

ACTION

1. Shoulder Abduction
2. Upward Rotation
3. Elbow Extension

PLANE OF MOTION

1. Frontal
2. Frontal
3. Frontal

6.24 UPRIGHT ROW

SUMMARY

The Upright Row is a compound exercise, which focuses on improving the synergy of the neuro-muscular system, strengthening the shoulder girdle & shoulder abductor musculature, improving body control & coordination and flexibility as well as improving skill & balance foundation for complex movements.

Note: Exercise can also be performed with dumbbells!

PURPOSE

1. Improving transfer of energy; synergy of neuro-muscular system
2. Strengthening of **shoulder girdle** (rhomboids primary; trapezius secondary) & **shoulder abductor** (deltoids) musculature
3. Improving body control & coordination by enhancing stabilizers and gliding neutralizers
4. Improving flexibility
5. Improving skill and balance foundation for complex movements

DESCRIPTION

1. Position barbell hip level on the rack; add resistance (plates) and attach safety clips
2. Take an **athletic stance**; stand straight, **feet are shoulder-width apart**; knees slightly flexed; toes point forward
3. Use a pronated grip (palms facing down) and place hands slightly wider than shoulder-width apart on the bar; wrists remain neutral and are in line with elbows; elbows remain close to the torso; lift barbell off the rack and take a step back
4. In athletic stance, **adduct scapulae** (push shoulder blades together) first, then abduct shoulders to 90° and pull barbell upward to xiphoid process of sternum (~ nipple level); barbell remains close to the body; elbows are flexed and at shoulder level; maintain neutral pelvis and spine position; look forward
5. Slowly adduct shoulder and extend elbows thereby returning barbell to starting position

KEY FACTORS

- Focus on perfect movement mechanics and range of motion
- Initiate movement by adducting scapulae, not elbow flexion
- Hands are just outside shoulders on the bar
- Wrists remain neutral and in line with elbows
- Maintain neutral spine position
- Maintain neutral pelvis position

DEGREE OF DIFFICULTY

- 1

REQUIRED EQUIPMENT

- 1 Rack
- 1 Barbell
- Plates
- 2 Safety Clips

RELEVANCE

- It is used to enhance strength of the deltoids/trapezius/levator scapula and to develop trunk musculature as stabilizer. It is an assistive lift since it has transfer in the lifting progression (e.g. high pull phase during power clean) and hence must be used in the Teaching/Hypertrophy Training Phase.
- Aids in injury prevention for the shoulder joint (e.g. impingement) due to improved muscle balance
- Results in more powerful stroke production due to more efficient energy transfer

ID: 624

RECOMMENDED EXERCISES

Deltoid Flexibility

1. 2 Racquet Serves
2. Dumbbell Bench Press
3. Anterior Deltoid

COMMON ERRORS

- Narrow grip is being used
- Shoulder abduction/elbow flexion initiates movement
- Shoulder abduction past 90°; elbows point up
- Wrist flexion occurs
- Excessive extension (arching) of the spinal column during pressing phase

BREATH IN & OUT

- IN: Before Shoulder Flexion
- OUT: During Shoulder Flexion

TARGETED MUSCULATURE

1. Rhomboids
2. Trapezius
3. Deltoids

ACTION	PLANE OF MOTION
1. Scapulae Adduction/Shoulder Horizontal Abduction	1. Frontal
2. Shoulder Abduction	2. Frontal
3. Shoulder Abduction	3. Frontal

6.25 BEND-OVER ROW

SUMMARY

The Bend-Over Row is a compound exercise, which focuses on improving the synergy of the neuro-muscular system, strengthening the shoulder girdle, shoulder abductor, and elbow flexor musculature, improving body control & coordination and flexibility as well as improving skill & balance foundation for complex movements.

Note: Exercise can also be performed with dumbbells!

PURPOSE

1. Improving transfer of energy; synergy of neuro-muscular system
2. Strengthening of **shoulder girdle** (rhomboids primary; trapezius secondary), **shoulder abductor** (deltoids), and elbow flexor (biceps) musculature
3. Improving body control & coordination by enhancing stabilizers and gliding neutralizers
4. Improving flexibility
5. Improving skill and balance foundation for complex movements

DESCRIPTION

1. Position barbell hip level on the rack; add resistance (plates) and attach safety clips
2. Take an **athletic stance**; stand straight, **feet are shoulder-width apart**; knees slightly flexed; toes point forward
3. Use a pronated grip (palms facing down) and place hands slightly wider than shoulder-width apart on the bar; wrists remain neutral and are in line with elbows; elbows remain close to the torso; lift barbell off the rack and take a step back
4. In athletic stance, flex hips to 90°, then flex the abdominals
5. **Retract scapulae** (push shoulder blades together) first, then abduct shoulders to 90° and pull barbell upward towards xiphoid process of sternum (barbell should be between belly button & chest); maintain neutral spine position; look forward
6. Slowly adduct shoulder and extend elbows thereby returning barbell to starting position

KEY FACTORS

- Focus on perfect movement mechanics and range of motion
- "Lock" the trunk by flexing abdominals
- Initiate movement by retracting scapulae, not elbow flexion
- Hands are just outside shoulders on the bar
- Wrists remain neutral and in line with elbows
- Maintain neutral spine position
- Maintain neutral pelvis position

ID: 625

DEGREE OF DIFFICULTY

- 1

REQUIRED EQUIPMENT

- 1 Rack
- 1 Barbell
- Plates
- 2 Safety Clips

RELEVANCE

- It is used to enhance strength of the rhomboids/trapezius/deltoids/biceps and to develop trunk musculature as stabilizer. It requires a strong trunk (erector spinae group; abdominals/obliques) musculature for stabilization. It is very limited as an assistive lift since it doesn't transfer in the lifting progression. Generally, it is used up to Basic Strength Training Phase.
- Aids in injury prevention for the shoulder joint (e.g. impingement) due to improved muscle balance
- Results in more powerful stroke production due to more efficient energy transfer

RECOMMENDED EXERCISES

Deltoid Flexibility

1. 2 Racquet Serves
2. Dumbbell Bench Press
3. Posterior Deltoid

COMMON ERRORS

- Hip flexion less than 90°
- Shoulder abduction/elbow flexion initiates movement
- Flexion of lumbar & thoracic spine (rounded back)

BREATH IN & OUT

- IN: Before Shoulder Flexion
- OUT: During Shoulder Flexion

TARGETED MUSCULATURE	ACTION	PLANE OF MOTION
1. Rhomboids	1. Horizontal Abduction	1. Frontal
2. Trapezius	2. Horizontal Abduction	2. Frontal
3. Deltoids	3. Horizontal Abduction	3. Frontal
4. Biceps	4. Elbow Flexion	4. Sagittal

6.26 HORIZONTAL PULL-UP/CHIN-UP

SUMMARY

The Horizontal Pull-Up/Chin-Up is a compound exercise, which focuses on improving the synergy of the neuro-muscular system, strengthening the shoulder girdle, shoulder abductor, and elbow flexor musculature, improving body control & coordination and flexibility as well as improving skill & balance foundation for complex movements.

Note: Use pronated grip for Pull-Up and supinated grip for Chin-Up.

PURPOSE

1. Improving transfer of energy; synergy of neuro-muscular system
2. Strengthening of **shoulder girdle** (rhomboids primary; trapezius secondary), **shoulder abductor** (deltoids), and elbow flexor (biceps) musculature
3. Improving body control & coordination by enhancing stabilizers and gliding neutralizers
4. Improving flexibility
5. Improving skill and balance foundation for complex movements

DESCRIPTION

1. Position barbell belly-button level on the rack; physio ball is in front of the rack
2. Use a pronated grip (palms facing down/forward), place hands slightly wider than shoulder-width apart on the bar and feet on top of the physio ball; elbows are extended; bar is on chest level; hips remain neutral pelvic position; wrists remain neutral and are in line with elbows
3. **Retract scapulae** (push shoulder blades together) first, then flex elbows to 90° and pull upper body closely towards barbell; maintain neutral spine and pelvis position; look up
4. Extend elbows and return to starting position; maintain neutral spine and pelvis position; look up

KEY FACTORS

- Focus on perfect movement mechanics and range of motion
- Maintain neutral pelvis position
- Maintain neutral spine position
- Initiate movement by retracting scapulae, not elbow flexion
- Hands are just outside shoulders on the bar
- Wrists remain neutral and in line with elbows

DEGREE OF DIFFICULTY

- 1

REQUIRED EQUIPMENT

- 1 Rack
- 1 Barbell
- 1 Physio Ball

RELEVANCE

- It is used to enhance strength of the rhomboids/trapezius/deltoids/biceps and to develop trunk musculature as stabilizer. It requires a strong trunk (erector spinae group; abdominals/obliques) musculature for stabilization. It is very limited as an assistive lift since it doesn't transfer in the lifting progression. Generally, it is used up to Basic Strength Training Phase.
- Aids in injury prevention for the shoulder joint (e.g. impingement) due to improved muscle balance
- Results in more powerful stroke production due to more efficient energy transfer

RECOMMENDED EXERCISES

Deltoid Flexibility

1. 2 Racquet Serves
2. Dumbbell Bench Press
3. Anterior Deltoid

COMMON ERRORS

- Excessive swinging occurs during movement
- Hip flexion occurs
- Elbow flexion initiates movement
- Flexion of lumbar & thoracic spine (rounded back)

BREATH IN & OUT

- IN: Before Elbow Flexion
- OUT: During Elbow Flexion

TARGETED MUSCULATURE

1. Rhomboids
2. Trapezius
3. Deltoids
4. Biceps

ACTION

1. Horizontal Abduction
2. Horizontal Abduction
3. Horizontal Abduction
4. Elbow flexion

PLANE OF MOTION

1. Frontal
2. Frontal
3. Frontal
4. Sagittal

6.27 MODIFIED PULL-UP/CHIN-UP

SUMMARY

The Modified Pull-Up/Chin-Up is a compound exercise, which focuses on improving the synergy of the neuro-muscular system, strengthening the shoulder girdle, shoulder extensor and elbow flexor musculature, improving body control & coordination and flexibility as well as improving skill & balance foundation for complex movements.

Note: Use pronated grip for Pull-Up and supinated grip for Chin-Up.

PURPOSE

1. Improving transfer of energy; synergy of neuro-muscular system
2. Strengthening of **shoulder girdle** (rhomboids), **shoulder extensor** (latissimus dorsi), and elbow flexor (biceps) musculature
3. Improving body control & coordination by enhancing stabilizers and gliding neutralizers
4. Improving flexibility
5. Improving skill and balance foundation for complex movements

DESCRIPTION

1. Position barbell chest level on the rack; physio ball is in front of the rack
2. Use a pronated grip (palms facing down/forward), place hands slightly wider than shoulder-width apart on the bar, flex hips to ~90° and position feet on top of the physio ball; elbows are extended; bar is on chest level; trunk is underneath the barbell; wrists remain neutral and are in line with elbows; maintain neutral spine position (push chest out); look forward
3. Flex elbows, which extends shoulder, and pull upper body upwards until chin is above barbell; maintain neutral spine position (push chest out); look forward
4. Extend elbows and return to starting position; maintain neutral spine position; look forward

KEY FACTORS

- Focus on perfect movement mechanics and range of motion
- Maintain neutral spine position
- Initiate movement by flexing elbows and extending shoulders
- Hands are just outside shoulders on the bar
- Wrists remain neutral and in line with elbows

DEGREE OF DIFFICULTY

- 2

REQUIRED EQUIPMENT

- 1 Rack
- 1 Barbell
- 1 Physio Ball

RELEVANCE

- It is used to enhance strength of the rhomboids/latissimus dorsi/biceps and to develop trunk musculature as stabilizer. It requires a strong trunk (erector spinae group; abdominals/obliques) musculature for stabilization. It is very limited as an assistive lift since it doesn't transfer in the lifting progression. Generally, it is used up to Basic Strength Training Phase.
- Aids in injury prevention for the shoulder joint (e.g. impingement) due to improved muscle balance
- Results in more powerful stroke production due to more efficient energy transfer

ID: 627

RECOMMENDED EXERCISES

1. Horizontal Pull-Up/Chin-Up

COMMON ERRORS

- Excessive swinging occurs during movement
- Flexion of lumbar & thoracic spine (rounded back)

BREATH IN & OUT

- IN: Before Elbow Flexion
- OUT: During Elbow Flexion

TARGETED MUSCULATURE	ACTION	PLANE OF MOTION
1. Latissimus Dorsi	1. Shoulder Extension	1. Sagittal
2. Deltoids (posterior)	2. Shoulder Extension	2. Sagittal
3. Trapezius	3. Shoulder Extension	3. Sagittal
4. Biceps	4. Elbow Flexion	4. Sagittal
5. Rhomboids	5. Horizontal Abduction	5. Frontal

6.28 LATERAL SQUAT WITH DIAGONAL ROTATION

SUMMARY

The Lateral Squat with Diagonal Rotation is a compound exercise, which focuses on improving the synergy of the neuro-muscular system, hip abductor and trunk rotator strength, hip and knee extensor strength, body control & coordination, flexibility as well as improving skill & balance foundation for complex movements.

Note: If the athlete has flexibility issues and/ or for teaching purposes, a stance wider than shoulder-width is warranted.

PURPOSE

1. Improving transfer of energy; synergy of neuro-muscular system
2. Strengthening of **hip abductors** & **trunk rotators** (primary), hip extensors & knee extensor (secondary) musculature
3. Improving **flexibility** for complex movements
4. Improving body control & coordination by enhancing stabilizers and gliding neutralizers
5. Improving skill and balance foundation for complex movements

DESCRIPTION

1. Take an **athletic stance**; stand straight, **feet are shoulder-width apart**; knees slightly flexed; toes point slightly outward (10°-20°)
2. Hold plate with both hands
3. In athletic stance step sideways to the right, **quickly** drop hips in the center into the squat, and rotate trunk so that plate is on hip level; knees are **outside** shoulders; keep weight on heels
4. Push off with the right foot returning to athletic stance while rotating trunk and diagonally moving plate to shoulder level
5. Repeat and switch sides

DEGREE OF DIFFICULTY

- 3

REQUIRED EQUIPMENT

- 1 Plate

RELEVANCE

- Results in more powerful stroke production and agility on the court due to more efficient energy transfer

KEY FACTORS

- Focus on perfect movement mechanics and range of motion
- Keep knees outside shoulders
- Distribute weight through heels
- Maintain neutral head position

ID: 628

RECOMMENDED EXERCISES

Hamstring Flexibility

1. Straight leg Kicks
2. Romanian Deadlift
3. Supine Towel Hamstring

Gluteal Flexibility

1. Lateral Squat
2. Back Squat
3. Supine Cross-Over

COMMON ERRORS

- Posterior pelvic tilt occurs
- Elbows flexion and shoulder flexion occur during squat movement
- Flexion of thoracic spine (rounded back) during motion
- Weight distribution occurs through the toes

BREATH IN & OUT

- IN: Before Hip Flexion
- OUT: During Hip Extension

TARGETED MUSCULATURE	ACTION	PLANE OF MOTION
1. Gluteus Medius & Minimus	1. Hip Abduction	1. Frontal
2. Obliques	2. Lumbar (Trunk) Rotation	2. Transverse
3. Gluteus Maximus	3. Hip Extension	3. Sagittal
4. Hamstrings	4. Hip Extension	4. Sagittal
5. Quadriceps	5. Knee Extension	5. Sagittal

6.29 LATERAL LUNGE W. DIAGONAL TRUNK ROTATION

SUMMARY

The Lateral Lunge with Diagonal Trunk Rotation is a compound exercise, which focuses on improving the synergy of the neuro-muscular system, strengthening the hip abductors, hip extensor & knee extensor musculature, improving body control & coordination, flexibility and adductor dynamic range, as well as improving skill & balance foundation for complex movements.

Note: If the athlete has flexibility issues and/ or for teaching purposes, a wider stance is warranted. If athlete has good flexibility a narrower grip is desirable. Exercise can also be performed by using body weight only!

PURPOSE

1. Improving transfer of energy; synergy of neuro-muscular system
2. Strengthening of **hip abductors** (primary), hip extensors & knee extensor (secondary) musculature
3. Improving body control & coordination by enhancing trunk & hip stabilizers and gliding neutralizers
4. Improving flexibility and adductor dynamic range
5. Improving skill and balance foundation for complex movements

DESCRIPTION

1. Take an **athletic stanc**e; stand straight, **feet are just wider than shoulder-width apart**; knees slightly flexed; toes point slightly outward (10°-20°)
2. Hold plate in both hands
3. Step sideways with the left foot, bend the left knee until left knee is at 90° and right leg is straight, and rotate trunk so that plate is on hip level; keep weight on heels; knee must not move beyond toes; toes point slightly outward (10°-20°)
4. Push-off with the left foot, return to athletic stance, while diagonally rotating trunk and moving plate to shoulder level
5. Step out of the lunge position to the left back to athletic stance

DEGREE OF DIFFICULTY

- 3

REQUIRED EQUIPMENT

- 1 Plate

RELEVANCE

- Results in faster running speed and better agility (change of direction) on the court due to more efficient energy transfer
- Improved accuracy and power when athlete is out of position during groundstroke production

KEY FACTORS

- Focus on perfect movement mechanics and range of motion
- Keep knees outside shoulders
- Distribute weight through heels
- Maintain neutral spine position
- Maintain neutral head position

ID: 629

RECOMMENDED EXERCISES

Hamstring Flexibility

1. Straight leg Kicks
2. Romanian Deadlift
3. Supine Towel Hamstring

Gluteal Flexibility

1. Lateral Squat
2. Back Squat
3. Supine Cross-Over

COMMON ERRORS

- Posterior pelvic tilt occurs; buttocks "tucks under"
- Bar is placed on top of cervical spine
- Flexion of thoracic spine (rounded back) during motion
- Athlete loses balance

BREATH IN & OUT

- IN: Before Hip Flexion
- OUT: During Hip Extension

TARGETED MUSCULATURE

1. Gluteus Medius & Minimus
2. Obliques
3. Gluteus Maximus
4. Hamstrings
5. Quadriceps

ACTION

1. Hip Abduction
2. Lumbar (Trunk) Rotation
3. Hip Extension
4. Hip Extension
5. Knee Extension

PLANE OF MOTION

1. Frontal
2. Transverse
3. Sagittal
4. Sagittal
5. Sagittal

6.30 ROMANIAN DEADLIFT TO HIGH RECEIVE

SUMMARY

The Romanian Deadlift (RDL) to High Receive is a compound exercise, which focuses on improving the synergy of the neuro-muscular system, strengthening the hip extensor & trunk extensor musculature, improving body control & coordination, pelvis flexibility as well as improving skill & balance foundation for complex movements.

Note: If flexion of lumbar spine (rounding of lower back) occurs during hip extension then decrease resistance immediately!

PURPOSE

1. Improving transfer of energy; synergy of neuro-muscular system
2. Strengthening of **hip extensor** (hamstrings primary) and **trunk extensor** (erector spinae) musculature
3. Improving body control & coordination by enhancing stabilizers (e.g. lower back) and gliding neutralizers
4. Improving pelvis flexibility
5. Improving skill and balance foundation for complex movements

DESCRIPTION

1. Position barbell on the rack; add resistance (plates) and attach safety clips; place barbell on the ground
2. Take an **athletic stance**; stand straight, **feet are shoulder-width apart**; knees slightly flexed; toes point slightly outward (10°-20°)
3. Use a **pronated grip** (palms facing down) and place hands just wider than shoulder-width on the bar; take barbell off the rack; stand up straight
4. First flex hips (~45°) to 90° (or as far as possible) **without** additional knee flexion; distribute weight through the heels; keep knees inside shoulders; maintain neutral spine position (push chest out and scapulae [shoulder blades] together; maintain neutral head position [look forward])
5. Extend the hips while maintaining neutral spine position
6. Once barbell moves past the knees **2nd pulling phase** occurs; explosively extend the hips and simultaneously jump vertical (plantar flexion) while shrugging the shoulders and flexing the elbows while abducting shoulders to 90° (upright row); barbell remains close to the body and reaches sternum (~ nipple) level; elbows point sideways
7. When barbell is at sternum level, flip the wrists (wrist extension), internally rotate and flex elbows under the bar, and receive the barbell on top of the chest; shoulder is flexed at 90°; elbows are flexed and pointing forward; maintain neutral spine and head position

ID: 630

DEGREE OF DIFFICULTY

- 2

REQUIRED EQUIPMENT

- 1 Rack
- 1 Barbell
- Plates
- 2 Safety Clips

RELEVANCE

- It is used to facilitate synergy of neuro-muscular system
- It is used to enhance explosiveness of the hip extensors (hamstrings) and to develop trunk musculature as stabilizer. It is an assistive lift since it has transfer in the lifting progression (e.g. 1st & 2nd pulling phase during power clean from the floor).

KEY FACTORS

- Focus on perfect movement mechanics and range of motion
- Keep knees inside shoulders
- Distribute weight through heels
- Maintain neutral spine position
- Maintain neutral head position

RECOMMENDED EXERCISES

Hamstring Flexibility

1. Straight leg Kicks
2. MB Sagittal Reach (I)
3. Supine Towel Hamstring

COMMON ERRORS

- Explosive hip extension occurs before barbell is past knees
- Additional knee flexion occurs
- Flexion of thoracic spine (rounded back) during motion

BREATH IN & OUT

- IN: Before Hip Extension
- OUT: During Hip Extension

FUNCTIONAL RANGE LIMITING FACTORS

1. Poor Back Strength
2. Hip Flexibility (tight hamstrings)

COMPENSATORY ACTION

1. Kyphotic spine position (rounding of lower back)
2. Additional knee flexion during hip flexion occurs

TARGETED MUSCULATURE

1. Hamstrings
2. Erector Spinae
3. Calves (gastrocnemius & soleus)
4. Trapezius
5. Deltoid

ACTION

1. Hip Extension
2. Trunk Extension
3. Plantar Flexion
4. Shoulder Abduction
5. Shoulder Abduction

PLANE OF MOTION

1. Sagittal
2. Sagittal
3. Sagittal
4. Frontal
5. Frontal

6.31 FRONT SQUAT TO PRESS

SUMMARY

The Front Squat to Press is a compound exercise, which focuses on improving the synergy of the neuro-muscular system, strengthening the knee extensor & hip extensor musculature, improving body control & coordination and flexibility as well as improving skill & balance foundation for complex movements.

Note: If the athlete has flexibility issues and/ or for teaching purposes, a stance wider than shoulder-width is warranted.

PURPOSE

1. Improving transfer of energy; synergy of neuro-muscular system
2. Strengthening of **knee extensor** (quadriceps primary), **hip extensor** (glutes/hamstrings secondary), and **shoulder** musculature
3. Improving body control & coordination by enhancing stabilizers and gliding neutralizers
4. Improving flexibility for complex movements (e.g. triceps flexibility for high receive)
5. Improving skill (hip flexion/extension) and balance foundation for complex movements

DESCRIPTION

1. Position barbell chest level on the rack; add resistance (plates) and attach safety clips
2. Take an **athletic stance**; stand straight, **feet are shoulder-width apart**; knees slightly flexed; toes point slightly outward (10°-20°)
3. Use a pronated grip (palms facing down) and place hands slightly wider than shoulder-width apart on the bar
4. Move elbows underneath the barbell and position barbell on top of the chest and shoulders; shoulders are flexed at 90°; elbow are flexed and point forward
5. First flex hips (~45°) and then knees until knees are flexed to 90° (or as far as possible); maintain neutral pelvic position; keep knees inside shoulders; distribute weight through the heels; maintain neutral spine position (push chest out and scapulae [shoulder blades] together; maintain neutral head position (look forward)
6. Extend the knees and hips and use the momentum to **extend hips rapidly** and drive arms upwards by pushing barbell upwards and extending the elbows; knees must not protrude past toes; look forward

KEY FACTORS

- Focus on perfect movement mechanics and range of motion
- Keep elbows up high; 90 °shoulder flexion
- Keep knees inside shoulders
- Distribute weight through heels
- Maintain neutral spine position
- Maintain neutral head position

ID: 631

RELEVANCE

- Enhances synergy of neuro-muscular system, which leads to more powerful stroke production and agility
- It is used to enhance strength of the quadriceps/ hamstrings and to develop trunk/lower back musculature as stabilizer. It is an assistive lift since it has transfer in the lifting progression (e.g. catching phase during power clean from the floor)

DEGREE OF DIFFICULTY

- 3

RECOMMENDED EXERCISES

Triceps Flexibility

1. Hang Clean
2. 2 Racquet Serves
3. Overhead Triceps

Hamstring Flexibility

1. Straight leg Kicks
2. Romanian Deadlift
3. Supine Towel Hamstring

Glutes Flexibility

1. High Knee Pulls
2. Deadlift
3. Supine Knee to Chest

TARGETED MUSCULATURE

1. Quadriceps
2. Hastrings
3. Glutes
4. Trapezius
5. Deltoid
6. Tricep

ACTION

1. Knee Extension
2. Hip Extension
3. Hip Extension
4. Shoulder Abduction
5. Shoulder Abduction
6. Elbow Extension

PLANE OF MOTION

1. Sagittal
2. Sagittal
3. Sagittal
4. Frontal
5. Frontal
6. Sagittal

BREATH IN & OUT

- IN: Before Hip Flexion
- OUT: During Hip Extension

REQUIRED EQUIPMENT

- 1 Rack
- 1 Barbell
- Plates
- 2 Safety Clips

COMMON ERRORS

- Posterior pelvic tilt occurs
- Elbows drop and bar is placed in front of the chest
- Flexion of thoracic spine (rounded back) during motion
- Weight distribution occurs through the toes

6.32 LATERAL SQUAT TO PRESS

SUMMARY

The Lateral Squat to Press is a compound exercise, which focuses on improving the synergy of the neuro-muscular system, strengthening the hip abductor & hip extensor, knee extensor, and shoulder musculature, improving body control & coordination and flexibility as well as improving skill & balance foundation for complex movements.

Note: If the athlete has flexibility issues and/ or for teaching purposes, a stance wider than shoulder-width is warranted.

PURPOSE

1. Improving transfer of energy; synergy of neuro-muscular system
2. Strengthening of **hip abductors** (gluteus medius & minimus), **hip extensor** (glutes/hamstrings secondary), **knee extensor** (quadriceps primary), and **shoulder** musculature
3. Improving body control & coordination by enhancing stabilizers and gliding neutralizers
4. Improving flexibility for complex movements (e.g. triceps flexibility for high receive)
5. Improving skill (hip flexion/extension) and balance foundation for complex movements

DESCRIPTION

1. Position barbell chest level on the rack; add resistance (plates) and attach safety clips
2. Take an **athletic stance**; stand straight, **feet are shoulder-width apart**; knees slightly flexed; toes point slightly outward (10°-20°)
3. Use a pronated grip (palms facing down) and place hands slightly wider than shoulder-width apart on the bar
4. Move elbows underneath the barbell and position barbell on top of the chest and shoulders; shoulders are flexed at 90°; elbow are flexed and point forward
5. In athletic stance step sideways to the right, **quickly** drop hips in the center into the squat (knees flexed at 90°); maintain neutral pelvic position; keep knees inside shoulders; distribute weight through the heels; maintain neutral spine position (push chest out and scapulae [shoulder blades] together; maintain neutral head position (look forward)
6. Push off with the right foot and extend the knees and hips; use the momentum to **extend hips rapidly** and drive arms upwards by pushing barbell upward and extending the elbows; knees must not protrude past toes; look forward

DEGREE OF DIFFICULTY

- 3

REQUIRED EQUIPMENT

- 1 Rack
- 1 Barbell
- Plates
- 2 Safety Clips

RELEVANCE

- Enhances synergy of neuro-muscular system, which leads to more powerful stroke production and agility
- It is used to enhance strength of the hip abductors for lateral movement, quadriceps/hamstrings and to develop trunk/lower back musculature as stabilizer. It is an assistive lift since it has transfer in the lifting progression (e.g. catching phase during power clean from the floor)

KEY FACTORS

- Focus on perfect movement mechanics and range of motion
- Keep elbows up high; 90 °shoulder flexion
- Keep knees inside shoulders
- Distribute weight through heels
- Maintain neutral spine position
- Maintain neutral head position

ID: 632

TARGETED MUSCULATURE

1. Hip Abductors (Gluteus Medius & Minimus)
2. Gluteus Maximus
3. Hamstrings
4. Quadriceps
5. Trapezius
6. Deltoid
7. Triceps

ACTION

1. Hip Abduction & Extension
2. Hip Extension
3. Hip Extension
4. Knee Extension
5. Shoulder Abduction
6. Shoulder Abduction
7. Elbow Extension

PLANE OF MOTION

1. Frontal
2. Sagittal
3. Sagittal
4. Sagittal
5. Frontal
6. Frontal
7. Sagittal

RECOMMENDED EXERCISES

Gluteal Flexibility

1. Lateral Squat
2. Back Squat
3. Supine Cross-Over

Quadriceps Flexibility

1. Buttocks Kicks
2. Knee Extension
3. Side-Lying Quad

COMMON ERRORS

- Posterior pelvic tilt occurs
- Elbows drop and bar is placed in front of the chest
- Flexion of thoracic spine (rounded back) during motion
- Weight distribution occurs through the toes

BREATH IN & OUT

- IN: Before Hip Flexion
- OUT: During Hip Extension

6.33 HANG CLEAN TO PRESS

SUMMARY

The Hang Clean to Press is a compound exercise, which focuses on improving the synergy of the neuromuscular system, improving explosiveness of hip extensor musculature, strengthening the shoulder musculature, improving body control & coordination and flexibility as well as improving skill & balance foundation for complex movements.

Note: If the athlete has flexibility issues, a stance wider than shoulder-width is warranted.

PURPOSE

1. Improving transfer of energy; synergy of neuromuscular system
2. Improving explosiveness of **hip extensor** (hamstrings primary; glutes secondary) musculature (applying force vertically) and strengthening shoulder musculature
3. Improving body control & coordination by enhancing stabilizers and gliding neutralizers
4. Improving flexibility
5. Improving skill and balance foundation for complex movements

DESCRIPTION

1. Position barbell hip level on the rack; add resistance (plates) and attach safety clips
2. Take an **athletic stance**; stand straight, **feet are shoulder-width apart**; knees slightly flexed; toes point forward
3. Use a pronated grip (palms facing down) and place hands shoulder-width apart on the bar
4. Lift barbell off the rack; take a few steps back
5. In athletic stance, keep elbows extended, slightly flex hips until chest is over barbell; generally barbell will be touching the legs within the lower 1/3 of the thigh (above knee); maintain neutral spine position (push chest out and scapulae [shoulder blades] together; maintain neutral head position (look forward)
6. Explosively extend the hips and simultaneously jump vertically (plantar flexion) while shrugging the shoulders and flexing the elbows while abducting shoulders to 90° (upright row); barbell remains close to the body and reaches sternum (~ nipple) level; elbows point sideways
7. When barbell is at sternum level, flip the wrists (wrist extension), internally rotate and flex elbows under the bar, and receive the barbell on top of the chest; shoulder is flexed at 90°; elbows are flexed and pointing forward; high receive occurs without knee and hip flexion; maintain neutral spine and head position
8. Slightly flex the hips (without excessive knee flexion), then **extend hips rapidly** and drive arms upwards by pushing barbell upwards and extending the elbows; knees must not protrude past toes; look forward

ID: 633

DEGREE OF DIFFICULTY

- 3

REQUIRED EQUIPMENT

- 1 Rack
- 1 Barbell
- Plates
- 2 Safety Clips

RELEVANCE

- Teaches efficient vertical application of force, including the high receive, by improving synergy of lower extremities, trunk, and upper extremities; **2nd pulling phase only**
- Improves explosiveness of the hip extensors (hamstrings) and strength of shoulder musculature
- Results in faster running speed and more powerful stroke production (e.g. serve) on the court due to more efficient energy transfer

PRE-REQUISITE EXERCISES

1. Jump Shrug (Floor)
2. Upright Row
3. Hang Clean to High Receive
4. Push-Press

TARGETED MUSCULATURE

1. Hip Extensors (hamstrings)
2. Calves (gastrocnemius, soleus)
3. Trapezius
4. Deltoid
5. Tricep

ACTION

1. Hip Extension
2. Plantar Flexion
3. Shoulder Abduction
4. Shoulder Abduction
5. Elbow Extension

PLANE OF MOTION

1. Sagittal
2. Sagittal
3. Frontal
4. Frontal
5. Sagittal

KEY FACTORS

- Focus on perfect movement mechanics and range of motion
- Use narrow grip (under shoulders)
- 2nd pulling phase is explosive
- Bar remains close to the body during upright row; elbows point sideways
- Elbows point forward after receive
- Receive occurs in standing position
- Maintain neutral spine position
- Maintain neutral head position

COMMON ERRORS

- Wide grip and stance are used
- Bar remains more than 2.5 inches away from the body during high pull
- No shoulder abduction during high receive; elbows never point sideways
- Flexion of thoracic & lumbar spine occurs (rounded back) during motion
- Athlete loses balance

BREATH IN & OUT

- IN: Before Knee/Hip Extension
- OUT: During Knee/Hip Extension

6.34 SINGLE ARM SNATCH TO OVERHEAD SQUAT

SUMMARY

The Single Arm Snatch to Overhead Squat is a compound exercise, which focuses on improving the synergy of the neuro-muscular system, learning the snatch receive (improving hip flexor speed), improving explosiveness of hip extensor musculature while transitioning into shoulder shrug, improving body control & coordination and flexibility as well as improving skill & balance foundation for complex movements.

Note: Athlete must have good **hamstring** flexibility to receive the dumbbell at 90° of knee flexion with a narrow stance.

PURPOSE

1. Improving transfer of energy; synergy of neuro-muscular system
2. Learning the snatch receive (90° knee flexion); improving hip flexor speed
3. Improving explosiveness of **hip extensor** (hamstrings primary; glutes secondary) musculature while transitioning into the snatch receive; applying force vertically
4. Improving body control & coordination by enhancing stabilizers and gliding neutralizers
5. Improving flexibility
6. Improving skill and balance foundation for complex movements

DESCRIPTION

1. Take an **athletic stance**; stand straight, **feet are shoulder-width apart**; knees slightly flexed; toes point forward
2. Use a pronated grip, take dumbbell in one hand, keep elbow extended and flex hips till dumbbell is in the center of the legs on knee level; maintain neutral spine position (push chest out and scapulae [shoulder blades] together; maintain neutral head position (look forward)
3. Explosively extend the hips and simultaneously jump vertical (plantar flexion) while shrugging the shoulders and flexing the elbow while abducting shoulder to 90° (upright row); barbell remains close to the body and reaches sternum (~ nipple) level; elbows point sideways
4. When dumbbell reaches neutral gravity (no movement), explosively flex the hips and knees, flip the wrists (wrist extension) and extend the elbow; knees are flexed at 90° (or as low as possible); feet remain within shoulder-width; shoulder is in full flexion; maintain neutral spine and head position
5. Extend hips (~45°) and knees until standing up straight; maintain neutral pelvic position; distribute weight through the heels; maintain neutral spine position (push chest out and scapulae [shoulder blades] together; maintain neutral head position (look forward)

DEGREE OF DIFFICULTY

- 4

REQUIRED EQUIPMENT

- 1 Dumbbell

RELEVANCE

- Exercise is being used to learn efficient vertical application of force, including the snatch receive, by improving synergy of lower extremities, trunk, and upper extremities; **2nd pulling phase only**
- Improves hip flexor speed and explosiveness of the hip extensors (hamstrings).
- Results in faster running speed and more powerful stroke production (e.g. serve) on the court due to more efficient energy transfer

ID: 634

PRE-REQUISITE EXERCISES

1. Overhead Squat
2. Hang Snatch

KEY FACTORS

- Focus on perfect movement mechanics and range of motion
- Use medial grip (between legs)
- 2nd pulling phase is explosive
- Dumbbell remains close to the body during upright row; elbow points sideways
- Keep knees within shoulders
- Rapidly flex knees to receive and decelerate the dumbbells
- Elbows are extended after receive
- Maintain neutral spine position
- Maintain neutral head position

COMMON ERRORS

- Wide stance is used
- Legs jump out past shoulders
- Dumbbell remains more than 2.5 inches away from the body during high pull
- No shoulder abduction during high receive; elbows never point sideways
- Flexion of thoracic & lumbar spine occurs (rounded back) during motion
- Athlete loses balance

BREATH IN & OUT

- IN: Before Knee/Hip Extension
- OUT: During Knee/Hip Flexion

6.35 PUSH-PRESS

SUMMARY

The Push-Press is a compound exercise, which focuses on improving the synergy of the neuro-muscular system, creating momentum through rapid hip extension, improving body control & coordination and flexibility as well as improving skill & balance foundation for complex movements.

Note: Exercise can also be performed by using dumbbells!

PURPOSE

1. Improving transfer of energy; synergy of neuro-muscular system
2. Creating momentum via **rapid hip extension** to move barbell past the head (pushing phase) before extending elbows (pressing phase)
3. Improving body control & coordination by enhancing stabilizers and gliding neutralizers
4. Improving flexibility
5. Improving skill (rapid hip extension) and balance foundation for complex movements

DESCRIPTION

1. Position barbell chest level on the rack; add resistance (plates) and attach safety clips
2. Take an **athletic stance**; stand straight, **feet are shoulder-width apart**; knees slightly flexed; toes point forward
3. Use a pronated grip (palms facing down) and place hands slightly wider than shoulder-width apart on the bar; wrists remain neutral and are in line with elbows; elbows remain close to the torso and point towards the ground; lift barbell off the rack and take a step back
4. Slightly flex the hips (without excessive knee flexion), then **extend hips rapidly** and drive arms upwards by pushing barbell upward and extending the elbows; knees must not protrude past toes; look forward
5. Flex elbows, move head slightly back, and return barbell to starting position

DEGREE OF DIFFICULTY

- 1

REQUIRED EQUIPMENT

- 1 Rack
- 1 Barbell
- Plates
- 2 Safety Clips

RELEVANCE

- It is used to enhance speed of hip extensors (hamstring), deltoids/trapezius/triceps and to develop trunk musculature as stabilizer. It is an assistive lift since it has transfer in the lifting progression (e.g. overhead phase during power clean) and hence should be used in the Strength & Power Training Phase.
- Results in more powerful stroke production due to more efficient energy transfer

KEY FACTORS

- Focus on perfect movement mechanics and range of motion
- Hip flexion to rapid hip extension without excessive knee flexion
- Hands are just outside shoulders on the bar
- Wrists remain neutral and in line with elbows
- Maintain neutral spine position
- Move head out of the way

ID: 635

PRE-REQUISITE EXERCISES

1. Front Squat
2. Standing Military Press

COMMON ERRORS

- Wide grip is used
- Excessive knee flexion occurs during hip flexion to create momentum
- Wrist flexion occurs; elbows point forward
- Excessive extension (arching) of the spinal column during pressing phase
- Resistance remains in front of the body

BREATH IN & OUT

- IN: Before Shoulder Flexion
- OUT: During Shoulder Flexion

TARGETED MUSCULATURE

1. Hamstring
2. Trapezius
3. Deltoid
4. Tricep

ACTION

1. Hip Extension
2. Scapulae Upward Rotation
3. Shoulder Abduction
4. Elbow Extension

PLANE OF MOTION

1. Sagittal
2. Fontal
3. Frontal
4. Sagittal

6.36 FORWARD LUNGE TO PRESS

SUMMARY

The Forward Lunge to Press is a compound exercise, which focuses on improving the synergy of the neuro-muscular system, strengthening the knee extensor, hip extensor, and shoulder musculature, improving body control & coordination and flexibility as well as improving skill & balance foundation for complex movements.

Note: If the athlete has flexibility issues and/ or for teaching purposes, a stance wider than shoulder-width is warranted.

PURPOSE

1. Improving transfer of energy; synergy of neuro-muscular system
2. Strengthening of **knee extensor** (quadriceps primary), **hip extensor** (glutes/hamstrings secondary), and **shoulder** musculature
3. Improving body control & coordination by enhancing stabilizers and gliding neutralizers
4. Improving flexibility for complex movements
5. Improving skill (hip flexion/extension) and balance foundation for complex movements

DESCRIPTION

1. Position barbell chest level on the rack; add resistance (plates) and attach safety clips
2. Take an **athletic stance**; stand straight, **feet are shoulder-width apart**; knees slightly flexed; toes point slightly outward (10°-20°)
3. Use a pronated grip (palms facing down) and place hands slightly wider than shoulder-width apart on the bar
4. Move elbows underneath the barbell and position barbell on top of the chest and shoulders; shoulders are flexed at 90°; elbow are flexed and point forward
5. Step into a forward lunge while simultaneously pressing the barbell over the head; distribute weight through the heel of the front foot; maintain neutral spine position (push chest out and scapulae [shoulder blades] together; maintain neutral head position (look forward)
6. Push-off with the front foot and return to starting position while simultaneously lowering the barbell back towards the chest

DEGREE OF DIFFICULTY

- 3

REQUIRED EQUIPMENT

- 1 Rack
- 1 Barbell
- Plates
- 2 Safety Clips

RELEVANCE

- Enhances synergy of neuro-muscular system, which leads to more powerful stroke production and agility
- It is used to enhance strength of the quadriceps/ hamstrings and to develop trunk/lower back musculature as stabilizer. It is an assistive lift since it has transfer in the lifting progression (e.g. catching phase during clean & jerk)

KEY FACTORS

- Focus on perfect movement mechanics and range of motion
- Distribute weight through heel
- Maintain neutral spine position
- Maintain neutral head position

ID: 636

RECOMMENDED EXERCISES

Hamstring Flexibility

1. Straight leg Kicks
2. Romanian Deadlift
3. Supine Towel Hamstring

Glutes Flexibility

1. High Knee Pulls
2. Deadlift
3. Supine Knee to Chest

COMMON ERRORS

- Flexion of thoracic spine (rounded back) occurs during motion
- Weight distribution occurs through the toes

BREATH IN & OUT

- IN: Before Hip Flexion
- OUT: During Hip Extension

TARGETED MUSCULATURE

1. Glutes
2. Hamstring
3. Quadriceps
4. Trapezius
5. Deltoid
6. Tricep

ACTION

1. Hip Extension
2. Hip Extension
3. Knee Extension
4. Scapulae Upward Rotation
5. Shoulder Abduction
6. Elbow Extension

PLANE OF MOTION

1. Sagittal
2. Sagittal
3. Sagittal
4. Frontal
5. Frontal
6. Sagittal

6.37 DEADLIFT TO UPRIGHT ROW

SUMMARY

The Deadlift to Upright Row is a compound exercise, which focuses on improving the synergy of the neuro-muscular system, enhancing the explosiveness of the hip extensor musculature while transitioning into shoulder shrug, improving body control & coordination and flexibility as well as improving skill & balance foundation for complex movements.

Note: If the athlete has flexibility issues and/ or for teaching purposes, a stance wider than shoulder-width is warranted.

PURPOSE

1. Improving transfer of energy; synergy of neuro-muscular system
2. **Strengthening** of **knee extensor** (quadriceps primary) & **hip extensor** (hamstrings secondary) musculature as well as strengthening of **shoulder girdle** (rhomboids primary; trapezius secondary) & **shoulder abductor** (deltoids) musculature
3. Improving body control & coordination by enhancing stabilizers and gliding neutralizers
4. Improving flexibility
5. Improving skill and balance foundation for complex movements

DESCRIPTION

1. Position barbell hip level on the rack; add resistance (plates) and attach safety clips
2. Use a pronated grip (palms facing down) and place hands shoulder-width apart on the bar
3. Lift barbell off the rack; take a few steps back and position barbell on the floor
4. Take an **athletic stance**; stand straight, **feet are shoulder-width apart**; knees slightly flexed; toes point slightly outward (10°-20°)
5. Assume deadlift starting position; flex the transverse abdominis (abs) before moving the barbell; maintain neutral spine and head position; look forward
6. **1st pulling phase**: Extend hips and knees in controlled fashion; keep neutral spine position (push chest out and scapulae [shoulder blades] together); maintain neutral head position (look forward)
7. **2nd Pulling Phase**: In athletic stance, adduct scapulae (push shoulder blades together) first, then abduct shoulders to 90° and pull barbell upwards to xiphoid process of sternum (~ nipple level); barbell remains close to the body; elbows are flexed and on shoulder level; maintain neutral pelvis and spine position; look forward
8. Slowly adduct shoulder and extend elbows thereby returning barbell to starting position

ID: 637

DEGREE OF DIFFICULTY

- 1

REQUIRED EQUIPMENT

- 1 Rack
- 1 Barbell
- Plates
- 2 Safety Clips

RELEVANCE

- Exercise is used to learn efficient vertical application of force by improving synergy of lower extremities, trunk, and upper extremities; 1st & 2nd pulling phase
- Improves strength of knee extensor (quadriceps primary) & hip extensor (hamstrings secondary) musculature as well as strengthens the shoulder girdle (rhomboids primary; trapezius secondary) & shoulder abductor (deltoids) musculature
- It is an assistive lift since it has transfer in the lifting progression (e.g. 2nd pulling phase during power clean from the floor) and hence must be used in the Teaching/Hypertrophy -, and Strength Training Phase.

COMMON ERRORS

- Wide grip and stance are used
- 1st pulling phase is done explosively from the floor
- Flexion of thoracic & lumbar spine occurs (rounded back) during motion
- Athlete loses balance

PRE-REQUISITE EXERCISES

1. Traditional Deadlift
2. Upright Row

BREATH IN & OUT

- IN: Before Hip Flexion
- OUT: During Hip Extension

KEY FACTORS

- Focus on perfect movement mechanics and range of motion
- Use narrow grip (under shoulders)
- Flex transverse abdominis
- 1st pulling phase is slow: Initiate exercise via controlled knee/hip extension
- 2nd pulling phase is slow
- Maintain neutral spine position
- Maintain neutral head position

TARGETED MUSCULATURE

1. Gluteus Maximus
2. Hamstrings
3. Quadriceps
4. Rhomboids
5. Trapezius
6. Deltoid

ACTION

1. Hip Extension
2. Hip Extension
3. Knee Extension
4. Scapulae Adduction
5. Shoulder Abduction
6. Shoulder Abduction

PLANE OF MOTION

1. Sagittal
2. Sagittal
3. Sagittal
4. Frontal
5. Frontal
6. Frontal

6.38 JUMP SHRUG

SUMMARY

The Jump Shrug is a compound exercise, which focuses on improving the synergy of the neuro-muscular system, enhancing the explosiveness of the hip extensor musculature while transitioning into shoulder shrug, improving body control & coordination and flexibility as well as improving skill & balance foundation for complex movements.

Note: If the athlete has flexibility issues, a stance wider than shoulder-width is warranted. Exercise can also be performed with dumbbells.

PURPOSE

1. Improving transfer of energy; synergy of neuro-muscular system
2. Improving explosiveness of **hip extensor** (hamstrings primary; glutes secondary) musculature while transitioning into shrugging the shoulders; applying force vertically
3. Improving body control & coordination by enhancing stabilizers and gliding neutralizers
4. Improving flexibility
5. Improving skill and balance foundation for complex movements

DESCRIPTION

1. Position barbell hip level on the rack; add resistance (plates) and attach safety clips
2. Take an **athletic stance**; stand straight, **feet are shoulder-width apart**; knees slightly flexed; toes point forward
3. Use a pronated grip (palms facing down) and place hands shoulder-width apart on the bar
4. Lift barbell off the rack; take a few steps back
5. In athletic stance, keep elbows extended, slightly flex hips until chest is over barbell; generally barbell will be touching the legs within the lower 1/3 of the thigh (above knee); maintain neutral spine position (push chest out and scapulae [shoulder blades] together); maintain neutral head position (look forward)
6. Forcefully extend the hips and simultaneously jump vertically (plantar flexion) while shrugging the shoulders; elbows remain extended throughout the movement

KEY FACTORS

- Focus on perfect movement mechanics and range of motion
- Use narrow grip (under shoulders)
- Initiate exercise via rapid hip extension
- Maintain neutral spine position
- Maintain neutral head position

DEGREE OF DIFFICULTY

- 1

REQUIRED EQUIPMENT

- 1 Rack
- 1 Barbell
- Plates
- 2 Safety Clips

RELEVANCE

- Exercise is used to learn efficient vertical application of force by improving synergy of lower extremities, trunk, and upper extremities; **2nd pulling phase only**
- Improves explosiveness of the hip extensors (hamstrings). It is an assistive lift since it has transfer in the lifting progression (e.g. 2nd pulling phase during power clean from the floor) and hence must be used in the Teaching/Hypertrophy Training Phase..
- Results in faster running speed and more powerful stroke production on the court due to more efficient energy transfer

ID: 638

RECOMMENDED EXERCISES

Hamstring Flexibility

1. Straight Leg Kicks
2. Romanian Deadlift
3. Supine Towel Hamstring

Gluteal Flexibility

1. High Knee Pulls
2. Deadlift
3. Supine Knee to Chest

COMMON ERRORS

- Wide grip and stance are used
- Movement segments are done separately; e.g. hip extension then shrugging
- Flexion of thoracic spine (rounded back) during motion
- Athlete loses balance

BREATH IN & OUT

- IN: Before Hip Flexion
- OUT: During Hip Extension

TARGETED MUSCULATURE

1. Hip Extensors (hamstrings & glutes)
2. Calves (gastrocnemius & soleus)
3. Shoulder Girdle (Trapezius & Levator Scapula)

ACTION

1. Hip Extension
2. Plantar Flexion
3. Scapula Elevation

PLANE OF MOTION

1. Sagittal
2. Sagittal
3. Frontal

INTEGRATED STRENGTH & INTEGRATED POWER PHASES

The integrated strength & integrated power phases are considered **strength training for performance**, which is the application of strength as it relates to conditioning, which means that the athlete needs to transfer energy through various muscle groups effectively in order to optimize performance. It is the application of force couples rather than isolated force. This is different than high resistance strength training (weight lifting), where the focus is on maximizing force production! Instead, the athlete learns how to efficiently transfer energy to apply force at the point of manifestation. This can be seen in the example of tennis: when the athlete hits a ball with a racquet, the amount of force generated upon the ball from the racquet depends on force generated and transferred up through the different body segments (lower extremities, trunk and upper extremities); force is being transferred from one body segment to another segment, where the force is either further accelerated or decelerated depending on the efficiency of the system.

Bodybuilders are usually very inefficient at force transfer. Even though they have huge muscles and can generate a lot of force (in a single movement plane) when the action is isolated and stabilized, they can't get that applicable force out of the muscle when the environment is dynamic (actively stabilized action; no machines) instead of static (passively stabilized actions; machines). In the case of a dynamic environment, body positions change depending on the situation, whereas in a static environment body positions remain unchanged. When playing tennis, body positions constantly change and the athlete has to stabilize the body while applying force (hitting the ball). Sometimes stability is being compromised during shot production due to velocity changes. Therefore, during strength for performance training, the focus is on using the different muscle groups in synchronicity so that the joints can create more force or becomes more effective at creating/transferring the appropriate amount of force to either stabilize or control the body while doing something else (e.g. hitting a tennis ball).

WHY INTEGRATED STRENGTH FOR PERFORMANCE TRAINING MAKES SENSE

There are three (3) main reasons why strength for performance training is important:

1. Reduces Strength Imbalances
2. Increases Joint Force Production Capacity
3. Enhances Agility through Effective Deceleration

The effective transfer of energy is the focus during strength for performance training (integrated strength & integrated power phase). This is accomplished by reducing muscular strength imbalances; strength imbalances decrease force production capabilities and increase the risk of injuries. This makes the uniting of force couples very important because the athlete needs to have muscular strength balance for an effective transfer of energy to occur. If the athlete is in motion and has muscular strength imbalances, the effectiveness of the antagonists, which are muscles compensating the action, are compromised, which causes **translation** (sliding within the joint capsule; e.g. shoulder, humeral head) in the joint capsule. The more translation there is within the joint, the less energy that can be transferred. Therefore, if a tennis player does not have very good muscular strength balance in his/her shoulders, he/she is not going to be able to generate a lot of force upon release of the ball during, for instance, the serve. That might account for the difference between a 120 mph (192 km/h) and 130 mph (208 km/h) serve; there is a huge difference between having to return a 130 mph serve versus a 120 mph serve!

Improving total force production of a particular body segment is the goal of high resistance strength training (weight lifting) but during strength for performance training the goal is to increase the total force production of the entire joint! For example, if the athlete were to only do weightlifting (resistance strength training), the best weightlifter would also be the best athlete but that's simply not the case. In tennis, the athlete is constantly changing body positions and moving in different directions, while having to hit a tennis ball (exerting force) - which is very challenging. Therefore the goal must be to enhance the neural pathways (nervous system) so as to be able to transfer energy through various body segments in order to increase maximum force output in a controlled fashion.

The ability to change direction effectively (agility) is very important because it allows the athlete to do more with the ball. How precisely and powerfully the athlete can hit the ball during a rally depends on how efficiently he/she can change direction and this depends on the athlete's ability to accommodate center of mass (body) deceleration during the hitting of the ball (applying force) in another direction. If the athlete cannot decelerate effectively, the risk of injury increases because center of mass management is limited. So, if the athlete moves in one direction (e.g. forehand side) but the ball (tracking device) goes in the opposite direction, he/she has to shift and accelerate the center of mass to get to the ball (in the backhand corner). The longer that action takes, the harder it will be to do anything with the ball. If the athlete knows where the ball is going but cannot get there quickly enough, his/her anticipation' is useless, isn´t it?

DEVELOPING THE CORE

Developing the core is a key component to effective energy transfer. Four (4) areas are important in core development:

1. Thoracolumbar Fascia (creates rigidity at the spine/low back)
2. Transverse Abdominis
3. Pelvic Floor
4. Diaphragm

The thoracolumbar fascia creates rigidity at the spine (back), the transverse abdominis in the front and sides, the pelvic floor at the "bottom", and the diaphragm produces compression at the top. When the transverse abdominis and diaphragm compress while the pelvic floor and thoracolumbar fascia are rigid, pressure within the core increases, which pushes against the spine, which in turn causes the spine to become more rigid as well.

Consequently, the spine becomes more stable and effective transfer of energy can occur because there is no area for energy "leakage". Other muscle groups such as lateral flexors, rotators of the obliques, and the rectus abdominis also contribute. The rectus abdominis is rather postural, whereas the obliques (lateral flexors & trunk rotators) are power generating muscles as a result of their dominant fast twitch fiber consistency. It is important to understand that the oblique musculature doesn´t just stabilize an action but generates most of the power as well because most of the force generated results from a rotational component (e.g. hip rotation). That's why the musculature is designed that way. In other words, the body is designed to rotate and the rotation occurs without a "locked" hip but with all body segments working together in sync. When a body segment stops, energy is transferred to the next segment and so on. How effective the athlete can transfer energy becomes evident in the force velocity (power) at the end of the terminal limb (e.g. arm). Therefore, developing core transverse stability is most important; the transverse abdominis must be able to create rapid rigidity. Rapid rigidity enables the spine to essentially lock in place, thereby enhancing energy transferability.

Research indicates that during explosive hip/trunk rotation (firing rate of less than 0.3 seconds) the transverse abdominis needs to be engaged, otherwise there is not enough core stability, which can produce sheer forces at the vertebral column, and this can cause damage to the intervertebral discs. Compression of the intervertebral discs can even cause disc impingement! Also, when the transverse abdominis doesn't engage, a lack of rigidity will result, which causes other muscles to compensate, which in turn can cause an agonist (prime mover) to become a stabilizer but the muscle cannot do both actions simultaneously in an efficient manner. Therefore, the muscle's ability to transfer energy efficiently is lost because it is too busy trying to stabilize an action rather than generating more power. In other words, when the transverse abdominis is not engaged during rapid hip/trunk rotation, there is going to be inefficiency during energy transfer.

When the motor units (muscle signals) are in sync and working in a coordinated fashion, power output can be maximized. This phenomenon is analogous to team rowing. If all the athletes row at the same time, the movement will be very efficient compared to that attained by people rowing whenever each one of them is ready (because firing rates are not in sync)! If one can increase the firing rates by recruiting the fastest muscle fibers, force will be generated with synchronicity and maximum speed.

When one takes a closer look at the most powerful hitters, significant trunk rotation can be observed; it is, in fact, controlled trunk rotation with excellent range of motion. Some people believe that the more flexible they are, the weaker they are but that's not necessarily the case because one can take advantage of the viscoelastic properties of elongated muscle tissue, which doesn't decrease its force output. Athletes with limited range of motion (ROM) don't have maximum force capabilities because of limited motor unit recruitment; the higher the ROM, the more motor unit can be recruited. Oftentimes athletes use heavier weights when lifting because they think that force output in a limited ROM is better. One can observe an athlete doing a rowing exercise pulling 200 lb but will he be able to function better in tennis where full ROM is required?

Also, if an athlete has muscular imbalances, multi-joint actions will be inefficient in terms of energy transfer and that imbalance needs to be corrected first via isolated resistance strength training. If the athlete were to engage in holistic strength training, compensation would occur, whereby the "weak" muscle will cause other muscles to compensate during the action and there is still going to be a deficiency. Therefore, deficiencies must be addressed first using a coordinated pattern, where a simpler movement is used to put stress on a particular area. For example, let's assume the lower hamstring is the problem. During physio ball leg curls the lower hamstring is isolated but the hip extensors (glutes) and upper-hamstring - plus all trunk stabilizers - are also engaged at the same time!

It is also important to point out that there is no such thing as a **weak muscle** because muscles have potential. It is the muscle's **display** that is "weak". Muscles have significant potential to exert force but they may not be able to reach their potential because of inefficient muscle fiber recruitment. It is thus the case that athletes can easily improve their force output by 10% - 15% with minimal training and without any additional muscle mass. Many athletes do not tap into their potential because they are not trained properly.

TRAINING PROGRAM CONSIDERATIONS FOR STRENGTH TRAINING FOR PERFORMANCE

The athlete needs to learn how to forward lunge, reverse lunge, lateral lunge, back squat, front squat, lateral squat, and overhead press during the skill acquisition and hypertrophy phases for motor patterning purposes. Once the athlete is proficient, the exercises presented in the Lunge & Presses section, Asymmetrical Loading & Squatting section, Transverse Exercise section, and Low Back section can be used during the integration phases. As a general rule of thumb: When the athlete increases the speed of the exercise, the resistance/weight decreases.

The **Lunge & Press** section **(see Lunge & Press on page 262)** seeks to prepare the athlete for the controlling of resistance during the more complex movements found in later training phases. Therefore, the resistance used is lighter than during the basic strength phase. For example, the Forward Lunge & Press uses rather light resistance (e.g. 45 lb barbell only), which is less weight than would be used during the Push-Press (basic strength phase), but the Forward Lunge & Press also prepares the athlete for the Split-Jerk, which will be part of the power training phase. So what we have is an integrated approach, whereby the trunk & shoulders are required to stabilize while the athlete performs a landing in a split-stance position.

The **Asymmetrical Loading & Squatting section** **(see Asymmetrical Loading & Squatting on page 277)** presents barbell exercises that dynamically challenge the trunk because of the way that they load. They are also assistive and can be loaded with as much weight as needed because the athlete holds the bar high so that the weights stack up over the shoulders. Athletes will find that these exercises are still challenging even if lighter resistances or bars (e.g. 25 lb) are used.

The **Transverse Exercises** section **(see Transverse Exercises on page 291)** presents exercises with a rotational component. Use caution when performing the transverse exercises and do not use heavy resistance. For most athletes 2-8 lb weighted bars will suffice. Every time speed of movement increases, resistance/weight decreases! By using a straight bar the rotational inertia dramatically increases the challenge to the trunk, particularly the obliques and serratus anterior, as they relate to the posterior aspects of the trunk.

During **Low Back training (see Low Back on page 303)**, spinal alignment is the focal point in order to ensure efficient energy transfer while playing tennis. The spine is categorized into five segments:

1. Cervical Spine (C1-C7 vertebrae)
2. Thoracic Spine (T1-T12 vertebrae)
3. Lumbar Spine (L1-L5 vertebrae)
4. Sacrum (S1-S5)
5. Coccyx

Although the **sacrum** is composed of five (5) different vertebrae, in adults the vertebrae have been fused together to form one large segment. The coccyx, otherwise known as the tailbone, forms the end of the spine.

The **lumbar spine** is the area that causes problems for many athletes. Most injuries occur between the L4 & L5 vertebrae or the L5 & S1 vertebrae. For this reason, the low back training section aims to strengthen the lumbar and sacrum region, the lumbar-sacral complex and its motion segments; a motion segment consists of two (2) vertebrae and an intervening disc.

Pelvic Positions

Since the lumbar spine curvature is directly influenced by the athlete's pelvic position, the coach and/or athlete must pay attention to proper pelvic tilting during exercise. Improper pelvic tilting and/or spinal curvature will decrease energy transfer efficiency, which will result in sub-maximal performance outcomes.

The **iliac crest** and **anterior superior iliac spine** (ASIS) of the hip are used as reference points to determine pelvic positioning. There are three (3) different pelvic positions:

1. Anterior Pelvic Tilt
2. Neutral Pelvic Tilt
3. Posterior Pelvic Tilt

Looking from the side, during anterior pelvic tilting the iliac crest and ASIS shift forward (anteriorly) while during posterior pelvic tilting the reference points shift backwards (posteriorly). Neutral pelvic tilting during exercise is desirable because proper muscular alignment maintains joint integrity and efficient energy transfer of the lumbar-sacral complex.

Anterior or posterior pelvic tilting often occurs because of poor range of motion (ROM) in the hip extensor or hip flexor muscle groups and/or supportive connective tissues. Another factor can be strength deficiencies between hip flexors & extensors and/or trunk flexors & extensors. Therefore, dynamic and static stretching of the aforementioned muscle groups should be deployed regularly and strengthening exercises should also be included regularly into the athlete's workout regimen.

6.39 FORWARD LUNGE & PRESS

SUMMARY

The Forward Lunge & Press is a strength for performance exercise, which focuses on improving power production capabilities during stroke production, improving flexibility of lower and upper body musculature as well as stability of legs, trunk and shoulders using appropriate resistance (bar + weights).

PURPOSE

1. Improving power production capabilities for stroke production (effective energy transfer)
2. Improving flexibility of lower and upper body musculature
3. Improving stability (legs, trunk, shoulders)

DESCRIPTION

1. Stand in **athletic stance** (feet are shoulder-width apart; knees are slightly bent)
2. Hold barbell in both hands and slightly wider than shoulder-width apart
3. Place barbell on top of your chest and raise elbows horizontally until shoulder is at 90° or as far as possible
4. Use a little hitch (hip movement) to initiate the lunge
5. Step into a lunge; keep weight on the heel of the front foot
6. Extend arms until barbell is above your ears
7. Return to starting position
8. Alternate lunge movement

REQUIRED EQUIPMENT

- Barbell
- Weights (if applicable)

DEGREE OF DIFFICULTY

- 1

PRE-REQUISITE EXERCISES

1. Forward/Reverse Lunge (Dynamic Warm-up)
2. Forward Lunge & Overhead Reach (Dynamic Warm-up)
3. Push-Press (Resistance Training)

ID: 639

COMMON ERRORS

- Athlete loses stability during movement
- Arms are not fully extended and above the head/ears
- Bar is placed in front of – or behind the head

SOLUTION

- Decrease weight of bar or refer to pre-requisite exercises
- Use a wider grip

KEY FACTORS

- Use athlete-appropriate resistance; no loss of stability during movement
- Make sure you have enough space in front of you
- Use alternate lunge movement
- Maintain balance and land in same location during lunging

RELEVANCE

- Prepares you for next training phase (strength/power phase)
- Improves stability during groundstroke execution
- Improves accuracy and speed of groundstrokes
- If "Stability Pad Lunge Test" show deficiency, implement this exercise into the Resistance Training Routine

6.40 LUNGE PUSH-OFF TO OVERHEAD PRESS

SUMMARY

The Lunge Push-Off to Overhead Press is a strength for performance exercise, which focuses on improving power production capabilities during stroke production, improving flexibility of lower and upper body musculature as well as stability of legs, trunk and shoulders using appropriate resistance (bar + weights).

PURPOSE

1. Improving power production capabilities for stroke production (effective energy transfer)
2. Improving flexibility of lower and upper body musculature
3. Improving stability (legs, trunk, shoulders)

DESCRIPTION

1. Start from the lunge position; knee must not protrude past toes
2. Hold barbell in both hands and slightly wider than shoulder-width apart
3. Place barbell on top of your chest and raise elbows horizontally until shoulder is at 90° or as far as possible
4. Forcefully push-off with the front foot and return to standing position
5. During push-off extend arms until barbell is above your ears
6. Return to starting position
7. Alternate lunge movement

PRE-REQUISITE EXERCISES

1. Forward/Reverse Lunge (Dynamic Warm-up)
2. Forward Lunge & Overhead Reach (Dynamic Warm-up)
3. Push-Press (Resistance Training)
4. Forward Lunge & Press

DEGREE OF DIFFICULTY

- 2

REQUIRED EQUIPMENT

- Barbell
- Weights (if applicable)

RELEVANCE

- Prepares you for next training phase (strength/power phase)
- Improves stability during groundstroke execution
- Improves accuracy and speed of groundstrokes
- If "Stability Pad Lunge Test" show deficiency, implement this exercise into the Resistance Training Routine

ID: 640

COMMON ERRORS

- Athlete loses stability during movement
- Arms are not fully extended and above the head/ears
- Bar is placed in front of – or behind the head

SOLUTION

- Decrease weight of bar or refer to pre-requisite exercises
- Use a wider grip

KEY FACTORS

- Use athlete-appropriate resistance; no loss of stability during movement
- Make sure you have enough space in front of you
- Use alternate lunge movement
- Maintain balance and land in same location during lunging

6.41 LUNGE PUSH-OFF TO POWER PRESS

SUMMARY

The Lunge Push-Off to Power Press is a strength for performance exercise, which focuses on improving power production capabilities during stroke production, improving flexibility of lower and upper body musculature as well as stability of legs, trunk and shoulders using appropriate resistance (bar + weights).

PURPOSE

1. Improving power production capabilities for stroke production (effective energy transfer)
2. Improving flexibility of lower and upper body musculature
3. Improving stability (legs, trunk, shoulders)
4. Improving hip extensor speed

DESCRIPTION

1. Start from the lunge position; knee must not protrude past toes
2. Hold barbell in both hands and slightly wider than shoulder-width apart
3. Place barbell on top of your chest and raise elbows horizontally until shoulder is at 90° or as far as possible
4. **Explosively** push-off with the front foot and land on both feet
5. During push-off extend arms until barbell is above your ears
6. Return to starting position
7. Alternate lunge movement

PRE-REQUISITE EXERCISES

1. Forward/Reverse Lunge (Dynamic Warm-up)
2. Forward Lunge & Overhead Reach (Dynamic Warm-up)
3. Push-Press (Resistance Training)
4. Forward Lunge & Press

COMMON ERRORS

- Athlete loses stability during movement
- Arms are not fully extended and above the head/ears
- Bar is placed in front of – or behind the head

SOLUTION

- Decrease weight of bar or refer to pre-requisite exercises
- Use a wider grip

DEGREE OF DIFFICULTY

- 3

REQUIRED EQUIPMENT

- Barbell
- Weights (if applicable)

RELEVANCE

- Prepares you for next training phase (power phase)
- Improves stability during groundstroke execution
- Improves accuracy and speed of groundstrokes
- If "Stability Pad Lunge Test" show deficiency, implement this exercise into your Resistance Training Routine

KEY FACTORS

- Use athlete-appropriate resistance; no loss of stability during movement
- Make sure you have enough space in front of you
- Use alternate lunge movement
- Maintain balance and land in same location during lunging

ID: 641

6.42 FORWARD LUNGE SA BB OVERHEAD PRESS

SUMMARY

The Forward Lunge to Single-Arm Barbell Overhead Press is a strength for performance exercise, which focuses on improving power production capabilities during stroke production, improving flexibility of lower and upper body musculature as well as stability of legs, trunk and shoulders using appropriate resistance (dumbbell).

PURPOSE

1. Improving power production capabilities for stroke production (effective energy transfer)
2. Improving flexibility of lower and upper body musculature
3. Improving stability (legs, trunk, especially **shoulders**)
4. Improving hip lateral flexion

DESCRIPTION

1. Hold barbell (BB) centered in your right hand and flex the elbow so that BB touches your shoulder and elbow is close to/touching the body
2. From **athletic stance** position (feet are shoulder-width apart; knees are slightly bent) use left leg and step into a forward lunge
3. Simultaneously extend elbow and press BB over your head
4. **Forcefully** push-off with the front foot and return to neutral stance
5. Hold BB centered in your left hand and step into a lunge with your right leg
6. Simultaneously extend elbow and press BB over your head
7. **Forcefully** push-off with the front foot and return to neutral stance

DEGREE OF DIFFICULTY

- 4

REQUIRED EQUIPMENT

- Barbell (use appropriate weight)

RELEVANCE

- Prepares you for next training phase (strength/power phase)
- Improves stability during groundstroke execution
- Improves accuracy and speed of groundstrokes
- If "Shoulder Mobility Test" and/or "Stability Pad Lunge Test" show deficiency, implement this exercise into the Resistance Training Routine

COMMON ERRORS

- Athlete loses stability during movement
- Arms are not fully extended and above the head/ears
- BB is placed in front of – or behind the head
- Elbows don't remain close to the body

SOLUTION

- Decrease weight of bar or refer to pre-requisite exercises
- Use a wider grip
- Decrease weight

PRE-REQUISITE EXERCISES

1. Forward/Reverse Lunge (Dynamic Warm-up)
2. Forward Lunge & Overhead Reach (Dynamic Warm-up)
3. Forward Lunge & Heel Reach (Dynamic Warm-up)
4. Push-Press (Resistance Training)
5. Forward Lunge & Press
6. Forward Lunge to Single-Arm Dumbbell Overhead Press

KEY FACTORS

- Use athlete-appropriate resistance; no loss of stability during movement
- Make sure you have enough space in front of you
- Use alternate lunge movement
- Maintain balance and land in same location during lunging

ID: 642

6.43 FORWARD LUNGE SA DB OVERHEAD PRESS

SUMMARY

The Forward Lunge to Single-Arm Dumbbell Overhead Press is a strength for performance exercise, which focuses on improving power production capabilities during stroke production, improving flexibility of lower and upper body musculature as well as stability of legs, trunk and shoulders using appropriate resistance (dumbbell).

PURPOSE

1. Improving power production capabilities for stroke production (effective energy transfer)
2. Improving flexibility of lower and upper body musculature
3. Improving stability (legs, trunk, shoulders)
4. Improving hip lateral flexion

DESCRIPTION

1. Hold dumbbell (DB) in your right hand and flex the elbow so that BB touches your shoulder and elbow is close to/touching the body
2. From **athletic stance** position (feet are shoulder-width apart; knees are slightly bent) use left leg and step into a forward lunge
3. Simultaneously extend elbow and press DB over your head
4. **Forcefully** push-off with the front foot and return to neutral stance
5. Hold DB in your left hand and step into a lunge with your right leg
6. Simultaneously extend elbow and press DB over your head
7. **Forcefully** push-off with the front foot and return to neutral stance

PRE-REQUISITE EXERCISES

1. Forward/Reverse Lunge (Dynamic Warm-up)
2. Forward Lunge & Overhead Reach (Dynamic Warm-up)
3. Forward Lunge & Heel Reach (Dynamic Warm-up)
4. Push-Press (Resistance Training)
5. Forward Lunge & Press

DEGREE OF DIFFICULTY

- 3

REQUIRED EQUIPMENT

- 1 Dumbbell

RELEVANCE

- Prepares you for next training phase (strength/power phase)
- Improves stability during groundstroke execution
- Improves accuracy and speed of groundstrokes
- If "Shoulder Mobility Test" and/or "Stability Pad Lunge Test" show deficiency, implement this exercise into the Resistance Training Routine

ID: 643

COMMON ERRORS

- Athlete loses stability during movement
- Arms are not fully extended and above the head/ears
- DB is placed in front of – or behind the head
- Elbows don't remain close to the body

SOLUTION

- Decrease weight of bar or refer to pre-requisite exercises
- Use a wider grip
- Decrease weight

KEY FACTORS

- Use athlete-appropriate resistance; no loss of stability during movement
- Make sure you have enough space in front of you
- Use alternate lunge movement
- Maintain balance and land in same location during lunging

6.44 FRONT SQUAT & PRESS

SUMMARY

The Front Squat & Press is a strength for performance exercise, which focuses on improving power production capabilities during stroke production, improving flexibility of lower and upper body musculature as well as stability of legs, trunk and shoulders using appropriate resistance (bar + weights).

PURPOSE

1. Improving power production capabilities for stroke production (hip flexion & effective energy transfer)
2. Improving flexibility of lower and upper body musculature
3. Improving stability (legs, trunk, shoulders)

DESCRIPTION

1. Stand in **athletic stance** (feet are shoulder-width apart; knees are slightly bent)
2. Hold barbell in both hands and slightly wider than shoulder-width apart
3. Place barbell on top of your chest and raise elbows horizontally until shoulder is at 90° or as far as possible
4. Flex hips until knees are at 90°; keep weight on the heels of the feet
5. Extend hips until you are standing
6. Extend arms until barbell is above your ears
7. Lower barbell back towards the chest

RELEVANCE

- Prepares you for next training phase (strength/power phase)
- Improves stability during groundstroke execution
- Improves accuracy and speed of groundstrokes
- If "Shoulder Mobility Test" show deficiency, implement this exercise into the Resistance Training Routine

DEGREE OF DIFFICULTY

- 1

REQUIRED EQUIPMENT

- Barbell
- Weights (if applicable)

PRE-REQUISITE EXERCISES

1. Squat (Dynamic Warm-up)
2. Squat & Overhead Reach (Dynamic Warm-up)
3. Overhead Squat (Resistance Training)
4. Front Squat (Resistance Training)
5. Push-Press (Resistance Training)

ID: 644

COMMON ERRORS

- Athlete loses stability during movement
- Arms are not fully extended and above the head/ears
- Bar is placed in front of – or behind the head

SOLUTION

- Decrease weight of bar or refer to pre-requisite exercises
- Use a wider grip

KEY FACTORS

- Use athlete-appropriate resistance; no loss of stability during movement or excessive curvature of the back
- Make sure knees go over the toes but stay inside shoulders during squat
- Maintain balance and land in same location during lunging

6.45 FRONT SQUAT TO PRESS

SUMMARY

The Front Squat to Press is a strength for performance exercise, which focuses on improving power production capabilities during stroke production, improving flexibility of lower and upper body musculature as well as stability of legs, trunk and shoulders using appropriate resistance (bar + weights).

PURPOSE

1. Improving power production capabilities for stroke production (hip flexion & effective energy transfer)
2. Improving flexibility of lower and upper body musculature
3. Improving stability (legs, trunk, shoulders)

DESCRIPTION

1. Stand in **athletic stance** (feet are shoulder-width apart; knees are slightly bent)
2. Hold barbell in both hands and slightly wider than shoulder-width apart
3. Place barbell on top of your chest and raise elbows horizontally until shoulder is at 90° or as far as possible
4. Flex hips until knees are at 90°; keep weight on the heels of the feet
5. Extend hips and simultaneously extend arms until barbell is above your ears
6. Lower barbell back towards the chest
7. Repeat

PRE-REQUISITE EXERCISES

1. Squat (Dynamic Warm-up)
2. Squat & Overhead Reach (Dynamic Warm-up)
3. Overhead Squat (Resistance Training)
4. Front Squat (Resistance Training)
5. Push-Press (Resistance Training)

KEY FACTORS

- Use athlete-appropriate resistance; no loss of stability during movement or excessive curvature of the back
- Make sure knees go over the toes but stay inside shoulders during squat
- Maintain balance and land in same location during lunging

DEGREE OF DIFFICULTY

- 2

REQUIRED EQUIPMENT

- Barbell
- Weights (if applicable)

RELEVANCE

- Prepares you for next training phase (strength/power phase)
- Improves stability during groundstroke execution
- Improves accuracy and speed of groundstrokes
- If "Shoulder Mobility Test" show deficiency, implement this exercise into the Resistance Training Routine

ID: 645

COMMON ERRORS

- Athlete loses stability during movement
- Arms are not fully extended and above the head/ears
- Bar is placed in front of – or behind the head

SOLUTION

- Decrease weight of bar or refer to pre-requisite exercises
- Use a wider grip

6.46 SQUAT TO SA DB OVERHEAD PRESS

SUMMARY

The Squat to Single-Arm Dumbbell Overhead Press is a strength for performance exercise, which focuses on improving power production capabilities during stroke production, improving flexibility of lower and upper body musculature as well as stability of legs, trunk and shoulders using appropriate resistance (dumbbell).

PURPOSE

1. Improving power production capabilities for stroke production (effective energy transfer)
2. Improving flexibility of lower and upper body musculature
3. Improving stability (legs, trunk, especially **shoulders)**
4. Improving hip lateral flexion

DESCRIPTION

1. Hold dumbbell (DB) in your right hand and flex the elbow so that DB touches your shoulder and elbow is close to/touching the body
2. From **athletic stance** position (feet are shoulder-width apart; knees are slightly bent) perform a squat
3. Extend hips to return to neutral stance while simultaneously extending elbow, pressing DB over the head
4. Switch hands and repeat

PRE-REQUISITE EXERCISES

1. Squat (Dynamic Warm-up)
2. Squat & Overhead Reach (Dynamic Warm-up)
3. Overhead Squat (Resistance Training)
4. Front Squat (Resistance Training)
5. Push-Press (Resistance Training)

DEGREE OF DIFFICULTY

- 3

REQUIRED EQUIPMENT

- Dumbbell (use appropriate weight)

RELEVANCE

- Prepares you for next training phase (strength/power phase)
- Improves stability during groundstroke execution
- Improves accuracy and speed of groundstrokes
- If "Shoulder Mobility Test" and/or "Stability Pad Squat Test" show deficiency, implement this exercise into the Resistance Training Routine

ID: 646

COMMON ERRORS

- Athlete loses stability during movement
- Arms are not fully extended and above the head/ears
- DB is placed in front of – or behind the head
- Elbows don't remain close to the body

SOLUTION

- Decrease weight of bar or refer to pre-requisite exercises
- Use a wider grip
- Decrease weight

KEY FACTORS

- Use athlete-appropriate resistance; no loss of stability during movement or excessive curvature of the back
- Make sure knees go over the toes but stay inside shoulders during squat
- Maintain balance and land in same location during lunging

6.47 SQUAT TO SA BARBELL OVERHEAD PRESS

SUMMARY

The Squat to Single-Arm Barbell Overhead Press is a strength for performance exercise, which focuses on improving power production capabilities during stroke production, improving flexibility of lower and upper body musculature as well as stability of legs, trunk and shoulders using appropriate resistance (dumbbell).

PURPOSE

1. Improving power production capabilities for stroke production (effective energy transfer)
2. Improving flexibility of lower and upper body musculature
3. Improving stability (legs, trunk, especially **shoulders**)
4. Improving hip lateral flexion

DESCRIPTION

1. Hold barbell (BB) centered in your right hand and flex the elbow so that BB touches your shoulder and elbow is close to/touching the body
2. From **athletic stance** position (feet are shoulder-width apart; knees are slightly bent) perform a squat
3. Extend hips returning to neutral stance while simultaneously extending the elbow, pressing BB over the head
4. Switch hands and hold BB centered in your left hand and perform a squat
5. Extend hips returning to neutral stance while simultaneously extending the elbow, pressing BB over the head

PRE-REQUISITE EXERCISES

1. Squat (Dynamic Warm-up)
2. Squat & Overhead Reach (Dynamic Warm-up)
3. Overhead Squat (Resistance Training)
4. Front Squat (Resistance Training)
5. Push-Press (Resistance Training)
6. Squat to Single –Arm Dumbbell Overhead Press

COMMON ERRORS

- Athlete loses stability during movement
- Arms are not fully extended and above the head/ears
- BB is placed in front of – or behind the head
- Elbows don't remain close to the body

DEGREE OF DIFFICULTY

- 4

ID: 647

REQUIRED EQUIPMENT

- Barbell (use appropriate weight)

RELEVANCE

- Prepares you for next training phase (strength/power phase)
- Improves stability during groundstroke execution
- Improves accuracy and speed of groundstrokes
- If "Shoulder Mobility Test" and/or "Stability Pad Squat Test" show deficiency, implement this exercise into the Resistance Training Routine

KEY FACTORS

- Use athlete-appropriate resistance; no loss of stability during movement or excessive curvature of the back
- Make sure knees go over the toes but stay inside shoulders during squat
- Maintain balance and land in same location during lunging

SOLUTION

- Decrease weight of bar or refer to pre-requisite exercises
- Use a wider grip
- Decrease weight

6.48 SQUAT TO FORWARD PRESS (I)

SUMMARY

The Squat to Forward Press (I) is a strength for performance exercise, which focuses on improving power production capabilities during stroke production, improving flexibility of lower body musculature as well as stability of legs, trunk and shoulders using appropriate resistance (bar + weights).

PURPOSE

1. Improving power production capabilities for stroke production (dynamically challenging trunk & effective energy transfer)
2. Improving flexibility of lower body musculature
3. Improving stability (legs, trunk, shoulders)

DESCRIPTION

1. Stand in **athletic stance** (feet are shoulder-width apart; toes point forward; knees are slightly bent)
2. Place barbell on the ground approximately 2 feet in front of you
3. Hold barbell in both hands and extend your arms so that shoulder is at 90°
4. Bend knees until they are at 90° and simultaneously bend elbows, thereby bringing bar closer to shoulder; lean buttocks back and keep weight on the heels of the feet
5. Keep knees inside the shoulders
6. Extend hips and knees and press barbell forward simultaneously

PRE-REQUISITE EXERCISES

1. Squat (Dynamic Warm-up)
2. Squat & Overhead Reach (Dynamic Warm-up)

DEGREE OF DIFFICULTY

- 1

REQUIRED EQUIPMENT

- Barbell (use appropriate weight)

RELEVANCE

- Improves stability during groundstroke execution
- Improves accuracy and speed of groundstrokes

KEY FACTORS

- Use athlete-appropriate resistance; no loss of stability during movement or excessive curvature of the back
- Make sure knees go over the toes but stay inside shoulders during squat

COMMON ERRORS

- Knees are moving towards each other during squat
- Arms are not fully extended

SOLUTION

- Use squat dynamic stretch: use wider stance if necessary
- Decrease weight of bar or refer to pre-requisite exercises

ID: 648

6.49 BILATERAL SQUAT TO FORWARD PRESS (II)

SUMMARY

The Bilateral Squat to Forward Press (II) is a strength for performance exercise, which focuses on improving power production capabilities during stroke production, improving flexibility of lower body musculature as well as stability of legs, trunk and shoulders using appropriate resistance (bar + weights).

PURPOSE

1. Improving power production capabilities for stroke production (dynamically challenging trunk & effective energy transfer) and change of direction (agility)
2. Improving flexibility of lower body musculature
3. Improving stability (legs, trunk, shoulders)

DESCRIPTION

1. Stand straight with feet close together
2. Place barbell on the ground approximately 2 feet in front of you
3. Hold barbell in both hands, extend your arms so that shoulder is at 90°
4. Step sideways with the left foot until both feet are shoulder-width apart
5. Bend knees until they are at 90° and simultaneously bend elbows, thereby bringing bar closer to shoulder; lean buttocks back and keep weight on the heels of the feet
6. Keep knees inside the shoulders
7. Extend hips and knees, step sideways, and press barbell forward simultaneously
8. Repeat stepping sideways with the right foot now

PRE-REQUISITE EXERCISES

1. Bilateral Squat (Dynamic Warm-up)
2. Bilateral Squat w. Trunk Rotation (Dynamic Warm-up)

COMMON ERRORS

- Knees are moving towards each other during squat
- Arms are not fully extended

REQUIRED EQUIPMENT

- 1 Barbell
- Weights (if applicable)

RELEVANCE

- Improves stability during groundstroke execution
- Improves accuracy and speed of groundstrokes

KEY FACTORS

- Use athlete-appropriate resistance; no loss of stability during movement or excessive curvature of the back
- Make sure knees go over the toes but stay inside shoulders during squat

SOLUTION

- Use squat dynamic stretch: use wider stance if necessary
- Decrease weight of bar or refer to pre-requisite exercises

DEGREE OF DIFFICULTY

- 2

ID: 649

6.50 BILATERAL SQUAT TO PRESS W. HIP FLEXION (III)

SUMMARY

The Bilateral Squat to Forward Press with Hip Flexion (III) is a strength for performance exercise, which focuses on improving power production capabilities during stroke production, improving flexibility of lower body musculature as well as stability of legs, trunk and shoulders using appropriate resistance (bar + weights).

PURPOSE

1. Improving power production capabilities for stroke production (dynamically challenging trunk & effective energy transfer) and change of direction (agility)
2. Improving flexibility of lower body musculature
3. Improving stability (legs, trunk, shoulders)

DESCRIPTION

1. Stand straight with feet close together
2. Place barbell on the ground approximately 2 feet in front of you
3. Hold barbell in both hands, extend your arms so that shoulder is at 90°
4. Step sideways with the left foot until both feet are shoulder-width apart
5. Bend knees until they are at 90° and simultaneously bend elbows, thereby bringing bar closer to shoulder; lean buttocks back and keep weight on the heels of the feet
6. Keep knees inside the shoulders
7. Extend hips and knees, bring left foot forward so that knee is at hip level and bend at 90°, and press barbell forward simultaneously; you end up standing on your right foot
8. Repeat stepping sideways with the right foot now and bend the left knee when you come up

DEGREE OF DIFFICULTY

- 3

REQUIRED EQUIPMENT

- 1 Barbell
- Weights (if applicable)

RELEVANCE

- Improves stability during groundstroke execution
- Improves accuracy and speed of groundstrokes

KEY FACTORS

- Use athlete-appropriate resistance; no loss of stability during movement or excessive curvature of the back
- Make sure knees go over the toes but stay inside shoulders during squat

PRE-REQUISITE EXERCISES

1. Bilateral Squat (Dynamic Warm-up)
2. Bilateral Squat w. Trunk Rotation (Dynamic Warm-up)
3. Bilateral Squat to Forward Press (II)

COMMON ERRORS

- Knees are moving towards each other during squat
- Arms are not fully extended

SOLUTION

- Use squat dynamic stretch: use wider stance if necessary
- Decrease weight of bar or refer to pre-requisite exercises

ID: 650

6.51 BILATERAL SQUAT TO PRESS HIP FLEXION TO ROT.

SUMMARY

The Bilateral Squat to Forward Press with Hip Flexion to Rotation (IV) is a strength for performance exercise, which focuses on improving power production capabilities during stroke production, improving flexibility of lower body musculature as well as stability of legs, trunk and shoulders using appropriate resistance (bar + weights).

PURPOSE

1. Improving power production capabilities for stroke production (dynamically challenging trunk & effective energy transfer) and change of direction (agility)
2. Improving flexibility of lower body musculature
3. Improving stability (legs, trunk, shoulders)

DESCRIPTION

1. Stand straight with feet close together
2. Place barbell on the ground approximately 2 feet in front of you
3. Hold barbell in both hands, extend your arms so that shoulder is at 90°
4. Step sideways with the left foot until both feet are shoulder-width apart
5. Bend knees until they are at 90° and simultaneously bend elbows, thereby bringing bar closer to shoulder; lean buttocks back and keep weight on the heels of the feet
6. Keep knees inside the shoulders
7. Extend hips and knees, bring left foot forward so that knee is at hip level and bend at 90°, and rotate barbell to the right simultaneously; you end up standing on your right foot and barbell is just outside your right shoulder
8. Repeat stepping sideways with the right foot now and bend the left knee when you come up and rotate barbell to the left side

PRE-REQUISITE EXERCISES

1. Bilateral Squat (Dynamic Warm-up)
2. Bilateral Squat w. Trunk Rotation (Dynamic Warm-up)
3. Bilateral Squat to Forward Press (II)
4. Bilateral Squat to Forward Press with Hip Flexion (III)

DEGREE OF DIFFICULTY

- 4

REQUIRED EQUIPMENT

- 1 Barbell
- Weights (if applicable)

RELEVANCE

- Improves stability during groundstroke execution
- Improves accuracy and speed of groundstrokes

KEY FACTORS

- Use athlete-appropriate resistance; no loss of stability during movement or excessive curvature of the back
- Make sure knees go over the toes but stay inside shoulders during squat

ID: 651

COMMON ERRORS

- Knees are moving towards each other during squat
- Arms are not fully extended

SOLUTION

- Use squat dynamic stretch: use wider stance if necessary
- Decrease weight of bar or refer to pre-requisite exercises

6.52 REVERSE LUNGE TO FORWARD PRESS (I)

SUMMARY

The Reverse Lunge to Forward Press (I) is a strength for performance exercise, which focuses on improving power production capabilities during groundstrokes, improving flexibility, as well as stability of trunk and leg musculature using a barbell (BB).

PURPOSE

1. Improving power production capabilities for groundstrokes
2. Improving flexibility
3. Improving stability of trunk and leg musculature

DESCRIPTION

1. Place barbell on the ground approximately 2 feet in front of you and hold it in your right hand
2. Step into a reverse lunge with the right foot; keep weight on the heel of the front foot; left knee is at 90°
3. Hold BB in right hand close to the shoulder; elbow is bent and maintains contact with rib cage
4. Push through the heel of the front foot, extend hips, and push BB forward by extending the elbow
5. Return to starting position and repeat
6. Switch leg and arm

PRE-REQUISITE EXERCISES

1. Forward/Reverse Lunge (Dynamic Warm-up)
2. Forward Lunge with Heel Reach (Dynamic Warm-up)
3. Squat to Forward Press

COMMON ERRORS

- Athlete loses stability during movement

DEGREE OF DIFFICULTY

- 1

REQUIRED EQUIPMENT

- 1 barbell (BB)
- Weights (if applicable)

KEY FACTORS

- Maintain balance during exercise
- Knee must not protrude beyond toes during lunge
- Maintain straight upper body during movement
- Use appropriately weighted bar; no loss of stability during movement
- Maintain balance and land in same location during lunging

RELEVANCE

- Prepares you for next training phase (strength/power phase)
- Improves stability during groundstroke execution
- Improves accuracy and speed of groundstrokes
- If "Stability Pad Squat Test" show deficiency, implement this exercise into the Resistance Training Routine

SOLUTION

- Decrease weight of bar and/or refer to pre-requisite exercises

ID: 652

6.53 REV. LUNGE TO FORWARD PRESS TO STANCE (II)

SUMMARY

The Reverse Lunge to Forward Press to Stance (II) is a strength for performance exercise, which focuses on improving power production capabilities during groundstrokes, improving flexibility, as well as stability of trunk and leg musculature using a barbell (BB).

PURPOSE

1. Improving power production capabilities for groundstrokes
2. Improving flexibility
3. Improving stability of trunk and leg musculature

DESCRIPTION

1. Place barbell on the ground approximately 2 feet in front of you and hold it with your right hand
2. Step into a reverse lunge with the right foot; keep weight on the heel of the front foot; left knee is at 90°
3. Hold BB in right hand close to the shoulder; elbow is bent and maintains contact with rib cage
4. Push through the heel of the front foot, extend hips, push BB forward by extending the elbow, and finish in **athletic stance** position (feet are shoulder-width apart; knees are slightly bent)
5. Return to starting position and repeat
6. Switch leg and arm

PRE-REQUISITE EXERCISES

1. Forward/Reverse Lunge (Dynamic Warm-up)
2. Forward Lunge with Heel Reach (Dynamic Warm-up)
3. Squat to Forward Press
4. Reverse Lunge to Forward Press

DEGREE OF DIFFICULTY

- 2

REQUIRED EQUIPMENT

- 1 barbell (BB)
- Weights (if applicable)

RELEVANCE

- Prepares you for next training phase (strength/power phase)
- Improves stability during groundstroke execution
- Improves accuracy and speed of groundstrokes
- If "Stability Pad Squat Test" show deficiency, implement this exercise into the Resistance Training Routine

KEY FACTORS

- Maintain balance during exercise
- Knee must not protrude beyond toes during lunge
- Maintain straight upper body during movement
- Use appropriately weighted bar; no loss of stability during movement
- Maintain balance and land in same location during lunging

ID: 653

COMMON ERRORS

- Athlete loses stability during movement

SOLUTION

- Decrease weight of bar and/or refer to pre-requisite exercises

6.54 REV. LUNGE FORWARD PRESS W. HIP FLEXION (III)

SUMMARY

The Reverse Lunge to Forward Press with Hip Flexion (III) is a strength for performance exercise, which focuses on improving power production capabilities during groundstrokes, improving flexibility, as well as stability of trunk and leg musculature using a barbell (BB).

PURPOSE

1. Improving power production capabilities for groundstrokes
2. Improving flexibility
3. Improving stability of trunk and leg musculature

DESCRIPTION

1. Place barbell on the ground approximately 2 feet in front of you and hold it with your right hand
2. Step into a reverse lunge with the right foot; keep weight on the heel of the front foot; left knee is at 90°
3. Hold BB in right hand close to the shoulder; elbow is bent and maintains contact with rib cage
4. Push through the heel of the front foot, extend hips, push BB forward by extending the elbow, flex the right hip and knee to 90°, and finish standing on the left leg
5. Step back into reverse lunge (starting position) and repeat
6. Switch leg and arm

PRE-REQUISITE EXERCISES

1. Forward/Reverse Lunge (Dynamic Warm-up)
2. Forward Lunge with Heel Reach (Dynamic Warm-up)
3. Squat to Forward Press
4. Reverse Lunge to Forward Press
5. Reverse Lunge to Forward Press to Stance

DEGREE OF DIFFICULTY

- 3

REQUIRED EQUIPMENT

- 1 barbell (BB)
- Weights (if applicable)

RELEVANCE

- Prepares you for next training phase (strength/power phase)
- Improves stability during groundstroke execution
- Improves accuracy and speed of groundstrokes
- If "Stability Pad Squat Test" show deficiency, implement this exercise into the Resistance Training Routine

KEY FACTORS

- Maintain balance during exercise
- Knee must not protrude beyond toes during lunge
- Maintain straight upper body during movement
- Use appropriately weighted bar; no loss of stability during movement
- Maintain balance and land in same location during lunging

COMMON ERRORS

- Athlete loses stability during movement

SOLUTION

- Decrease weight of bar and/or refer to pre-requisite exercises

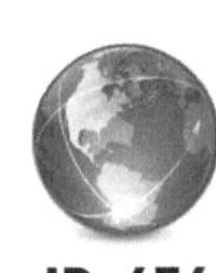

ID: 654

6.55 REV. LUNGE TO FORWARD PRESS W. ROTATION

SUMMARY

The Reverse Lunge to Forward Press with Rotation (IV) is a strength for performance exercise, which focuses on improving power production capabilities during groundstrokes, improving flexibility, as well as stability of trunk and leg musculature using a barbell (BB).

PURPOSE

1. Improving power production capabilities for groundstrokes
2. Improving flexibility
3. Improving stability of trunk and leg musculature

DESCRIPTION

1. Place barbell on the ground approximately 2 feet in front of you and hold it with your right hand
2. Step into a reverse lunge with the right foot; keep weight on the heel of the front foot; left knee is at 90°
3. Hold BB in right hand close to the shoulder; elbow is bent and maintains contact with rib cage
4. Push through the heel of the front foot, extend hips, push BB forward by extending the elbow, flex the right hip and knee to 90°, and simultaneously rotate the bar using **both hands** and finish standing on both legs (athletic position)
5. Step back into reverse lunge (starting position) and repeat
6. Switch leg and arm

PRE-REQUISITE EXERCISES

1. Forward/Reverse Lunge (Dynamic Warm-up)
2. Forward Lunge with Heel Reach (Dynamic Warm-up)
3. Squat to Forward Press
4. Reverse Lunge to Forward Press
5. Reverse Lunge to Forward Press to Stance
6. Reverse Lunge to Forward Press with Hip Flexion

DEGREE OF DIFFICULTY

- 4

REQUIRED EQUIPMENT

- 1 barbell (BB)
- Weights (if applicable)

RELEVANCE

- Prepares you for next training phase (strength/power phase)
- Improves stability during groundstroke execution
- Improves accuracy and speed of groundstrokes
- If "Stability Pad Squat Test" show deficiency, implement this exercise into the Resistance Training Routine

KEY FACTORS

- Maintain balance during exercise
- Knee must not protrude beyond toes during lunge
- Maintain straight upper body during movement
- Use appropriately weighted bar; no loss of stability during movement
- Maintain balance and land in same location during lunging

ID: 655

COMMON ERRORS

- Athlete loses stability during movement

SOLUTION

- Decrease weight of bar and/or refer to pre-requisite exercises

6.56 REV. LUNGE TO PRESS W. ROTATION: SINGLE LEG

SUMMARY

The Reverse Lunge to Forward Press with Rotation (V) is a strength for performance exercise, which focuses on improving power production capabilities during groundstrokes, improving flexibility, as well as stability of trunk and leg musculature using a barbell (BB).

PURPOSE

1. Improving power production capabilities for groundstrokes
2. Improving flexibility
3. Improving stability of trunk and leg musculature

DESCRIPTION

1. Place barbell on the ground approximately 2 feet in front of you and hold it with your right hand
2. Step into a reverse lunge with the right foot; keep weight on the heel of the front foot; left knee is at 90°
3. Hold BB in right hand close to the shoulder; elbow is bent and maintains contact with rib cage
4. Push through the heel of the front foot, extend hips, push BB forward by extending the elbow, flex the right hip and knee to 90°, and simultaneously rotate the bar using **both hands** and finish standing on the **left leg**
5. Step back into reverse lunge (starting position) and repeat
6. Switch leg and arm

PRE-REQUISITE EXERCISES

1. Forward/Reverse Lunge (Dynamic Warm-up)
2. Forward Lunge with Heel Reach (Dynamic Warm-up)
3. Squat to Forward Press
4. Reverse Lunge to Forward Press
5. Reverse Lunge to Forward Press to Stance
6. Reverse Lunge to Forward Press with Hip Flexion

DEGREE OF DIFFICULTY

- 5

REQUIRED EQUIPMENT

- 1 barbell (BB)
- Weights (if applicable)

RELEVANCE

- Prepares you for next training phase (strength/power phase)
- Improves stability during groundstroke execution
- Improves accuracy and speed of groundstrokes
- If "Stability Pad Squat Test" show deficiency, implement this exercise into the Resistance Training Routine

KEY FACTORS

- Maintain balance during exercise
- Knee must not protrude beyond toes during lunge
- Maintain straight upper body during movement
- Use appropriately weighted bar; no loss of stability during movement
- Maintain balance and land in same location during lunging

COMMON ERRORS

- Athlete loses stability during movement

SOLUTION

- Decrease weight of bar and/or refer to pre-requisite exercises

ID: 656

6.57 LATERAL SQUAT W. BARBELL ROTATION

SUMMARY

The Lateral Squat with Barbell Rotation (IV) is a strength for performance exercise, which focuses on improving power production capabilities during groundstrokes, improving flexibility, improving agility capability, as well as stability of trunk and leg musculature using a barbell (BB).

PURPOSE

1. Improving power production capabilities for groundstrokes
2. Improving flexibility
3. Improving agility capability
4. Improving stability of trunk and leg musculature

DESCRIPTION

1. Place barbell on the ground approximately 2 feet in front of you and hold it in **both hands**
2. Feet are close together
3. Hold BB in **both hands** in front of your chest; elbows are bent
4. Step sideways into a lateral squat with the right foot; keep weight on the heel of the foot; right knee is at 90°
5. Push through the heel of the right foot, extend hips, and simultaneously rotate the bar using **both hands** towards the left shoulder and finish in neutral position
6. Step back into lateral squat and repeat
7. Switch leg

DEGREE OF DIFFICULTY

- 4

RELEVANCE

- Prepares you for next training phase (strength/power phase)
- Improves stability during groundstroke execution
- Improves accuracy and speed of groundstrokes
- If "Trunk Rotation Test" and/or "Stability Pad Squat Test" show deficiency, implement this exercise into the Resistance Training Routine

PRE-REQUISITE EXERCISES

1. Lateral Squat (Dynamic Warm-up)
2. Lateral Squat with Rotation (Dynamic Warm-up)

COMMON ERRORS

- Athlete loses stability during movement

SOLUTION

- Decrease weight of bar and/or refer to pre-requisite exercises

KEY FACTORS

- Maintain balance during exercise
- Knee must not protrude beyond toes during squat
- Maintain straight upper body during movement
- Use appropriately weighted bar; no loss of stability during movement
- Maintain balance and land in same location during squatting

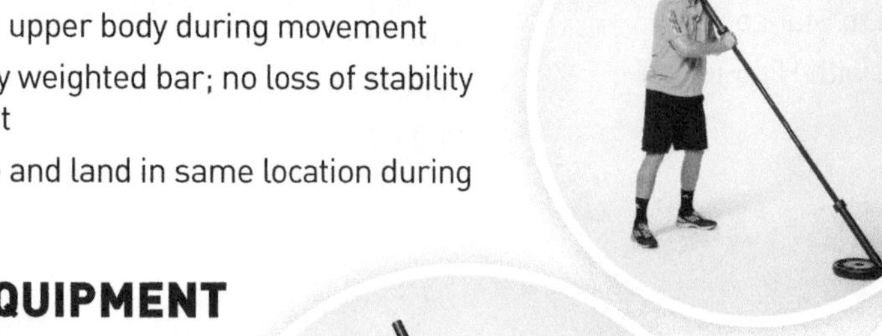

REQUIRED EQUIPMENT

- 1 barbell (BB)
- Weights (if applicable)

ID: 657

6.58 LATERAL SQUAT TO HIP FLEXION W. BB ROTATION

SUMMARY

The Lateral Squat to Hip Flexion with Barbell Rotation (V) is a strength for performance exercise, which focuses on improving power production capabilities during groundstrokes, improving flexibility, improving agility capability, as well as stability of trunk and leg musculature using a barbell (BB).

PURPOSE

1. Improving power production capabilities for groundstrokes
2. Improving flexibility
3. Improving agility capability
4. Improving stability of trunk and leg musculature

DESCRIPTION

1. Place barbell on the ground approximately 2 feet in front of you and hold it in **both hands**
2. Feet are close together
3. Hold BB in **both hands** in front of your chest; elbows are bent
4. Step sideways into a lateral squat with the right foot; keep weight on the heel of the foot; right knee is at 90°
5. Push through the heel of the right foot, extend hips, simultaneously rotate the bar using **both hands** outside the left shoulder, bend right hip and knee to 90° and finish standing on the left leg
6. Step back into lateral squat and repeat
7. Switch leg

PRE-REQUISITE EXERCISES

1. Lateral Squat (Dynamic Warm-up)
2. Lateral Squat with Rotation (Dynamic Warm-up)
3. Lateral Squat to Barbell Rotation

DEGREE OF DIFFICULTY

- 5

REQUIRED EQUIPMENT

- 1 barbell (BB)
- Weights (if applicable)

RELEVANCE

- Prepares you for next training phase (strength/power phase)
- Improves stability during groundstroke execution
- Improves accuracy and speed of groundstrokes
- If "Trunk Rotation Test" and/or "Stability Pad Squat Test" show deficiency, implement this exercise into the Resistance Training Routine

KEY FACTORS

- Maintain balance during exercise
- Knee must not protrude beyond toes during lunge
- Maintain straight upper body during movement
- Use appropriately weighted bar; no loss of stability during movement
- Maintain balance and land in same location during lunging

COMMON ERRORS

- Athlete loses stability during movement

SOLUTION

- Decrease weight of bar and/or refer to pre-requisite exercises

ID: 658

6.59 LATERAL LUNGE WITH BARBELL ROTATION

SUMMARY

The Lateral Lunge with Barbell Rotation (IV) is a strength for performance exercise, which focuses on improving power production capabilities during groundstrokes, improving flexibility, improving agility capability, as well as stability of trunk and leg musculature using a barbell (BB).

PURPOSE

1. Improving power production capabilities for groundstrokes
2. Improving flexibility
3. Improving agility capability
4. Improving stability of trunk and leg musculature

DESCRIPTION

1. Place barbell on the ground approximately 2 feet in front of you and hold it in **both hands**
2. Feet are close together
3. Hold BB in **both hands** in front of your chest; elbows are bent
4. Step sideways into a lateral lunge with the right foot; keep weight on the heel of the foot; right knee is at 90°
5. Push through the heel of the right foot, extend hips, and simultaneously rotate the bar using **both hands** towards the left shoulder and finish in neutral position
6. Step back into lateral lunge and repeat
7. Switch leg

PRE-REQUISITE EXERCISES

1. Lateral Lunge (Dynamic Warm-up)
2. Lateral Lunge with Rotation (Dynamic Warm-up)
3. Lateral Squat to Barbell Rotation
4. Lateral Squat to Hip Flexion with Rotation

DEGREE OF DIFFICULTY

- 4

REQUIRED EQUIPMENT

- 1 barbell (BB)
- Weights (if applicable)

RELEVANCE

- Prepares you for next training phase (strength/power phase)
- Improves stability during groundstroke execution
- Improves accuracy and speed of groundstrokes
- If "Trunk Rotation Test" and/or "Stability Pad Squat Test" show deficiency, implement this exercise into the Resistance Training Routine

KEY FACTORS

- Maintain balance during exercise
- Knee must not protrude beyond toes during lunge
- Maintain straight upper body during movement
- Use appropriately weighted bar; no loss of stability during movement
- Maintain balance and land in same location during lunging

ID: 659

COMMON ERRORS

- Athlete loses stability during movement

SOLUTION

- Decrease weight of bar and/or refer to pre-requisite exercises

6.60 LATERAL LUNGE HIP FLEX. W. BB ROTATION (V)

SUMMARY

The Lateral Lunge to Hip Flexion with Barbell Rotation: Single Leg (V) is a strength for performance exercise, which focuses on improving power production capabilities during groundstrokes, improving flexibility, improving agility capability, as well as stability of trunk and leg musculature using a barbell (BB).

PURPOSE

1. Improving power production capabilities for groundstrokes
2. Improving flexibility
3. Improving agility capability
4. Improving stability of trunk and leg musculature

DESCRIPTION

1. Place barbell on the ground approximately 2 feet in front of you and hold it in **both hands**
2. Feet are close together
3. Hold BB in **both hands** in front of your chest; elbows are bent
4. Step sideways into a lateral lunge with the right foot; keep weight on the heel of the foot; right knee is at 90°
5. Push through the heel of the right foot, extend hips, simultaneously rotate the bar using both hands outside the left shoulder, bend right hip and knee to 90° and finish standing on the **left leg**
6. Step back into lateral lunge and repeat
7. Switch leg

PRE-REQUISITE EXERCISES

1. Lateral Lunge (Dynamic Warm-up)
2. Lateral Lunge with Rotation (Dynamic Warm-up)
3. Lateral Squat to Barbell Rotation
4. Lateral Squat to Hip Flexion with Rotation
5. Lateral Lunge with Barbell Rotation

DEGREE OF DIFFICULTY

- 5

REQUIRED EQUIPMENT

- 1 barbell (BB)
- Weights (if applicable)

RELEVANCE

- Prepares you for next training phase (strength/power phase)
- Improves stability during groundstroke execution
- Improves accuracy and speed of groundstrokes
- If "Trunk Rotation Test" and/or "Stability Pad Squat Test" show deficiency, implement this exercise into the Resistance Training Routine

KEY FACTORS

- Maintain balance during exercise
- Knee must not protrude beyond toes during lunge
- Maintain straight upper body during movement
- Use appropriately weighted bar; no loss of stability during movement
- Maintain balance and land in same location during lunging

ID: 660

COMMON ERRORS

- Athlete loses stability during movement

SOLUTION

- Decrease weight of bar and/or refer to pre-requisite exercises

6.61 LATERAL LUNGE WITH BAR ROTATION

SUMMARY

The Lateral Lunge with Bar Rotations is a strength for performance exercise, which focuses on improving power production capabilities during groundstrokes, improving flexibility of trunk musculature, as well as stability & coordination using a weighted bar.

PURPOSE

1. Improving power production capabilities for groundstrokes
2. Improving flexibility of trunk musculature
3. Improving stability & coordination

DESCRIPTION

Athlete holds a weighted bar (2-10 lb) and needs to:

1. Hold weighted bar in both hands about shoulder-width apart
2. Step sideways with the left foot and bend the left knee until left knee is at 90° and right leg is straight; knee must not move beyond toes
3. Rotate trunk to the left, then to the right
4. Push-off with the left foot and lunge to the right side until right knee is at 90° and left leg is straight; knee must not move beyond toes
5. Rotate trunk to the left, then to the right

PRE-REQUISITE EXERCISES

1. Bilateral Lunges (Dynamic Warm-up)
2. Bilateral Lunges with Trunk Rotation (Dynamic Warm-up)

COMMON ERRORS

- Athlete loses stability during movement
- Arms are flexed during rotation

REQUIRED EQUIPMENT

- 1 Weighted Bar

DEGREE OF DIFFICULTY

- 3

RELEVANCE

- Prepares you for next training phase (strength/power phase)
- Improves stability during groundstroke execution
- Improves accuracy and speed of groundstrokes
- Improves change of direction ability (agility)
- If "Trunk Rotator Test" and/or "Bilateral Lunge Test" show deficiency, implement this exercise into the Resistance Training Routine

KEY FACTORS

- Arms remain straight during rotation
- Keep the bar up in front of the body during rotation
- Knees must not protrude past toes during the lunge
- Use appropriately weighted bar; no loss of stability during movement
- Maintain balance and land in same location during lunging

SOLUTION

- Decrease weight of bar or refer to pre-requisite exercises
- Initiate rotation with the trunk instead of using arms to move the bar

ID: 661

6.62 BILATERAL LUNGE WITH BAR ROTATION

SUMMARY

The Bilateral Lunge with Bar Rotations is a strength for performance exercise, which focuses on improving power production capabilities during groundstrokes, improving flexibility of trunk musculature, as well as stability & coordination using a weighted bar.

PURPOSE

1. Improving power production capabilities for groundstrokes
2. Improving flexibility of trunk musculature
3. Improving stability & coordination

DESCRIPTION

Athlete holds a weighted bar (2-10 lb) and needs to:

1. Hold weighted bar in both hands about shoulder-width apart
2. Step sideways with the left foot and bend the left knee until left knee is at 90° and right leg is straight; knee must not move beyond toes
3. Rotate trunk to the left, then to the right
4. Push-off with the left foot, side-step, and lunge to the right side until right knee is at 90° and left leg is straight; knee must not move beyond toes
5. Rotate trunk to the left, then to the right

PRE-REQUISITE EXERCISES

1. Bilateral Lunges (Dynamic Warm-up)
2. Bilateral Lunges w. Trunk Rotation (Dynamic Warm-up)
3. Lateral Lunge w. Bar Rotation

DEGREE OF DIFFICULTY

- 4

REQUIRED EQUIPMENT

- 1 Weighted Bar

RELEVANCE

- Prepares you for next training phase (strength/power phase)
- Improves stability during groundstroke execution
- Improves accuracy and speed of groundstrokes
- Improves change of direction ability (agility)
- If "Trunk Rotator Test" and/or "Bilateral Lunge Test" show deficiency, implement this exercise into the Resistance Training Routine

KEY FACTORS

- Arms remain straight during rotation
- Keep the bar up in front of the body during rotation
- Knees must not protrude past toes during the lunge
- Use appropriately weighted bar; no loss of stability during movement
- Maintain balance and land in same location during lunging

ID: 662

DVD

COMMON ERRORS

- Athlete loses stability during movement
- Arms are flexed during rotation

SOLUTION

- Decrease weight of bar or refer to pre-requisite exercises
- Initiate rotation with the trunk instead of using arms to move the bar

6.63 SQUAT WITH BAR ROTATIONS

SUMMARY

The Squat with Bar Rotations is a strength for performance exercise, which focuses on improving power production capabilities during groundstrokes, improving flexibility of trunk musculature, as well as stability & coordination using a weighted bar.

PURPOSE

1. Improving power production capabilities for groundstrokes
2. Improving flexibility of trunk musculature
3. Improving stability & coordination

DESCRIPTION

Athlete holds a weighted bar (2-10 lb) and needs to:

1. Hold weighted bar in both hands about shoulder-width apart
2. Step into a squat; keep weight on the heel of the front foot
3. Keep arms straight and rotate trunk from left to right and right to left; bar should be at chest-level during rotations

PRE-REQUISITE EXERCISES

1. Bilateral Squat (Dynamic Warm-up)
2. Bilateral Squat w. Trunk Rotation (Dynamic Warm-up)

COMMON ERRORS

- Athlete loses stability during movement
- Arms are flexed during rotation

REQUIRED EQUIPMENT

- 1 Weighted Bar

RELEVANCE

- Prepares you for next training phase (strength/power phase)
- Improves stability during groundstroke execution
- Improves accuracy and speed of groundstrokes
- If "Trunk Rotator Test" and/or "Stability Pad Squat Test" show deficiency, implement this exercise into the Resistance Training Routine

KEY FACTORS

- Arms remain straight during rotation
- Keep the bar up in front of the body during rotation
- Knees must not protrude past toes during the lunge
- Use appropriately weighted bar; no loss of stability during movement
- Maintain balance and land in same location during lunging

SOLUTION

- Decrease weight of bar or refer to pre-requisite exercises
- Initiate rotation with the trunk instead of using arms to move the bar

DEGREE OF DIFFICULTY

- 3

ID: 663

6.64 BILATERAL SQUAT WITH BAR ROTATIONS

SUMMARY

The Bilateral Squat with Bar Rotations is a strength for performance exercise, which focuses on improving power production capabilities during groundstrokes, improving flexibility of trunk musculature, as well as stability & coordination using a weighted bar.

PURPOSE

1. Improving power production capabilities for groundstrokes
2. Improving flexibility of trunk musculature
3. Improving stability & coordination

DESCRIPTION

Athlete holds a weighted bar (2-10 lb) and needs to:

1. Hold weighted bar in both hands about shoulder-width apart
2. Step to the left into lateral squat; knee must not move beyond toes
3. Rotate trunk to the left, then to the right
4. Push off with left foot
5. Side-Step
6. Step to the right into lateral squat; knee must not move beyond toes
7. Rotate trunk to the left, then to the right
8. Push off with left foot
9. Return to starting position

PRE-REQUISITE EXERCISES

1. Bilateral Squat (Dynamic Warm-up)
2. Bilateral Squat w. Trunk Rotation (Dynamic Warm-up)
3. Squat w. Bar Rotation

COMMON ERRORS

- Athlete loses stability during movement
- Arms are flexed during rotation

DEGREE OF DIFFICULTY

- 4

REQUIRED EQUIPMENT

- 1 Weighted Bar

RELEVANCE

- Prepares you for next training phase (strength/power phase)
- Improves stability during groundstroke execution
- Improves accuracy and speed of groundstrokes
- Improves change of direction ability (agility)
- If "Trunk Rotator Test" and/or "Bilateral Lunge Test" show deficiency, implement this exercise into the Resistance Training Routine

KEY FACTORS

- Arms remain straight during rotation
- Keep the bar up in front of the body during rotation
- Knees must not protrude past toes during the lunge
- Use appropriately weighted bar; no loss of stability during movement
- Maintain balance and land in same location during lunging

SOLUTION

- Decrease weight of bar or refer to pre-requisite exercises
- Initiate rotation with the trunk instead of using arms to move the bar

ID: 664

6.65 LUNGE WITH BAR ROTATIONS

SUMMARY

The Lunge with Bar Rotations is a strength for performance exercise, which focuses on improving power production capabilities during groundstrokes, improving flexibility of trunk musculature, as well as stability & coordination using a weighted bar.

PURPOSE

1. Improving power production capabilities for groundstrokes
2. Improving flexibility of trunk musculature
3. Improving stability & coordination

DESCRIPTION

Athlete holds a weighted bar (2-10 lb) and needs to:

1. Hold weighted bar in both hands about shoulder-width apart
2. Step into a lunge; keep weight on the heel of the front foot
3. Keep arms straight and rotate trunk from left to right and right to left; bar should be at chest-level during rotations

PRE-REQUISITE EXERCISES

1. Cross-Over Lunge (Dynamic Warm-up)
2. Cross-Over Lunge with Heel Reach (Dynamic Warm-up)

REQUIRED EQUIPMENT

- 1 Weighted Bar

DEGREE OF DIFFICULTY

- 3

RELEVANCE

- Prepares you for next training phase (strength/power phase)
- Improves stability during groundstroke execution
- Improves accuracy and speed of groundstrokes
- If "Trunk Rotator Test" and/or "Stability Pad Squat Test" show deficiency, implement this exercise into the Resistance Training Routine

ID: 665

COMMON ERRORS

- Athlete loses stability during movement
- Arms are flexed during rotation

SOLUTION

- Decrease weight of bar or refer to pre-requisite exercises
- Initiate rotation with the trunk instead of using arms to move the bar

KEY FACTORS

- Arms remain straight during rotation
- Keep the bar up in front of the body during rotation
- Knees must not protrude past toes during the lunge
- Use appropriately weighted bar; no loss of stability during movement
- Maintain balance and land in same location during lunging

6.66 CROSS-OVER LUNGE BAR ROTATIONS

SUMMARY

The Cross-Over Lunge Bar Rotations is a strength for performance exercise, which focuses on improving power production capabilities during groundstrokes, improving flexibility of trunk musculature, as well as stability & coordination using a weighted bar.

PURPOSE

1. Improving power production capabilities for groundstrokes
2. Improving flexibility of trunk musculature
3. Improving stability & coordination

DESCRIPTION

Athlete holds a weighted bar (2-10 lb) and needs to:

1. Stand up straight, feet shoulder-width apart, holding weighted bar shoulder-width apart in both hands
2. Perform a cross-over move; right leg crosses over behind the left foot, stepping into a lunge while arms are straight and trunk rotates to the left
3. Keep weight on the heel of front foot (left foot)
4. Move trailing foot (right foot) in line (parallel) with left foot; feet are shoulder-width apart
5. Cross-over with left foot behind the right foot, stepping into a lunge while arms are straight and trunk rotates to the right
6. Keep weight on the heel of front foot (right foot)
7. Move trailing foot (left foot) in line (parallel) with right foot; feet are shoulder-width apart
8. Perform a cross-over move; right leg crosses over behind the left foot, stepping into a lunge while arms are straight and trunk rotates to the left

DEGREE OF DIFFICULTY

- 4

RELEVANCE

- Prepares you for next training phase (strength/power phase)
- Improves stability during groundstroke execution
- Improves accuracy and speed of groundstrokes
- If "Trunk Rotator Test" and/or "Stability Pad Squat Test" show deficiency, implement this exercise into the Resistance Training Routine

KEY FACTORS

- Arms remain straight during rotation
- Keep the bar up in front of the body during rotation
- Knees must not protrude past toes during the lunge
- Use appropriately weighted bar; no loss of stability during movement
- Maintain balance and land in same location during lunging

COMMON ERRORS

- Athlete loses stability during movement
- Arms are flexed during rotation

SOLUTION

- Decrease weight of bar or refer to pre-requisite exercises
- Initiate rotation with the trunk instead of using arms to move the bar

PRE-REQUISITE EXERCISES

1. Cross-Over Lunges (Dynamic Warm-up)
2. Cross-Over Lunge with Heel Reaches (Dynamic Warm-up)
3. Lunge with Bar Rotations
4. Lateral Squat with Bar Rotations
5. Lateral Lunge with Bar Rotations

ID: 666

DVD

REQUIRED EQUIPMENT

- 1 Weighted Bar

6.67 FORWARD LUNGE & DB REACH TO OH PRESS

SUMMARY

The Forward Lunge & Dumbbell Reach to Overhead Press is a strength for performance exercise, which focuses on improving power production capabilities during stroke production, improving flexibility of lower and upper body musculature as well as stability of legs, trunk and shoulders using appropriate resistance (start light).

PURPOSE

1. Improving power production capabilities for stroke production (effective energy transfer)
2. Improving flexibility of lower and upper body musculature
3. Improving stability (legs, trunk, shoulders)

DESCRIPTION

1. Stand in **athletic stance** (feet are shoulder-width apart; knees are slightly bent)
2. Hold 1 dumbbell (DB) in each hand
3. Step into a forward lunge with the left foot
4. Rotate trunk to your left and move DB next to your hips (or as far as you can rotate)
5. Push off with the front foot and simultaneously push DB over the head
6. Return to starting position
7. Step into a forward lunge with the left foot again
8. Rotate trunk to your right and move DB next to your hips (or as far as you can rotate)
9. Push off with the front foot and simultaneously push DB over the head
10. Repeat same movement with right leg

RELEVANCE

- Prepares you for next training phase (strength/power phase)
- Improves stability during groundstroke execution
- Improves accuracy and speed of groundstrokes
- If "Trunk Rotator Test" and/or "Bilateral Lunge Test" show deficiency, implement this exercise into your Resistance Training Routine

KEY FACTORS

- Use athlete-appropriate resistance; no loss of stability during movement
- Make sure you have enough space in front of you
- Use alternate lunge movement
- Maintain balance and land in same location during lunging

COMMON ERRORS

- Athlete loses stability during movement
- Arms are not fully extended and above the head/ears
- DB is placed in front of – or behind the head

SOLUTION

- Decrease weight of bar or refer to pre-requisite exercises
- Use a wider grip

PRE-REQUISITE EXERCISES

1. Forward/Reverse Lunge (Dynamic Warm-up)
2. Forward Lunge & Overhead Reach (Dynamic Warm-up)
3. Push-Press (Resistance Training)
4. Forward Lunge & DB Reach THEN Overhead Press

REQUIRED EQUIPMENT

- 2 Dumbbells

ID: 667

DEGREE OF DIFFICULTY

- 2

6.68 FORWARD LUNGE & DB REACH THEN OH PRESS

SUMMARY

The Forward Lunge & Dumbbell Reach Then Overhead Press is a strength for performance exercise, which focuses on improving power production capabilities during stroke production, improving flexibility of lower and upper body musculature as well as stability of legs, trunk and shoulders using appropriate resistance (start light).

PURPOSE

1. Improving power production capabilities for stroke production (effective energy transfer)
2. Improving flexibility of lower and upper body musculature
3. Improving stability (legs, trunk, shoulders)

DESCRIPTION

1. Stand in **athletic stance** (feet are shoulder-width apart; knees are slightly bent)
2. Hold 1 dumbbell (DB) in each hand
3. Step into a forward lunge with the left foot
4. Rotate trunk to your left and move DB next to your hips (or as far as you can rotate)
5. Push off with the front foot and return to starting position
6. Push DB over your head
7. Return to starting position
8. Step into a forward lunge with the left foot again
9. Rotate trunk to your right and move DB next to your hips (or as far as you can rotate)
10. Push off with the front foot and return to starting position
11. Push DB over your head
12. Repeat same movement with right leg

PRE-REQUISITE EXERCISES

1. Forward/Reverse Lunge (Dynamic Warm-up)
2. Forward Lunge & Overhead Reach (Dynamic Warm-up)
3. Push-Press (Resistance Training)

DEGREE OF DIFFICULTY

- 1

REQUIRED EQUIPMENT

- 2 Dumbbells

RELEVANCE

- Prepares you for next training phase (strength/power phase)
- Improves stability during groundstroke execution
- Improves accuracy and speed of groundstrokes
- If "Trunk Rotator Test" and/or "Bilateral Lunge Test" show deficiency, implement this exercise into the Resistance Training Routine

KEY FACTORS

- Use athlete-appropriate resistance; no loss of stability during movement
- Make sure you have enough space in front of you
- Use alternate lunge movement
- Maintain balance and land in same location during lunging

COMMON ERRORS

- Athlete loses stability during movement
- Arms are not fully extended and above the head/ears
- DB is placed in front of – or behind the head

SOLUTION

- Decrease weight of bar or refer to pre-requisite exercises
- Use a wider grip

ID: 668

6.69 ALTERNATING LUNGE & DB REACH TO OH PRESS

SUMMARY

The Alternating Lunge & Dumbbell Reach to Overhead Press is a strength for performance exercise, which focuses on improving power production capabilities during stroke production, improving flexibility of lower and upper body musculature as well as stability of legs, trunk and shoulders using appropriate resistance (start light).

PURPOSE

1. Improving power production capabilities for stroke production (effective energy transfer)
2. Improving flexibility of lower and upper body musculature
3. Improving stability (legs, trunk, shoulders)

DESCRIPTION

1. Stand in **athletic stance** (feet are shoulder-width apart; knees are slightly bent)
2. Hold 1 dumbbell (DB) in each hand
3. Step into a forward lunge with the left foot
4. Rotate trunk to your left and move DB next to your hips (or as far as you can rotate)
5. Push off with the front foot and simultaneously push DB over the head
6. Return to starting position
7. Step into a forward lunge with the right foot
8. Rotate trunk to your right and move DB next to your hips (or as far as you can rotate)
9. Push off with the front foot and simultaneously push DB over the head
10. Return to starting position
11. Step into a forward lunge with the left foot
12. Rotate trunk to your right and move DB next to your hips (or as far as you can rotate)
13. Push off with the front foot and simultaneously push DB over the head
14. Return to starting position
15. Step into a forward lunge with the right foot
16. Rotate trunk to your left and move DB next to your hips (or as far as you can rotate)

RELEVANCE

- Prepares you for next training phase (strength/power phase)
- Improves stability during groundstroke execution
- Improves accuracy and speed of groundstrokes
- If "Trunk Rotator Test" and/or "Bilateral Lunge Test" show deficiency, implement this exercise into the Resistance Training Routine

KEY FACTORS

- Use athlete-appropriate resistance; no loss of stability during movement
- Make sure you have enough space in front of you
- Use alternate lunge movement
- Maintain balance and land in same location during lunging

PRE-REQUISITE EXERCISES

1. Forward/Reverse Lunge (Dynamic Warm-up)
2. Forward Lunge & Overhead Reach (Dynamic Warm-up)
3. Push-Press (Resistance Training)
4. Forward Lunge & DB Reach to Overhead Press

COMMON ERRORS

- Athlete loses stability during movement
- Arms are not fully extended and above the head/ears
- DB is placed in front of – or behind the head

SOLUTION

- Decrease weight of bar or refer to pre-requisite exercises
- Use a wider grip

ID: 669

DVD

DEGREE OF DIFFICULTY

- 3

REQUIRED EQUIPMENT

- 2 Dumbbells

6.70 SUPINE BRIDGING

SUMMARY

The Supine Bridging I is a low back exercise, which focuses on improving hip extensor strength, trunk extensor strength and improving skill and strength foundation for more complex movements.

PURPOSE

1. Improving hip-extensor strength
2. Improving trunk extensor strength
3. Improving skill and strength foundation for complex movements

DESCRIPTION

1. Place floor mat on the ground
2. Lie flat on the floor mat (face up) with arms close to the trunk (palms down)
3. Knees are in line with shoulders
4. Bring heels toward the buttocks until knees are flexed at 90°
5. Extend hips upwards to neutral pelvic position; hold position for 1 second
6. Descend hips back to the ground

BREATH IN & OUT

- IN: When descending
- OUT: During Hip Extension

TARGETED MUSCLES

1. Low Back Extensors
2. Hip Extensors

DEGREE OF DIFFICULTY

- 1

REQUIRED EQUIPMENT

- 1 Floor Mat

RELEVANCE

- General strengthening of the lower back to prevent injuries
- Low back injuries/discomfort can occur due to repetitive jumping activities (e.g. ballistic/plyometric activities); supine bridging can alleviate low back pain thereby allowing for proper training volume and intensity

ID: 670

6.71 SINGLE-LEG SUPINE BRIDGING

SUMMARY

The Single-Leg Supine Bridging is a low back exercise, which focuses on improving hip extensor strength, trunk extensor strength and skill and strength foundation for more complex movements as well as trunk stabilization capabilities.

PURPOSE

1. Improving hip-extensor strength
2. Improving trunk extensor strength
3. Improving skill and strength foundation for complex movements
4. Improving trunk stabilization capabilities

DESCRIPTION

1. Place floor mat on the ground
2. Lie flat on the floor mat (face up) with arms close to the trunk (palms down)
3. Knees are in line with shoulders
4. Bring heels toward the buttocks until knees are flexed at 90°
5. Extend left leg
6. Extend right hip upwards to neutral pelvic position; hold position for 1 second
7. Descend right hip back to the ground
8. Extend left leg and repeat

PRE-REQUISITE EXERCISES

1. Supine Bridging

BREATH IN & OUT

- IN: When descending
- OUT: During Hip Extension

DEGREE OF DIFFICULTY

- 2

REQUIRED EQUIPMENT

- 1 Floor Mat

TARGETED MUSCLES

1. Low Back Extensors
2. Hip Extensors

RELEVANCE

- General strengthening of the lower back to prevent injuries
- Low back injuries/discomfort can occur due to repetitive jumping activities (e.g. ballistic/plyometric/serving activities); supine bridging can alleviate low back pain thereby allowing for proper training volume and intensity
- Strengthening the trunk stabilizers allows for better energy transfer, which results in more powerful stroke production

ID: 671

6.72 SL SUPINE BRIDGING W. CL HIP FLEXION

SUMMARY

The Single-Leg Supine Bridging with Contra-Lateral Hip Flexion is a low back exercise, which focuses on improving hip extensor strength, trunk extensor strength and skill and strength foundation for more complex movements as well as trunk stabilization capabilities.

PURPOSE

1. Improving hip-extensor strength
2. Improving trunk extensor strength
3. Improving skill and strength foundation for complex movements
4. Improving trunk stabilization capabilities

DESCRIPTION

1. Place floor mat on the ground
2. Lie flat on the floor mat (face up) with arms close to the trunk (palms down)
3. Knees are in line with shoulders
4. Bring heels toward the buttocks until knees are flexed at 90°
5. Extend left leg and flex hip; toes point upward
6. Extend right hip upwards to neutral pelvic position; hold position for 1 second
7. Descend right hip back to the ground
8. Extend left leg, flex hip, and repeat

PRE-REQUISITE EXERCISES

1. Supine Bridging
2. Single-Leg Supine Bridging

BREATH IN & OUT

- IN: When descending
- OUT: During Hip Extension

TARGETED MUSCLES

1. Low Back Extensors
2. Hip Extensors

DEGREE OF DIFFICULTY

- 3

REQUIRED EQUIPMENT

- 1 Floor Mat

RELEVANCE

- General strengthening of the lower back to prevent injuries
- Low back injuries/discomfort can occur due to repetitive jumping activities (e.g. ballistic/plyometric activities/serving); supine bridging can alleviate low back pain thereby allowing for proper training volume and intensity
- Strengthening the trunk stabilizers allows for better energy transfer, which results in more powerful stroke production

ID: 672

6.73 ASSISTED PHYSIO BALL SUPINE BRIDGING

SUMMARY

The Assisted Physio Ball Supine Bridging is a low back exercise, which focuses on improving hip extensor strength, trunk extensor strength and skill and strength foundation for more complex movements as well as trunk stabilization capabilities.

PURPOSE

1. Improving hip-extensor strength
2. Improving trunk extensor strength
3. Improving skill and strength foundation for complex movements
4. Improving trunk stabilization capabilities

DESCRIPTION

Coach assists the athlete by holding the physio ball in place.

1. Place floor mat on the ground and the physio ball towards the lower end on the ground
2. Lie flat on the floor mat (face up) with arms ~45° (abducted) away from the trunk (palms down), put both feet on top of the physio ball, and **flex knees**
3. Knees are in line with shoulders°
4. Extend the hips upwards to neutral pelvic position; only the shoulder blades and head touch the ground; hold position for 1 second
5. Descend hips back to the ground; **don't lie flat on the ground**; only touch with buttocks

PRE-REQUISITE EXERCISES

1. Supine Bridging
2. Single-Leg Supine Bridging
3. Single-Leg Supine Bridging with contra-lateral hip flexion

BREATH IN & OUT

- IN: When descending
- OUT: During Hip Extension

DEGREE OF DIFFICULTY

- 1

REQUIRED EQUIPMENT

- 1 Floor Mat
- 1 Physio Ball (55cm-65cm)

RELEVANCE

- General strengthening of the lower back to prevent injuries
- Low back injuries/discomfort can occur due to repetitive jumping activities (e.g. ballistic/plyometric activities/serving); supine bridging can alleviate low back pain thereby allowing for proper training volume and intensity
- Strengthening the trunk stabilizers allows for better energy transfer, which results in more powerful stroke production

TARGETED MUSCLES

1. Low Back Extensors
2. Hip Extensors

ID: 673

6.74 PHYSIO BALL SUPINE BRIDGING

SUMMARY

The Physio Ball Supine Bridging is a low back exercise, which focuses on improving hip extensor strength, trunk extensor strength and skill and strength foundation for more complex movements as well as trunk stabilization capabilities.

PURPOSE

1. Improving hip-extensor strength
2. Improving trunk extensor strength
3. Improving skill and strength foundation for complex movements
4. Improving trunk stabilization capabilities

DESCRIPTION

1. Place floor mat on the ground and the physio ball towards the lower end on the ground
2. Lie flat on the floor mat (face up) with arms ~45° (abducted) away from the trunk (palms down), put both feet on top of the physio ball, and **flex knees**
3. Knees are in line with shoulders°
4. Extend the hips upwards to neutral pelvic position; only the shoulder blades and head touch the ground; hold position for 1 second
5. Descend hips back to the ground; **don't lie flat on the ground**; only touch with buttocks

RELEVANCE

- General strengthening of the lower back to prevent injuries
- Low back injuries/discomfort can occur due to repetitive jumping activities (e.g. ballistic/plyometric activities/serving); supine bridging can alleviate low back pain thereby allowing for proper training volume and intensity
- Strengthening the trunk stabilizers allows for better energy transfer, which results in more powerful stroke production

BREATH IN & OUT

- IN: When descending
- OUT: During Hip Extension

DEGREE OF DIFFICULTY

- 2

REQUIRED EQUIPMENT

- 1 Floor Mat
- 1 Physio Ball (55cm-65cm)

TARGETED MUSCLES

1. Low Back Extensors
2. Hip Extensors

PRE-REQUISITE EXERCISES

1. Assisted Physio Ball Supine Bridging

ID: 674

6.75 SINGLE-LEG PHYSIO BALL SUPINE BRIDGING

SUMMARY

The Single-Leg Physio Ball Supine Bridging is a low back exercise, which focuses on improving hip extensor strength, trunk extensor strength, skill and strength foundation for more complex movements and trunk stabilization capabilities.

PURPOSE

1. Improving hip-extensor strength
2. Improving trunk extensor strength
3. Improving skill and strength foundation for complex movements
4. Improving trunk stabilization capabilities

DESCRIPTION

1. Place floor mat on the ground and the physio Ball towards the lower end on the ground
2. Lie flat on the floor mat (face up) with arms ~45° (abducted) away from the trunk (palms down), put both feet on top of the physio Ball, and **flex knees**
3. Knees are in line with shoulders
4. Extend left leg and flex hip; toes point upward
5. Extend the right hip upwards to neutral pelvic position; only the shoulder blades and head touch the ground; hold position for 1 second
6. Descend hips back to the ground; **don't lie flat on the ground**; only touch with buttocks

BREATH IN & OUT

- IN: When descending
- OUT: During Hip Extension

PRE-REQUISITE EXERCISES

1. Assisted Physio Ball Supine Bridging
2. Physio Ball Supine Bridging

DEGREE OF DIFFICULTY

- 3

REQUIRED EQUIPMENT

- 1 Floor Mat
- 1 Physio Ball (55cm-65cm)

TARGETED MUSCLES

1. Low Back Extensors
2. Hip Extensors

RELEVANCE

- General strengthening of the lower back to prevent injuries
- Low back injuries/discomfort can occur due to repetitive jumping activities (e.g. ballistic/plyometric activities/serving); supine bridging can alleviate low back pain thereby allowing for proper training volume and intensity
- Strengthening the trunk stabilizers allows for better energy transfer, which results in more powerful stroke production

ID: 675

6.76 PRONE CL SINGLE-LEG & SINGLE-ARM RAISES

SUMMARY

The Prone Contra-Lateral Single-Leg & Single-Arm Raises is a low back exercise, which focuses on improving hip extensor strength, trunk extensor strength and improving skill and strength foundation for more complex movements.

PURPOSE

1. Improving hip-extensor strength
2. Improving trunk extensor strength
3. Improving skill and strength foundation for complex movements
4. Improving skill and strength foundation for complex movements

DESCRIPTION

1. Place floor mat on the ground
2. Lie flat on the floor mat (face down) with arms and legs extended (palms down)
3. Knees are in line with shoulders
4. Raise the opposite arm & leg simultaneously; hold 1 second
5. Descend and raise the other arm and leg simultaneously

BREATH IN & OUT

- IN: When descending
- OUT: During When raising

TARGETED MUSCLES

1. Low Back Extensors
2. Hip Extensors
3. Trunk Stabilizers

DEGREE OF DIFFICULTY

- 1

REQUIRED EQUIPMENT

- 1 Floor Mat

RELEVANCE

- General strengthening of the lower back to prevent injuries
- Low back injuries/discomfort can occur due to repetitive jumping activities (e.g. ballistic/plyometric activities); prone limb raises can alleviate low back pain thereby allowing for proper training volume and intensity

ID: 676

6.77 4-POINT PRONE SINGLE-LIMB RAISES

SUMMARY

The 4 Point Prone Single-Limb Raises is a low back exercise, which focuses on improving hip extensor strength, trunk extensor strength, skill and strength foundation for more complex movements, and trunk stabilization capabilities.

PURPOSE

1. Improving hip-extensor strength
2. Improving trunk extensor strength
3. Improving skill and strength foundation for complex movements
4. Improving trunk stabilization, balance and proprioception capabilities

DESCRIPTION

1. Place floor mat on the ground
2. Position hands and knees on the floor mat (face down) with arms extended and hips & legs flexed at 90° (palms down); arms are underneath the shoulders and knees are in line with shoulders
3. Raise each limb at a time; hold 1 second; extend chest and retract the scapular throughout the movement; keep looking **forward** during movements

PRE-REQUISITE EXERCISES

1. Prone Contra-Lateral Single-Leg & Single-Arm Raises

BREATH IN & OUT

- IN: When descending
- OUT: During When raising

DEGREE OF DIFFICULTY

- 1

REQUIRED EQUIPMENT

- 1 Floor Mat

RELEVANCE

- General strengthening of the lower back to prevent injuries
- Low back injuries/discomfort can occur due to repetitive jumping activities (e.g. ballistic/plyometric activities); prone limb raises can alleviate low back pain thereby allowing for proper training volume and intensity

TARGETED MUSCLES

1. Low Back Extensors
2. Hip Extensors
3. Trunk Stabilizers

ID: 677

6.78 4-POINT PRONE CONTRA-LATERAL LIMB RAISES

SUMMARY

The 4 Point Prone Contra-Lateral Limb Raises is a low back exercise, which focuses on improving hip extensor strength, trunk extensor strength, skill and strength foundation for more complex movements and trunk stabilization, balance and proprioception capabilities.

PURPOSE

1. Improving hip-extensor strength
2. Improving trunk extensor strength
3. Improving skill and strength foundation for complex movements
4. Improving trunk stabilization, balance and proprioception capabilities

DESCRIPTION

1. Place floor mat on the ground
2. Position hands and knees on the floor mat (face down) with arms extended and hips & legs flexed at 90° (palms down); arms are underneath the shoulders and knees are in line with shoulders
3. Raise opposite limbs (arm & leg) simultaneously; extend chest and retract the scapular throughout the movement; hold 1 second and descend; keep looking **forward** during movements

REQUIRED EQUIPMENT

- 1 Floor Mat

TARGETED MUSCLES

1. Low Back Extensors
2. Hip Extensors
3. Trunk Stabilizers

PRE-REQUISITE EXERCISES

1. Prone Contra-Lateral Single-Leg & Single-Arm Raises
2. 4-Point Prone Single-Limb Raises

BREATH IN & OUT

- IN: When descending
- OUT: During When raising

RELEVANCE

- General strengthening of the lower back to prevent injuries
- Low back injuries/discomfort can occur due to repetitive jumping activities (e.g. ballistic/plyometric activities); prone limb raises can alleviate low back pain thereby allowing for proper training volume and intensity

DEGREE OF DIFFICULTY

- 2

ID: 678

6.79 4-POINT PRONE ALTERNATING CL LIMB RAISE

SUMMARY

The 4 Point Alternating Prone Contra-Lateral Limb Raises is a low back exercise, which focuses on improving hip extensor strength, trunk extensor strength and trunk stabilization, balance and proprioception capabilities.

PURPOSE

1. Improving hip-extensor strength
2. Improving trunk extensor strength
3. Improving skill and strength foundation for complex movements
4. Improving trunk stabilization, balance and proprioception capabilities

DESCRIPTION

1. Place floor mat on the ground
2. Position hands and knees on the floor mat (face down) with arms extended and hips & legs flexed at 90° (palms down); arms are underneath the shoulders and knees are in line with shoulders
3. Raise opposite limbs (arm & leg) simultaneously in alternating fashion; hold 1 second and descend; extend chest and retract the scapular throughout the movement; keep looking **forward** during movement

PRE-REQUISITE EXERCISES

1. Prone Contra-Lateral Single-Leg & Single-Arm Raises
2. 4-Point Prone Contra-Lateral Limb Raises

BREATH IN & OUT

- IN: When descending
- OUT: During When raising

DEGREE OF DIFFICULTY

- 3

REQUIRED EQUIPMENT

- 1 Floor Mat

RELEVANCE

- General strengthening of the lower back to prevent injuries
- Low back injuries/discomfort can occur due to repetitive jumping activities (e.g. ballistic/plyometric activities); prone limb raises can alleviate low back pain thereby allowing for proper training volume and intensity

TARGETED MUSCLES

1. Low Back Extensors
2. Hip Extensors
3. Trunk Stabilizers

ID: 679

6.80 4-POINT PRONE PHYSIO BALL SINGLE-LIMB RAISE

SUMMARY

The 4 Point Prone Physio Ball Single-Limb Raise is a low back exercise, which focuses on improving hip extensor strength, trunk extensor strength and trunk stabilization, balance and proprioception capabilities.

PURPOSE

1. Improving hip-extensor strength
2. Improving trunk extensor strength
3. Improving skill and strength foundation for complex movements
4. Improving trunk stabilization, balance and proprioception capabilities

DESCRIPTION

1. Lie on top of the physio ball with the hips and trunk
2. Position hands and knees on the ground (face down) with arms and legs extended; arms are underneath the shoulders and knees are in line with shoulders
3. Raise each limb one at a time; hold 1 second; extend chest and retract the scapular throughout the movement; keep looking **forward** during movements

PRE-REQUISITE EXERCISES

1. 4-Point Prone Alternating Contra-Lateral Limb Raises

BREATH IN & OUT

- IN: When descending
- OUT: During When raising

TARGETED MUSCLES

1. Low Back Extensors
2. Hip Extensors
3. Trunk Stabilizers

DEGREE OF DIFFICULTY

- 1

REQUIRED EQUIPMENT

- 1 Physio Ball (55cm-65cm)

RELEVANCE

- General strengthening of the lower back to prevent injuries
- Low back injuries/discomfort can occur due to repetitive jumping activities (e.g. ballistic/plyometric activities); prone limb raises can alleviate low back pain thereby allowing for proper training volume and intensity

ID: 680

6.81 4-POINT PRONE PHYSIO BALL CL LIMB RAISE

SUMMARY

The 4 Point Prone Physio Ball Contra-Lateral Limb Raises is a low back exercise, which focuses on improving hip extensor strength, trunk extensor strength and trunk stabilization, balance and proprioception capabilities.

PURPOSE

1. Improving hip-extensor strength
2. Improving trunk extensor strength
3. Improving skill and strength foundation for complex movements
4. Improving trunk stabilization, balance and proprioception capabilities

DESCRIPTION

1. Lie on top of the physio ball with the hips and trunk
2. Position hands and knees on the ground (face down) with arms and legs extended; arms are underneath the shoulders and knees are in line with shoulders
3. Raise opposite limbs (arm & leg) simultaneously; hold 1 second and descend; extend chest and retract the scapular throughout the movement; keep looking **forward** during movements

PRE-REQUISITE EXERCISES

1. 4-Point Prone Alternating Contra-Lateral Limb Raises
2. 4-Point Prone Physio Ball Single-Limb Raises

BREATH IN & OUT

- IN: When descending
- OUT: During When raising

DEGREE OF DIFFICULTY

- 2

REQUIRED EQUIPMENT

- 1 Physio Ball (55cm-65cm)

RELEVANCE

- General strengthening of the lower back to prevent injuries
- Low back injuries/discomfort can occur due to repetitive jumping activities (e.g. ballistic/plyometric activities); prone limb raises can alleviate low back pain thereby allowing for proper training volume and intensity

TARGETED MUSCLES

1. Low Back Extensors
2. Hip Extensors
3. Trunk Stabilizers

ID: 681

6.82 4-POINT PRONE PB ALTERNATING CL-LIMB RAISE

SUMMARY

The 4 Point Prone Physioball Alternating Contra-Lateral Limb Raise is a low back exercise, which focuses on improving hip extensor strength, trunk extensor strength and trunk stabilization, balance and proprioception capabilities.

PURPOSE

1. Improving hip-extensor strength
2. Improving trunk extensor strength
3. Improving skill and strength foundation for complex movements
4. Improving trunk stabilization, balance and proprioception capabilities

DESCRIPTION

1. Lie on top of the physio Ball with the hips and trunk
2. Position hands and knees on the ground (face down) with arms and legs extended; arms are underneath the shoulders and knees are in line with shoulders
3. Raise opposite limbs (arm & leg) simultaneously in alternating fashion; hold 1 second and descend; extend chest and retract the scapular throughout the movement; keep looking **forward** during movements

PRE-REQUISITE EXERCISES

1. 4-Point Prone Alternating Contra-Lateral Limb Raises
2. 4-Point Prone Physio ball Single-Limb Raises
3. 4-Point Prone Physio ball Contra-Lateral Limb Raises

BREATH IN & OUT

- IN: When descending
- OUT: During When raising

DEGREE OF DIFFICULTY

- 3

REQUIRED EQUIPMENT

- 1 Physio Ball (55cm-65cm)

RELEVANCE

- General strengthening of the lower back to prevent injuries
- Low back injuries/discomfort can occur due to repetitive jumping activities (e.g. ballistic/plyometric activities); prone limb raises can alleviate low back pain thereby allowing for proper training volume and intensity

TARGETED MUSCLES

1. Low Back Extensors
2. Hip Extensors
3. Trunk Stabilizers

ID: 682

6.83 4-POINT PRONE PB ALTERN. UNILAT. LIMB RAISE

SUMMARY

The 4 Point Prone Physio Ball Alternating Unilateral Raise is a low back exercise, which focuses on improving hip extensor strength, trunk extensor strength and trunk stabilization, balance and proprioception capabilities.

PURPOSE

1. Improving hip-extensor strength
2. Improving trunk extensor strength
3. Improving skill and strength foundation for complex movements
4. Improving trunk stabilization, balance and proprioception capabilities

DESCRIPTION

1. Lie on top of the physio ball with the hips and trunk
2. Position hands and knees on the ground (face down) with arms and legs extended; arms are underneath the shoulders and knees are in line with shoulders
3. Raise same-side limbs (arm & leg) simultaneously in alternating fashion; hold 1 second and descend; extend chest and retract the scapular throughout the movement; keep looking **forward** during movements

PRE-REQUISITE EXERCISES

1. 4-Point Prone Alternating Contra-Lateral Limb Raises
2. 4-Point Prone Physio ball Single-Limb Raises
3. 4-Point Prone Physio ball Contra-Lateral Limb Raises
4. 4-Point Prone Physio ball Alternating Contra-Lateral Limb Raises

BREATH IN & OUT

- IN: When descending
- OUT: During When raising

DEGREE OF DIFFICULTY

- 4

REQUIRED EQUIPMENT

- 1 Physio Ball (55cm-65cm)

RELEVANCE

- General strengthening of the lower back to prevent injuries
- Low back injuries/discomfort can occur due to repetitive jumping activities (e.g. ballistic/plyometric activities); prone limb raises can alleviate low back pain thereby allowing for proper training volume and intensity

TARGETED MUSCLES

1. Low Back Extensors
2. Hip Extensors
3. Trunk Stabilizers

ID: 683

6.84 ASSISTED PRONE PHYSIO BALL TRUNK EXTENSION

SUMMARY

The Assisted Prone Physio Ball Trunk Extension is a low back exercise, which focuses on improving hip extensor strength, trunk extensor strength and trunk stabilization, balance and proprioception capabilities.

PURPOSE

1. Improving hip-extensor strength
2. Improving trunk extensor strength
3. Improving skill and strength foundation for complex movements
4. Improving trunk stabilization, balance and proprioception capabilities

DESCRIPTION

Coach stabilizes lower-extremities (legs).

1. Lie on top of the physio ball with the hips and trunk
2. Fold hands in front of the chest and extend legs; knees are in line with shoulders
3. Raise upper-body; hold 1 second; extend chest and retract the scapular throughout the movement; keep looking **forward** during movements

BREATH IN & OUT

- IN: When descending
- OUT: During When raising

TARGETED MUSCLES

1. Low Back Extensors
2. Hip Extensors
3. Trunk Stabilizers

DEGREE OF DIFFICULTY

- 1

REQUIRED EQUIPMENT

- 1 Physio Ball (55cm-65cm)

RELEVANCE

- General strengthening of the lower back to prevent injuries
- Low back injuries/discomfort can occur due to repetitive jumping activities (e.g. ballistic/plyometric activities); prone limb raises can alleviate low back pain thereby allowing for proper training volume and intensity

ID: 684

6.85 PRONE PHYSIO BALL TRUNK EXTENSION

SUMMARY

The Prone Physioball Trunk Extension is a low back exercise, which focuses on improving hip extensor strength, trunk extensor strength and trunk stabilization, balance and proprioception capabilities.

PURPOSE

1. Improving hip-extensor strength
2. Improving trunk extensor strength
3. Improving skill and strength foundation for complex movements
4. Improving trunk stabilization, balance and proprioception capabilities

DESCRIPTION

Coach stabilizes lower-extremities (legs).

1. Lie on top of the physio ball with the hips and trunk
2. Fold hands in front of the chest and extend legs; knees are in line with shoulders
3. Raise upper-body; hold 1 second; extend chest and retract the scapular throughout the movement; keep looking **forward** during movements

PRE-REQUISITE EXERCISES

1. Assisted Prone Physio Ball Trunk Extension

BREATH IN & OUT

- IN: When descending
- OUT: During When raising

DEGREE OF DIFFICULTY

- 2

REQUIRED EQUIPMENT

- 1 Physio Ball (55cm-65cm)

RELEVANCE

- General strengthening of the lower back to prevent injuries
- Low back injuries/discomfort can occur due to repetitive jumping activities (e.g. ballistic/plyometric activities); prone limb raises can alleviate low back pain thereby allowing for proper training volume and intensity

TARGETED MUSCLES

1. Low Back Extensors
2. Hip Extensors
3. Trunk Stabilizers

ID: 685

6.86 ASSISTED PRONE PB UNILATERAL LEG EXTENSION

SUMMARY

The Assisted Prone Physio Ball Unilateral Leg Extension is a low back exercise, which focuses on improving hip extensor strength, trunk extensor strength and trunk stabilization, balance and proprioception capabilities.

PURPOSE

1. Improving hip-extensor strength
2. Improving trunk extensor strength
3. Improving skill and strength foundation for complex movements
4. Improving trunk stabilization, balance and proprioception capabilities

DESCRIPTION

Coach stabilizes physio ball.

1. Lie on top of the physio ball with the hips and trunk
2. Place elbows and hands on the ground; knees are in line with shoulders
3. One leg maintains ground contact; raise other leg to neutral spine position; hold 1 second; extend chest and retract the scapular throughout the movement; keep looking **forward** during movements

DEGREE OF DIFFICULTY

- 1

REQUIRED EQUIPMENT

- 1 Physio Ball (55cm-65cm)

RELEVANCE

- General strengthening of the lower back to prevent injuries
- Low back injuries/discomfort can occur due to repetitive jumping activities (e.g. ballistic/plyometric activities); prone limb raises can alleviate low back pain thereby allowing for proper training volume and intensity

PRE-REQUISITE EXERCISES

1. 4-Point Prone Physio Ball Alternating Unilateral Limb Raises

BREATH IN & OUT

- IN: When descending
- OUT: When raising

TARGETED MUSCLES

1. Low Back Extensors
2. Hip Extensors
3. Trunk Stabilizers

ID: 686

6.87 PRONE PHYSIO BALL UNILATERAL LEG EXTENSION

SUMMARY

The Prone Physio Ball Unilateral Leg Extension is a low back exercise, which focuses on improving hip extensor strength, trunk extensor strength and trunk stabilization, balance and proprioception capabilities.

PURPOSE

1. Improving hip-extensor strength
2. Improving trunk extensor strength
3. Improving skill and strength foundation for complex movements
4. Improving trunk stabilization, balance and proprioception capabilities

DESCRIPTION

1. Lie on top of the physio ball with the hips and trunk
2. Place elbows and hands on the ground; knees are in line with shoulders
3. One leg maintains ground contact; raise other leg to neutral spine position; hold 1 second; extend chest and retract the scapular throughout the movement; keep looking **forward** during movements

PRE-REQUISITE EXERCISES

1. Assisted Prone Physio Ball Uni-Lateral Leg Extension

BREATH IN & OUT

- IN: When descending
- OUT: During When raising

DEGREE OF DIFFICULTY

- 2

REQUIRED EQUIPMENT

- 1 Physio Ball (55cm-65cm)

RELEVANCE

- General strengthening of the lower back to prevent injuries
- Low back injuries/discomfort can occur due to repetitive jumping activities (e.g. ballistic/plyometric activities); prone limb raises can alleviate low back pain thereby allowing for proper training volume and intensity

TARGETED MUSCLES

1. Low Back Extensors
2. Hip Extensors
3. Trunk Stabilizers

ID: 687

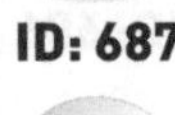

6.88 PRONE PB ALTERNATING LEG EXTENSION

SUMMARY

The Prone Physio Ball Alternating Leg Extension is a low back exercise, which focuses on improving hip extensor strength, trunk extensor strength and trunk stabilization, balance and proprioception capabilities.

PURPOSE

1. Improving hip-extensor strength
2. Improving trunk extensor strength
3. Improving skill and strength foundation for complex movements
4. Improving trunk stabilization, balance and proprioception capabilities

DESCRIPTION

1. Lie on top of the physio ball with the hips and trunk
2. Place elbows and hands on the ground; knees are in line with shoulders
3. Raise legs in alternating fashion to neutral spine position; hold 1 second; extend chest and retract the scapular throughout the movement; keep looking **forward** during movements

PRE-REQUISITE EXERCISES

1. Prone Physio Ball Unilateral Leg Extension

BREATH IN & OUT

- IN: When descending
- OUT: During When raising

TARGETED MUSCLES

1. Low Back Extensors
2. Hip Extensors
3. Trunk Stabilizers

DEGREE OF DIFFICULTY

- 3

REQUIRED EQUIPMENT

- 1 Physio Ball (55cm-65cm)

RELEVANCE

- General strengthening of the lower back to prevent injuries
- Low back injuries/discomfort can occur due to repetitive jumping activities (e.g. ballistic/plyometric activities); prone limb raises can alleviate low back pain thereby allowing for proper training volume and intensity

ID: 688

6.89 PRONE PHYSIO BALL BILATERAL LEG EXTENSION

SUMMARY

The Prone Physio Ball Bilateral Leg Extension is a low back exercise, which focuses on improving hip extensor strength, trunk extensor strength and trunk stabilization, balance and proprioception capabilities.

PURPOSE

1. Improving hip-extensor strength
2. Improving trunk extensor strength
3. Improving trunk stabilization, balance and proprioception capabilities

DESCRIPTION

1. Lie on top of the physio ball with the hips and trunk
2. Place elbows and hands on the ground; knees are in line with shoulders
3. Raise legs simultaneously to neutral spine position; hold 1 second; extend chest and retract the scapular throughout the movement; keep looking **forward** during movements

PRE-REQUISITE EXERCISES

1. Prone Physio Ball Alternating Leg Extension

BREATH IN & OUT

- IN: When descending
- OUT: When raising

TARGETED MUSCLES

1. Low Back Extensors
2. Hip Extensors
3. Trunk Stabilizers

DEGREE OF DIFFICULTY

- 4

REQUIRED EQUIPMENT

- 1 Physio Ball (55cm-65cm)

RELEVANCE

- General strengthening of the lower back to prevent injuries
- Low back injuries/discomfort can occur due to repetitive jumping activities (e.g. ballistic/plyometric activities); prone limb raises can alleviate low back pain thereby allowing for proper training volume and intensity

ID: 689

6.90 ASSISTED SEATED PB HIP FLEXION TO EXTENSION

SUMMARY

The Assisted Seated Physio Ball Hip Flexion to Extension is a low back exercise, which focuses on improving hip extensor strength, trunk extensor strength and trunk stabilization, balance and proprioception capabilities.

PURPOSE

1. Improving hip-extensor strength
2. Improving trunk extensor strength
3. Improving skill and strength foundation for complex movements
4. Improving trunk stabilization, balance and proprioception capabilities

DESCRIPTION

Coach kneels on the ground and assists movement via elastic band.

1. Sit upright on top of the physio ball; hips and legs flexed at 90°; knees are outside shoulders
2. Hold elastic band in both hands; arms remain straight during movement
3. Coach pulls elastic band towards himself/herself; athlete simultaneously flexes hips and maintains neutral spine position during movement; hold 1 second; extend chest and retract the scapular throughout the movement; keep looking **forward** during movements
4. Athlete extends hips thereby returning to seated position; coach provides resistance

BREATH IN & OUT

- IN: When descending
- OUT: When raising

DEGREE OF DIFFICULTY

- 1

REQUIRED EQUIPMENT

- 1 Physio Ball (55cm-65cm)
- Elastic Band

RELEVANCE

- General strengthening of the lower back to prevent injuries
- Low back injuries/discomfort can occur due to repetitive jumping activities (e.g. ballistic/plyometric activities); prone limb raises can alleviate low back pain thereby allowing for proper training volume and intensity

TARGETED MUSCLES

1. Low Back Extensors
2. Hip Extensors
3. Trunk Stabilizers

ID: 690

6.91 STANDING HIP FLEXION TO EXTENSION

SUMMARY

The Standing Hip Flexion to Extension is a low back exercise, which focuses on improving hip extensor strength, trunk extensor strength and trunk stabilization, balance and proprioception capabilities.

PURPOSE

1. Improving hip-extensor strength
2. Improving trunk extensor strength
3. Improving skill and strength foundation for complex movements
4. Improving trunk stabilization, balance and proprioception capabilities

DESCRIPTION

1. Stand upright in athletic stance; knees are slightly flexed and under the shoulders
2. Cross arms in front of the chest
3. Knees remain in position but will flex automatically; flex hips and lower upper-body towards the ground and hold 1 second; extend chest and retract the scapular throughout the movement; keep looking **forward** during movements
4. Return back to starting position

PRE-REQUISITE EXERCISES

1. Assisted Seated Physio Ball Hip Flexion to Extension

BREATH IN & OUT

- IN: When descending
- OUT: When raising

DEGREE OF DIFFICULTY

- 2

RELEVANCE

- General strengthening of the lower back to prevent injuries
- Low back injuries/discomfort can occur due to repetitive jumping activities (e.g. ballistic/plyometric activities); prone limb raises can alleviate low back pain thereby allowing for proper training volume and intensity

TARGETED MUSCLES

1. Low Back Extensors
2. Hip Extensors
3. Trunk Stabilizers

ID: 691

6.92 STANDING MB HIP FLEXION TO EXTENSION

SUMMARY

The Standing MB Hip Flexion to Extension is a low back exercise, which focuses on improving hip extensor strength, trunk extensor strength and trunk stabilization, balance and proprioception capabilities.

PURPOSE

1. Improving hip-extensor strength
2. Improving trunk extensor strength
3. Improving skill and strength foundation for complex movements
4. Improving trunk stabilization, balance and proprioception capabilities

DESCRIPTION

1. Stand upright in athletic stance; knees are slightly flexed and under the shoulders
2. Hold medicine ball close to the chest
3. Knees remain in position but will flex automatically; flex hips and lower upper-body towards the ground and hold 1 second; extend chest and retract the scapular throughout the movement; keep looking **forward** during movements
4. Return back to starting position

PRE-REQUISITE EXERCISES

1. Standing Hip Flexion to Extension

BREATH IN & OUT

- IN: When descending
- OUT: When raising

DEGREE OF DIFFICULTY

- 3

REQUIRED EQUIPMENT

- 1 Medicine Ball (4lb-10lb)

RELEVANCE

- General strengthening of the lower back to prevent injuries
- Low back injuries/discomfort can occur due to repetitive jumping activities (e.g. ballistic/plyometric activities); prone limb raises can alleviate low back pain thereby allowing for proper training volume and intensity

TARGETED MUSCLES

1. Low Back Extensors
2. Hip Extensors
3. Trunk Stabilizers

ID: 692

6.93 STANDING PB HIP FLEXION TO EXTENSION

SUMMARY

The Standing Physio Ball Hip Flexion to Extension is a low back exercise, which focuses on improving hip extensor strength, trunk extensor strength and trunk stabilization, balance and proprioception capabilities.

PURPOSE

1. Improving hip-extensor strength
2. Improving trunk extensor strength
3. Improving skill and strength foundation for complex movements
4. Improving trunk stabilization, balance and proprioception capabilities

DESCRIPTION

1. Stand upright in athletic stance; knees are slightly flexed and under the shoulders
2. Extend arms forward and hold physio ball
3. Knees remain in position but will flex automatically; flex hips and lower upper-body towards the ground and hold 1 second; extend chest and retract the scapular throughout the movement; keep looking **forward** during movements
4. Return back to starting position

PRE-REQUISITE EXERCISES

1. Standing Medicine Ball Hip Flexion to Extension

BREATH IN & OUT

- IN: When descending
- OUT: When raising

TARGETED MUSCLES

1. Low Back Extensors
2. Hip Extensors
3. Trunk Stabilizers

REQUIRED EQUIPMENT

- 1 Physio Ball (55cm-65cm)

DEGREE OF DIFFICULTY

- 4

RELEVANCE

- General strengthening of the lower back to prevent injuries
- Low back injuries/discomfort can occur due to repetitive jumping activities (e.g. ballistic/plyometric activities); prone limb raises can alleviate low back pain thereby allowing for proper training volume and intensity

ID: 693

FUNCTIONAL TRAINING

Before the athlete engages in any of the exercises presented in this section, ensure that he/she can perform the pre-requisite exercises properly. Generally, pre-requisite exercises should be included during the high resistance preparation phase of the training program because the exercises are used to prepare the athlete for the next training phases. For example, the forward lunge & press is a pre-requisite for the split-jerk exercises. The advantage of the functional strength for performance exercises is that the resistance decreases while the challenge increases.

Therefore, exercises can also be used during competition if the volume is adjusted properly; volume depends on a few factors such as time off between matches and available energy reserves.

Function-based training should be used in conjunction with strength training because that will enhance overall strength of the athlete, which then will ultimately enhance power training; to only commit to function-based training is inefficient because the resistance is too light for athletic development.

RATIONALE FOR FUNCTIONAL TRAINING

The purpose of functional training is to optimize synchronicity of the neuromuscular system in order to improve movement patterns and sport-specific activities; it is not used for muscle training! While moving on the court the neuromuscular system works in sync from head to toe, which means that every muscle receives signals from the nervous system and has some responsibility for the movement, either as a prime mover, secondary (assistive) mover, stabilizer, or gliding neutralizer (for summary see "Under the Microscope: Responsibility of Muscle during Movement"). As the athlete progresses through each of the movement phases, there will be some muscles that will have to deal with undesirable actions because of movement or kinetic chain inefficiencies (e.g. poor running economy). Remember that a state of equilibrium/stability can only be attained when the center of mass is within the base of support. During movement the center of gravity is constantly shifting while trying to maintain ideal position with respect to the base of support. Oftentimes stabilizers try to maintain the center of gravity in this "ideal" position but each time the center of gravity deviates/shifts, the stabilizers have to work twice as hard to return it back to ideal position. Functional training aims to improve center of gravity management during movements.

IDENTIFYING RESPONSIBILITIES OF THE MUSCLES

As previously mentioned, muscles work together to allow body movements and they play different roles during those movements, depending on their responsibilities. Here is a quick review.

The **prime mover** (also called agonist) is the main muscle responsible for the joint movement. It produces the majority of the force so that an object (mass) can travel a certain distance. For example, during bench pressing the pectoralis major (chest) is the prime mover; it generates the most amount of force during the pressing phase.

The **secondary**, or **assistive**, **mover** will assist the prime mover by also producing some force to allow for the movement to occur. Back to the bench press example: the triceps is needed to assist the pectoralis (prime mover) because without the triceps (and shoulder) the arm cannot be extended.

Guiding neutralizers help to prevent or at least neutralize undesirable movement or action while stabilizers stabilize the joint at the place where the movement or action occurs.

Undesirable movement/action occurs when movement economy is poor or inefficient. This can result in injury and must be avoided. For example, the shoulder joint handles significant forces during tennis. When taking a closer look at the shoulder (glenohumeral joint), one can observe that the head of the humerus connects with the shallow glenoid fossa. Whenever the head of the humerus moves out of position (translates) inside the joint capsule, there is a significant risk of injury when the joint is under significant force (pressure); minimal translation decreases movement efficiency while larger translation causes injury!

UNDER THE MICROSCOPE

RESPONSIBILITY OF MUSCLES DURING MOVEMENT

- Prime Mover: Major Force Producer
- Secondary Mover: Minor Force Producer
- Guiding Neutralizer: Prevents undesirable action
- Stabilizer: Stabilization of the Joint where action occurs

EXAMPLE: ALTERNATING CABLE PRESS

Prime Mover

- Pectoralis Major

Secondary Movers

- Triceps
- Anterior Deltoid
- Obliques

Guiding Neutralizers

- Hip flexors
- Rectus Abdominis
- Hip Adductor

Stabilizers

- Transverse Abdominis

For example, if the athlete shows poor movement economy during bench press exercises, his/her ability to press heavy resistance will be less and the risk of injury will increase as well.

TRAINING PROGRAM CONSIDERATIONS

The athlete needs to learn how to do push-ups, bench presses, Russian twists, forward lunges, reverse lunges, deadlifts (Romanian; RDL) and single-leg squats during the skill acquisition and hypertrophy phase for motor patterning purposes. Once the athlete is proficient, the exercises presented here can be used during the integration phases. As a general rule of thumb: When the athlete increases the speed of the exercise, the resistance/weight decreases.

6.94 PUSH-UP TO SINGLE LIMB RAISE (I)

SUMMARY

The Push-Up to Single Limb Raise (I) is a functional training exercise, which focuses on improving the synergy of the neuro-muscular system, trunk stability, body control & coordination as well as improving skill & balance foundation for complex movements.

PURPOSE

1. Improving synergy of neuro-muscular system
2. Improving trunk stability for more efficient transfer of energy
3. Improving body control & coordination by enhancing stabilizers and gliding neutralizers
4. Improving skill and balance foundation for complex movements

DESCRIPTION

1. Face down and position arms and feet shoulder-width apart; place palm of the hand underneath the shoulders; extend elbows; hips are in neutral pelvic position; look forward
2. Place tennis ball on the ground at sternum (nipple) level
3. Flex elbows and lower upper-body until chest touches the tennis ball; maintain neutral pelvic position; look forward
4. Extend elbows and elevate upper-body away from the ground; maintain neutral pelvic position; look forward
5. Raise **one limb** off the ground
6. Hold position for 1 second before returning to starting position
7. Repeat but raise another limb

KEY FACTORS

- Focus on perfect movement mechanics and range of motion
- Maintain neutral pelvis position
- Maintain neutral spine position
- Maintain stability

PRE-REQUISITE EXERCISES

1. Push-Up

DEGREE OF DIFFICULTY

- 1

RELEVANCE

- Results in more powerful stroke production on the court
- Results in overall change of direction (agility) improvements on the court

COMMON ERRORS

- Pelvic repositioning occurs (e.g. hip flexion)
- Flexion of thoracic spine (rounded back) during motion
- Athlete loses balance

BREATH IN & OUT

- IN: Before Elbow Flexion
- OUT: During Limb Raise

REQUIRED EQUIPMENT

- 1 Tennis Ball

ID: 694

6.95 PUSH-UP TO CONTRALATERAL LIMB RAISE (II)

SUMMARY

The Push-Up to Contralateral Limb Raise (II) is a functional training exercise, which focuses on improving the synergy of the neuro-muscular system, trunk stability, body control & coordination as well as improving skill & balance foundation for complex movements.

PURPOSE

1. Improving synergy of neuro-muscular system
2. Improving trunk stability for more efficient transfer of energy
3. Improving body control & coordination by enhancing stabilizers and gliding neutralizers
4. Improving skill and balance foundation for complex movements

DESCRIPTION

1. Face down and position arms and feet shoulder-width apart; place palm of the hand underneath the shoulders; extend elbows; hips are in neutral pelvic position; look forward
2. Place tennis ball on the ground at sternum (nipple) level
3. Flex elbows and lower upper-body until chest touches the tennis ball; maintain neutral pelvic position; look forward
4. Extend elbows and elevate upper-body away from the ground; maintain neutral pelvic position; look forward
5. Raise **contralateral limbs** off the ground; maintain neutral pelvic position; look forward
6. Hold position for 1 second before returning to starting position
7. Repeat and raise the opposite limbs

PRE-REQUISITE EXERCISES

1. Push-Up to Single Limb Raise

COMMON ERRORS

- Pelvic repositioning occurs (e.g. hip flexion)
- Flexion of thoracic spine (rounded back) during motion
- Athlete loses balance

BREATH IN & OUT

- IN: Before Elbow Flexion
- OUT: During Limb Raise

DEGREE OF DIFFICULTY

- 2

REQUIRED EQUIPMENT

- 1 Tennis Ball

RELEVANCE

- Results in more powerful stroke production on the court
- Results in overall change of direction (agility) improvements on the court

KEY FACTORS

- Focus on perfect movement mechanics and range of motion
- Maintain neutral pelvis position
- Maintain neutral spine position
- Maintain stability

ID: 695

6.96 PUSH-UP TO CL LIMB RAISE TO FLEXION (III)

SUMMARY

The Push-Up to Contralateral Limb Raise to Flexion (III) is a functional training exercise, which focuses on improving the synergy of the neuro-muscular system, trunk stability, body control & coordination as well as improving skill & balance foundation for complex movements.

PURPOSE

1. Improving synergy of neuro-muscular system
2. Improving trunk stability for more efficient transfer of energy
3. Improving body control & coordination by enhancing stabilizers and gliding neutralizers
4. Improving skill and balance foundation for complex movements

DESCRIPTION

1. Face down and position arms and feet shoulder-width apart; place palm of the hand underneath the shoulders; extend elbows; hips are in neutral pelvic position; look forward
2. Place tennis ball on the ground at sternum (nipple) level
3. Flex elbows and lower upper-body until chest touches the tennis ball; maintain neutral pelvic position; look forward
4. Extend elbows and elevate upper-body away from the ground; maintain neutral pelvic position; look forward
5. Raise **contralateral limbs** off the ground; maintain neutral pelvic position; look forward
6. Hold position for 1 second
7. Bring contralateral limbs **close together** (knee & elbow) and hold position for 1 second
8. Repeat and raise the opposite limbs

PRE-REQUISITE EXERCISES

1. Push-Up to Contralateral Limb Raise II

COMMON ERRORS

- Pelvic repositioning occurs (e.g. hip flexion)
- Flexion of thoracic spine (rounded back) during motion
- Athlete loses balance

BREATH IN & OUT

- IN: Before Elbow Flexion
- OUT: During Limb Flexion

DEGREE OF DIFFICULTY

- 3

REQUIRED EQUIPMENT

- 1 Tennis Ball

RELEVANCE

- Results in more powerful stroke production on the court
- Results in overall change of direction (agility) improvements on the court

KEY FACTORS

- Focus on perfect movement mechanics and range of motion
- Maintain neutral pelvis position
- Maintain neutral spine position
- Maintain stability

ID: 696

6.97 PUSH-UP TO IPSIL. ARM & LEG CEILING RAISE (IV)

SUMMARY

The Push-Up to Ipsilateral Arm & Ceiling Reach is a functional training exercise, which focuses on improving the synergy of the neuro-muscular system, trunk stability, body control & coordination as well as improving skill & balance foundation for complex movements.

PURPOSE

1. Improving synergy of neuro-muscular system
2. Improving trunk stability for more efficient transfer of energy
3. Improving body control & coordination by enhancing stabilizers and gliding neutralizers
4. Improving skill and balance foundation for complex movements

DESCRIPTION

1. Face down and position arms and feet shoulder-width apart; place palm of the hand underneath the shoulders; extend elbows; hips are in neutral pelvic position; look forward
2. Place tennis ball on the ground at sternum (nipple) level
3. Flex elbows and lower upper-body until chest touches the tennis ball; maintain neutral pelvic position; look forward
4. Extend elbows and elevate upper-body away from the ground; maintain neutral pelvic position; look forward
5. Raise **ipsilateral limbs** off the ground and reach towards the ceiling; maintain neutral pelvic position; look forward
6. Hold position for 1 second before returning to starting position
7. Repeat and raise the opposite limbs

DEGREE OF DIFFICULTY

- 4

REQUIRED EQUIPMENT

- 1 Tennis Ball

RELEVANCE

- Results in more powerful stroke production on the court
- Results in overall change of direction (agility) improvements on the court

KEY FACTORS

- Focus on perfect movement mechanics and range of motion
- Maintain neutral head position
- Maintain stability

PRE-REQUISITE EXERCISES

1. Push-Up to Contralateral Limb Raise to Flexion III

COMMON ERRORS

- Weight distribution occurs at the toes
- Flexion of thoracic spine (rounded back) during motion
- Athlete loses balance

BREATH IN & OUT

- IN: Before Elbow Flexion
- OUT: During Ceiling Reach

ID: 697

6.98 PHYSIO BALL LEG CURL (I)

SUMMARY

The Physio Ball Leg Curl (I) I is a functional training exercise, which focuses on improving the synergy of the neuro-muscular system, trunk stability, body control & coordination as well as improving skill & balance foundation for complex movements.

PURPOSE

1. Improving synergy of neuro-muscular system
2. Improving trunk stability for more efficient transfer of energy
3. Improving body control & coordination by enhancing stabilizers and gliding neutralizers
4. Improving skill and balance foundation for complex movements

DESCRIPTION

1. Place floor mat on the ground and lie down in supine position (face up); place physio ball in front of the feet
2. Extend knees and keep legs close together; move heels centered and on top of the physio ball; move arms out wide until shoulder is 90° horizontally abducted;
3. Elevate the trunk (hips) up high to neutral pelvic position (higher center of gravity)
4. Keep extending the hips and flex the knees
5. Keep trunk (hips) in elevated position and extend knees
6. Repeat

BREATH IN & OUT

- IN: Before Knee Flexion
- OUT: During Knee Flexion

COMMON ERRORS

- Trunk elevation is low (low center of gravity)
- Head comes off the ground during motion
- Athlete loses balance

REQUIRED EQUIPMENT

- 1 Floor Matt
- 1 Physio Ball

RELEVANCE

- Results in more powerful stroke production on the court
- Results in overall change of direction (agility) improvements on the court

KEY FACTORS

- Focus on perfect movement mechanics and range of motion
- Maintain neutral pelvis position during movement
- Maintain stability

DEGREE OF DIFFICULTY

- 1

ID: 698

6.99 PHYSIO BALL LEG CURL (II): SHOULDER FLEXION

SUMMARY

The Physio Ball Leg Curl (II) I is a functional training exercise, which focuses on improving the synergy of the neuro-muscular system, trunk stability, body control & coordination as well as improving skill & balance foundation for complex movements.

PURPOSE

1. Improving synergy of neuro-muscular system
2. Improving trunk stability for more efficient transfer of energy
3. Improving body control & coordination by enhancing stabilizers and gliding neutralizers
4. Improving skill and balance foundation for complex movements

DESCRIPTION

1. Place floor mat on the ground and lie down in supine position (face up); place physio ball in front of the feet
2. Extend knees and keep legs close together; move heels centered and on top of the physio ball; extend arms and move them behind the head holding straight bar;
3. Elevate the trunk (hips) up high to neutral pelvic position (higher center of gravity)
4. Keep hips extended, flex knees and **simultaneously** flex the shoulders thereby bringing the bar towards the knees
5. Keep trunk (hips) in elevated position, extend knees and **simultaneously** extend shoulders until bar is behind the head
6. Repeat

PRE-REQUISITE EXERCISES

1. Physio Ball Leg Curl I

BREATH IN & OUT

- IN: Before Shoulder Flexion
- OUT: During Shoulder Flexion

REQUIRED EQUIPMENT

- 1 Floor Mat
- 1 Physio Ball
- 1 Straight Bar (8lb-45lb; or equivalent object)

DEGREE OF DIFFICULTY

- 2

RELEVANCE

- Results in more powerful stroke production on the court
- Results in overall change of direction (agility) improvements on the court

KEY FACTORS

- Focus on perfect movement mechanics and range of motion
- Maintain neutral pelvis position during movement
- Maintain stability

COMMON ERRORS

- Trunk elevation is low (low center of gravity)
- Head comes off the ground during motion
- Athlete loses balance

ID: 699

6.100 PHYSIO BALL LEG CURL (III): SINGLE LEG

SUMMARY

The Physio Ball Leg Curl (III) is a functional training exercise, which focuses on improving the synergy of the neuro-muscular system, trunk stability, body control & coordination as well as improving skill & balance foundation for complex movements.

PURPOSE

1. Improving synergy of neuro-muscular system
2. Improving trunk stability for more efficient transfer of energy
3. Improving body control & coordination by enhancing stabilizers and gliding neutralizers
4. Improving skill and balance foundation for complex movements

DESCRIPTION

1. Place floor mat on the ground and lie down in supine position (face up); place physio ball in front of the feet
2. Extend knees and keep legs close together; move the heel of the right foot centered and on top of the physio ball; left leg remains parallel but off the physio ball; move arms out wide until shoulder is 90° horizontally abducted;
3. Elevate the trunk (hips) up high to neutral pelvic position (higher center of gravity)
4. Keep hips extended and flex the right knee while the left knee remains extended and off the physio ball
5. Keep trunk (hips) in elevated position and extend right knee
6. Repeat and switch legs

PRE-REQUISITE EXERCISES

1. Physio Ball Leg Curl II: Shoulder Flexion

COMMON ERRORS

- Trunk elevation is low (low center of gravity)
- Head comes off the ground during motion
- Athlete loses balance

DEGREE OF DIFFICULTY

- 3

BREATH IN & OUT

- IN: Before Knee Flexion
- OUT: During Knee Flexion

REQUIRED EQUIPMENT

- 1 Floor Mat
- 1 Physio Ball

RELEVANCE

- Results in more powerful stroke production on the court
- Results in overall change of direction (agility) improvements on the court

KEY FACTORS

- Focus on perfect movement mechanics and range of motion
- Maintain neutral pelvis position during movement
- Maintain stability

ID: 6100

6.101 PB LEG CURL (IV): SINGLE LEG W. CL HIP FLEXION

SUMMARY

The Physio Ball Leg Curl (IV) is a functional training exercise, which focuses on improving the synergy of the neuro-muscular system, trunk stability, body control & coordination as well as improving skill & balance foundation for complex movements.

PURPOSE

1. Improving synergy of neuro-muscular system
2. Improving trunk stability for more efficient transfer of energy
3. Improving body control & coordination by enhancing stabilizers and gliding neutralizers
4. Improving skill and balance foundation for complex movements

DESCRIPTION

1. Lie down on the ground in supine position (face up); place physio ball in front of the feet
2. Extend knees and keep legs close together; move the heel of the **right** foot centered and on top of the physio ball; **left** leg remains parallel but off the ground **next** to the physio ball; move arms out wide until shoulder is 45° horizontally abducted
3. Elevate the trunk (hips) up high to neutral pelvic position (higher center of gravity)
4. Keep hips extended, flex the **right** knee while **simultaneously** kicking the **left** leg (extended) upwards thereby flexing the left hip
5. Keep trunk (hips) in elevated position, extend right knee, and extend left hip back to starting position
6. Repeat and switch legs

PRE-REQUISITE EXERCISES

1. Physio Ball Leg Curl III: Single Leg

BREATH IN & OUT

- IN: Before Knee Flexion
- OUT: During Knee Flexion

DEGREE OF DIFFICULTY

- 4

REQUIRED EQUIPMENT

- 1 Physio Ball

RELEVANCE

- Results in more powerful stroke production on the court
- Results in overall change of direction (agility) improvements on the court

KEY FACTORS

- Focus on perfect movement mechanics and range of motion
- Maintain neutral pelvis position during movement
- Keep extended leg off the ground
- Maintain stability

COMMON ERRORS

- Trunk elevation is low (low center of gravity)
- Head comes off the ground during motion
- Extended leg touches the ground during hip extension or knee flexion occurs
- Athlete loses balance

ID: 6101

6.102 PB LEG CURL (V): SL W. CL HIP FLEXION - NO ARMS

SUMMARY

The Physio Ball Leg Curl (V) is a functional training exercise, which focuses on improving the synergy of the neuro-muscular system, trunk stability and body control & coordination.

PURPOSE

1. Improving synergy of neuro-muscular system
2. Improving trunk stability for more efficient transfer of energy
3. Improving body control & coordination by enhancing stabilizers and gliding neutralizers

DESCRIPTION

1. Lie down on the ground in supine position (face up); place physio ball in front of the feet
2. Extend knees and keep legs close together; move the heel of the **right** foot centered and on top of the physio ball; **left** leg remains parallel but off the ground **next** to the physio ball; **cross arms on top of the chest**
3. Elevate the trunk (hips) up high to neutral pelvic position (higher center of gravity)
4. Keep hips extended, flex the **right** knee while **simultaneously** kicking the **left** leg (extended) upwards thereby flexing the left hip
5. Keep trunk (hips) in elevated position, extend right knee, and extend left hip back to starting position
6. Repeat and switch legs

PRE-REQUISITE EXERCISES

1. Physio Ball Leg Curl IV: Single Leg with Contralateral Hip Flexion

BREATH IN & OUT

- IN: Before Knee Flexion
- OUT: During Knee Flexion

DEGREE OF DIFFICULTY

- 5

REQUIRED EQUIPMENT

- 1 Physio Ball

RELEVANCE

- Results in more powerful stroke production on the court
- Results in overall change of direction (agility) improvements on the court

KEY FACTORS

- Focus on perfect movement mechanics and range of motion
- Maintain neutral pelvis position during movement
- Keep extended leg off the ground
- Maintain stability

COMMON ERRORS

- Trunk elevation is low (low center of gravity)
- Head comes off the ground during motion
- Extended Leg touches the ground during hip extension or knee flexion occurs
- Athlete loses balance

ID: 6102

6.103 PHYSIO BALL SUPINE DB PRESS (I)

SUMMARY

The Physio Ball Supine DB Press (I) is a functional training exercise, which focuses on improving the synergy of the neuro-muscular system, trunk stability, body control & coordination as well as improving skill & balance foundation for complex movements.

Note: If you have to spot because the athlete cannot maintain balance, **spot the ball**, not the athlete!

PURPOSE

1. Improving synergy of neuro-muscular system
2. Improving trunk stability for more efficient transfer of energy
3. Improving body control & coordination by enhancing stabilizers and gliding neutralizers
4. Improving skill and balance foundation for complex movements

DESCRIPTION

1. Place physio ball on the ground and lie on top of the physio ball in supine position (face up); **cervical spine**, **scapulae**, and **head** maintain contact with the physio ball
2. Legs are shoulder-width apart; knees flexed at 90°
3. Hold dumbbells (DB) in each hand
4. Elevate the trunk (hips) up high to neutral pelvic position (higher center of gravity)
5. Horizontally abduct the shoulders to 90° and flex elbows to 90°
6. Extend elbows and press DB upward until DB are **above the head**; maintain trunk in neutral pelvic position during movement
7. Flex elbows and return to starting position; keep trunk in neutral pelvic position during movement
8. Repeat

PRE-REQUISITE EXERCISES

1. Bench Press

BREATH IN & OUT

- IN: Before Shoulder Adduction
- OUT: During Shoulder Adduction

DEGREE OF DIFFICULTY

- 1

REQUIRED EQUIPMENT

- 1 Physio Ball (small; 55cm or less)
- 2 Dumbbells (DB)

RELEVANCE

- Results in more powerful stroke production on the court
- Results in overall change of direction (agility) improvements on the court

KEY FACTORS

- Focus on perfect movement mechanics and range of motion
- Maintain neutral pelvis position during movement
- Press DB over the head
- Maintain stability

COMMON ERRORS

- Trunk elevation is low (low center of gravity)
- Head comes off the physio ball during motion
- Athlete loses balance

ID: 6103

6.104 PHYSIO BALL SUPINE DB PRESS (II): SINGLE ARM

SUMMARY

The Physio Ball Supine DB Press (II) is a functional training exercise, which focuses on improving the synergy of the neuro-muscular system, trunk stability, body control & coordination as well as improving skill & balance foundation for complex movements.

Note: If you have to spot because the athlete cannot maintain balance, **spot the ball**, not the athlete!

PURPOSE

1. Improving synergy of neuro-muscular system
2. Improving trunk stability for more efficient transfer of energy
3. Improving body control & coordination by enhancing stabilizers and gliding neutralizers
4. Improving skill and balance foundation for complex movements

DESCRIPTION

1. Place physio ball on the ground and lie on top of the physio ball in supine position (face up); **cervical spine**, **scapulae**, and **head** maintain contact with the physio ball
2. Legs are shoulder-width apart; knees flexed at 90°
3. Hold dumbbell (DB) in one hand; other hand remains close to the trunk (or also horizontally abducted shoulder = easier)
4. Elevate the trunk (hips) up high to neutral pelvic position (higher center of gravity)
5. Horizontally abduct the shoulder to 90° and flex elbow to 90°
6. Extend elbow and press DB upward until DB is **above the head**; keep trunk in neutral pelvic position during movement
7. Flex elbow and return to starting position; keep trunk in neutral pelvic position during movement
8. Repeat and switch arms

PRE-REQUISITE EXERCISES

1. Physio Ball Supine DB Press I

BREATH IN & OUT

- IN: Before Shoulder Adduction (Pressing)
- OUT: During Shoulder Adduction (Pressing)

COMMON ERRORS

- Trunk elevation is low (low center of gravity)
- Head comes off the physio ball during motion
- Athlete loses balance

KEY FACTORS

- Focus on perfect movement mechanics and range of motion
- Maintain neutral pelvis position during movement
- Press DB over the head
- Maintain stability

REQUIRED EQUIPMENT

- 1 Physio Ball (small; 55cm or less)
- 2 Dumbbells (DB)

RELEVANCE

- Results in more powerful stroke production on the court
- Results in overall change of direction (agility) improvements on the court

DEGREE OF DIFFICULTY

- 2

ID: 6104

6.105 PB SUPINE DB PRESS TO REACH (III): SINGLE ARM

SUMMARY

The Physio Ball Supine DB Press to Reach (III) is a functional training exercise, which focuses on improving the synergy of the neuro-muscular system, trunk stability, body control & coordination as well as improving skill & balance foundation for complex movements.

Note: If you have to spot because the athlete cannot maintain balance, **spot the ball**, not the athlete!

PURPOSE

1. Improving synergy of neuro-muscular system
2. Improving trunk stability for more efficient transfer of energy
3. Improving body control & coordination by enhancing stabilizers and gliding neutralizers
4. Improving skill and balance foundation for complex movements

DESCRIPTION

1. Place physio ball on the ground and lie on top of the physio ball in supine position (face up); **cervical spine**, **scapulae**, and **head** maintain contact with the physio ball
2. Legs are shoulder-width apart; knees flexed at 90°
3. Hold dumbbell (DB) in one hand; other hand remains close to the trunk (or horizontally abducted shoulder = easier)
4. Elevate the trunk (hips) up high to neutral pelvic position (higher center of gravity)
5. Horizontally abduct the shoulder to 90° and flex elbow to 90°
6. Extend elbow, press DB upward, **reach high** until DB is **above the head** and **internally rotate the trunk**; upper-body is perpendicular to the ball (or as far as possible); **only shoulder maintains contact with the ball**
7. Flex elbow, externally rotate trunk and return to starting position;
8. Repeat and switch arms

PRE-REQUISITE EXERCISES

1. Physio Ball Supine DB Press II

BREATH IN & OUT

- IN: Before Shoulder Adduction (Pressing)
- OUT: During Shoulder Adduction (Pressing)

DEGREE OF DIFFICULTY

- 3

REQUIRED EQUIPMENT

- 1 Physio Ball (small; 55cm or less)
- 1 Dumbbell (DB)

RELEVANCE

- Results in more powerful stroke production on the court
- Results in overall change of direction (agility) improvements on the court

KEY FACTORS

- Focus on perfect movement mechanics and range of motion (trunk rotation)
- Rotate trunk and reach until upper-body is perpendicular to the ball
- Press DB over the head
- Maintain stability

COMMON ERRORS

- Trunk elevation is low (low center of gravity)
- Athlete loses balance

ID: 6105

6.106 PB SUPINE DB PRESS TO REACH (IV): ALTERNATING

SUMMARY

The Physio Ball Supine DB Press to Reach (IV) is a functional training exercise, which focuses on improving the synergy of the neuro-muscular system, trunk stability as well as body control & coordination.

Note: If you have to spot because the athlete cannot maintain balance, **spot the ball**, not the athlete!

PURPOSE

1. Improving synergy of neuro-muscular system
2. Improving trunk stability for more efficient transfer of energy
3. Improving body control & coordination by enhancing stabilizers and gliding neutralizers

DESCRIPTION

1. Place physio ball on the ground and lie on top of the physio ball in supine position (face up); **cervical spine**, **scapulae**, and **head** maintain contact with the physio ball
2. Legs are shoulder-width apart; knees flexed at 90°
3. Hold dumbbells (DB) in each hand;
4. Elevate the trunk (hips) up high to neutral pelvic position (higher center of gravity)
5. Horizontally abduct the shoulders to 90° and flex elbows to 90°
6. Extend elbow, press DB upward, **reach high** until DB is **above the head**, and **internally rotate the trunk**; upper-body is perpendicular to the ball (or as far as possible); **only shoulder maintains contact with the ball**
7. Flex elbow, externally rotate trunk, and return to starting position
8. Extend other elbow, press DB upward, **reach high** until DB is **above the head** and **internally rotate the trunk**; upper-body is perpendicular to the ball (or as far as possible); **only shoulder maintains contact with the ball**
9. Flex elbow, externally rotate trunk and return to starting position
10. Repeat

PRE-REQUISITE EXERCISES

1. Physio Ball Supine DB Press to Reach III

REQUIRED EQUIPMENT

- 1 Physio Ball (small; 55cm or less)
- 2 Dumbbells (DB)

RELEVANCE

- Results in more powerful stroke production on the court
- Results in overall change of direction (agility) improvements on the court

KEY FACTORS

- Focus on perfect movement mechanics and range of motion (trunk rotation)
- Rotate trunk and reach until upper-body is perpendicular to the ball
- Press DB over the head
- Maintain stability

COMMON ERRORS

- Trunk elevation is low (low center of gravity)
- Athlete loses balance

DEGREE OF DIFFICULTY

- 4

BREATH IN & OUT

- IN: Before Shoulder Adduction
- OUT: During Shoulder Adduction

ID: 6106

6.107 PHYSIO BALL PUSH-UP TO SINGLE LIMB RAISE I

SUMMARY

The Physio Ball Push-Up to Single Limb Raise I is a functional training exercise, which focuses on improving the synergy of the neuro-muscular system, trunk stability, body control & coordination as well as improving skill & balance foundation for complex movements

Note: If you have to spot because the athlete cannot maintain balance, **spot the ball**, not the athlete!

PURPOSE

1. Improving synergy of neuro-muscular system
2. Improving trunk stability for more efficient transfer of energy
3. Improving body control & coordination by enhancing stabilizers and gliding neutralizers
4. Improving skill and balance foundation for complex movements

DESCRIPTION

1. Face down and position arms and feet shoulder-width apart; place palm of the hand underneath the shoulders; extend elbows; hips are in neutral pelvic position; feet are on top of the physio ball; look forward
2. Place tennis ball on the ground at sternum (nipple) level
3. Flex elbows and lower upper-body until chest touches the tennis ball; maintain neutral pelvic position; look forward
4. Extend elbows and elevate upper-body away from the ground; maintain neutral pelvic position; look forward
5. Raise **one limb** off the ground
6. Hold position for 1 second before returning to starting position
7. Repeat but **raise another** limb

PRE-REQUISITE EXERCISES

1. Push-Up to Single Limb Raise I

BREATH IN & OUT

- IN: Before Elbow Flexion
- OUT: During Limb Raise

DEGREE OF DIFFICULTY

- 1

REQUIRED EQUIPMENT

- 1 Tennis Ball
- 1 Physio Ball

RELEVANCE

- Results in more powerful stroke production on the court
- Results in overall change of direction (agility) improvements on the court

KEY FACTORS

- Focus on perfect movement mechanics and range of motion
- Maintain neutral pelvis position
- Maintain neutral spine position
- Maintain stability

COMMON ERRORS

- Pelvic repositioning occurs (e.g. hip flexion)
- Flexion of thoracic spine (rounded back) during motion
- Athlete loses balance

ID: 6107

6.108 PB PUSH-UP TO CONTRALATERAL LIMB RAISE II

SUMMARY

The Physio Ball Push-Up to Contralateral Limb Raise II is a functional training exercise, which focuses on improving the synergy of the neuro-muscular system, trunk stability, body control & coordination as well as improving skill & balance foundation for complex movements.

Note: If you have to spot because the athlete cannot maintain balance, **spot the ball**, not the athlete!

PURPOSE

1. Improving synergy of neuro-muscular system
2. Improving trunk stability for more efficient transfer of energy
3. Improving body control & coordination by enhancing stabilizers and gliding neutralizers
4. Improving skill and balance foundation for complex movements

DESCRIPTION

1. Face down and position arms and feet shoulder-width apart; place palm of the hand underneath the shoulders; extend elbows; hips are in neutral pelvic position; feet are on top of the physio ball (PB); look forward
2. Place tennis ball on the ground at sternum (nipple) level
3. Flex elbows and lower upper-body until chest touches the tennis ball; maintain neutral pelvic position; look forward
4. Extend elbows and elevate upper-body away from the ground; maintain neutral pelvic position; look forward
5. Raise **contralateral limbs** off the ground & PB; maintain neutral pelvic position; look forward
6. Hold position for 1 second before returning to starting position
7. Repeat and raise the opposite limbs

PRE-REQUISITE EXERCISES

1. Push-Up to Single Limb Raise II

BREATH IN & OUT

- IN: Before Elbow Flexion
- OUT: During Limb Raise

DEGREE OF DIFFICULTY

- 2

REQUIRED EQUIPMENT

- 1 Tennis Ball
- 1 Physio Ball (PB)

RELEVANCE

- Results in more powerful stroke production on the court
- Results in overall change of direction (agility) improvements on the court

KEY FACTORS

- Focus on perfect movement mechanics and range of motion
- Maintain neutral pelvis position
- Maintain neutral spine position
- Maintain stability

COMMON ERRORS

- Pelvic repositioning occurs (e.g. hip flexion)
- Flexion of thoracic spine (rounded back) during motion
- Athlete loses balance

ID: 6108

6.109 PB PUSH-UP TO CL LIMB RAISE TO FLEXION (III)

SUMMARY

The Physio Ball Push-Up to Contralateral Limb Raise to Flexion (III) is a functional training exercise, which focuses on improving the synergy of the neuro-muscular system, trunk stability, body control & coordination as well as improving skill & balance foundation for complex movements.

Note: If you have to spot because the athlete cannot maintain balance, **spot the ball**, not the athlete!

PURPOSE

1. Improving synergy of neuro-muscular system
2. Improving trunk stability for more efficient transfer of energy
3. Improving body control & coordination by enhancing stabilizers and gliding neutralizers
4. Improving skill and balance foundation for complex movements

DESCRIPTION

1. Face down and position arms and feet shoulder-width apart; place palm of the hand underneath the shoulders; extend elbows; hips are in neutral pelvic position; feet are on top of the physio ball (PB); look forward
2. Place tennis ball on the ground at sternum (nipple) level
3. Flex elbows and lower upper-body until chest touches the tennis ball; maintain neutral pelvic position; look forward
4. Extend elbows and elevate upper-body away from the ground; maintain neutral pelvic position; look forward
5. Raise **contralateral** limbs off the ground & MB: maintain neutral pelvic position; look forward
6. Hold position for 1 second
7. Bring contralateral limbs **close together** (knee & elbow) and hold position for 1 second
8. Repeat and raise the opposite limbs

PRE-REQUISITE EXERCISES

1. 4 Point Prone Contralateral Limb Raises
2. Push-Up to Contralateral Limb Raise to Flexion (III)

BREATH IN & OUT

- IN: Before Elbow Flexion
- OUT: During Limb Raise

ID: 6109

REQUIRED EQUIPMENT

- 1 Tennis Ball
- 1 Physio Ball (PB)

DEGREE OF DIFFICULTY

- 3

RELEVANCE

- Results in more powerful stroke production on the court
- Results in overall change of direction (agility) improvements on the court

KEY FACTORS

- Focus on perfect movement mechanics and range of motion
- Maintain neutral pelvis position
- Maintain neutral spine position
- Maintain stability

COMMON ERRORS

- Pelvic repositioning occurs (e.g. hip flexion)
- Flexion of thoracic spine (rounded back) during motion
- Athlete loses balance

6.110 PB PUSH-UP TO IPSIL. ARM & LEG CEILING RAISE (IV)

SUMMARY

The Physio Ball Push-Up to Ipsilateral Arm & Ceiling Reach (IV) is a functional training exercise, which focuses on improving the synergy of the neuro-muscular system, trunk stability, body control & coordination as well as improving skill & balance foundation for complex movements.

PURPOSE

1. Improving synergy of neuro-muscular system
2. Improving trunk stability for more efficient transfer of energy
3. Improving body control & coordination by enhancing stabilizers and gliding neutralizers
4. Improving skill and balance foundation for complex movements

DESCRIPTION

1. Face down and position arms and feet shoulder-width apart; place palm of the hand underneath the shoulders; extend elbows; hips are in neutral pelvic position; feet are on top of the physio ball (PB); look forward
2. Place tennis ball on the ground at sternum (nipple) level
3. Flex elbows and lower upper-body until chest touches the tennis ball; maintain neutral pelvic position; look forward
4. Extend elbows and elevate upper-body away from the ground; maintain neutral pelvic position; look forward
5. Raise **ipsilateral limbs** off the ground and reach towards the ceiling; maintain neutral pelvic position; look forward
6. Hold position for 1 second before returning to starting position
7. Repeat and raise the opposite limbs

PRE-REQUISITE EXERCISES

1. Push-Up to Ipsilateral Arm & Leg Raise IV

BREATH IN & OUT

- IN: Before Elbow Flexion
- OUT: During Limb Raise

DEGREE OF DIFFICULTY

- 4

REQUIRED EQUIPMENT

- 1 Tennis Ball
- 1 Physio Ball (PB)

RELEVANCE

- Results in more powerful stroke production on the court
- Results in overall change of direction (agility) improvements on the court

KEY FACTORS

- Focus on perfect movement mechanics and range of motion
- Maintain neutral head position
- Maintain stability

COMMON ERRORS

- Weight distribution occurs at the toes
- Flexion of thoracic spine (rounded back) during motion
- Athlete loses balance

ID: 6110

6.111 PHYSIO BALL PUSH-UP TO TRUNK ROTATION

SUMMARY

The Physio Ball Push-Up to Trunk Rotation is a functional training exercise, which focuses on improving the synergy of the neuro-muscular system, trunk stability, body control & coordination as well as improving flexibility of trunk rotators.

Note: Monitor the speed of the trunk rotation and increase the speed accordingly as the athlete becomes more proficient with the exercise dynamics.

PURPOSE

1. Improving synergy of neuro-muscular system
2. Improving trunk stability for more efficient transfer of energy
3. Improving body control & coordination by enhancing stabilizers and gliding neutralizers
4. Improving flexibility of trunk rotators

DESCRIPTION

1. Face down, position arms outside the shoulders and feet close together; extend elbows; hips are in neutral pelvic position; thighs are on top of the physio ball; look forward
2. Flex knees to 90°
3. Rotate trunk, move knees to the left side, and flex elbows to lower upper-body close to the ground; look forward
4. Extend elbows and elevate upper-body away from the ground; look forward
5. Rotate trunk, move knees to the right side, and flex elbows to lower upper-body close to the ground; look forward
6. Extend elbows and elevate upper-body away from the ground; look forward

PRE-REQUISITE EXERCISES

1. Physio Ball Supine DB Press to Reach III

BREATH IN & OUT

- IN: Before Elbow Flexion
- OUT: During Trunk Rotation

REQUIRED EQUIPMENT

- 1 Physio Ball

DEGREE OF DIFFICULTY

- 5

RELEVANCE

- Results in more powerful stroke production on the court
- Results in overall change of direction (agility) improvements on the court

KEY FACTORS

- Focus on perfect movement mechanics and range of motion
- Maintain neutral head position
- Maintain stability

COMMON ERRORS

- Weight distribution occurs at the toes
- Flexion of thoracic spine (rounded back) during motion
- Athlete loses balance

ID: 6111

6.112 PHYSIO BALL TRUNK ROTATION III

SUMMARY

The Physio Ball Trunk Rotation III is a functional training exercise, which focuses on improving the synergy of the neuro-muscular system, trunk stability, body control & coordination as well as improving flexibility of trunk rotators.

Note: Monitor the speed of the trunk rotation and increase the speed accordingly as the athlete becomes more proficient with the exercise dynamics.

PURPOSE

1. Improving synergy of neuro-muscular system
2. Improving trunk stability for more efficient transfer of energy
3. Improving body control & coordination by enhancing stabilizers and gliding neutralizers
4. Improving flexibility of trunk rotators

DESCRIPTION

1. Face down, position arms outside the shoulders and feet close together; extend elbows; hips are in neutral pelvic position; thighs are on top of the physio ball; look forward
2. Flex knees to 90°
3. Rotate trunk and move knees to the left side; look forward
4. Return to starting position
5. Repeat and switch sides

BREATH IN & OUT

- IN: Before Trunk Rotation
- OUT: During Trunk Rotation

COMMON ERRORS

- Flexion of thoracic spine (rounded back) during motion
- Athlete loses balance

REQUIRED EQUIPMENT

- 1 Physio Ball

DEGREE OF DIFFICULTY

- 3

RELEVANCE

- Results in more powerful stroke production on the court
- Results in overall change of direction (agility) improvements on the court

KEY FACTORS

- Focus on perfect movement mechanics and range of motion
- Maintain neutral head position
- Maintain stability

ID: 6112

6.113 PHYSIO BALL TRUNK ROTATION IV: ALTERNATING

SUMMARY

The Physio Ball Trunk Rotation IV is a functional training exercise, which focuses on improving the synergy of the neuro-muscular system, trunk stability, body control & coordination as well as improving flexibility of trunk rotators.

Note: Monitor the speed of the trunk rotation and increase the speed accordingly as the athlete becomes more proficient with the exercise dynamics.

PURPOSE

1. Improving synergy of neuro-muscular system
2. Improving trunk stability for more efficient transfer of energy
3. Improving body control & coordination by enhancing stabilizers and gliding neutralizers
4. Improving flexibility of trunk rotators

DESCRIPTION

1. Face down, position arms outside the shoulders and feet close together; extend elbows; hips are in neutral pelvic position; thighs are on top of the physio ball; look forward
2. Flex knees to 90°
3. Rotate trunk and move knees to the left side; look forward
4. Return to starting position but don't stop
5. Rotate trunk and move knees to the right side; look forward

PRE-REQUISITE EXERCISES

1. Physio Ball Trunk Rotation III

BREATH IN & OUT

- IN: Before Trunk Rotation
- OUT: During Trunk Rotation

REQUIRED EQUIPMENT

- 1 Physio Ball

DEGREE OF DIFFICULTY

- 4

RELEVANCE

- Results in more powerful stroke production on the court
- Results in overall change of direction (agility) improvements on the court

KEY FACTORS

- Focus on perfect movement mechanics and range of motion
- Maintain neutral head position
- Maintain stability

COMMON ERRORS

- Flexion of thoracic spine (rounded back) during motion
- Athlete loses balance

ID: 6113

6.114 PHYSIO BALL ROLL-OUT

SUMMARY

The Physio Ball Roll-Out is a functional training exercise, which focuses on improving the synergy of the neuro-muscular system, trunk stability, body control & coordination as well as improving skill & balance foundation for complex movements.

Note: If athlete cannot maintain neutral pelvic position during movement increase the starting position distance between body and physio ball; move hands **on top** of the physio ball.

PURPOSE

1. Improving synergy of neuro-muscular system
2. Improving trunk stability for more efficient transfer of energy
3. Improving body control & coordination by enhancing stabilizers and gliding neutralizers
4. Improving skill and balance foundation for complex movements

DESCRIPTION

1. Place floor mat on the ground and physio ball in front of the mat
2. Kneel on the knees; position knees and feet shoulder-width apart; place palms of the hand in front of the physio ball; extend elbows; hips are in neutral pelvic position; look forward
3. Maintain neutral pelvic, spine and head position, **extend shoulders** and roll physio ball forward to elbow level
4. Hold position for 1 second
5. **Flex shoulders** and roll physio ball back to starting position; maintain neutral pelvic position

PRE-REQUISITE EXERCISES

1. Russian Lean

BREATH IN & OUT

- IN: Before Shoulder Extension
- OUT: During Shoulder Flexion

DEGREE OF DIFFICULTY

- 4

REQUIRED EQUIPMENT

- 1 Floor Mat
- 1 Physio Ball

RELEVANCE

- Results in more powerful stroke production on the court
- Results in overall change of direction (agility) improvements on the court

KEY FACTORS

- Focus on perfect movement mechanics and range of motion
- Maintain neutral pelvic, spine and head position
- Maintain stability

COMMON ERRORS

- Hip Flexion occurs during movement
- Elbow flexion occurs during movement
- Flexion of thoracic spine (rounded back) during motion
- Athlete loses balance

ID: 6114

6.115 LUNGE TO MB DIAGONAL REACH (I)

SUMMARY

The Lunge to MB Diagonal Reach (I) is a functional training exercise, which focuses on improving the synergy of the neuro-muscular system, trunk stability, body control & coordination as well as improving skill & balance foundation for complex movements.

PURPOSE

1. Improving synergy of neuro-muscular system
2. Improving trunk stability for more efficient transfer of energy
3. Improving body control & coordination by enhancing stabilizers and gliding neutralizers
4. Improving skill and balance foundation for complex movements

DESCRIPTION

1. Take an athletic stance; stand straight, feet are shoulder-width apart; knees slightly flexed
2. Hold medicine ball naturally in both hands; push chest forward
3. Step into a **lunge** with the **left foot** and externally rotate trunk to the **right**; lean forward with upper-body, elbows are extended; spine and head are in neutral position; MB is lateral to the **right** hip
4. Internally rotate trunk, extend the shoulders, thereby raising MB diagonally across the chest and over the **left** shoulder; MB is to the left of the head
5. Repeat and switch sides

PRE-REQUISITE EXERCISES

1. Forward/Reverse Lunge

BREATH IN & OUT

- IN: Before Lunge Position
- OUT: During Diagonal MB Reach

DEGREE OF DIFFICULTY

- 1

REQUIRED EQUIPMENT

- 1 Medicine Ball (2lb – 14lb)

RELEVANCE

- Results in more powerful stroke production on the court
- Results in overall change of direction (agility) improvements on the court

KEY FACTORS

- Focus on perfect movement mechanics and range of motion
- Maintain neutral spine and head position
- Maintain stability

COMMON ERRORS

- Elbow flexion occurs during movement
- Flexion of thoracic spine (rounded back) during motion
- Athlete loses balance

ID: 6115

6.116 REVERSE LUNGE TO MB DIAGONAL REACH (II)

SUMMARY

The Reverse Lunge to MB Diagonal Reach (II) is a functional training exercise, which focuses on improving the synergy of the neuro-muscular system, trunk stability, body control & coordination as well as improving skill & balance foundation for complex movements.

PURPOSE

1. Improving synergy of neuro-muscular system
2. Improving trunk stability for more efficient transfer of energy
3. Improving body control & coordination by enhancing stabilizers and gliding neutralizers
4. Improving skill and balance foundation for complex movements

DESCRIPTION

1. Take an athletic stance; stand straight, feet are shoulder-width apart; knees slightly flexed
2. Hold medicine ball naturally in both hands; push chest forward
3. Step into a **reverse lunge** with the **right** foot and externally rotate trunk to the **right**; lean forward with upper-body, elbows are extended; spine and head are in neutral position; MB is lateral to the right hip
4. Push through the heel of the front foot, returning to starting position, while **simultaneously** internally rotating trunk, extending the shoulders, thereby raising MB diagonally across the chest and over the left shoulder; MB is to the **left** of the head
5. Repeat and switch sides

PRE-REQUISITE EXERCISES

1. Lunge to MB Diagonal Reach I

BREATH IN & OUT

- IN: Before Lunge Position
- OUT: During Diagonal MB Reach

DEGREE OF DIFFICULTY

- 2

REQUIRED EQUIPMENT

- 1 Medicine Ball (2lb – 14lb)

RELEVANCE

- Results in more powerful stroke production on the court
- Results in overall change of direction (agility) improvements on the court

KEY FACTORS

- Focus on perfect movement mechanics and range of motion
- Maintain neutral spine and head position
- Maintain stability

COMMON ERRORS

- Elbow flexion occurs during movement
- Flexion of thoracic spine (rounded back) during motion
- Athlete loses balance

ID: 6116

6.117 REV. LUNGE TO MB DIAG. REACH (III): ALTERNATING

SUMMARY

The Reverse Lunge to MB Diagonal Reach (III) is a functional training exercise, which focuses on improving the synergy of the neuro-muscular system, trunk stability, body control & coordination as well as improving skill & balance foundation for complex movements.

PURPOSE

1. Improving synergy of neuro-muscular system
2. Improving trunk stability for more efficient transfer of energy
3. Improving body control & coordination by enhancing stabilizers and gliding neutralizers
4. Improving skill and balance foundation for complex movements

DESCRIPTION

1. Take an athletic stance; stand straight, feet are shoulder-width apart; knees slightly flexed
2. Hold medicine ball naturally in both hands; push chest forward
3. Step into a **reverse lunge** with the **right** foot and externally rotate trunk to the **right**; lean forward with upper-body, elbows are extended; spine and head are in neutral position; MB is lateral to the right hip
4. Push through the heel of the front foot, returning to starting position, while **simultaneously** internally rotating trunk, extending the shoulders, thereby raising MB diagonally across the chest and over the **left** shoulder; MB is to the **left** of the head
5. Step into a **reverse lunge** with the **left** foot and externally rotate trunk to the **left**; lean forward with upper-body, elbows are extended; spine and head are in neutral position; MB is lateral to the right hip
6. Push through the heel of the front foot, returning to starting position, while **simultaneously** internally rotating trunk, extending the shoulders, and thereby raising MB diagonal across the chest and over the **right** shoulder; MB is to the **right** of the head
7. Repeat and switch sides

DEGREE OF DIFFICULTY

- 3

PRE-REQUISITE EXERCISES

1. Reverse Lunge to MB Diagonal Reach II

COMMON ERRORS

- Elbow flexion occurs during movement
- Flexion of thoracic spine (rounded back) during motion
- Athlete loses balance

ID: 6117

REQUIRED EQUIPMENT

- 1 Medicine Ball (2lb – 14lb)

RELEVANCE

- Results in more powerful stroke production on the court
- Results in overall change of direction (agility) improvements on the court

KEY FACTORS

- Focus on perfect movement mechanics and range of motion
- Maintain neutral spine and head position
- Maintain stability

BREATH IN & OUT

- IN: Before Lunge Position
- OUT: During Diagonal MB Reach

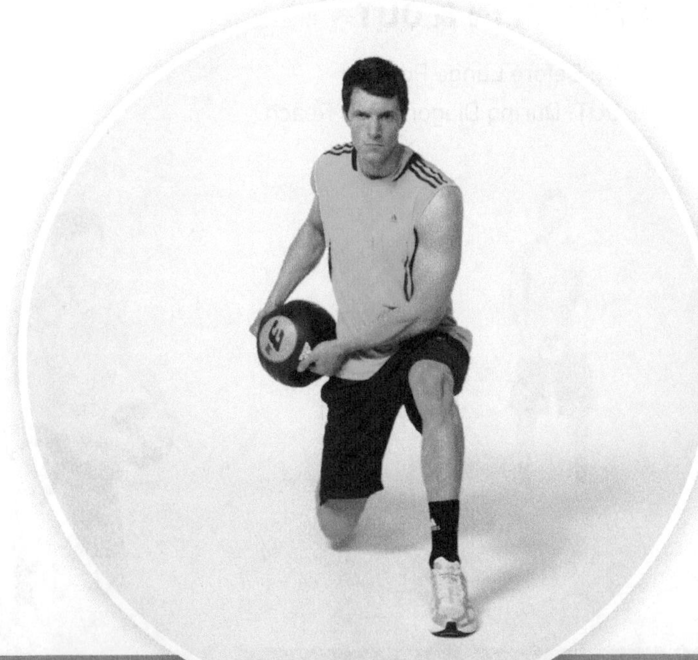

6.118 REV. LUNGE TO MB DIAG. REACH (IV): ALTERN. JUMP

SUMMARY

The Reverse Lunge to MB Diagonal Reach (IV) is a functional training exercise, which focuses on improving the synergy of the neuro-muscular system, trunk stability, body control & coordination as well as improving skill & balance foundation for complex movements.

PURPOSE

1. Improving synergy of neuro-muscular system
2. Improving trunk stability for more efficient transfer of energy
3. Improving body control & coordination by enhancing stabilizers and gliding neutralizers
4. Improving skill and balance foundation for complex movements

DESCRIPTION

1. Take an athletic stance; stand straight, feet are shoulder-width apart; knees slightly flexed
2. Hold medicine ball naturally in both hands; push chest forward
3. Step into a **reverse lunge** with the **right** foot and externally rotate trunk to the **right**; lean forward with upper-body, elbows are extended; spine and head are in neutral position; MB is lateral to the right hip
4. Push through the heel of the front foot, **jump vertical**, while **simultaneously** internally rotating trunk, **extending the shoulders**, and thereby raising MB diagonally across the chest and over the **left** shoulder; MB is to the **left** of the head
5. Land into a **reverse lunge** with the **left** foot and externally rotate trunk to the **left**; lean forward with upper-body, elbows are extended; spine and head are in neutral position; MB is lateral to the right hip
6. Push through the heel of the front foot, **jump vertically**, while **simultaneously** internally rotating trunk, **extending the shoulders**, and thereby raising MB diagonally across the chest and over the **right** shoulder; MB is to the **right** of the head
7. Land into a **reverse lunge** with the **right** foot and externally rotate trunk to the **right**
8. Repeat and switch sides

REQUIRED EQUIPMENT

- 1 Medicine Ball (2lb – 14lb)

DEGREE OF DIFFICULTY

- 4

RELEVANCE

- Results in more powerful stroke production on the court
- Results in overall change of direction (agility) improvements on the court

KEY FACTORS

- Focus on perfect movement mechanics and range of motion
- Maintain neutral spine and head position
- Maintain stability

COMMON ERRORS

- Elbow flexion occurs during movement
- Flexion of thoracic spine (rounded back) during motion
- Athlete loses balance

PRE-REQUISITE EXERCISES

1. Reverse Lunge to MB Diagonal Reach III

BREATH IN & OUT

- IN: Before Lunge Position
- OUT: During During Diagonal MB Reach

ID: 6118

6.119 PRONE ABDUCTOR LATERAL KICKS

SUMMARY

The Prone Abductor Lateral Kicks is a functional training exercise, which focuses on improving the synergy of the neuro-muscular system, trunk stability, body control & coordination as well as improving skill & balance foundation for complex movements.

Note: If athlete cannot maintain neutral pelvic position during movement, decrease the speed of hip abduction/adduction. To increase degree of difficulty, increase the speed of hip abduction/adduction.

PURPOSE

1. Improving synergy of neuro-muscular system
2. Improving trunk stability for more efficient transfer of energy
3. Improving body control & coordination by enhancing stabilizers and gliding neutralizers
4. Improving skill and balance foundation for complex movements

DESCRIPTION

1. Face down and position arms shoulder-width apart and feet close together; place palm of the hand underneath the shoulders; extend elbows; hips are in neutral pelvic position; look forward
2. Abduct the left hip by kicking out the left leg as far as possible; maintain neutral pelvic position; look forward
3. Adduct the left hip, thereby swing left leg back into starting position; maintain neutral pelvic position; look forward
4. As soon as left foot touches the right foot, abduct the right hip by kicking out the right leg as far as possible; maintain neutral pelvic position; look forward
5. Adduct the right hip, thereby swing right leg back into starting position; maintain neutral pelvic position; look forward

DEGREE OF DIFFICULTY

- 1

RELEVANCE

- Results in more powerful stroke production on the court
- Results in overall change of direction (agility) improvements on the court

KEY FACTORS

- Focus on perfect movement mechanics and range of motion
- Maintain neutral pelvis position
- Maintain neutral spine position
- Maintain stability

ID: 6119

PRE-REQUISITE EXERCISES

1. 4 Point Prone Single Limb Raises I

COMMON ERRORS

- Pelvic repositioning occurs (e.g. hip flexion)
- Flexion of thoracic spine (rounded back) during motion
- Athlete loses balance

BREATH IN & OUT

- IN: Before Hip Abduction
- OUT: During Hip Abduction/Adduction

6.120 MB SAGITTAL REACH (I)

SUMMARY

The Medicine Ball (MB) Sagittal Reach (I) is a functional training exercise, which focuses on improving the synergy of the neuro-muscular system, trunk stability, body control & coordination as well as improving skill & balance foundation for complex movements.

PURPOSE

1. Improving synergy of neuro-muscular system
2. Improving trunk stability for more efficient transfer of energy
3. Improving hamstrings flexibility
4. Improving body control & coordination by enhancing stabilizers and gliding neutralizers
5. Improving skill and balance foundation for complex movements

DESCRIPTION

1. Take an athletic stance; stand straight, feet are shoulder-width apart; knees slightly flexed
2. Hold medicine ball naturally in both hands; push chest forward
3. Flex the hips to 90 ° (or as far as possible) and reach MB forward towards the ground; elbows are extended; spine and head remain in neutral position; look forward
4. Extend hips, simultaneously **extend the shoulders**, and reach MB over the head; elbows are extended; spine and head remain in neutral position; look forward

PRE-REQUISITE EXERCISES

1. Romanian Deadlift

BREATH IN & OUT

- IN: Before Hip Flexion
- OUT: During Hip Flexion

DEGREE OF DIFFICULTY

- 1

REQUIRED EQUIPMENT

- 1 Medicine Ball (2lb – 14lb)

RELEVANCE

- Results in more powerful stroke production on the court
- Results in overall change of direction (agility) improvements on the court

KEY FACTORS

- Focus on perfect movement mechanics and range of motion
- Maintain neutral spine and head position
- Maintain stability

COMMON ERRORS

- Elbow flexion occurs during movement
- Flexion of thoracic spine (rounded back) during motion
- Athlete loses balance

ID: 6120

6.121 MB SAGITTAL REACH (III): SINGLE LEG PIRIFORMIS

SUMMARY

The MB Sagittal Reach (III) is a functional training exercise, which focuses on improving the synergy of the neuro-muscular system, trunk stability, body control & coordination as well as improving skill & balance foundation for complex movements.

PURPOSE

1. Improving synergy of neuro-muscular system
2. Improving trunk stability for more efficient transfer of energy
3. Improving piriformis & hamstrings flexibility
4. Improving body control & coordination by enhancing stabilizers and gliding neutralizers
5. Improving skill and balance foundation for complex movements

DESCRIPTION

1. Take an athletic stance; stand straight, feet are shoulder-width apart; knees slightly flexed
2. Hold medicine ball naturally in both hands; push chest forward
3. Stand on the **right** leg, flex the **left** knee, externally rotate the **left** leg, and position the **left** ankle over the **right** knee
4. Flex the hips to 90 ° (or as far as possible) and reach MB forward towards the ground; elbows are extended; spine and head remain in neutral position; look forward
5. Extend hips, simultaneously extend the shoulders, and reach MB over the head; knee remains over toes; elbows are extended; spine and head remain in neutral position; look forward
6. Repeat and switch legs

PRE-REQUISITE EXERCISES

1. Single Leg Romanian Deadlift

BREATH IN & OUT

- IN: Before Hip Flexion
- OUT: During Hip Flexion

DEGREE OF DIFFICULTY

- 3

REQUIRED EQUIPMENT

- 1 Medicine Ball (2lb – 14lb)

RELEVANCE

- Results in more powerful stroke production on the court
- Results in overall change of direction (agility) improvements on the court

KEY FACTORS

- Focus on perfect movement mechanics and range of motion
- Knee remains over toes
- Maintain neutral spine and head position
- Maintain stability

COMMON ERRORS

- Knee protrudes past the toes during movement
- Elbow flexion occurs during movement
- Flexion of thoracic spine (rounded back) during motion
- Athlete loses balance

ID: 6121

6.122 CLEAN PULL (FLOOR)

SUMMARY

The Clean Pull is a compound exercise, which focuses on improving the synergy of the neuro-muscular system, explosiveness of hip extensor musculature while transitioning into shoulder shrug, body control & coordination, flexibility as well as improving skill & balance foundation for complex movements.

Note: If the athlete has flexibility issues, a stance wider than shoulder-width is warranted.

DESCRIPTION

1. Position barbell hip level on the rack; add resistance (plates) and attach safety clips
2. Use a pronated grip (palms facing down) and place hands shoulder-width apart on the bar
3. Lift barbell off the rack; take a few steps back and position barbell on the floor
4. Take an **athletic stance**; stand straight, **feet are shoulder-width apart**; knees slightly flexed; toes point slightly outward (10°-20°)
5. Assume deadlift starting position; **flex the transverse abdominis** (abs) before moving the barbell; maintain neutral spine – and head position; look position, look forward
6. **1st pulling phase**; extend hips and knees in controlled fashion; maintain neutral spine position (push chest out and scapulae [shoulder blades] together); maintain neutral head position (look forward)
7. Once barbell moves past the knees **2nd pulling phase** occurs; explosively extend the hips and simultaneously jump vertically (plantar flexion) while shrugging the shoulders; elbows remain extended throughout the movement

KEY FACTORS

- Focus on perfect movement mechanics and range of motion
- Use narrow grip (under shoulders)
- Flex transverse abdominis
- 1st pulling phase is slow: Initiate exercise via controlled knee/hip extension
- 2nd pulling phase is explosive
- Maintain neutral spine position
- Maintain neutral head position

ID: 6122

PURPOSE

1. Improving transfer of energy; synergy of neuro-muscular system
2. Improving explosiveness of **hip extensor** (hamstrings primary; glutes secondary) musculature while transitioning into shrugging the shoulders; applying force vertically
3. Improving body control & coordination by enhancing stabilizers and gliding neutralizers
4. Improving flexibility
5. Improving skill and balance foundation for complex movements

REQUIRED EQUIPMENT

- 1 Rack
- 1 Barbell
- Plates
- 2 Safety Clips

DEGREE OF DIFFICULTY

- 2

RELEVANCE

- Exercise is being used to learn efficient vertical application of force by improving synergy of lower extremities, trunk, and upper extremities; 1st & 2nd pulling phase
- Improves explosiveness of the hip extensors (hamstrings). It is an assistive lift since it has transfer in the lifting progression (e.g. 2nd pulling phase during power clean from the floor) and hence must be used in the Teaching/Hypertrophy Training Phase.
- Results in faster running speed and more powerful stroke production (e.g. serve) on the court due to more efficient energy transfer

COMMON ERRORS

- Wide grip and stance are used
- 1st pulling phase is done explosively from the floor
- Flexion of thoracic & lumbar spine occurs (rounded back) during motion
- Athlete loses balance

BREATH IN & OUT

- IN: Before Knee/Hip Extension
- OUT: During Knee/Hip Extension

PRE-REQUISITE EXERCISES

1. Deadlift
2. Jump Shrug

TARGETED MUSCLES

- Hamstrings
- Glutes
- Quadriceps
- Calves (gastrocnemius, soleus)
- Shoulder Girdle (Traps & Levator Scapula)

ACTION

- Hip Extension
- Hip Extension
- Knee Extension
- Plantar Flexion
- Scapula Elevation

PLANE OF MOTION

- Sagittal
- Sagittal
- Sagittal
- Sagittal
- Frontal

6.123 HIGH PULL (FLOOR)

SUMMARY

The High Pull is a compound exercise, which focuses on improving the synergy of the neuro-muscular system, explosiveness of hip extensor musculature while transitioning into shoulder shrug, body control & coordination, flexibility as well as improving skill & balance foundation for complex movements.

Note: If the athlete has flexibility issues, a stance wider than shoulder-width is warranted.

PURPOSE

1. Improving transfer of energy; synergy of neuro-muscular system
2. Improving explosiveness of **hip extensor** (hamstrings primary; glutes secondary) musculature while transitioning into shrugging the shoulders; applying force vertically
3. Improving body control & coordination by enhancing stabilizers and gliding neutralizers
4. Improving flexibility
5. Improving skill and balance foundation for complex movements

DESCRIPTION

1. Position barbell hip level on the rack; add resistance (plates) and attach safety clips
2. Use a pronated grip (palms facing down) and place hands shoulder-width apart on the bar
3. Lift barbell off the rack; take a few steps back and position barbell on the floor
4. Take an **athletic stance**; stand straight, **feet are shoulder-width apart**; knees slightly flexed; toes point slightly outward (10°-20°)
5. Assume deadlift starting position; **flex the transverse abdominis** (abs) before moving the barbell; maintain neutral spine and head position; look forward
6. **1st pulling phase**; extend hips and knees in controlled fashion; maintain neutral spine position (push chest out and scapulae [shoulder blades] together); maintain neutral head position (look forward)
7. Once barbell moves past the knees **2nd pulling phase** occurs; explosively extend the hips and simultaneously jump vertically (plantar flexion) while shrugging the shoulders and flexing the elbows while abducting shoulders to 90° (**upright row**); barbell remains close to the body and reaches sternum (~ nipple) level; elbows point sideways

PRE-REQUISITE EXERCISES

1. Deadlift
2. Jump Shrug
3. Upright Row

ID: 6123

REQUIRED EQUIPMENT

- 1 Rack
- 1 Barbell
- Plates
- 2 Safety Clips

DEGREE OF DIFFICULTY

- 2

RELEVANCE

- Exercise is being used to learn efficient vertical application of force by improving synergy of lower extremities, trunk, and upper extremities; 1st & 2nd pulling phase
- Improves explosiveness of the hip extensors (hamstrings). It is an assistive lift since it has transfer in the lifting progression (e.g. 2nd pulling phase during power clean from the floor) and hence must be used in the Teaching/Hypertrophy Training Phase.
- Results in faster running speed and more powerful stroke production (e.g. serve) on the court due to more efficient energy transfer

COMMON ERRORS

- Wide grip and stance are used
- 1st pulling phase is done explosively from the floor
- Flexion of thoracic - & lumbar spine occurs (rounded back) during motion
- Athlete loses balance

TARGETED MUSCLES	ACTION	PLANE OF MOTION
Hamstrings	Hip Extension	Sagittal
Glutes	Hip Extension	Sagittal
Quadriceps	Knee Extension	Sagittal
Calves (gastrocnemius, soleus)	Plantar Flexion	Sagittal
Shoulder Girdle (Traps & Levator Scapula)	Scapula Elevation	Frontal
Deltoid	Shoulder Abduction	Frontal

BREATH IN & OUT

- IN: Before Knee/Hip Extension
- OUT: During Knee/Hip Extension

KEY FACTORS

- Focus on perfect movement mechanics and range of motion
- Use narrow grip (under shoulders)
- Flex transverse abdominis
- 1st pulling phase is slow: Initiate exercise via controlled knee/hip extension
- 2nd pulling phase is explosive
- Bar remains close to the body during upright row exercise; elbows point sideways
- Maintain neutral spine position
- Maintain neutral head position

6.124 HIGH RECEIVE (FLOOR)

SUMMARY

The High Receive is a compound exercise, which focuses on improving the synergy of the neuromuscular system, learning the high receive, improving explosiveness of hip extensor musculature while transitioning into shoulder shrug, body control & coordination, flexibility as well as improving skill & balance foundation for complex movements.

Note: If the athlete has flexibility issues, a stance wider than shoulder-width is warranted.

PURPOSE

1. Improving transfer of energy; synergy of neuromuscular system
2. Learning the high receive
3. Improving explosiveness of **hip extensor** (hamstrings primary; glutes secondary) musculature while transitioning into shrugging the shoulders; applying force vertically
4. Improving body control & coordination by enhancing stabilizers and gliding neutralizers
5. Improving flexibility
6. Improving skill and balance foundation for complex movements

DESCRIPTION

1. Position barbell hip level on the rack; add resistance (plates) and attach safety clips
2. Use a pronated grip (palms facing down) and place hands shoulder-width apart on the bar
3. Lift barbell off the rack; take a few steps back and position barbell on the floor
4. Take an **athletic stance**; stand straight, **feet are shoulder-width apart**; knees slightly flexed; toes point slightly outward (10°-20°)
5. Assume deadlift starting position; **flex the transverse abdominis** (abs) before moving the barbell; maintain neutral spine and head position; look forward
6. **1st pulling phase**; extend hips and knees in controlled fashion; maintain neutral spine position (push chest out and scapulae [shoulder blades] together); maintain neutral head position (look forward)
7. Once barbell moves past the knees **2nd pulling phase** occurs; explosively extend the hips and simultaneously jump vertically (plantar flexion) while shrugging the shoulders and flexing the elbows while abducting shoulders to 90° (upright row); barbell remains close to the body and reaches sternum (~ nipple) level; elbows point sideways
8. When barbell is at sternum level, flip the wrists (wrist extension), internally rotate and flex elbows under the bar and receive the barbell on top of the chest; shoulder is flexed at 90°; elbows are flexed and pointing forward; maintain neutral spine and head position

ID: 6124

REQUIRED EQUIPMENT

- 1 Rack
- 1 Barbell
- Plates
- 2 Safety Clips

DEGREE OF DIFFICULTY

- 3

RELEVANCE

- Exercise is being used to learn efficient vertical application of force by improving synergy of lower extremities, trunk, and upper extremities; 1st & 2nd pulling phase
- Improves explosiveness of the hip extensors (hamstrings). It is an assistive lift since it has transfer in the lifting progression (e.g. 2nd pulling phase during power clean from the floor) and hence must be used in the Teaching/Hypertrophy Training Phase.
- Results in faster running speed and more powerful stroke production (e.g. serve) on the court due to more efficient energy transfer

PRE-REQUISITE EXERCISES

1. High Pull (Floor)

COMMON ERRORS

- Wide grip and stance are used
- 1st pulling phase is done explosively from the floor
- Bar remains more than 2.5 inches away from the body during upright row
- No shoulder abduction during high receive; elbows never point sideways
- Flexion of thoracic & lumbar spine occurs (rounded back) during motion
- Athlete loses balance

BREATH IN & OUT

- IN: Before Knee/Hip Extension
- OUT: During Knee/Hip Extension

KEY FACTORS

- Focus on perfect movement mechanics and range of motion
- Use narrow grip (under shoulders)
- Flex transverse abdominis
- 1st pulling phase is slow: Initiate exercise via controlled knee/hip extension
- 2nd pulling phase is explosive
- Bar remains close to the body during upright row exercise; elbows point sideways
- Elbows point forward after receive
- Maintain neutral spine position
- Maintain neutral head position

TARGETED MUSCLES	ACTION	PLANE OF MOTION
Hamstrings	Hip Extension	Sagittal
Glutes	Hip Extension	Sagittal
Quadriceps	Knee Extension	Sagittal
Calves (gastrocnemius, soleus)	Plantar Flexion	Sagittal
Shoulder Girdle (Traps & Levator Scapula)	Scapula Elevation	Frontal
Deltoid	Shoulder Abduction	Frontal

6.125 HANG CLEAN TO HIGH RECEIVE

SUMMARY

The Hang Clean to High Receive is a compound exercise, which focuses on improving the synergy of the neuro-muscular system, learning the high receive, improving explosiveness of hip extensor musculature while transitioning into shoulder shrug, body control & coordination, flexibility as well as improving skill & balance foundation for complex movements.

Note: If the athlete has flexibility issues, a stance wider than shoulder-width is warranted.

PURPOSE

1. Improving transfer of energy; synergy of neuro-muscular system
2. Learning the high receive
3. Improving explosiveness of **hip extensor** (hamstrings primary; glutes secondary) musculature while transitioning into the high receive; applying force vertically
4. Improving body control & coordination by enhancing stabilizers and gliding neutralizers
5. Improving flexibility
6. Improving skill and balance foundation for complex movements

DESCRIPTION

1. Position barbell hip level on the rack; add resistance (plates) and attach safety clips
2. Take an **athletic stance**; stand straight, **feet are shoulder-width apart**; knees slightly flexed; toes point forward
3. Use a pronated grip (palms facing down) and place hands shoulder-width apart on the bar
4. Lift barbell off the rack; take a few steps back
5. Take an athletic stance, keep elbows extended, slightly flex hips until **chest is over barbell**; generally barbell will be touching the legs within the lower 1/3 of the thigh (above knee); maintain neutral spine position (push chest out and scapulae [shoulder blades] together; maintain neutral head position (look forward)
6. Explosively extend the hips and simultaneously jump vertically (plantar flexion) while shrugging the shoulders and flexing the elbows while abducting shoulders to 90° (upright row); barbell remains close to the body and reaches sternum (~ nipple) level; elbows point sideways
7. When barbell is at sternum level flip the wrists (wrist extension), internally rotate and flex elbows under the bar and receive the barbell on top of the chest; shoulder is flexed at 90°; elbows are flexed and pointing forward; high receive occurs without knee and hip flexion; maintain neutral spine and head position

ID: 6125

DEGREE OF DIFFICULTY

- 2

REQUIRED EQUIPMENT

- 1 Rack
- 1 Barbell
- Plates
- 2 Safety Clips

RELEVANCE

- Exercise is being used to learn efficient vertical application of force, including the high receive, by improving synergy of lower extremities, trunk, and upper extremities; **2nd pulling phase only**
- Improves explosiveness of the hip extensors (hamstrings). It is an assistive lift since it has transfer in the lifting progression (e.g. 2nd pulling phase during power clean from the floor) and hence must be used in the Teaching/Hypertrophy Training Phase.
- Results in faster running speed and more powerful stroke production (e.g. serve) on the court due to more efficient energy transfer

PRE-REQUISITE EXERCISES

1. Jump Shrug (Hang)
2. Upright Row

COMMON ERRORS

- Wide grip and stance are used
- Bar remains more than 2.5 inches away from the body during high pull
- No shoulder abduction during high receive; elbows never point sideways
- Flexion of thoracic & lumbar spine occurs (rounded back) during motion
- Athlete loses balance

KEY FACTORS

- Focus on perfect movement mechanics and range of motion
- Use narrow grip (under shoulders)
- 2nd pulling phase is explosive
- Bar remains close to the body during upright row exercise; elbows point sideways
- Elbows point forward after receive
- Receive occurs in standing position
- Maintain neutral spine position
- Maintain neutral head position

BREATH IN & OUT

- IN: Before Knee/Hip Extension
- OUT: During Knee/Hip Extension

TARGETED MUSCLES

- Hamstrings
- Calves (gastrocnemius, soleus)
- Shoulder Girdle (Traps & Levator Scapula)
- Deltoid

ACTION

- Hip Extension
- Plantar Flexion
- Scapula Elevation
- Shoulder Abduction

PLANE OF MOTION

- Sagittal
- Sagittal
- Sagittal
- Frontal

6.126 HANG CLEAN TO POWER RECEIVE

SUMMARY

The Hang Clean to Power Receive is a compound exercise, which focuses on improving the synergy of the neuro-muscular system, learning the power receive (improving hip flexor speed), improving explosiveness of hip extensor musculature while transitioning into shoulder shrug, body control & coordination, flexibility as well as improving skill & balance foundation for complex movements.

Note: Athlete must have good **hamstring** flexibility to receive the barbell at 90° of knee flexion with a narrow stance.

PURPOSE

1. Improving transfer of energy; synergy of neuro-muscular system
2. Learning the power receive (90° knee flexion); improving **hip flexor** speed
3. Improving explosiveness of **hip extensor** (hamstrings primary; glutes secondary) musculature while transitioning into the power receive; applying force vertically
4. Improving body control & coordination by enhancing stabilizers and gliding neutralizers
5. Improving flexibility
6. Improving skill and balance foundation for complex movements

DESCRIPTION

1. Position barbell hip level on the rack; add resistance (plates) and attach safety clips
2. Take an **athletic stance**; stand straight, **feet are shoulder-width apart**; knees slightly flexed; toes point forward
3. Use a pronated grip (palms facing down) and place hands shoulder-width apart on the bar
4. Lift barbell off the rack; take a few steps back
5. Take an athletic stance, keep elbows extended, slightly flex hips until chest is over barbell; generally barbell will be touching the legs within the lower 1/3 of the thigh (above knee); maintain neutral spine position (push chest out and scapulae [shoulder blades] together; maintain neutral head position (look forward)
6. Explosively extend the hips and simultaneously jump vertically (plantar flexion) while shrugging the shoulders and flexing the elbows while abducting shoulders to 90° (upright row); barbell remains close to the body and reaches sternum (~ nipple) level; elbows point sideways
7. When barbell reaches neutral gravity (no movement) flip the wrists (wrist extension), internally rotate and flex elbows under the bar and rapidly flex the hips to receive the barbell on top of the chest; knees are flexed at 90° (or as low as possible); shoulder is flexed at 90°; elbows are flexed and pointing forward; power receive occurs with knee and hip flexion; maintain neutral spine and head position

DEGREE OF DIFFICULTY

- 3

REQUIRED EQUIPMENT

- 1 Rack
- 1 Barbell
- Plates
- 2 Safety Clips

RELEVANCE

- Exercise is being used to learn efficient vertical application of force, including the power receive, by improving synergy of lower extremities, trunk, and upper extremities; **2nd pulling phase only**
- Improves hip flexor speed and explosiveness of the hip extensors (hamstrings). It is an assistive lift since it has transfer in the lifting progression (e.g. 2nd receiving phase during power clean from the floor) and hence must be used in the Teaching/Hypertrophy Training Phase.
- Results in faster running speed and more powerful stroke production (e.g. serve) on the court due to more efficient energy transfer

PRE-REQUISITE EXERCISES

1. Front Squat
2. Hang Clean to High Receive

ID: 6126

COMMON ERRORS

- Wide grip and stance are used
- Bar remains more than 2.5 inches away from the body during high pull
- No shoulder abduction during high receive; elbows never point sideways
- Flexion of thoracic & lumbar spine occurs (rounded back) during motion
- Athlete loses balance

BREATH IN & OUT

- IN: Before Knee/Hip Extension
- OUT: During Knee/Hip Extension

KEY FACTORS

- Focus on perfect movement mechanics and range of motion
- Use narrow grip (under shoulders)
- 2nd pulling phase is explosive
- Bar remains close to the body during upright row exercise; elbows point sideways
- Rapidly flex knees to receive and decelerate the barbell
- Elbows point forward after receive
- Maintain neutral spine position
- Maintain neutral head position

TARGETED MUSCLES	ACTION	PLANE OF MOTION
Hamstrings	Hip Extension	Sagittal
Glutes	Hip Extension	Sagittal
Quadriceps	Knee Extension/Hip Flexion	Sagittal
Iliopsoas	Hip Flexion	Hip Flexion
Calves (gastrocnemius, soleus)	Plantar Flexion	Sagittal
Shoulder Girdle (Trapezius & Levator Scapula)	Scapula Elevation	Frontal
Deltoid	Shoulder Abduction	Frontal

6.127 SINGLE ARM SNATCH

SUMMARY

The Single Arm Snatch is a compound exercise, which focuses on improving the synergy of the neuro-muscular system, learning the snatch receive (improving hip flexor speed), improving explosiveness of hip extensor musculature while transitioning into shoulder shrug, improving body control & coordination, flexibility as well as improving skill & balance foundation for complex movements.

Note: Athlete must have good **hamstring** flexibility to receive the dumbbell at 90° of knee flexion with a narrow stance.

PURPOSE

1. Improving transfer of energy; synergy of neuro-muscular system
2. Learning the **snatch receive** (90° knee flexion); improving **hip flexor** speed
3. Improving explosiveness of **hip extensor** (hamstrings primary; glutes secondary) musculature while transitioning into the snatch receive; applying force vertically
4. Improving body control & coordination by enhancing stabilizers and gliding neutralizers
5. Improving flexibility (e.g. latissimus dorsi)
6. Improving skill and balance foundation for complex movements

DESCRIPTION

1. Take an **athletic stance**; stand straight, **feet are shoulder-width apart**; knees slightly flexed; toes point forward
2. Use a pronated grip, take dumbbell in one hand, keep elbow extended and flex hips till dumbbell is in the center of the legs at knee level; maintain neutral spine position (push chest out and scapulae [shoulder blades] together; maintain neutral head position (look forward)
3. Explosively extend the hips and simultaneously jump vertically (plantar flexion) while shrugging the shoulders and flexing the elbow while abducting shoulder to 90° (upright row); dumbbell remains close to the body and reaches sternum (~ nipple) level; elbows point sideways
4. When dumbbell reaches neutral gravity (no movement) explosively flex the hips and knees, flip the wrists (wrist extension) and extend the elbow; knees are flexed at 90° (or as low as possible); shoulder is in full flexion; maintain neutral spine and head position

COMMON ERRORS

- Wide stance is being used
- Dumbbell remains more than 2.5 inches away from the body during high pull
- No shoulder abduction during high receive; elbows never point sideways
- Flexion of thoracic & lumbar spine occurs (rounded back) during motion
- Athlete loses balance

ID: 6127

DEGREE OF DIFFICULTY

- 4

REQUIRED EQUIPMENT

- 1 Dumbbell

RELEVANCE

- Exercise is being used to learn efficient vertical application of force, including the snatch receive, by improving synergy of lower extremities, trunk, and upper extremities; **2nd pulling phase only**
- Improves hip flexor speed and explosiveness of the hip extensors (hamstrings). It is an assistive lift since it has transfer in the lifting progression (e.g. 2nd receiving phase during the snatch from the floor) and hence must be used in the Teaching/Hypertrophy Training Phase.
- Results in faster running speed and more powerful stroke production (e.g. serve) on the court due to more efficient energy transfer

PRE-REQUISITE EXERCISES

1. Hang Snatch

TARGETED MUSCLES

- Glutes
- Hamstrings
- Quadriceps
- Iliopsoas
- Calves (gastrocnemius, soleus)
- Shoulder Girdle (Trapezius & Levator Scapula)
- Deltoid

ACTION

- Hip Extension
- Hip Extension
- Knee Extension/Hip Flexion
- Hip Flexion
- Plantar Flexion
- Scapula Elevation
- Shoulder Abduction

PLANE OF MOTION

- Sagittal
- Sagittal
- Sagittal
- Sagittal
- Sagittal
- Frontal
- Frontal

BREATH IN & OUT

- IN: Before Knee/Hip Extension
- OUT: During Knee/Hip Extension

KEY FACTORS

- Focus on perfect movement mechanics and range of motion
- Use medial grip (between legs)
- 2nd pulling phase is explosive
- Dumbbell remains close to the body during upright row exercise; elbow points sideways
- Rapidly flex knees and hips to receive and decelerate the dumbbell
- Elbow is extended after receive
- Maintain neutral spine position
- Maintain neutral head position

6.128 PLATE SNATCH

SUMMARY

The Plate Snatch is a compound exercise, which focuses on improving the synergy of the neuromuscular system, learning the snatch receive (improving hip flexor speed), improving explosiveness of hip extensor musculature while transitioning into shoulder shrug, improving body control & coordination, flexibility as well as improving skill & balance foundation for complex movements.

Note: Athlete must have good **hamstring** flexibility to receive the dumbbell at 90° of knee flexion with a narrow stance.

PURPOSE

1. Improving transfer of energy; synergy of neuromuscular system
2. Learning the **snatch receive** (90° knee flexion); improving **hip flexor** speed
3. Improving explosiveness of **hip extensor** (hamstrings primary; glutes secondary) musculature while transitioning into the snatch receive; applying force vertically
4. Improving body control & coordination by enhancing stabilizers and gliding neutralizers
5. Improving flexibility (e.g. latissimus dorsi)
6. Improving skill and balance foundation for complex movements

DESCRIPTION

1. Take an **athletic stance**; stand straight, **feet are shoulder-width apart**; knees slightly flexed; toes point forward
2. Use a pronated grip, take plate in both hands, keep elbows extended and flex hips till plate is in the center of the legs; maintain neutral spine position (push chest out and scapulae [shoulder blades] together; maintain neutral head position (look forward)
3. Explosively extend the hips and simultaneously jump vertically (plantar flexion) while shrugging the shoulders and flexing the elbows while abducting shoulders to 90° (upright row); plate remains close to the body and reaches sternum (~ nipple) level; elbows point sideways
4. When plate reaches neutral gravity (no movement), explosively flex the hips and knees, flip the wrists (wrist extension), extend the elbows, and **land in narrow stance** (feet remain within shoulders); knees are flexed at 90° (or as low as possible); shoulder is in full flexion; maintain neutral spine and head position
5. Extend the hips and knees and stand up straight

DEGREE OF DIFFICULTY

- 2

REQUIRED EQUIPMENT

- 1 Bumper Plate (rubber-made plate)

RELEVANCE

- Teaches efficient vertical application of force, including the snatch receive, by improving synergy of lower extremities, trunk, and upper extremities; **2nd pulling phase only**
- Improves hip flexor speed and explosiveness of the hip extensors (hamstrings). It is an assistive lift since it has transfer in the lifting progression (e.g. 2nd receiving phase during the snatch from the floor).
- Results in faster running speed and more powerful stroke production (e.g. serve) on the court due to more efficient energy transfer

PRE-REQUISITE EXERCISES

1. Overhead Squat

ID: 6128

TARGETED MUSCLES	ACTION	PLANE OF MOTION
• Glutes	• Hip Extension	• Sagittal
• Hamstrings	• Hip Extension	• Sagittal
• Quadriceps	• Knee Extension/Hip Flexion	• Sagittal
• Iliopsoas	• Hip Flexion	• Sagittal
• Calves (gastrocnemius, soleus)	• Plantar Flexion	• Sagittal
• Shoulder Girdle (Trapezius & Levator Scapula)	• Scapula Elevation	• Frontal
• Deltoid	• Shoulder Abduction	• Frontal

KEY FACTORS

- Focus on perfect movement mechanics and range of motion
- 2nd pulling phase is explosive
- Plate remains close to the body during upright row; elbow points sideways
- Rapidly flex knees and hips to receive and decelerate the plate
- Elbows are extended after receive
- Maintain neutral spine position
- Maintain neutral head position

COMMON ERRORS

- Wide stance is being used
- Plate remains more than 2.5 inches away from the body during high pull
- No shoulder abduction during high receive; elbows never point sideways
- Flexion of thoracic & lumbar spine occurs (rounded back) during motion
- Athlete loses balance

BREATH IN & OUT

- IN: Before Knee/Hip Extension
- OUT: During Knee/Hip Extension

6.129 HANG SNATCH

SUMMARY

The Hang Snatch is a compound exercise, which focuses on improving the synergy of the neuromuscular system, learning the snatch receive (improving hip flexor speed), improving explosiveness of hip extensor musculature while transitioning into shoulder shrug, improving body control & coordination, flexibility as well as improving skill & balance foundation for complex movements.

Note: Athlete must have good **hamstring** & **latissimus dorsi** (shoulder) flexibility to receive the dumbbell at 90° of knee flexion with a narrow stance. If shoulder flexibility is an issue, do the Plate Snatch instead. With heavy resistance do not catch the bar on the way down in wide grip position - it will pull the shoulders out!

PURPOSE

1. Improving transfer of energy; synergy of neuromuscular system
2. Learning the **snatch receive** (90° knee flexion); improving **hip flexor** speed
3. Improving explosiveness of **hip extensor** (hamstrings primary; glutes secondary) musculature while transitioning into the snatch receive; applying force vertically
4. Improving body control & coordination by enhancing stabilizers and gliding neutralizers
5. Improving flexibility (e.g. latissimus dorsi)
6. Improving skill and balance foundation for complex movements

DESCRIPTION

1. Take an **athletic stance**; stand straight, **feet are shoulder-width apart**; knees slightly flexed; toes point forward
2. Use a pronated grip, take barbell in both hands using the snatch grip (hands past 2nd key), keep elbows extended and flex hips till barbell is in the center of the legs above knee level; maintain neutral spine position (push chest out and scapulae [shoulder blades] together; maintain neutral head position (look forward)
3. Explosively extend the hips and simultaneously jump vertically (plantar flexion) while shrugging the shoulders and flexing the elbows while abducting shoulders to 90° (upright row); barbell remains close to the body and reaches sternum (~ nipple) level; elbows point sideways
4. When barbell reaches neutral gravity (no movement) explosively flex the hips and knees, flip the wrists (wrist extension), extend the elbows and **land in narrow stance** (feet remain within shoulders); knees are flexed at 90° (or as low as possible); shoulder is in full flexion; maintain neutral spine and head position
5. Extend the hips and knees and stand up straight

ID: 6129

DEGREE OF DIFFICULTY

- 3

REQUIRED EQUIPMENT

- 1 Barbell
- Bumper Plates (rubber-made plates)
- 2 Safety Clips

RELEVANCE

- Teaches efficient vertical application of force, including the snatch receive, by improving synergy of lower extremities, trunk, and upper extremities; **2nd pulling phase only**
- Improves hip flexor speed and explosiveness of the hip extensors (hamstrings). It is an assistive lift since it has transfer in the lifting progression (e.g. 2nd receiving phase during the snatch from the floor).
- Results in faster running speed and more powerful stroke production (e.g. serve) on the court due to more efficient energy transfer

PRE-REQUISITE EXERCISES

1. Overhead Squat
2. Plate Snatch

BREATH IN & OUT

- IN: Before Knee/Hip Extension
- OUT: During Knee/Hip Extension

TARGETED MUSCLES

- Glutes
- Hamstrings
- Quadriceps
- Iliopsoas
- Calves (gastrocnemius, soleus)
- Shoulder Girdle (Trapezius & Levator Scapula)
- Deltoid

ACTION

- Hip Extension
- Hip Extension
- Knee Extension/Hip Flexion
- Hip Flexion
- Plantar Flexion
- Scapula Elevation
- Shoulder Abduction

PLANE OF MOTION

- Sagittal
- Sagittal
- Sagittal
- Sagittal
- Sagittal
- Frontal
- Frontal

COMMON ERRORS

- Wide stance is being used
- Barbell remains more than 2.5 inches away from the body during high pull
- No shoulder abduction during high receive; elbows never point sideways
- Flexion of thoracic & lumbar spine occurs (rounded back) during motion
- Athlete loses balance

KEY FACTORS

- Focus on perfect movement mechanics and range of motion
- Use snatch grip (hands past 2nd key)
- 2nd pulling phase is explosive
- Barbell remains close to the body during upright row exercise; elbow points sideways
- Rapidly flex knees and hips to receive and decelerate the barbell
- Elbows are extended after receive
- Maintain neutral spine position
- Maintain neutral head position

6.130 PUSH-JERK

SUMMARY

The Push-Jerk is a compound exercise, which focuses on improving the synergy of the neuro-muscular system, improving hip flexor speed, improving body control & coordination, flexibility as well as improving skill & balance foundation for complex movements.

Note: For most athletes the Push-Jerk is difficult due to flexibility requirements in the **latissimus dorsi**. Exercise can also be performed with dumbbells!

PURPOSE

1. Improving transfer of energy; synergy of neuro-muscular system
2. Improving **hip flexor speed** (iliopsoas, rectus femoris, sartorius, gluteus minimus); the conversion of rapid hip extension into rapid hip flexion
3. Improving body control & coordination by enhancing stabilizers and gliding neutralizers
4. Improving flexibility
5. Improving skill (rapid hip flexion) and balance foundation for complex movement

DESCRIPTION

1. Position barbell chest level on the rack; add resistance (plates) and attach safety clips
2. Take an **athletic stance**; stand straight, **feet are under the shoulders**; knees slightly flexed; toes point forward
3. Use a pronated grip (palms facing down) and place hands slightly wider than shoulder-width apart on the bar; position barbell on top of the chest, move elbow underneath barbell and flex shoulder to 90°; elbows point forward; lift barbell off the rack and take a step back
4. Slightly flex the hips (without excessive knee flexion) then **extend hips rapidly** to move barbell vertically off the chest and immediately **flex hips rapidly** to get under the barbell and extend the elbows; **feet must stay within shoulders**; knees must not protrude past toes; look forward
5. Stand up straight, flex elbows, move head slightly back and return barbell to starting position

DEGREE OF DIFFICULTY

- 4

REQUIRED EQUIPMENT

- 1 Rack
- 1 Barbell
- Plates
- 2 Safety Clips

RELEVANCE

- It is used to enhance speed of hip flexors (iliopsoas, rectus femoris, sartorius, gluteus minimus) and to develop neutral pelvic position since the hip flexors are attached to the iliac spine and also the lumbar spine
- Results in more powerful jumping and better agility and stroke production capabilities

ID: 6130

COMMON ERRORS

- Wide grip is used
- Athlete jumps out wide (feet outside shoulders)
- Excessive knee flexion occurs before hip extension to create momentum
- Excessive extension (arching) of the spinal column during pressing phase
- Resistance remains in front of the body

KEY FACTORS

- Focus on perfect movement mechanics and range of motion
- Slight hip flexion to rapid hip extension without excessive knee flexion
- Hands are just outside shoulders on the bar
- Maintain neutral spine position
- Move head out of the way

PRE-REQUISITE EXERCISES

1. Overhead Squat
2. Push-Press

BREATH IN & OUT

- IN: Before Hip Flexion
- OUT: During Hip Flexion

TARGETED MUSCLES

- Hip Flexors (iliopsoas, rectus femoris, sartorius, gluteus minimus)

ACTION

- Hip Flexion

PLANE OF MOTION

- Sagittal

6.131 SPLIT-JERK

SUMMARY

The Split-Jerk is a compound exercise, which focuses on improving the synergy of the neuro-muscular system, improving split-stance hip flexor speed, improving body control & coordination, flexibility as well as improving skill & balance foundation for complex movements.

Note: Exercise can also be performed using dumbbells!

PURPOSE

1. Improving transfer of energy; synergy of neuro-muscular system
2. Improving **split-stance hip flexor speed** (iliopsoas, rectus femoris, sartorius, gluteus minimus); the conversion of rapid hip extension into rapid split-stance hip flexion
3. Improving body control & coordination by enhancing stabilizers and gliding neutralizers
4. Improving flexibility
5. Improving skill (rapid hip flexion) and balance foundation for complex movements

DESCRIPTION

1. Position barbell chest level on the rack; add resistance (plates) and attach safety clips
2. Take an **athletic stance**; stand straight, **feet are under the shoulders**; knees slightly flexed; toes point forward
3. Use a pronated grip (palms facing down) and place hands slightly wider than shoulder-width apart on the bar; position barbell on top of the chest, move elbow underneath barbell and flex shoulder to 90°; elbows point forward; lift barbell off the rack and take a step back
4. Slightly flex the hips (without excessive knee flexion) then **extend hips rapidly** to move barbell vertically off the chest and immediately **flex hips rapidly** to get under the barbell and extend the elbows; **feet must stay within shoulders**; knees must not protrude past toes; look forward
5. Stand up straight, flex elbows, move head slightly back, and return barbell to starting position
6. Switch legs

DEGREE OF DIFFICULTY

- 3

REQUIRED EQUIPMENT

- 1 Rack
- 1 Barbell
- Plates
- 2 Safety Clips

RELEVANCE

- It is used to enhance speed of hip flexors (iliopsoas, rectus femoris, sartorius, gluteus minimus) for split-stance action and to develop neutral pelvic position since the hip flexors are attached to the iliac spine and also the lumbar spine
- Results in more powerful jumping –, agility -, and stroke production capabilities

ID: 6131

COMMON ERRORS

- Wide grip is used
- Athlete jumps out wide (feet outside shoulders)
- Excessive knee flexion occurs before hip extension to create momentum
- Excessive extension (arching) of the spinal column during pressing phase
- Resistance remains in front of the body

KEY FACTORS

- Focus on perfect movement mechanics and range of motion
- Slight hip flexion to rapid hip extension without excessive knee flexion
- Hands are just outside shoulders on the bar
- Maintain neutral spine position
- Move head out of the way

BREATH IN & OUT

- IN: Before Hip Flexion
- OUT: During Hip Flexion

PRE-REQUISITE EXERCISES

1. Forward Lunge to Press

TARGETED MUSCLES

- Hip Flexors (iliopsoas, rectus femoris, sartorius, gluteus minimus)

ACTION

- Hip Flexion

PLANE OF MOTION

- Sagittal

No doubt, when one thinks of a competitive tennis match, the first performance attributes that come to mind are speed, reaction time, agility, and power. Tennis is a power dominant sport, where high-intensity short duration bouts constitute the majority of play. Researchers have estimated that 95% of the energy utilized in competitive play comes from anaerobic sources such as the adenosine triphosphate creatinephosphate (ATP-CP) system and glycolysis; only 5% is purported to be attributed through aerobic means.

INTRODUCTION

According to the majority of available research, the average length of a point during a tennis match is less than 15 seconds, with trends showing that point durations have dropped within the past decade considerably (1).

This means that developing quickness, while demonstrating agility in an efficient manner, is crucial to success in competitive tennis. These demonstrations of athletic ability must be repeated with maximal rest time of 20 seconds between bouts according to the rules of tennis. A player must be fast and powerful, and have the endurance to maintain these qualities during an entire match (1).

Speed is defined as the ability to produce force rapidly to move at a high velocity. However, there are multiple aspects to speed:

- **Speed Economy**: assures that minimal excess energy is expended (wasted) to perform the athletic movement
- **Speed-Strength**: provides for production of rapidly implemented force
- **Speed Endurance**: allows the athlete to perform the action repeatedly

Generally, speed economy improvements are realized through flexibility – and stability/balance training. Improving speed-strength is the focus in the weight room, while speed endurance training takes place on the court or on the running track.

These aforementioned components of speed can be enhanced by implementing the drills and exercises into the training program.

In general, many think of **linear speed** (one plane) when they want to improve speed, such as a 100 m sprint event. Speed in tennis however occurs in multiple planes (directions), so the speed must be complemented in a successful athlete with an equal dose of agility. **Agility** is defined as the ability to move quickly and to change direction rapidly. An athlete who is agile can rapidly accelerate in one direction, quickly decelerate, and speedily accelerate in a different direction.

Balance, the attainment of static equilibrium against all external forces, is a crucial component of agility. An athlete must have the ability to balance his/her body weight against the forces of acceleration and deceleration in order to quickly change direction. For example, tennis players who can balance on one leg while decelerating and simultaneously change the direction of their hips to accelerate in a different direction are demonstrating the aspects of optimal agility. Many of the presented exercises will help the athlete train the body and nervous system to perform these actions.

Quickness is the overall integration of speed, agility, and balance that allows the athlete to cover ground efficiently on the court. An integration of the selected plyometrics/ballistics, speed ladder drills, and agility drills in this section will aid in improving an athlete's level of quickness.

SPEED TRAINING

Speed, as generally applied to human beings, refers to the ability to move at maximum speed for a short duration of time or at a set velocity; one doesn't always move at maximum speed and one certainly controls how fast to move.

Speed is defined as work x distance/time.

Speed = (Work x Distance)/Time

According to Newton, **work** is defined as force x distance and power is defined as work/time, which can be expressed as (force x distance)/time.

Power = Work / Time

= (Force x Distance) / Time

Therefore, since power is a component of speed (and vice versa) one should work on enhancing power by improving flexibility, balance (stability) and speed. Because stability and flexibility are key components in improving **speed economy**, one should focus on improving these components first! If one can improve speed economy then overall speed (speed-strength & speed endurance) will improve because less resistive forces are counteractive and if overall speed improves, one becomes more powerful! Therefore, in order to become more powerful, training should initially focus on:

1. Improving flexibility
2. Improving stability/balance
3. Improving speed economy

In general, if one has poor economy in upper-body movement mechanics then it will affect lower-body speed economy and hence reduce maximum speed output. But in tennis, since one is holding a racquet in both hands while running over the tennis court, upper-body movement mechanics are less important in optimizing speed than they are during a 100m sprint event. For more information read: **"Under the Microscope: How Proper Upper-Body Movement Mechanics Will Improve Sprint Times"**.

NEED FOR SPEED

If the goal is to move faster on the tennis court, one must improve certain factors in training that will yield positive results during competition. These factors are:

1. Sustaining Power Output
2. Improving Neural Pathway Efficiency
3. Enhancing Muscle Balance
4. Optimizing Movement Mechanics
5. Maximizing Energy-System Efficiency
6. Improving Energy System Thresholds

Next we will explore each of these components in more detail.

UNDER THE MICROSCOPE

HOW PROPER UPPER-BODY MOVEMENT MECHANICS WILL IMPROVE SPRINT TIMES

Most people use their arms to remain balanced during jogging or sprinting but arm swings can be used effectively to improve speed economy and hence maximum speed. In fact, one can lift their own body off the ground just by swinging the arms so that the elbows remain in a straight line.

- Sit down on the ground; legs remain straight and parallel in front of you
- Perform fast alternate arm swings so that elbows travel in a straight line (palm of your hand move from cheek of your buttocks to cheek of your face)
- Buttocks will lift off the ground, causing vertical displacement (body moves upward)

When one sprints, performing the same alternate arm swings at maximum speed will also cause vertical displacement, which will enhance stride length, causing one to cover more distance with each step (horizontal displacement), thereby improving sprint times!

SUSTAINED POWER OUTPUT

Being able to sustain high power output is a necessity if one wants to remain powerful during an entire match or practice session; in short, this refers to one's ability to exert force in a fast manner for a prolonged period of time (e.g. duration of a match). If the athlete can do something really well only once but has to repeat the action over and over again during a match then performance is going to decline because the athlete runs out of energy. Since a tennis match can last anywhere between 50-180 minutes (conditioning force) with (on average) 15 seconds of maximum power output during points (applied force) and 20 seconds rest intervals between points, the athlete needs to commit to strength training (applied force) and conditioning (conditioning force) respectively.

NEURAL PATHWAY EFFICIENCY

Type II muscle fibers are the fast twitch fibers, which allow for the very rapid contractions necessary for burst speed but they only contribute to force output for about 5-7 minutes of work. As a result, it is recommended not to exceed 7-9 minutes (up to 9 minutes also has positive effect on speed endurance) of work for speed training purposes since the recruitment of fast twitch muscle fibers is the focus. If one engages in prolonged high intensity speed training (10+ minutes of work), slow twitch muscle fibers will be recruited instead because fast twitch fibers will have become fatigued. Additionally, energy system efficiency will be compromised since ATP-CP system and anaerobic metabolism energy contributions will decrease while aerobic metabolism energy contributions will increase. Therefore, speed will be reduced and slow twitch muscle fibers will be predominantly recruited.

Due to the fact that tennis requires repeat performances of jumping, acceleration, deceleration and change of direction activities, energy system efficiency is vital to success on the court; whoever can perform these activities the best will be able to do more with the ball. Therefore, it is important to consider the speed-strength component itself but also how to enhance speed endurance! One of the key concepts contributing to just that is to optimize speed economy by reducing the waste of energy; this can be achieved by enhancing **neural pathway efficiency** and **movement economy**. If one is not wasting any energy, that energy can be used to improve performance.

MUSCLE BALANCE

Muscle balance enables proper alignment with regards to kinetic chain efficiency. Muscle imbalance creates unequal force couples, which will reduce effective transfer of energy through the kinetic chain and even lead to injuries. Apart from significant force couple problems, limited range of motion (ROM) can also cause injury.

For example, if the hamstrings are tight (limited ROM) then full hip flexion cannot be attained, which negatively impacts running and jumping capabilities. Also, if hip extensors are tight, full hip flexion and/or optimization of hip flexors cannot occur.

MOVEMENT MECHANICS

The enhancement of movement mechanics refers to improving speed economy, which has a positive effect on speed-strength and endurance. If less energy is being wasted, more energy is available, which allows for faster movements (speed-strength) while delaying the onset of fatigue (speed endurance).

MAXIMIZING ENERGY SYSTEM EFFICIENCY

This endeavor affects speed endurance capabilities because the more effective the energy systems work the better the buffering capabilities (removal of hydrogen ions), which is where the rest-to-work ratios come into play. If rest intervals are too short, energy system optimization is impossible because overloading capability is compromised, which is necessary to improve energy system efficiency. In other words, conditioning is the key concept in maximizing energy system efficiency. That's why there is a big problem when one returns from serious (knee) injury because fitness levels have deteriorated due to inactivity. Instead of being able to work on speed economy and speed endurance, a lot of time is spent on returning to previous fitness levels. This also explains why the best athlete is the one that remains healthy!

IMPROVING ENERGY SYSTEM THRESHOLD

Speed training can be used to push energy system thresholds, thereby improving speed endurance. First, focus on learning movement mechanics, then use some resistance when performing the drills (loading the action) in anticipation of increasing the challenge (e.g. resistance goes down, rest intervals shorten). Essentially, energy system thresholds can be improved by using the progression concept employed during strength training.

Recall from the introduction that **speed economy** assures that minimal excess energy is expended (wasted) to perform the athletic movement by reducing resistive forces along the movement path. Therefore, optimizing movement/speed economy will improve **speed-strength**, which is the ability to produce force at high velocities (rapidly). If the athlete improves in stabilizing and managing his/her center of gravity, the amount of force required to change direction decreases too, which is why improving balance/stabilization is a pre-requisite for improving speed. Therefore, it is imperative to focus on **movement technique** before challenging the movement (e.g. increasing weight)!

IMPROVING SPEED

As previously mentioned, strength training in the gym must complement speed training in order to maximize results and produce improved performance on the tennis court.

IMPROVING GENERAL CONDITIONING

The goal is to optimize movement patterns but before the athlete can engage in these activities he/she should take part in a fitness assessment, introduced in Chapter 4 (see Chapter 4: Fitness Assessment on page 61), to find out which deficiencies need to be addressed! For example, if the athlete shows poor results in the "Bilateral Knee Extension Test", hamstring flexibility issues need to be addressed before he/she can engage in speed training.

IMPROVING FORCE OUTPUT

Ballistic exercises are being used to maximize force output. **Force** can be defined as (mass x distance)/time, and distance/time is speed. Therefore, force is mass x speed.

Force (J) = (mass {kg} x distance {m})/time (s)

= mass x speed

Therefore, the goal is to increase the speed of the movement and/or the acceleration of an object or resistance.

IMPROVING TRANSFER OF ENERGY

The emphasis here is the effective transfer of energy from the ground through the body in order to exert force. In other words, the focus is the improvement of kinetic chain efficiency; the effective transfer of ground reaction forces through the body.

Functional exercises (see Functional Training on page 327) and **strength for performance exercises** (see Lunge & Press on page 262) include lunge & press activities, asymmetrical loading & squatting, transverse plane (trunk rotation) activities and various medicine ball based activities, where the focus is more on endurance than on power, which means that the resistance is lower but the volume is higher.

ACCELERATED SPEED

During plyometric training the emphasis is on optimizing neural pathways, where the athlete accelerates the speed of the movement so that it almost becomes reflexive in nature. To do this the resistance has to be lower than that used during ballistic exercises but the time between repetitions is kept to a minimum, leading to faster turnovers.

IMPROVING SPEED ENDURANCE

Sport loading consists of resisted high-speed activities, which can be in a single direction (parachute drag) or multiple directions (resistance band drills). These types of exercises really challenge the energy systems (metabolism), while generating a lot of force, which allows the athlete to really push **speed endurance** capabilities. Attention must be paid to proper sprint/running form because it affects movement (speed) economy, which in turn affects speed endurance.

IMPROVING MAXIMUM SPEED

During over-speed training the athlete focuses on optimizing the ATP-CP energy system and the nervous system; peak performance of both components is required for maximum speed. The goal is to get the athlete to move faster than is possible unaided so that the nervous system learns to move faster. This can be accomplished by the use of different devices (e.g. sling-shot) and/or running on declines. It is important for the athlete to have full recovery (e.g. 3-4 minutes recovery for 15 seconds of work) between repetitions because the nervous system needs to be able to function properly at maximum capacity. For example, if the athlete is slingshotted into a sprint, he/she will require neural and metabolic recovery so that each repetition can be performed at maximum ability. This scenario also translates to the weight room during power exercises. If the athlete performs hang snatches, 3-5 repetitions are the maximum that can be performed in good form because power exercises are so fast and athletic that they require optimal nervous system (neural) performance.

It is important to focus on maximum speed while maintaining good form and not just maximizing speed! Over-speed training is often used in error because it is focused to much on simply making movements faster instead of concentrating on the form of the movement as well. If the focus is just on movement speed, the economy of the movement can suffer and the athlete starts training the wrong neural patterns! For example, if down-hill sprinting has too much of a decline, the athlete actually has to decelerate because he/she is moving too fast and cannot maintain stability!

HOW ABOUT AEROBIC CONDITIONING?

Since tennis is definitely not an aerobic dominant sport in any sense of the word, does that mean there is no need for aerobic conditioning? The answer is: there is certainly a need not but only when it makes sense. If it appears that an athlete lacks a general aerobic base to perform the anaerobic bouts of play seen in a match, long, slow endurance training should be implemented during a preparation stage (Skill Acquisition/Hypertrophy Phase) of training. This would be during the first and maybe second week of training. From a sports science aspect it wouldn't make much sense for the athlete to go jogging 60 minutes 4/5 times per week because the aerobic energy system is mainly supplemental, whereas the ATP-CP energy system and anaerobic glycolytic energy system predominate during tennis. From a psychological standpoint though (meaning that the athlete can use it a way to relax from mental pressure before or after a match), 20-30 minutes of light jogging would make sense. Generally speaking, the athlete can be conditioned by, ideally, maximizing anaerobic power and endurance with adequate recovery time because lactic acid build up can be managed; the athlete manages lactic acid by buffering it into lactate. More precisely, the athlete can take lactate and diffuse into the cells without the help of insulin. Most of the lactate will be transported to the heart but some will go to the anaerobic cells and into the Krebs cycle. In that case the athlete needs to be in good shape to actually utilize that energy (lactate) for fuel. It would be ideal to condition the athlete by improving anaerobic power without producing too much aerobic enzymes (limited mitochondria density).

Therefore, producing higher capillary activity and stroke volume is desirable; this can be accomplished through sprint training with short rest intervals (work to rest ratio is 1:3 [ATP-CP energy system], 1:2 [glycolytic energy system], 1:1 [aerobic energy system]). If the athlete wants to have the capacity to go at high rates of speed for a longer period of time, the athlete's heart needs to be stronger in order to pump more blood since blood transports oxygen. The goal is to enhance the properties of the type II (fast twitch) muscle fibers, instead of recruiting type I (slow twitch) muscle fibers, which would be the case with steady state (endurance running) training due to improved mitochondrial density being produced. Therefore, use logic when attempting to maintain your aerobic base and condition, keeping in mind the requirements specific to tennis. Interval training using sport distances and movement patterns will metabolically prepare an athlete for the sport, without resorting to long distance running because no sport really calls for sustained endurance, except triathlons and similar long distance races.

INTEGRATED PERIODIZATION MODEL (IPM)

Following the integrated periodization model (IPM) for speed, agility, and quickness (SAQ) training, which is used to complement strength resistance training, will produce maximum improvements in athletic performance. Therefore, it is important that High Resistance Training (weight lifting component) complements Low Resistance Training (SAQ training), otherwise overall training outcomes are not as positive as they could be and the athlete ends up wasting time. The focus of this chapter is the SAQ training component. It is recommended that you use the information provided here in conjunction with the strength & conditioning component (High Resistance Training). For High Resistance Training refer to Chapter 6 **(see Chapter 6: Strength & Conditioning - Resistance Training on page 171)**. For example, when the athlete is engaging in Olympic lifts during the High Resistance Power Training, one needs to complement those activities (in the gym) with appropriate Low Resistance Power Training (SAQ training) activities (e.g. MB Trunk Twist Passes) in order to improve overall conditioning.

It is important to utilize a developmental approach with respect to speed, agility, and quickness (SAQ) training because the risk of injury is elevated because activities are being performed at maximum effort. In general, the focus must be on proper form instead of focusing on the total amount of resistance being moved. For example, before the athlete engages in any heavy medicine ball throws, he/she needs to learn how to perform the movement effectively. Otherwise they are reinforcing bad habits, which is counterproductive for performance on the court. The same holds true for agility drills, where the athlete needs to know how to change direction properly before moving at maximum speed.

In general, the SAQ training program is divided into three (3) main categories that correspond to the aspects of speed; speed economy, speed-strength, and speed endurance. The main categories complement the eight (8) training phases that are being used during the High Resistance Training program.

Developing Speed Economy

1. Skill Acquisition Phase
2. Hypertrophy Phase
3. Basic Strength Phase

Developing Speed-strength

4. Integrated Strength Phase
5. Strength-Power Phase
6. Integrated Power Phase
7. Power Phase

Developing Speed Endurance

8. Power Performance Phase

The various exercises of the Speed Economy and Speed-strength sections are divided into categories based on their purpose (categories; e.g. speed economy), degree of difficulty and corresponding goals.

DEVELOPING SPEED ECONOMY

Before any speed training commences, the athlete should complete the flexibility – and performance tests provided in Chapter 4 **(see Chapter 4: Fitness Assessment on page 61)** in order to determine any possible deficiencies that need to be addressed. Failure to do so can expose the athlete to an elevated risk of possible injury and reinforce undesirable movement patterns that are difficult to correct at a later stage. To address flexibility issues, refer to the appropriate stretching exercises provided in the performance preparation chapter 5 **(see Chapter 5: Performance Preparation on page 111).**

The speed economy section entails the following subcategories:

- Balance & Stability Training
- Stride Length & Frequency Training

BALANCE & STABILITY TRAINING

Balance can be defined as the ability to maintain body equilibrium, where all force couples equal zero (cancel each other out); it can be thought of as "static equilibrium". On the other hand, **stability** can be defined as the ability of an object (e.g. athlete) to maintain body equilibrium while in motion; it can be thought of as "dynamic equilibrium" or "dynamic balance". Dynamic balance allows for agility by establishing force & counter-force couples but oftentimes people think of balance training as the attempt of someone to hold a steady position, which is the state of static equilibrium, and all force couples equal zero (0). While playing tennis the athlete is almost always in motion and hence needs to deal with dynamic balance, maintaining dynamic equilibrium. During dynamic equilibrium all force couples are controlled to a point of stability. The force couples don't have to be equal to zero, which is where the athlete is completely static, but the differential has to be small enough that the athlete can control the center of mass/gravity within the base of support (legs) to maintain stability.

Since **agility** can be defined as the ability to change direction, it is obvious that maintaining stability during directional change depends on how well the athlete can manage his/her body and maintain balance. That explains why agility and stability (dynamic balance) are directly related to each other and why an athlete needs to have good balance and dynamic stability capabilities in order to change direction on the court effectively. Since balance/stability is a pre-requisite for agility drills, balance/stability drills will be addressed early on in the preparation phase.

Unfortunately, it is not uncommon for athletes and/or coaches to separate balance and agility exercises conceptually because they think of balance as a static activity and agility as the application of speed during change of direction. In reality, balance in sports is dynamic (non-static) and being able to manage dynamic equilibrium is essential in order to perform well on the tennis court because the athlete needs to be in control during stroke production. Also, whoever can manage and maintain dynamic equilibrium on the court will be the better player and that's why balance training should be part of any tennis player's daily workout program.

Also, proper biomechanics require all components to be applied equally, which is why muscle balance is essential; this is where the performance and flexibility tests provided in chapter 4 **(see Chapter 4: Fitness Assessment on page 61)** come into play. Generally speaking, if the athlete is stronger on one side than on the other, performance will be negatively affected because fatigue will result from the bad muscle balance. Good muscle balance makes fatigue much less of a factor because less energy will be wasted in trying to correct imbalances, thereby extending the time before fatigue sets in.

COMPONENTS AFFECTING BALANCE

Balance is important for optimal performance on the tennis court and it is helpful for the athlete to understand what factors affect balance. The center for balance is located in the brain, the inner ear to be precise; it is called the **vestibular apparatus**. The vestibular apparatus receives **visual data**, processes the information, and sends a signal to the appropriate organs and muscles. Visual data is important because it communicates depth perception as well as speed and location of objects (e.g. a tennis ball).

Also important is **proprioception**, which is an endogenous control system that conveys information regarding muscle length and tension for stability purposes.

More precisely, muscle stimuli are constantly communicating in order to allow the athlete to have the most efficient movement mechanics that the body can produce at any given time based on its experience and rate of fatigue. Therefore, it is important to prevent muscle fatigue and that's where balance endurance and strength training come into play. The longer that muscles function properly the better the performance on the court will be because fatigued muscles can't stabilize any action/movement and when the athlete fatigues stroke production suffers. Thus, being able to maintain stability for a long time is important and that's why the athlete needs to have some level of training where stability endurance is being addressed (see provided Balance Exercises).

Head movement affects balance. Keeping the head stable during stroke production will improve accuracy of the vestibular apparatus, which impacts general equilibrium. The more stable the athlete is during shots the better it is for shot accuracy and speed. When people experience sea-sickness, communication via the vestibular circuit (vestibular apparatus to cerebellum to brain stem via nuclei to muscles) is compromised and maintaining stability is challenging.

Tactile awareness refers to ground contact communication; it is the ability to use surface contact for balance. To improve tactile awareness various types of equipment can be used, including balance boards, BOSU, or other stability challenging devices.

Postural stabilizers are very important because the strength of an athlete and how well he/she can maintain balance depends on endurance, strength, and overall efficiency of the stabilizers. Stabilizer strength is related to how strong the athlete is overall. For example, if the athlete can squat under load in good form, he/she will also have good strength in the stabilizers related to that action because the trunk has good control. When it comes to stabilizer endurance it is important how long the athlete can manage that postural stability. If the athlete has efficiency but is not training well then he/she ends up losing stabilizer efficiency, which means he/she can't exert prime mover force well. Therefore, prime mover force capabilities are secondary; the primary consideration is that the athlete can stabilize the action/movement so that force can be exerted! Postural stabilizer efficiency depends on how well the athlete can utilize force, which depends on how much energy is being used (or not wasted). So, if the athlete becomes energy efficient, more energy is being preserved, which then can be used to stabilize the action/movement longer because muscles don't fatigue as quickly. This will have positive implications during practice and competition.

TRAINING PROGRAM CONSIDERATIONS

The athlete needs to learn how to forward lunge, single-leg Romanian deadlift and squat during the skill acquisition and hypertrophy phases for motor patterning purposes. Once the athlete has achieved proficiency, the exercises presented here can be used during the integration phases. As a general rule of thumb: When the athlete increases the speed of the exercise, the resistance/weight should decrease.

7.01 SIDE-STEP TO DIAGONAL LUNGE

SUMMARY

The Side-Step to Diagonal Lunge is a stability exercise, which focuses on improving stability, optimizing power-production capabilities, flexibility, as well as improving skill & balance foundation for complex movements.

DESCRIPTION

1. Stand with feet close together
2. Side-step to the left
3. Step into diagonal lunge position with the right foot; push chest out and look **forward**;
4. Return to "Ready Position"
5. Side-step to the right
6. Step into diagonal lunge position with the left foot; push chest out and look **forward**;
7. Return to "Ready Position"

PRE-REQUISITE EXERCISES

1. Forward/Reverse Lunge
2. Bilateral Squat

COMMON ERRORS

- Athlete distributes weight through the ball of the foot (toes); knees protrude past the toes during the lunge
- Athlete loses stability

BREATH IN & OUT

- IN: Before Lunge position
- OUT: During lunge position

DEGREE OF DIFFICULTY

- 1

PURPOSE

1. Improving body control & coordination
2. Optimizing power-production capabilities of musculature
3. Improving flexibility
4. Improving skill and balance foundation for complex movements

RELEVANCE

- Warms-up musculature of lower extremities used during groundstrokes
- If "Bilateral Knee Extension Test" shows deficiency, implement this exercise into the warm-up routine
- If "Stability Pad Squat Test" shows deficiency, implement this exercise into the Resistance Training Program
- If the athlete loses stability during **groundstrokes** he/she should regularly do this exercise; it will improve their balance and power during shots

KEY FACTORS

- Focus on perfect movement mechanics and range of motion
- Feet remain flat-footed during movement
- Maintain balance during movement

ID: 701

7.02 SIDE-STEP TO DIAGONAL SINGLE LEG RDL

SUMMARY

The Side-Step to Diagonal Single Leg RDL is a stability exercise, which focuses on improving stability, optimizing power-production capabilities, flexibility, as well as improving skill & balance foundation for complex movements.

DESCRIPTION

1. Stand with feet close together
2. Side-step to the left
3. Step into a diagonal Single Leg Romanian Deadlift (SL RDL) with the right foot; push chest out and look **forward**;
4. Return to "Ready Position"
5. Side-step to the right
6. Step into diagonal SL RDL with the left foot; push chest out and look **forward**;
7. Return to "Ready Position"

PRE-REQUISITE EXERCISES

1. Forward/Reverse Lunge
2. Single-Leg RDL

BREATH IN & OUT

- IN: Before Lunge position
- OUT: During lunge position

DEGREE OF DIFFICULTY

- 1

PURPOSE

1. Improving body control & coordination
2. Optimizing power-production capabilities of musculature
3. Improving flexibility
4. Improving skill and balance foundation for complex movements

RELEVANCE

- Warms-up musculature of lower extremities used during groundstrokes
- If "Bilateral Knee Extension Test" shows deficiency, implement this exercise into the warm-up routine
- If "Stability Pad Squat Test" shows deficiency, implement this exercise into the Resistance Training Program
- If the athlete loses stability during **groundstrokes** he/she should regularly do this exercise; it will improve their balance and power during shots

KEY FACTORS

- Focus on perfect movement mechanics and range of motion
- Feet remain flat-footed during movement
- Maintain balance during movement

COMMON ERRORS

- Athlete distributes weight through the ball of the foot (toes); knees protrude past the toes during the SL RDL
- Athlete loses stability

ID: 702

7.03 SINGLE LEG SQUAT

SUMMARY

The Single-Leg Squat is a balance exercise, which focuses on improving stability, optimizing power-production capabilities, flexibility, as well as improving skill & balance foundation for complex movements.

PURPOSE

1. Improving body control & coordination
2. Optimizing power-production capabilities of musculature
3. Improving flexibility
4. Improving skill and balance foundation for complex movements

DESCRIPTION

1. Take on **athletic stance** position; knees and hips are slightly flexed; upper-body is straight
2. Stand on the one leg
3. Maintain erect posture; shoulders remain over hips; push chest out and look forward; arms remain straight and close to the side of the body
4. Flex **non-weight bearing** knee to 90°
5. Flex **weight bearing** knee to ~45°; remain erect posture; maintain chest over the toes; hold position for 1 second
6. Extend weight bearing knee to starting position
7. Switch legs

PRE-REQUISITE DRILLS

Squat, SL RDL, Lunge

BREATH IN & OUT

- IN: Before Single Leg Squat
- OUT: During Single Leg Squat

DEGREE OF DIFFICULTY

1

RELEVANCE

- Warms-up musculature of lower extremities used during groundstrokes
- If "Bilateral Knee Extension Test" shows deficiency, implement this exercise into the warm-up routine
- If "Stability Pad Squat Test" shows deficiency, implement this exercise into the Resistance Training Program
- If the athlete loses stability during **groundstrokes** he/she should regularly do this exercise; it will improve their balance and power during shots

KEY FACTORS

- Focus on perfect movement mechanics and range of motion
- Feet remain flat-footed during movement
- Maintain balance during movement

COMMON ERRORS

- Athlete distributes weight through the ball of the foot (toes); knees protrude past the toes during the single leg squat
- Athlete loses stability
- Athlete leans too far forward (chest is past the toes)

ID: 703

7.04 MB TRUNK ROTATION (I)

SUMMARY

The Medicine Ball (MB) Trunk Rotation (I) is a balance exercise, which focuses on improving body control, balance & coordination, power-production capabilities, flexibility as well as improving skill & balance foundation for complex movements.

Note: If athlete cannot maintain balance during rotation, flex elbows and move MB closer to the chest.

DESCRIPTION

1. Place 2 agility rings parallel and shoulder-width apart on the ground; face an object/partner
2. Step inside agility rings
3. Hold a medicine ball (MB) naturally in both hands in front of the trunk
4. Take on **athletic stance** position; knees and hips are slightly flexed; upper-body is straight
5. Raise arms to shoulder-level and hold a medicine ball (MB) in both hands in front of the trunk; elbows are slightly flexed
6. Rotate the trunk all the way to the **left** until shoulders are perpendicular to the object/partner(or as far as possible); both elbows remain in initial position; maintain neutral head position; keep **looking forward**
7. Hold position for 1 second
8. Rotate the trunk all the way to the **right** until shoulders are perpendicular to the object/partner(or as far as possible); maintain neutral head position; keep **looking forward**
9. Hold position for 1 second
10. Return to starting position

REQUIRED EQUIPMENT

- Object/Partner
- 1 Medicine ball (4 lb – 10 lb)
- 2 Agility rings

BREATH IN & OUT

- IN: Before Trunk Rotation
- OUT: During Trunk Rotation

PURPOSE

1. Improving body control & coordination
2. Optimizing power-production capabilities of musculature
3. Improving flexibility
4. Improving skill and balance foundation for complex movements

DEGREE OF DIFFICULTY

1

RELEVANCE

- Warms-up musculature of upper extremities and trunk used during groundstrokes
- If "Trunk Rotator Test" shows deficiency, implement this exercise into the warm-up routine

KEY FACTORS

- Focus on perfect movement mechanics (initiate rotation by the trunk) and range of motion (90° external trunk rotation)
- Feet remain flat-footed during movement
- Maintain balance inside agility rings during rotation

COMMON ERRORS

- Athlete initiates rotation via arms
- Athlete moves feet during rotation
- Athlete flexes elbows during rotation

ID: 704

7.05 MB TRUNK ROTATION (II): DIAGONAL LUNGE

SUMMARY

The Medicine Ball (MB) Trunk Rotation (II) is a balance exercise, which focuses on improving body control, balance & coordination, power-production capabilities, flexibility, as well as improving skill & balance foundation for complex movements.

Note: If athlete cannot maintain balance during rotation, flex elbows and move MB closer to the chest.

PURPOSE

1. Improving body control & coordination
2. Optimizing power-production capabilities of musculature
3. Improving flexibility
4. Improving skill and balance foundation for complex movements

DESCRIPTION

1. Hold a medicine ball (MB) naturally in both hands in front of the trunk
2. Take on **diagonal lunge position** with the **right** foot; distribute weight through the heel (flat footed); knees and hips are flexed at 90°; back remains straight; maintain neutral head position; keep **looking forward**
3. Raise arms to shoulder-level and hold a medicine ball (MB) in both hands in front of the trunk; elbows are slightly flexed; **lean forward** with the upper-body
4. Rotate the trunk all the way to the **left** until shoulders are perpendicular to the object/partner(or as far as possible); both elbows remain in initial position; maintain neutral head position; keep **looking forward**
5. Hold position for 1 second
6. Rotate the trunk all the way to the **right** until shoulders are perpendicular to the object/partner (or as far as possible); maintain neutral head position; keep **looking forward**
7. Hold position for 1 second
8. Return to starting position; switch feet

PRE-REQUISITE DRILLS

- Forward/Reverse Lunge
- MB Trunk Rotation

DEGREE OF DIFFICULTY

2

RELEVANCE

- Warms-up musculature of lower and upper extremities and trunk used during groundstrokes
- If "Trunk Rotator Test" and/or "Single-Leg Stability Test" show deficiency, implement this exercise into the warm-up routine

KEY FACTORS

- Focus on perfect movement mechanics (initiate rotation by the trunk) and range of motion (90° external trunk rotation)
- Distribute weight through the heel of the front foot
- Rotate trunk to initiate rotation
- Lean forward during rotation
- Maintain stability

COMMON ERRORS

- Athlete initiates rotation via arms
- Athlete distributes weight through the ball of the foot (toes)
- Athlete loses stability (upper-body leans backwards)

ID: 705

REQUIRED EQUIPMENT

- Object/Partner
- 1 Medicine ball (4 lb – 10 lb)

BREATH IN & OUT

- IN: Before Trunk Rotation
- OUT: During Trunk Rotation

7.06 MB TRUNK ROTATION (III): SINGLE LEG

SUMMARY

The Medicine Ball (MB) Trunk Rotation (III) is a balance exercise, which focuses on improving body control, balance & coordination, power-production capabilities, flexibility, as well as improving skill & balance foundation for complex movements.

Note: If athlete cannot maintain balance during rotation, flex elbows and move MB closer to the chest.

PURPOSE

1. Improving body control & coordination
2. Optimizing power-production capabilities of musculature
3. Improving flexibility
4. Improving skill and balance foundation for complex movements

DESCRIPTION

1. Hold a medicine ball (MB) naturally in both hands in front of the trunk
2. Take on **diagonal single leg stance** position; knee and hip are slightly flexed; non-weight bearing knee is flexed at 90°; back remains straight; **lean forward** with the upper-body
3. Rotate the trunk all the way to the **left** until shoulders are perpendicular to the object/partner (or as far as possible); both elbows remain in initial position; maintain neutral head position; keep **looking forward**
4. Hold position for 1 second
5. Rotate the trunk all the way to the **right** until shoulders are perpendicular to the object/partner (or as far as possible); maintain neutral head position; keep **looking forward**
6. Hold position for 1 second
7. Return to starting position

PRE-REQUISITE DRILLS

- Single-Leg Squat
- MB Trunk Rotation II

DEGREE OF DIFFICULTY

3

RELEVANCE

- Warms-up musculature of lower and upper extremities and trunk used during groundstrokes
- If "Trunk Rotator Test" and/or "Single-Leg Stability Test" show deficiency, implement this exercise into the warm-up routine

KEY FACTORS

- Focus on perfect movement mechanics (initiate rotation by the trunk) and range of motion (90° external trunk rotation)
- Feet remain flat-footed during movement
- Rotate trunk to initiate rotation
- Lean forward during rotation
- Maintain stability

COMMON ERRORS

- Athlete initiates rotation via arms
- Athlete moves feet during rotation
- Athlete loses stability (upper-body leans backwards)

ID: 706

REQUIRED EQUIPMENT

- Object/Partner
- 1 Medicine ball (4 lb – 10 lb)

BREATH IN & OUT

- IN: Before Trunk Rotation
- OUT: During Trunk Rotation

7.07 MB TRUNK ROT. (IV): ALTERNATE DIAGONAL LUNGE

SUMMARY

The Medicine Ball (MB) Trunk Rotation (IV) is a stability exercise, which focuses on improving body control, balance & coordination, power-production capabilities, flexibility, as well as improving skill & balance foundation for complex movements.

Note: If athlete cannot maintain balance during rotation, flex elbows and move MB closer to the chest.

PURPOSE

1. Improving body control & coordination
2. Optimizing power-production capabilities of musculature
3. Improving flexibility
4. Improving skill and balance foundation for complex movements

DESCRIPTION

1. Hold a medicine ball (MB) naturally in both hands in front of the trunk
2. Take on **athletic stance** position; knees and hips are slightly flexed; upper-body is straight
3. Side-Step to the **left**
4. Step into **diagonal lunge** position with the **right** foot; distribute weight through the heel (flat footed); knees and hips are flexed at 90°; back remains straight; maintain neutral head position; keep **looking forward**
5. Raise arms to shoulder-level and hold a medicine ball (MB) in both hands in front of the trunk; elbows are slightly flexed; **lean forward** with the upper-body
6. Rotate the trunk all the way to the **left** until shoulders are perpendicular to the object/partner(or as far as possible); both elbows remain in initial position; maintain neutral head position; keep **looking forward**
7. Hold position for 1 second
8. Rotate the trunk all the way to the **right** until shoulders are perpendicular to the object/partner (or as far as possible); maintain neutral head position; keep **looking forward**
9. Hold position for 1 second
10. Return to starting position; switch feet

PRE-REQUISITE DRILLS

- Side-Step to Diagonal Lunge
- MB Trunk Rotation III

REQUIRED EQUIPMENT

- Object/Partner
- 1 Medicine ball (4 lb – 10 lb)

DEGREE OF DIFFICULTY

4

RELEVANCE

- Warms-up musculature of lower and upper extremities and trunk used during groundstrokes
- If "Trunk Rotator Test" and/or "Single-Leg Stability Test" show deficiency, implement this exercise into the warm-up routine

KEY FACTORS

- Focus on perfect movement mechanics (initiate rotation by the trunk) and range of motion (90° external trunk rotation)
- Distribute weight through the heel of the front foot
- Rotate trunk to initiate rotation
- Lean forward during rotation
- Maintain stability

COMMON ERRORS

- Athlete initiates rotation via arms
- Athlete distributes weight through the ball of the foot (toes)
- Athlete loses stability (upper-body leans backwards)

BREATH IN & OUT

- IN: Before Trunk Rotation
- OUT: During Trunk Rotation

ID: 707

7.08 MB TRUNK ROTATION (V): ALTERNATE SINGLE LEG

SUMMARY

The Medicine Ball (MB) Trunk Rotation (V) is a stability exercise, which focuses on improving body control, balance & coordination, power-production capabilities, and flexibility.

Note: If athlete cannot maintain balance during rotation, flex elbows and move MB closer to the chest.

PURPOSE

1. Improving body control & coordination
2. Optimizing power-production capabilities of musculature
3. Improving flexibility

DESCRIPTION

1. Hold a medicine ball (MB) naturally in both hands in front of the trunk
2. Take on **athletic stance** position; knees and hips are slightly flexed; upper-body is straight
3. Side-Step to the **left**
4. Step into **diagonal single leg stance** position; knee and hip are slightly flexed; non-weight bearing knee is flexed at 90°; back remains straight; **lean forward** with the upper-body
5. Rotate the trunk all the way to the **left** until shoulders are perpendicular to the object/partner (or as far as possible); both elbows remain in initial position; maintain neutral head position; keep **looking forward**
6. Hold position for 1 second
7. Rotate the trunk all the way to the **right** until shoulders are perpendicular to the object/partner (or as far as possible); maintain neutral head position; keep **looking forward**
8. Hold position for 1 second
9. Return to starting position; switch legs

PRE-REQUISITE DRILLS

- Side-Step to Diagonal Single Leg RDL
- MB Trunk Rotation III

REQUIRED EQUIPMENT

- Object/Partner
- 1 Medicine ball (4 lb – 10 lb)

DEGREE OF DIFFICULTY

5

RELEVANCE

- Warms-up musculature of lower and upper extremities and trunk used during groundstrokes
- If "Trunk Rotator Test" and/or "Single-Leg Stability Test" show deficiency, implement this exercise into the warm-up routine

KEY FACTORS

- Focus on perfect movement mechanics (initiate rotation by the trunk) and range of motion (90° external trunk rotation)
- Feet remain flat-footed during movement
- Rotate trunk to initiate rotation
- Lean forward during rotation
- Maintain stability

COMMON ERRORS

- Athlete initiates rotation via arms
- Athlete moves feet during rotation
- Athlete loses stability (upper-body leans backwards)

BREATH IN & OUT

- IN: Before Trunk Rotation
- OUT: During Trunk Rotation

ID: 708

7.09 OVERHEAD MB PULL-OVER (I)

SUMMARY

The Overhead Medicine Ball (MB) Pull-Over (I) is a balance exercise, which focuses on improving body control, balance & coordination, power-production capabilities, flexibility, as well as improving skill & balance foundation for complex movements.

Note: If athlete cannot maintain balance during pull-over, flex elbows and move MB closer to the body.

PURPOSE

1. Improving body control & coordination
2. Optimizing power-production capabilities of upper-body musculature
3. Improving flexibility
4. Improving skill and balance foundation for complex movements

DESCRIPTION

1. Hold a medicine ball (MB) in both hands behind the head; remain 2-3 feet away from the object/partner
2. Take on athletic stance position; knees are slightly flexed; upper-body remains straight; face the object/partner; maintain neutral head position; keep looking forward
3. Flex the shoulders, keep elbows slightly flexed, and pull the MB over the head to chest-level (90° of shoulder flexion)
4. Hold position for 1 second
5. Extend the shoulder with extended elbows until the MB is over the head, then flex the elbows and return MB to starting position

COMMON ERRORS

- Elbows are fully extended (locked) during pull-over
- Flexion of thoracic spine (rounded back) during pull-over

DEGREE OF DIFFICULTY

1

RELEVANCE

- Warms-up musculature of lower and upper extremities and trunk used during the serve
- If "Shoulder Mobility Test" and/or "Trunk Extension Test" show deficiency, implement this exercise into the warm-up routine

REQUIRED EQUIPMENT

- 1 Medicine ball (4 lb – 14 lb)

KEY FACTORS

- Focus on perfect movement mechanics and range of motion
- Maintain neutral head position
- Flex shoulders with slight elbow flexion
- Extend shoulder with extended elbows until MB is over the head
- Maintain stability

BREATH IN & OUT

- IN: Before Shoulder Flexion
- OUT: During Shoulder Flexion

ID: 709

7.10 OVERHEAD MB PULL-OVER (II): LUNGE POSITION

SUMMARY

The Overhead Medicine Ball (MB) Pull-Over (II) is a balance exercise, which focuses on improving body control, balance & coordination, power-production capabilities, flexibility, as well as improving skill & balance foundation for complex movements.

Note: If athlete cannot maintain balance during pull-over, flex elbows and move MB closer to the body.

DESCRIPTION

1. Hold a medicine ball (MB) in both hands behind the head; remain 2-3 feet away from the object/partner
2. Take on a **forward lunge position** with the **right** foot; distribute weight through the heel (flat footed); knees and hips are flexed at 90°; back remains straight; face the object/partner; maintain neutral head position; keep **looking forward**
3. Maintain neutral pelvic position, flex the shoulders, keep elbows slightly flexed, and pull the MB over the head to chest-level (90° of shoulder flexion)
4. Hold position for 1 second
5. Extend the shoulder with extended elbows until the MB is over the head, then flex the elbows and return MB to starting position

PRE-REQUISITE DRILLS

- Forward/Reverse Lunge
- Overhead MB Pull-Over I

DEGREE OF DIFFICULTY

2

REQUIRED EQUIPMENT

- 1 Medicine ball (4 lb – 14 lb)

BREATH IN & OUT

- IN: Before Shoulder Flexion
- OUT: During Shoulder Flexion

PURPOSE

1. Improving body control & coordination
2. Optimizing power-production capabilities of upper-body musculature
3. Improving flexibility
4. Improving skill and balance foundation for complex movements

RELEVANCE

- Warms-up musculature of lower and upper extremities and trunk used during the serve
- If "Hip Flexion Test" and/or "Trunk Extension Test" show deficiency, implement this exercise into the warm-up routine

KEY FACTORS

- Focus on perfect movement mechanics and range of motion
- Distribute weight through the heel of the front foot
- Maintain neutral head position
- Flex shoulders with slight elbow flexion
- Extend shoulder with extended elbows until MB is over the head
- Maintain stability

COMMON ERRORS

- Elbows are fully extended (locked) during pull-over
- Flexion of thoracic spine (rounded back) during pull-over
- Athlete distributes weight through the ball of the foot (toes)
- Athlete loses balance

ID: 710

7.11 OVERHEAD MB PULL-OVER (III): SINGLE LEG

SUMMARY

The Overhead Medicine Ball (MB) Pull-Over (II) is a balance exercise, which focuses on improving body control, balance & coordination, power-production capabilities, flexibility, as well as improving skill & balance foundation for complex movements.

Note: If athlete cannot maintain balance during pull-over, flex elbows and move MB closer to the body.

PURPOSE

1. Improving body control & coordination
2. Optimizing power-production capabilities of upper-body musculature
3. Improving flexibility
4. Improving skill and balance foundation for complex movements

DESCRIPTION

1. Hold a medicine ball (MB) in both hands behind the head
2. Take on **single leg stance** position; knee and hip are slightly flexed; non-weight bearing knee is flexed at 90°; back remains straight; face the object/partner; maintain neutral head position; keep **looking forward**
3. Maintain neutral pelvic position, flex the shoulders, keep elbows slightly flexed, and pull the MB over the head to chest-level (90° of shoulder flexion)
4. Hold position for 1 second
5. Extend the shoulder with extended elbows until the MB is over the head, then flex the elbows and return MB to starting position;

PRE-REQUISITE DRILLS

- Single-Leg Squat
- Overhead MB Pull-Over II

REQUIRED EQUIPMENT

- 1 Medicine ball (4 lb – 14 lb)

BREATH IN & OUT

- IN: Before Shoulder Flexion
- OUT: During Shoulder Flexion

COMMON ERRORS

- Elbows are fully extended (locked) during pull-over
- Flexion of thoracic spine (rounded back) during pull-over
- Athlete loses balance

DEGREE OF DIFFICULTY

3

RELEVANCE

- Warms-up musculature of lower and upper extremities and trunk used during the serve
- If "Single Leg Stability Test" and/or "Trunk Extension Test" show deficiency, implement this exercise into the warm-up routine

KEY FACTORS

- Focus on perfect movement mechanics and range of motion
- Maintain neutral head position
- Flex shoulders with slight elbow flexion
- Extend shoulder with extended elbows until MB is over the head
- Maintain stability

ID: 711

7.12 OVERHEAD MB PULL OVER (IV): ALTERNATE LUNGE

SUMMARY

The Overhead Medicine Ball (MB) Pull-Over (IV) is a stability exercise, which focuses on improving body control, balance & coordination, power-production capabilities, flexibility, as well as improving skill & balance foundation for complex movements.

Note: If athlete cannot maintain balance during pull-over, flex elbows and move MB closer to the body.

PURPOSE

1. Improving body control & coordination
2. Optimizing power-production capabilities of upper-body musculature
3. Improving flexibility
4. Improving skill and balance foundation for complex movements

DESCRIPTION

1. Hold a medicine ball (MB) in both hands behind the head
2. Take on **athletic stance** position; knees are slightly flexed; upper-body is straight
3. Side-Step to the **left**
4. Step into a **diagonal lunge position** with the **right** foot; distribute weight through the heel (flat footed); knees and hips are flexed at 90°; back remains straight; face the object/partner; maintain neutral head position; keep **looking forward**
5. Maintain neutral pelvic position, flex the shoulders, keep elbows slightly flexed, and pull the MB over the head to chest-level (90° of shoulder flexion)
6. Extend the shoulder with extended elbows until the MB is over the head, then flex the elbows and return MB to starting position
7. Side-step to the **right**
8. Step into diagonal lunge position with left foot and repeat

PRE-REQUISITE DRILLS

- Side-Step to Diagonal Lunge
- Overhead MB Pull-Over II

REQUIRED EQUIPMENT

- 1 Medicine ball (4 lb – 14 lb)

BREATH IN & OUT

- IN: Before Shoulder Flexion
- OUT: During Shoulder Flexion

DEGREE OF DIFFICULTY

4

RELEVANCE

- Warms-up musculature of lower and upper extremities and trunk used during the serve
- If "Single Leg Stability Test" and/or "Hip Flexion Test" show deficiency, implement this exercise into the warm-up routine

KEY FACTORS

- Focus on perfect movement mechanics and range of motion
- Maintain neutral head position
- Distribute weight through the heel of the front foot
- Flex shoulders with slight elbow flexion
- Maintain neutral pelvic position during pull-over
- Extend shoulder with extended elbows until MB is over the head
- Maintain stability

COMMON ERRORS

- Elbows are fully extended (locked) during pull-over
- Flexion of thoracic spine (rounded back) during pull-over
- Athlete distributes weight through the ball of the foot (toes)
- Athlete loses balance

ID: 712

7.13 OVERHEAD MB PULL OVER (V): ALTERNATE SL

SUMMARY

The Overhead Medicine Ball (MB) Pull-Over (V) is a stability exercise, which focuses on improving body control, balance & coordination, power-production capabilities, and flexibility.

Note: If athlete cannot maintain balance during pull-over, flex elbows and move MB closer to the body.

PURPOSE

1. Improving body control & coordination
2. Optimizing power-production capabilities of upper-body musculature
3. Improving flexibility

DESCRIPTION

1. Hold a medicine ball (MB) in both hands behind the head
2. Take on **athletic stance** position; knees and hips are slightly flexed; upper-body is straight
3. Side-Step to the **left**
4. Step into a **diagonal single leg stance** position; knee and hip are slightly flexed; non-weight bearing knee is flexed at 90°; back remains straight; face the object/partner; maintain neutral head position; keep **looking forward**
5. Maintain neutral pelvic position, flex the shoulders, keep elbows slightly flexed, and pull the MB over the head to chest-level (90° of shoulder flexion)
6. Extend the shoulder with extended elbows until the MB is over the head, then flex the elbows and return MB to starting position
7. Side-step to the **right**
8. Step into diagonal single-leg stance position with **left** foot and repeat

PRE-REQUISITE DRILLS

- Side-Step to Diagonal Single-Leg RDL
- Overhead MB Pull-Over III

REQUIRED EQUIPMENT

- 1 Medicine ball (4 lb – 14 lb)

BREATH IN & OUT

- IN: Before Shoulder Flexion
- OUT: During Shoulder Flexion

DEGREE OF DIFFICULTY

5

RELEVANCE

- Warms-up musculature of lower and upper extremities and trunk used during the serve
- If "Single Leg Stability Test" and/or "Trunk Extension Test" show deficiency, implement this exercise into the warm-up routine

KEY FACTORS

- Focus on perfect movement mechanics and range of motion
- Maintain neutral head position
- Flex shoulders with slight elbow flexion
- Maintain neutral pelvic position during pull-over
- Extend shoulder with extended elbows until MB is over the head
- Maintain stability

COMMON ERRORS

- Elbows are fully extended (locked) during pull-over
- Flexion of thoracic spine (rounded back) during pull-over
- Athlete loses balance

ID: 713

7

7.14 3-WAY HAND REACHES (I)

SUMMARY

The 3 Way Hand Reaches (I) is a balance exercise, which focuses on improving balance & coordination, power-production capabilities, flexibility, as well as improving skill & balance foundation for complex movements.

PURPOSE

1. Improving body control & coordination
2. Optimizing power-production capabilities of upper-body musculature
3. Improving flexibility
4. Improving skill and balance foundation for complex movements

DESCRIPTION

1. Place three (3) cones (targets) in a semi-circle 1-2 feet in front of you
2. Take on **athletic stance** position; feet are shoulder-width apart; knees and hips are slightly flexed; upper-body is straight; **look forward**
3. Move hands together, extend arms, push chest out; look forward
4. Flex hips to 90° (or as far as possible) and reach towards the cones without losing stability; feet maintain ground contact
5. Extend hips to neutral position before reaching for next cone

PRE-REQUISITE DRILLS

- Squat
- Romanian Deadlift (RDL)

DEGREE OF DIFFICULTY

1

RELEVANCE

- Warms-up musculature of lower extremities and trunk used during groundstrokes
- If "Bilateral Knee Extension Test" shows deficiency, implement this exercise into the warm-up routine
- If "Stability Pad Squat Test" shows deficiency, implement this exercise into the Resistance Training Program
- If the athlete loses stability during the **serve** he/she should regularly do this exercise because it will improve balance and power during shots

KEY FACTORS

- Focus on perfect movement mechanics and range of motion
- Maintain neutral head position
- Maintain stability

COMMON ERRORS

- No hip extension occurs after each reach
- Flexion of thoracic spine (rounded back) during reaches
- Athlete loses balance

ID: 714

REQUIRED EQUIPMENT

- 3 Cones

BREATH IN & OUT

- IN: Before Hand Reach
- OUT: During Hand Reach

7.15 3-WAY HAND REACHES (II): SINGLE LEG

SUMMARY

The 3 Way Hand Reaches (II): Single Leg is a balance exercise, which focuses on improving balance & coordination, power-production capabilities, flexibility, as well as improving skill & balance foundation for complex movements.

PURPOSE

1. Improving body control & coordination
2. Optimizing power-production capabilities of upper-body musculature
3. Improving flexibility
4. Improving skill and balance foundation for complex movements

DESCRIPTION

1. Place three (3) cones (targets) in a semi-circle 1-2 feet in front of you
2. Take on **single leg stance** position; knee and hip are slightly flexed; non-weight bearing knee is flexed at 90°; back remains straight; face the cones; maintain neutral head position; keep **looking forward**
3. Flex hips to 90° (or as far as possible), move hands together, extend elbows, and reach towards the cones without losing stability; feet maintain ground contact
4. Extend hips to neutral position before reaching for next cone
5. Switch legs

PRE-REQUISITE DRILLS

- 3 Way Hand Reaches (I)
- Single Leg RDL
- Lunge

DEGREE OF DIFFICULTY

2

RELEVANCE

- Warms-up musculature of lower extremities and trunk used during groundstrokes
- If "Bilateral Knee Extension Test" shows deficiency, implement this exercise into the warm-up routine
- If "Stability Pad Squat Test" shows deficiency, implement this exercise into the Resistance Training Program
- If the athlete loses stability during the **serve** he/she should regularly do this exercise because it will improve balance and power during shots

KEY FACTORS

- Focus on perfect movement mechanics and range of motion
- Maintain neutral head position
- Maintain stability

COMMON ERRORS

- No hip extension occurs after each reach
- Flexion of thoracic spine (rounded back) during reaches
- Athlete loses balance

ID: 715

REQUIRED EQUIPMENT

- 3 Cones

BREATH IN & OUT

- IN: Before Hand Reach
- OUT: During Hand Reach

7.16 3 WAY HAND REACHES (III): SL SH CROSS-OVER

SUMMARY

The 3 Way Hand Reaches (III): Single Leg Single Hand Cross-Over is a balance exercise, which focuses on improving balance & coordination, power-production capabilities, flexibility, as well as improving skill & balance foundation for complex movements.

PURPOSE

1. Improving body control & coordination
2. Optimizing power-production capabilities of upper-body musculature
3. Improving flexibility
4. Improving skill and balance foundation for complex movements

DESCRIPTION

1. Place three (3) cones (targets) in a semi-circle 1-2 feet in front of you
2. Take on **single leg stance** position; knee and hip are slightly flexed; non-weight bearing knee is flexed at 90°; back remains straight; face the cones; maintain neutral head position; keep **looking forward**
3. Use **right** hand, extend arm, and reach towards the cone in front of you (cone #2) without losing stability
4. Cross over and reach the cone to the left (cone #1) with the **right** hand
5. Use the **left** hand and cross over to touch the cone to the right (cone #3)
6. Switch legs and start with the **left** hand

PRE-REQUISITE DRILLS

- 3 Way Hand Reaches (II)

DEGREE OF DIFFICULTY

3

BREATH IN & OUT

- IN: Before Hand Reach
- OUT: During Hand Reach

RELEVANCE

- Warms-up musculature of lower extremities and trunk used during groundstrokes
- If "Bilateral Knee Extension Test" shows deficiency, implement this exercise into the warm-up routine
- If "Stability Pad Squat Test" shows deficiency, implement this exercise into the Resistance Training Program
- If the athlete loses stability during **groundstrokes** he/she should regularly do this exercise because it will improve balance and power during shots

KEY FACTORS

- Focus on perfect movement mechanics and range of motion
- Maintain neutral head position
- Maintain stability

COMMON ERRORS

- No hip extension occurs after each reach
- Flexion of thoracic spine (rounded back) during reaches
- Athlete loses balance

REQUIRED EQUIPMENT

- 3 Cones

ID: 716

7.17 3-WAY HEEL REACH (I): SINGLE LEG HOLD

SUMMARY

The 3 Way Heel Reach (I) is a balance exercise, which focuses on improving balance & coordination, power-production capabilities, flexibility, as well as improving skill & balance foundation for complex movements.

PURPOSE

1. Improving body control & coordination
2. Optimizing power-production capabilities of upper-body musculature
3. Improving flexibility
4. Improving skill and balance foundation for complex movements

DESCRIPTION

1. Place three (3) cones (targets) in a semi-circle 1-2 feet in front of you
2. Take on **single leg stance** position (**left** leg); knee and hip are slightly flexed; non-weight bearing knee is extended; back remains straight; face the cones; maintain neutral head position; keep **looking forward**
3. Use **right** leg and point the heel towards the cone in front of you (cone #2) without losing stability
4. Hold position 5 seconds
5. Cross over and reach the cone to the left (cone #1) with the **right** foot heel
6. Hold position 5 seconds
7. Cross over to reach the cone to the right (cone #3)
8. Hold position 5 seconds
9. Switch legs

RELEVANCE

- Warms-up musculature of lower extremities and trunk used during groundstrokes
- If "Bilateral Knee Extension Test" shows deficiency, implement this exercise into the warm-up routine
- If "Stability Pad Squat Test" shows deficiency, implement this exercise into the Resistance Training Program
- If the athlete loses stability during **groundstrokes** he/she should regularly do this exercise because it will improve balance and power during shots

KEY FACTORS

- Focus on perfect movement mechanics and range of motion
- Maintain neutral head position
- Maintain stability

COMMON ERRORS

- No hip extension occurs after each reach
- Flexion of thoracic spine (rounded back) during reaches
- Athlete loses balance

DEGREE OF DIFFICULTY

2

PRE-REQUISITE DRILLS

- Single Leg Romanian Deadlift

REQUIRED EQUIPMENT

- 3 Cones

BREATH IN & OUT

- IN: Before Heel Reach
- OUT: During Heel Reach

7.18 3-WAY HEEL REACH (II): SINGLE LEG REACH

SUMMARY

The 3 Way Heel Reach (II) is a balance exercise, which focuses on improving balance & coordination, power-production capabilities, flexibility, as well as improving skill & balance foundation for complex movements.

PURPOSE

1. Improving body control & coordination
2. Optimizing power-production capabilities of upper-body musculature
3. Improving flexibility
4. Improving skill and balance foundation for complex movements

DESCRIPTION

1. Place three (3) cones (targets) in a semi-circle 1-2 feet in front of you
2. Take on **single leg stance** position (left leg); knee and hip are slightly flexed; non-weight bearing knee is extended; back remains straight; face the cones; maintain neutral head position; keep **looking forward**
3. Use **right** leg and point the heel towards the cone in front of you (cone #2) without losing stability
4. Cross over and reach the cone to the left (cone #1) with the **right** foot heel
5. Cross over to reach the cone to the right (cone #3)
6. Switch legs

PRE-REQUISITE DRILLS

- 3 Way Heel Reaches (I): Single Leg Holds

DEGREE OF DIFFICULTY

2

RELEVANCE

- Warms-up musculature of lower extremities and trunk used during groundstrokes
- If "Bilateral Knee Extension Test" shows deficiency, implement this exercise into the warm-up routine
- If "Stability Pad Squat Test" shows deficiency, implement this exercise into the Resistance Training Program
- If the athlete loses stability during **groundstrokes** he/she should regularly do this exercise because it will improve balance and power during shots

KEY FACTORS

- Focus on perfect movement mechanics and range of motion
- Maintain neutral head position
- Maintain stability

COMMON ERRORS

- No hip extension occurs after each reach
- Flexion of thoracic spine (rounded back) during reaches
- Athlete loses balance

ID: 718

REQUIRED EQUIPMENT

- 3 Cones

BREATH IN & OUT

- IN: Before Heel Reach
- OUT: During Heel Reach

7.19 3-WHR (III): SINGLE LEG RANDOM REACH

SUMMARY

The 3 Way Heel Reaches (III) is a balance exercise, which focuses on improving balance & coordination, power-production capabilities, and flexibility.

Coach/partner randomly calls out cone numbers that athlete needs to reach.

DESCRIPTION

1. Place three (3) cones (targets) in a semi-circle 1-2 feet in front of you
2. Take on **single leg stance** position (**left** leg); knee and hip are slightly flexed; non-weight bearing knee is extended; back remains straight; face the cones; maintain neutral head position; keep **looking forward**
3. Use **right** leg and point the heel towards the cone that is being called out by the coach (e.g. cone #2) without losing stability
4. Switch legs

PRE-REQUISITE DRILLS

- 3 Way Heel Reaches (II): Single Leg Reaches

COMMON ERRORS

- No hip extension occurs after each reach
- Flexion of thoracic spine (rounded back) during reaches
- Athlete loses balance

REQUIRED EQUIPMENT

- Coach/Partner
- 3 Cones

BREATH IN & OUT

- IN: Before Heel Reach
- OUT: During Heel Reach

KEY FACTORS

- Focus on perfect movement mechanics and range of motion
- Maintain neutral head position
- Maintain stability

ID: 719

PURPOSE

1. Improving body control & coordination
2. Optimizing power-production capabilities of upper-body musculature
3. Improving flexibility

DEGREE OF DIFFICULTY

3

RELEVANCE

- Warms-up musculature of lower extremities and trunk used during groundstrokes
- If "Bilateral Knee Extension Test" shows deficiency, implement this exercise into the warm-up routine
- If "Stability Pad Squat Test" shows deficiency, implement this exercise into the Resistance Training Program
- If the athlete loses stability during **groundstrokes** he/she should regularly do this exercise because it will improve their balance and power during shots

7.20 STABILITY-PAD SQUAT

SUMMARY

The Stability-Pad Squat is a balance exercise, which focuses on improving balance & coordination, power-production capabilities, flexibility, as well as improving skill & balance foundation for complex movements.

DESCRIPTION

1. Setup 2 stability pads shoulder-width apart on a non-sliding, even surface
2. Stand on both pads; toes pointing forward;
3. Take on **athletic stance**; knees and hips are slightly flexed; back remains straight; maintain neutral head position; keep **looking forward**
4. Distribute weight evenly through your feet and squat (flex your knees & hips until they reach 90°)
5. Extend your knees & hips until you stand erect

DEGREE OF DIFFICULTY

1

PRE-REQUISITE DRILLS

- Squat, Deadlift, Lunge

BREATH IN & OUT

- IN: Before Single Leg Squat
- OUT: During Single Leg Squat

REQUIRED EQUIPMENT

- 2 Stability pads

PURPOSE

1. Improving body control & coordination
2. Optimizing power-production capabilities of upper-body musculature
3. Improving flexibility
4. Improving skill and balance foundation for complex movements

RELEVANCE

- Warms-up musculature of lower extremities and trunk used during groundstrokes
- If "Stability-Pad Squat Test" shows deficiency, implement this exercise into the warm-up routine
- If "Stability Pad Squat Test" shows deficiency, implement this exercise into the Resistance Training Program
- If the athlete loses stability during **groundstrokes** he/she should regularly do this exercise because it will improve balance and power during shots

KEY FACTORS

- Focus on perfect movement mechanics and range of motion
- Maintain neutral head position
- Maintain stability

COMMON ERRORS

- Weight distribution occurs at the toes
- Flexion of thoracic spine (rounded back) during motion
- Athlete loses balance

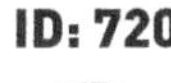

7.21 STABILITY-PAD LUNGE

SUMMARY

The Stability-Pad Lunge is a balance exercise, which focuses on improving balance & coordination, power-production capabilities, flexibility, as well as improving skill & balance foundation for complex movements.

PURPOSE

1. Improving body control & coordination
2. Optimizing power-production capabilities of upper-body musculature
3. Improving flexibility
4. Improving skill and balance foundation for complex movements

DESCRIPTION

1. Set up 2 stability pads two shoulder-widths apart on a non-sliding, even surface
2. Stand in the center of the 2 pads and move ~3 feet in front of the pads;
3. Take on **athletic stance**; knees and hips are slightly flexed; back remains straight; maintain neutral head position; keep **looking forward**
4. Take a big step diagonally onto the pad, heels first; toes pointing diagonally in line with knee
5. Distribute weight evenly through the foot and lunge (bend knees until they reach 90°)
6. Extend knees and push off the pad
7. Return to starting position and switch legs

PRE-REQUISITE DRILLS

- Lunge
- Squat
- Single Leg RDL

REQUIRED EQUIPMENT

- 2 Stability pad

BREATH IN & OUT

- IN: Before Lunge Position
- OUT: During Lunge Position

DEGREE OF DIFFICULTY

1

RELEVANCE

- Warms-up musculature of lower extremities and trunk used during groundstrokes
- If "Stability-Pad Squat Test" shows deficiency, implement this exercise into the warm-up routine
- If "Stability Pad Squat Test" shows deficiency, implement this exercise into the Resistance Training Program
- If the athlete loses stability during **groundstrokes** he/she should regularly do this exercise because it will improve balance and power during shots

KEY FACTORS

- Focus on perfect movement mechanics and range of motion
- Maintain neutral head position
- Maintain stability

COMMON ERRORS

- Weight distribution occurs at the toes
- Flexion of thoracic spine (rounded back) during motion
- Athlete loses balance

ID: 721

STRIDE LENGTH & FREQUENCY EXERCISES

In this section speed ladder exercises are being presented that will help the athlete to optimize movement economy, which translates into improving foot speed. If the athlete becomes more proficient at stabilizing the action and managing the center of gravity effectively, the amount of energy required to produce force and change direction will be reduced.

Therefore, the ability to move at top speed on the court will be enhanced, which allows the athlete a greater variety in shot selection and reduces the time for the opponent to react. For that reason it is imperative to focus on technique!

Consequently, the exercises are categorized and try to duplicate movement patterns that occur when playing tennis. They are presented in a developmental fashion according to their respective degrees of difficulty:

1. Introductory
2. Intermediate
3. Advanced
4. Professional

Initially the athlete will need to become proficient in **Speed Ladder Drills** before moving on to the **Integrated Speed, Agility**, and Reaction Drills.

7.22 FAST FEET I

SUMMARY

The Fast Feet I is an introductory speed ladder exercise, which focuses on improving footwork for groundstrokes, utilizing a speed ladder.

PURPOSE

1. Improving footwork for groundstrokes

DESCRIPTION

1. Stand directly in front of the 1st rung
2. Place both feet inside each square, starting with the left or right foot
3. Keep body weight on the balls of the feet (toes)
4. Progress down the ladder in a rapid fashion while **looking at the feet**

KEY FACTORS

- Stay on balls of the feet; toes
- Hit the center of the squares
- Initiate exercise with the right foot & the left foot, respectively

REQUIRED EQUIPMENT

- 1 Speed Ladder

COMMON ERRORS

- Whole foot is on the ground (flat-footed)
- Exercise is initiated only using the left foot

DEGREE OF DIFFICULTY

1

ID: 722

7.23 FAST FEET II

SUMMARY

The Fast Feet II is an intermediate speed ladder exercise, which focuses on improving footwork for groundstrokes, utilizing the speed ladder while holding a racquet.

PURPOSE

1. Improving footwork for groundstrokes

DESCRIPTION

1. Stand directly in front of the 1st rung
2. Hold the **racquet** in both hands – ready position
3. Place both feet inside each square, starting with the left or right foot
4. Keep body weight on the balls of the feet (toes)
5. Progress down the ladder in a rapid fashion while **looking at the feet**

REQUIRED EQUIPMENT

- 1 Speed Ladder
- 1 Racquet

DEGREE OF DIFFICULTY

2

KEY FACTORS

- Stay on balls of the feet; toes
- Hit the center of the squares
- Initiate exercise with the right foot & the left foot, respectively

COMMON ERRORS

- Whole foot is on the ground (flat-footed)
- Exercise is initiated only using the left foot

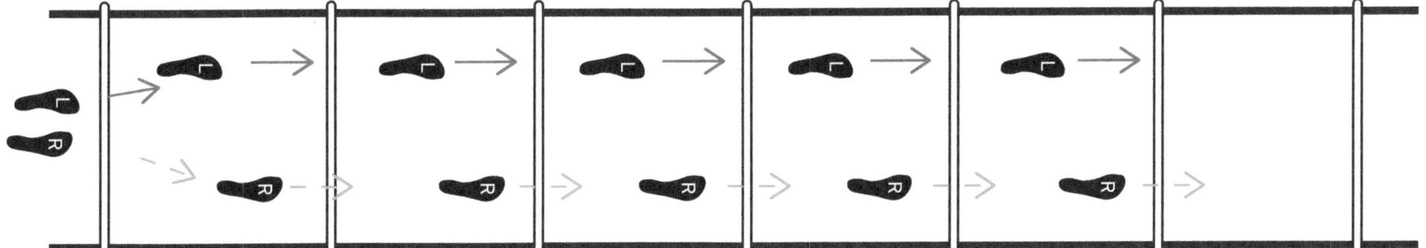

ID: 723

7.24 FAST FEET III

SUMMARY

The Fast Feet III is an advanced speed ladder exercise, which focuses on improving footwork for groundstrokes, utilizing the speed ladder while holding a racquet.

PURPOSE

1. Improving footwork for groundstrokes

DESCRIPTION

1. Stand directly in front of the 1st rung
2. Hold the **racquet** in both hands – ready position
3. Place both feet inside each square, starting with the left or right foot
4. Keep body weight on the balls of the feet (toes)
5. Progress down the ladder in a rapid fashion while **looking forward**

KEY FACTORS

- Stay on balls of the feet; toes
- Hit the center of the squares
- Initiate exercise with the right foot & the left foot, respectively

COMMON ERRORS

- Whole foot is on the ground (flat-footed)
- Exercise is initiated only using the left foot

PRE-REQUISITE DRILLS

- Fast Feet II

REQUIRED EQUIPMENT

- 1 Speed Ladder
- 1 Racquet

DEGREE OF DIFFICULTY

3

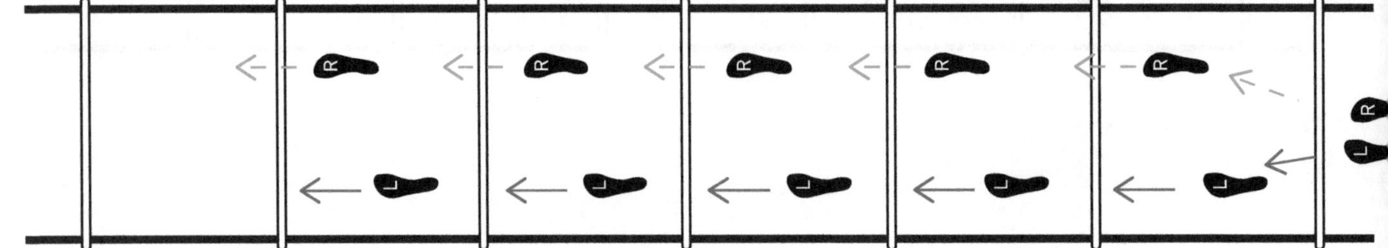

ID: 724

7.25 FAST FEET IV

SUMMARY

The Fast Feet IV is a professional speed ladder exercise, which focuses on improving footwork for groundstrokes, utilizing the speed ladder while holding a racquet and tracking an opponent.

PURPOSE

1. Improving footwork for groundstrokes

DESCRIPTION

1. Stand directly in front of the 1st rung
2. Hold the **racquet** in both hands – ready position
3. Place both feet inside each square, starting with the left or right foot
4. Keep body weight on the balls of the feet (toes)
5. Progress down the ladder in a rapid fashion while looking forward **tracking an opponent**

KEY FACTORS

- Stay on balls of the feet; toes
- Hit the center of the squares
- Initiate exercise with the right foot & the left foot, respectively

COMMON ERRORS

- Whole foot is on the ground (flat-footed)
- Exercise is initiated only using the left – or right foot

PRE-REQUISITE DRILLS

- Fast Feet III

REQUIRED EQUIPMENT

- 1 Speed Ladder
- 1 Racquet

DEGREE OF DIFFICULTY

4

ID: 725

7.26 JUMP-OVER FAST FEET I

SUMMARY

The Jump-Over Fast Feet I is an introductory speed ladder exercise, which focuses on improving footwork for transition game and quick start capability, utilizing a speed ladder.

PURPOSE

1. Improving footwork for transition game
2. Improving quick start capability

DESCRIPTION

1. Stand directly in front of the 1st rung
2. **Jump over** the rung in front of you and land into the 2nd rung, leading with the **left** foot
3. Step **backwards** into the 1st rung, leading with the **left** foot
4. **Jump over** the rung in front of you and land into the 3rd rung, leading with the **left** foot
5. Step **backwards** into the 2nd rung, leading with the left foot
6. Keep body weight on the balls of the feet (toes)
7. Progress down the ladder in a rapid fashion while **looking at the feet**

REQUIRED EQUIPMENT

- 1 Speed Ladder

KEY FACTORS

- Stay on balls of the feet; toes
- Hit the center of the squares
- Initiate exercise with the right foot & the left foot, respectively

COMMON ERRORS

- Whole foot is on the ground (flat-footed)
- Exercise is initiated only using the left foot

DEGREE OF DIFFICULTY

1

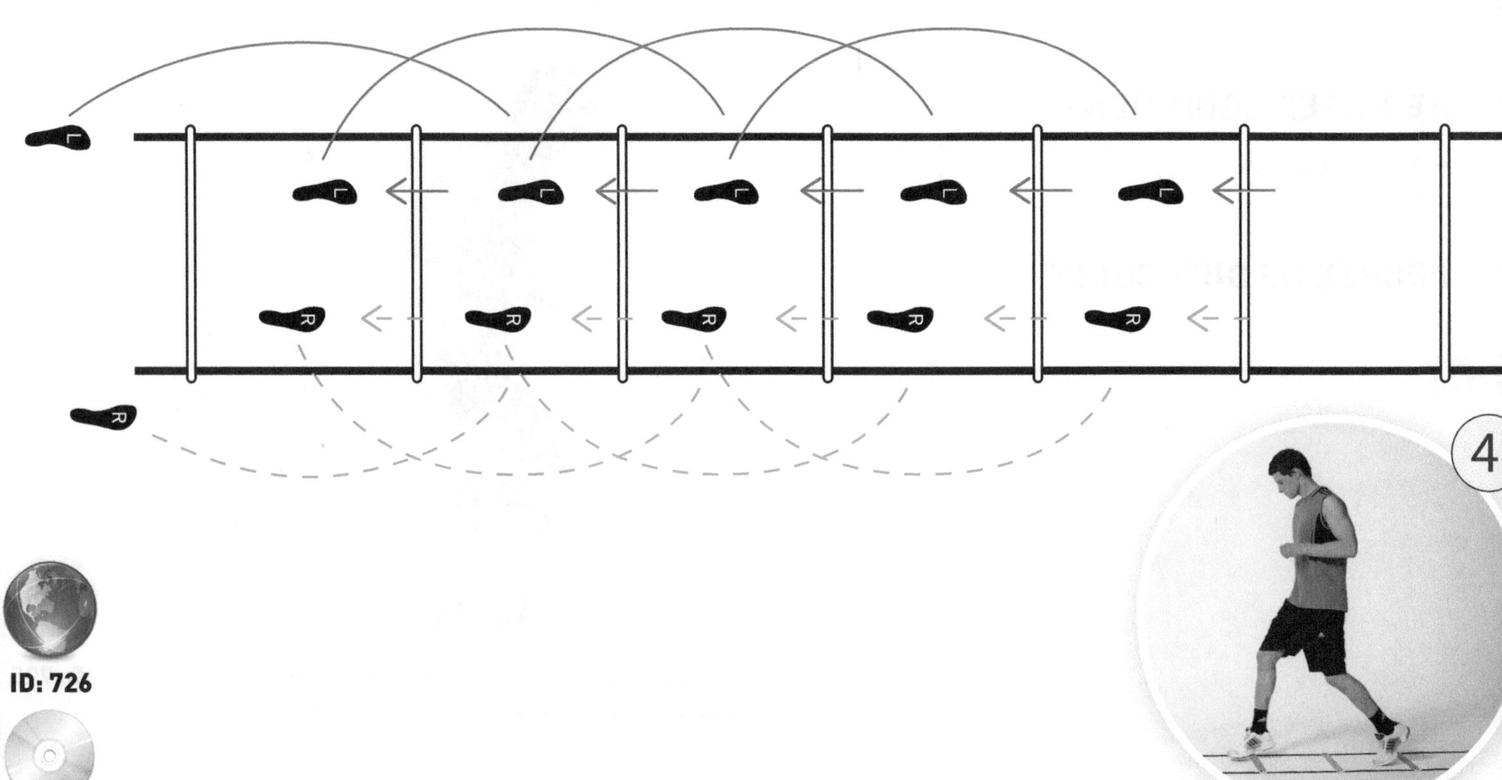

7.27 JUMP-OVER FAST FEET II

SUMMARY

The Jump-Over Fast Feet II is an intermediate speed ladder exercise, which focuses on improving footwork for transition game and quick start capability, utilizing a speed ladder.

PURPOSE

1. Improving footwork for transition game
2. Improving quick start capability

DESCRIPTION

1. Stand directly in front of the 1st rung holding a **tennis racquet** in both hands
2. Jump over the rung in front of you and land into the 2nd rung, leading with the left foot
3. Step backwards into the 1st rung, leading with the left foot
4. Jump over the rung in front of you and land into the 3rd rung, leading with the left foot
5. Step backwards into the 2nd rung, leading with the left foot
6. Keep body weight on the balls of the feet (toes)
7. Progress down the ladder in a rapid fashion while **looking at the feet**

DEGREE OF DIFFICULTY

2

KEY FACTORS

- Stay on balls of the feet; toes
- Hit the center of the squares
- Initiate exercise with the right foot & the left foot, respectively

COMMON ERRORS

- Whole foot is on the ground (flat-footed)
- Exercise is initiated only using the left foot

PRE-REQUISITE DRILLS

- Jump-Over Fast Feet I

REQUIRED EQUIPMENT

- 1 Speed Ladder
- 1 Racquet

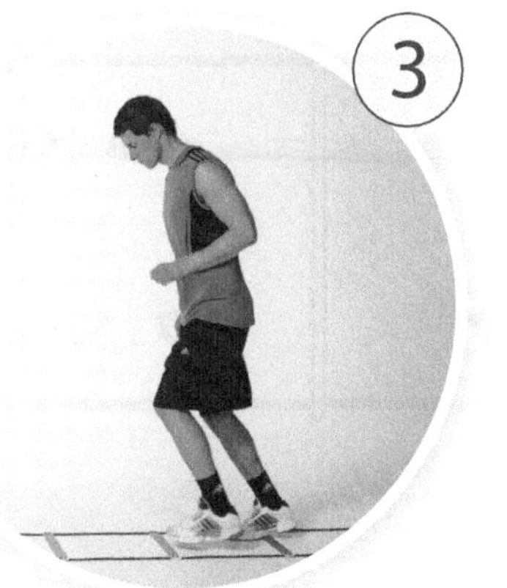

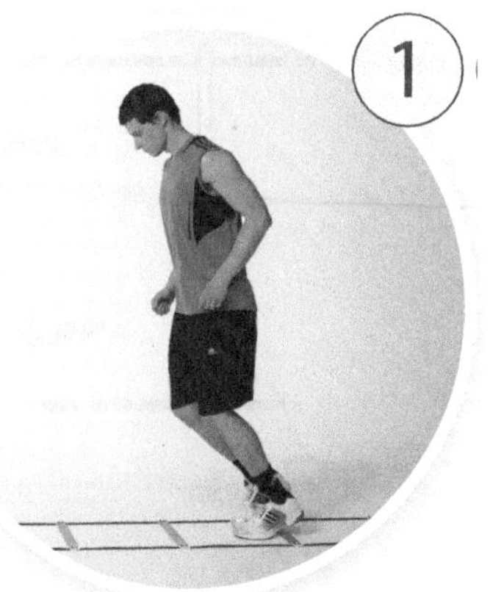

ID: 727

7.28 JUMP-OVER FAST FEET III

SUMMARY

The Jump-Over Fast Feet III is an advanced speed ladder exercise, which focuses on improving footwork for transition game and quick start capability, utilizing a speed ladder.

PURPOSE

1. Improving footwork for transition game
2. Improving quick start capability

DESCRIPTION

1. Stand directly in front of the 1st rung holding a **tennis racquet** in both hands
2. Jump over the rung in front of you and land into the 2nd rung, leading with the left foot
3. Step backwards into the 1st rung, leading with the left foot
4. Jump over the rung in front of you and land into the 3rd rung, leading with the left foot
5. Step backwards into the 2nd rung, leading with the left foot
6. Keep body weight on the balls of the feet (toes)
7. Progress down the ladder in a rapid fashion while **looking forward**

DEGREE OF DIFFICULTY

3

KEY FACTORS

- Stay on balls of the feet; toes
- Hit the center of the squares
- Initiate exercise with the right foot & the left foot, respectively

COMMON ERRORS

- Whole foot is on the ground (flat-footed)
- Exercise is initiated only using the left foot

PRE-REQUISITE DRILLS

- Jump-Over Fast Feet II

REQUIRED EQUIPMENT

- 1 Speed Ladder,
- 1 Racquet

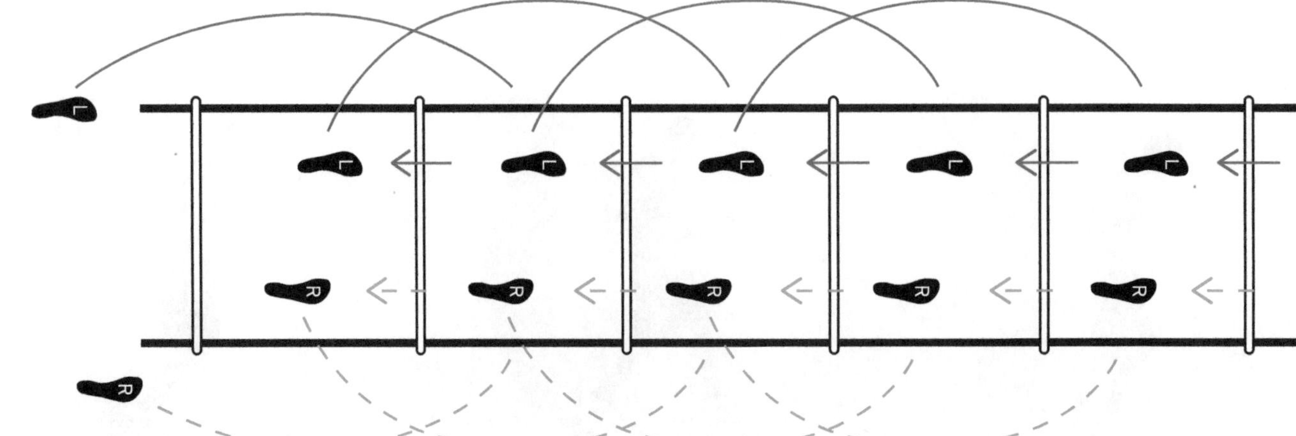

ID: 728

7.29 JUMP-OVER FAST FEET IV

SUMMARY

The Jump-Over Fast Feet IV is a professional speed ladder exercise, which focuses on improving footwork for transition game and quick start capability, utilizing a speed ladder.

PURPOSE

1. Improving footwork for transition game
2. Improving quick start capability

DESCRIPTION

1. Stand directly in front of the 1st rung holding a **tennis racquet** in both hands
2. Jump over the rung in front of you and land into the 2nd rung, leading with the left foot
3. Step backwards into the 1st rung, leading with the left foot
4. Jump over the rung in front of you and land into the 3rd rung, leading with the left foot
5. Step backwards into the 2nd rung, leading with the left foot
6. Keep body weight on the balls of the feet (toes)
7. Progress down the ladder in a rapid fashion while **tracking the coach**

PRE-REQUISITE DRILLS

- Jump-Over Fast Feet III

KEY FACTORS

- Stay on balls of the feet; toes
- Hit the center of the squares
- Initiate exercise with the right foot & the left foot, respectively

COMMON ERRORS

- Whole foot is on the ground (flat-footed)
- Exercise is initiated only using the left foot

REQUIRED EQUIPMENT

- 1 Speed Ladder,
- 1 Racquet

DEGREE OF DIFFICULTY

4

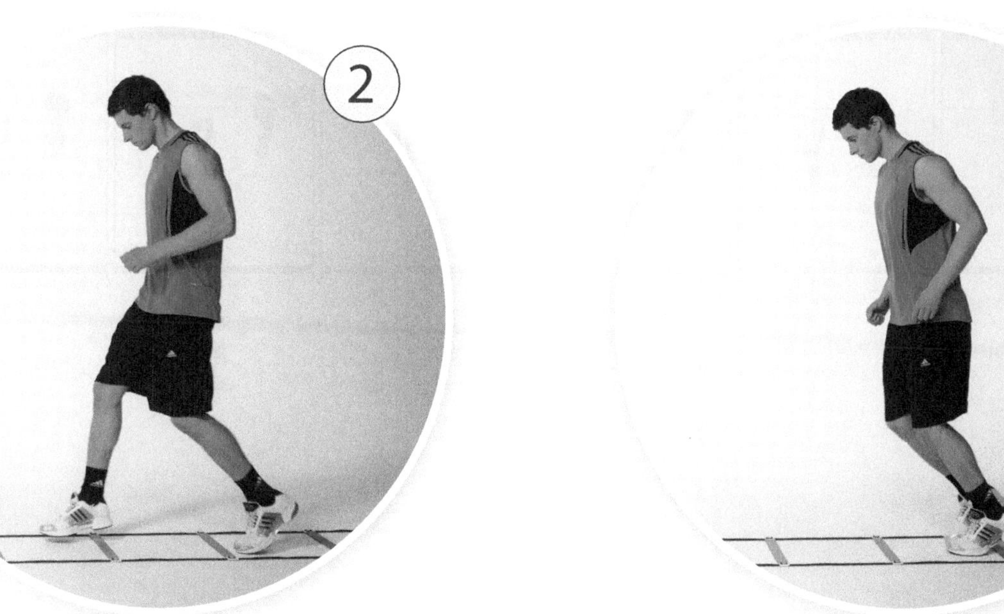

ID: 729

7.30 LATERAL FAST FEET I

SUMMARY

The Lateral Fast Feet I is an introductory speed ladder exercise, which focuses on improving footwork for groundstrokes, utilizing a speed ladder.

PURPOSE

1. Improving footwork for groundstrokes

DESCRIPTION

1. Stand **sideways** in front of the 1st rung
2. Place both feet inside each square, starting with the left or right foot
3. Keep body weight on the balls of the feet (toes)
4. Progress down the ladder in a rapid fashion while **looking at the feet**

KEY FACTORS

- Stay on balls of the feet; toes
- Hit the center of the squares
- Initiate exercise with the right foot & the left foot, respectively

COMMON ERRORS

- Whole foot is on the ground (flat-footed)
- Exercise is initiated only using the left foot

REQUIRED EQUIPMENT

- 1 Speed Ladder

DEGREE OF DIFFICULTY

1

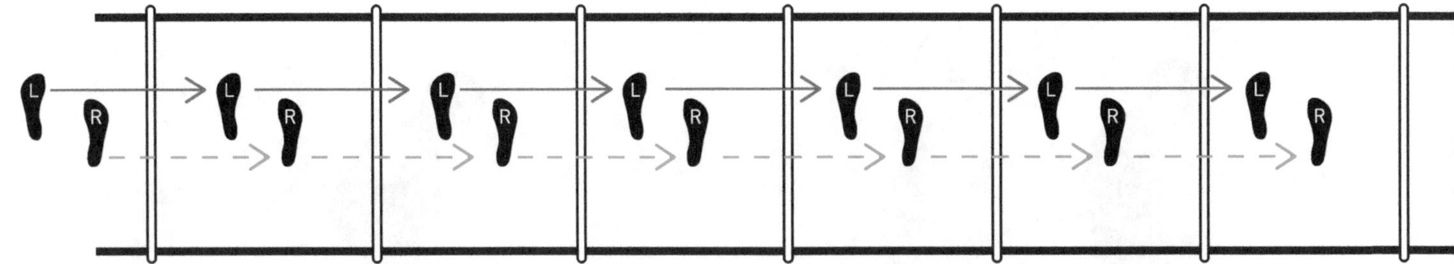

ID: 730

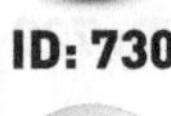

7.31 LATERAL FAST FEET II

SUMMARY

The Lateral Fast Feet II is an intermediate speed ladder exercise, which focuses on improving footwork for groundstrokes, utilizing the speed ladder while holding a racquet.

PURPOSE

1. Improving footwork for groundstrokes

DESCRIPTION

1. Stand **sideways** in front of the 1st rung
2. **Hold the racquet** in both hands – ready position
3. Place both feet inside each square, starting with the left or right foot
4. Keep body weight on the balls of the feet (toes)
5. Progress down the ladder in a rapid fashion while **looking at the feet**

KEY FACTORS

- Stay on balls of the feet; toes
- Hit the center of the squares
- Initiate exercise with the right foot & the left foot, respectively

COMMON ERRORS

- Whole foot is on the ground (flat-footed)
- Exercise is initiated only using the left foot

PRE-REQUISITE DRILLS

- Lateral Fast Feet I

REQUIRED EQUIPMENT

- 1 Speed Ladder
- 1 Racquet

DEGREE OF DIFFICULTY

2

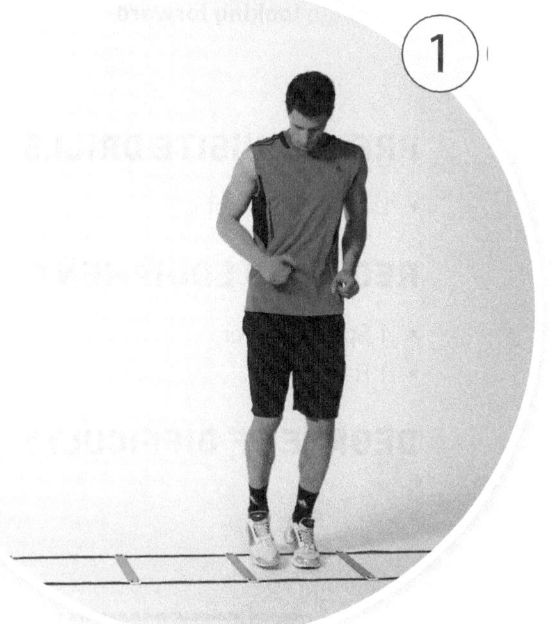

1

2

3

ID: 731

7.32 LATERAL FAST FEET III

SUMMARY

The Lateral Fast Feet III is an advanced speed ladder exercise, which focuses on improving footwork for groundstrokes, utilizing the speed ladder while holding a racquet.

PURPOSE

1. Improving footwork for groundstrokes

DESCRIPTION

1. Stand **sideways** in front of the 1st rung
2. **Hold the racquet** in both hands – ready position
3. Place both feet inside each square, starting with the left or right foot
4. Keep body weight on the balls of the feet (toes)
5. Progress down the ladder in a rapid fashion while **looking forward**

KEY FACTORS

- Stay on balls of the feet; toes
- Hit the center of the squares
- Initiate exercise with the right foot & the left foot, respectively

COMMON ERRORS

- Whole foot is on the ground (flat-footed)
- Exercise is initiated only using the left foot

PRE-REQUISITE DRILLS

- Lateral Fast Feet II

REQUIRED EQUIPMENT

- 1 Speed Ladder
- 1 Racquet

DEGREE OF DIFFICULTY

3

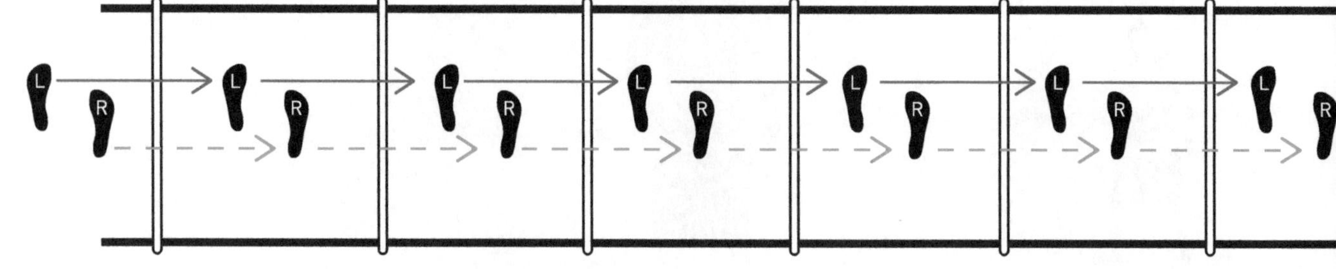

ID: 732

7.33 LATERAL FAST FEET IV

SUMMARY

The Lateral Fast Feet IV is a professional speed ladder exercise, which focuses on improving footwork for groundstrokes, utilizing the speed ladder while holding a racquet and tracking an opponent.

PURPOSE

1. Improving footwork for groundstrokes

DESCRIPTION

1. Stand **sideways** in front of the 1st rung
2. **Hold the racquet** in both hands – ready position
3. Place both feet inside each square, starting with the left or right foot
4. Keep body weight on the balls of the feet (toes)
5. Progress down the ladder in a rapid fashion while looking forward **tracking an opponent**

KEY FACTORS

- Stay on balls of the feet; toes
- Hit the center of the squares
- Initiate exercise with the right foot & the left foot, respectively

COMMON ERRORS

- Whole foot is on the ground (flat-footed)
- Exercise is initiated only using the left – or right foot

PRE-REQUISITE DRILLS

- Lateral Fast Feet III

REQUIRED EQUIPMENT

- 1 Speed Ladder
- 1 Racquet

DEGREE OF DIFFICULTY

4

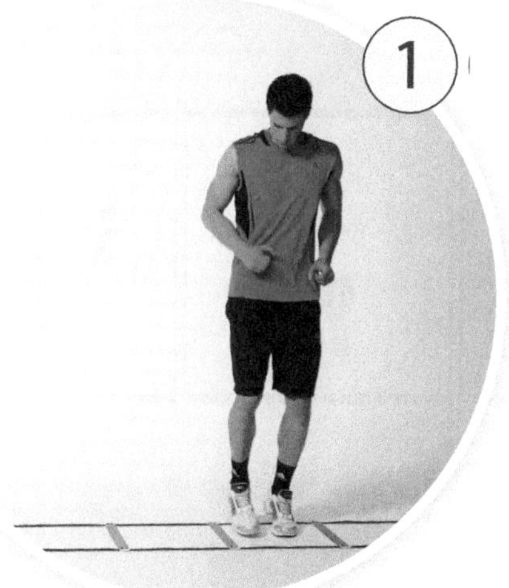

ID: 733

7.34 INSIDE-OUT FAST FEET I

SUMMARY

The Inside-Out Fast Feet I is an introductory speed ladder exercise, which focuses on improving footwork for the inside-out forehand, utilizing a speed ladder.

PURPOSE

1. Improving footwork for inside-out forehand

DESCRIPTION

1. Stand **sideways** in front of the 1st rung
2. Place both feet inside each square, starting with the left - or right foot
3. Keep body weight on the balls of the feet (toes)
4. Progress down the ladder in a rapid fashion while **looking at the feet**
5. When approaching the last square move the **trailing foot** behind the **leading leg** into the last square
6. Push off with the **trailing foot**, landing diagonally in front of the speed ladder with the **leading foot**

REQUIRED EQUIPMENT

- 1 Speed Ladder

KEY FACTORS

- Stay on balls of the feet; toes
- Hit the center of the squares
- Initiate exercise with the right foot & the left foot, respectively

COMMON ERRORS

- Whole foot is on the ground (flat-footed)
- Exercise is initiated only using the left foot

PRE-REQUISITE DRILLS

- Lateral Fast Feet I
- Posterior Cross-Over

DEGREE OF DIFFICULTY

1

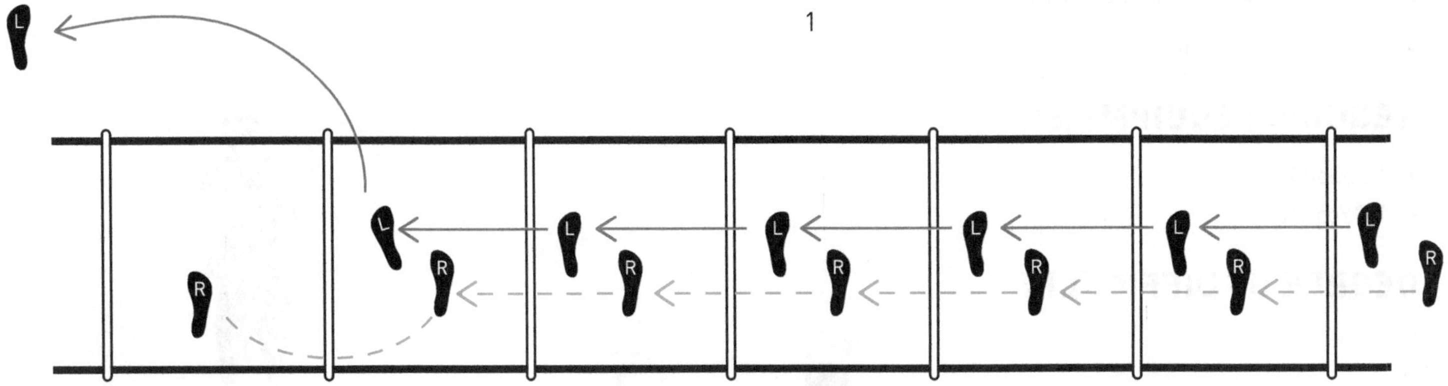

ID: 734

7.35 INSIDE-OUT FAST FEET II

SUMMARY

The Inside-Out Fast Feet II is an intermediate speed ladder exercise, which focuses on improving footwork for the inside-out forehand, utilizing a speed ladder.

PURPOSE

1. Improving footwork for inside-out forehand

DESCRIPTION

1. Stand **sideways** in front of the 1st rung
2. **Hold a racquet** in both hands (ready position)
3. Place both feet inside each square, starting with the left or right foot
4. Keep body weight on the balls of the feet (toes)
5. Progress down the ladder in a rapid fashion while **looking at the feet**
6. When approaching the last square move the trailing foot behind the leading leg into the last square
7. Push off with the trailing foot, landing diagonally in front of the speed ladder with the leading foot

KEY FACTORS

- Stay on balls of the feet; toes
- Hit the center of the squares
- Initiate exercise with the right foot & the left foot, respectively

COMMON ERRORS

- Whole foot is on the ground (flat-footed)
- Exercise is initiated only using the left foot

PRE-REQUISITE DRILLS

- Lateral Fast Feet I
- Posterior Cross-Over

REQUIRED EQUIPMENT

- 1 Speed Ladder
- 1 Racquet

DEGREE OF DIFFICULTY

2

ID: 735

7.36 INSIDE-OUT FAST FEET III

SUMMARY

The Inside-Out Fast Feet III is an advanced speed ladder exercise, which focuses on improving footwork for the inside-out forehand, utilizing a speed ladder.

PURPOSE

1. Improving footwork for inside-out forehand

DESCRIPTION

1. Stand **sideways** in front of the 1st rung
2. **Hold a racquet** in both hands (ready position)
3. Place both feet inside each square, starting with the left or right foot
4. Keep body weight on the balls of the feet (toes)
5. Progress down the ladder in a rapid fashion while l**ooking forward**
6. When approaching the last square move the trailing foot behind the leading leg into the last square
7. Push off with the trailing foot, landing diagonally in front of the speed ladder with the leading foot

PRE-REQUISITE DRILLS

- Lateral Fast Feet II
- Posterior Cross-Over

KEY FACTORS

- Stay on balls of the feet; toes
- Hit the center of the squares
- Initiate exercise with the right foot & the left foot, respectively

COMMON ERRORS

- Whole foot is on the ground (flat-footed)
- Exercise is initiated only using the left foot

REQUIRED EQUIPMENT

- 1 Speed Ladder
- 1 Racquet

DEGREE OF DIFFICULTY

3

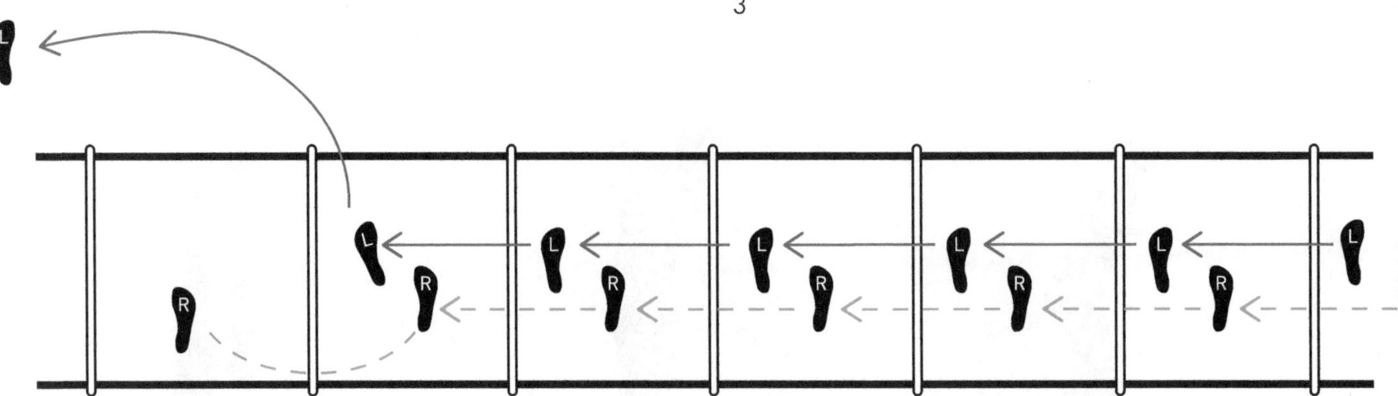

ID: 736

7.37 INSIDE-OUT FAST FEET IV

SUMMARY

The Inside-Out Fast Feet IV is a professional speed ladder exercise, which focuses on improving footwork for the inside-out forehand, utilizing a speed ladder.

PURPOSE

1. Improving footwork for inside-out forehand

DESCRIPTION

1. Stand **sideways** in front of the 1st rung
2. **Hold a racquet** in both hand (ready position)
3. Place both feet inside each square, starting with the left or right foot
4. Keep body weight on the balls of the feet (toes)
5. Progress down the ladder in a rapid fashion while **tracking the coach**
6. When approaching the last square move the trailing foot behind the leading leg into the last square
7. Push off with the trailing foot, landing diagonally in front of the speed ladder with the leading foot

KEY FACTORS

- Stay on balls of the feet; toes
- Hit the center of the squares
- Initiate exercise with the right foot & the left foot, respectively

COMMON ERRORS

- Whole foot is on the ground (flat-footed)
- Exercise is initiated only using the left foot

PRE-REQUISITE DRILLS

- Lateral Fast Feet III
- Lateral Posterior Cross-Over

REQUIRED EQUIPMENT

- 1 Speed Ladder
- 1 Racquet

DEGREE OF DIFFICULTY

4

ID: 737

7.38 LATERAL ANTERIOR CROSS-OVER I

SUMMARY

The Lateral Anterior Cross-Over I is an introductory speed ladder exercise, which focuses on improving footwork for groundstrokes, utilizing a speed ladder.

PURPOSE

1. Improving footwork for groundstrokes

DESCRIPTION

1. Stand **sideways**; place **left** foot into the 1st square and the **right** foot into 2nd square
2. **Keep hips neutral** during movement
3. Move the left foot in front of the right foot into the 3rd square then move right foot into 4th square
4. Keep body weight on the balls of the feet (toes)
5. Progress down the ladder in a rapid fashion while **looking at the feet**
6. When getting to the end of the ladder "switch legs" and perform same movement going back

DEGREE OF DIFFICULTY

1

KEY FACTORS

- Hips remain neutral
- Stay on balls of the feet; toes
- Hit the center of the squares
- Initiate exercise with the right foot & the left foot, respectively

COMMON ERRORS

- Excessive hip rotation
- Whole foot is on the ground (flat-footed)
- Exercise is initiated only using the left foot

REQUIRED EQUIPMENT

- 1 Speed Ladder

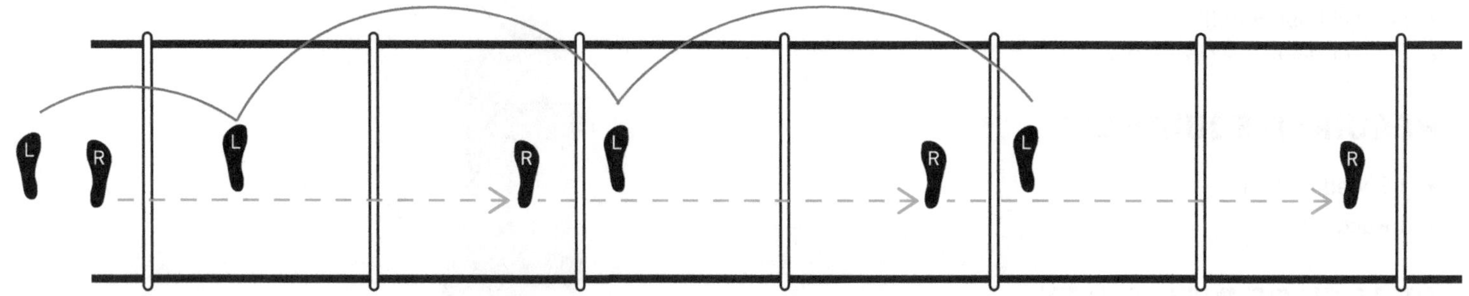

ID: 738

7.39 LATERAL ANTERIOR CROSS-OVER II

SUMMARY

The Lateral Anterior Cross-Over II is an intermediate speed ladder exercise, which focuses on improving footwork for groundstrokes, utilizing a speed ladder.

PURPOSE

1. Improving footwork for groundstrokes

DESCRIPTION

1. **Hold a racquet** in both hands and stand sideways; place left foot into the 1st square and the right foot into 2nd square
2. **Keep hips neutral** during movement
3. Move the left foot in front of the right foot into the 3rd square then move right foot into 4th square
4. Keep body weight on the balls of the feet (toes)
5. Progress down the ladder in a rapid fashion while **looking at the feet**
6. When getting to the end of the ladder "switch legs" and perform same movement going back

PRE-REQUISITE DRILLS

- Lateral Anterior Cross-Over I

REQUIRED EQUIPMENT

- 1 Speed Ladder
- 1 Racquet

KEY FACTORS

- Hips remain neutral
- Stay on balls of the feet; toes
- Hit the center of the squares
- Initiate exercise with the right foot & the left foot, respectively

COMMON ERRORS

- Excessive hip rotation
- Whole foot is on the ground (flat-footed)
- Exercise is initiated only using the left foot

DEGREE OF DIFFICULTY

2

ID: 739

7.40 LATERAL ANTERIOR CROSS-OVER III

SUMMARY

The Lateral Anterior Cross-Over III is an advanced speed ladder exercise, which focuses on improving footwork for groundstrokes, utilizing a speed ladder.

PURPOSE

1. Improving footwork for groundstrokes

DESCRIPTION

1. **Hold a racquet** in both hands and stand sideways; place left foot into the 1st square and the right foot into 2nd square
2. **Keep hips neutral** during movement
3. Move the left foot in front of the right foot into the 3rd square then move right foot into 4th square
4. Keep body weight on the balls of the feet (toes)
5. Progress down the ladder in a rapid fashion while **looking forward**
6. When getting to the end of the ladder "switch legs" and perform same movement going back

PRE-REQUISITE DRILLS

- Lateral Anterior Cross-Over II

KEY FACTORS

- Hips remain neutral
- Stay on balls of the feet; toes
- Hit the center of the squares
- Initiate exercise with the right foot & the left foot, respectively

COMMON ERRORS

- Excessive hip rotation
- Whole foot is on the ground (flat-footed)
- Exercise is initiated only using the left foot

REQUIRED EQUIPMENT

- 1 Speed Ladder
- 1 Racquet

DEGREE OF DIFFICULTY

3

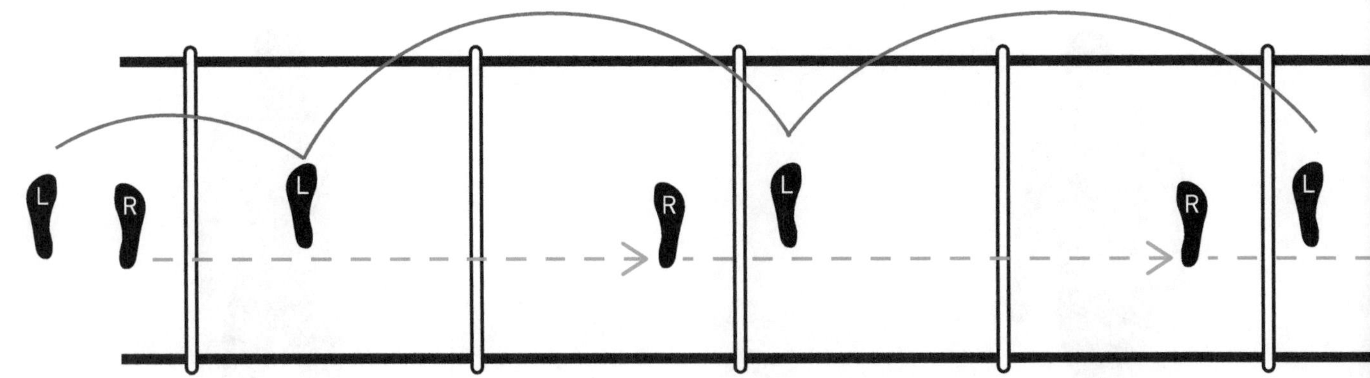

ID: 740

7.41 LATERAL ANTERIOR CROSS-OVER IV

SUMMARY

The Lateral Anterior Cross-Over IV is a professional speed ladder exercise, which focuses on improving footwork for groundstrokes, utilizing a speed ladder.

PURPOSE

1. Improving footwork for groundstrokes

DESCRIPTION

1. **Hold a racquet** in both hands and stand sideways; place left foot into the 1st square and the right foot into 2nd square
2. **Keep hips neutral** during movement
3. Move the left foot in front of the right foot into the 3rd square then move right foot into 4th square
4. Keep body weight on the balls of the feet (toes)
5. Progress down the ladder in a rapid fashion while **tracking the coach**
6. When getting to the end of the ladder "switch legs" and perform same movement going back

PRE-REQUISITE DRILLS

- Lateral Anterior Cross-Over III

KEY FACTORS

- Hips remain neutral
- Stay on balls of the feet; toes
- Hit the center of the squares
- Initiate exercise with the right foot & the left foot, respectively

COMMON ERRORS

- Excessive hip rotation
- Whole foot is on the ground (flat-footed)
- Exercise is initiated only using the left foot

REQUIRED EQUIPMENT

- 1 Speed Ladder
- 1 Racquet

DEGREE OF DIFFICULTY

4

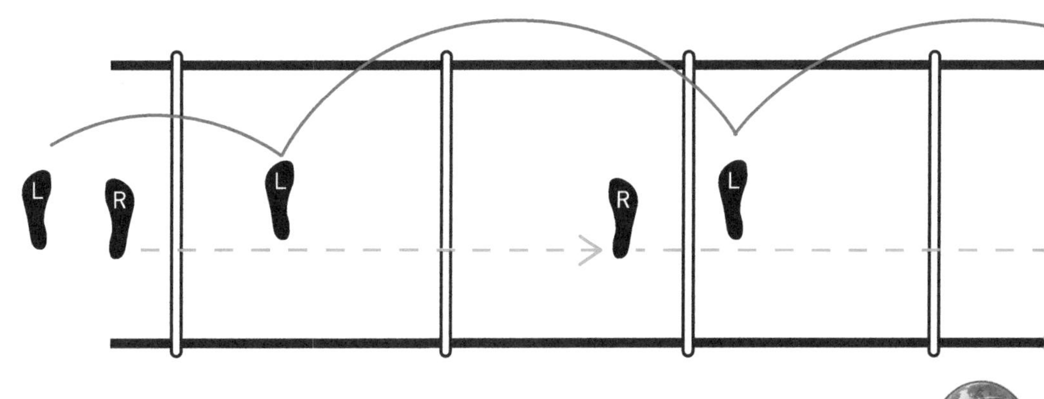

ID: 741

7.42 LATERAL POSTERIOR CROSS-OVER I

SUMMARY

The Lateral Posterior Cross-Over I is an introductory speed ladder exercise, which focuses on improving footwork for groundstrokes, utilizing a speed ladder.

PURPOSE

1. Improving footwork for groundstrokes

DESCRIPTION

1. Stand **sideways**; place **left** foot into the 1st square and the **right** foot into 2nd square
2. **Keep hips neutral** during movement
3. Move the left foot behind the right foot into the 3rd square then move right foot into 4th square
4. Keep body weight on the balls of the feet (toes)
5. Progress down the ladder in a rapid fashion while **looking at the feet**
6. When getting to the end of the ladder "switch legs" and perform same movement going back

REQUIRED EQUIPMENT

- 1 Speed Ladder

KEY FACTORS

- Hips remain neutral
- Stay on balls of the feet; toes
- Hit the center of the squares
- Initiate exercise with the right foot & the left foot, respectively

COMMON ERRORS

- Excessive hip rotation
- Whole foot is on the ground (flat-footed)
- Exercise is initiated only using the left foot

DEGREE OF DIFFICULTY

1

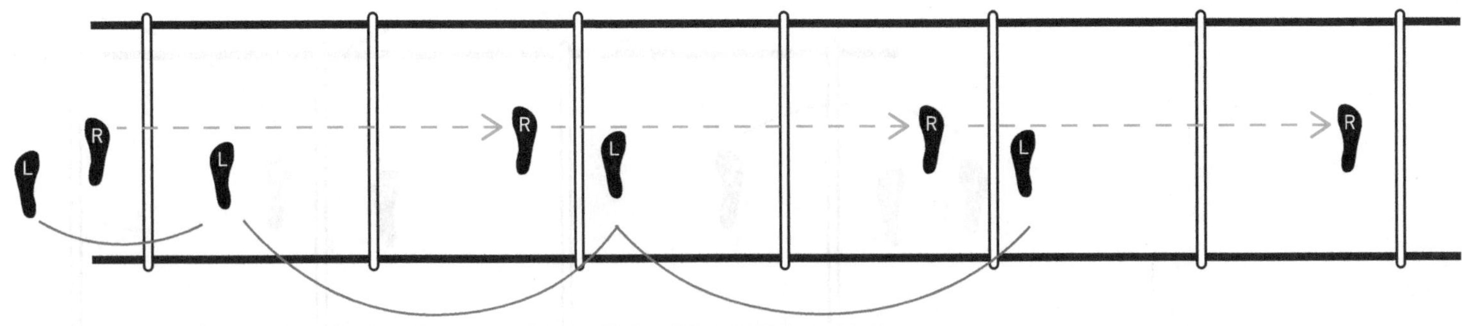

ID: 742

7.43 LATERAL POSTERIOR CROSS-OVER II

SUMMARY

The Lateral Posterior Cross-Over II is an intermediate speed ladder exercise, which focuses on improving footwork for groundstrokes, utilizing a speed ladder.

PURPOSE

1. Improving footwork for groundstrokes

DESCRIPTION

1. **Hold a racquet** in both hands and stand sideways; place left foot into the 1st square and the right foot into 2nd square
2. **Keep hips neutral** during movement
3. Move the left foot behind the right foot into the 3rd square then move right foot into 4th square
4. Keep body weight on the balls of the feet (toes)
5. Progress down the ladder in a rapid fashion while **looking at the feet**
6. When getting to the end of the ladder "switch legs" and perform same movement going back

PRE-REQUISITE DRILLS

- Lateral Posterior Cross-Over I

KEY FACTORS

- Hips remain neutral
- Stay on balls of the feet; toes
- Hit the center of the squares
- Initiate exercise with the right foot & the left foot, respectively

COMMON ERRORS

- Excessive hip rotation
- Whole foot is on the ground (flat-footed)
- Exercise is initiated only using the left foot

REQUIRED EQUIPMENT

- 1 Speed Ladder
- 1 Racquet

DEGREE OF DIFFICULTY

2

ID: 743

7.44 LATERAL POSTERIOR CROSS-OVER III

SUMMARY

The Lateral Posterior Cross-Over III is an advanced speed ladder exercise, which focuses on improving footwork for groundstrokes, utilizing a speed ladder.

PURPOSE

1. Improving footwork for groundstrokes

DESCRIPTION

1. **Hold a racquet** in both hands and stand sideways; place left foot into the 1st square and the right foot into 2nd square
2. **Keep hips neutral** during movement
3. Move the left foot behind the right foot into the 3rd square then move right foot into 4th square
4. Keep body weight on the balls of the feet (toes)
5. Progress down the ladder in a rapid fashion while **looking at the feet**
6. When getting to the end of the ladder "switch legs" and perform same movement going back

PRE-REQUISITE DRILLS

- Lateral Posterior Cross-Over II

KEY FACTORS

- Hips remain neutral
- Stay on balls of the feet; toes
- Hit the center of the squares
- Initiate exercise with the right foot & the left foot, respectively

COMMON ERRORS

- Excessive hip rotation
- Whole foot is on the ground (flat-footed)
- Exercise is initiated only using the left foot

REQUIRED EQUIPMENT

- 1 Speed Ladder
- 1 Racquet

DEGREE OF DIFFICULTY

3

ID: 744

7.45 LATERAL POSTERIOR CROSS-OVER IV

SUMMARY

The Lateral Posterior Cross-Over IV is a professional speed ladder exercise, which focuses on improving footwork for groundstrokes, utilizing a speed ladder.

PURPOSE

1. Improving footwork for groundstrokes

DESCRIPTION

1. **Hold a racquet** in both hands and stand sideways; place left foot into the 1st square and the right foot into 2nd square
2. **Keep hips neutral** during movement
3. Move the left foot behind the right foot into the 3rd square then move right foot into 4th square
4. Keep body weight on the balls of the feet (toes)
5. Progress down the ladder in a rapid fashion while **tracking the coach**
6. When getting to the end of the ladder "switch legs" and perform same movement going back

PRE-REQUISITE DRILLS

- Lateral Posterior Cross-Over III

KEY FACTORS

- Hips remain neutral
- Stay on balls of the feet; toes
- Hit the center of the squares
- Initiate exercise with the right foot & the left foot, respectively

COMMON ERRORS

- Excessive hip rotation
- Whole foot is on the ground (flat-footed)
- Exercise is initiated only using the left foot

REQUIRED EQUIPMENT

- 1 Speed Ladder
- 1 Racquet

DEGREE OF DIFFICULTY

4

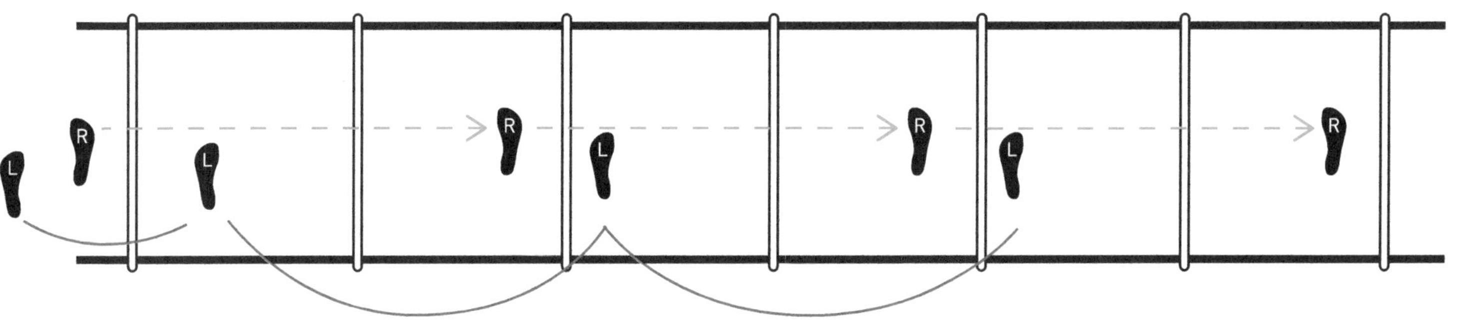

ID: 745

7.46 CARIOCA I

SUMMARY

The Carioca I is an introductory speed ladder exercise, which focuses on improving footwork for groundstrokes, utilizing a speed ladder.

PURPOSE

1. Improving footwork for groundstrokes

DESCRIPTION

1. Stand **sideways**; place **left** foot into the 1st square and the **right** foot into 2nd square
2. **Keep hips neutral** during movement
3. Move the **left** foot behind the right foot into the 3rd square, then move **right** foot into 4th square, move the left foot in front of the right foot into the 5th square, and the **right** foot into the 6th square
4. Keep body weight on the balls of the feet (toes)
5. Progress down the ladder in a rapid fashion while **looking at the feet**
6. When getting to the end of the ladder "switch legs" and perform same movement going back

PRE-REQUISITE DRILLS

- Lateral Anterior Cross-Over I
- Lateral Posterior Cross-Over I

KEY FACTORS

- Hips remain neutral
- Stay on balls of the feet; toes
- Hit the center of the squares
- Initiate exercise with the right foot & the left foot, respectively

COMMON ERRORS

- Excessive hip rotation
- Whole foot is on the ground (flat-footed)
- Exercise is initiated only using the left foot

REQUIRED EQUIPMENT

- 1 Speed Ladder

DEGREE OF DIFFICULTY

1

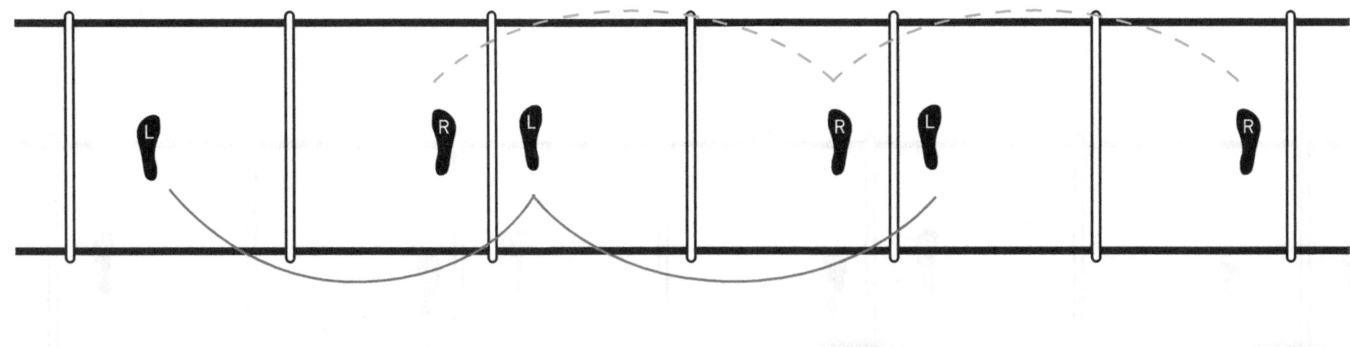

ID: 746

7.47 CARIOCA II

SUMMARY

The Carioca II is an intermediate speed ladder exercise, which focuses on improving footwork for groundstrokes, utilizing a speed ladder.

DESCRIPTION

1. Stand **sideways** and **hold a racquet** in both hands; place left foot into the 1st square and the right foot into 2nd square
2. **Keep hips neutral** during movement
3. Move the left foot behind the right foot into the 3rd square, then move the right foot into 4th square, move the left foot in front of the right foot into the 5th square, and the right foot into the 6th square
4. Keep body weight on the balls of the feet (toes)
5. Progress down the ladder in a rapid fashion while **looking at the feet**
6. When getting to the end of the ladder "switch legs" and perform same movement going back

PRE-REQUISITE DRILLS

- Lateral Anterior Cross-Over II
- Lateral Posterior Cross-Over II

PURPOSE

1. Improving footwork for groundstrokes

KEY FACTORS

- Hips remain neutral
- Stay on balls of the feet; toes
- Hit the center of the squares
- Initiate exercise with the right foot & the left foot, respectively

COMMON ERRORS

- Excessive hip rotation
- Whole foot is on the ground (flat-footed)
- Exercise is initiated only using the left foot

REQUIRED EQUIPMENT

- 1 Speed Ladder
- 1 Racquet

DEGREE OF DIFFICULTY

2

ID: 747

7.48 CARIOCA III

SUMMARY

The Carioca III is an advanced speed ladder exercise, which focuses on improving footwork for groundstrokes, utilizing a speed ladder.

PURPOSE

1. Improving footwork for groundstrokes

DESCRIPTION

1. Stand **sideways** and **hold a racquet** in both hands; place left foot into the 1st square and the right foot into 2nd square
2. **Keep hips neutral** during movement
3. Move the left foot behind the right foot into the 3rd square, then move the right foot into 4th square, move the left foot in front of the right foot into the 5th square, and the right foot into the 6th square
4. Keep body weight on the balls of the feet (toes)
5. Progress down the ladder in a rapid fashion while **looking forward** (eyes don't look at feet)
6. When getting to the end of the ladder "switch legs" and perform same movement going back

PRE-REQUISITE DRILLS

- Lateral Anterior Cross-Over III
- Lateral Posterior Cross-Over III

KEY FACTORS

- Hips remain neutral
- Stay on balls of the feet; toes
- Hit the center of the squares
- Initiate exercise with the right foot & the left foot, respectively

COMMON ERRORS

- Excessive hip rotation
- Whole foot is on the ground (flat-footed)
- Exercise is initiated only using the left foot

REQUIRED EQUIPMENT

- 1 Speed Ladder
- 1 Racquet

DEGREE OF DIFFICULTY

3

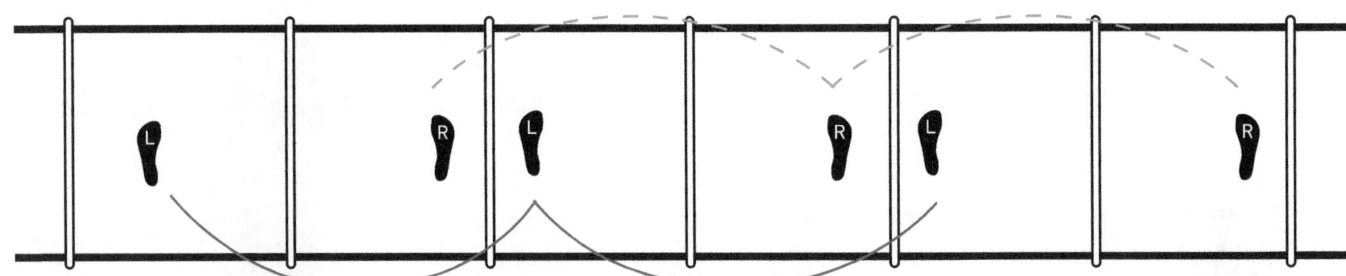

ID: 748

7.49 CARIOCA IV

SUMMARY

The Carioca IV is a professional speed ladder exercise, which focuses on improving footwork for groundstrokes, utilizing a speed ladder.

PURPOSE

1. Improving footwork for groundstrokes

DESCRIPTION

1. Stand **sideways** and **hold a racquet** in both hands; place left foot into the 1st square and the right foot into 2nd square
2. **Keep hips neutral** during movement
3. Move the left foot behind the right foot into the 3rd square, then move the right foot into 4th square, move the left foot in front of the right foot into the 5th square, and the right foot into the 6th square
4. Keep body weight on the balls of the feet (toes)
5. Progress down the ladder in a rapid fashion while **tracking the coach** (eyes don't look at feet)
6. When getting to the end of the ladder "switch legs" and perform same movement going back

PRE-REQUISITE DRILLS

- Lateral Anterior Cross-Over IV
- Lateral Posterior Cross-Over IV

KEY FACTORS

- Hips remain neutral
- Stay on balls of the feet; toes
- Hit the center of the squares
- Initiate exercise with the right foot & the left foot, respectively

COMMON ERRORS

- Excessive hip rotation
- Whole foot is on the ground (flat-footed)
- Exercise is initiated only using the left foot

DEGREE OF DIFFICULTY

4

REQUIRED EQUIPMENT

- 1 Speed Ladder
- 1 Racquet

ID: 749

7.50 LATERAL FAST FEET GROUNDSTROKE STEP-INS (I)

SUMMARY

The Lateral Fast Feet Groundstroke Step-ins (I) is an introductory integrated speed exercise, which focuses on improving lateral baseline movement, foot speed for groundstrokes and stability & coordination for stroke production utilizing a short speed ladder and 2 agility rings.

PURPOSE

1. Improving lateral baseline movement
2. Improving foot speed for groundstrokes
3. Improving stability & coordination for stroke production

DESCRIPTION

No balls are being fed by the teaching pro. The player stands behind the baseline in the center and:

1. Moves through a speed ladder via "**Lateral Fast Feet**" toward **deuce-court** while **looking down** at speed ladder
2. Simulates hitting 1 groundstroke by stepping inside agility ring with the **left** foot, swinging, then rotating forward with the **right** foot, transitioning the body inside the baseline
3. Transitions through speed ladder via "**Lateral Fast Feet**" while **looking down** at speed ladder
4. Simulates hitting 1 groundstroke by stepping inside agility ring with the **right** foot, then rotating forward with the **left** foot, transitioning the body inside the baseline
5. Transition back via "**Lateral Fast Feet**" while **looking down** at speed ladder

PRE-REQUISITE DRILLS

- Lateral Fast Feet I

REQUIRED EQUIPMENT

- 1 Short Speed Ladder
- 2 Agility Rings

DEGREE OF DIFFICULTY

1

KEY FACTORS

- Footwork ► movement towards the individual shots should be initiated by side-steps
- Intensity ► groundstrokes need to be hit forcefully so that the player's body keeps moving towards the net
- Quickness ► player needs to move sideways quickly through speed ladder after hitting groundstrokes

COMMON ERRORS

- Player fails to transition body weight through the shots
- Player doesn't transition through speed ladder correctly

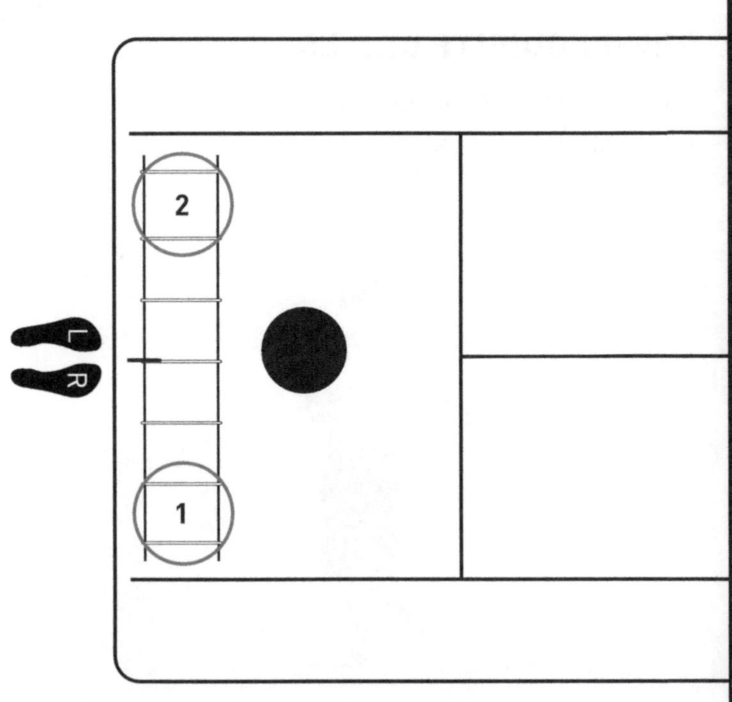

ID: 750

7.51 LATERAL FAST FEET GS STEP IN (II): RACQUET

SUMMARY

The Lateral Fast Feet Groundstroke Step-ins (II) is an intermediate integrated speed exercise, which focuses on improving lateral baseline movement, foot speed for groundstrokes and stability & coordination for stroke production utilizing a short speed ladder, 2 agility rings and a tennis racquet.

PURPOSE

1. Improving lateral baseline movement
2. Improving foot speed for groundstrokes
3. Improving stability & coordination for stroke production

DESCRIPTION

No balls are being fed by the teaching pro. The player, **holding a racquet**, stands behind the baseline in the center and:

1. Moves through a speed ladder via "Lateral Fast Feet" toward deuce-court while **looking down** at speed ladder
2. SImulates hitting 1 groundstroke by stepping inside agility ring with the left foot, swinging, then rotating forward with the right foot, transitioning the body inside the baseline
3. Transitions through speed ladder via "Lateral Fast Feet" while **looking forward**
4. Simulates hitting 1 groundstroke by stepping inside agility ring with the right foot, then rotating forward with the left foot, transitioning the body inside the baseline
5. Transition back via "Lateral Fast Feet" while **loo-king down** at speed ladder

PRE-REQUISITE DRILLS

- Lateral Fast Feet II
- Lateral Fast Feet Groundstroke Step-Ins I

DEGREE OF DIFFICULTY

2

KEY FACTORS

- Footwork movement towards the individual shots should be initiated by side-steps
- Intensity groundstrokes need to be hit forcefully so that the player's body keeps moving towards the net
- Quickness player needs to move sideways quickly through speed ladder after hitting groundstrokes

COMMON ERRORS

- Player fails to transition body weight through the shots
- Player doesn't transition through speed ladder correctly

REQUIRED EQUIPMENT

- 1 Racquet
- 1 Short Speed Ladder
- 2 Agility Rings

ID: 751

7.52 LATERAL FAST FEET GS STEP IN (III): RACQUET

SUMMARY

The Lateral Fast Feet Groundstroke Step-ins (III) is an advanced integrated speed exercise, which focuses on improving lateral baseline movement, foot speed for groundstrokes and stability & coordination for stroke production utilizing a short speed ladder, tennis racquet and balls.

PURPOSE

1. Improving lateral baseline movement
2. Improving foot speed for groundstrokes
3. Improving stability & coordination for stroke production

DESCRIPTION

2 balls are being fed by the teaching pro. The player, **holding a racquet**, stands behind the baseline in the center and:

1. Moves through a speed ladder via "Lateral Fast Feet" toward deuce-court while **looking forward** at the opposite baseline
2. Hits 1 groundstroke by stepping inside agility ring with the left foot, then rotating forward with the right foot, transitioning the body inside the baseline
3. Transitions through speed ladder via "Lateral Fast Feet" while **looking forward** at the opposite baseline
4. Hits 1 groundstroke by stepping inside agility ring with the right foot, then rotating forward with the left foot, transitioning the body inside the baseline
5. Transition back via "Lateral Fast Feet" while **looking forward** at the opposite baseline

DEGREE OF DIFFICULTY

3

KEY FACTORS

- Footwork ▸ movement towards the individual shots should be initiated by side-steps
- Intensity ▸ groundstrokes need to be hit forcefully so that the player's body keeps moving towards the net
- Quickness ▸ player needs to move sideways quickly through speed ladder after hitting groundstrokes

COMMON ERRORS

- Player fails to transition body weight through the shots
- Player transitions through speed ladder incorrectly

REQUIRED EQUIPMENT

- 1 Racquet
- 1 Short Speed Ladder
- Tennis Balls
- 2 Agility Rings

PRE-REQUISITE DRILLS

- Lateral Fast Feet III
- Lateral Fast Feet Groundstroke Step-Ins II

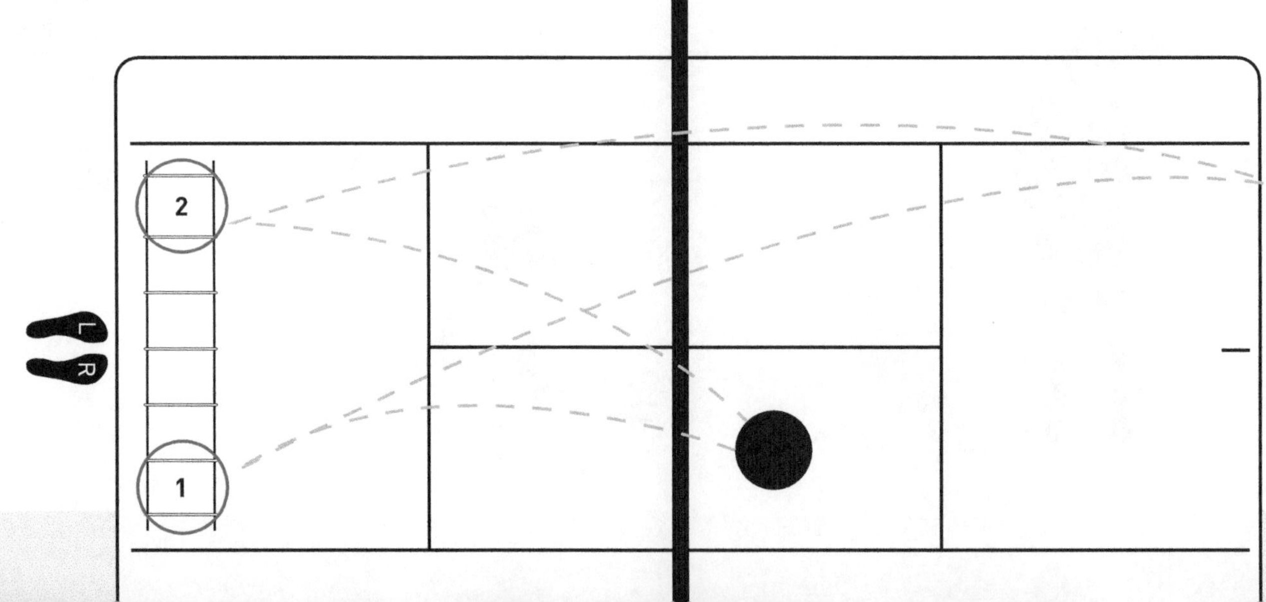

ID: 752

7.53 LATERAL FAST FEET GS STEP IN (IV)

SUMMARY

The Lateral Fast Feet Groundstroke Step-ins (IV) is a professional integrated speed exercise, which focuses on improving lateral baseline movement, foot speed for groundstrokes, stability & coordination for stroke production, and improving shot accuracy utilizing a short speed ladder, tennis racquet and balls, and 4 cones.

DESCRIPTION

Teaching pro sets up a target area using 4 cones and feeds 2 balls. The player, **holding a racquet**, stands behind the baseline in the center and:

1. Moves through a speed ladder via "Lateral Fast Feet" toward deuce-court while **looking forward** at the opposite baseline
2. Hits 1 groundstroke into a **target area** by stepping inside agility ring with the left foot, then rotating forward with the right foot, transitioning the body inside the baseline
3. Transitions through speed ladder via "Lateral Fast Feet" while **looking forward** at the opposite baseline
4. Hits 1 groundstroke into a **target area** by stepping inside agility ring with the right foot, then rotating forward with the left foot, transitioning the body inside the baseline
5. Transition back via "Lateral Fast Feet" while **looking forward** at the opposite baseline

PRE-REQUISITE DRILLS

- Lateral Fast Feet III
- Lateral Fast Feet Groundstroke Step-Ins III

PURPOSE

1. Improving lateral baseline movement
2. Improving foot speed for groundstrokes
3. Improving stability & coordination for stroke production
4. Improving shot accuracy

KEY FACTORS

- Footwork movement towards the individual shots should be initiated by side-steps
- Intensity groundstrokes need to be hit forcefully so that the player's body keeps moving towards the net
- Quickness player needs to move sideways quickly through speed ladder after hitting groundstrokes
- Accuracy Player should hit at least 30% of all shots into target area

COMMON ERRORS

- Player fails to transition body weight through the shots
- Player doesn't transition through speed ladder correctly

REQUIRED EQUIPMENT

- 1 Racquet
- 1 Short Speed Ladder
- Tennis Balls
- 2 Agility Rings
- 4 Cones

DEGREE OF DIFFICULTY

4

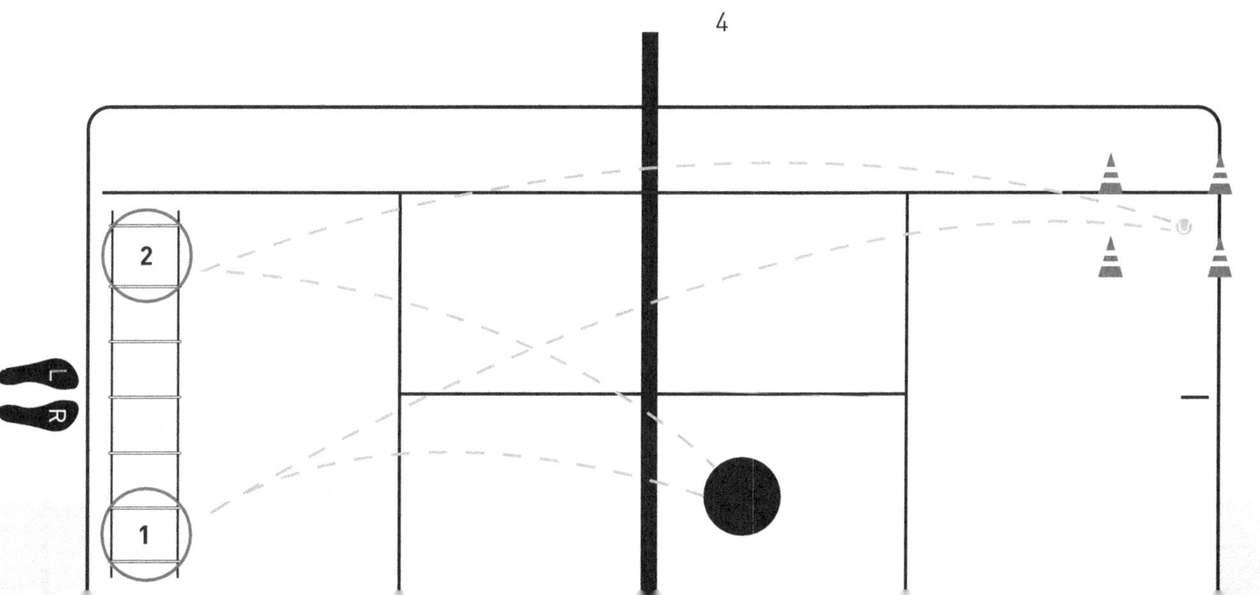

ID: 753

7.54 LAT. POSTERIOR X-OVER TO DIAGONAL LUNGE (I)

SUMMARY

The Lateral Posterior Cross-Over to Diagonal Lunge (I) is an introductory integrated speed exercise, which focuses on improving body control & coordination and footwork for volleys utilizing a speed ladder and 1 agility ring.

PURPOSE

1. Improving body control & coordination
2. Improving footwork for the volley

DESCRIPTION

1. Place speed ladder on an even, solid, non-sliding surface (e.g. clay court)
2. Position agility ring ~3 feet in front of the speed ladder, parallel to the 2nd square
3. Take on **athletic stance** position standing inside the 2nd & 3rd square; knees and hips are slightly flexed; upper-body is straight; **look down** towards the feet during movement
4. Move the **right** foot behind the left foot inside the 1st square (posterior cross-over); hips remain neutral (face forward) during cross-over
5. Push off the **right** foot and step into the agility ring with the **left** foot into a **diagonal lunge**; maintain straight upper-body but lean slightly forward so that chest is above the knee
6. Push off with the **left** foot and return to starting position
7. Side-step to the **right**
8. Move agility ring to the opposite side, switch legs, and repeat

RELEVANCE

- Utilize this exercise when the athlete has trouble maintaining balance during the volley when the ball comes straight at the body

KEY FACTORS

- Focus on perfect movement mechanics
- Maintain neutral pelvic position during cross-over
- Maintain stability during lunge; knee must not protrude past the knee

COMMON ERRORS

- Flexion of thoracic spine (rounded back) during lunge
- Knee protrudes past the toes during lunge
- Athlete loses balance

PRE-REQUISITE DRILLS

- Lateral Posterior Cross-Over I
- MB Trunk Rotation II: Diagonal Lunge

REQUIRED EQUIPMENT

- 1 Speed Ladder
- 1 Agility Ring

BREATH IN & OUT

- IN: Before Diagonal Lunge
- OUT: During Diagonal Lunge

DEGREE OF DIFFICULTY

1

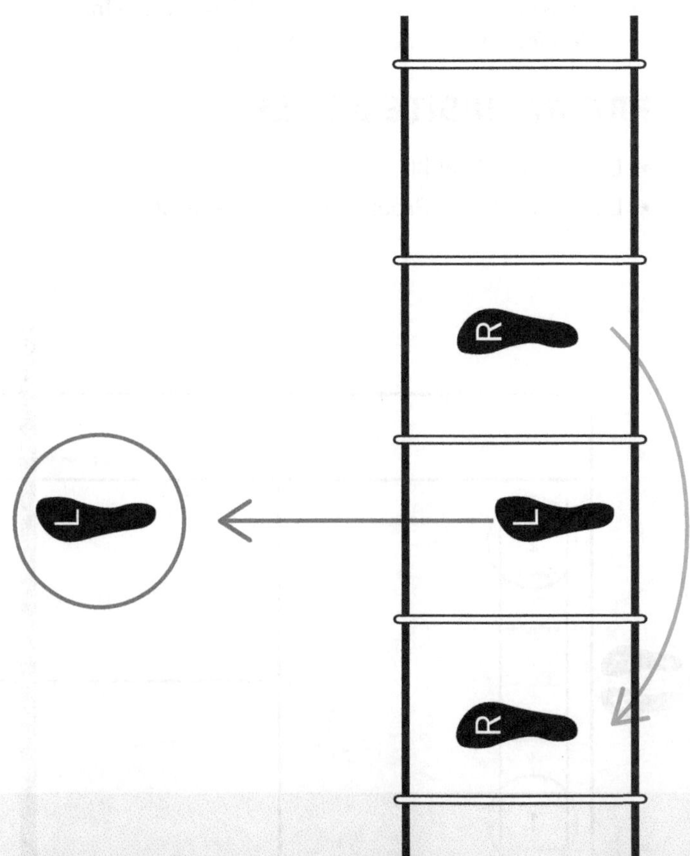

ID: 754

7.55 LAT. POST. X-OVER TO DIAG. LUNGE (II): RACQUET

SUMMARY

The Lateral Posterior Cross-Over to Diagonal Lunge (II) is an intermediate integrated speed exercise, which focuses on improving body control & coordination and footwork for volleys utilizing a speed ladder, 1 agility ring and a tennis racquet.

PURPOSE

1. Improving body control & coordination
2. Improving footwork for the volley

DESCRIPTION

1. Place speed ladder on an even, solid, non-sliding surface (e.g. clay court)
2. Position agility ring ~3 feet in front of the speed ladder, parallel to the 2nd square
3. **Hold a racquet** in both hands
4. Take on **athletic stance** position standing inside the 2nd & 3rd square; knees and hips are slightly flexed; upper-body is straight; **look down** towards the feet during movement
5. Move the right foot behind the left foot inside the 1st square (posterior cross-over); hips remain neutral (face forward) during cross-over
6. Push off the right foot and step into the agility ring with the left foot into a diagonal lunge; maintain straight upper-body but lean slightly forward so that chest is above the knee
7. **Swing the racquet** simulating a volley
8. Push off with the left foot and return to starting position
9. Side-step to the right
10. Move agility ring to the opposite side, switch legs, and repeat

DEGREE OF DIFFICULTY

2

RELEVANCE

- Utilize this exercise when the athlete has trouble maintaining balance during the volley when the ball comes straight at the body

KEY FACTORS

- Focus on perfect movement mechanics
- Maintain neutral pelvic position during cross-over
- Maintain stability during lunge; knee must not protrude past the knee

COMMON ERRORS

- Flexion of thoracic spine (rounded back) during lunge
- Knee protrudes past the toes during lunge
- Athlete loses balance

PRE-REQUISITE DRILLS

- Lateral Posterior Cross-Over II
- MB Trunk Rotation II: Diagonal Lunge

REQUIRED EQUIPMENT

- 1 Speed Ladder
- 1 Agility Ring
- 1 Racquet

BREATH IN & OUT

- IN: Before Diagonal Lunge
- OUT: During Diagonal Lunge

7.56 LAT. POST . X-OVER TO DIAGONAL LUNGE (III)

SUMMARY

The Lateral Posterior Cross-Over to Diagonal Lunge (III) is an advanced integrated speed exercise, which focuses on improving body control & coordination and footwork for volleys utilizing a speed ladder, agilitz ring, tennis racquet, tennis balls and a partner.

PURPOSE

1. Improving body control & coordination
2. Improving footwork for the volley

DESCRIPTION

1. Place speed ladder on an even, solid, non-sliding surface (e.g. clay court)
2. Position agility ring ~3 feet in front of the speed ladder, parallel to the 2nd square
3. **Hold a racquet** in both hands
4. Take on **athletic stance** position standing inside the 2nd & 3rd square; knees and hips are slightly flexed; upper-body is straight; **look forward** during movement
5. Move the right foot behind the left foot inside the 1st square (posterior cross-over); hips remain neutral (face forward) during cross-over
6. Push off the right foot and step into the agility ring with the left foot into a diagonal lunge; maintain straight upper-body but lean slightly forward so that chest is above the knee
7. **Coach/partner feeds a tennis ball**
8. Swing the racquet **hitting a volley**
9. Push off with the left foot and return to starting position
10. Side-step to the right
11. Move agility ring to the opposite side, switch legs, and repeat

PRE-REQUISITE DRILLS

- Lateral Posterior Cross-Over III
- MB Trunk Rotation II: Diagonal Lunge

DEGREE OF DIFFICULTY

3

BREATH IN & OUT

- IN: Before Diagonal Lunge
- OUT: During Diagonal Lunge

REQUIRED EQUIPMENT

- 1 Speed Ladder
- 1 Agility Ring
- 1 Racquet
- Tennis Balls
- Coach/Partner

RELEVANCE

- Utilize this exercise when the athlete has trouble maintaining balance during the volley when the ball comes straight at the body

KEY FACTORS

- Focus on perfect movement mechanics
- Maintain neutral head position during movement
- Maintain neutral pelvic position during cross-over
- Maintain stability during lunge; knee must not protrude past the knee

COMMON ERRORS

- Flexion of thoracic spine (rounded back) during lunge
- Knee protrudes past the toes during lunge
- Athlete loses balance

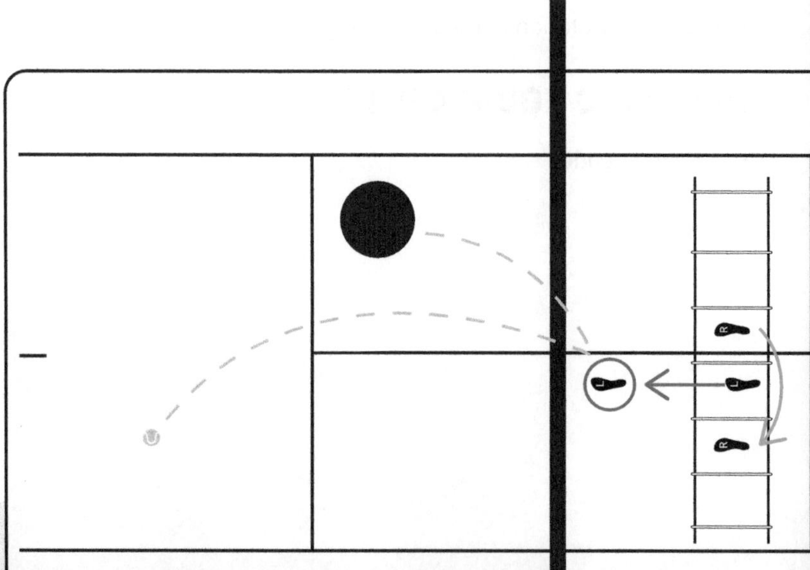

ID: 756

7.57 LAT. POST. X-OVER TO DIAG. LUNGE (IV): TARGET

SUMMARY

The Lateral Posterior Cross-Over to Diagonal Lunge (IV) is a professional integrated speed exercise, which focuses on improving body control & coordination and footwork for volleys utilizing a speed ladder, agility ring, tennis racquet and balls, 4 cones and a partner.

DESCRIPTION

1. Place speed ladder on an even, solid, non-sliding surface (e.g. clay court) and **setup target area** with 4 cones
2. Position agility ring ~3 feet in front of the speed ladder, parallel to the 2nd square
3. **Hold a racquet** in both hands
4. Take on **athletic stance** position standing inside the 2nd & 3rd square; knees and hips are slightly flexed; upper-body is straight; look forward and **track the coach/partner** during movement
5. Move the right foot behind the left foot inside the 1st square (posterior cross-over); hips remain neutral (face forward) during cross-over
6. Push off the right foot and step into the agility ring with the left foot into a diagonal lunge; maintain straight upper-body but lean slightly forward so that chest is above the knee
7. Coach/Partner feeds a tennis ball
8. Swing the racquet hitting a volley into **target area**
9. Push off with the left foot and return to starting position
10. Side-step to the right
11. Move agility ring to the opposite side, switch legs, and repeat

PRE-REQUISITE DRILLS

- Lateral Posterior Cross-Over III
- MB Trunk Rotation II: Diagonal Lunge

DEGREE OF DIFFICULTY

4

RELEVANCE

- Utilize this exercise when the athlete has trouble maintaining balance during the volley when the ball comes straight at the body

PURPOSE

1. Improving body control & coordination
2. Improving footwork for the volley

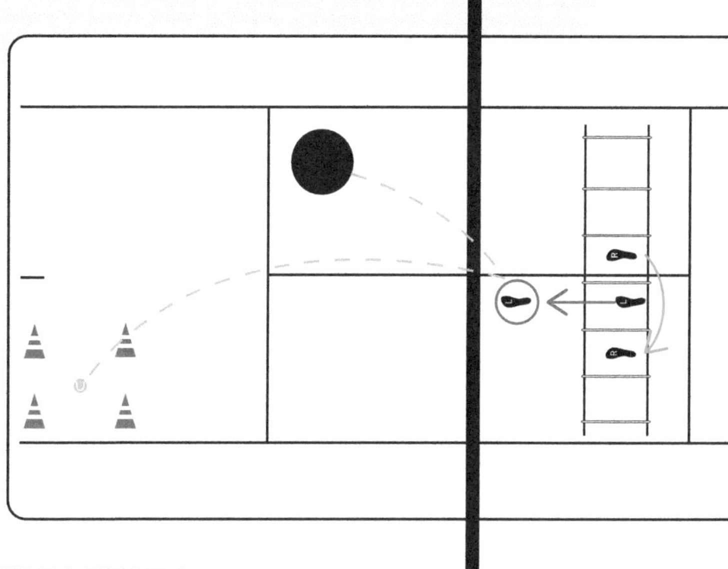

KEY FACTORS

- Focus on perfect movement mechanics
- Maintain neutral head position during movement
- Maintain neutral pelvic position during cross-over
- Maintain stability during lunge; knee must not protrude past the knee

COMMON ERRORS

- Flexion of thoracic spine (rounded back) during lunge
- Knee protrudes past the toes during lunge
- Athlete loses balance

BREATH IN & OUT

- IN: Before Diagonal Lunge
- OUT: During Diagonal Lunge

REQUIRED EQUIPMENT

- 1 Speed Ladder
- 1 Agility Ring
- 1 Racquet
- 4 Cones
- Tennis Balls
- Coach/Partner

ID: 757

7.58 LATERAL FAST FEET TO BALL-DROP & REACT (I)

SUMMARY

The Lateral Fast Feet to Ball-Drop & React I is an introductory integrated speed, agility & reaction exercise, which focuses on improving lateral baseline movement, foot speed for groundstrokes, reaction time for transition game, and hand-eye coordination utilizing a short speed ladder and tennis balls.

PURPOSE

1. Improving lateral baseline movement
2. Improving foot speed for groundstrokes
3. Improving reaction time for transition game
4. Improving hand-eye coordination

DESCRIPTION

1 ball is being fed by the teaching pro. The player stands behind the baseline in the center of the speed ladder and:

1. Needs to move through a speed ladder via "**Lateral Fast Feet**" while **looking down** at speed ladder
2. **Sprints** towards the service line when teaching pro gives an **audible signal**
3. **Catches** the ball before the 2nd bounce

The Teaching Pro:

1. Stands at top of the service T holding a tennis ball in each hand
2. Raises both arms 5´10" (shoulder/ear level)
3. **Shouts** when releasing 1 tennis ball

PRE-REQUISITE DRILLS

- Lateral Fast Feet I
- Jump-Over Fast Feet I

DEGREE OF DIFFICULTY

1

REQUIRED EQUIPMENT

- 1 Short Speed Ladder
- 2 Tennis Balls

KEY FACTORS

- Footwork ► movement through speed ladder via "Lateral Fast Feet"
- Coordination ► player needs to catch the ball
- Quickness ► on audible signal, player needs to move forward quickly and get to the ball

COMMON ERRORS

- Player doesn't transition through speed ladder correctly
- Player doesn't reach the ball before 2nd bounce

ID: 758

7.59 LATERAL FAST FEET TO BALL-DROP & REACT (II)

SUMMARY

The Lateral Fast Feet to Ball-Drop & React II is an intermediate integrated speed, agility & reaction exercise, which focuses on improving lateral baseline movement, foot speed for groundstrokes, reaction time for transition game, and hand-eye coordination utilizing a short speed ladder, tennis balls and racquet.

PURPOSE

1. Improving lateral baseline movement
2. Improving foot speed for groundstrokes
3. Improving reaction time for transition game
4. Improving hand-eye coordination

DESCRIPTION

1 ball is being fed by the teaching pro. The player **holds a racquet**, stands behind the baseline in the center of the speed ladder and:

1. Needs to move through a speed ladder via "Lateral Fast Feet" while **looking down** at speed ladder
2. **Sprints** towards the service line when teaching pro gives an **audible signal**
3. **Catches** the ball with the **racquet** before the 2nd bounce

The Teaching Pro:

1. Stands at top of the service T holding a tennis ball in each hand
2. Raises both arms 5´10" (shoulder/ear level)
3. **Shouts** when releasing 1 tennis ball

PRE-REQUISITE DRILLS

- Lateral Fast Feet II
- Jump-Over Fast Feet II

DEGREE OF DIFFICULTY

2

REQUIRED EQUIPMENT

- 1 Short Speed Ladder
- 2 Tennis Balls
- 1 Racquet

KEY FACTORS

- Footwork movement through speed ladder via "Lateral Fast Feet"
- Coordination player needs to catch the ball
- Quickness on audible signal, player needs to move forward quickly and get to the ball

COMMON ERRORS

- Player doesn't transition through speed ladder correctly
- Player doesn't reach the ball before 2nd bounce

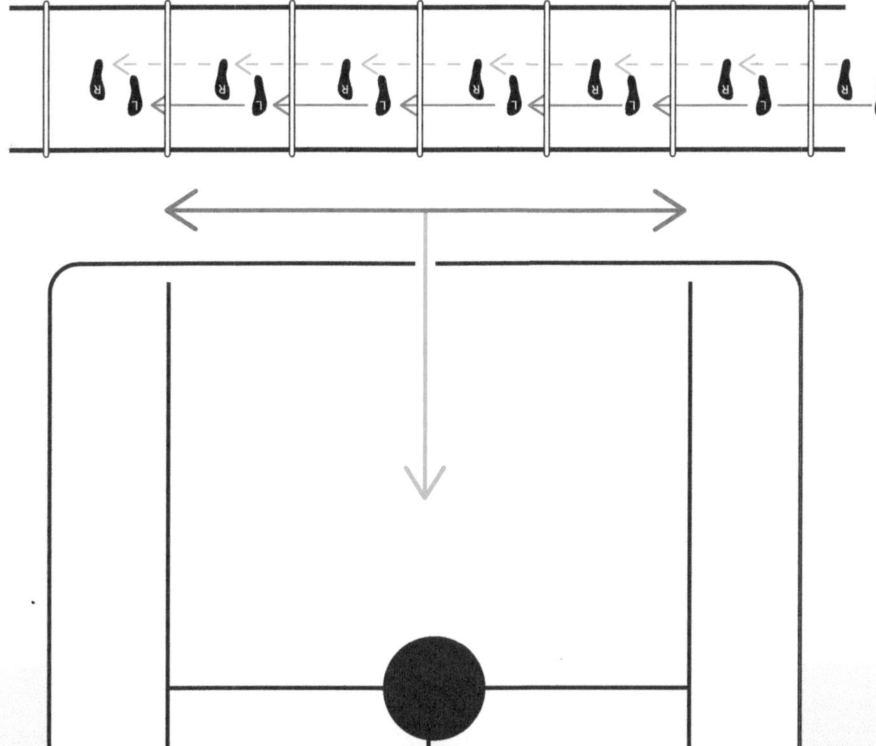

ID: 759

7.60 LATERAL FAST FEET TO BALL-DROP & REACT (III)

SUMMARY

The Lateral Fast Feet to Ball-Drop & React III is an advanced integrated speed, agility & reaction exercise, which focuses on improving lateral baseline movement, foot speed for groundstrokes, reaction time for transition game, and hand-eye coordination utilizing a short speed ladder, tennis balls and racquet.

PURPOSE

1. Improving lateral baseline movement
2. Improving foot speed for groundstrokes
3. Improving reaction time for transition game
4. Improving hand-eye coordination

DESCRIPTION

1 ball is being fed by the teaching pro. The player **holds a racquet** and is standing behind the baseline in the center of the speed ladder and:

1. Moves through a speed ladder via "Lateral Fast Feet" while **looking forward** towards the net
2. **Sprints** towards the service line when teaching pro gives a **visual signal** (ball drop)
3. **Hits the ball** with the racquet before the 2nd bounce

The Teaching Pro:

1. Stands at top of the service T holding a tennis ball in each hand
2. Raises both arms 5"10" (shoulder/ear level)
3. **Releases** 1 tennis ball

PRE-REQUISITE DRILLS

- Lateral Fast Feet III
- Jump-Over Fast Feet III

COMMON ERRORS

- Player doesn't transition through speed ladder correctly
- Player doesn't reach the ball before 2nd bounce

DEGREE OF DIFFICULTY

3

REQUIRED EQUIPMENT

- 1 Short Speed Ladder
- 2 Tennis Balls
- 1 Racquet

KEY FACTORS

- Footwork » movement through speed ladder via "Lateral Fast Feet"
- Coordination » player needs to hit the ball
- Quickness » on visual signal, player needs to move forward quickly and get to the ball

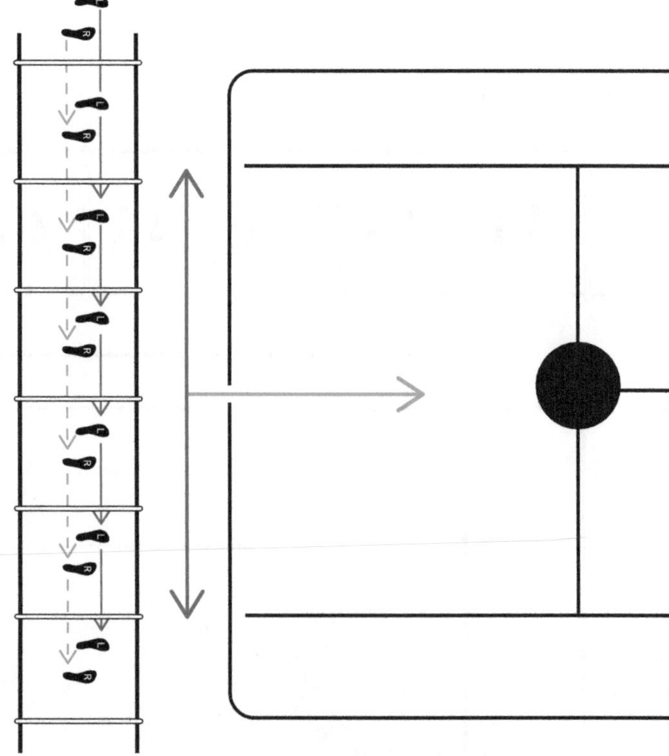

ID: 760

7.61 LATERAL FAST FEET TO BALL-DROP & REACT (IV)

SUMMARY

The Lateral Fast Feet to Ball-Drop & React IV is a professional integrated speed, agility & reaction exercise, which focuses on improving lateral baseline movement, foot speed for groundstrokes, reaction time for transition game, hand-eye coordination, and accuracy utilizing a short speed ladder, tennis balls and racquet, and 4 cones.

PURPOSE

1. Improving lateral baseline movement
2. Improving foot speed for groundstrokes
3. Improving reaction time for transition game
4. Improving hand-eye coordination
5. Improving accuracy

DESCRIPTION

1 ball is being fed by the teaching pro. The player **holds a racquet** and is standing behind the baseline in the center of the speed ladder and:

1. Needs to move through a speed ladder via "Lateral Fast Feet" while **tracking** the coach
2. **Sprints** towards the service line when teaching pro gives a **visual signal** (feeds ball)
3. **Hits** the ball into a **target area** before the 2nd bounce

The Teaching Pro:

1. Stands at center of the opposite baseline, holding a racquet and tennis ball
2. **Randomly** feeds a ball towards the opposing service line

PRE-REQUISITE DRILLS

- Lateral Fast Feet IV
- Jump-Over Fast Feet IV

DEGREE OF DIFFICULTY

4

REQUIRED EQUIPMENT

- 1 Short Speed Ladder
- 2 Tennis Balls
- 1 Racquet
- 4 Cones

KEY FACTORS

- Footwork – movement through speed ladder via "Lateral Fast Feet"
- Coordination – player needs to hit the ball
- Quickness – on visual signal, player needs to move forward quickly and get to the ball
- Accuracy – player needs to hit >60% into target area

COMMON ERRORS

- Player doesn't transition through speed ladder correctly
- Player doesn't reach the ball before 2nd bounce
- Player misses target area

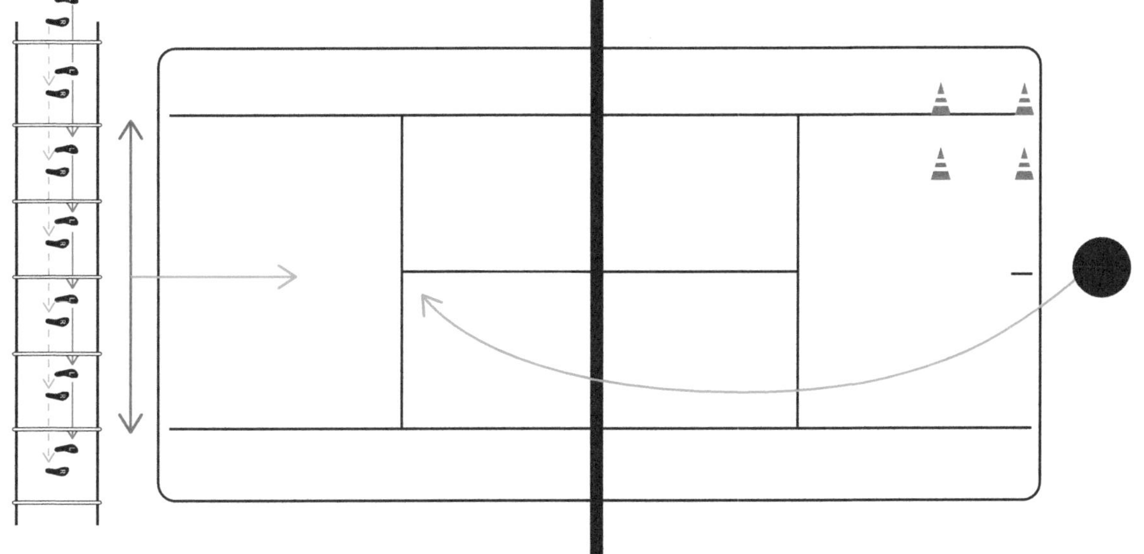

ID: 761

7

7.62 INSIDE-OUT FAST FEET I

SUMMARY

The Inside-Out Fast Feet I is an introductory integrated speed & agility exercise, which focuses on improving the inside-out forehand and footwork for the inside-out forehand by utilizing a speed ladder. and tennis balls.

PURPOSE

1. Improving footwork for inside-out forehand
2. Improving inside-out forehand

DESCRIPTION

1 ball is being fed by the coach towards the last square of the speed ladder. Athlete needs to:

1. Stand **sideways** in front of the 1st rung
2. Place both feet inside each square, starting with the left or right foot
3. Keep body weight on the balls of the feet (toes)
4. Progress down the ladder in a rapid fashion while **looking down** towards the speed ladder
5. When approaching the last square move the **trailing foot** behind the **leading leg** into the last square
6. Push off with the **trailing foot**, landing diagonally in front of the speed ladder with the **leading foot**
7. **Catch and throw** the ball back to the teaching pro

PRE-REQUISITE DRILLS

- Lateral Fast Feet III
- Posterior Cross-Over III

DEGREE OF DIFFICULTY

1

REQUIRED EQUIPMENT

- 1 Speed Ladder
- Tennis Balls

KEY FACTORS

- Stay on balls of the feet; toes
- Hit the center of the squares
- Initiate exercise with the right foot & the left foot, respectively

COMMON ERRORS

- Whole foot is on the ground (flat-footed)
- Exercise is initiated only using the left foot

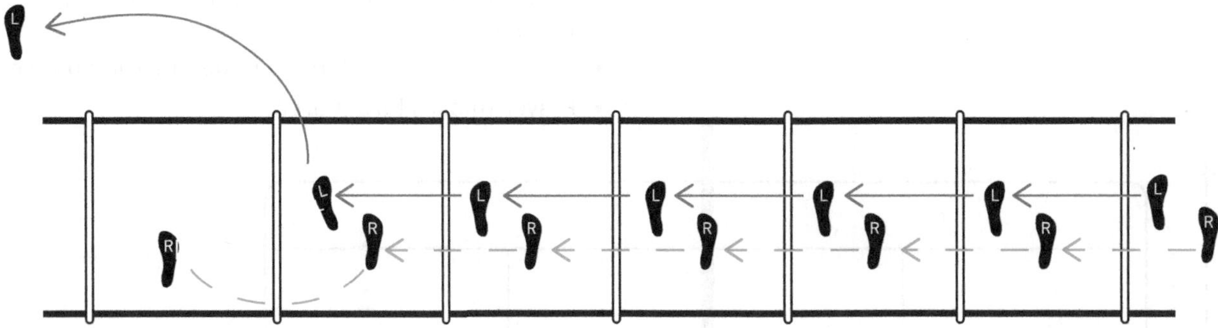

ID: 762

7.63 INSIDE-OUT FAST FEET II: RACQUET

SUMMARY

The Inside-Out Fast Feet II is an intermediate integrated speed & agility exercise, which focuses on improving the inside-out forehand and footwork for the inside-out forehand, utilizing a speed ladder, tennis racquet and balls.

PURPOSE

1. Improving footwork for inside-out forehand
2. Improving inside-out forehand

DESCRIPTION

1 ball must be fed by the coach towards the last square of the speed ladder. Athlete is **holding a racquet** and needs to:

1. Stand **sideways** in front of the 1st rung
2. Place both feet inside each square, starting with the left or right foot
3. Keep body weight on the balls of the feet (toes)
4. Progress down the ladder in a rapid fashion while **looking down** towards the speed ladder
5. When approaching the last square move the trailing foot behind the leading leg into the last square
6. Push off with the trailing foot, landing diagonally in front of the speed ladder with the leading foot
7. **Hit an inside-out forehand**

DEGREE OF DIFFICULTY

2

REQUIRED EQUIPMENT

- 1 Speed Ladder
- 1 Racquet
- Tennis Balls

KEY FACTORS

- Stay on balls of the feet; toes
- Hit the center of the squares
- Initiate exercise with the right foot & the left foot, respectively

COMMON ERRORS

- Whole foot is on the ground (flat-footed)
- Exercise is initiated only using the left foot

PRE-REQUISITE DRILLS

- Lateral Fast Feet III
- Lateral Posterior Cross-Over III

ID: 763

7.64 INSIDE-OUT FAST FEET III

SUMMARY

The Inside-Out Fast Feet III is an advanced integrated speed & agility exercise, which focuses on improving the inside-out forehand and footwork for the inside-out forehand by utilizing a speed ladder, tennis racquet and balls.

PURPOSE

1. Improving footwork for inside-out forehand
2. Improving inside-out forehand

DESCRIPTION

1 ball must be fed by the coach towards the last square of the speed ladder. Athlete is **holding a racquet** and needs to:

1. Stand **sideways** in front of the 1st rung
2. Place both feet inside each square, starting with the left or right foot
3. Keep body weight on the balls of the feet (toes)
4. Progress down the ladder in a rapid fashion while **looking forward** towards opposite baseline
5. When approaching the last square move the trailing foot behind the leading leg into the last square
6. Push off with the trailing foot, landing diagonally in front of the speed ladder with the leading foot
7. **Hit an inside-out forehand**

PRE-REQUISITE DRILLS

- Lateral Fast Feet III
- Lateral Posterior Cross-Over III

DEGREE OF DIFFICULTY

3

REQUIRED EQUIPMENT

- 1 Speed Ladder
- 1 Racquet
- Tennis Balls

KEY FACTORS

- Stay on balls of the feet; toes
- Hit the center of the squares
- Initiate exercise with the right foot & the left foot, respectively

COMMON ERRORS

- Whole foot is on the ground (flat-footed)
- Exercise is initiated only using the left foot

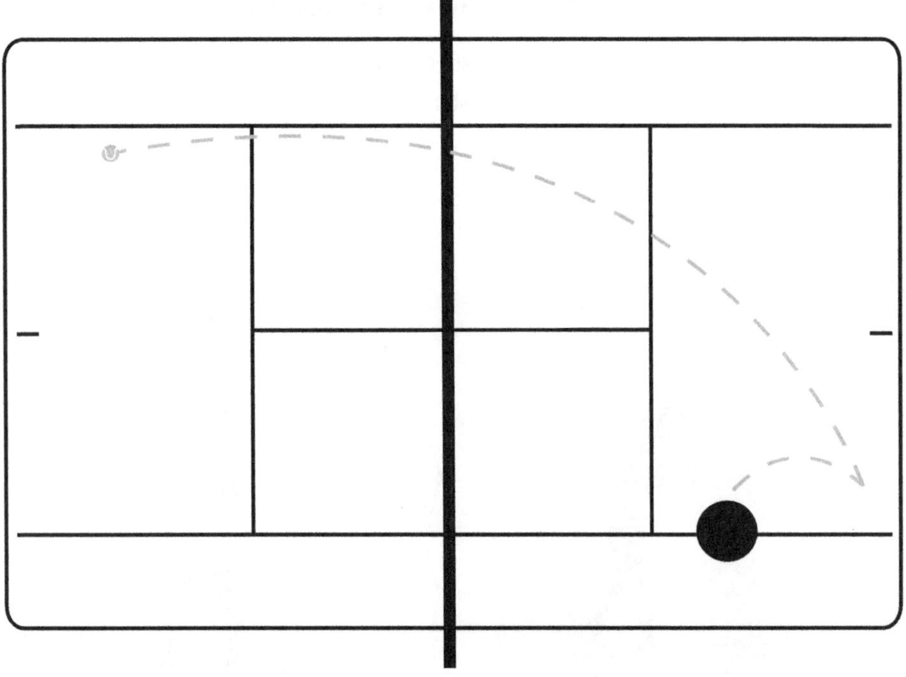

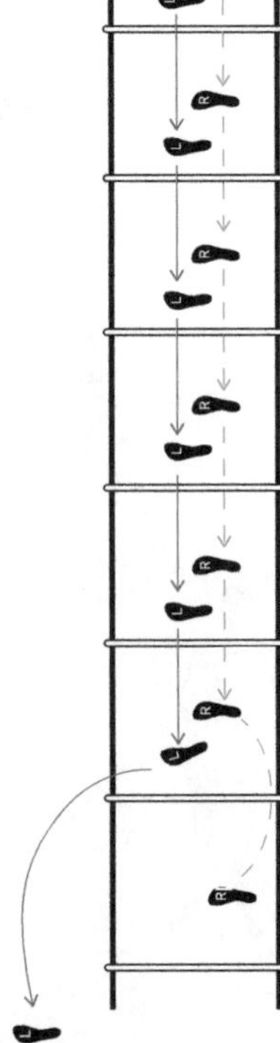

ID: 764

7.65 INSIDE-OUT FAST FEET IV: TARGET

SUMMARY

The Inside-Out Fast Feet VI is a professional integrated speed & agility exercise, which focuses on improving the inside-out forehand stroke, its accuracy, and footwork for the inside-out forehand, utilizing a speed ladder, 4 cones, tennis racquet and balls.

PURPOSE

1. Improving footwork for inside-out forehand
2. Improving inside-out forehand
3. Improving accuracy

DESCRIPTION

Coach sets up a **target area** (4 cones). 1 ball must be fed by the coach towards the last square of the speed ladder. Athlete is **holding a racquet** and needs to:

1. Stand **sideways** in front of the 1st rung
2. Place both feet inside each square, starting with the left or right foot
3. Keep body weight on the balls of the feet (toes)
4. Progress down the ladder in a rapid fashion while **tracking** the coach
5. When approaching the last square move the trailing foot behind the leading leg into the last square
6. Push off with the trailing foot, landing diagonally in front of the speed ladder with the leading foot
7. Hit an inside-out forehand into the **target area**

PRE-REQUISITE DRILLS

- Lateral Fast Feet IV
- Lateral Posterior Cross-Over IV

DEGREE OF DIFFICULTY

4

REQUIRED EQUIPMENT

- 1 Speed Ladder
- 1 Racquet
- Tennis Balls
- 4 Cones

KEY FACTORS

- Stay on balls of the feet; toes
- Hit the center of the squares
- Initiate exercise with the right foot & the left foot, respectively
- At least 30% of shots made need to be inside target area

COMMON ERRORS

- Whole foot is on the ground (flat-footed)
- Exercise is initiated only using the left foot

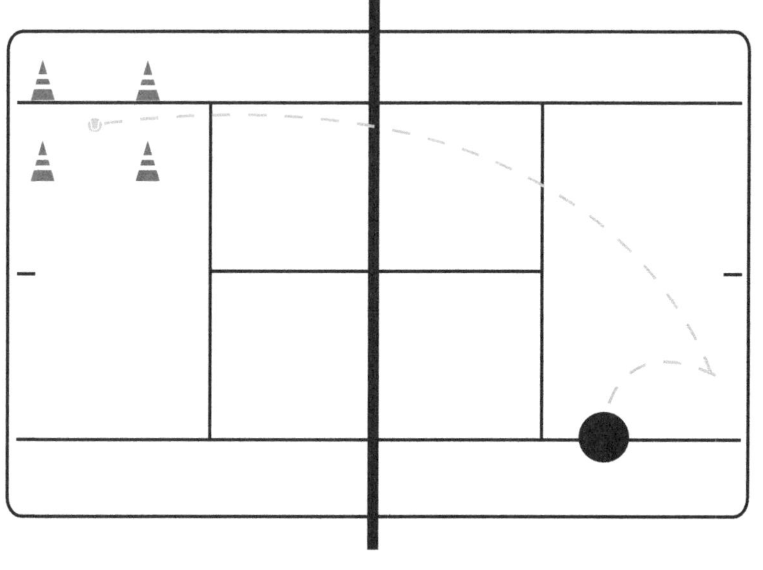

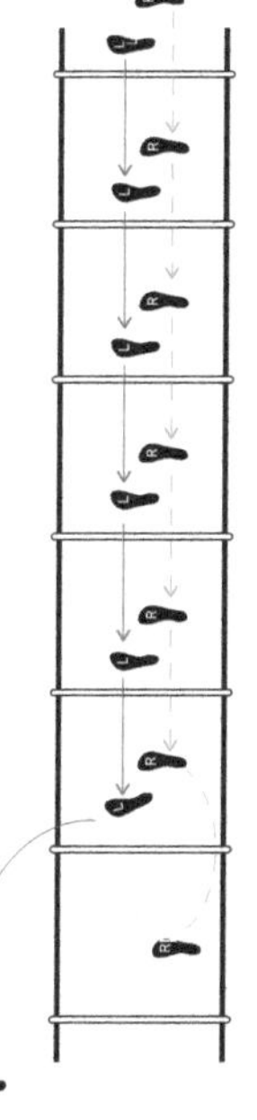

ID: 765

7

7.66 2 SHOTS & LADDER + VOLLEY (I)

SUMMARY

The 2 Shots & Ladder + Volley I is an introductory integrated speed & agility exercise, which focuses on improving footwork for groundstrokes, improving agility for transition game, getting the player used to transition from base-line to service-line, improving foot speed for approach shot, split-stepping and hitting an aggressive volley utilizing a short speed ladder and 6 agility rings.

PURPOSE

1. Improving footwork for groundstrokes
2. Improving agility for transition game
3. Improving foot speed for approach shot
4. Improving split-step
5. Improving 1st volley

DESCRIPTION

No balls are being fed by the teaching pro. The player stands behind the baseline in the center and needs to:

1. Move quickly via **side-step** to the rubber ring at deuce-court
2. Jump inside the ring with the **right** foot
3. Stick the landing (1/4 squat)
4. Push-off with the **right** foot
5. Move quickly via **side-step** to the rubber ring at ad-court
6. Jump inside the ring with the **left** foot
7. Stick the landing (1/4 squat)
8. Push-off with the **left** foot
9. Move quickly via **side-step** to the center baseline
10. Transition forward through speed ladder via "**Fast Feet**" while **looking down** at speed ladder
11. **Split-step** into 2 rubber rings inside service box
12. Perform a forehand or backhand **lunge-volley**

DEGREE OF DIFFICULTY

1

REQUIRED EQUIPMENT

- 6 Agility Rings
- 1 Short Speed Ladder

KEY FACTORS

- Footwork ► movement towards the individual shots should be initiated by side-steps & split-step before the volley
- Intensity ► approach shot needs to be hit forcefully so that the player's body keeps moving towards the net and volley needs to be struck aggressively (no drop-shot volleys)
- Quickness ► player needs to move forward quickly through speed ladder after hitting groundstrokes
- Agility ► player needs to change direction quickly (baseline movement to transition game)

COMMON ERRORS

- After reaching ring #2, player runs directly diagonalLY towards the speed ladder before side-stepping back toward the center baseline.
- Player doesn't transition through speed ladder correctly
- Player neglects to split-step before hitting the volley (3rd shot)

PRE-REQUISITE DRILLS

- Fast Feet I
- 2 Shots & Forehand Slam + Volley

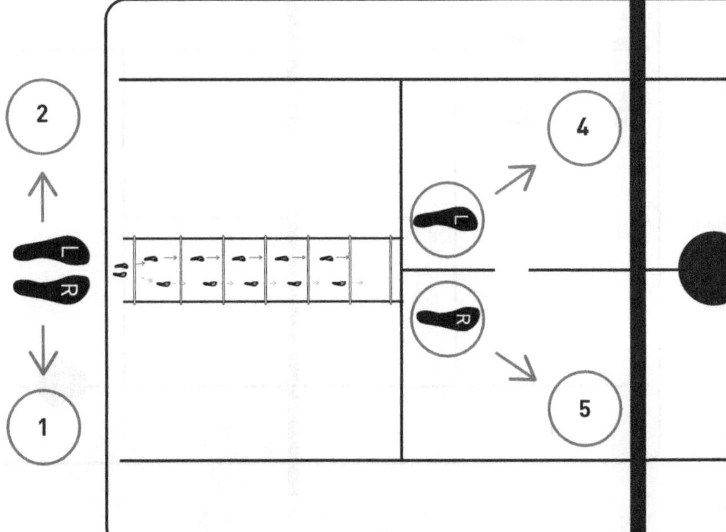

ID: 766

7.67 2 SHOTS & LADDER + VOLLEY (II)

SUMMARY

The 2 Shots & Ladder + Volley II is an intermediate integrated speed & agility exercise, which focuses on improving footwork for groundstrokes, improving agility for transition game, getting the player used to transition from base-line to service-line, improving foot speed for approach shot, split-stepping and hitting an aggressive volley utilizing a short speed ladder, 6 agility rings and a tennis racquet.

DESCRIPTION

0 balls are being fed by the teaching pro. The player, **holding a racquet**, stands behind the baseline in the center and needs to:

1. Move quickly via **side-step** to the rubber ring at deuce-court
2. Jump inside the ring with the **right** foot
3. Stick the landing (1/4 squat)
4. Push-off with the **right** foot
5. Move quickly via **side-step** to the rubber ring at ad-court
6. Jump inside the ring with the **left** foot
7. Stick the landing (1/4 squat)
8. Push-off with the **left** foot
9. Move quickly via **side-step** to the center baseline
10. Transition forward through speed ladder via "Fast Feet" while **looking down** at speed ladder
11. **Split-step i**nto 2 rubber rings inside service box
12. Perform a forehand or backhand **lunge-volley**

PRE-REQUISITE DRILLS

- Fast Feet II
- 2 Shots & Ladder + Volley I

PURPOSE

1. Improving footwork for groundstrokes
2. Improving agility for transition game
3. Improving foot speed for approach shot
4. Improving split-step
5. Improving 1st volley

DEGREE OF DIFFICULTY

2

REQUIRED EQUIPMENT

- 1 Racquet
- 6 Agility Rings
- 1 Short Speed Ladder

KEY FACTORS

- Footwork movement towards the individual shots should be initiated by side-steps & split-step before the volley
- Intensity approach shot needs to be hit forcefully so that the player's body keeps moving towards the net and volley needs to be struck aggressively (no drop-shot volleys)
- Quickness player needs to move forward quickly through speed ladder after hitting groundstrokes
- Agility player needs to change direction quickly (baseline movement to transition game)

COMMON ERRORS

- After reaching ring #2, player runs directly diagonally towards the speed ladder before side-stepping back toward the center baseline.
- Player doesn't transition through speed ladder correctly
- Player neglects to split-step before hitting the volley (3rd shot)

ID: 767

7.68 2 SHOTS & LADDER + VOLLEY (III)

SUMMARY

The 2 Shots & Ladder + Volley III is an advanced integrated speed & agility exercise, which focuses on improving footwork for groundstrokes, improving agility for transition game, getting the player used to transition from base-line to service-line, improving foot speed for approach shot, split-stepping and hitting an aggressive 1st volley, utilizing 6 rubber rings, short speed ladder, racquet and tennis balls.

PURPOSE

1. Improving footwork for groundstrokes
2. Improving agility for transition game
3. Improving foot speed for approach shot
4. Improving split-step
5. Improving 1st volley

DESCRIPTION

3 balls are being fed by the teaching pro. The player, **holding a racquet**, stands behind the baseline in the center and needs to:

1. Move quickly via side-step to the rubber ring at deuce-court
2. Jump inside the ring with the right foot
3. Stick the landing (1/4 squat)
4. **Hit a groundstroke**
5. Push-off with the right foot
6. Move quickly via side-step to the rubber ring at ad-court
7. Jump inside the ring with the left foot
8. Stick the landing (1/4 squat)
9. **Hit a groundstroke**
10. Push-off with the left foot
11. Move quickly via side-step to the center baseline
12. Transition forward through speed ladder via "Fast Feet" while **looking forward** at opposite base line
13. Split-step into 2 rubber rings inside service box
14. **Hit** a forehand or backhand lunge-volley

Teaching pro feeds:

1. Shot to the player's forehand side
2. Shot to the player's backhand side
3. Shot to player's forehand OR backhand for a volley

COMMON ERRORS

- After reaching ring #2, player runs directly diagonalLY towards the speed ladder before side-stepping back toward the center baseline.
- Player doesn't transition through speed ladder correctly
- Player neglects to split-step before hitting the volley (3rd shot)

ID: 768

DEGREE OF DIFFICULTY

3

KEY FACTORS

- Footwork » movement towards the individual shots should be initiated by side-steps & split-step before the volley
- Intensity » approach shot needs to be hit forcefully so that the player's body keeps moving towards the net and volley needs to be struck aggressively (no drop-shot volleys)
- Quickness » player needs to move forward quickly through speed ladder after hitting groundstrokes
- Agility » player needs to change direction quickly (baseline movement to transition game

REQUIRED EQUIPMENT

- 1 Racquet
- 6 Agility Rings
- 1 Short Speed Ladder
- Tennis Balls

PRE-REQUISITE DRILLS

- Fast Feet III
- 2 Shots & Ladder + Volley II

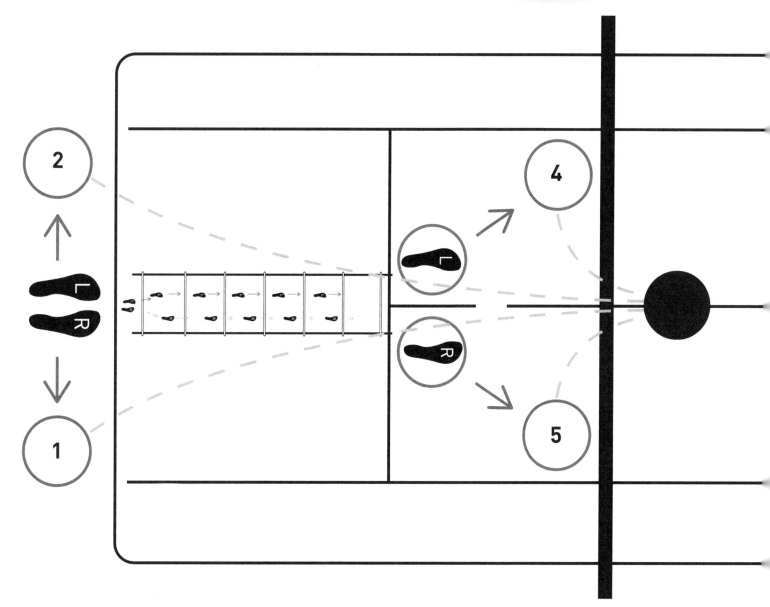

7.69 2 SHOTS & LADDER + VOLLEY (IV)

SUMMARY

The 2 Shots & Ladder + Volley IV is a professional integrated speed & agility exercise, which focuses on improving footwork for groundstrokes, improving agility for transition game, getting the player used to transition from base-line to service-line, improving foot speed for approach shot, split-stepping and hitting an aggressive 1st volley, utilizing 6 rubber rings, 4 cones, short speed ladder, racquet and tennis balls.

DESCRIPTION

3 balls are being fed by the teaching pro. The player, **holding a racquet**, stands behind the baseline in the center and needs to:

1. Move quickly via side-step to the rubber ring at deuce-court
2. Jump inside the ring with the right foot
3. Stick the landing (1/4 squat)
4. Hit a groundstroke
5. Push-off with the right foot
6. Move quickly via side-step to the rubber ring at ad-court
7. Jump inside the ring with the left foot
8. Stick the landing (1/4 squat)
9. Hit a groundstroke
10. Push-off with the left foot
11. Move quickly via side-step to the center baseline
12. Transition forward through speed ladder via "Fast Feet" while **tracking** the coach
13. **Split-step** into 2 rubber rings inside service box
14. **Hit** a forehand or backhand lunge-volley into the **target area**

Teaching pro **sets up a target area** (4 cones) and feeds:

1. Shot to the player's forehand side
2. Shot to the player's backhand side
3. Shot to player's forehand OR backhand for a volley

PRE-REQUISITE DRILLS

- Fast Feet IV
- 2 Shots & Ladder + Volley III

ID: 769

PURPOSE

1. Improving footwork for groundstrokes
2. Improving agility for transition game
3. Improving foot speed for approach shot
4. Improving split-step
5. Improving accuracy of 1st volley

KEY FACTORS

- Footwork ► movement towards the individual shots should be initiated by side-steps & split-step before the volley
- Intensity ► approach shot needs to be hit forcefully so that the player's body keeps moving towards the net and volley needs to be struck aggressively (no drop-shot volleys)
- Quickness ► player needs to move forward quickly through speed ladder after hitting groundstrokes
- Agility ► player needs to change direction quickly (baseline movement to transition game)

COMMON ERRORS

- After reaching ring #2, player runs directly diagonally towards the speed ladder before side-stepping back toward the center baseline.
- Player doesn't transition through speed ladder correctly
- Player neglects to split-step before hitting the volley (3rd shot

REQUIRED EQUIPMENT

- 1 Racquet
- 6 Agility Rings
- 1 Short Speed Ladder
- Tennis Balls
- 4 Cones

DEGREE OF DIFFICULTY

4

BASIC CONCEPTS OF TRAINING TO IMPROVE POWER: SPEED-STRENGTH

Power, which can be expressed as (force x distance)/time), is commonly referred to as **speed-strength** and is the factor behind performing work in a quick (short) period of time; in other words, power is the time rate of work (work/time). Being a powerful athlete means being able to exert force in order to handle the resistance of one's own body weight to performing explosive movements in a coordinated and athletic manner. High power enables the athlete to perform a strong serve, change directions quickly, dive and return serves effectively, perform vertical and lateral jumps, and accelerate about the court in an efficient manner.

Improving power has two aspects. On the one hand, the athlete performs high resistance power training exercises in the gym; strength for power (strength-power) and power exercises **(see Chapter 6: Strength & Conditioning - Resistance Training on page 171)**. On the other hand, the athlete does speed-strength (power) conditioning drills on the court, which can be thought of as low resistance power training exercises. It is important to point out that the strength/power resistance training exercises must complement the speed-strength conditioning exercises to achieve optimal results. Whether the athlete focuses on the weight lifting or the conditioning depends on the overall training emphasis and whether the athlete is in competition or not. Generally, when the athlete is in or close to competition, the training emphasis should be on conditioning.

Also, the athlete should have corrected any speed economy deficiencies before focusing on the various speed-strength conditioning exercises. Doing so ensures effective speed-strength conditioning training since less resistive forces are working against the athlete's effort.

Speed-strength (power) training revolves around developing the body's synchronized activation of motor neurons and fast-twitch muscle fibers. This means that power exercises train the nervous system to collaborate effectively with the muscular system. To describe it simply, potential energy developed in power exercises is converted to enhance the speed with which an athlete can perform work or an athletic movement.

STRENGTH FOR POWER

According to Newton's 2nd law of motion, **force** (F) can be expressed as mass (m) of an object x acceleration (a) of the object; F = m x a.

Generally, if a force acts upon an object and causes the **displacement** of the object, **work** occurred upon the object. In other words, in order for a force to qualify as having done work on an object, the force must cause its displacement. Also, the force must be applied in the same direction as the displacement to be considered positive work; a vertical force cannot cause a horizontal displacement. This is referred to as **strength** with respect to exercise. For example, during bench pressing the athlete lies flat on a bench and applies force vertically to move the bar off the chest. Once the bar moves vertically, work is being done to move the bar. If the bar doesn't move then no work is being done! In other words, **work** (W) can be expressed as force (F) x displacement (d); W = F · d. With respect to exercise, strength is the equivalent to physical work, since **strength** (S) is defined as force x distance; S = F x d, which = m · a · d.

Since power is the time rate of work ([force · distance]/time), and work (force · distance) is the equivalent to strength, then maximizing the athlete's force output will also cause maximum power output, which is why strength training precedes power training!

In order to maximize the athlete's **strength** (S = m · a · d), force output (F = m · a) must be maximized, which means that the resistance (m) should increase while the velocity of the movement (a) decreases and the distance (d) remains the same. Slower velocity with heavier resistance leads to greater muscle fiber recruitment. Also, stabilization properties are going to improve due to the prolonged motor unit control mechanism.

It is important to understand that absolute muscular strength development is not the goal. Instead, the focus must be on maximizing body mass adjusted muscular strength because it is highly related to peak performance. This means that the athlete must be strong for his/her size. While playing tennis the athlete needs to control the body (weight) during stroke production, which means controlling dynamic stability while applying force and moving in different directions.

If a tennis player is trained like a body builder (hypertrophy training only), the athlete will become too heavy (too much muscle mass), which decreases his/her ability

to change direction (center of mass) effectively. In other words, if the athlete is too big they don't have the ability to move as fluently as they need to.

During power training (P = [force · distance/time] = F · a), the speed at which work can be performed is going to be maximized, which means high movement velocity. High velocities reduce overall force output due to muscle fiber recruitment limitations but also neural control mechanisms are reduced as well because there is no time to think during the action.

HOW STRENGTH BENEFITS POWER

There are a few different ways that strength enhances power. Strength benefits power by improving:

1. Force production capabilities
2. Stabilization
3. Neural patterns

Proper strength training allows for greater force production capabilities of fast twitch muscle fibers, which allows for a greater application of power. When the athlete can generate more force (higher strength levels), the higher force application in combination with higher movement velocities translates into more power since strength is maximizing force output and power is generating force rapidly. Therefore the athlete requires adequate strength levels in order to generate more power. This does not mean that the athlete needs to maximize strength levels to generate more power! Instead, the focus is on optimizing the balance between strength and power (body mass adjusted muscular strength underlying power development) in order to optimize performance on the court.

Also, strength training can improve muscle balance, which enhances the control of body segments by enhancing stabilization properties. Improved muscle balance also allows for greater functional range of motion at a particular joint since the body segments are more in sync.

When the athlete engages in different exercises under load, it has a positive effect on neural patterns due to efficient fast twitch muscle recruitment; it speeds up the signal transmission and recruits powerful muscle fibers.

In general, power exercises are **ballistic**, which means that they are accelerated movements, where the force production is greater than simply moving an object from point A to B.

Therefore, the focus is on improving strength (maximum force output), and using that strength to move the athlete's center of mass effectively. This is where balance/stability properties become an issue because if the athlete cannot transfer energy effectively throughout the body (e.g. during change of direction), energy cannot be transferred very rapidly either because of the inherent loss of energy. Recall that strength is simply the ability to generate a contractile force, which is quantifiable and either has a joint angle change (isotonic contraction; concentric eccentric component) or it does not (isometric contraction). Isometric force production is used to enhance stabilization properties. When one muscle group generates force and contracts to stabilize the action, another muscle group can apply that force to move body segments. Therefore, the athlete's strength levels depend on the strength of the stabilizers, otherwise there is going to be a loss in maximum force production due to "leakage". In other words, if only certain body segments are strong but the muscles connecting the body segments are weak, there will be a loss in the athlete's ability to apply strength. So, segmentally the athlete may be strong but as far as connecting factors are concerned the athlete will be limited to whatever stabilizer strength capacity he possesses. If those stabilizing muscles have never been exposed to transferring energy through the heels all the way up through the body up through the bar, the athlete will be inefficient when trying to generate maximum power. So, in other words, any weakness will result in a loss in the athlete's ability to apply strength. For this reason we employ an integrated approach with integrated movement patterns. This is also the reason why athletes (e.g. tennis players) need to be able to do power clean lifts!

STRENGTH TRAINING CONCEPTS FOR PERFORMANCE

Take a look at the Strength Training for Performance segment and exercises presented in the "Speed Economy" section of this book **(see Strength Training for Performance on page 260)**. The athlete should be familiar with those exercises before shifting the focus to developing speed-strength.

Also, the exercises in the resistance training chapter **(see Chapter 6: Strength & Conditioning - Resistance Training on page 171)**, should be used in conjunction with the strength exercises for conditioning because they enhance the integrity of the trunk.

If the athlete cannot transfer energy effectively through the trunk, it doesn't matter what happens at the extremities (e.g. hands). For example, during the standing Push-Press the athlete cannot lift as much weight as when doing a seated Push-Press because the chair stabilizes the action and all the athlete needs to do is exert force upwards in a single plane; during the standing Push-Press the muscles of the trunk have to stabilize the action. Therefore, if the athlete only commits to resistance strength training (e.g. seated push-press), where maximum force output is the focus, the integrity of the trunk will be underdeveloped.

During strength training for conditioning the focus is on training movements, not muscles; the athlete has to become proficient in the movement. As previously mentioned, developing the core (trunk) before the extremities makes sense with regards to kinetic energy transfer. Since energy is 100% at the ground, the athlete´s lower extremities need to be developed through closed-chain compound activities because they will also develop the trunk (core).

Contrast training, a strength and power training concept, will be introduced next. During contrast training the athlete engages in controlled heavy lifting (strength resistance training exercise) immediately followed by a plyometric/ballistic exercise. So, the athlete will do a 6 repetition squat close to volitional failure, but not until no further repetitions can be performed, before transitioning right into a plyometric/ballistic exercise, adding the accelerated component. This mixture of heavy strength resistance exercise followed by an explosive strength for conditioning exercise doesn't change recruitment characteristics because the high resistance stimulates the motor units that respond to the afferent pathways of heavy loading and then the high velocity ballistic/plyometric exercise changes those pathways slightly to recruit other fast twitch muscle fibers because of the speed of the action. Therefore, the maximum amount of fast twitch fibers can be recruited, which leads to maximum power output. In other words, when a strength resistance training exercises precedes a ballistic/plyometric exercise, power output is enhanced due to neural pathway enhancements associated with the progression from pre-fatigue to high-rate fast twitch fiber recruitment. When only going to pre-fatigue, the athlete retains some level of energy within the energy system, but then challenges the energy system with a lightweight explosive movement, which leads to fastest twitch fiber recruitment.

If, on the other hand, the athlete goes to volitional failure during the strength exercise, that will cause an increase in motor unit (muscle fiber) recruitment patterns. As some motor units (muscle fibers) fatigue, others are going to be recruited. But when the athlete uses the strength exercise to cause complete failure (no more reps possible), the fast twitch motor units (muscle fibers) which needed to be recruited for the explosive exercise will not be available. Therefore, during contrast training, the athlete is pre-fatiguing the fast twitch muscle fibers during the strength exercise phase but the fastest twitch muscle fibers are then recruited during the ballistic/plyometric portion.

Research has shown that doing power training following power training is ineffective. Therefore, do not combine high resistance power training with low resistance power training (e.g. plyometrics); it is too much stress on the nervous system!

POWER TRAINING: HIGH RESISTANCE POWER & LOW RESISTANCE POWER

There are two different types of power training:

1. High Resistance Power Training
2. Low Resistance Power Training

The high resistance power training occurs predominantly during resistance training in the weight room, where the athlete lifts heavier loads. On the other hand, low resistance power training often occurs during conditioning drills on the court or in the gym, where lighter loads are being used; light resistance can be moved faster. Just to clarify: the difference between the 2 kinds of power training is not the location where the exercises are being performed but how much resistance is being moved and which energy systems are more predominant in supplying the energy.

The difference in the resistance being moved also causes a shift in the predominant energy system being used during each of the power training applications. During heavier loads (High Resistance Power Training) the **phosphagen system** (ATP-CP system) provides the energy to generate power, whereas the glycolytic pathways (anaerobic glycolysis) provide the power for lighter resistance during that power conditioning training (Low Resistance Power Training).

Consequently, during power cleans in the strength room the athlete performs 3-5 repetitions before the phosphagen energy system is drained. Also, resistance doesn't always refer to an external load (e.g. dumbbells); body weight can also be used as resistance. For instance, take a 200 lb (~91kg) athlete performing a high box jump onto a 30-inch (~75cm) box. Even though the athlete is not using an external resistance, the high box jump cannot be performed by the athlete in a rebound fashion because the resistance being moved is already very high (200 lb ~ 91kg), which means that energy is predominantly being provided by the ATP-CP system. This is why it is recommended to step off the box and wait 5 seconds between high box jumps to allow for a measure of recovery.

If the glycolytic pathways were providing the energy during high box jumps, the athlete could jump on and off the box in a rebound fashion. In reality, after the 2nd jump people would have scars all over their legs and wouldn´t be able to continue because there is a reduction in force output due to lactic acid build up in the glycolytic pathways.

On the other hand, when the athlete does medicine ball (MB) chest passes as fast as possible against a wall with a 6lb (~3kg) medicine ball that rebounds, the glycolytic energy system is predominantly responsible for the supply of energy when doing 3 sets at 10-15 repetitions in a set period of time. It is the glycolytic energy system because the resistance is low, the velocity is high, and there is an endurance component to it as well.

POWER TRAINING SUMMARY TABLE

	High Resistance Power	Low Resistance Power
Energy System:	ATP/CP	Glycolytic
Dominant Muscle Action:	Concentric Contraction	Stretch-Shortening Cycle
Intensity in 1RM	70 – 90% intensity	45 – 60% intensity
Repetitions:	< 6 reps	8 – 20 reps
Rest between sets:	90 – 120 seconds	60 – 90 seconds
Volume:	Low	High

Another thing to consider during rapid movements is the amount of fatigue to the nervous system. During fast movements the central nervous system (CNS) is completely responsible for maintaining dynamic equilibrium. So, if the CNS cannot maintain the velocity, the movement will be out of control. If the CNS cannot control the athlete's movements, the athlete's performance level will decrease significantly. This phenomenon can also be observed during agility drills where some of the athletes cannot control the center of mass and hence lose stability and sometimes even fall to the ground. This can cause embarrassment in the athlete because the agility drill cannot be completed because of their lack of dynamic equilibrium at the highest speed; they cannot control their center of mass within the base of support, which causes an unstable environment.

Generally speaking, during most land-based sports, athletes have to move their center of mass over the base of support to an outside point, which basically means that they lose stability and have to regain it. This is the scenario that allows for effective locomotion (moving from one place to another). The more efficiently that athletes can manage their center of mass, the farther and faster they can move. If they have deficiencies in controlling their center of mass, they will be unable to move very fast regardless of the direction they are going.

This phenomenon also applies to the tennis court. One of the big issues for tennis players is the ability to decelerate and neutralize the center of mass (body) before each stroke in order to hit a controlled and powerful shot - but oftentimes that is precisely where errors occur. Athletes can create high velocity movements but that doesn't mean that they can control them. For instance, there are athletes that can hit very powerful groundstrokes during warm-up when they don't have to move as much but once the match starts and they have to move at maximum speed during rallies, they cannot duplicate those powerful shots on the court; they cannot do it because their velocity is too high.

This is where the strength-power training phase comes into play. The strength-power training benefits power training because it benefits those stabilization segments. By only committing to strength training the athlete limits his power output. Strength training should be used to complement power training!

BALLISTIC TRAINING VS. PLYOMETRIC TRAINING

Ballistics are used to improve the strength (force output) of the athlete and **plyometrics** are used to improve overall power output; ballistics do not partake of the benefits arising from the **stretch-shortening cycle** (SSC; explained on page 580) but plyometrics do!

Plyometric and ballistic exercises include:

- Jumps
- Throws
- Passes
- Many other assorted body weight or medicine ball drills

One should note that this is not a comprehensive list as many other drills can be devised using hurdles, agility rings, etc.

The **speed ladder** and **cone drills** (agility drills) can be utilized to improve agility, foot speed, balance and coordination. When implementing these three types of exercises into an exclusive speed, agility, and quickness (SAQ) training session, it is suggested that the exercises be performed in the following order:

1. Plyometrics/ballistics
2. Speed ladder drills
3. Agility drills

This is just a rule of thumb however; it depends on the complexity of the drills selected for a given training session and the primary goal of the training. Metabolic speed conditioning or additional aerobic training should be performed at the very end of the session.

TRAINING PROGRAM CONSIDERATIONS

The proper time to introduce power training into the workout session depends on the goal of the training, the complexity and intensity of the power training exercises that are planned (High Resistance Power Exercises & Low Resistance Power Exercises), and whatever other goals the session wants to achieve. If one is combining power exercises with traditional resistance training exercises during the same session, it is suggested that all heavy ballistics be performed before anything else, and that any low resistance plyometrics/ballistics be performed at the end of the session – perhaps in **superset** fashion (instant transition from one exercise to another exercise thereby combining the two to effectively create one).

Complex and intense power training (High Resistance Power Training) should be performed first (such as Power Clean or Push Jerks) because it places the greatest demand on the nervous system. If intense squats, deadlifts or other compound exercises are performed first, the athlete's neural efficiency will be diminished before he begins to deal with the greatest challenge to the nervous system.

If the athlete is training simply for power on a given day, he should start with the heavy ballistics, transition to complex plyometrics, and finish with easier plyometrics and lower resistance ballistics (such as heavy medicine ball throws) that can involve a high number of repetitions. This is only a basic guideline. There can be many variations depending on the entire list of exercises chosen for a given training session.

Level of Proficiency	# of Ground Contacts/Session	# of Ground Contacts/Week
Beginner	80 – 100	160 - 200
Intermediate	100 – 120	200 - 240
Advanced	120 – 140	240 - 280
Professional	140 – 160	280 - 320

TRAINING VOLUME, RECOVERY, AND FREQUENCY

The risk of overtraining during power training is very high because the muscular system is under a lot of stress due to the high movement velocities and the high levels of stability required to perform the exercises in good form. Therefore, overall volume should be adjusted to match the proficiency of the athletes. In general, the volume pertains to the number of jumps or repetitions, usually referred to as contacts; the term "contacts" can also refer to high resistance power training exercises (e.g. power clean)! Each time the athlete comes in contact with the ground during power exercises, there is a jarring of the joints and considerable force to be absorbed by the targeted musculature. Therefore, it is recommended that the athlete be able to squat 1.5x their body weight before attempting any aggressive lower body plyometrics, especially box drops and the like.

This is to ensure that the individual has adequate muscular strength and joint stability. For a beginner, the suggested limit is 80 -100 contacts per session. For an intermediate, 100 -120 contacts per session is acceptable. For an athlete with advanced power training status, 120 -140 contacts per session may be appropriate. A weekly total of approximately 300 contacts would indicate that an upper limit of volume has been reached. It is important to adhere to these recommendations because, for instance, if someone is new to plyometric exercise without having proper muscular strength and/or balance, the likelihood of injury increases due to overtraining.

Recovery periods between sets of numerous power exercises should be similar to that of resistance strength training. As a rule of thumb 90 – 120 seconds is suitable for the Olympic Lifts and most heavy ballistics. For lighter resistance plyometrics and ballistics, a rest period of around 60 - 90 seconds is appropriate. You have to think logically; for example, if you are performing a set of 6 high box jumps, you may want to rest 15 seconds between jumps and about 75 – 90 seconds between sets. High box jumps don't provide significant external resistance, but the exercise itself can be challenging (and if you don't make a jump your shins will find it hard to forgive you). Therefore, smaller boxes are used so that the athlete can step down from the box instead of jumping down because it preserves energy for consecutive jumps. If the athlete jumps off the box, deceleration of the body weight has to occur; this requires energy.

If true power-type sets are being performed, the athlete should be allowed about 2 minutes rest between sets; perform only 5-6 jumps when jumping for max height. If the athlete tries more repetitions than that, the shins will feel it because the athlete only has enough energy for 5-6 jumps. There is not much of a difference between making a jump and not making it; oftentimes one foot will make it but the other won´t. Therefore, the athlete needs to take these jumps seriously otherwise injuries can occur. Also, there shouldn´t be any superman syndrome where the athletes try to outdo one another!

It should also be noted that power training challenges the athlete's nervous system as well as the targeted musculature. The athletes need neural recovery to keep the speed of each set at a level conducive to optimal power production. On the other hand, if the athlete is working on power endurance at the tail end of an exercise session, super-setting two or more exercises with 45 – 60 seconds rest periods could be appropriate for increasing anaerobic endurance.

With regards to frequency, it depends on how plyometrics are being used. Plyometrics can be:

1. Integrated with strength training
2. Isolated in running programs that are being used during conditioning
3. Integrated with speed work

Generally, plyometrics should be performed 1-3 days per week on non-consecutive days depending on whether upper and lower body activities (jumps & throws) are being performed. With the integrated approach athletes can do ~300 contacts/week if they are just doing plyometrics that week but no one ever just does plyometrics because they have to be integrated into strength training and/or conditioning. When plyometrics are integrated with strength training, the athlete works out 2x/week.

SAFETY CONSIDERATIONS

Athletes often get hurt doing plyometric/ballistic exercises because of the superman syndrome, not because plyometrics are so dangerous; the real reason is that the exercises are fun and tend to encourage competition! With plyometric/ballistic training there is a tendency for people to want to compete much more than they do during resistance training exercises.

Carefully follow the exercise descriptions in order to avoid injuries like:

1. Ankle rolls
2. Shin trauma
3. Plantar fasciitis
4. Jumpers knee (patella tendinitis)

Always check the box height and ensure that the boxes are locked. Also check and clean any surface area (on top of the box and on the ground) for dust and liquids (e.g. water, sweat) because they can become slippery. Proper footwear is a must! Do not wear any sandals, flip flops, or shoes without proper arch support.

Some exercises (e.g. tuck jumps) can also be performed in shallow water (1-3 feet deep) because it reduces the risk of injury but if the focus is on maximizing power output, the land-based applications work best.

BALLISTICS

The ballistic exercises presented focus on improving the athlete's explosiveness. During a ballistic exercise the athlete accelerates an object faster than necessary, moving its center of mass quickly from point A to point B; the velocity of the required movement needs to be high. More precisely, ballistics consists of a concentric acceleration phase and an eccentric deceleration phase with ground contact time (amortization phase) lasting longer than 0.25 seconds. Therefore, all Olympic lifts (e.g. power clean, snatch) are ballistic in nature.

Generally, it is recommended to engage in ballistics prior to plyometrics training **(see Plyometrics on page 580)** since ballistics are a good preparation for plyometrics because of the additional weight being used (which results in the amortization phase being > 0.25 seconds). Oftentimes athletes cannot do plyometric exercises in true plyometric fashion because they are too slow. Since plyometrics require a ground contact time of less than 0.25 seconds, resistance (weight) has to be on the lower end; otherwise the athlete wastes time decelerating and hence exceeds 0.25 seconds of ground contact. It is very practical to have athletes do ballistic exercises using heavier resistance to improve plyometrics using lighter resistance.

It is important to ensure that before the athlete starts doing the exercises at maximum effort they are being done correctly with regards to form. Therefore, try to carefully follow the exercise descriptions.

The ballistic exercises in this section have the following subcategories:

- Loaded Counter-Movement Box Jumps & Box Rebounds
- Heavy Concentric Medicine Ball Throws
- Loaded Rebounds
- Bounds

For effective athletic development the exercises have been categorized according to degree of difficulty:

1. Beginner
2. Intermediate
3. Advanced
4. Professional

LOADED COUNTER-MOVEMENT BOX JUMPS & BOX REBOUNDS

Depths jumps consist of the athlete stepping off a box of particular height, landing on the ground, and then using the energy to jump onto another object or in another direction. The athlete is going to accelerate the body, thereby maximizing nervous system efficiency for a single repetition with duplicable repetitions to follow; they are "controlled" jumps since they are isolated jumps. Box rebounds, on the other hand, require the athlete to jump in place and repeatedly stabilize unstable movements.

Depth jumps are extremely effective at neural pathway development for concentric acceleration, eccentric deceleration, and overall foot speed.

It is important to note that single leg depth jumps are much more difficult and warrant lower boxes; use boxes as low as 2 inches for single-leg activity during skill acquisition phase. Exercises are shown on **page 473.**

HEAVY CONCENTRIC THROWS

During heavy concentric throws the focus is on explosiveness, rather than the total amount of resistance being used; emphasis is on the speed of the action and control of the body. Some of the selected exercises duplicate movement patterns seen in the weight room during resistance training. For example, the "Plate Jacks" mimic the "Snatch" movement since the athlete has to jump up by extending the hips, then explosively flex the hips and catch the resistance in overhead position, before jumping down again. Take a look at **page 508** for heavy concentric throw exercise.

LOW-SPEED LOADED REBOUNDS

The low-speed loaded rebounds focus on improving the athlete's explosiveness. They are also developmental and vary in the height of the jumps; they range from low (below hip level) , to medium (hip level), to high (above hip level). Stabilization and transfer of energy requirements increase with the height of the jumps.

When the athlete moves around when jumping, transfer of energy is inefficient; center of mass control is weak. Refer to **page 534** for low-speed loaded rebounds.

BOUNDS

Bounds, also known as broad jumps or long jumps, are ballistic in nature and are excellent for developing explosive hip flexion and hip extension capabilities, which will translate into faster speed on the court and more explosive starts and jumps. They use a mild vertical component with a heavy horizontal component.

Effective utilization of the body is key not only during stroke production but also when moving around the court. In other words, the effective transfer of energy is important for powerful stroke production and explosiveness on the court; whoever has the greatest ability to maintain dynamic equilibrium (stability) during stroke production will win the match.

During double & triple broad jumps the athlete must manage the body (center of mass), accelerate it forward rapidly, and control the center of mass during landing before accelerating forward again. Generally, the person with the greatest ability to reach full hip extension with rapid hip flexion will travel the farthest distance because they maximize the utilization of the body. During the Olympic long jump event athletes attain full hip extension in-flight and land into full hip flexion.

In the case of double & triple bounds the landing is very important. Most athletes have a very good 1st jump but the 2nd jump won't be as good because they control the 1st bound but lose some of the dynamic equilibrium going into the 2nd bound and lose even more dynamic equilibrium going into the 3rd. The 3rd bound is significant because it shows how well the athlete "controls" the energy.

The bound exercises **page 570** will help the athlete in to use his/her body to enhance the dynamic equilibrium (stability) needed during stroke production.

7.70 LOADED LL DEPTH JUMP TO FULL EXTENSION (I)

SUMMARY

The Loaded Low-Level Depth Jump to Full Extension I is a ballistic exercise, which focuses on developing neural pathways for explosive jumping, body control & coordination as well as improving skill and strength foundation for complex movements utilizing a box, 2 agility rings, and ankle weights.

DESCRIPTION

Athlete wears **ankle weights**.

1. Place box onto solid, non-sliding surface
2. Place 2 agility rings in front of the box
3. Step onto the box; athlete stands up straight and positions the feet under the shoulders
4. Step off the box with **one (1) foot**
5. Land with **both feet simultaneously** into agility rings
6. Immediately **jump upwards** with both legs simultaneously while **looking down** at the ground; extend hips, use arm swing to generate force and raise arms over the head
7. Land inside the **agility rings**

BREATH IN & OUT

- IN: Before Step Off
- OUT: During Jumping

PURPOSE

1. Developing neural pathways for explosive jumping capability (neurological feedback loop)
2. Improving balance (body control) & coordination
3. Improving skill and strength foundation for complex movements

DEGREE OF DIFFICULTY

1

REQUIRED EQUIPMENT

- 6 – 8 Inch Box
- 2 Agility Rings
- 5-10 lb Ankle Weights

KEY FACTORS

- Focus on perfect movement mechanics and explosiveness (maximum height)
- Step off the box with one (1) foot
- Land on both feet simultaneously inside agility rings
- Jump vertically with both feet simultaneously
- Maintain balance; land in same location inside agility rings

COMMON ERRORS

- Athlete lands outside agility rings

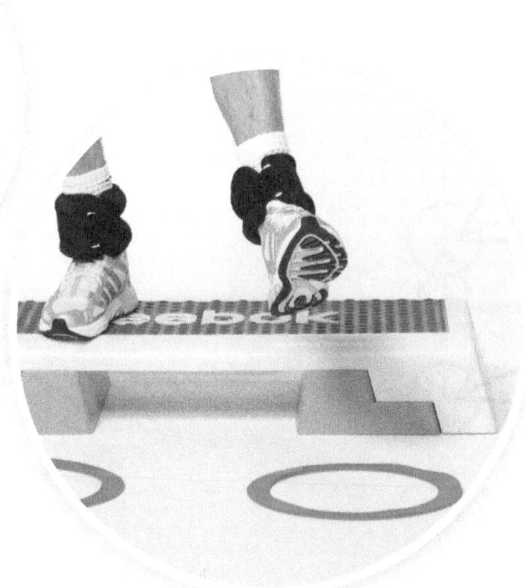

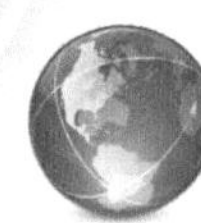

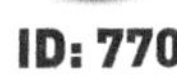

7.71 LOADED LL DEPTH JUMP TO FULL EXTENSION (II)

SUMMARY

The Loaded Low-Level Depth Jump to Full Extension II is a ballistic exercise, which focuses on developing neural pathways for explosive jumping, body control & coordination as well as improving skill and strength foundation for complex movements utilizing a box, 2 agility rings, and ankle weights.

PURPOSE

1. Developing neural pathways for explosive jumping capability (neurological feedback loop)
2. Improving balance (body control) & coordination
3. Improving skill and strength foundation for complex movements

DESCRIPTION

Athlete wears **ankle weights**.

1. Place box onto solid, non-sliding surface
2. Place 2 agility rings in front of the box
3. Step onto the box; athlete stands up straight and positions the feet under the shoulders
4. Step off the box with **one (1) foot; look forward**
5. Land with **both feet simultaneously** into agility rings
6. Immediately **jump upwards** with both legs simultaneously while **looking forward**; extend hips, use arm swing to generate force and raise arms over the head
7. Land inside the **agility rings**

PRE-REQUISITE DRILLS

- Loaded Low-Level Depth Jump to Full Extension (I)

BREATH IN & OUT

- IN: Before Step Off
- OUT: During Jumping

DEGREE OF DIFFICULTY

2

REQUIRED EQUIPMENT

- 6 – 8 Inch Box
- 2 Agility Rings
- 5-10 lb Ankle Weights

KEY FACTORS

- Focus on perfect movement mechanics and explosiveness (maximum height)
- Step off the box with one (1) foot; look forward
- Land on both feet simultaneously inside agility rings
- Jump vertically with both feet simultaneously
- Maintain balance; land in same location inside agility rings

COMMON ERRORS

- Athlete lands outside agility rings

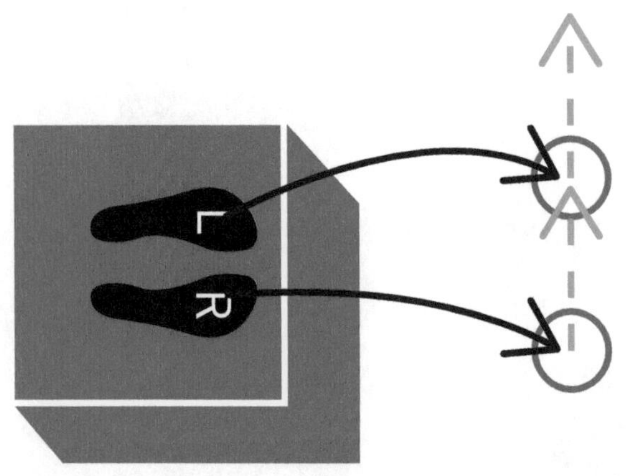

ID: 771

7.72 LOADED LL DEPTH JUMP TO HIGH TUCK JUMP (I)

SUMMARY

The Loaded Low-Level Depth Jump to High Tuck Jump I is a ballistic exercise, which focuses on improving neural pathways for explosive jumping, body control & coordination, skill and strength foundation as well as improving flexibility utilizing a box, 2 agility rings, and ankle weights.

PURPOSE

1. Developing neural pathways for explosive jumping capability (neurological feedback loop)
2. Improving balance (body control) & coordination
3. Improving skill and strength foundation for complex movements
4. Improving flexibility (Glutes & Hamstrings)

DESCRIPTION

Athlete wears **ankle weights**.

1. Place box onto solid, non-sliding surface
2. Place 2 agility rings in front of the box
3. Step onto the box; athlete stands up straight and positions the feet under the shoulders
4. Step off the box with **one (1) foot**
5. Land with both feet **simultaneously** into agility rings
6. Immediately jump upwards into a **high tuck jump** with both legs **simultaneously** while **looking down** at the ground
7. Land inside the **agility rings**

PRE-REQUISITE DRILLS

- Loaded Low-Level Depth Jump to Full Extension (I)
- Loaded High-Level Tuck Jump (I)

BREATH IN & OUT

- IN: Before Step Off
- OUT: During Jumping

DEGREE OF DIFFICULTY

1

REQUIRED EQUIPMENT

- 6 – 8 Inch Box
- 2 Agility Rings
- 5-10 lb Ankle Weights

KEY FACTORS

- Focus on perfect movement mechanics and explosiveness (maximum height)
- Step off the box with one (1) foot
- Land on both feet simultaneously inside agility rings
- Jump vertically with both feet simultaneously
- Maintain balance; land in same location inside agility ring

COMMON ERRORS

- Athlete lands outside agility rings

ID: 772

7.73 LOADED LL DEPTH JUMP TO HIGH TUCK JUMP (II)

SUMMARY

The Loaded Low-Level Depth Jump to High Tuck Jump II is a ballistic exercise, which focuses on improving neural pathways for explosive jumping, body control & coordination, skill and strength foundation as well as improving flexibility utilizing a box, 2 agility rings, and ankle weights.

PURPOSE

1. Developing neural pathways for explosive jumping capability (neurological feedback loop)
2. Improving balance (body control) & coordination
3. Improving skill and strength foundation for complex movements
4. Improving flexibility (Glutes & Hamstrings)

DESCRIPTION

Athlete wears **ankle weights**.

1. Place box onto solid, non-sliding surface
2. Place 2 agility rings in front of the box
3. Step onto the box; athlete stands up straight and positions the feet under the shoulders
4. Step off the box with **one (1) foot; look forward**
5. Land with both feet **simultaneously** into agility rings
6. Immediately jump upwards into a high tuck jump with both legs simultaneously while **looking forward**
7. Land inside the agility rings

PRE-REQUISITE DRILLS

- Loaded Low-Level Depth Jump to Full Extension (I)
- Loaded High-Level Tuck Jump (I)

BREATH IN & OUT

- IN: Before Step Off
- OUT: During Jumping

DEGREE OF DIFFICULTY

2

REQUIRED EQUIPMENT

- 6 – 8 Inch Box
- 2 Agility Rings
- 5-10 lb Ankle Weights

KEY FACTORS

- Focus on perfect movement mechanics and explosiveness (maximum height)
- Step off the box with one (1) foot; look forward
- Land on both feet simultaneously inside agility rings
- Jump vertically with both feet simultaneously
- Maintain balance; land in same location inside agility rings

COMMON ERRORS

- Athlete lands outside agility rings

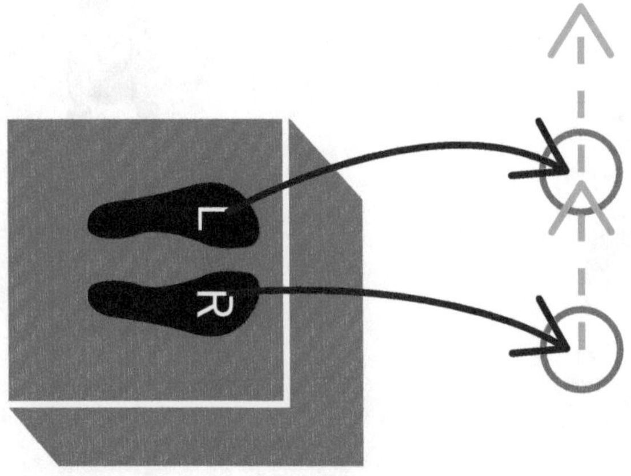

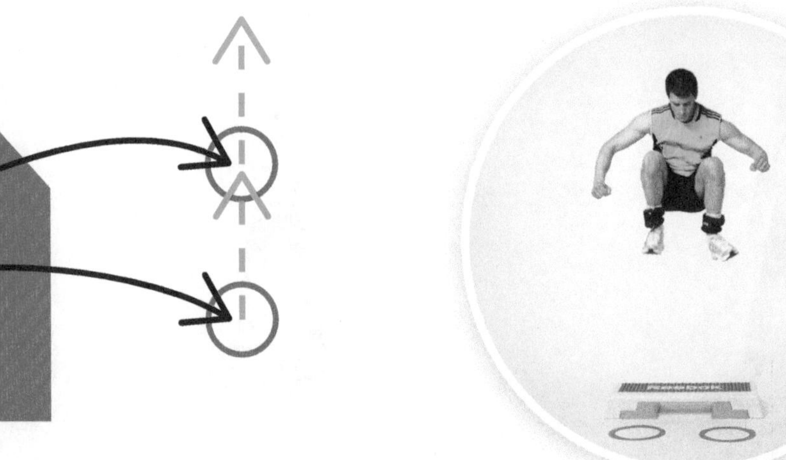

ID: 773

7.74 L LL SL DEPTH JUMP TO SL HIGH TUCK JUMP (III)

SUMMARY

The Loaded Low-Level Single-Leg Depth Jump to Single-Leg High Tuck Jump III is a ballistic exercise, which focuses on improving neural pathways for explosive jumping, body control & coordination, skill and strength foundation as well as improving flexibility utilizing a box, 2 agility rings, and ankle weights.

PURPOSE

1. Developing neural pathways for explosive jumping capability (neurological feedback loop)
2. Improving balance (body control) & coordination
3. Improving skill and strength foundation for complex movements
4. Improving flexibility (Glutes & Hamstrings)

DESCRIPTION

Athlete wears **ankle weights**.

1. Place box onto solid, non-sliding surface
2. Place 2 agility rings in front of the box
3. Step onto the box; athlete stands up straight and positions the feet under the shoulders
4. Step off the box with **right** foot
5. Land with **right** foot into agility ring; **look down** to the ground
6. Immediately jump upwards into a high tuck jump with **right** leg
7. Land inside the **agility ring**
8. Switch legs

COMMON ERRORS

- Athlete lands outside agility rings

REQUIRED EQUIPMENT

- 2 – 6 Inch Box
- 2 Agility Rings
- 5-10 lb Ankle Weights

KEY FACTORS

- Focus on perfect movement mechanics and explosiveness (maximum height)
- Step off the box with one (1) foot
- Land on one foot inside agility ring
- Jump vertically with one foot
- Maintain balance; land in same location inside agility ring

PRE-REQUISITE DRILLS

- Loaded Low-Level Depth Jump to Full Extension (I)
- Loaded Single-Leg High-Level Tuck Jump (I)

BREATH IN & OUT

- IN: Before Step Off
- OUT: During Jumping

DEGREE OF DIFFICULTY

3

ID: 774

7.75 L LL SL DEPTH JUMP TO SL HIGH TUCK JUMP (IV)

SUMMARY

The Loaded Low-Level Single-Leg Depth Jump to Single-Leg High Tuck Jump IV is a ballistic exercise, which focuses on improving neural pathways for explosive jumping, body control & coordination, skill and strength foundation as well as improving flexibility utilizing a box and ankle weights.

PURPOSE

1. Developing neural pathways for explosive jumping capability (neurological feedback loop)
2. Improving balance (body control) & coordination
3. Improving skill and strength foundation for complex movements
4. Improving flexibility (Glutes & Hamstrings)

DESCRIPTION

Athlete wears ankle weights.

1. Place box onto solid, non-sliding surface
2. Step onto the box; athlete stands up straight and positions the feet under the shoulders
3. Step off the box with **right** foot
4. Land with **right** foot; **look forward** during landing
5. Immediately jump upwards into a high tuck jump with **right** leg
6. Land in the same spot
7. Switch legs

PRE-REQUISITE DRILLS

- Loaded Low-Level Depth Jump to Full Extension (II)
- Loaded Single-Leg High-Level Tuck Jump (II)

BREATH IN & OUT

- IN: Before Step Off
- OUT: During Jumping

DEGREE OF DIFFICULTY

4

REQUIRED EQUIPMENT

- 2 – 6 inch Box
- 5-10 lb Ankle Weights

KEY FACTORS

- Focus on perfect movement mechanics and explosiveness (maximum height)
- Step off the box with one (1) foot
- Land on one foot
- Jump vertically with one foot
- Maintain balance; land in same location

COMMON ERRORS

- Athlete moves around; doesn't land in same location

ID: 775

7.76 LOADED LL DEPTH JUMP TO LATERAL BOX JUMP (I)

SUMMARY

The Loaded Low-Level Depth Jump to Lateral Box Jump I is a ballistic exercise, which focuses on developing neural pathways for explosive jumping during the serve, body control & coordination as well as improving skill and strength foundation for complex movements utilizing 2 boxes, 2 agility rings, and ankle weights.

DESCRIPTION

Athlete wears **ankle weights**.

1. Place boxes onto solid, non-sliding surface
2. Place 2 agility rings in front of box #1; box #2 is perpendicular to box #1
3. Step onto box #1; athlete takes on stance as if to begin his/her **service motion**; generally position the feet under the shoulders
4. Step off the box with the **leading** foot
5. Land with both feet **simultaneously** into agility rings
6. Immediately **jump laterally** (sideways) with both legs **simultaneously**, performing a mid-level lateral tuck jump, onto box #2; **look down** at the ground during ground contact
7. Land on top of box #2

PRE-REQUISITE DRILLS

- Loaded Low-Level Depth Jump to Full Extension (I)
- Loaded Mid-Level Lateral Tuck Jump (I)

PURPOSE

1. Developing neural pathways for explosive jumping capability (neurological feedback loop) for the **Serve**
2. Improving balance (body control) & coordination
3. Improving skill and strength foundation for complex movements

DEGREE OF DIFFICULTY

1

KEY FACTORS

- Focus on perfect movement mechanics and explosiveness (maximum height)
- Step off box #1 with the leading foot
- Land on both feet simultaneously inside agility rings
- Jump laterally with both feet simultaneously
- Maintain balance; land on top of Box #2

COMMON ERRORS

- Athlete lands outside agility rings

REQUIRED EQUIPMENT

- Two 6 – 8 Inch Boxes
- 2 Agility Rings
- 5-10 lb Ankle Weights

BREATH IN & OUT

- IN: Before Step Off
- OUT: During Jumping

ID: 776

7.77 LOADED LL DEPTH JUMP TO LATERAL BOX JUMP (II)

SUMMARY

The Loaded Low-Level Depth Jump to Lateral Box Jump II is a ballistic exercise, which focuses on developing neural pathways for explosive jumping during the serve, body control & coordination as well as improving skill and strength foundation for complex movements utilizing 2 boxes, 2 agility rings, and ankle weights.

PURPOSE

1. Developing neural pathways for explosive jumping capability (neurological feedback loop) for the **Serve**
2. Improving balance (body control) & coordination
3. Improving skill and strength foundation for complex movements

DESCRIPTION

Athlete wears **ankle weights**.

1. Place boxes onto solid, non-sliding surface
2. Place 2 agility rings in front of box #1; box #2 is perpendicular to box #1
3. Step onto the box #1; athlete takes on stance as if to begin his/her service motion; generally position the feet under the shoulders
4. Step off the box with the **leading** foot
5. Land with both feet **simultaneously** into agility rings
6. Immediately jump laterally (sideways) with both legs **simultaneously**, performing a mid-level lateral tuck jump, onto box #2; **look forward** during jump and ground contact
7. Land on top of box #2

PRE-REQUISITE DRILLS

- Loaded Low-Level Depth Jump to Full Extension (II)
- Loaded Mid-Level Lateral Tuck Jump (II)

BREATH IN & OUT

- IN: Before Step Off
- OUT: During Jumping

DEGREE OF DIFFICULTY

2

REQUIRED EQUIPMENT

- Two 6 – 8 Inch Boxes
- 2 Agility Rings
- 5-10 lb Ankle Weights

KEY FACTORS

- Focus on perfect movement mechanics and explosiveness (maximum height)
- Step off box #1 with the leading foot
- Land on both feet simultaneously inside agility rings
- Jump laterally with both feet simultaneously
- Maintain balance; land on top of Box #2

COMMON ERRORS

- Athlete lands outside agility rings

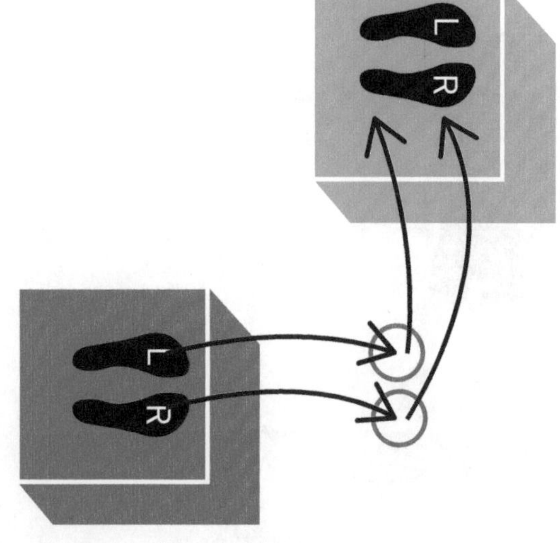

ID: 777

7.78 LLLDEPTHJUMPTOLAT.BOXJUMP:SLLANDING(III)

SUMMARY

The Loaded Low-Level Depth Jump to Lateral Box Jump: Single-Foot Landing III is a ballistic exercise, which focuses on developing neural pathways for explosive jumping during the serve, body control & coordination as well as improving skill and strength foundation for complex movements utilizing 2 boxes, 2 agility rings, and ankle weights.

PURPOSE

1. Developing neural pathways for explosive jumping capability (neurological feedback loop) for the **Serve**
2. Improving balance (body control) & coordination
3. Improving skill and strength foundation for complex movements (e.g. serve)

DESCRIPTION

Athlete wears **ankle weights**.

1. Place boxes onto solid, non-sliding surface
2. Place 2 agility rings in front of box #1; box #2 is perpendicular to box #1
3. Step onto the box #1; athlete takes on stance as if to begin his/her service motion; generally position the feet under the shoulders
4. Step off the box with the **leading** foot
5. Land with both feet simultaneously into agility rings; **look forward** during jump and ground contact
6. Immediately jump laterally (sideways) with both legs simultaneously, performing a mid-level lateral tuck jump, onto box #2
7. Land on top of box #2 with the **leading** foot; **look down** during landing

PRE-REQUISITE DRILLS

- Loaded Low-Level Depth Jump to Full Extension (II)
- Loaded Mid-Level Lateral Tuck Jump (II)
- Loaded Single-Leg Mid-Level Tuck Jump (II)

DEGREE OF DIFFICULTY

3

KEY FACTORS

- Focus on perfect movement mechanics and explosiveness (maximum height)
- Step off box #1 with the leading foot
- Land on both feet simultaneously inside agility rings
- Jump laterally with both feet simultaneously
- Maintain balance; land on top of Box #2 with the leading foot

COMMON ERRORS

- Athlete lands outside agility rings

REQUIRED EQUIPMENT

- Two 6 – 8 Inch Boxes
- 2 Agility Rings
- 5-10 lb Ankle Weights

BREATH IN & OUT

- IN: Before Step Off
- OUT: During Jumping

ID: 778

7

7.79 LLL DEPTH JUMP TO LAT. BOX JUMP: SL LANDING (IV)

SUMMARY

The Loaded Low-Level Depth Jump to Lateral Box Jump: Single-Foot Landing IV is a ballistic exercise, which focuses on developing neural pathways for explosive jumping during the serve, body control & coordination as well as improving skill and strength foundation for complex movements utilizing 2 boxes, 2 agility rings, and ankle weights.

PURPOSE

1. Developing neural pathways for explosive jumping capability (neurological feedback loop) for the **Serve**
2. Improving balance (body control) & coordination
3. Improving skill and strength foundation for complex movements (e.g. serve)

DESCRIPTION

Athlete wears **ankle weights**.

1. Place boxes onto solid, non-sliding surface
2. Place 2 agility rings in front of box #1; box #2 is perpendicular to box #1
3. Step onto the box #1; athlete takes on stance as if to begin his/her service motion; generally position the feet under the shoulders
4. Step off the box with the **leading** foot
5. Land with both feet simultaneously into agility rings; **look forward** during jump and ground contact
6. Immediately jump laterally (sideways) with both legs simultaneously, performing a mid-level lateral tuck jump, onto box #2
7. Land on top of box #2 with the **leading** foot; **look forward** during landing

PRE-REQUISITE DRILLS

- Loaded Low-Level Depth Jump to Full Extension (III)
- Loaded Mid-Level Lateral Tuck Jump (III)
- Loaded Single-Leg Mid-Level Tuck Jump (III)

BREATH IN & OUT

- IN: Before Step Off
- OUT: During Jumping

DEGREE OF DIFFICULTY

4

REQUIRED EQUIPMENT

- Two 6 – 8 Inch Boxes
- 2 Agility Rings
- 5-10 lb Ankle Weights

KEY FACTORS

- Focus on perfect movement mechanics and explosiveness (short ground contact)
- Step off box #1 with the leading foot
- Land on both feet simultaneously inside agility rings
- Jump laterally with both feet simultaneously
- Maintain balance; land on top of Box #2 with the leading foot

COMMON ERRORS

- Athlete lands outside agility rings

ID: 779

7.80 LOADED LL DEPTH JUMP TO DIAGONAL BOX JUMP (I)

SUMMARY

The Loaded Low-Level Depth Jump to Diagonal Box Jump I is a ballistic exercise, which focuses on developing neural pathways for explosive change of direction during the return & volley, body control & coordination as well as improving skill and strength foundation for complex movements utilizing 2 boxes, 2 agility rings, and ankle weights.

PURPOSE

1. Developing neural pathways for explosive change of direction capability (neurological feedback loop) for the **Return & Volley**
2. Improving balance (body control) & coordination
3. Improving skill and strength foundation for complex movements

DESCRIPTION

Athlete wears **ankle weights**.

1. Place boxes onto solid, non-sliding surface
2. Place 2 agility rings in front of box #1; box #2 is diagonal to box #1
3. Step onto box #1; athlete takes on stance similar to the **return**; generally position the feet under the shoulders
4. Step off the box **one (1) foot**
5. Land with both feet **simultaneously** into agility rings; **look down** at the ground during ground contact
6. Immediately jump diagonally (1st to the right side then to the left side) with both legs **simultaneously**, performing a mid-level lateral tuck jump, onto box #2
7. Land on top of box #2 with both legs

DEGREE OF DIFFICULTY

1

REQUIRED EQUIPMENT

- Two 6 – 8 Inch Boxes
- 2 Agility Rings
- 5-10 lb Ankle Weights

KEY FACTORS

- Focus on perfect movement mechanics and explosiveness (maximum height)
- Step off box #1 with the leading foot
- Land on both feet simultaneously inside agility rings
- Jump laterally with both feet simultaneously
- Maintain balance; land on top of Box #2 with both legs

PRE-REQUISITE DRILLS

- Loaded Low-Level Depth Jump to Full Extension (I)
- Loaded Mid-Level Lateral Tuck Jump (I)
- Loaded Low-Level Depths Jump to Long Jump (I)

COMMON ERRORS

- Athlete lands outside agility rings

BREATH IN & OUT

- IN: Before Step Off
- OUT: During Jumping

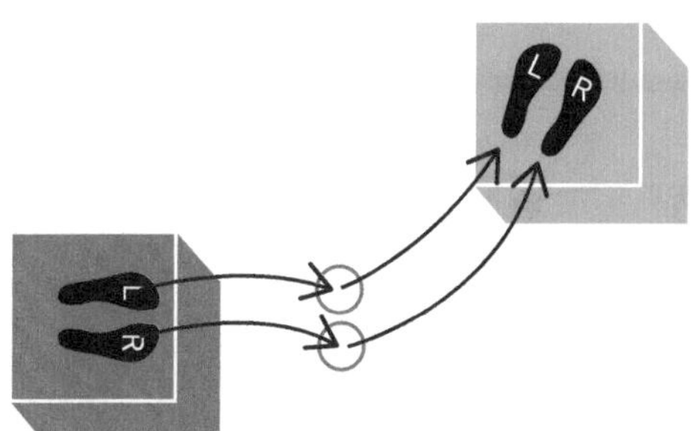

ID: 780

7.81 LOADED LL DEPTH JUMP TO DIAG. BOX JUMP (II)

SUMMARY

The Loaded Low-Level Depth Jump to Diagonal Box Jump II is a ballistic exercise, which focuses on developing neural pathways for explosive change of direction during the return & volley, body control & coordination as well as improving skill and strength foundation for complex movements utilizing 2 boxes, 2 agility rings, and ankle weights.

PURPOSE

1. Developing neural pathways for explosive change of direction capability (neurological feedback loop) for the **Return & Volley**
2. Improving balance (body control) & coordination
3. Improving skill and strength foundation for complex movements

DESCRIPTION

Athlete wears **ankle weights**.

1. Place boxes onto solid, non-sliding surface
2. Place 2 agility rings in front of box #1; box #2 is diagonal to box #1
3. Step onto the box #1; athlete takes on stance similar to the **return**; generally position the feet under the shoulders
4. Step off the box **one (1) foot**
5. Land with both feet **simultaneously** into agility rings; **look forward** during ground contact
6. Immediately jump diagonally (1st to the right side then to the left side) with both legs **simultaneously**, performing a mid-level lateral tuck jump, onto box #2
7. Land on top of box #2 with both legs

PRE-REQUISITE DRILLS

- Loaded Low-Level Depth Jump to Full Extension (II)
- Loaded Mid-Level Lateral Tuck Jump (II)
- Low-Level Depths Jump to Long Jump (II)

BREATH IN & OUT

- IN: Before Step Off
- OUT: During Jumping

DEGREE OF DIFFICULTY

2

REQUIRED EQUIPMENT

- Two 6 – 8 Inch Boxes
- 2 Agility Rings
- 5-10 lb Ankle Weights

KEY FACTORS

- Focus on perfect movement mechanics and explosiveness (maximum height)
- Step off box #1 with the leading foot
- Land on both feet simultaneously inside agility rings
- Jump laterally with both feet simultaneously
- Maintain balance; land on top of Box #2 with both legs

COMMON ERRORS

- Athlete lands outside agility rings

ID: 781

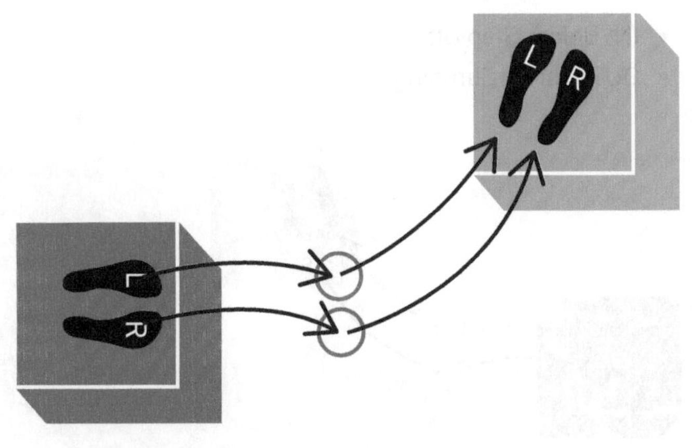

7.82 L LL DEPTH JUMP TO DIAG. BOX JUMP: SL LAND. (III)

SUMMARY

The Loaded Low-Level Depth Jump to Diagonal Box Jump III is a ballistic exercise, which focuses on developing neural pathways for explosive change of direction during the return & volley, body control & coordination as well as improving skill and strength foundation for complex movements utilizing 2 boxes, 2 agility rings, and ankle weights.

DESCRIPTION

Athlete wears **ankle weights**.

1. Place boxes onto solid, non-sliding surface
2. Place 2 agility rings in front of box #1; box #2 is diagonal to box #1
3. Step onto the box #1; athlete takes on stance similar to the **return**; generally position the feet under the shoulders
4. Step off the box one (1) foot
5. Land with both feet simultaneously into agility rings; **look forward** during ground contact
6. Immediately jump diagonally(1st to the right side then to the left side) with both legs simultaneously, performing a mid-level lateral tuck jump, onto box #2
7. Land on top of box #2 with the left leg (right side jumping) and the right leg (left side jumping); **look down** during landing

PRE-REQUISITE DRILLS

- Loaded Low-Level Depth Jump to Full Extension (II)
- Loaded Mid-Level Lateral Tuck Jump (II)
- Loaded Low-Level Depths Jump to Long Jump (II)

BREATH IN & OUT

- IN: Before Step Off
- OUT: During Jumping

PURPOSE

1. Developing neural pathways for explosive change of direction capability (neurological feedback loop) for the **Return & Volley**
2. Improving balance (body control) & coordination
3. Improving skill and strength foundation for complex movements

DEGREE OF DIFFICULTY

3

REQUIRED EQUIPMENT

- Two 6 – 8 Inch Boxes
- 2 Agility Rings
- 5-10 lb Ankle Weights

KEY FACTORS

- Focus on perfect movement mechanics and explosiveness (short ground contact)
- Step off box #1 with the leading foot
- Land on both feet simultaneously inside agility rings
- Jump laterally with both feet simultaneously
- Maintain balance; land on top of Box #2 with one leg

COMMON ERRORS

- Athlete lands outside agility rings

ID: 782

7.83 L LL DEPTH JUMP TO DIAG. BOX JUMP: SL LAND. (IV)

SUMMARY

The Loaded Low-Level Depth Jump to Diagonal Box Jump IV is a ballistic exercise, which focuses on developing neural pathways for explosive change of direction during the return & volley, body control & coordination as well as improving skill and strength foundation for complex movements utilizing 2 boxes, 2 agility rings, and ankle weights.

PURPOSE

1. Developing neural pathways for explosive change of direction capability (neurological feedback loop) for the **Return & Volley**
2. Improving balance (body control) & coordination
3. Improving skill and strength foundation for complex movement

DESCRIPTION

Athlete wears **ankle weights**.

1. Place boxes onto solid, non-sliding surface
2. Place 2 agility rings in front of box #1; box #2 is diagonal to box #1
3. Step onto the box #1; athlete takes on stance similar to the **return**; generally position the feet under the shoulders
4. Step off the box one (1) foot
5. Land with both feet simultaneously into agility rings; **look forward** during ground contact
6. Immediately jump diagonally (1st to the right side then to the left side) with both legs simultaneously, performing a mid-level lateral tuck jump, onto box #2
7. Land on top of box #2 with the left leg (right side jumping) and the right leg (left side jumping); **look forward** during landing

PRE-REQUISITE DRILLS

- Loaded Low-Level Depth Jump to Full Extension (II)
- Loaded Mid-Level Lateral Tuck Jump (II)
- Loaded Low-Level Depths Jump to Long Jump (II)

BREATH IN & OUT

- IN: Before Step Off
- OUT: During Jumping

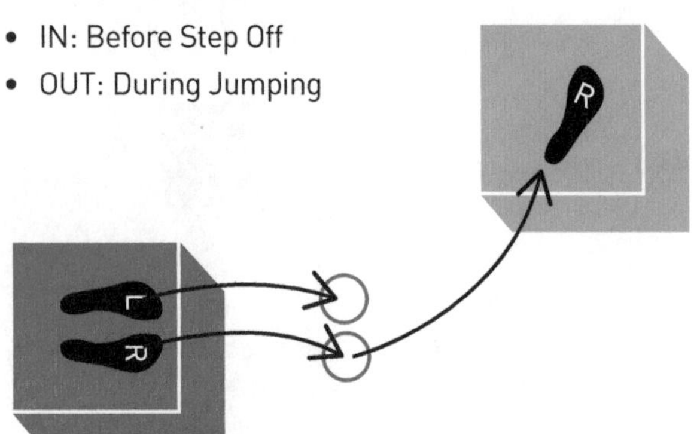

ID: 783

DEGREE OF DIFFICULTY

4

REQUIRED EQUIPMENT

- Two 6 – 8 Inch Boxes
- 2 Agility Rings
- 5-10 lb Ankle Weights

KEY FACTORS

- Focus on perfect movement mechanics and explosiveness (maximum height)
- Step off box #1 with the leading foot
- Land on both feet simultaneously inside agility rings
- Jump laterally with both feet simultaneously
- Maintain balance; land on top of Box #2 with one leg

COMMON ERRORS

- Athlete lands outside agility rings

7.84 LOADED LOW-LEVEL DEPTH JUMP TO LONG JUMP (I)

SUMMARY

The Loaded Low-Level Depth Jump to Long Jump I is a ballistic exercise, which focuses on developing neural pathways for explosive jumping, body control & coordination, flexibility as well as improving skill and strength foundation for complex movements utilizing 2 boxes, 2 agility rings, 2 cones and ankle weights.

PURPOSE

1. Developing neural pathways for explosive jumping capability (neurological feedback loop)
2. Improving balance (body control) & coordination
3. Improving skill and strength foundation for complex movements
4. Improving flexibility (Glutes & Hamstrings)

DESCRIPTION

Athlete wears **ankle weights**.

1. Place box onto solid, non-sliding surface
2. Place 2 agility rings in front of the box and 2 cones ~8 feet in front of the box
3. Step onto the box; athlete stands up straight and positions the feet under the shoulders
4. Step off the box with **one (1) foot**
5. Land with both feet **simultaneously** into agility rings; **look down** at the ground
6. Immediately jump forward with both legs **simultaneously**; extend hips and land in **squat** position
7. Jump past the 2 cones

KEY FACTORS

- Focus on perfect movement mechanics and explosiveness (maximum height & distance)
- Step off the box with one (1) foot
- Land on both feet simultaneously inside agility rings
- Jump forward with both feet simultaneously
- Maintain balance during landing

REQUIRED EQUIPMENT

- 6 – 8 Inch Box
- 2 Agility Rings
- 2 Cones
- 5-10 lb Ankle Weights

BREATH IN & OUT

- IN: Before Step Off
- OUT: During Jumping

COMMON ERRORS

- Athlete looses balance during landing

DEGREE OF DIFFICULTY

1

ID: 784

7.85 LOADED LOW-LEVEL DEPTH JUMP TO LONG JUMP (II)

SUMMARY

The Loaded Low-Level Depth Jump to Long Jump II is a ballistic exercise, which focuses on developing neural pathways for explosive jumping, body control & coordination, flexibility as well as improving skill and strength foundation for complex movements utilizing 2 boxes, 2 agility rings, 2 cones and ankle weights.

PURPOSE

1. Developing neural pathways for explosive jumping capability (neurological feedback loop)
2. Improving balance (body control) & coordination
3. Improving skill and strength foundation for complex movements
4. Improving flexibility (Glutes & Hamstrings)

DESCRIPTION

Athlete wears **ankle weights**.

1. Place box onto solid, non-sliding surface
2. Place 2 agility rings in front of the box and 2 cones ~6 feet in front of the box
3. Step onto the box; athlete stands up straight and positions the feet under the shoulders
4. Step off the box with one (1) foot
5. Land with both feet simultaneously into agility rings; **look forward**
6. Immediately jump forward with both legs simultaneously; extend hips and land in **squat** position
7. Jump past the 2 cones

BREATH IN & OUT

- IN: Before Step Off
- OUT: During Jumping

PRE-REQUISITE DRILLS

- Loaded Low-Level Depth Jump to Long Jump (I)

DEGREE OF DIFFICULTY

2

REQUIRED EQUIPMENT

- 6 – 8 Inch Box
- 2 Agility Rings
- 2 Cones
- 5-10 lb Ankle Weights

KEY FACTORS

- Focus on perfect movement mechanics and explosiveness (maximum height & distance)
- Step off the box with one (1) foot
- Land on both feet simultaneously inside agility rings
- Jump forward with both feet simultaneously
- Maintain balance during landing

COMMON ERRORS

- Athlete looses balance during landing

7.86 LOADED LL DJ TO LONG JUMP: SL LANDING (III)

SUMMARY

The Loaded Low-Level Depth Jump to Long Jump: Single-Leg Landing III is a ballistic exercise, which focuses on developing neural pathways for explosive jumping, body control & coordination, flexibility as well as improving skill and strength foundation for complex movements utilizing 2 boxes, 2 agility rings, 2 cones and ankle weights.

PURPOSE

1. Developing neural pathways for explosive jumping capability (neurological feedback loop)
2. Improving balance (body control) & coordination
3. Improving skill and strength foundation for complex movements
4. Improving flexibility (Glutes & Hamstrings)

DESCRIPTION

Athlete wears **ankle weights**.

1. Place box onto solid, non-sliding surface
2. Place 2 agility rings in front of the box and 2 cones ~6 feet in front of the box
3. Step onto the box; athlete stands up straight and positions the feet under the shoulders
4. Step off the box with one (1) foot
5. Land with both feet simultaneously into agility rings; **look forward**
6. Immediately jump forward with both legs simultaneously; extend hips and land in **single-leg squat** position; **look down** during landing
7. Jump past the 2 cones

PRE-REQUISITE DRILLS

- Loaded Low-Level Depth Jump to Long Jump (II)

DEGREE OF DIFFICULTY

3

KEY FACTORS

- Focus on perfect movement mechanics and explosiveness (maximum height & distance)
- Step off the box with one (1) foot
- Land on both feet simultaneously inside agility rings
- Jump forward with both feet simultaneously
- Maintain balance during landing

COMMON ERRORS

- Athlete looses balance during landing

REQUIRED EQUIPMENT

- 6 – 8 Inch Box
- 2 Agility Rings
- 2 Cones
- 5-10 lb Ankle Weights

BREATH IN & OUT

- IN: Before Step Off
- OUT: During Jumping

ID: 786

7.87 LOADED LL DJ TO LONG JUMP: SL LANDING (IV)

SUMMARY

The Loaded Low-Level Depth Jump to Long Jump: Single-Leg Landing IV is a ballistic exercise, which focuses on developing neural pathways for explosive jumping, body control & coordination, flexibility as well as improving skill and strength foundation for complex movements utilizing 2 boxes, 2 cones and ankle weights.

PURPOSE

1. Developing neural pathways for explosive jumping capability (neurological feedback loop)
2. Improving balance (body control) & coordination
3. Improving skill and strength foundation for complex movements
4. Improving flexibility (Glutes & Hamstrings)

DESCRIPTION

Athlete wears **ankle weights**.

1. Place box onto solid, non-sliding surface
2. Step onto the box; athlete stands up straight and positions the feet under the shoulders
3. Step off the box with one (1) foot
4. Land with both feet simultaneously on the ground; **look forward**
5. Immediately jump forward with both legs simultaneously; extend hips and land in **single-leg squat** position; **look forward** during landing
6. Jump past the 2 cones

BREATH IN & OUT

- IN: Before Step Off
- OUT: During Jumping

PRE-REQUISITE DRILLS

- Loaded Low-Level Depth Jump to Long Jump: Single-Leg Landing (III)

COMMON ERRORS

- Athlete looses balance during landing

DEGREE OF DIFFICULTY

4

REQUIRED EQUIPMENT

- 6 – 8 Inch Box
- 5-10 lb Ankle Weights
- 2 Cones

KEY FACTORS

- Focus on perfect movement mechanics and explosiveness (maximum height & distance)
- Step off the box with one (1) foot
- Land on both feet simultaneously on the ground
- Jump forward with both feet simultaneously
- Maintain balance during landing

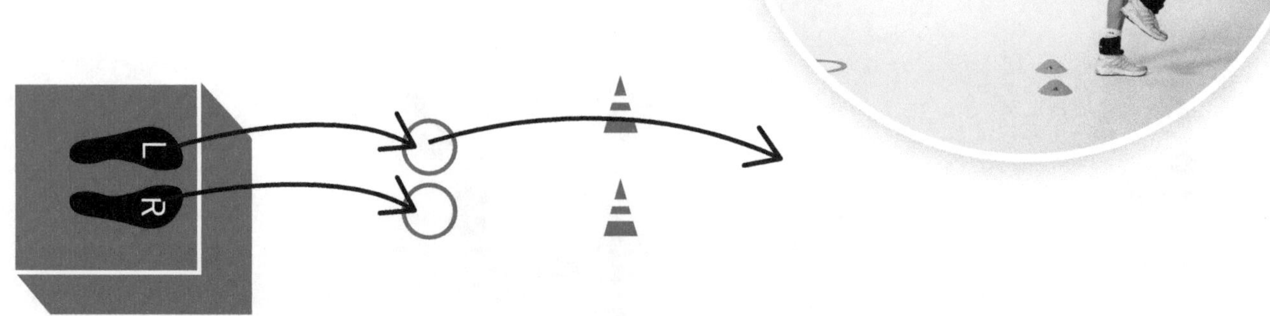

7.88 LOADED LOW-LEVEL BOX JUMP REBOUNDS (I)

SUMMARY

The Loaded Low-Level Box Jump Rebounds I is a ballistic exercise, which focuses on developing neural pathways for explosive jumping, body control & coordination as well as improving skill and strength foundation for complex movements utilizing a box, 4 agility rings and ankle weights.

PURPOSE

1. Developing neural pathways for explosive jumping capability (neurological feedback loop)
2. Improving reaction time for lower extremities (legs)
3. Improving balance (body control) & coordination
4. Improving skill and strength foundation for complex movements

DESCRIPTION

Athlete wears **ankle weights**.

1. Place box onto solid, non-sliding surface ~2 feet apart
2. Place 4 agility rings shoulder-width apart on the ground; 2 in front and 2 behind the box
3. Step into agility rings in front of the box
4. Jump on top of the box with both legs **simultaneously**, use arm swing to generate force
5. Land with both feet **simultaneously**
6. Immediately jump off the box with both legs **simultaneously** while **looking down** at the ground
7. Immediately jump backwards on top of the box with both legs **simultaneously** while **looking down**
8. Land
9. Jump off, landing inside the **agility rings**

BREATH IN & OUT

- IN: Before Jumping
- OUT: During Jumping

DEGREE OF DIFFICULTY

1

REQUIRED EQUIPMENT

- 2 – 6 Inch Boxes
- 4 Agility Rings
- 5-10 lb Ankle Weights

KEY FACTORS

- Focus on perfect movement mechanics and explosiveness (maximum height)
- Land on both feet simultaneously inside agility rings
- Jump forward/backward with both feet simultaneously
- Maintain balance; land in same location inside agility rings and on top of the boxes

COMMON ERRORS

- Athlete lands outside agility rings
- Athlete looses balance during landing

ID: 788

7.89 LOADED LOW-LEVEL BOX JUMP REBOUNDS (II)

SUMMARY

The Loaded Low-Level Box Jump Rebounds II is a ballistic exercise, which focuses on developing neural pathways for explosive jumping, body control & coordination as well as improving skill and strength foundation for complex movements utilizing a box, 4 agility rings and ankle weights.

PURPOSE

1. Developing neural pathways for explosive jumping capability (neurological feedback loop)
2. Improving reaction time for lower extremities (legs)
3. Improving balance (body control) & coordination
4. Improving skill and strength foundation for complex movements

DESCRIPTION

Athlete wears **ankle weights**.

1. Place box onto solid, non-sliding surface ~2 feet apart
2. Place 4 agility rings shoulder-width apart on the ground; 2 in front and 2 behind the box
3. Step into agility rings in front of the box
4. Jump on top of the box with both legs simultaneously, use arm swing to generate force
5. Land with both feet simultaneously
6. Immediately jump off the box with both legs simultaneously while **looking forward**
7. Immediately jump backwards on top of the box with both legs simultaneously while **looking forward**
8. Land
9. Jump off, landing inside the **agility rings**

PRE-REQUISITE DRILLS

- Loaded Low-Level Depth Jump Rebounds (I)

BREATH IN & OUT

- IN: Before Jumping
- OUT: During Jumping

DEGREE OF DIFFICULTY

2

REQUIRED EQUIPMENT

- 2 – 6 Inch Boxes
- 4 Agility Rings
- 5-10 lb Ankle Weights

KEY FACTORS

- Focus on perfect movement mechanics and explosiveness (maximum height)
- Land on both feet simultaneously inside agility rings
- Jump forward/backward with both feet simultaneously
- Maintain balance; land in same location inside agility rings and on top of the boxes

COMMON ERRORS

- Athlete lands outside agility rings
- Athlete looses balance during landing

ID: 789

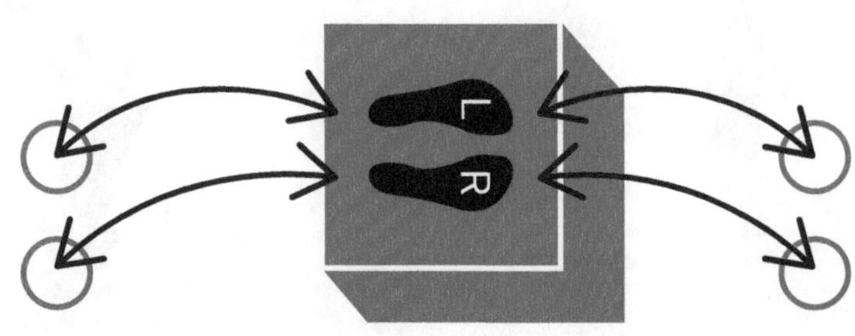

7.90 LOADED LL BOX JUMP SINGLE-LEG REBOUNDS (III)

SUMMARY

The Loaded Low-Level Box Jump Single-Leg Rebounds III is a ballistic exercise, which focuses on developing neural pathways for explosive jumping, body control & coordination as well as improving skill and strength foundation for complex movements utilizing a box, 2 agility rings and ankle weights.

DESCRIPTION

Athlete wears **ankle weights**.

1. Place box onto solid, non-sliding surface ~2 feet apart
2. Place 2 agility rings on the ground; 1 in front and 1 behind the box
3. Step into agility ring with **one (1) leg**; the one in front of the box
4. Jump on top of the box with one leg; use arm swing to generate force
5. Land with **one (1) foot**
6. Immediately jump off the box with **one (1) leg** while **looking down** at the ground
7. Immediately jump backwards on top of the box with **one (1) leg** while **looking down**
8. Land
9. Jump off, landing inside the **agility ring**
10. Switch leg

PRE-REQUISITE DRILLS

- Loaded Low-Level Depth Jump Rebounds (II)

BREATH IN & OUT

- IN: Before Jumping
- OUT: During Jumping

PURPOSE

1. Developing neural pathways for explosive jumping capability (neurological feedback loop)
2. Improving reaction time for lower extremities (legs)
3. Improving balance (body control) & coordination
4. Improving skill and strength foundation for complex movements

DEGREE OF DIFFICULTY

3

REQUIRED EQUIPMENT

- 2 – 6 Inch Box
- 2 Agility Rings
- 5-10 lb Ankle Weights

KEY FACTORS

- Focus on perfect movement mechanics and explosiveness (maximum height)
- Land on one foot inside agility ring
- Jump forward/backward with one foot
- Maintain balance; land in same location inside agility ring and on top of the box

COMMON ERRORS

- Athlete lands outside agility rings
- Athlete looses balance during landing

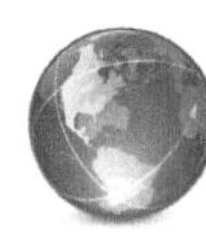

ID: 790

7.91 LOADED LL BOX JUMP SINGLE-LEG REBOUNDS (IV)

SUMMARY

The Loaded Low-Level Box Jump Single-Leg Rebounds IV is a ballistic exercise, which focuses on developing neural pathways for explosive jumping, body control & coordination as well as improving skill and strength foundation for complex movements utilizing a box, 2 agility rings and ankle weights.

PURPOSE

1. Developing neural pathways for explosive jumping capability (neurological feedback loop)
2. Improving reaction time for lower extremities (legs)
3. Improving balance (body control) & coordination
4. Improving skill and strength foundation for complex movements

DESCRIPTION

Athlete wears ankle weights.

1. Place box onto solid, non-sliding surface ~2 feet apart
2. Place 2 agility rings on the ground; 1 in front and 1 behind the box
3. Step into agility ring with one (1) leg; the one in front of the box
4. Jump on top of the box with one leg; use arm swing to generate force
5. Land with one (1) foot
6. Immediately jump off the box with one (1) leg while **looking forward**
7. Immediately jump backwards on top of the box with one leg while **looking forward**
8. Land
9. Jump off, landing inside the **agility ring**
10. Switch leg

PRE-REQUISITE DRILLS

- Loaded Low-Level Depth Jump Single-Leg Rebounds (III)

BREATH IN & OUT

- IN: Before Jumping
- OUT: During Jumping

DEGREE OF DIFFICULTY

4

REQUIRED EQUIPMENT

- 2 – 6 Inch Box
- 2 Agility Rings
- 5-10 lb Ankle Weights

KEY FACTORS

- Focus on perfect movement mechanics and explosiveness (maximum height)
- Land on one foot inside agility ring
- Jump forward/backward with one foot
- Maintain balance; land in same location inside agility ring and on top of the box

COMMON ERRORS

- Athlete lands outside agility rings
- Athlete looses balance during landing

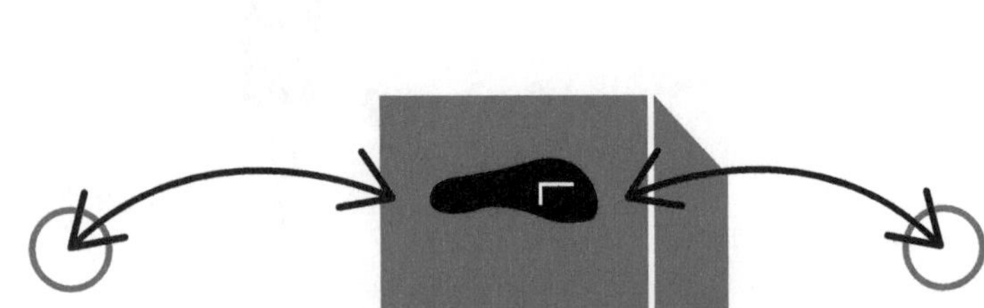

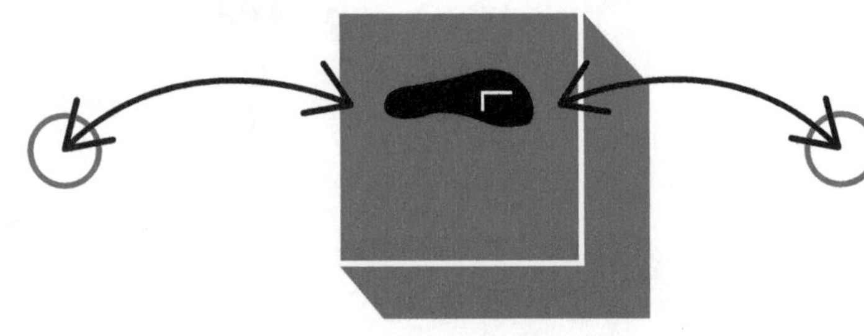

ID: 791

7.92 LOADED LL LATERAL BOX JUMP REBOUNDS (I)

SUMMARY

The Loaded Low-Level Lateral Box Jump Rebounds I is a ballistic exercise, which focuses on developing neural pathways for explosive jumping, body control & coordination as well as improving skill and strength foundation for complex movements utilizing a box, 4 agility rings and ankle weights.

DESCRIPTION

Athlete wears **ankle weights**.

1. Place box onto solid, non-sliding surface ~2 feet apart
2. Place 4 agility rings laterally (sideways) shoulder-width apart on the ground; 2 in front and 2 behind the box
3. Step into agility rings in front of the box
4. Jump on top of the box with both legs **simultaneously**, use arm swing to generate force
5. Land with both feet **simultaneously**; **look down** during landing
6. Immediately jump off the box with both legs **simultaneously** while **looking down** at the ground
7. Immediately jump back on top of the box with both legs **simultaneously** while **looking down**
8. Land
9. Jump off, landing inside the **agility rings**

BREATH IN & OUT

- IN: During Landing
- OUT: During Landing

PURPOSE

1. Developing neural pathways for explosive jumping capability (neurological feedback loop)
2. Improving balance (body control) & coordination
3. Improving skill and strength foundation for complex movements

DEGREE OF DIFFICULTY

1

REQUIRED EQUIPMENT

- 2 – 6 Inch Boxes
- 4 Agility Rings
- 5-10 lb Ankle Weights

KEY FACTORS

- Focus on perfect movement mechanics and explosiveness (maximum height)
- Land on both feet simultaneously inside agility rings
- Jump laterally with both feet simultaneously
- Maintain balance; land in same location inside agility rings and on top of the boxes

COMMON ERRORS

- Athlete lands outside agility rings
- Athlete looses balance during landing

ID: 792

7.93 LOADED LL LATERAL BOX JUMP REBOUNDS (II)

SUMMARY

The Loaded Low-Level Lateral Box Jump Rebounds II is a ballistic exercise, which focuses on developing neural pathways for explosive jumping, body control & coordination as well as improving skill and strength foundation for complex movements utilizing a box, 4 agility rings and ankle weights.

PURPOSE

1. Developing neural pathways for explosive jumping capability (neurological feedback loop)
2. Improving balance (body control) & coordination
3. Improving skill and strength foundation for complex movements

DESCRIPTION

Athlete wears **ankle weights**.

1. Place box onto solid, non-sliding surface ~2 feet apart
2. Place 4 agility rings laterally (sideways) shoulder-width apart on the ground; 2 in front and 2 behind the box
3. Step into agility rings in front of the box
4. Jump on top of the box with both legs simultaneously, use arm swing to generate force
5. Land with both feet simultaneously; **look forward** during landing
6. Immediately jump off the box with both legs simultaneously while **looking forward**
7. Immediately jump back on top of the box with both legs simultaneously while **looking forward**
8. Land
9. Jump off, landing inside the **agility rings**

PRE-REQUISITE DRILLS

- Loaded Low-Level Lateral Box Jump Rebounds (I)

BREATH IN & OUT

- IN: During Landing
- OUT: During Jumping

DEGREE OF DIFFICULTY

2

REQUIRED EQUIPMENT

- 2 – 6 Inch Boxes
- 4 Agility Rings
- 5-10 lb Ankle Weights

KEY FACTORS

- Focus on perfect movement mechanics and explosiveness (maximum height)
- Land on both feet simultaneously inside agility rings
- Jump laterally with both feet simultaneously
- Maintain balance; land in same location inside agility rings and on top of the box

COMMON ERRORS

- Athlete lands outside agility rings
- Athlete looses balance during landing

ID: 793

7.94 LOADED LL SL LATERAL BOX JUMP REBOUNDS (III)

SUMMARY

The Loaded Low-Level Single-Leg Lateral Box Jump Rebounds III is a ballistic exercise, which focuses on developing neural pathways for explosive jumping, body control & coordination as well as improving skill and strength foundation for complex movements utilizing a box, 2 agility rings and ankle weights.

PURPOSE

1. Developing neural pathways for explosive jumping capability (neurological feedback loop)
2. Improving balance (body control) & coordination
3. Improving skill and strength foundation for complex movements

DESCRIPTION

Athlete wears **ankle weights**.

1. Place box onto solid, non-sliding surface ~2 feet apart
2. Place 2 agility rings laterally (sideways); 1 in front and 1 behind the box
3. Step into agility ring in front of the box with one (1) leg
4. Jump on top of the box with **one (1) leg**; use arm swing to generate force
5. Land on the same foot; **look down** during landing
6. Immediately jump off the box with one (1) leg while **looking down**
7. Immediately jump back on top of the box with one leg while **looking down**
8. Land
9. Jump off, landing inside the **agility ring**

DEGREE OF DIFFICULTY

3

REQUIRED EQUIPMENT

- 2 – 6 Inch Boxes
- 2 Agility Rings
- 5-10 lb Ankle Weights

KEY FACTORS

- Focus on perfect movement mechanics and explosiveness (maximum height)
- Land on one foot inside agility ring
- Jump laterally with one foot
- Maintain balance; land in same location inside agility ring and on top of the box

COMMON ERRORS

- Athlete lands outside agility rings
- Athlete looses balance during landing

PRE-REQUISITE DRILLS

- Loaded Low-Level Lateral Box Jump Rebounds (II)

BREATH IN & OUT

- IN: During landing
- OUT: During Jumping

ID: 794

7.95 LOADED LL SL LATERAL BOX JUMP REBOUNDS (IV)

SUMMARY

The Loaded Low-Level Single-Leg Lateral Box Jump Rebounds IV is a ballistic exercise, which focuses on developing neural pathways for explosive jumping, body control & coordination as well as improving skill and strength foundation for complex movements utilizing a box, 2 agility rings and ankle weights.

PURPOSE

1. Developing neural pathways for explosive jumping capability (neurological feedback loop)
2. Improving balance (body control) & coordination
3. Improving skill and strength foundation for complex movements

DESCRIPTION

Athlete wears **ankle weights**.

1. Place box onto solid, non-sliding surface ~2 feet apart
2. Place 2 agility rings laterally (sideways); 1 in front and 1 behind the box
3. Step into agility ring in front of the box with **one (1) leg**
4. Jump on top of the box with one (1) leg; use arm swing to generate force
5. Land on the same foot; **look forward** during lan-ding
6. Immediately jump off the box with one (1) leg while **looking forward**
7. Immediately jump back on top of the box with one leg while **looking forward**
8. Land
9. Jump off, landing inside the agility ring

PRE-REQUISITE DRILLS

- Loaded Low-Level Lateral Box Jump Rebounds (III)

BREATH IN & OUT

- IN: During landing
- OUT: During Jumping

DEGREE OF DIFFICULTY

4

REQUIRED EQUIPMENT

- 2 – 6 Inch Boxes
- 2 Agility Rings
- 5-10 lb Ankle Weights

KEY FACTORS

- Focus on perfect movement mechanics and explosi-veness (maximum height)
- Land on one foot inside agility ring
- Jump laterally with one foot
- Maintain balance; land in same location inside agility ring and on top of the box

COMMON ERRORS

- Athlete lands outside agility rings
- Athlete looses balance during landing

ID: 795

7.96 ML ABDUC./ADDUC. BOX JUMP REBOUNDS (I)

SUMMARY

The Mid-Level Abductor/Adductor Box Jump Rebounds I is a ballistic exercise, which focuses on developing neural pathways for explosive lateral change of direction capability, reaction time, body control & coordination as well as improving skill and strength foundation for complex movements utilizing a box and 2 agility rings.

PURPOSE

1. Developing neural pathways for explosive lateral change of direction capability (neurological feedback loop)
2. Improving balance (body control) & coordination
3. Improving skill and strength foundation for complex movements

DESCRIPTION

1. Place box onto solid, non-sliding surface
2. Place 2 agility rings shoulder-width apart on the ground; 1 to the left side and 1 to the right side of the box
3. Step on top of the box; feet are close together
4. **Step off** the box with both legs **simultaneously**
5. Land with both feet **simultaneously** inside agility rings; **look down** to the ground during landing
6. Immediately jump on top of the box with both legs **simultaneously** while **looking down** at the box
7. Repeat

BREATH IN & OUT

- IN: Before Step Off
- OUT: During Jumping

DEGREE OF DIFFICULTY

1

REQUIRED EQUIPMENT

- 10 - 15 Inch Box (width smaller than shoulder-width)
- 2 Agility Rings

KEY FACTORS

- Focus on perfect movement mechanics and explosiveness (maximum height)
- Step off the box with both feet simultaneously
- Land on both feet simultaneously inside agility rings
- Jump upwards with both feet simultaneously
- Maintain balance; land in same location inside agility rings and on top of the box

COMMON ERRORS

- Athlete lands outside agility rings

ID: 796

7.97 ML ABDUC./ADDUC. BOX JUMP REBOUNDS (II)

SUMMARY

The Mid-Level Abductor/Adductor Box Jump Rebounds II is a ballistic exercise, which focuses on developing neural pathways for explosive lateral change of direction capability, reaction time, body control & coordination as well as improving skill and strength foundation for complex movements utilizing a box and 2 agility rings.

PURPOSE

1. Developing neural pathways for explosive lateral change of direction capability (neurological feedback loop)
2. Improving balance (body control) & coordination
3. Improving skill and strength foundation for complex movements

DESCRIPTION

1. Place box onto solid, non-sliding surface
2. Place 2 agility rings shoulder-width apart on the ground; 1 to the left side and 1 to the right side of the box
3. Step on top of the box; feet are close together
4. Step off the box with both legs simultaneously
5. Land with both feet simultaneously inside agility rings; **look forward** during landing
6. Immediately jump on top of the box with both legs simultaneously while **looking forward** during landing
7. Repeat

PRE-REQUISITE DRILLS

- Mid-Level Abductor/Adductor Box Jump Rebounds (I)

BREATH IN & OUT

- IN: Before Step Off
- OUT: During Jumping

DEGREE OF DIFFICULTY

2

REQUIRED EQUIPMENT

- 10 - 15 Inch Box (width smaller than shoulder-width)
- 2 Agility Rings

KEY FACTORS

- Focus on perfect movement mechanics and explosiveness (maximum height)
- Step off the box with both feet simultaneously
- Land on both feet simultaneously inside agility rings
- Jump upwards with both feet simultaneously
- Maintain balance; land in same location inside agility rings and on top of the box

COMMON ERRORS

- Athlete lands outside agility rings

ID: 797

7.98 ML ABDUC./ADDUC. BOX JUMP REB. (III): SL LAND.

SUMMARY

The Mid-Level Abductor/Adductor Box Jump Rebound: Single-Leg Landing III is a ballistic exercise, which focuses on developing neural pathways for explosive lateral change of direction capability, reaction time, body control & coordination as well as improving skill and strength foundation for complex movements utilizing a box and 2 agility rings.

DESCRIPTION

1. Place box onto solid, non-sliding surface
2. Place 2 agility rings shoulder-width apart on the ground; 1 to the left side and 1 to the right side of the box
3. Step on top of the box; feet are close together
4. Step off the box with both legs simultaneously
5. Land with both feet simultaneously inside agility rings; **look forward** during landing
6. Immediately jump on top of the box **landing on the right leg**; **look down** during landing
7. Repeat; also perform drill landing on **left** leg

PRE-REQUISITE DRILLS

- Single-Leg Squat
- Mid-Level Abductor/Adductor Box Jump Rebounds (II)

BREATH IN & OUT

- IN: Before Step Off
- OUT: During Jumping

PURPOSE

1. Developing neural pathways for explosive lateral change of direction capability (neurological feedback loop)
2. Improving balance (body control) & coordination
3. Improving skill and strength foundation for complex movements

DEGREE OF DIFFICULTY

3

REQUIRED EQUIPMENT

- 10 - 15 Inch Box (width smaller than shoulder-width)
- 2 Agility Rings

KEY FACTORS

- Focus on perfect movement mechanics and explosiveness (maximum height)
- Step off the box with both feet
- Land on both feet simultaneously inside agility rings
- Jump upwards with both feet simultaneously
- Maintain balance; land in same location inside agility rings and on top of the box (**single-leg stance**)

COMMON ERRORS

- Athlete lands outside agility rings
- Athlete looses balance during landing

ID: 798

7 7.99 ML ABDUC./ADDUC. BOX JUMP REB. (IV): SL LAND.

SUMMARY

The Mid-Level Abductor/Adductor Box Jump Rebounds: Single-Leg Landing IV is a ballistic exercise, which focuses on developing neural pathways for explosive lateral change of direction capability, reaction time, body control & coordination as well as improving skill and strength foundation for complex movements utilizing a box and 2 agility rings.

PURPOSE

1. Developing neural pathways for explosive lateral change of direction capability (neurological feedback loop)
2. Improving balance (body control) & coordination
3. Improving skill and strength foundation for complex movements

DESCRIPTION

1. Place box onto solid, non-sliding surface
2. Place 2 agility rings shoulder-width apart on the ground; 1 to the left side and 1 to the right side of the box
3. Step on top of the box; feet are close together
4. Jump off the box with both legs simultaneously
5. Land with both feet simultaneously inside agility rings; **look forward** during landing
6. Immediately jump on top of the box landing on the right leg; **look forward** during landing
7. Repeat; also perform drill landing on **left** leg

PRE-REQUISITE DRILLS

- Single-Leg Squat
- Mid-Level Abductor/Adductor Box Jump Rebounds (III)

BREATH IN & OUT

- IN: Before Step Off
- OUT: During Jumping

DEGREE OF DIFFICULTY

4

REQUIRED EQUIPMENT

- 10 - 15 Inch Box (width smaller than shoulder-width)
- 2 Agility Rings

KEY FACTORS

- Focus on perfect movement mechanics and explosiveness (maximum height)
- Step off the box with both feet
- Land on both feet simultaneously inside agility rings
- Jump upwards with both feet simultaneously
- Maintain balance; land in same location inside agility rings and on top of the box (**single-leg stance**)

COMMON ERRORS

- Athlete lands outside agility rings
- Athlete looses balance during landing

ID: 799

7.100 ML ABDUC./ADDUC. BJ REB. (V): ALTERN. SL LAND.

SUMMARY

The Mid-Level Abductor/Adductor Box Jump Rebounds: Alternate Single-Leg Landing V is a ballistic exercise, which focuses on developing neural pathways for explosive lateral change of direction capability, reaction time, body control & coordination as well as improving skill and strength foundation for complex movements utilizing a box and 2 agility rings.

PURPOSE

1. Developing neural pathways for explosive lateral change of direction capability (neurological feedback loop)
2. Improving balance (body control) & coordination
3. Improving skill and strength foundation for complex movements

DESCRIPTION

1. Place box onto solid, non-sliding surface
2. Place 2 agility rings shoulder-width apart on the ground; 1 to the left side and 1 to the right side of the box
3. Step on top of the box; feet are close together
4. Jump off the box with both legs simultaneously
5. Land with both feet simultaneously inside agility rings; **look forward** during landing
6. Immediately jump on top of the box landing on the **right** leg; **look forward** during landing
7. Jump off the box, land, and jump onto the box landing on **left** leg

PRE-REQUISITE DRILLS

- Single-Leg Squat
- Mid-Level Abductor/Adductor Box Jump Rebounds (IV)

BREATH IN & OUT

- IN: Before Step Off
- OUT: During Jumping

DEGREE OF DIFFICULTY

5

REQUIRED EQUIPMENT

- 10 - 15 Inch Box (width smaller than shoulder-width)
- 2 Agility Rings

KEY FACTORS

- Focus on perfect movement mechanics and explosiveness (short ground contact)
- Step off the box with both feet
- Land on both feet simultaneously inside agility rings
- Jump upwards with both feet simultaneously
- Maintain balance; land in same location inside agility rings and on top of the box (**single-leg stance**)

COMMON ERRORS

- Athlete lands outside agility rings
- Athlete looses balance during landing

ID: 7100

7.101 SQUAT BOX JUMP REBOUNDS (I)

SUMMARY

The Squat Box Jump Rebounds I is a ballistic exercise, which focuses on developing neural pathways for explosive lateral & vertical change of direction capability, reaction time, body control & coordination as well as improving skill and strength foundation for complex movements utilizing a box and 2 agility rings.

PURPOSE

1. Developing neural pathways for explosive lateral & vertical change of direction capability (Abductors/ Adductors; neurological feedback loop)
2. Improving balance (body control) & coordination
3. Improving skill and strength foundation for complex movements

DESCRIPTION

1. Place box onto solid, non-sliding surface
2. Place 2 agility rings shoulder-width apart on the ground; 1 to the left side and 1 to the right side of the box
3. **Stand over the box** and inside the agility rings
4. Jump on top of the box; feet are close together
5. Jump off the box with both legs **simultaneously** into a **squat** (knees at 90°)
6. Land with both feet **simultaneously** inside agility rings; **look down** to the ground during landing
7. Immediately jump on top of the box with both legs **simultaneously** while **looking down** at the box
8. Repeat

COMMON ERRORS

- Athlete lands outside agility rings
- Athlete looses balance during landing

BREATH IN & OUT

- IN: Before Step Off
- OUT: During Jumping

PRE-REQUISITE DRILLS

- Squat

DEGREE OF DIFFICULTY

1

REQUIRED EQUIPMENT

- 10 - 15 Inch Box (width smaller than shoulder-width)
- 2 Agility Rings

KEY FACTORS

- Focus on perfect movement mechanics and explosiveness (maximum height)
- Jump off the box with both feet simultaneously
- Land on both feet simultaneously inside agility rings
- Jump upwards with both feet simultaneously
- Maintain balance; land in same location inside agility rings and on top of the box

ID: 7101

7.102 SQUAT BOX JUMP REBOUNDS (II)

SUMMARY

The Squat Box Jump Rebounds II is a ballistic exercise, which focuses on developing neural pathways for explosive lateral & vertical change of direction capability, reaction time, body control & coordination as well as improving skill and strength foundation for complex movements utilizing a box and 2 agility rings.

PURPOSE

1. Developing neural pathways for explosive lateral & vertical change of direction capability (Abductors/ Adductors; neurological feedback loop)
2. Improving balance (body control) & coordination
3. Improving skill and strength foundation for complex movements

DESCRIPTION

1. Place box onto solid, non-sliding surface
2. Place 2 agility rings shoulder-width apart on the ground; 1 to the left side and 1 to the right side of the box
3. **Stand over the box** and inside the agility rings
4. Jump on top of the box; feet are close together
5. Jump off the box with both legs simultaneously into a **squat** (knees at 90°)
6. Land with both feet simultaneously inside agility rings; **look forward** to the ground during landing
7. Immediately jump on top of the box with both legs simultaneously while **looking forward** at the box
8. Repeat

PRE-REQUISITE DRILLS

- Squat Jump
- Squat Box Jump Rebounds (I)

BREATH IN & OUT

- IN: Before Step Off
- OUT: During Jumping

COMMON ERRORS

- Athlete lands outside agility rings
- Athlete looses balance during landing

DEGREE OF DIFFICULTY

2

REQUIRED EQUIPMENT

- 10 - 15 Inch Box (width smaller than shoulder-width)
- 2 Agility Rings

KEY FACTORS

- Focus on perfect movement mechanics and explosiveness (maximum height)
- Jump off the box with both feet simultaneously
- Land on both feet simultaneously inside agility rings
- Jump upwards with both feet simultaneously
- Maintain balance; land in same location inside agility rings and on top of the box

ID: 7102

7.103 SL EXPLOSIVE LATERAL REBOUND PRESS (III)

SUMMARY

The Single-Leg Explosive Lateral Rebound Press III is a ballistic exercise, which focuses on improving energy transfer for more powerful stroke production, body control, balance & coordination, explosiveness of lower extremities (legs), as well as improving skill & strength foundation for complex movements utilizing a box, an agility ring and a dumbbell.

PURPOSE

1. Improving energy transfer for more powerful stroke production (e.g. the serve; recovery after serving) and reaction time
2. Improving body control, balance, and coordination
3. Improving explosiveness of lower extremities (neurological feedback loop)
4. Improving skill and strength foundation for complex movements

DESCRIPTION

1. Place 1 agility ring diagonal in front of the box on the ground
2. Put one leg on op of the box (hip & knee flexed at 90°); place other leg inside the ring
3. Hold the dumbbell in the opposite hand close to the shoulder; **look forward**
4. Explosively push off with the leg on top of the box and **simultaneously** press the dumbbell (DB) over the head; arm is extended
5. Land inside agility ring
6. **Hold 1 second** and repeat

COMMON ERRORS

- Athlete moves back and forth during jumps
- Athlete jumps at sub-maximal height
- Athlete lands outside agility ring

PRE-REQUISITE DRILLS

- Single-Leg Squat
- Overhead Squat
- Single-Leg Explosive Vertical Jump to Single-Arm DB Snatch (II)

BREATH IN & OUT

- IN: When landing
- OUT: During Jumping

DEGREE OF DIFFICULTY

3

REQUIRED EQUIPMENT

- 1 Agility Ring
- 1 Dumbbell (5 lb – 35 lb)
- 1 Box (10 – 20 inch height)

KEY FACTORS

- Focus on perfect movement mechanics, explosiveness (maximum height), and body control (landing)
- Jump with one foot, land on one foot
- Maintain balance: land in same location inside agility ring

ID: 7103

7.104 SL EXPLOSIVE LATERAL REBOUND PRESS (IV)

SUMMARY

The Single-Leg Explosive Lateral Rebound Press IV is a ballistic exercise, which focuses on improving energy transfer for more powerful stroke production, body control, balance & coordination, explosiveness of lower extremities (legs), as well as improving skill & strength foundation for complex movements utilizing a box, an agility ring and a dumbbell.

PURPOSE

1. Improving energy transfer for more powerful stroke production (e.g. the serve; recovery after serving) and reaction time
2. Improving body control, balance, and coordination
3. Improving explosiveness of lower extremities (neurological feedback loop)
4. Improving skill and strength foundation for complex movements

DESCRIPTION

1. Place 1 agility ring diagonal in front of the box on the ground
2. Put one leg on op of the box (hip & knee flexed at 90°); place other leg inside the ring
3. Hold the dumbbell in the opposite hand close to the shoulder; **look forward**
4. Explosively push off with the leg on top of the box and simultaneously press the dumbbell (DB) over the head; arm is extended
5. Land inside agility ring
6. **Immediately** repeat

DEGREE OF DIFFICULTY

4

REQUIRED EQUIPMENT

- 1 Agility Ring
- 1 Dumbbell (5 lb – 35 lb)
- 1 Box (10 – 20 inch height)

KEY FACTORS

- Focus on perfect movement mechanics, explosiveness (maximum height), and body control (landing)
- Jump with one foot, land on one foot
- Maintain balance: land in same location inside agility ring

COMMON ERRORS

- Athlete moves back and forth during jumps
- Athlete jumps at sub-maximal height
- Athlete lands outside agility ring

BREATH IN & OUT

- IN: When landing
- OUT: During Jumping

PRE-REQUISITE DRILLS

- Single-Leg Squat
- Overhead Squat
- Single-Leg Explosive Vertical Jump to Single-Arm DB Snatch (III)

ID: 7104

7.105 JUMP-SERVE OVERHEAD MB THROW (I)

SUMMARY

The Jump Serve Overhead Medicine Ball (MB) Throw (I) is a ballistic exercise, which focuses on improving energy transfer for more powerful stroke production, body control, balance & coordination, explosiveness of lower extremities (legs), as well as improving skill & strength foundation for complex movements utilizing a medicine ball and agility rings.

PURPOSE

1. Improving energy transfer for more powerful stroke production (e.g. the serve)
2. Improving body control & coordination
3. Improving explosiveness of lower extremities (neurological feedback loop); foot speed-strength for diagonal movement (diagonal jump during serve)
4. Improving skill and strength foundation for complex movements

DESCRIPTION

1. Place 1 agility ring ~1 foot inside the baseline; place 2 agility rings where feet are located during serve and step inside rings
2. Hold a medicine ball (MB) in both hands behind the head
3. Stand in ready position to begin the **serve**, perpendicular to the baseline
4. Bend the knees and jump vertically & horizontally(diagonally) with both feet **simultaneously** inside the baseline and perform an overhead MB throw towards the appropriate (diagonal) service box
5. Land inside the 1 agility ring with the **leading** foot; **look down** to the ground during landing

PRE-REQUISITE DRILLS

- Lateral Box Jump
- Overhead MB Throw

COMMON ERRORS

- Athlete jumps vertically
- Athlete releases MB early
- Athlete lands outside the agility ring

BREATH IN & OUT

- IN: When bending knees
- OUT: During Jump & Throw

DEGREE OF DIFFICULTY

1

REQUIRED EQUIPMENT

- 1 Medicine Ball (4 lb – 20 lb)
- 3 Agility Rings

KEY FACTORS

- Focus on perfect movement mechanics and explosiveness (maximum height)
- Jump diagonal with both feet simultaneously
- Jump at ~45°
- Release MB at highest point in the air
- Maintain balance: land in same location inside the agility ring

ID: 7105

7.106 JUMP-SERVE OVERHEAD MB THROW (II)

SUMMARY

The Jump Serve Overhead Medicine Ball (MB) Throw (II) is a ballistic exercise, which focuses on improving energy transfer for more powerful stroke production, body control, balance & coordination, explosiveness of lower extremities (legs), as well as improving skill & strength foundation for complex movements utilizing a medicine ball and agility rings.

PURPOSE

1. Improving energy transfer for more powerful stroke production (e.g. the serve)
2. Improving body control & coordination
3. Improving explosiveness of lower extremities (neurological feedback loop); foot speed-strength for diagonal movement (diagonal jump during serve)
4. Improving skill and strength foundation for complex movements

DESCRIPTION

1. Place 1 agility ring ~1 foot inside the baseline; place 2 agility rings where feet are located during serve and step inside rings
2. Hold a medicine ball (MB) in both hands behind the head
3. Stand in ready position to begin the **serve**, perpendicular to the baseline
4. Bend the knees and jump vertically & horizontally (diagonally) with both feet **simultaneously** inside the baseline and perform an overhead MB throw towards the appropriate (diagonal) service box; **look forward** during movement
5. Land inside the 1 agility ring with the **leading** foot; **look forward** during landing

DEGREE OF DIFFICULTY

2

REQUIRED EQUIPMENT

- 1 Medicine Ball (4 lb – 20 lb)
- 3 Agility Rings

KEY FACTORS

- Focus on perfect movement mechanics and explosiveness (maximum height)
- Jump diagonal with both feet simultaneously
- Jump at ~45°
- Release MB at highest point in the air
- Maintain balance: land in same location inside the agility ring

COMMON ERRORS

- Athlete jumps vertically
- Athlete releases MB early
- Athlete lands outside the agility ring

PRE-REQUISITE DRILLS

- Jump-Serve Overhead MB Throw (I)

BREATH IN & OUT

- IN: When bending knees
- OUT: During Jump & Throw

ID: 7106

7.107 JUMP-SERVE OH MB THROW (III): SL LANDING

SUMMARY

The Jump Serve Overhead Medicine Ball (MB) Throw: Single-Leg Landing (III) is a ballistic exercise, which focuses on improving energy transfer for more powerful stroke production, body control, balance & coordination, explosiveness of lower extremities (legs), as well as improving skill & strength foundation for complex movements utilizing a medicine ball and agility rings.

PURPOSE

1. Improving energy transfer for more powerful stroke production (e.g. the serve)
2. Improving balance, body control & coordination
3. Improving explosiveness of lower extremities (neurological feedback loop); foot speed-strength for diagonal movement (diagonal jump during serve)
4. Improving skill and strength foundation for complex movements

DESCRIPTION

1. Place 2 agility rings where feet are located during serve and step inside rings; place 1 agility ring in line with agility ring of the leading foot ~1 foot inside the baseline
2. Hold a medicine ball (MB) in both hands behind the head
3. Stand in ready position to begin the **serve**, perpendicular to the baseline
4. Bend the knees and jump vertically & horizontally (diagonally) with both feet simultaneously inside the baseline and perform an overhead MB throw towards the appropriate (diagonal) service box; **look forward** during movement
5. Land inside the 1 agility ring with the leading foot and **stick the landing**; **look down** to the ground during landing

PRE-REQUISITE DRILLS

- Jump-Serve Overhead MB Throw (II)

BREATH IN & OUT

- IN: When bending knees
- OUT: During Jump & Throw

DEGREE OF DIFFICULTY

3

REQUIRED EQUIPMENT

- 1 Medicine Ball (4 lb – 20 lb)
- 3 Agility Rings

KEY FACTORS

- Focus on perfect movement mechanics and explosiveness (maximum height)
- Jump diagonal with both feet simultaneously
- Jump at ~45°
- Release MB at highest point in the air
- Maintain balance: land in same location inside the agility ring with leading foot

COMMON ERRORS

- Athlete jumps vertically
- Athlete releases MB early
- Athlete lands outside the agility ring
- Athlete doesn't stick the landing: loss of stability

ID: 7107

7.108 JUMP-SERVE OH MB THROW (IV): SL LANDING

SUMMARY

The Jump Serve Overhead Medicine Ball (MB) Throw: Single-Leg Landing (IV) is a ballistic exercise, which focuses on improving energy transfer for more powerful stroke production, body control, balance & coordination, explosiveness of lower extremities (legs), as well as improving skill & strength foundation for complex movements utilizing a medicine ball and agility rings.

DESCRIPTION

1. Place 2 agility rings where feet are located during serve and step inside rings; place 1 agility ring in line with agility ring of the leading foot ~1 foot inside the baseline
2. Hold a medicine ball (MB) in both hands behind the head
3. Stand in ready position to begin the **serve**, perpendicular to the baseline
4. Bend the knees and jump vertically & horizontally (diagonally) with both feet simultaneously inside the baseline and perform an overhead MB throw towards the appropriate (diagonal) service box; **look forward** during movement
5. Land inside the 1 agility ring with the **leading** foot and **stick the landing**; **look forward** during landing

PURPOSE

1. Improving energy transfer for more powerful stroke production (e.g. the serve)
2. Improving balance, body control & coordination
3. Improving explosiveness of lower extremities (neurological feedback loop); foot speed-strength for diagonal movement (diagonal jump during serve)
4. Improving skill and strength foundation for complex movements

DEGREE OF DIFFICULTY

4

REQUIRED EQUIPMENT

- 1 Medicine Ball (4 lb – 20 lb)
- 3 Agility Rings

KEY FACTORS

- Focus on perfect movement mechanics and explosiveness (maximum height)
- Jump diagonal with both feet simultaneously
- Jump at ~45°
- Release MB at highest point in the air
- Maintain balance: land in same location inside the agility ring with leading foot

COMMON ERRORS

- Athlete jumps vertically
- Athlete releases MB early
- Athlete lands outside the agility ring
- Athlete doesn't stick the landing: loss of stability

PRE-REQUISITE DRILLS

- Jump-Serve Overhead MB Throw (III)

BREATH IN & OUT

- IN: When bending knees
- OUT: During Jump & Throw

7.109 MEDICINE BALL TRUNK TWIST THROW (I)

SUMMARY

The Medicine Ball (MB) Trunk Twist Throw (I) is a ballistic exercise, which focuses on improving energy transfer for more powerful stroke production, body control, balance & coordination, explosiveness of the trunk, as well as improving skill & strength foundation for complex movements utilizing a medicine ball and agility rings.

This exercise can also be performed with a partner instead of the wall.

PURPOSE

1. Improving energy transfer for more powerful stroke production (e.g. groundstrokes)
2. Improving body control (balance) & coordination
3. Improving explosiveness of the trunk by enhancing synergy of lower extremities and the trunk (neurological feedback loop); rotational power training for transverse movement (trunk rotation during groundstrokes)
4. Improving skill and strength foundation for complex movements

DESCRIPTION

1. Place 2 agility rings parallel and ~8 feet away from the concrete wall; rings should be shoulder-width apart
2. Step inside agility rings
3. Hold a medicine ball (MB) naturally in both hands in front of the trunk
4. Take on **athletic stance** position; knees and hips are slightly flexed; upper-body is straight
5. Rotate the trunk outwardly until shoulders are perpendicular to the wall (or as far as possible); maintain neutral head position; keep **looking forward**
6. Initiate the throw with the **hips** and **trunk**, not the arms
7. Extend the hips until standing on the balls of the feet, lean forward with the upper-body, and simultaneously rotate trunk inwardly until shoulders are nearly parallel to the wall
8. Explosively release MB at hip-level and throw MB against the wall; maintain neutral head position; keep **looking forward**
9. Do **NOT** catch the rebound

PRE-REQUISITE DRILLS

- Medicine Ball Trunk Rotation

DEGREE OF DIFFICULTY

1

KEY FACTORS

- Focus on perfect movement mechanics and explosiveness (maximum distance)
- Maintain neutral head position; keep looking forward
- Extend hips and rotate trunk to initiate external rotation and throw
- Release MB at hip level
- Maintain balance: stay inside agility rings during throw

COMMON ERRORS

- Athlete initiates throw via arms
- Athlete loses balance
- Athlete releases MB early
- Athlete catches rebound in the air

REQUIRED EQUIPMENT

- Concrete Wall/Partner
- 1 Medicine Ball (10 lb – 25 lb)
- 2 Agility Rings

BREATH IN & OUT

- IN: Before Rotation
- OUT: During MB release

ID: 7109

7.110 MB TRUNK TWIST THROW (II): DIAGONAL LUNGE

SUMMARY

The Medicine Ball (MB) Trunk Twist Throw (II) is a ballistic exercise, which focuses on improving energy transfer for more powerful stroke production, body control, balance & coordination, explosiveness of the trunk, as well as improving skill & strength foundation for complex movements.

This exercise can also be performed with a partner instead of the wall.

PURPOSE

1. Improving energy transfer for more powerful stroke production (e.g. groundstrokes)
2. Improving body control (balance) & coordination
3. Improving explosiveness of the trunk by enhancing synergy of lower extremities and the trunk (neurological feedback loop); rotational power training for transverse movement (trunk rotation during groundstrokes)
4. Improving skill and strength foundation for complex movements

DESCRIPTION

1. Hold a medicine ball (MB) naturally in both hands in front of the trunk
2. Take on **diagonal lunge position**; distribute weight through the heel (flat footed); knees and hips are flexed at 90°; back remains straight; maintain neutral head position; keep **looking forward**
3. Rotate the trunk outwardly until shoulders are perpendicular to the wall (or as far as possible); maintain neutral head position; keep looking forward
4. Initiate the throw with the **hips** and **trunk**, not the arms
5. Rotate trunk inwardly until shoulders are nearly parallel to the wall
6. **Lean forward** with the upper-body and explosively release MB at hip-level and throw MB against the wall; maintain neutral head position; keep **looking forward**
7. Do **NOT** catch the rebound

PRE-REQUISITE DRILLS

- Forward/Reverse Lunge
- Medicine Ball Trunk Rotation II
- MB Trunk Twist Throw

DEGREE OF DIFFICULTY

2

KEY FACTORS

- Focus on perfect movement mechanics and explosiveness (maximum distance)
- Distribute weight through the heel of the front foot
- Rotate trunk to initiate throw
- Maintain neutral head position; keep looking forward
- Lean forward during throw
- Release MB at hip level
- Maintain balance

COMMON ERRORS

- Athlete initiates throw via arms
- Athlete distributes weight through the ball of the foot (toes)
- Athlete releases MB early
- Athlete loses balance (upper-body leans backwards)
- Athlete catches rebound in the air

REQUIRED EQUIPMENT

- Concrete Wall/Partner
- 1 Medicine Ball (10 lb – 25 lb)

BREATH IN & OUT

- IN: Before Rotation
- OUT: During MB release

ID: 7110

7.111 MB TRUNK TWIST THROW (III): SINGLE-LEG

SUMMARY

The Medicine Ball (MB) Trunk Twist Throw (III) is a ballistic exercise, which focuses on improving energy transfer for more powerful stroke production, body control, balance & coordination, explosiveness of the trunk, as well as improving skill & strength foundation for complex movements.

This exercise can also be performed with a partner instead of the wall.

PURPOSE

1. Improving energy transfer for more powerful stroke production (e.g. groundstrokes)
2. Improving body control (balance) & coordination
3. Improving explosiveness of the trunk by enhancing synergy of lower extremities and the trunk (neurological feedback loop); rotational power training for transverse movement (trunk rotation during groundstrokes)
4. Improving skill and strength foundation for complex movements

DESCRIPTION

1. Hold a medicine ball (MB) naturally in both hands in front of the trunk
2. Take on **diagonal single-leg stance** position; knee and hip are slightly flexed; non-weight bearing knee is flexed at 90°; back remains straight
3. Rotate the trunk outwardly until shoulders are perpendicular to the wall (or as far as possible); maintain neutral head position; keep **looking forward**
4. Initiate the throw with the **hips** and **trunk**, not the arms
5. Rotate trunk inwardly until shoulders are nearly parallel to the wall
6. **Lean forward** with the upper-body and explosively release MB at hip-level and throw MB against the wall; maintain neutral head position; keep **looking forward**
7. Do NOT catch the rebound
8. Maintain stability after the throw

PRE-REQUISITE DRILLS

- Single-Leg Squat
- MB Trunk Rotation III
- MB Trunk Twist Throw II

DEGREE OF DIFFICULTY

3

KEY FACTORS

- Focus on perfect movement mechanics and explosiveness (maximum distance)
- Rotate trunk to initiate throw
- Maintain neutral head position; keep looking forward
- Lean forward during throw
- Release MB at hip level
- Maintain balance

COMMON ERRORS

- Athlete initiates throw via arms
- Athlete releases MB early
- Athlete loses balance (e.g. upper-body leans backwards)
- Athlete catches rebound in the air

REQUIRED EQUIPMENT

- Concrete Wall/Partner
- 1 Medicine Ball (10 lb – 25 lb)

BREATH IN & OUT

- IN: Before Rotation
- OUT: During MB release

ID: 7111

7.112 MB TRUNK TWIST THR. (IV): ALTERN. DIAG. LUNGE

SUMMARY

The Medicine Ball (MB) Trunk Twist Throw (IV) is a ballistic exercise, which focuses on improving energy transfer for more powerful stroke production, body control, balance & coordination, explosiveness of the trunk, as well as improving skill & strength foundation for complex movements.

This exercise can also be performed with a partner instead of the wall.

PURPOSE

1. Improving energy transfer for more powerful stroke production (e.g. groundstrokes)
2. Improving body control (stability) & coordination
3. Improving explosiveness of the trunk by enhancing synergy of lower extremities and the trunk (neurological feedback loop); rotational power training for transverse movement (trunk rotation during groundstrokes)
4. Improving skill and strength foundation for complex movements

DESCRIPTION

1. Hold a medicine ball (MB) naturally in both hands in front of the trunk
2. Side-Step to the **left**
3. Step into a **diagonal lunge position** with the **right** foot; distribute weight through the heel (flat footed); knees and hips are flexed at 90°; back remains straight
4. Rotate the trunk outwardly until shoulders are perpendicular to the wall (or as far as possible); maintain neutral head position; keep **looking forward**
5. Initiate the throw with the **hips** and **trunk**, not the arms
6. Rotate trunk inwardly until shoulders are nearly parallel to the wall
7. **Lean forward** with the upper-body, explosively release MB at hip-level, rotate non-weight bearing hip forward, land on the left foot, and throw MB against the wall; maintain neutral head position; keep **looking forward**
8. Pick up the MB and **side-step** to the other side
9. Step into **diagonal lunge** with the **left** foot and repeat

PRE-REQUISITE DRILLS

- MB Trunk Rotation IV
- MB Trunk Twist Throw II

DEGREE OF DIFFICULTY

4

KEY FACTORS

- Focus on perfect movement mechanics and explosiveness (maximum distance)
- Distribute weight through the heel of the front foot
- Rotate trunk to initiate throw
- Maintain neutral head position; keep looking forward
- Lean forward during throw
- Release MB at hip level
- Rotate non-weight bearing hip forward
- Maintain stability

COMMON ERRORS

- Athlete initiates throw via arms
- Athlete distributes weight through the ball of the foot (toes)
- Athlete releases MB early
- Athlete loses stability (e.g. upper-body leans backwards)
- Athlete catches rebound in the air

BREATH IN & OUT

- IN: Before Rotation
- OUT: During MB release

REQUIRED EQUIPMENT

- Concrete Wall/Partner
- 1 Medicine Ball (10 lb – 25 lb)

ID: 7112

7.113 MB TRUNK TWIST THROW (V): ALTERNATE SL

SUMMARY

The Medicine Ball (MB) Trunk Twist Throw (V) is a ballistic exercise, which focuses on improving energy transfer for more powerful stroke production, body control, balance & coordination, and explosiveness of the trunk.

This exercise can also be performed with a partner instead of the wall.

PURPOSE

1. Improving energy transfer for more powerful stroke production (e.g. groundstrokes)
2. Improving body control (stability) & coordination
3. Improving explosiveness of the trunk by enhancing synergy of lower extremities and the trunk (neurological feedback loop); rotational power training for transverse movement (trunk rotation during groundstrokes)

DESCRIPTION

1. Hold a medicine ball (MB) naturally in both hands in front of the trunk
2. Side-Step to the **left**
3. Step into a **diagonal single-leg stance** position with the **right** foot; knee and hip are slightly flexed; non-weight bearing knee is flexed at 90°; back remains straight
4. Rotate the trunk outwardly until shoulders are perpendicular to the wall (or as far as possible); maintain neutral head position; keep **looking forward**
5. Initiate the throw with the **hips** and **trunk**, not the arms
6. Rotate trunk inwardly until shoulders are nearly parallel to the wall
7. **Lean forward** with the upper-body and explosively release MB at hip-level and throw MB against the wall; maintain neutral head position; keep **looking forward**
8. Rotate non-weight bearing hip forward and land on the other leg
9. Pick up the MB and **side-step** to the other side
10. Step into **diagonal single-leg stance** position with the **left** foot and repeat

PRE-REQUISITE DRILLS

- MB Trunk Rotation IV
- MB Trunk Twist Throw III

BREATH IN & OUT

- IN: Before Rotation
- OUT: During MB release

DEGREE OF DIFFICULTY

5

REQUIRED EQUIPMENT

- Concrete Wall/Partner
- 1 Medicine Ball (10 lb – 25 lb)

KEY FACTORS

- Focus on perfect movement mechanics and explosiveness (maximum distance)
- Rotate trunk to initiate throw
- Maintain neutral head position; keep looking forward
- Lean forward during throw
- Release MB at hip level
- Rotate non-weight bearing hip forward
- Maintain stability

COMMON ERRORS

- Athlete initiates throw via arms
- Athlete releases MB early
- Athlete loses stability (e.g. upper-body leans backwards)
- Athlete catches rebound in the air

ID: 7113

7.114 OVERHEAD MEDICINE BALL THROW (I)

SUMMARY

The Overhead Medicine Ball (MB) Throw (I) is a ballistic exercise, which focuses on improving energy transfer for more powerful stroke production, body control, balance & coordination, explosiveness of the trunk, as well as improving skill & strength foundation for complex movements.

This exercise can also be performed with a partner instead of the wall.

PURPOSE

1. Improving energy transfer for more powerful stroke production (e.g. the serve)
2. Improving body control (balance) & coordination
3. Improving explosiveness of the trunk by enhancing synergy of upper extremities and the trunk (neurological feedback loop); hip flexion and elbow extension speed-strength for sagittal movement (hip flexion and elbow extension during serve)
4. Improving skill and strength foundation for complex movements

DESCRIPTION

1. Hold a medicine ball (MB) in both hands behind the head; remain 6-8 feet away from the wall/partner
2. Take on **athletic stance** position; knees and hips are slightly flexed; upper-body remains straight; face the wall/partner; maintain neutral head position; keep looking forward
3. Extend the hips forward and explosively throw the MB **forward** towards the wall/partner
4. Receive bounce pass from wall/partner; do NOT catch MB in the air
5. Repeat

PRE-REQUISITE DRILLS

- Overhead MB Pull-Over I

REQUIRED EQUIPMENT

- 1 Medicine Ball (10 lb – 25 lb)
- Concrete Wall/Partner

BREATH IN & OUT

- IN: When extending hips
- OUT: During Throw

DEGREE OF DIFFICULTY

1

KEY FACTORS

- Focus on perfect movement mechanics and explosiveness (maximum distance)
- Maintain neutral head position
- Extend hips
- Release MB over the head
- Maintain balance

COMMON ERRORS

- Athlete throws MB without prior hip extension
- Athlete loses balance
- Athlete releases MB early
- Athlete catches rebound in the air

ID: 7114

7.115 OVERHEAD MB THROW (II): LUNGE POSITION

SUMMARY

The Overhead Medicine Ball (MB) Throw (II) is a ballistic exercise, which focuses on improving energy transfer for more powerful stroke production, body control, balance & coordination, explosiveness of the trunk, as well as improving skill & strength foundation for complex movements.

This exercise can also be performed with a partner instead of the wall.

PURPOSE

1. Improving energy transfer for more powerful stroke production (e.g. the serve)
2. Improving body control (balance) & coordination
3. Improving explosiveness of the trunk by enhancing synergy of upper extremities and the trunk (neurological feedback loop); hip flexion and elbow extension speed-strength for sagittal movement (hip flexion and elbow extension during serve)
4. Improving skill and strength foundation for complex movements

DESCRIPTION

1. Hold a medicine ball (MB) in both hands behind the head; remain 6-8 feet away from the wall/partner
2. Take on a **forward lunge position** with the **right** foot; distribute weight through the heel (flat footed); knees and hips are flexed at 90°; back remains straight; face the wall/partner; maintain neutral head position; keep **looking forward**
3. Extend the hips forward, flex the hips and explosively throw the MB **forward** towards the wall/partner
4. Receive bounce pass from wall/partner; do NOT catch MB in the air
5. Switch legs and repeat

PRE-REQUISITE DRILLS

- Forward/Reverse Lunge
- Overhead MB Pull-Over II

REQUIRED EQUIPMENT

- 1 Medicine Ball (10 lb – 25 lb)
- Concrete Wall/Partner

BREATH IN & OUT

- IN: When extending hips
- OUT: During Throw

DEGREE OF DIFFICULTY

2

KEY FACTORS

- Focus on perfect movement mechanics and explosiveness (maximum distance)
- Distribute weight through the heel of the front foot
- Maintain neutral head position
- Extend hips
- Release MB over the head
- Maintain balance

COMMON ERRORS

- Athlete throws MB without prior hip extension
- Athlete distributes weight through the ball of the foot (toes)
- Athlete loses balance
- Athlete releases MB early
- Athlete catches rebound in the air

ID: 7115

7.116 OVERHEAD MB THROW (III): SINGLE-LEG

SUMMARY

The Overhead Medicine Ball (MB) Throw (III) is a ballistic exercise, which focuses on improving energy transfer for more powerful stroke production, body control, balance & coordination, explosiveness of the trunk, as well as improving skill & strength foundation for complex movements.

This exercise can also be performed with a partner instead of the wall.

PURPOSE

1. Improving energy transfer for more powerful stroke production (e.g. the serve)
2. Improving body control (balance) & coordination
3. Improving explosiveness of the trunk by enhancing synergy of upper extremities and the trunk (neurological feedback loop); hip flexion and elbow extension speed-strength for sagittal movement (hip flexion and elbow extension during serve)
4. Improving skill and strength foundation for complex movements

DESCRIPTION

1. Hold a medicine ball (MB) in both hands behind the head; remain 6-8 feet away from the wall/partner
2. Take on **single-leg stance** position; knee and hip are slightly flexed; non-weight bearing knee is flexed at 90°; back remains straight; face the wall/partner; maintain neutral head position; keep **looking forward**
3. Extend the hip forward, flex the hip and explosively throw the MB **forward** towards the wall/partner
4. Receive bounce pass from wall/partner; do NOT catch MB in the air
5. Repeat

PRE-REQUISITE DRILLS

- Single-Leg Squat
- Overhead MB Pull-Over III

REQUIRED EQUIPMENT

- 1 Medicine Ball (10 lb – 25 lb)
- Concrete Wall/Partner

BREATH IN & OUT

- IN: When extending hips
- OUT: During Throw

DEGREE OF DIFFICULTY

3

KEY FACTORS

- Focus on perfect movement mechanics and explosiveness (maximum distance)
- Maintain neutral head position
- Extend hip
- Release MB over the head
- Maintain balance

COMMON ERRORS

- Athlete loses balance
- Athlete releases MB early
- Athlete catches rebound in the air

ID: 7116

7.117 OH MB THROW (II): ALTERN. LUNGE POSITION

SUMMARY

The Overhead Medicine Ball (MB) Throw (IV) is a ballistic exercise, which focuses on improving energy transfer for more powerful stroke production, body control, balance & coordination, explosiveness of the trunk, as well as improving skill & strength foundation for complex movements.

This exercise can also be performed with a partner instead of the wall.

PURPOSE

1. Improving energy transfer for more powerful stroke production (e.g. the serve)
2. Improving body control (stability) & coordination
3. Improving explosiveness of the trunk by enhancing synergy of upper extremities and the trunk (neurological feedback loop); hip flexion and elbow extension speed-strength for sagittal movement (hip flexion and elbow extension during serve)
4. Improving skill and strength foundation for complex movements

DESCRIPTION

1. Hold a medicine ball (MB) in both hands behind the head; remain 6-8 feet away from the wall/partner
2. Side-Step to the **left**
3. Step into a **forward lunge position** with the **right** foot; distribute weight through the heel (flat footed); knees and hips are flexed at 90°; back remains straight; face the wall/partner; maintain neutral head position; keep **looking forward**
4. Extend the hips forward, flex the hips, rotate non-weight bearing hip forward, explosively throw the MB **forward** towards the wall/partner, and land on the **left** foot
5. Receive bounce pass from wall/partner; do NOT catch MB in the air
6. Side-step to the **right**
7. Step into forward lunge position with **left** foot and repeat

DEGREE OF DIFFICULTY

4

KEY FACTORS

- Focus on perfect movement mechanics and explosiveness (maximum distance)
- Distribute weight through the heel of the front foot
- Maintain neutral head position
- Extend hips
- Release MB over the head
- Rotate non-weight bearing hip forward
- Maintain stability

COMMON ERRORS

- Athlete loses stability
- Athlete distributes weight through the ball of the foot (toes)
- Athlete releases MB early
- Athlete catches rebound in the air

PRE-REQUISITE DRILLS

- Overhead MB Pull-Over II
- Overhead MB Throw II

REQUIRED EQUIPMENT

- 1 Medicine Ball (10 lb – 25 lb)
- Concrete Wall/Partner

BREATH IN & OUT

- IN: When extending hips
- OUT: During Throw

ID: 7117

7.118 OVERHED MB THROW (V): ALTERNATE SL

SUMMARY

The Overhead Medicine Ball (MB) Throw (V) is a ballistic exercise, which focuses on improving energy transfer for more powerful stroke production, body control, balance & coordination, and explosiveness of the trunk.

This exercise can also be performed with a partner instead of the wall.

PURPOSE

1. Improving energy transfer for more powerful stroke production (e.g. the serve)
2. Improving body control (stability) & coordination
3. Improving explosiveness of the trunk by enhancing synergy of upper extremities and the trunk (neurological feedback loop); hip flexion and elbow extension speed-strength for sagittal movement (hip flexion and elbow extension during serve)

DESCRIPTION

1. Hold a medicine ball (MB) in both hands behind the head; remain 6-8 feet away from the wall/partner
2. Side-Step to the **left**
3. Step into **single-leg stance** position with the **right** foot; knee and hip are slightly flexed; non-weight bearing knee is flexed at 90°; back remains straight; face the wall/partner; maintain neutral head position; keep **looking forward**
4. Extend the hip forward, flex the hip, rotate non-weight bearing hip forward, explosively throw the MB **forward** towards the wall/partner, and land on the **left** foot
5. Receive bounce pass from wall/partner; do NOT catch MB in the air
6. Side-step to the **right**
7. Step into **single-leg stance** position with the **left** foot and repeat

DEGREE OF DIFFICULTY

5

KEY FACTORS

- Focus on perfect movement mechanics and explosiveness (maximum distance)
- Maintain neutral head position
- Extend hip
- Release MB over the head
- Rotate non-weight bearing hip forward
- Maintain stability

COMMON ERRORS

- Athlete loses stability
- Athlete releases MB early
- Athlete catches rebound in the air

PRE-REQUISITE DRILLS

- MB Trunk Rotation V
- MB Trunk Twist Throw III

BREATH IN & OUT

- IN: When extending hips
- OUT: During Throw

REQUIRED EQUIPMENT

- 1 Medicine Ball (10 lb – 25 lb)
- Concrete Wall/Partner

ID: 7118

7.119 PLATE JACKS I

SUMMARY

The Plate Jacks I is a ballistic exercise, which focuses on improving energy transfer for more powerful stroke production, body control & coordination, explosiveness of lower extremities (legs), as well as improving skill & strength foundation for complex movements.

PURPOSE

1. Improving energy transfer for more powerful stroke production (e.g. the serve)
2. Improving body control & coordination
3. Improving explosiveness of lower extremities (neurological feedback loop); foot speed-strength for lateral movement (side step)
4. Improving skill and strength foundation for complex movements

DESCRIPTION

1. Place 2 agility rings just wider than shoulder-width apart on the ground and step inside
2. Hold the plate in both hands close to the body
3. Drop into a **squat position** thereby lowering the plate between your legs; arms are extended
4. Explosively jump upwards, move feet together, and raise plate above your head; feet should be between agility rings
5. **Hold for 1 second**
6. Jump inside agility rings, drop down into squat position, and lower plate between the legs; **look down** to the ground during landing

PRE-REQUISITE DRILLS

- Squat
- Overhead Squat

BREATH IN & OUT

- IN: When landing
- OUT: During Jumping

DEGREE OF DIFFICULTY

1

REQUIRED EQUIPMENT

- 2 Agility Rings
- 10 lb – 45 lb Plate

KEY FACTORS

- Focus on perfect movement mechanics and explosiveness (maximum height)
- Jump with both feet simultaneously
- Maintain balance: land in same location inside - and in between agility rings

COMMON ERRORS

- Athlete moves back and forth during jumps
- Athlete jumps at sub-maximal height
- Athlete lands outside agility rings

ID: 7119

7.120 PLATE JACKS II

SUMMARY

The Plate Jacks II is a ballistic exercise, which focuses on improving energy transfer for more powerful stroke production, body control & coordination, explosiveness of lower extremities (legs), as well as improving skill & strength foundation for complex movements.

PURPOSE

1. Improving energy transfer for more powerful stroke production (e.g. the serve)
2. Improving body control & coordination
3. Improving explosiveness of lower extremities (neurological feedback loop); foot speed-strength for lateral movement (side step)
4. Improving skill and strength foundation for complex movements

DESCRIPTION

1. Place 2 agility rings just wider than shoulder-width apart on the ground and step inside
2. Hold the plate in both hands close to the body
3. Drop into a squat position thereby lowering the plate between your legs; arms are extended
4. Explosively jump upwards, move feet together, and raise plate above your head; feet should be between agility rings
5. **Instantly** jump inside agility rings, drop down into squat position, and lower plate between the legs; **look forward** during landing

PRE-REQUISITE DRILLS

- Squat
- Overhead Squat
- Plate Jacks (I)

DEGREE OF DIFFICULTY

2

REQUIRED EQUIPMENT

- 2 Agility Rings
- 10 lb – 45 lb Plate

KEY FACTORS

- Focus on perfect movement mechanics and explosiveness (maximum height)
- Jump with both feet simultaneously
- Maintain balance: land in same location inside - and in between agility rings

COMMON ERRORS

- Athlete moves back and forth during jumps
- Athlete jumps at sub-maximal height
- Athlete lands outside agility rings

BREATH IN & OUT

- IN: When landing
- OUT: During Jumping

ID: 7120

7.121 MEDICINE BALL CHOPS (I)

SUMMARY

The Medicine Ball Chops I is a ballistic exercise, which focuses on improving energy transfer for more powerful stroke production, body control & coordination, explosiveness of upper extremities, as well as improving skill & strength foundation for complex movements.

PURPOSE

1. Improving energy transfer for more powerful stroke production (e.g. the groundstrokes)
2. Improving body control & coordination
3. Improving explosiveness of upper extremities (neurological feedback loop); upper-body strength for stroke production (e.g. volley)
4. Improving skill and strength foundation for complex movements

DESCRIPTION

1. Hold the medicine ball (MB) in both hands close to the trunk
2. Take on **athletic stance** position (feet are in line with shoulders); **look forward** during exercise
3. Take MB behind the head and fully extend the trunk
4. Explosively flex the trunk and slam the MB into the ground; **get head out of the way** during MB rebound
5. Catch MB and use speed of the MB rebound to accelerate **trunk extension/flexion**

BREATH IN & OUT

- IN: During Catching
- OUT: During Slamming

DEGREE OF DIFFICULTY

1

REQUIRED EQUIPMENT

- 8 lb – 25 lb Medicine Ball

KEY FACTORS

- Focus on perfect movement mechanics and explosiveness (maximum **force generation & speed**)
- Maintain balance

COMMON ERRORS

- Athlete moves back and forth during slamming
- Athlete achieves sub-maximal explosiveness and/or speed with MB

ID: 7121

7.122 MEDICINE BALL DIAGONAL CHOPS (II)

SUMMARY

The Medicine Ball Diagonal Chops II is a ballistic exercise, which focuses on improving energy transfer for more powerful stroke production, body control & coordination, explosiveness of upper extremities, as well as improving skill & strength foundation for complex movements.

PURPOSE

1. Improving energy transfer for more powerful stroke production (e.g. the groundstrokes)
2. Improving body control & coordination
3. Improving explosiveness of upper extremities (neurological feedback loop); upper-body strength for stroke production (e.g. volley)
4. Improving skill and strength foundation for complex movements

DESCRIPTION

Coach/partner stands behind the athlete and tosses medicine Ball (MB) over the athlete's shoulder. Athlete needs to:

1. Take on **athletic stance** position (feet are in line with shoulders); **look over the shoulder** during catching phase
2. Catch MB over the shoulder with both hands
3. Immediately **rotate the trunk** to the other side
4. Explosively slam the MB into the ground (bounce-pass) back to the coach/partner
5. Rotate trunk back to the other side and **catch MB**

PRE-REQUISITE DRILLS

- MB Chops (I)

DEGREE OF DIFFICULTY

2

REQUIRED EQUIPMENT

- 8 lb – 25 lb Medicine Ball

KEY FACTORS

- Focus on perfect movement mechanics and explosiveness (maximum **force generation & speed**)
- Maintain balance

COMMON ERRORS

- Athlete loses stability during slamming
- Athlete achieves sub-maximal explosiveness and/or speed with MB

BREATH IN & OUT

- IN: During Catching
- OUT: During Slamming

ID: 7122

7.123 PLATE BLOCKS I

SUMMARY

The Plate Blocks I is a ballistic exercise, which focuses on improving energy transfer for more powerful stroke production, body control & coordination, explosiveness of upper extremities, as well as improving skill & strength foundation for complex movements utilizing a medicine ball and weight plate.

PURPOSE

1. Improving energy transfer for more powerful stroke production (e.g. the groundstrokes)
2. Improving body control & coordination
3. Improving explosiveness of upper extremities (neurological feedback loop); upper-body strength for stroke production (e.g. volley)
4. Improving skill and strength foundation for complex movements

DESCRIPTION

Coach/partner stands in front of athlete, holds a medicine ball (MB) in both hands and chest passes it towards the athlete.

1. Athlete holds the plate in both hands close to the chest
2. Athlete takes **serving position** (trailing foot is in front of leading foot); **look forward** during exercise
3. Coach/partner chest-passes MB towards chest of the athlete
4. Athlete explosively extends arms forward, hits MB with the plate, thereby returning MB to coach
5. Athlete returns plate toward chest
6. Coach **holds** the MB for **1 second** before passing it back to the athlete

PRE-REQUISITE DRILLS

- Bench Press

REQUIRED EQUIPMENT

- 4 lb – 12 lb Medicine Ball
- 10 lb – 45 lb Plate

DEGREE OF DIFFICULTY

1

KEY FACTORS

- Focus on perfect movement mechanics and explosiveness (maximum **distance**)
- Maintain balance

COMMON ERRORS

- Athlete moves back and forth during plate blocks
- Athlete achieves sub-maximal distance with MB
- Athlete loses stability during movement

BREATH IN & OUT

- IN: During Elbow Flexion
- OUT: During Elbow Extension

ID: 7123

7.124 PLATE BLOCKS II

SUMMARY

The Plate Blocks II is a ballistic exercise, which focuses on improving energy transfer for more powerful stroke production, body control & coordination, explosiveness of upper extremities, as well as improving skill & strength foundation for complex movements utilizing a medicine ball and weight plate.

PURPOSE

1. Improving energy transfer for more powerful stroke production (e.g. the groundstrokes)
2. Improving body control & coordination
3. Improving explosiveness of upper extremities (neurological feedback loop); Upper-body strength for stroke production (e.g. volley)
4. Improving skill and strength foundation for complex movements

DESCRIPTION

Coach/partner stands in front of athlete, holds a medicine ball (MB) in both hands and chest passes it towards the athlete.

1. Athlete holds the plate in both hands close to the chest
2. Athlete takes **serving position** (trailing foot is in front of leading foot); look forward during exercise
3. Coach/partner chest-passes MB towards chest of the athlete
4. Athlete explosively extends arms forwards, hits MB with the plate, thereby returning MB to coach
5. Athlete returns plate toward chest
6. Coach **instantly** returns the MB back to the athlete

BREATH IN & OUT

- IN: During Elbow Flexion
- OUT: During Elbow Extension

DEGREE OF DIFFICULTY

2

REQUIRED EQUIPMENT

- 4 lb – 12 lb Medicine Ball
- 10 lb – 45 lb Plate

KEY FACTORS

- Focus on perfect movement mechanics and explosiveness (maximum **distance**)
- Maintain balance

COMMON ERRORS

- Athlete moves back and forth during plate blocks
- Athlete achieves sub-maximal distance with MB
- Athlete loses stability during movement

PRE-REQUISITE DRILLS

- Plate Blocks I

ID: 7124

7.125 DIAGONAL LUNGE TO PLATE BLOCKS (III)

SUMMARY

The Diagonal Lunge to Plate Blocks III is a ballistic exercise, which focuses on improving energy transfer for more powerful stroke production, body control & coordination, explosiveness of upper extremities, as well as improving skill & strength foundation for complex movements utilizing a medicine ball and weight plate.

PURPOSE

1. Improving energy transfer for more powerful stroke production (e.g. the groundstrokes)
2. Improving body control & coordination
3. Improving explosiveness of upper extremities (neurological feedback loop); upper-body strength for stroke production (e.g. volley)
4. Improving skill and strength foundation for complex movements

DESCRIPTION

Coach/partner stands in front of athlete, holds a medicine ball (MB) in both hands and chest passes it towards the athlete.

1. Athlete holds the plate in both hands close to the chest
2. Athlete drops into a **diagonal lunge position**; **look forward** during exercise
3. Coach/partner chest-passes MB towards chest of the athlete
4. Athlete explosively extends arms forwards, hits MB with the plate, thereby returning MB to coach
5. Athlete returns plate toward chest
6. Coach **holds** the MB for **1 second** before passing it back to the athlete

PRE-REQUISITE DRILLS

- Lunge & Twist
- Plate Blocks (II)

REQUIRED EQUIPMENT

- 4 lb – 12 lb Medicine Ball
- 10 lb – 45 lb Plate

BREATH IN & OUT

- IN: During Elbow Flexion
- OUT: During Elbow Extension

DEGREE OF DIFFICULTY

3

KEY FACTORS

- Focus on perfect movement mechanics and explosiveness (maximum **distance**)
- Maintain balance

COMMON ERRORS

- Athlete moves back and forth during plate blocks
- Athlete achieves sub-maximal distance with MB
- Athlete loses stability during movement

ID: 7125

7.126 DIAGONAL LUNGE TO PLATE BLOCKS (IV)

SUMMARY

The Diagonal Lunge to Plate Blocks (IV) is a ballistic exercise, which focuses on improving energy transfer for more powerful stroke production, body control & coordination, explosiveness of upper extremities, as well as improving skill & strength foundation for complex movements utilizing a medicine ball and weight plate.

PURPOSE

1. Improving energy transfer for more powerful stroke production (e.g. the groundstrokes)
2. Improving body control & coordination
3. Improving explosiveness of upper extremities (neurological feedback loop); upper-body strength for stroke production (e.g. volley)
4. Improving skill and strength foundation for complex movements

DESCRIPTION

Coach/partner stands in front of athlete, holds a medicine ball (MB) in both hands and chest passes it towards the athlete.

1. Athlete holds the plate in both hands close to the chest
2. Athlete drops into a diagonal lunge position; look forward during exercise
3. Coach/partner chest-passes MB towards chest of the athlete
4. Athlete explosively extends arms forwards, hits MB with the plate, thereby returning MB to coach
5. Athlete quickly returns plate toward chest
6. Coach **instantly** returns the MB back to the athlete

DEGREE OF DIFFICULTY

4

REQUIRED EQUIPMENT

- 4 lb – 12 lb Medicine Ball
- 10 lb – 45 lb Plate

KEY FACTORS

- Focus on perfect movement mechanics and explosiveness (maximum **distance**)
- Maintain balance

COMMON ERRORS

- Athlete moves back and forth during plate blocks
- Athlete achieves sub-maximal distance with MB
- Athlete loses stability during movement

PRE-REQUISITE DRILLS

- Diagonal Lunge to Plate Blocks (III)

BREATH IN & OUT

- IN: During Elbow Flexion
- OUT: During Elbow Extension

ID: 7126

7.127 LOADED LOW-LEVEL TUCK JUMP I

SUMMARY

The Loaded Low-Level Tuck Jump I is a ballistic exercise, which focuses on improving quick start sequence, body control & coordination, foot speed-strength, as well as improving skill and strength foundation for complex movements utilizing agility rings and ankle weights.

PURPOSE

1. Improving quick start sequence (split-step to 1st step)
2. Improving body control & coordination
3. Improving foot speed-strength (neurological feedback loop)
4. Improving skill and strength foundation for complex movements

DESCRIPTION

Athlete wears ankle weights, stands up straight and needs to:

1. Position the feet under the shoulders
2. Place 2 agility rings in front of feet
3. Step into agility rings
4. Jump up with both legs **simultaneously** while **looking down** at the feet; flex knees **below** hip level
5. Land inside the agility rings

DEGREE OF DIFFICULTY

1

KEY FACTORS

- Focus on perfect movement mechanics and speed
- Jump with both feet simultaneously
- Keep knees below hip level
- Maintain balance – land in same location inside agility rings

COMMON ERRORS

- Athlete moves back and forth inside agility rings during jumps
- Athlete jumps at sub-maximal speed
- Athlete lands outside agility rings

BREATH IN & OUT

- IN: When landing
- OUT: During Jumping

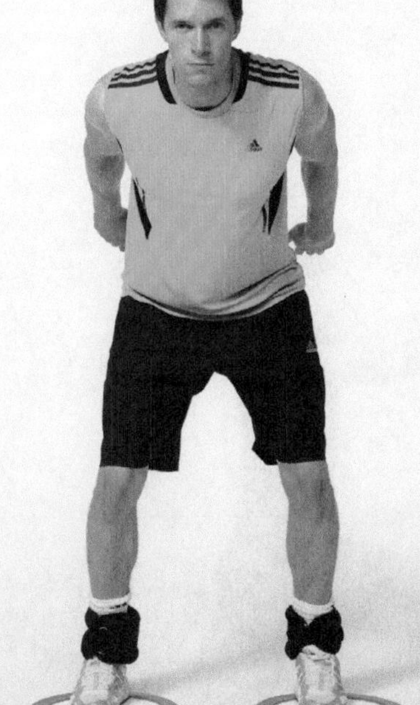

REQUIRED EQUIPMENT

ID: 7127

- 2 Agility Rings
- 5-10 lb Ankle Weights

7.128 LOADED LOW-LEVEL TUCK JUMP II

SUMMARY

The Loaded Low-Level Tuck Jump II is a ballistic exercise, which focuses on improving quick start sequence, body control & coordination, foot speed-strength, as well as improving skill and strength foundation for complex movements utilizing agility rings and ankle weights.

PURPOSE

1. Improving quick start sequence (split-step to 1st step)
2. Improving body control & coordination
3. Improving foot speed-strength (neurological feedback loop)
4. Improving skill and strength foundation for complex movements

DESCRIPTION

Athlete wears ankle weights stands up straight and needs to:

1. Position the feet under the shoulders
2. Place 2 agility rings in front of feet
3. Step into agility rings
4. Jump up with both legs simultaneously while **looking forward**; flex knees **below** hip level
5. Land inside the agility rings

PRE-REQUISITE DRILLS

- Loaded Low-Level Tuck Jumps I

DEGREE OF DIFFICULTY

2

KEY FACTORS

- Focus on perfect movement mechanics and speed
- Jump with both feet simultaneously
- Keep knees below hip level
- Maintain balance – land in same location inside agility rings

COMMON ERRORS

- Athlete looks down towards feet
- Athlete moves back and forth inside agility rings during jumps
- Athlete jumps at sub-maximal speed
- Athlete lands outside agility rings

BREATH IN & OUT

- IN: When landing
- OUT: During Jumping

REQUIRED EQUIPMENT

- 2 Agility Rings
- 5-10 lb Ankle Weights

7.129 LOADED LOW-LEVEL TUCK JUMP III

SUMMARY

The Loaded Low-Level Tuck Jump III is a ballistic exercise, which focuses on improving quick start sequence, body control & coordination as well as improving foot speed-strength utilizing a tennis ball and ankle weights.

PURPOSE

1. Improving quick start sequence (split-step to 1st step)
2. Improving body control & coordination
3. Improving foot speed-strength (neurological feedback loop)

DESCRIPTION

Coach throws tennis ball at athlete during jumps. Athlete wears ankle weights, stands up straight and needs to:

1. Position the feet under the shoulders
2. Jump up with both legs simultaneously while **looking forward**; flex knees below hip level
3. **Catch and return** tennis ball

PRE-REQUISITE DRILLS

- Loaded Low-Level Tuck Jumps II

BREATH IN & OUT

- IN: When landing
- OUT: During Jumping

DEGREE OF DIFFICULTY

3

REQUIRED EQUIPMENT

- Tennis Ball
- 5-10 lb Ankle Weights

KEY FACTORS

- Focus on perfect movement mechanics and speed
- Jump with both feet simultaneously
- Keep knees below hip level
- Maintain balance – land in same location

COMMON ERRORS

- Athlete looks down towards feet
- Athlete moves back and forth during jumps
- Athlete jumps at sub-maximal speed
- Athlete can't catch tennis ball

ID: 7129

7.130 LOADED MID-LEVEL TUCK JUMP I

SUMMARY

The Loaded Mid-Level Tuck Jump I is a ballistic exercise, which focuses on improving hip flexor speed, body control & coordination, foot speed-strength, as well as improving skill and strength foundation for complex movements utilizing agility rings and ankle weights.

PURPOSE

1. Improving sprinting and jumping capability (hip-flexor speed)
2. Improving body control & coordination
3. Improving foot speed-strength (neurological feedback loop)
4. Improving skill and strength foundation for complex movements

DESCRIPTION

Athlete wears ankle weights, stands up straight and needs to:

1. Position the feet under the shoulders
2. Place 2 agility rings in front of feet
3. Step into agility rings
4. Jump up with both legs **simultaneously** while **looking down** at the feet; flex knees **at hip level**
5. Land inside the agility rings

COMMON ERRORS

- Athlete keeps knees below hip level during jumping
- Athlete moves back and forth inside agility rings during jumps
- Athlete jumps at sub-maximal speed
- Athlete lands outside agility rings

DEGREE OF DIFFICULTY

1

REQUIRED EQUIPMENT

- 2 Agility Rings
- 5-10 lb Ankle Weights

KEY FACTORS

- Focus on perfect movement mechanics and speed
- Jump with both feet simultaneously
- Keep knees at hip level
- Maintain balance – land in same location inside agility rings

BREATH IN & OUT

- IN: When landing
- OUT: During Jumping

PRE-REQUISITE DRILLS

- Loaded Low-Level Tuck Jumps (I-III)

ID: 7130

7.131 LOADED MID-LEVEL TUCK JUMP II

SUMMARY

The Loaded Mid-Level Tuck Jump II is a ballistic exercise, which focuses on improving hip flexor speed, body control & coordination, foot speed-strength, as well as improving skill and strength foundation for complex movements utilizing agility rings and ankle weights.

PURPOSE

1. Improving sprinting and jumping capability (hip-flexor speed)
2. Improving body control & coordination
3. Improving foot speed-strength (neurological feedback loop)
4. Improving skill and strength foundation for complex movements

DESCRIPTION

Athlete wears ankle weights, stands up straight and needs to:

1. Position the feet under the shoulders
2. Place 2 agility rings in front of feet
3. Step into agility rings
4. Jump up with both legs simultaneously while **looking forward**; flex knees **at hip level**
5. Land inside the agility rings

PRE-REQUISITE DRILLS

- Loaded Mid-Level Tuck Jumps I

COMMON ERRORS

- Athlete looks down towards feet
- Athlete moves back and forth inside agility rings during jumps
- Athlete jumps at sub-maximal speed
- Athlete lands outside agility rings

BREATH IN & OUT

- IN: When landing
- OUT: During Jumping

DEGREE OF DIFFICULTY

2

REQUIRED EQUIPMENT

- 2 Agility Rings
- 5-10 lb Ankle Weights

KEY FACTORS

- Focus on perfect movement mechanics and speed
- Jump with both feet simultaneously
- Keep knees at hip level
- Maintain balance – land in same location inside agility rings

ID: 7131

7.132 LOADED MID-LEVEL TUCK JUMP III

SUMMARY

The Loaded Mid-Level Tuck Jump III is a ballistic exercise, which focuses on improving hip flexor speed, body control & coordination as well as improving foot speed-strength utilizing a tennis ball and ankle weights.

PURPOSE

1. Improving sprinting and jumping capability (hip-flexor speed)
2. Improving body control & coordination
3. Improving foot speed (neurological feedback loop)

DESCRIPTION

Coach throws tennis ball at athlete during jumps. Athlete wears ankle weights, stands up straight and needs to:

1. Position the feet under the shoulders
2. Jump up with both legs simultaneously while **looking forward**; flex knees **at hip level**
3. **Catch and return** tennis ball

PRE-REQUISITE DRILLS

- Loaded Low-Level Tuck Jumps II

BREATH IN & OUT

- IN: When landing
- OUT: During Jumping

DEGREE OF DIFFICULTY

3

REQUIRED EQUIPMENT

- Tennis Ball
- 5-10 lb Ankle Weights

KEY FACTORS

- Focus on perfect movement mechanics and speed
- Jump with both feet simultaneously
- Keep knees at hip level
- Maintain balance – land in same location

COMMON ERRORS

- Athlete looks down towards feet
- Athlete moves back and forth during jumps
- Athlete jumps at sub-maximal speed
- Athlete can't catch tennis ball

ID: 7132

7.133 LOADED HIGH-LEVEL TUCK JUMP I

SUMMARY

The Loaded High-Level Tuck Jump I is a ballistic exercise, which focuses on improving hip flexor speed, body control & coordination, foot speed-strength, flexibility, as well as improving skill and strength foundation for complex movements utilizing agility rings and ankle weights.

PURPOSE

1. Improving sprinting and jumping capability (hip-flexor speed)
2. Improving body control & coordination
3. Improving foot speed-strength (neurological feedback loop)
4. Improving flexibility (Glutes & Hamstrings)
5. Improving skill and strength foundation for complex movements

DESCRIPTION

Athlete wears ankle weights, stands up straight and needs to:

1. Position the feet under the shoulders
2. Place 2 agility rings in front of feet
3. Step into agility rings
4. Jump up with both legs **simultaneously** while **looking down** at the feet; flex knees **above hip level** (chest); don't go for maximum height but **speed**
5. Land inside the **agility rings**

COMMON ERRORS

- Athlete keeps knees below or at hip level during jumps
- Athlete moves back and forth inside agility rings during jumps
- Athlete jumps at sub-maximal speed
- Athlete lands outside agility rings

PRE-REQUISITE DRILLS

- Loaded Mid-Level Tuck Jumps (I-III)

BREATH IN & OUT

- IN: When landing
- OUT: During Jumping

DEGREE OF DIFFICULTY

1

REQUIRED EQUIPMENT

- 2 Agility Rings
- 5-10 lb Ankle Weights

KEY FACTORS

- Focus on perfect movement mechanics and speed
- Jump with both feet simultaneously
- Keep knees above hip level
- Maintain balance – land in same location inside agility rings

ID: 7133

7.134 LOADED HIGH-LEVEL TUCK JUMP II

SUMMARY

The Loaded High-Level Tuck Jump II is a ballistic exercise, which focuses on improving hip flexor speed, body control & coordination, foot speed-strength, flexibility, as well as improving skill and strength foundation for complex movements utilizing agility rings and ankle weights.

PURPOSE

1. Improving sprinting and jumping capability (hip-flexor speed)
2. Improving body control & coordination
3. Improving foot speed-strength (neurological feedback loop)
4. Improving flexibility (Glutes & Hamstrings)
5. Improving skill and strength foundation for complex movements

DESCRIPTION

Athlete wears ankle weights, stands up straight and needs to:

1. Position the feet under the shoulders
2. Place 2 agility rings in front of feet
3. Step into agility rings
4. Jump up with both legs simultaneously while **looking forward**; flex knees above hip level (chest); don't go for maximum height but speed
5. Land inside the agility rings

PRE-REQUISITE DRILLS

- Loaded Mid-Level Tuck Jumps (I)

DEGREE OF DIFFICULTY

2

REQUIRED EQUIPMENT

- 2 Agility Rings
- 5-10 lb Ankle Weights

KEY FACTORS

- Focus on perfect movement mechanics and speed
- Jump with both feet simultaneously
- Keep knees above hip level
- Maintain balance – land in same location inside agility rings

COMMON ERRORS

- Athlete keeps knees below or at hip level during jumps
- Athlete moves back and forth inside agility rings during jumps
- Athlete jumps at sub-maximal speed
- Athlete lands outside agility rings

BREATH IN & OUT

- IN: When landing
- OUT: During Jumping

ID: 7134

7.135 LOADED HIGH-LEVEL TUCK JUMP III

SUMMARY

The Loaded High-Level Tuck Jump III is a ballistic exercise, which focuses on improving hip flexor speed, body control & coordination, flexibility as well as improving foot speed-strength utilizing a tennis ball and ankle weights.

PURPOSE

1. Improving sprinting and jumping capability (hip-flexor speed)
2. Improving body control & coordination
3. Improving foot speed-strength (neurological feedback loop)
4. Improving flexibility (Glutes & Hamstrings)

DESCRIPTION

Coach throws tennis ball at athlete during jumps. Athlete wears ankle weights, stands up straight and needs to:

1. Position the feet under the shoulders
2. Jump up with both legs simultaneously while **looking forward**; flex knees above hip level (chest); don't go for maximum height but speed
3. **Catch and return** tennis ball

PRE-REQUISITE DRILLS

- Loaded Mid-Level Tuck Jump (II)

COMMON ERRORS

- Athlete keeps knees below or at hip level during jumps
- Athlete moves back and forth inside agility rings during jumps
- Athlete jumps at sub-maximal speed
- Athlete lands outside agility rings

DEGREE OF DIFFICULTY

3

REQUIRED EQUIPMENT

- 1 Tennis Ball
- 5-10 lb Ankle Weights

KEY FACTORS

- Focus on perfect movement mechanics and speed
- Jump with both feet simultaneously
- Keep knees above hip level
- Maintain balance – land in same location inside agility rings

BREATH IN & OUT

- IN: When landing
- OUT: During Jumping

ID: 7135

7.136 LOADED SINGLE-LEG LOW-LEVEL TUCK JUMP I

SUMMARY

The Loaded Single-Leg Low-Level Tuck Jump I is a ballistic exercise, which focuses on improving quick start sequence, body control & coordination, foot speed-strength, as well as improving skill and strength foundation for complex movements utilizing an agility ring and ankle weights.

PURPOSE

1. Improving quick start sequence (split-step to 1st step)
2. Improving body control & coordination
3. Improving foot speed-strength for low-height jumps (neurological feedback loop)
4. Improving skill and strength foundation for complex movements

DESCRIPTION

Athlete wears ankle weights, stands up straight and needs to:

1. Place 1 agility ring on the ground (flat surface)
2. Step into agility rings with one leg; other leg is off the ground
3. Jump up on 1 leg while **looking down** at the ground; flex knee **below hip level**
4. Land inside the agility ring
5. Switch leg and repeat

PRE-REQUISITE DRILLS

- Loaded Low-Level Tuck Jump (I)

BREATH IN & OUT

- IN: When landing
- OUT: During Jumping

DEGREE OF DIFFICULTY

1

REQUIRED EQUIPMENT

- 1 Agility Ring
- 5-10 lb Ankle Weights

KEY FACTORS

- Focus on perfect movement mechanics and speed
- Keep knees below hip level
- Maintain balance – land in same location inside agility rings

COMMON ERRORS

- Athlete moves back and forth inside agility ring during jumps
- Athlete jumps at sub-maximal speed
- Athlete lands outside agility ring

ID: 7136

7.137 LOADED SINGLE-LEG LOW-LEVEL TUCK JUMP II

SUMMARY

The Loaded Single-Leg Low-Level Tuck Jump II is a ballistic exercise, which focuses on improving quick start sequence, body control & coordination, foot speed-strength, as well as improving skill and strength foundation for complex movements utilizing an agility ring and ankle weights.

PURPOSE

1. Improving quick start sequence (split-step to 1st step)
2. Improving body control & coordination
3. Improving foot speed-strength for low-height jumps (neurological feedback loop)
4. Improving skill and strength foundation for complex movements

DESCRIPTION

Athlete wears ankle weights, stands up straight and needs to:

1. Place 1 agility ring on the ground (flat surface)
2. Step into agility rings with left leg; right leg is off the ground
3. Jump up on 1 leg while **looking forward**; flex knee below hip level
4. Land inside the agility ring
5. Switch leg and repeat

PRE-REQUISITE DRILLS

- Loaded Low-Level Tuck Jump (II)

BREATH IN & OUT

- IN: When landing
- OUT: During Jumping

DEGREE OF DIFFICULTY

2

REQUIRED EQUIPMENT

- 1 Agility Ring
- 5-10 lb Ankle Weights

KEY FACTORS

- Focus on perfect movement mechanics and speed
- Keep knees below hip level
- Maintain balance – land in same location inside agility rings

COMMON ERRORS

- Athlete moves back and forth inside agility ring during jumps
- Athlete jumps at sub-maximal speed
- Athlete lands outside agility ring

ID: 7137

7.138 LOADED SINGLE-LEG LOW-LEVEL TUCK JUMP III

SUMMARY

The Loaded Single-Leg Low-Level Tuck Jump II is a ballistic exercise, which focuses on improving quick start sequence, body control & coordination as well as improving foot speed-strength utilizing a tennis ball and ankle weights.

PURPOSE

1. Improving quick start sequence (split-step to 1st step)
2. Improving body control & coordination
3. Improving foot speed-strength for low-height jumps (neurological feedback loop)

DESCRIPTION

Coach throws tennis ball at athlete during jumps. Athlete wears ankle weights, stands up straight and needs to:

1. Start with the leg closest to the cone
2. Jump up on 1 leg while **looking forward**; flex knee below hip level
3. **Catch tennis ball and return**
4. Switch leg and repeat

PRE-REQUISITE DRILLS

- Loaded Low-Level Tuck Jump (III)

BREATH IN & OUT

- IN: When landing
- OUT: During Jumping

DEGREE OF DIFFICULTY

3

REQUIRED EQUIPMENT

- 1 Tennis Ball
- 5-10 lb Ankle Weights

KEY FACTORS

- Focus on perfect movement mechanics and speed
- Keep knees below hip level
- Maintain balance – land in same location inside agility rings

COMMON ERRORS

- Athlete moves back and forth inside agility ring during jumps
- Athlete jumps at sub-maximal speed
- Athlete lands outside agility ring

ID: 7138

7.139 LOADED SINGLE-LEG MID-LEVEL TUCK JUMP I

SUMMARY

The Loaded Single-Leg Mid-Level Tuck Jump I is a ballistic exercise, which focuses on improving quick start sequence, body control & coordination, foot speed-strength, as well as improving skill and strength foundation for complex movements utilizing an agility ring and ankle weights.

PURPOSE

1. Improving quick start sequence (split-step to 1st step)
2. Improving body control & coordination
3. Improving foot speed-strength for sub-maximal jumps (neurological feedback loop)
4. Improving skill and strength foundation for complex movements

DESCRIPTION

Athlete wears ankle weights, stands up straight and needs to:

1. Place 1 agility ring on the ground (flat surface)
2. Step into agility ring with left leg; right leg is off the ground
3. Jump up on 1 leg while **looking down** at the ground; flex knee **at hip level**
4. Land inside the **agility ring**
5. Switch leg and repeat

PRE-REQUISITE DRILLS

- Loaded Mid-Level Tuck Jump (I)

BREATH IN & OUT

- IN: When landing
- OUT: During Jumping

DEGREE OF DIFFICULTY

1

REQUIRED EQUIPMENT

- 1 Agility Ring
- 5-10 lb Ankle Weights

KEY FACTORS

- Focus on perfect movement mechanics and speed
- Keep knees at hip level
- Maintain balance – land in same location inside agility rings

COMMON ERRORS

- Athlete keeps knees below hip level during jumps
- Athlete moves back and forth inside agility rings during jumps
- Athlete jumps at sub-maximal speed
- Athlete lands outside agility rings

ID: 7139

7.140 LOADED SINGLE-LEG MID-LEVEL TUCK JUMP II

SUMMARY

The Loaded Single-Leg Mid-Level Tuck Jump II is a ballistic exercise, which focuses on improving quick start sequence, body control & coordination, foot speed-strength, as well as improving skill and strength foundation for complex movements utilizing an agility ring and ankle weights.

PURPOSE

1. mproving quick start sequence (split-step to 1st step)
2. Improving body control & coordination
3. Improving foot speed-strength for sub-maximal jumps (neurological feedback loop)
4. Improving skill and strength foundation for complex movement

DESCRIPTION

Athlete wears ankle weights, stands up straight and needs to:

1. Place 1 agility ring on the ground (flat surface)
2. Step into agility ring with left leg; right leg is off the ground
3. Jump up on 1 leg while **looking forward**; flex knee at hip level
4. Land inside the agility ring
5. Switch leg and repeat

PRE-REQUISITE DRILLS

- Loaded Mid-Level Tuck Jump (II)

BREATH IN & OUT

- IN: When landing
- OUT: During Jumping

DEGREE OF DIFFICULTY

2

REQUIRED EQUIPMENT

- 1 Agility Ring
- 5-10 lb Ankle Weights

KEY FACTORS

- Focus on perfect movement mechanics and speed
- Keep knees at hip level
- Maintain balance – land in same location inside agility rings

COMMON ERRORS

- Athlete keeps knees below hip level during jumps
- Athlete moves back and forth inside agility rings during jumps
- Athlete jumps at sub-maximal speed
- Athlete lands outside agility rings

ID: 7140

7.141 LOADED SINGLE-LEG MID-LEVEL TUCK JUMP III

SUMMARY

The Loaded Single-Leg Mid-Level Tuck Jump III is a ballistic exercise,which focuses on improving quick start sequence, body control & coordination as well as improving foot speed-strength utilizing a tennis ball and ankle weights.

PURPOSE

1. Improving quick start sequence (split-step to 1st step)
2. Improving body control & coordination
3. Improving foot speed-strength for sub-maximal jumps (neurological feedback loop)

DESCRIPTION

Coach throws tennis ball at athlete during jumps. Athlete wears ankle weights, stands up straight and needs to:

1. Jump up on 1 leg while **looking forward**; flex knee at hip level
2. **Catch tennis ball and return**
3. Switch leg and repeat

PRE-REQUISITE DRILLS

- Loaded Mid-Level Tuck Jump (III)

BREATH IN & OUT

- IN: When landing
- OUT: During Jumping

DEGREE OF DIFFICULTY

3

REQUIRED EQUIPMENT

- 1 Tennis Ball
- 5-10 lb Ankle Weights

KEY FACTORS

- Focus on perfect movement mechanics and speed
- Keep knee at hip level
- Maintain balance – land in same location inside agility rings

COMMON ERRORS

- Athlete keeps knees below hip level during jumps
- Athlete moves back and forth inside agility rings during jumps
- Athlete jumps at sub-maximal speed
- Athlete lands outside agility rings

ID: 7141

7.142 LOADED SINGLE-LEG HIGH-LEVEL TUCK JUMP I

SUMMARY

The Loaded Single-Leg High-Level Tuck Jump I is a ballistic exercise, which focuses on improving hip flexor speed, body control & coordination, foot speed-strength, flexibility, as well as improving skill and strength foundation for complex movements utilizing an agility ring and ankle weights.

PURPOSE

1. Improving hip-flexor speed
2. Improving body control & coordination
3. Improving foot speed-strength (neurological feedback loop)
4. Improving flexibility (Glutes & Hamstrings)
5. Improving skill and strength foundation for complex movements

DESCRIPTION

Athlete wears ankle weights, stands up straight and needs to:

1. Place 1 agility ring on the ground (flat surface)
2. Step into agility ring with left leg; right leg is off the ground
3. Jump up on 1 leg while **looking down** at the ground; flex knee **above hip level** (chest)
4. Land inside the **agility ring**
5. Switch leg and repeat

PRE-REQUISITE DRILLS

- Loaded High-Level Tuck Jump (I)

BREATH IN & OUT

- IN: When landing
- OUT: During Jumping

DEGREE OF DIFFICULTY

1

REQUIRED EQUIPMENT

- 1 Agility Ring
- 5-10 lb Ankle Weights

KEY FACTORS

- Focus on perfect movement mechanics and speed
- Keep knees above hip level
- Maintain balance – land in same location inside agility rings

COMMON ERRORS

- Athlete keeps knees below or at hip level during jumps
- Athlete moves back and forth inside agility rings during jumps
- Athlete jumps at sub-maximal speed
- Athlete lands outside agility rings

ID: 7142

7.143 LOADED SINGLE-LEG HIGH-LEVEL TUCK JUMP II

SUMMARY

The Loaded Single-Leg High-Level Tuck Jump II is a ballistic exercise, which focuses on improving hip flexor speed, body control & coordination, foot speed-strength, flexibility, as well as improving skill and strength foundation for complex movements utilizing an agility ring and ankle weights.

PURPOSE

1. Improving hip-flexor speed
2. Improving body control & coordination
3. Improving foot speed-strength (neurological feedback loop)
4. Improving flexibility (Glutes & Hamstrings)
5. Improving skill and strength foundation for complex movements

DESCRIPTION

Athlete wears ankle weight, stands up straight and needs to:

1. Place 1 agility ring on the ground (flat surface)
2. Step into agility ring with left leg; right leg is off the ground
3. Jump up on 1 leg while looking forward; flex knee above hip level (chest)
4. Land inside the agility ring
5. Switch leg and repeat

PRE-REQUISITE DRILLS

- Loaded High-Level Tuck Jump (II)

BREATH IN & OUT

- IN: When landing
- OUT: During Jumping

DEGREE OF DIFFICULTY

2

REQUIRED EQUIPMENT

- 1 Agility Ring
- 5-10 lb Ankle Weights

KEY FACTORS

- Focus on perfect movement mechanics and speed
- Keep knee above hip level
- Maintain balance – land in same location inside agility rings

COMMON ERRORS

- Athlete keeps knees below or at hip level during jumps
- Athlete moves back and forth inside agility rings during jumps
- Athlete jumps at sub-maximal speed
- Athlete lands outside agility rings

ID: 7143

7.144 LOADED SINGLE-LEG HIGH-LEVEL TUCK JUMP III

SUMMARY

The Loaded Single-Leg High-Level Tuck Jump III is a ballistic exercise, which focuses on improving hip flexor speed, body control & coordination, flexibility as well as improving foot speed-strength utilizing a tennis ball and ankle weights.

PURPOSE

1. Improving hip-flexor speed
2. Improving body control & coordination
3. Improving foot speed-strength (neurological feedback loop)
4. Improving flexibility (Glutes & Hamstrings)

DESCRIPTION

Coach throws tennis ball at athlete during jumps. Athlete wears ankle weights, stands up straight and needs to:

1. Jump up on 1 leg while **looking forward**; flex knee above hip level
2. **Catch tennis ball and return**
3. Switch leg and repeat

PRE-REQUISITE DRILLS

- Loaded High-Level Tuck Jump (III)

BREATH IN & OUT

- IN: When landing
- OUT: During Jumping

DEGREE OF DIFFICULTY

3

REQUIRED EQUIPMENT

- 1 Tennis Ball
- 5-10 lb Ankle Weights

KEY FACTORS

- Focus on perfect movement mechanics and speed
- Keep knee above hip level
- Maintain balance – land in same location inside agility rings

COMMON ERRORS

- Athlete keeps knees below or at hip level during jumps
- Athlete moves back and forth inside agility rings during jumps
- Athlete jumps at sub-maximal speed
- Athlete lands outside agility rings

ID: 7144

7.145 LOADED LOW-LEVEL LATERAL TUCK JUMP I

SUMMARY

The Loaded Low-Level Lateral Tuck Jump I is a ballistic exercise, which focuses on improving quick start sequence along the baseline, body control & coordination, foot speed-strength as well as improving skill and strength foundation for complex movements utilizing a cone, agility rings and ankle weights.

PURPOSE

1. Improving quick start sequence (split-step to 1st side-step)
2. Improving body control & coordination
3. Improving foot speed-strength (neurological feedback loop)
4. Improving skill and strength foundation for complex movements

DESCRIPTION

Athlete wears ankle weights, stands up straight and needs to:

1. Place 2 agility rings on the ground two shoulder-widths apart and put a cone in between the 2 rings
2. Place the **outside foot** inside the agility ring
3. Position the feet under the shoulders
4. Jump back and forth over the cone with both legs **simultaneously** while **looking down** at the feet; flex knees **below hip level**
5. **Outside foot** lands inside the agility rings

PRE-REQUISITE DRILLS

- Loaded Low-Level Tuck Jump (I)

BREATH IN & OUT

- IN: When landing
- OUT: During Jumping

DEGREE OF DIFFICULTY

1

REQUIRED EQUIPMENT

- 2 Agility Rings
- One 2 inch cone
- 5-10 lb Ankle Weights

KEY FACTORS

- Focus on perfect movement mechanics and speed; **raise knees to go over the cone**
- Maintain upper body over the cone during jumps
- Jump with both feet simultaneously
- Keep knees below hip level
- Maintain balance – land in same location inside agility rings

COMMON ERRORS

- Athlete moves heels towards buttocks instead of raising the knees when jumping over the cone
- Feet are too close together during jumps
- Athlete moves outside agility rings during jumps
- Athlete jumps at sub-maximal speed

ID: 7145

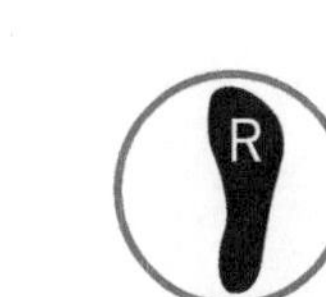

7.146 LOADED LOW-LEVEL LATERAL TUCK JUMP II

SUMMARY

The Loaded Low-Level Lateral Tuck Jump II is a ballistic exercise, which focuses on improving quick start sequence along the baseline, body control & coordination, foot speed-strength as well as improving skill and strength foundation for complex movements utilizing a cone, agility rings and ankle weights.

PURPOSE

1. Improving quick start sequence (split-step to 1st side-step)
2. Improving body control & coordination
3. Improving foot speed-strength (neurological feedback loop)
4. Improving skill and strength foundation for complex movements

DESCRIPTION

Athlete wears ankle weights, stands up straight and needs to:

1. Place 2 agility rings on the ground two shoulder-widths apart and put a cone in between the 2 rings
2. Place the outside foot inside the agility ring
3. Position the feet under the shoulders
4. Jump back and forth over the cone with both legs simultaneously while **looking forward**; flex knees below hip level
5. Outside foot lands inside the agility rings

PRE-REQUISITE DRILLS

- Loaded Low-Level Tuck Jump (II)

BREATH IN & OUT

- IN: When landing
- OUT: During Jumping

DEGREE OF DIFFICULTY

2

REQUIRED EQUIPMENT

- 2 Agility Rings
- One 2 inch cone
- 5-10 lb Ankle Weights

KEY FACTORS

- Focus on perfect movement mechanics and speed; raise knees to go over the cone
- Maintain upper body over the cone during jumps
- Jump with both feet simultaneously
- Keep knees below hip level
- Maintain balance – land in same location inside agility rings

COMMON ERRORS

- Athlete moves heels towards buttocks instead of raising the knees when jumping over the cone
- Feet are too close together during jumps
- Athlete moves outside agility rings during jumps
- Athlete jumps at sub-maximal speed

ID: 7146

7.147 LOADED LOW-LEVEL LATERAL TUCK JUMP III

SUMMARY

The Loaded Low-Level Lateral Tuck Jump III is a ballistic exercise, which focuses on improving quick start sequence along the baseline, body control & co-ordination as well as improving foot speed-strength utilizing a cone, tennis ball and ankle weights.

PURPOSE

1. Improving quick start sequence (split-step to 1st side-step)
2. Improving body control & coordination
3. Improving foot speed-strength (neurological feedback loop)

DESCRIPTION

Coach throws tennis ball at athlete during jumps. Athlete wears ankle weights, stands up straight and needs to:

1. Place a cone on the ground
2. Stand next to the cone
3. Position the feet under the shoulders
4. Jump back and forth over the cone with both legs simultaneously while **looking forward**; flex knees below hip level
5. **Catch and return tennis ball**

PRE-REQUISITE DRILLS

- Loaded Low-Level Tuck Jump (III)

BREATH IN & OUT

- IN: When landing
- OUT: During Jumping

DEGREE OF DIFFICULTY

3

REQUIRED EQUIPMENT

- 1 Tennis Ball
- One 2 inch cone
- 5-10 lb Ankle Weights

KEY FACTORS

- Focus on perfect movement mechanics and speed; raise knees to go over the cone
- Maintain upper body over the cone during jumps
- Jump with both feet simultaneously
- Keep knees below hip level
- Maintain balance – land in line with cones

COMMON ERRORS

- Athlete moves heels towards buttocks instead of raising the knees when jumping over the cone
- Feet are too close together during jumps
- Athlete doesn't land in same spot during jumps
- Athlete jumps at sub-maximal speed

ID: 7147

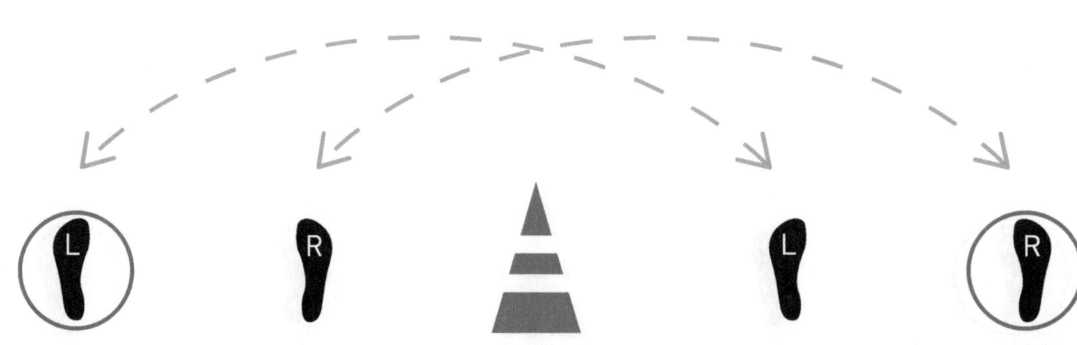

7.148 LOADED MID-LEVEL LATERAL TUCK JUMP I

SUMMARY

The Loaded Mid-Level Lateral Tuck Jump I is a ballistic exercise, which focuses on improving quick start sequence along the baseline, body control & coordination, foot speed-strength as well as improving skill and strength foundation for complex movements utilizing a cone, agility rings and ankle weights.

PURPOSE

1. Improving quick start sequence (split-step to 1st side-step)
2. Improving body control & coordination
3. Improving foot speed-strength (neurological feedback loop)
4. Improving skill and strength foundation for complex movements

DESCRIPTION

Athlete wears ankle weights, stands up straight and needs to:

1. Place 2 agility rings on the ground two shoulder-widths apart and put a cone in between the 2 rings
2. Place the outside foot inside the agility ring
3. Position the feet under the shoulders
4. Jump back and forth over the cone with both legs **simultaneously** while **looking down** at the feet; flex knees **at hip level**
5. Outside foot lands inside the agility rings

PRE-REQUISITE DRILLS

- Loaded Mid-Level Tuck Jump (I)

BREATH IN & OUT

- IN: When landing
- OUT: During Jumping

DEGREE OF DIFFICULTY

1

REQUIRED EQUIPMENT

- 2 Agility Rings
- One 4 inch cone
- 5-10 lb Ankle Weights

KEY FACTORS

- Focus on perfect movement mechanics and speed; raise knees to go over the cone
- Maintain upper body over the cone during jumps
- Jump with both feet simultaneously
- Keep knees at hip level
- Maintain balance – land in same location inside agility rings

COMMON ERRORS

- Athlete moves heels towards buttocks instead of raising the knees when jumping over the cone
- Feet are too close together during jumps
- Athlete moves outside agility rings during jumps
- Athlete jumps at sub-maximal speed

ID: 7148

7.149 LOADED MID-LEVEL LATERAL TUCK JUMP II

SUMMARY

The Loaded Mid-Level Lateral Tuck Jump II is a ballistic exercise, which focuses on improving quick start sequence along the baseline, body control & coordination, foot speed-strength as well as improving skill and strength foundation for complex movements utilizing a cone, agility rings and ankle weights.

PURPOSE

1. Improving quick start sequence (split-step to 1st side-step)
2. Improving body control & coordination
3. Improving foot speed-strength (neurological feedback loop)
4. Improving skill and strength foundation for complex movements

DESCRIPTION

Athlete wears ankle weights, stands up straight and needs to:

1. Place 2 agility rings on the ground two shoulder-widths apart and put a cone in between the 2 rings
2. Place the outside foot inside the agility ring
3. Position the feet under the shoulders
4. Jump back and forth over the cone with both legs simultaneously while **looking forward**; flex knees at hip level
5. Outside foot lands inside the agility rings

PRE-REQUISITE DRILLS

- Loaded Mid-Level Tuck Jump (II)

BREATH IN & OUT

- IN: When landing
- OUT: During Jumping

DEGREE OF DIFFICULTY

2

REQUIRED EQUIPMENT

- 2 Agility Rings
- One 4 inch cone
- 5-10 lb Ankle Weights

KEY FACTORS

- Focus on perfect movement mechanics and speed; raise knees to go over the cone
- Maintain upper body over the cone during jumps
- Jump with both feet simultaneously
- Keep knees at hip level
- Maintain balance – land in same location inside agility rings

COMMON ERRORS

- Athlete moves heels towards buttocks instead of raising the knees when jumping over the cone
- Feet are too close together during jumps
- Athlete moves outside agility rings during jumps
- Athlete jumps at sub-maximal speed

ID: 7149

7.150 LOADED MID-LEVEL LATERAL TUCK JUMP III

SUMMARY

The Loaded Mid-Level Lateral Tuck Jump III is a ballistic exercise, which focuses on improving quick start sequence along the baseline, body control & coordination as well as improving foot speed-strength utilizing a cone, tennis ball and ankle weights.

PURPOSE

1. Improving quick start sequence (split-step to 1st side-step)
2. Improving body control & coordination
3. Improving foot speed-strength (neurological feedback loop)

DESCRIPTION

Coach throws tennis ball at athlete during jumps. Athlete wears ankle weights, stands up straight and needs to:

1. Place a cone on the ground
2. Stand next to the cone
3. Position the feet under the shoulders
4. Jump back and forth over the cone with both legs simultaneously while **looking forward**; flex knees at hip level
5. **Catch and return tennis ball**

PRE-REQUISITE DRILLS

- Loaded Mid-Level Tuck Jump (III)

BREATH IN & OUT

- IN: When landing
- OUT: During Jumping

DEGREE OF DIFFICULTY

3

REQUIRED EQUIPMENT

- 1 Tennis Ball
- One 4 inch cone
- 5-10 lb Ankle Weights

KEY FACTORS

- Focus on perfect movement mechanics and speed; raise knees to go over the cone
- Maintain upper body over the cone during jumps
- Jump with both feet simultaneously
- Keep knees at hip level
- Maintain balance – land in line with cones

COMMON ERRORS

- Athlete moves heels towards buttocks instead of raising the knees when jumping over the cone
- Feet are too close together during jumps
- Athlete doesn't land in same spot during jumps
- Athlete jumps at sub-maximal speed

ID: 7150

7.151 LOADED HIGH-LEVEL LATERAL TUCK JUMP I

SUMMARY

The Loaded High-Level Lateral Tuck Jump I is a ballistic exercise, which focuses on improving quick start sequence along the baseline, body control & coordination, foot speed-strength as well as improving skill and strength foundation for complex movements utilizing a cone, agility rings and ankle weights.

PURPOSE

1. Improving quick start sequence (split-step to 1st side-step)
2. Improving body control & coordination
3. Improving foot speed-strength (neurological feedback loop)
4. Improving skill and strength foundation for complex movements

DESCRIPTION

Athlete wears ankle weights, stands up straight and needs to:

1. Place 2 agility rings on the ground two shoulder-widths apart and put a cone in between the 2 rings
2. Place the outside foot inside the agility ring
3. Position the feet under the shoulders
4. Jump back and forth over the cone with both legs **simultaneously** while **looking down** at the feet; flex knees **above hip level**
5. Outside foot lands inside the agility rings

PRE-REQUISITE DRILLS

- Loaded High-Level Tuck Jump (I)

BREATH IN & OUT

- IN: When landing
- OUT: During Jumping

DEGREE OF DIFFICULTY

1

REQUIRED EQUIPMENT

- 2 Agility Rings
- One 6 Inch Cone
- 5-10 lb Ankle Weights

KEY FACTORS

- Focus on perfect movement mechanics and speed; raise knees to go over the cone
- Maintain upper body over the cone during jumps
- Jump with both feet simultaneously
- Keep knees above hip level
- Maintain balance – land in same location inside agility rings

COMMON ERRORS

- Athlete moves heels towards buttocks instead of raising the knees when jumping over the cone
- Feet are too close together during jumps
- Athlete moves outside agility rings during jumps
- Athlete jumps at sub-maximal speed

ID: 7151

7.152 LOADED HIGH-LEVEL LATERAL TUCK JUMP II

SUMMARY

The Loaded High-Level Lateral Tuck Jump II is a ballistic exercise, which focuses on improving quick start sequence along the baseline, body control & coordination, foot speed-strength as well as improving skill and strength foundation for complex movements utilizing a cone, agility rings and ankle weights.

PURPOSE

1. Improving quick start sequence (split-step to 1st side-step)
2. Improving body control & coordination
3. Improving foot speed-strength (neurological feedback loop)
4. Improving skill and strength foundation for complex movements

DESCRIPTION

Athlete wears ankle weights, stands up straight an needs to:

1. Place 2 agility rings on the ground two shoulder-widths apart and put a cone in between the 2 rings
2. Place the outside foot inside the agility ring
3. Position the feet under the shoulders
4. Jump back and forth over the cone with both legs simultaneously while **looking forward**; flex knees above hip level
5. Outside foot lands inside the agility rings

PRE-REQUISITE DRILLS

- Loaded High-Level Tuck Jump (II)

BREATH IN & OUT

- IN: When landing
- OUT: During Jumping

DEGREE OF DIFFICULTY

2

REQUIRED EQUIPMENT

- 2 Agility Rings
- One 6 Inch Cone
- 5-10 lb Ankle Weights

KEY FACTORS

- Focus on perfect movement mechanics and speed; raise knees to go over the cone
- Maintain upper body over the cone during jumps
- Jump with both feet simultaneously
- Keep knees above hip level
- Maintain balance – land in same location inside agility rings

COMMON ERRORS

- Athlete moves heels towards buttocks instead of raising the knees when jumping over the cone
- Feet are too close together during jumps
- Athlete moves outside agility rings during jumps
- Athlete jumps at sub-maximal speed

ID: 7152

7.153 LOADED HIGH-LEVEL LATERAL TUCK JUMP III

SUMMARY

The Loaded High-Level Lateral Tuck Jump III is a ballistic exercise, which focuses on improving quick start sequence along the baseline, body control & co-ordination as well as improving foot speed-strength utilizing a cone, tennis ball and ankle weights.

PURPOSE

1. Improving quick start sequence (split-step to 1st side-step)
2. Improving body control & coordination
3. Improving foot speed-strength (neurological feedback loop)

DESCRIPTION

Coach throws tennis ball at athlete during jumps.

Athlete wears ankle weights, stands up straight and needs to:

1. Place a cone on the ground
2. Stand next to the cone
3. Position the feet under the shoulders
4. Jump back and forth over the cone with both legs simultaneously while **looking forward**; flex knees above hip level
5. **Catch and return tennis ball**

PRE-REQUISITE DRILLS

- Loaded High-Level Tuck Jump (III)

BREATH IN & OUT

- IN: When landing
- OUT: During Jumping

DEGREE OF DIFFICULTY

3

REQUIRED EQUIPMENT

- 1 Tennis Ball
- One 6 Inch Cone
- 5-10 lb Ankle Weights

KEY FACTORS

- Focus on perfect movement mechanics and speed; raise knees to go over the cone
- Maintain upper body over the cone during jumps
- Jump with both feet simultaneously
- Keep knees above hip level
- Maintain balance – land in line with cones

COMMON ERRORS

- Athlete moves heels towards buttocks instead of raising the knees when jumping over the cone
- Feet are too close together during jumps
- Athlete doesn't land in same spot during jumps
- Athlete jumps at sub-maximal speed

ID: 7153

7.154 LOADED SINGLE LEG LL LATERAL TUCK JUMP I

SUMMARY

The Loaded Single-Leg Low-Level Lateral Tuck Jump I is a ballistic exercise, which focuses on improving quick start sequence along the baseline, body control & coordination, foot speed-strength as well as improving skill and strength foundation for complex movements utilizing a cone, agility rings and ankle weights.

DESCRIPTION

Athlete wears ankle weights, stands up straight and needs to:

1. Place 2 agility rings on the ground shoulder-widths apart and put a cone in between the 2 rings
2. Stand on one leg (the leg closest to the cone) and place it inside the agility ring
3. Jump back and forth over the cone while **looking down** at the feet; flex knees **below hip level**

Note: Also perform exercise by jumping with the leg farthest away from the cone.

PRE-REQUISITE DRILLS

- Loaded Low-Level Tuck Jump (I)

BREATH IN & OUT

- IN: When landing
- OUT: During Jumping

PURPOSE

1. Improving quick start sequence (split-step to 1st side-step)
2. Improving body control & coordination
3. Improving foot speed-strength (neurological feedback loop)
4. Improving skill and strength foundation for complex movements

DEGREE OF DIFFICULTY

1

KEY FACTORS

- Focus on perfect movement mechanics and speed; raise knees to go over the cone
- Maintain upper body over the cone during jumps
- Keep knees below hip level
- Maintain balance – land inside agility ring

COMMON ERRORS

- Athlete moves heels towards buttocks instead of raising the knees when jumping over the cone
- Athlete moves outside agility rings during jumps
- Athlete jumps at sub-maximal speed

REQUIRED EQUIPMENT

- 2 Agility Rings
- One 2 Inch Cone
- 5-10 lb Ankle Weights

ID: 7154

7

7.155 LOADED SINGLE LEG LL LATERAL TUCK JUMP II

SUMMARY

The Loaded Single-Leg Low-Level Lateral Tuck Jump II is a ballistic exercise, which focuses on improving quick start sequence along the baseline, body control & coordination, foot speed-strength as well as improving skill and strength foundation for complex movements utilizing a cone, agility rings and ankle weights.

PURPOSE

1. Improving quick start sequence (split-step to 1st side-step)
2. Improving body control & coordination
3. Improving foot speed-strength (neurological feedback loop)
4. Improving skill and strength foundation for complex movements

DESCRIPTION

Athlete wears ankle weights, stands up straight and needs to:

1. Place 2 agility rings on the ground shoulder-widths apart and put a cone in between the 2 rings
2. Stand on one leg (the leg closest to the cone) and place it inside the agility ring
3. Jump back and forth over the cone while **looking forward**; flex knees below hip level

Note: Also perform exercise by jumping with the leg farthest away from the cone.

PRE-REQUISITE DRILLS

- Loaded Low-Level Tuck Jump (II)

BREATH IN & OUT

- IN: When landing
- OUT: During Jumping

DEGREE OF DIFFICULTY

2

REQUIRED EQUIPMENT

- 2 Agility Rings
- One 2 Inch Cone
- 5-10 lb Ankle Weights

KEY FACTORS

- Focus on perfect movement mechanics and speed; raise knees to go over the cone
- Maintain upper body over the cone during jumps
- Keep knees below hip level
- Maintain balance – land inside agility ring

COMMON ERRORS

- Athlete moves heels towards buttocks instead of raising the knees when jumping over the cone
- Athlete moves outside agility rings during jumps
- Athlete jumps at sub-maximal speed

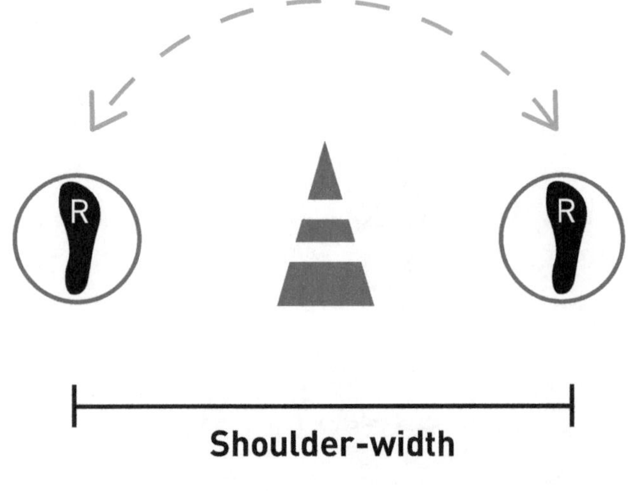

ID: 7155

7.156 LOADED SINGLE LEG LL LATERAL TUCK JUMP III

SUMMARY

The Loaded Single-Leg Low-Level Lateral Tuck Jump III is a ballistic exercise, which focuses on improving quick start sequence along the baseline, body control & coordination as well as improving foot speed-strength utilizing a cone, tennis ball and ankle weights.

PURPOSE

1. Improving quick start sequence (split-step to 1st side-step)
2. Improving body control & coordination
3. Improving foot speed-strength (neurological feedback loop)

DESCRIPTION

Coach throws tennis ball at athlete during jumps. Athlete wears ankle weights, stands up straight and needs to:

1. Place a cone on the ground
2. Stand on one leg (the leg closest to the cone)
3. Jump back and forth over the cone while **looking forward**; flex knees below hip level
4. **Catch and return tennis ball**

Note: Also perform exercise by jumping with the leg farthest away from the cone.

PRE-REQUISITE DRILLS

- Loaded Low-Level Tuck Jump (III)

BREATH IN & OUT

- IN: When landing
- OUT: During Jumping

DEGREE OF DIFFICULTY

3

REQUIRED EQUIPMENT

- 1 Tennis Ball
- One 2 Inch Cone
- 5-10 lb Ankle Weights

KEY FACTORS

- Focus on perfect movement mechanics and speed; raise knees to go over the cone
- Maintain upper body over the cone during jumps
- Keep knees below hip level
- Maintain balance – land inside agility ring

COMMON ERRORS

- Athlete moves heels towards buttocks instead of raising the knees when jumping over the cone
- Athlete doesn't land in same spot during jumps
- Athlete jumps at sub-maximal speed

ID: 7156

7.157 LOADED SINGLE LEG ML LATERAL TUCK JUMP I

SUMMARY

The Loaded Single-Leg Mid-Level Lateral Tuck Jump I is a ballistic exercise, which focuses on improving body control & coordination, foot speed-strength as well as improving skill and strength foundation for complex movements utilizing a cone, agility rings and ankle weights.

PURPOSE

1. Improving body control & coordination
2. Improving foot speed-strength (neurological feedback loop)
3. Improving skill and strength foundation for complex movements

DESCRIPTION

Athlete wears ankle weights, stands up straight and needs to:

1. Place 2 agility rings on the ground shoulder-widths apart and put a cone in between the 2 rings
2. Stand on one leg (the leg closest to the cone) and place it inside the agility ring
3. Jump back and forth over the cone while **looking down** at the feet; flex knees **at hip level**

Note: Also perform exercise by jumping with the leg farthest away from the cone.

PRE-REQUISITE DRILLS

- Loaded Mid-Level Tuck Jump (I)

BREATH IN & OUT

- IN: When landing
- OUT: During Jumping

DEGREE OF DIFFICULTY

1

REQUIRED EQUIPMENT

- 2 Agility Rings
- One 4 Inch Cone
- 5-10 lb Ankle Weights

KEY FACTORS

- Focus on perfect movement mechanics and speed; raise knees to go over the cone
- Maintain upper body over the cone during jumps
- Keep knees at hip level
- Maintain balance – land inside agility ring

COMMON ERRORS

- Athlete moves heels towards buttocks instead of raising the knees when jumping over the cone
- Athlete moves outside agility rings during jumps
- Athlete jumps at sub-maximal speed

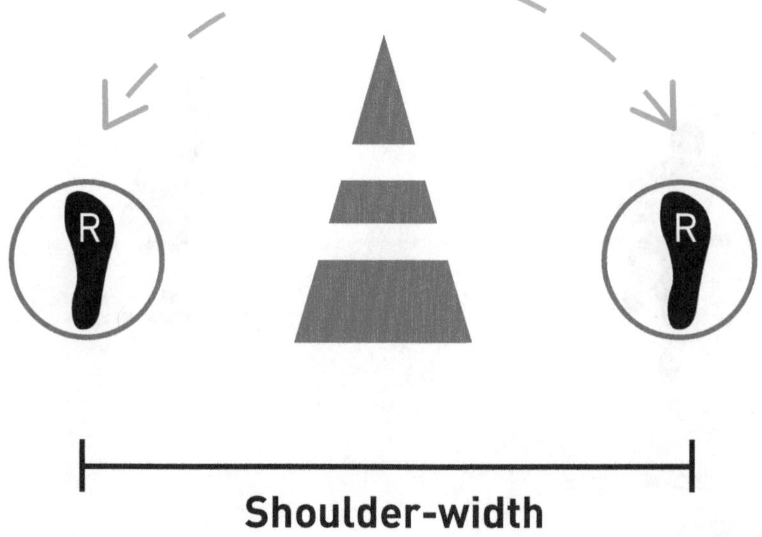

ID: 7157

7.158 LOADED SINGLE LEG ML LATERAL TUCK JUMP II

SUMMARY

The Loaded Single-Leg Mid-Level Lateral Tuck Jump II is a ballistic exercise, which focuses on improving body control & coordination, foot speed-strength as well as improving skill and strength foundation for complex movements utilizing a cone, agility rings and ankle weights.

PURPOSE

1. Improving body control & coordination
2. Improving foot speed-strength (neurological feedback loop)
3. Improving skill and strength foundation for complex movements

DESCRIPTION

Athlete wears ankle weights, stands up straight and needs to:

1. Place 2 agility rings on the ground shoulder-widths apart and put a cone in between the 2 rings
2. Stand on one leg (the leg closest to the cone) and place it inside the agility ring
3. Jump back and forth over the cone while **looking forward**; flex knees at hip level

Note: Also perform exercise by jumping with the leg farthest away from the cone.

PRE-REQUISITE DRILLS

- Loaded Mid-Level Tuck Jump (II)

BREATH IN & OUT

- IN: When landing
- OUT: During Jumping

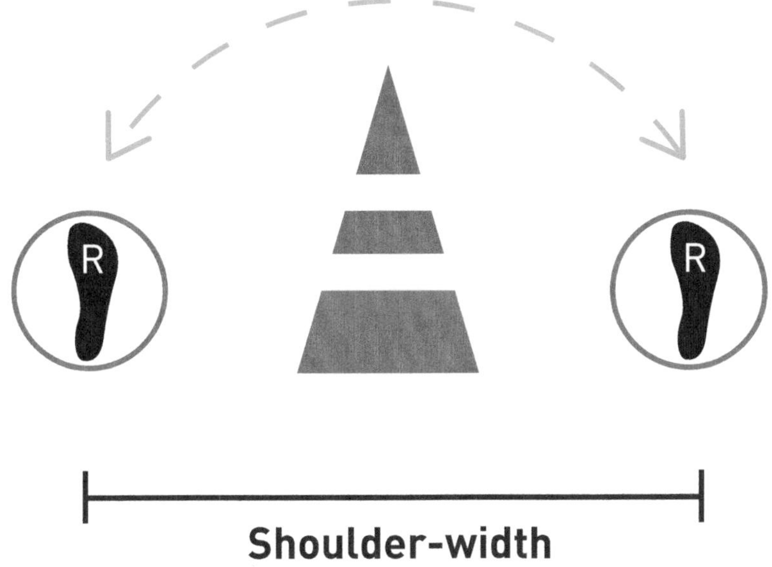

DEGREE OF DIFFICULTY

2

REQUIRED EQUIPMENT

- 2 Agility Rings
- One 4 Inch Cone
- 5-10 lb Ankle Weights

KEY FACTORS

- Focus on perfect movement mechanics and speed; raise knees to go over the cone
- Maintain upper body over the cone during jumps
- Keep knees at hip level
- Maintain balance – land inside agility ring

COMMON ERRORS

- Athlete moves heels towards buttocks instead of raising the knees when jumping over the cone
- Athlete moves outside agility rings during jumps
- Athlete jumps at sub-maximal speed

ID: 7158

7.159 LOADED SINGLE LEG ML LATERAL TUCK JUMP III

SUMMARY

The Loaded Single-Leg Mid-Level Lateral Tuck Jump III is a ballistic exercise, which focuses on improving body control & coordination as well as improving foot speed-strength utilizing a cone, tennis ball and ankle weights.

PURPOSE

1. Improving body control & coordination
2. Improving foot speed-strength (neurological feedback loop)

DESCRIPTION

Coach throws tennis ball at athlete during jumps. Athlete wears ankle weights, stands up straight and needs to:

1. Place a cone on the ground
2. Stand on one leg (the leg closest to the cone)
3. Jump back and forth over the cone while **looking forward**; flex knees at hip level
4. **Catch and return tennis ball**

Note: Also perform exercise by jumping with the leg farthest away from the cone.

PRE-REQUISITE DRILLS

- Loaded Mid-Level Tuck Jump (III)

BREATH IN & OUT

- IN: When landing
- OUT: During Jumping

DEGREE OF DIFFICULTY

3

REQUIRED EQUIPMENT

- 1 Tennis Ball
- One 4 Inch Cone
- 5-10 lb Ankle Weights

KEY FACTORS

- Focus on perfect movement mechanics and speed; raise knees to go over the cone
- Maintain upper body over the cone during jumps
- Keep knees at hip level
- Maintain balance – land inside agility ring

COMMON ERRORS

- Athlete moves heels towards buttocks instead of raising the knees when jumping over the cone
- Athlete doesn't land in same spot during jumps
- Athlete jumps at sub-maximal speed

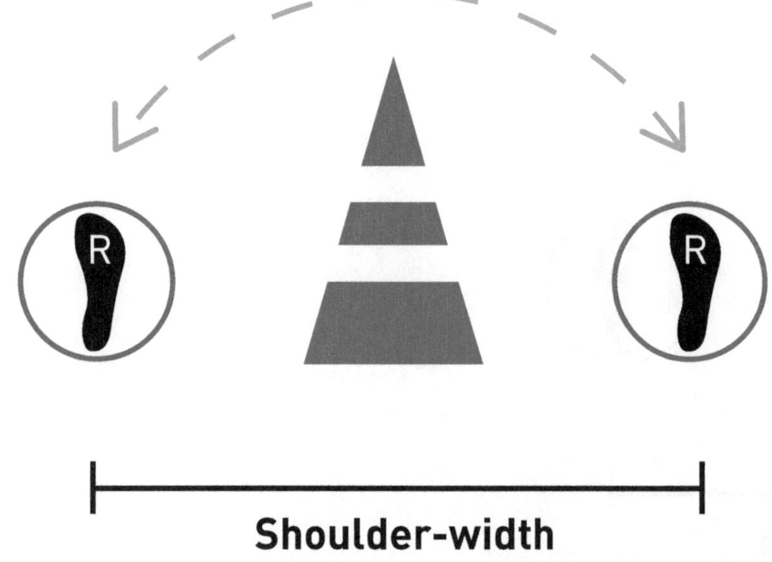

ID: 7159

7.160 LOADED SINGLE-LEG HL LATERAL TUCK JUMP I

SUMMARY

The Loaded Single-Leg High-Level Lateral Tuck Jump I is a ballistic exercise, which focuses on improving body control & coordination, foot speed-strength as well as improving skill and strength foundation for complex movements utilizing a cone, agility rings and ankle weights.

PURPOSE

1. Improving body control & coordination
2. Improving foot speed-strength (neurological feedback loop)
3. Improving skill and strength foundation for complex movements

DESCRIPTION

Athlete wears ankle weights, stands up straight and needs to:

1. Place 2 agility rings on the ground shoulder-widths apart and put a cone in between the 2 rings
2. Stand on one leg (the leg closest to the cone) and place it inside the agility ring
3. Jump back and forth over the cone while **looking down** at the feet; flex knees **above hip level** (chest)

Note: Also perform exercise by jumping with the leg farthest away from the cone.

DEGREE OF DIFFICULTY

1

REQUIRED EQUIPMENT

- 2 Agility Rings
- One 6 Inch Cone
- 5-10 lb Ankle Weight

KEY FACTORS

- Focus on perfect movement mechanics and speed; raise knees to go over the cone
- Maintain upper body over the cone during jumps
- Keep knees above hip level (chest)
- Maintain balance – land inside agility ring

PRE-REQUISITE DRILLS

- Loaded High-Level Tuck Jump (I)

BREATH IN & OUT

- IN: When landing
- OUT: During Jumping

COMMON ERRORS

- Athlete moves heels towards buttocks instead of raising the knees when jumping over the cone
- Athlete moves outside agility rings during jumps
- Athlete jumps at sub-maximal speed

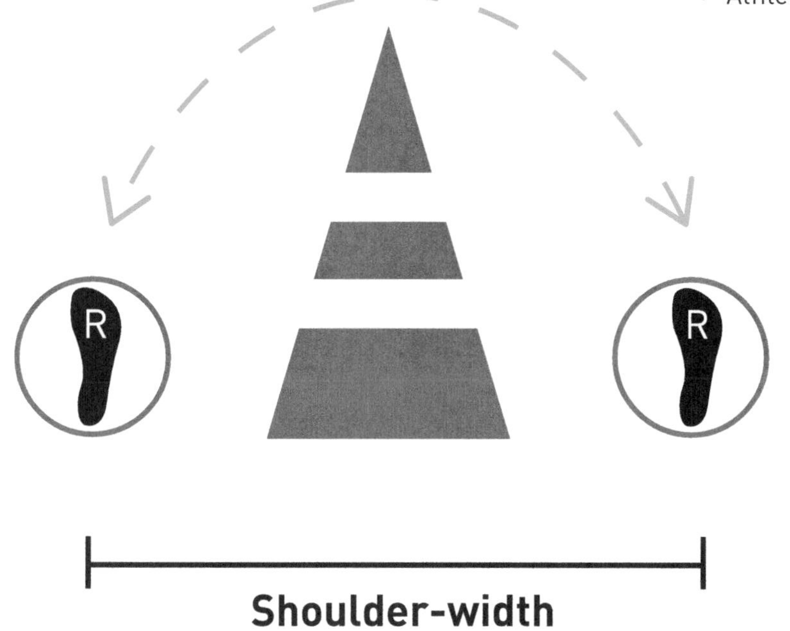

ID: 7160

7.161 LOADED SINGLE-LEG HL LATERAL TUCK JUMP II

SUMMARY

The Loaded Single-Leg High-Level Lateral Tuck Jump II is a plyometric exercise, which focuses on improving body control & coordination, foot speed-strength as well as improving skill and strength foundation for complex movements utilizing a cone, agility rings and ankle weights.

PURPOSE

1. Improving body control & coordination
2. Improving foot speed-strength (neurological feedback loop)
3. Improving skill and strength foundation for complex movements

DESCRIPTION

Athlete wears ankle weights, stands up straight and needs to:

1. Place 2 agility rings on the ground shoulder-widths apart and put a cone in between the 2 rings
2. Stand on one leg (the leg closest to the cone) and place it inside the agility ring
3. Jump back and forth over the cone while **looking forward**; flex knees above hip level

Note: Also perform exercise by jumping with the leg farthest away from the cone.

PRE-REQUISITE DRILLS

- Loaded High-Level Tuck Jump (II)

BREATH IN & OUT

- IN: When landing
- OUT: During Jumping

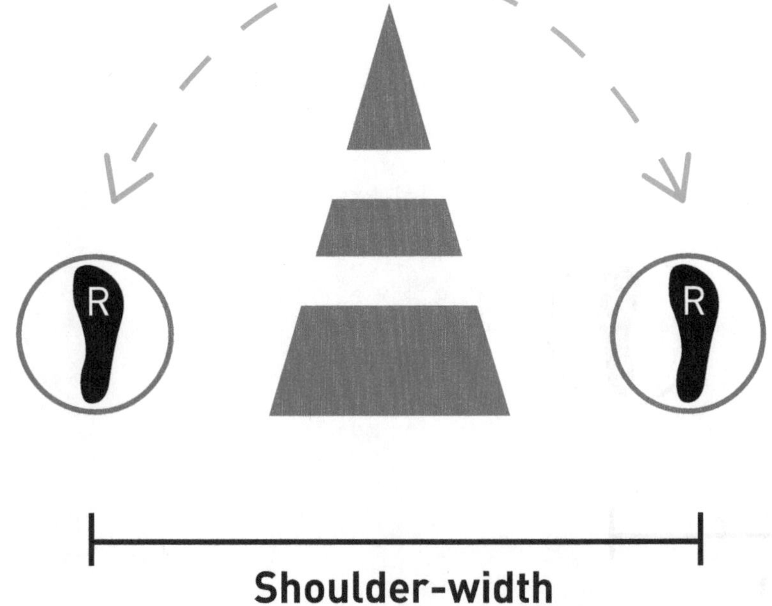

DEGREE OF DIFFICULTY

2

REQUIRED EQUIPMENT

- 2 Agility Rings
- One 6 Inch Cone
- 5-10 lb Ankle Weights

KEY FACTORS

- Focus on perfect movement mechanics and speed; raise knees to go over the cone
- Maintain upper body over the cone during jumps
- Keep knees above hip level
- Maintain balance – land inside agility ring

COMMON ERRORS

- Athlete moves heels towards buttocks instead of raising the knees when jumping over the cone
- Athlete moves outside agility rings during jumps
- Athlete jumps at sub-maximal speed

ID: 7161

7.162 LOADED SINGLE-LEG HL LATERAL TUCK JUMP III

SUMMARY

The Loaded Single-Leg High-Level Lateral Tuck Jump III is a plyometric exercise, which focuses on improving body control & coordination as well as improving foot speed utilizing a cone, tennis ball and ankle weights.

PURPOSE

1. Improving body control & coordination
2. Improving foot speed-strength (neurological feedback loop)

DESCRIPTION

Coach throws tennis ball at athlete during jumps. Athlete wears ankle weights, stands up straight and needs to:

1. Place a cone on the ground
2. Stand on one leg (the leg closest to the cone)
3. Jump back and forth over the cone while **looking forward**; flex knees above hip level
4. **Catch and return tennis ball**

Note: Also perform exercise by jumping with the leg farthest away from the cone.

PRE-REQUISITE DRILLS

- Loaded High-Level Tuck Jump (III)

BREATH IN & OUT

- IN: When landing
- OUT: During Jumping

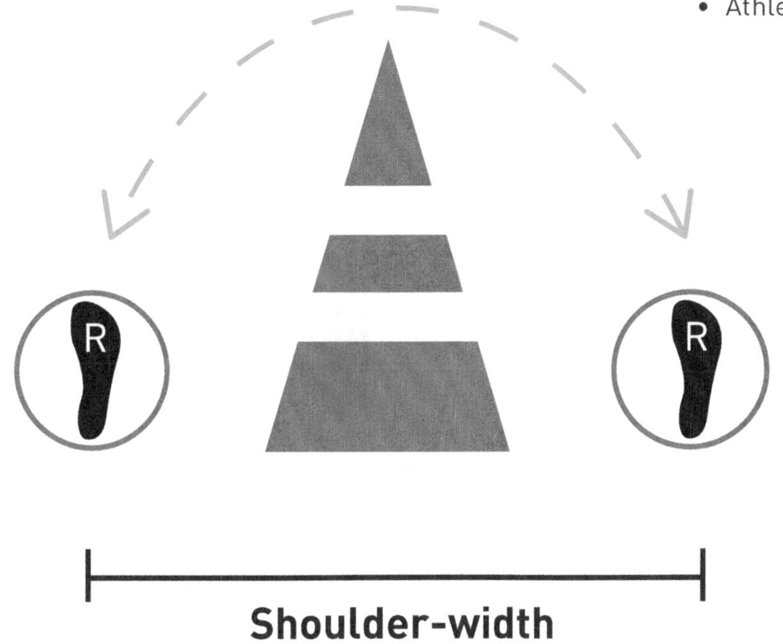

DEGREE OF DIFFICULTY

3

REQUIRED EQUIPMENT

- 1 Tennis Ball
- One 6 Inch Cone
- 5-10 lb Ankle Weights

KEY FACTORS

- Focus on perfect movement mechanics and speed; raise knees to go over the cone
- Maintain upper body over the cone during jumps
- Keep knees above hip level
- Maintain balance – land inside agility ring

COMMON ERRORS

- Athlete moves heels towards buttocks instead of raising the knees when jumping over the cone
- Athlete doesn't land in same spot during jumps
- Athlete jumps at sub-maximal speed

ID: 7162

7.163 BROAD JUMP (I)

SUMMARY

The Broad Jump I is a ballistic exercise, which focuses on developing neural pathways for explosive running, body control & coordination as well as improving skill and strength foundation for complex movements utilizing agility rings.

PURPOSE

1. Developing neural pathways for explosive running capability (neurological feedback loop)
2. Improving balance (body control) & coordination
3. Improving skill and strength foundation for complex movements

DESCRIPTION

1. Stand up straight and position the feet under the hips; arms remain close to the body
2. Place 2 agility rings in front of the feet and step inside
3. Flex hips while **simultaneously** swinging arms posterior (counter-move arm swing); **look forward**
4. Jump forcefully forward; swing arms anterior and **over the head**; fully extend hips
5. Land on both legs into a **squat** position; **look down** to the ground during landing; lean forward with upper body

DEGREE OF DIFFICULTY

1

REQUIRED EQUIPMENT

- 2 Agility Rings

PRE-REQUISITE DRILLS

- Squat

ID: 7163

KEY FACTORS

- Focus on perfect movement mechanics (hip flexion to full hip extension to hip flexion) not on distance; if full hip extension cannot be attained note what degree of extension can be achieved
- Maintain balance: land on both feet simultaneously into squat position
- Maintain balance – land inside agility ring

COMMON ERRORS

- Athlete leans back during landing and falls on the buttocks

BREATH IN & OUT

- IN: During initial hip flexion
- OUT: During Jumping

7.164 BROAD JUMP (II)

SUMMARY

The Broad Jump II is a ballistic exercise, which focuses on developing neural pathways for explosive running, body control & coordination as well as improving skill and strength foundation for complex movements utilizing agility rings.

PURPOSE

1. Developing neural pathways for explosive running capability (neurological feedback loop)
2. Improving balance (body control) & coordination
3. Improving skill and strength foundation for complex movements

DESCRIPTION

1. Stand up straight and position the feet under the hips; arms remain close to the body
2. Place 2 agility rings in front of the feet and step inside
3. Flex hips while simultaneously swinging arms posteriorly (counter-move arm swing); **look forward**
4. Jump forcefully forward; swing arms anteriorly and **over the head**; fully extend hips
5. Land on both legs into a squat position; **look forward** during landing; lean forward with upper body
6. Place 2 agility rings on the ground at initial landing position
7. Repeat and land inside agility rings

PRE-REQUISITE DRILLS

- Broad Jump (I)

BREATH IN & OUT

- IN: During initial hip flexion
- OUT: During Jumping

DEGREE OF DIFFICULTY

2

REQUIRED EQUIPMENT

- 4 Agility Rings

KEY FACTORS

- Focus on perfect movement mechanics (hip flexion to full hip extension to hip flexion) not on distance; if full hip extension cannot be attained note what degree of extension can be achieved
- Maintain balance: land on both feet simultaneously into squat position

COMMON ERRORS

- Athlete leans back during landing and falls on the buttocks
- Athlete lands outside agility rings

ID: 7164

7.165 BROAD JUMP: SINGLE-LEG LANDING (I)

SUMMARY

The Broad Jump: Single-Leg Landing I is a ballistic exercise, which focuses on developing neural pathways for explosive running, body control & coordination as well as improving skill and strength foundation for complex movements utilizing agility rings.

PURPOSE

1. Developing neural pathways for explosive running capability (neurological feedback loop)
2. Improving balance (body control) & coordination
3. Improving skill and strength foundation for complex movements

DESCRIPTION

1. Stand up straight and position the feet under the hips; arms remain close to the body
2. Place 2 agility rings in front of the feet and step inside
3. Flex hips while simultaneously swinging arms posteriorly (counter-move arm swing); **look forward**
4. Jump forcefully forward; swing arms anteriorly and over the head; fully extend hips
5. Land on one leg into a single-leg squat position; **look down** to the ground during landing; lean forward with upper body
6. Place 1 agility ring on the ground at initial landing position
7. Repeat and land inside agility ring

PRE-REQUISITE DRILLS

- Single-Leg Squat
- Broad Jump (II)

BREATH IN & OUT

- IN: During initial hip flexion
- OUT: During Jumping

DEGREE OF DIFFICULTY

1

REQUIRED EQUIPMENT

- 3 Agility Rings

KEY FACTORS

- Focus on perfect movement mechanics (hip flexion to full hip extension to hip flexion) not on distance; if full hip extension cannot be attained watch what degree of extension can be achieved
- Maintain balance: land on one foot into single-leg squat position

COMMON ERRORS

- Athlete leans back during landing and cannot maintain balance
- Athlete lands outside agility rings

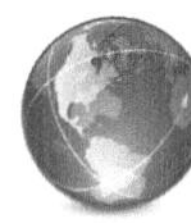

ID: 7165

7.166 BROAD JUMP: SINGLE-LEG LANDING (II)

SUMMARY

The Broad Jump: Single-Leg Landing II is a ballistic exercise, which focuses on developing neural pathways for explosive running, body control & coordination as well as improving skill and strength foundation for complex movements utilizing agility rings.

PURPOSE

1. Developing neural pathways for explosive running capability (neurological feedback loop)
2. Improving balance (body control) & coordination
3. Improving skill and strength foundation for complex movements

DESCRIPTION

1. Stand up straight and position the feet under the hips; arms remain close to the body
2. Place 2 agility rings in front of the feet and step inside
3. Flex hips while simultaneously swinging arms posteriorly (counter-move arm swing); **look forward**
4. Jump forcefully forward; swing arms anteriorly and **over the head**; fully extend hips
5. Land on one leg into a **single-leg squat** position; **look forward** during landing; lean forward with upper body
6. Place 1 agility ring on the ground at initial landing position
7. Repeat and land inside agility ring

PRE-REQUISITE DRILLS

- Broad Jump (III)

BREATH IN & OUT

- IN: During initial hip flexion
- OUT: During Jumping

DEGREE OF DIFFICULTY

2

REQUIRED EQUIPMENT

- 3 Agility Rings

KEY FACTORS

- Focus on perfect movement mechanics (hip flexion to full hip extension to hip flexion) not on distance; if full hip extension cannot be attained watch what degree of extension can be achieved
- Maintain balance: land on one foot into single-leg squat position

COMMON ERRORS

- Athlete leans back during landing and cannot maintain balance
- Athlete lands outside agility rings

ID: 7166

7.167 DOUBLE BROAD JUMP (III)

SUMMARY

The Double Broad Jump III is a ballistic exercise, which focuses on improving energy transfer for explosive running, stability & coordination as well as improving skill and strength foundation for complex movements utilizing agility rings.

DESCRIPTION

1. Stand up straight and position the feet under the hips; arms remain close to the body
2. Place 2 agility rings in front of the feet and step inside
3. Flex hips while simultaneously swinging arms posteriorly (counter-move arm swing); **look forward**
4. Jump forcefully forward; swing arms anteriorly and over the head; fully extend hips
5. Land on **both legs**
6. Instantly perform another broad jump
7. Land on **both legs** into a **squat position**; **look forward** during landing; lean forward with upper body
8. Place 2 agility rings on the ground at landing position
9. Repeat and land inside agility rings

PRE-REQUISITE DRILLS

- Broad Jump (II)

PURPOSE

1. Improving energy transfer for explosive running capability (neurological feedback loop)
2. Improving stability (body control) & coordination
3. Improving skill and strength foundation for complex movements

DEGREE OF DIFFICULTY

3

REQUIRED EQUIPMENT

- 4 Agility Rings

KEY FACTORS

- Focus on perfect movement mechanics (hip flexion to full hip extension to hip flexion) **and** distance
- Maintain balance: land on both feet simultaneously into squat position

COMMON ERRORS

- Athlete leans back during landing and falls on the buttocks
- Athlete lands outside agility rings

BREATH IN & OUT

- IN: During initial hip flexion
- OUT: During Jumping

ID: 7167

7.168 DOUBLE BROAD JUMP: SINGLE-LEG LANDING (IV)

SUMMARY

The Double Broad Jump IV is a ballistic exercise, which focuses on improving energy transfer for explosive running, stability & coordination as well as improving skill and strength foundation for complex movements utilizing agility rings.

PURPOSE

1. Improving energy transfer for explosive running capability (neurological feedback loop)
2. Improving stability (body control) & coordination
3. Improving skill and strength foundation for complex movements

DESCRIPTION

1. Stand up straight and position the feet under the hips; arms remain close to the body
2. Place 2 agility rings in front of the feet and step inside
3. Flex hips while simultaneously swinging arms posteriorly (counter-move arm swing); **look forward**
4. Jump forcefully forward; swing arms anteriorly and over the head; fully extend hips
5. Land on **both legs**
6. Instantly perform another broad jump
7. Land on **one leg** into a single-leg squat position; **look forward** during landing; lean forward with upper body
8. Place 1 agility ring on the ground at initial landing position
9. Repeat and land inside agility ring

BREATH IN & OUT

- IN: During initial hip flexion
- OUT: During Jumping

DEGREE OF DIFFICULTY

4

REQUIRED EQUIPMENT

- 3 Agility Rings

KEY FACTORS

- Focus on perfect movement mechanics (hip flexion to full hip extension to hip flexion) and distance
- Maintain balance: land on one foot into single-leg squat position

COMMON ERRORS

- Athlete leans back during landing and falls on the buttocks
- Athlete cannot maintain same distance during repetitions
- Athlete lands outside agility rings

PRE-REQUISITE DRILLS

- Broad Jump: Single-Leg Landing (II)

ID: 7168

7.169 DOUBLE BROAD JUMP: SINGLE-LEG (III)

SUMMARY

The Double Broad Jump: Single-Leg III is a ballistic exercise, which focuses on improving energy transfer for explosive running, stability & coordination as well as improving skill and strength foundation for complex movements utilizing agility rings.

PURPOSE

1. Improving energy transfer for explosive running capability (neurological feedback loop)
2. Improving stability (body control) & coordination
3. Improving skill and strength foundation for complex movements

DESCRIPTION

1. Stand up straight and position the feet under the hips; arms remain close to the body
2. Place 2 agility rings in front of the feet and step inside
3. Flex hips while simultaneously swinging arms posteriorly (counter-move arm swing); **look forward**
4. Jump forcefully forward; swing arms anteriorly and over the head; fully extend hips
5. Land on **one leg**
6. Instantly drive through with the same leg and perform another broad jump
7. Land on **both legs** into a squat position; **look forward** during landing; lean forward with upper body
8. Place 2 agility rings on the ground at landing position
9. Repeat and land inside agility rings

BREATH IN & OUT

- IN: During initial hip flexion
- OUT: During Jumping

DEGREE OF DIFFICULTY

3

REQUIRED EQUIPMENT

- 4 Agility Rings

KEY FACTORS

- Focus on perfect movement mechanics (hip flexion to full hip extension to hip flexion) and distance
- Maintain balance: land on both feet into single-leg squat position

COMMON ERRORS

- Athlete leans back during landing and falls on the buttocks
- Athlete cannot maintain same distance during repetitions
- Athlete lands outside agility ring

PRE-REQUISITE DRILLS

- Broad Jump: Single-Leg Landing (II)

ID: 7169

7.170 DOUBLE BROAD JUMP: SINGLE-LEG (IV)

SUMMARY

The Double Broad Jump: Single-Leg IV is a ballistic exercise, which focuses on improving energy transfer for explosive running, stability & coordination as well as improving skill and strength foundation for complex movements utilizing agility rings.

PURPOSE

1. Improving energy transfer for explosive running capability (neurological feedback loop)
2. Improving stability (body control) & coordination
3. Improving skill and strength foundation for complex movements

DESCRIPTION

1. Stand up straight and position the feet under the hips; arms remain close to the body
2. Place 2 agility rings in front of the feet and step inside
3. Flex hips while simultaneously swinging arms posteriorly (counter-move arm swing); **look forward**
4. Jump forcefully forward; swing arms anteriorly and over the head; fully extend hips
5. Land on **one leg**
6. Instantly drive through with the same leg and perform another broad jump
7. Land on **one leg** into a single-leg squat position; **look forward** during landing; lean forward with upper body
8. Place 1 agility ring on the ground at initial landing position
9. Repeat and land inside agility ring

PRE-REQUISITE DRILLS

- Double Broad Jump: Single-Leg Landing (III)

BREATH IN & OUT

- IN: During initial hip flexion
- OUT: During Jumping

DEGREE OF DIFFICULTY

4

REQUIRED EQUIPMENT

- 4 Agility Rings

KEY FACTORS

- Focus on perfect movement mechanics (hip flexion to full hip extension to hip flexion) and distance
- Maintain balance: land on one foot into single-leg squat position

COMMON ERRORS

- Athlete leans back during landing and falls on the buttocks
- Athlete cannot maintain same distance during repetitions
- Athlete lands outside agility ring

ID: 7170

7.171 TRIPLE BROAD JUMP (V)

SUMMARY

The Triple Broad Jump V is a ballistic exercise, which focuses on improving energy transfer for explosive running, stability & coordination as well as improving skill and strength foundation for complex movements utilizing agility rings.

PURPOSE

1. Improving energy transfer for explosive running capability (neurological feedback loop)
2. Improving stability (body control) & coordination
3. Improving skill and strength foundation for complex movements

DESCRIPTION

1. Stand up straight and position the feet under the hips; arms remain close to the body
2. Place 2 agility rings in front of the feet and step inside
3. Flex hips while simultaneously swinging arms posteriorly (counter-move arm swing); **look forward**
4. Jump forcefully forward; swing arms anteriorly and over the head; fully extend hips
5. Land on **one leg**
6. Instantly drive through with the same leg and perform another broad jump
7. Land on the **other** leg
8. Instantly drive through with the same leg and perform another broad jump
9. Land on **both legs** into a squat position; **look forward** during landing; lean forward with upper body
10. Place 2 agility rings on the ground at landing position
11. Repeat and land inside agility rings

DEGREE OF DIFFICULTY

5

REQUIRED EQUIPMENT

- 4 Agility Rings

KEY FACTORS

- Focus on perfect movement mechanics (hip flexion to full hip extension to hip flexion) and distance
- Maintain balance: land on both feet simultaneously into squat position

COMMON ERRORS

- Athlete leans back during landing and falls on the buttocks
- Athlete cannot maintain same distance during repetitions
- Athlete lands outside agility rings

PRE-REQUISITE DRILLS

- Double Broad Jump: Single-Leg (IV)

BREATH IN & OUT

- IN: During initial hip flexion
- OUT: During Jumping

ID: 7171

PLYOMETRICS

Plyometric training revolves around improving **contact transition speed** by exploiting the benefits of the **stretch-shortening cycle (SSC)**; the SSC is being used to enhance power production during a given jump, throw, pass, lift, etc. The SSC is initiated when the targeted muscle groups of a specific action undergo eccentric deceleration, such as the quadriceps and gluteals when landing from a jump. During eccentric deceleration, the muscle groups needed to accelerate the body away from that position, i.e. to jump back up off of the ground, are lengthened, while the muscle groups aiding in the smooth deceleration of the landing are shortened (hamstrings/hip flexors). Simply stated, this interaction of simultaneous shortening and lengthening produces a 'spring' of potential energy that can be unleashed during the concentric acceleration (the rebound jump) if the transition time, also referred to as **amortization phase**, between the landing and the rebound action is limited. Most research suggests the transition time needs to be less than ¼ (0.25 sec) of a second. In other words, during a plyometric exercise the athlete tries to accelerate an object (body) as fast as possible, moving its center of mass rapidly from point A to point B; velocity of the movement needs to be at a maximum. Therefore, the shorter the ground contacts, the faster the neural transfer. For optimal neural feedback development the amortization phase needs to be less than 0.25 seconds.

Oftentimes athletes cannot do plyometric exercises in true plyometric fashion because they are too slow. Since plyometrics require ground contact time of less than 0.25 seconds, resistance (weight) has to be on the lower end; otherwise the athlete wastes time decelerating and hence exceeds 0.25 seconds of ground contact.

It is important to ensure that before the athlete starts doing the exercises at maximum speed that the exercises are done correctly with regards to form. Therefore, try to carefully follow the exercise descriptions.

The plyometric exercises in this section have the following subcategories:

- Rapid Counter-Movement Box Jumps & Box Rebounds
- Light Concentric Medicine Ball Throws
- High-Speed Rebounds

For effective athletic development the exercises have been categorized based on degree of difficulty:

1. Beginner
2. Intermediate
3. Advanced
4. Professional

RAPID COUNTER-MOVEMENT BOX JUMPS & BOX REBOUNDS

Depth jumps consist of the athlete stepping off boxes of various heights, landing on the ground, and minimizing ground contact time to jump onto another object or in another direction. The athlete is going to accelerate the body, thereby maximizing nervous system efficiency for a single repetition with duplicable repetitions to follow; they are "controlled" jumps since they are isolated jumps. Box rebounds, on the other hand, require the athlete to jump in place and repeatedly stabilize unstable movements.

Depth jumps are extremely effective at neural pathway development for concentric acceleration, eccentric deceleration, and overall foot speed. It is desirable for athletes to have quick feet for running and jumping purposes and the various depth jumps and rebounds will aide in speed development. Also, single leg depth jumps are much more difficult and warrant lower boxes; use boxes as low as 2 inches for single-leg activity during skill acquisition phase. The single leg jumps are also very good for calf development and strengthening. Therefore they can be implemented as "plyo-calves" using rebounds of a different nature. It's more beneficial to use the jumps to work on the calves (plyo-calves) than simply doing plantar flexion calve raises at the end of a workout. It's not necessary to have a complete range of dorsi flexion to plantar flexion in order to work the calves because during running athletes don't have complete dorsi flexion (it's rather minimal). It's more beneficial to get the calves to have maximum force output from a flat surface! It doesn't mean that athletes should avoid complete range of motion during training; instead the goal is to combine the two.

Lateral jumps are more challenging for the athlete because there is a vertical component and a horizontal component. It's also more challenging because the athletes need the center of mass to hover, to the best of their ability, over the base of support (the end jump points).

So, if the athlete can keep the center of mass in between the jump points, the movement is going to be easier to control. For most athletes the center of mass will gravitate towards the terminal ends of the base of support during jumps. Therefore, it is going to be very challenging for them to get back over to the other side.

In general, box jumps are flexibility limited; the athlete should therefore be able to jump his/her hip/waist height before engaging in higher box jumps. Height itself is not an indicator of desirable speed.

An athlete´s being able to jump up on a 40 inch box is not necessarily that impressive because his/her relative size must be taken into account. When considering how high an athlete needs to raise his/her center of mass, it should be noted that a short person jumping up to 40 inches has to raise the center of mass higher than a basketball player who is 6"5'. During the jump the athlete needs to get the knees up and the heels over the box, which means flexibility is going to be an issue because if the athlete cannot bring the knees to the chest he/she will not be jumping very high – with the result that the athlete has to get the center of mass even higher to be able land on the box. Various exercises are shown on **page 582**.

LIGHT CONCENTRIC THROWS

During light concentric throws the focus is on speed rather than the total amount of resistance being used; emphasis is on rapid movements and control of the body. Athletes always need to be careful with single leg rotational and lateral movements because of the additional torque; athletes get hurt when they are not familiar with the situation. Consequently, they must learn the movement patterns first in a safe environment (slower speed); **it takes up to 3 weeks to get the motor patterning down**. Take a look at **page 650** for light concentric throw exercises.

HIGH-SPEED REBOUNDS

High-speed rebounds focus on improving the athlete's speed. They are also developmental and employ jumps at different heights, ranging from low (below hip level) , to medium (hip level), to high (above hip level). Stabilization and transfer of energy requirements increase with the height of the jumps. The athlete is being introduced to different stance positions, generally starting in a neutral stance. The exercises should be performed as true plyometrics but often athletes are unable to do them due to a lack of dynamic stability and control. The rebounds can, as a result, become very sloppy. The athlete needs to be able to perform the exercises within the targets (agility rings). If the athlete can do the exercises, this will indicate that he/she is capable of controlling vertical stability effectively. When the athlete moves around when jumping, the transfer of energy is inefficient; center of mass control is weak. Refer to **page 614** for high-speed rebounds.

7.172 LOW-LEVEL DEPTH JUMP TO FULL EXTENSION (I)

SUMMARY

The Low-Level Depth Jump to Full Extension I is a plyometric exercise, which focuses on developing neural pathways for explosive jumping, body control & coordination as well as improving skill and speed foundation for complex movements utilizing a box and agility rings.

PURPOSE

1. Developing neural pathways for explosive jumping capability (neurological feedback loop)
2. Improving balance (body control) & coordination
3. Improving skill and speed foundation for complex movements

DESCRIPTION

1. Place box onto solid, non-sliding surface
2. Place 2 agility rings in front of the box
3. Step onto the box; athlete stands up straight and positions the feet under the shoulders
4. Step off the box with one (1) foot
5. Land with both feet simultaneously into agility rings
6. Immediately jump upwards with both legs simultaneously while **looking down** at the ground; extend hips, use arm swing to generate force and raise arms over the head
7. Land inside the agility rings

BREATH IN & OUT

- IN: Before Step Off
- OUT: During Jumping

DEGREE OF DIFFICULTY

1

REQUIRED EQUIPMENT

- 6 – 8 Inch Box
- 2 Agility Rings

KEY FACTORS

- Focus on perfect movement mechanics and speed (short ground contact)
- Step off the box with one (1) foot
- Land on both feet simultaneously inside agility rings
- Jump vertically with both feet simultaneously
- Maintain balance; land in same location inside agility rings

COMMON ERRORS

- Athlete lands outside agility rings
- Athlete focuses on maximum height instead of minimizing ground contact time

ID: 7172

7.173 LOW-LEVEL DEPTH JUMP TO FULL EXTENSION (II)

SUMMARY

The Low-Level Depth Jump to Full Extension II is a plyometric exercise, which focuses on developing neural pathways for explosive jumping, body control & coordination as well as improving skill and speed foundation for complex movements utilizing a box and agility rings.

PURPOSE

1. Developing neural pathways for explosive jumping capability (neurological feedback loop)
2. Improving balance (body control) & coordination
3. Improving skill and speed foundation for complex movements

DESCRIPTION

1. Place box onto solid, non-sliding surface
2. Place 2 agility rings in front of the box
3. Step onto the box; athlete stands up straight and positions the feet under the shoulders
4. Step off the box with one (1) foot
5. Land with both feet simultaneously into agility rings
6. Immediately jump upwards with both legs simultaneously while **looking forward**; extend hips, use arm swing to generate force and raise arms over the head
7. Land inside the agility rings

PRE-REQUISITE DRILLS

- Low-Level Depth Jump to Full Extension (I)

BREATH IN & OUT

- IN: Before Step Off
- OUT: During Jumping

DEGREE OF DIFFICULTY

2

REQUIRED EQUIPMENT

- 6 – 8 Inch Box
- 2 Agility Rings

KEY FACTORS

- Focus on perfect movement mechanics and speed (short ground contact)
- Step off the box with one (1) foot
- Land on both feet simultaneously inside agility rings
- Jump vertically with both feet simultaneously
- Maintain balance; land in same location inside agility rings

COMMON ERRORS

- Athlete lands outside agility rings
- Athlete focuses on maximum height instead of minimizing ground contact time

ID: 7173

7.174 LOW-LEVEL DEPTH JUMP TO HIGH TUCK JUMP (I)

SUMMARY

The Low-Level Depth Jump to High Tuck Jump I is a plyometric exercise, which focuses on improving neural pathways for explosive jumping, body control & coordination, skill and speed foundation as well as improving flexibility utilizing a box and agility rings.

PURPOSE

1. Developing neural pathways for explosive jumping capability (neurological feedback loop)
2. Improving balance (body control) & coordination
3. Improving skill and speed foundation for complex movements
4. Improving flexibility (Glutes & Hamstrings)

DESCRIPTION

1. Place box onto solid, non-sliding surface
2. Place 2 agility rings in front of the box
3. Step onto the box; athlete stands up straight and positions the feet under the shoulders
4. Step off the box with one (1) foot
5. Land with both feet simultaneously into agility rings
6. Immediately jump upwards into a high tuck jump with both legs simultaneously while **looking down** at the ground
7. Land inside the agility rings

PRE-REQUISITE DRILLS

- Low-Level Depth Jump to Full Extension (I)
- High-Level Tuck Jump (I)

BREATH IN & OUT

- IN: Before Step Off
- OUT: During Jumping

DEGREE OF DIFFICULTY

1

REQUIRED EQUIPMENT

- 6 – 8 Inch Box
- 2 Agility Rings

KEY FACTORS

- Focus on perfect movement mechanics and speed (short ground contact)
- Step off the box with one (1) foot
- Land on both feet simultaneously inside agility rings
- Jump vertically with both feet simultaneously
- Maintain balance; land in same location inside agility rings

COMMON ERRORS

- Athlete lands outside agility rings
- Athlete focuses on maximum height instead of minimizing ground contact time

ID: 7174

7.175 LOW-LEVEL DEPTH JUMP TO HIGH TUCK JUMP (II)

SUMMARY

The Low-Level Depth Jump to High Tuck Jump II is a plyometric exercise, which focuses on improving neural pathways for explosive jumping, body control & coordination, skill and speed foundation as well as improving flexibility utilizing a box and agility rings.

PURPOSE

1. Developing neural pathways for explosive jumping capability (neurological feedback loop)
2. Improving balance (body control) & coordination
3. Improving skill and speed foundation for complex movements
4. Improving flexibility (Glutes & Hamstrings)

DESCRIPTION

1. Place box onto solid, non-sliding surface
2. Place 2 agility rings in front of the box
3. Step onto the box; athlete stands up straight and positions the feet under the shoulders
4. Step off the box with one (1) foot
5. Land with both feet simultaneously into agility rings
6. Immediately jump upwards into a high tuck jump with both legs simultaneously while **looking forward**
7. Land inside the agility rings

PRE-REQUISITE DRILLS

- Low-Level Depth Jump to Full Extension (I)
- High-Level Tuck Jump (I)

BREATH IN & OUT

- IN: Before Step Off
- OUT: During Jumping

DEGREE OF DIFFICULTY

2

REQUIRED EQUIPMENT

- 6 – 8 Inch Box
- 2 Agility Rings

KEY FACTORS

- Focus on perfect movement mechanics and speed (short ground contact)
- Step off the box with one (1) foot
- Land on both feet simultaneously inside agility rings
- Jump vertically with both feet simultaneously
- Maintain balance; land in same location inside agility rings

COMMON ERRORS

- Athlete lands outside agility rings
- Athlete focuses on maximum height instead of minimizing ground contact time

ID: 7175

7.176 LL SL DEPTH JUMP TO SL HIGH TUCK JUMP (III)

SUMMARY

The Low-Level Single-Leg Depth Jump to Single-Leg High Tuck Jump III is a plyometric exercise, which focuses on improving neural pathways for explosive jumping, body control & coordination, skill and speed foundation as well as improving flexibility utilizing a box and agility rings.

PURPOSE

1. Developing neural pathways for explosive jumping capability (neurological feedback loop)
2. Improving balance (body control) & coordination
3. Improving skill and speed foundation for complex movements
4. Improving flexibility (Glutes & Hamstrings)

DESCRIPTION

1. Place box onto solid, non-sliding surface
2. Place 2 agility rings in front of the box
3. Step onto the box; athlete stands up straight and positions the feet under the shoulders
4. Step off the box with right foot
5. Land with right foot into agility ring; **look down** to the ground
6. Immediately jump upwards into a high tuck jump with right leg
7. Land inside the agility ring
8. Switch legs

PRE-REQUISITE DRILLS

- Low-Level Depth Jump to Full Extension (I)
- Single-Leg High-Level Tuck Jump (I)

BREATH IN & OUT

- IN: Before Step Off
- OUT: During Jumping

DEGREE OF DIFFICULTY

3

KEY FACTORS

- Focus on perfect movement mechanics and speed (short ground contact)
- Step off the box with one (1) foot
- Land on one foot inside agility ring
- Jump vertically with one foot
- Maintain balance; land in same location inside agility ring

COMMON ERRORS

- Athlete lands outside agility rings
- Athlete focuses on maximum height instead of minimizing ground contact time

REQUIRED EQUIPMENT

- 2 – 6 Inch Box
- 2 Agility Rings

ID: 7176

7.177 LL SL DEPTH JUMP TO SL HIGH TUCK JUMP (IV)

SUMMARY

The Low-Level Single-Leg Depth Jump to Single-Leg High Tuck Jump IV is a plyometric exercise, which focuses on improving neural pathways for explosive jumping, body control & coordination, skill and speed foundation as well as improving flexibility utilizing a box.

PURPOSE

1. Developing neural pathways for explosive jumping capability (neurological feedback loop)
2. Improving balance (body control) & coordination
3. Improving skill and speed foundation for complex movements
4. Improving flexibility (Glutes & Hamstrings)

DESCRIPTION

1. Place box onto solid, non-sliding surface
2. Step onto the box; athlete stands up straight and positions the feet under the shoulders
3. Step off the box with right foot
4. Land with right foot; **look forward** during landing
5. Immediately jump upwards into a high tuck jump with right leg
6. Land in the same spot
7. Switch legs

PRE-REQUISITE DRILLS

- Low-Level Depth Jump to Full Extension (II)
- Single-Leg High-Level Tuck Jump (II)

BREATH IN & OUT

- IN: Before Step Off
- OUT: During Jumping

DEGREE OF DIFFICULTY

4

REQUIRED EQUIPMENT

- 2 – 6 Inch Box

KEY FACTORS

- Focus on perfect movement mechanics and speed (short ground contact)
- Step off the box with one (1) foot
- Land on one foot
- Jump vertically with one foot
- Maintain balance; land in same location

COMMON ERRORS

- Athlete moves around; doesn't land in same location
- Athlete focuses on maximum height instead of minimizing ground contact time

ID: 7177

7

7.178 LOW-LEVEL DEPTH JUMP TO LATERAL BOX JUMP (I)

SUMMARY

The Low-Level Depth Jump to Lateral Box Jump I is a plyometric exercise, which focuses on developing neural pathways for explosive jumping during the serve, body control & coordination as well as improving skill and speed foundation for complex movements utilizing boxes and agility rings.

PURPOSE

1. Developing neural pathways for explosive jumping capability (neurological feedback loop) for the **Serve**
2. Improving balance (body control) & coordination
3. Improving skill and speed foundation for complex movements

DESCRIPTION

1. Place boxes onto solid, non-sliding surface
2. Place 2 agility rings in front of box #1; box #2 is perpendicular to box #1
3. Step onto the box #1; athlete takes on stance used during his/her service; generally position the feet under the shoulders
4. Step off the box with the **leading** foot
5. Land with both feet simultaneously into agility rings
6. Immediately jump laterally (sideways) with both legs simultaneously, performing a mid-level lateral tuck jump, onto box #2; **look down** at the ground during ground contact
7. Land on top of box #2

PRE-REQUISITE DRILLS

- Low-Level Depth Jump to Full Extension (I)
- Mid-Level Lateral Tuck Jump (I)

BREATH IN & OUT

- IN: Before Step Off
- OUT: During Jumping

DEGREE OF DIFFICULTY

1

REQUIRED EQUIPMENT

- Two 6 – 8 Inch Boxes
- 2 Agility Rings

KEY FACTORS

- Focus on perfect movement mechanics and speed (short ground contact)
- Step off box #1 with the leading foot
- Land on both feet simultaneously inside agility rings
- Jump laterally with both feet simultaneously
- Maintain balance; land on top of Box #2

COMMON ERRORS

- Athlete lands outside agility rings
- Athlete focuses on maximum height instead of minimizing ground contact time

ID: 7178

7.179 LOW-LEVEL DEPTH JUMP TO LATERAL BOX JUMP (II)

SUMMARY

The Low-Level Depth Jump to Lateral Box Jump II is a plyometric exercise, which focuses on developing neural pathways for explosive jumping during the serve, body control & coordination as well as improving skill and speed foundation for complex movements utilizing boxes and agility rings.

PURPOSE

1. Developing neural pathways for explosive jumping capability (neurological feedback loop) for the **Serve**
2. Improving balance (body control) & coordination
3. Improving skill and speed foundation for complex movements

DESCRIPTION

1. Place boxes onto solid, non-sliding surface
2. Place 2 agility rings in front of box #1; box #2 is perpendicular to box #1
3. Step onto the box #1; athlete takes on stance used during his/her service; generally position the feet under the shoulders
4. Step off the box with the leading foot
5. Land with both feet simultaneously into agility rings
6. Immediately jump laterally (sideways) with both legs simultaneously, performing a mid-level lateral tuck jump, onto box #2; **look forward** during jump and ground contact
7. Land on top of box #2

PRE-REQUISITE DRILLS

- Low-Level Depth Jump to Full Extension (II)
- Mid-Level Lateral Tuck Jump (II)

BREATH IN & OUT

- IN: Before Step Off
- OUT: During Jumping

DEGREE OF DIFFICULTY

2

REQUIRED EQUIPMENT

- Two 6 – 8 Inch Boxes
- 2 Agility Rings

KEY FACTORS

- Focus on perfect movement mechanics and speed (short ground contact)
- Step off box #1 with the leading foot
- Land on both feet simultaneously inside agility rings
- Jump laterally with both feet simultaneously
- Maintain balance; land on top of Box #2

COMMON ERRORS

- Athlete lands outside agility rings
- Athlete focuses on maximum height instead of minimizing ground contact time

ID: 7179

7.180 LL DEPTH JUMP TO LAT. BOX JUMP: SL LANDING (III)

SUMMARY

The Low-Level Depth Jump to Lateral Box Jump: Single-Foot Landing III is a plyometric exercise, which focuses on developing neural pathways for explosive jumping during the serve, body control & coordination as well as improving skill and speed foundation for complex movements utilizing boxes and agility rings.

PURPOSE

1. Developing neural pathways for explosive jumping capability (neurological feedback loop) for the **Serve**
2. Improving balance (body control) & coordination
3. Improving skill and speed foundation for complex movements (e.g. serve)

DESCRIPTION

1. Place boxes onto solid, non-sliding surface
2. Place 2 agility rings in front of box #1; box #2 is perpendicular to box #1
3. Step onto the box #1; athlete takes on stance used during his/her service; generally position the feet under the shoulders
4. Step off the box with the **leading** foot
5. Land with both feet simultaneously into agility rings; **look forward** during jump and ground contact
6. Immediately jump laterally (sideways) with both legs simultaneously, performing a mid-level lateral tuck jump, onto box #2
7. Land on top of box #2 with the **leading foot**; **look down** during landing

PRE-REQUISITE DRILLS

- Low-Level Depth Jump to Full Extension (II)
- Mid-Level Lateral Tuck Jump (II)
- Single-Leg Mid-Level Tuck Jump (II)

DEGREE OF DIFFICULTY

3

BREATH IN & OUT

- IN: Before Step Off
- OUT: During Jumping

REQUIRED EQUIPMENT

- Two 6 – 8 Inch Boxes
- 2 Agility Rings

KEY FACTORS

- Focus on perfect movement mechanics and speed (short ground contact)
- Step off box #1 with the leading foot
- Land on both feet simultaneously inside agility rings
- Jump laterally with both feet simultaneously
- Maintain balance; land on top of Box #2 with the leading foot

COMMON ERRORS

- Athlete lands outside agility rings
- Athlete focuses on maximum height instead of minimizing ground contact time

ID: 7180

7.181 LL DEPTH JUMP TO LAT. BOX JUMP: SL LANDING (IV)

SUMMARY

The Low-Level Depth Jump to Lateral Box Jump: Single-Foot Landing IV is a plyometric exercise, which focuses on developing neural pathways for explosive jumping during the serve, body control & coordination as well as improving skill and speed foundation for complex movements utilizing boxes and agility rings.

PURPOSE

1. Developing neural pathways for explosive jumping capability (neurological feedback loop) for the **Serve**
2. Improving balance (body control) & coordination
3. Improving skill and speed foundation for complex movements (e.g. serve)

DESCRIPTION

1. Place boxes onto solid, non-sliding surface
2. Place 2 agility rings in front of box #1; box #2 is perpendicular to box #1
3. Step onto the box #1; athlete takes on stance used during his/her service; generally position the feet under the shoulders
4. Step off the box with the **leading foot**
5. Land with both feet simultaneously into agility rings; **look forward** during jump and ground contact
6. Immediately jump laterally (sideways) with both legs simultaneously, performing a mid-level lateral tuck jump, onto box #2
7. Land on top of box #2 with the **leading foot**; **look forward** during landing

PRE-REQUISITE DRILLS

- Low-Level Depth Jump to Full Extension (III)
- Mid-Level Lateral Tuck Jump (III)
- Single-Leg Mid-Level Tuck Jump (III)

BREATH IN & OUT

- IN: Before Step Off
- OUT: During Jumping

DEGREE OF DIFFICULTY

4

REQUIRED EQUIPMENT

- Two 6 – 8 Inch Boxes
- 2 Agility Rings

KEY FACTORS

- Focus on perfect movement mechanics and speed (short ground contact)
- Step off box #1 with the leading foot
- Land on both feet simultaneously inside agility rings
- Jump laterally with both feet simultaneously
- Maintain balance; land on top of Box #2 with the leading foot

COMMON ERRORS

- Athlete lands outside agility rings
- Athlete focuses on maximum height instead of minimizing ground contact time

ID: 7181

7.182 LL DEPTH JUMP TO DIAGONAL BOX JUMP (I)

SUMMARY

The Low-Level Depth Jump to Diagonal Box Jump I is a plyometric exercise, which focuses on developing neural pathways for explosive change of direction during the return & volley, body control & coordination as well as improving skill and speed foundation for complex movements utilizing boxes and agility rings.

PURPOSE

1. Developing neural pathways for explosive change of direction capability (neurological feedback loop) for the **Return & Volley**
2. Improving balance (body control) & coordination
3. Improving skill and speed foundation for complex movements

DESCRIPTION

1. Place boxes onto solid, non-sliding surface
2. Place 2 agility rings in front of box #1; box #2 is diagonal to box #1
3. Step onto the box #1; athlete takes on stance used during his/her service; generally position the feet under the shoulders
4. Step off the box one (1) foot
5. Land with both feet **simultaneously** into agility rings; **look down** at the ground during ground contact
6. Immediately jump diagonally (1st to the right side then to the left side) with both legs **simultaneously**, performing a mid-level lateral tuck jump, onto box #2
7. Land on top of box #2 with both legs

PRE-REQUISITE DRILLS

- Low-Level Depth Jump to Full Extension (I)
- Mid-Level Lateral Tuck Jump (I)
- Low-Level Depths Jump to Long Jump (I)

BREATH IN & OUT

- IN: Before Step Off
- OUT: During Jumping

DEGREE OF DIFFICULTY

1

REQUIRED EQUIPMENT

- Two 6 – 8 Inch Boxes
- 2 Agility Rings

KEY FACTORS

- Focus on perfect movement mechanics and speed (short ground contact)
- Step off box #1 with the leading foot
- Land on both feet simultaneously inside agility rings
- Jump laterally with both feet simultaneously
- Maintain balance; land on top of Box #2 with both legs

COMMON ERRORS

- Athlete lands outside agility rings
- Athlete focuses on maximum height instead of minimizing ground contact time

ID: 7182

7.183 LL DEPTH JUMP TO DIAGONAL BOX JUMP (II)

SUMMARY

The Low-Level Depth Jump to Diagonal Box Jump II is a plyometric exercise, which focuses on developing neural pathways for explosive change of direction during the return & volley, body control & coordination as well as improving skill and speed foundation for complex movements utilizing boxes and agility rings.

PURPOSE

1. Developing neural pathways for explosive change of direction capability (neurological feedback loop) for the **Return & Volley**
2. Improving balance (body control) & coordination
3. Improving skill and speed foundation for complex movements

DESCRIPTION

1. Place boxes onto solid, non-sliding surface
2. Place 2 agility rings in front of box #1; box #2 is diagonal to box #1
3. Step onto the box #1; athlete takes on stance used during his/her service; generally position the feet under the shoulders
4. Step off the box one (1) foot
5. Land with both feet simultaneously into agility rings; **look forward** during ground contact
6. Immediately jump diagonally (1st to the right side then to the left side) with both legs simultaneously, performing a mid-level lateral tuck jump, onto box #2
7. Land on top of box #2 with both legs

DEGREE OF DIFFICULTY

2

REQUIRED EQUIPMENT

- Two 6 – 8 Inch Boxes
- 2 Agility Rings

KEY FACTORS

- Focus on perfect movement mechanics and speed (short ground contact)
- Step off box #1 with the leading foot
- Land on both feet simultaneously inside agility rings
- Jump laterally with both feet simultaneously
- Maintain balance; land on top of Box #2 with both legs

PRE-REQUISITE DRILLS

- Low-Level Depth Jump to Full Extension (II)
- Mid-Level Lateral Tuck Jump (II)
- Low-Level Depths Jump to Long Jump (II)

COMMON ERRORS

- Athlete lands outside agility rings
- Athlete focuses on maximum height instead of minimizing ground contact time

BREATH IN & OUT

- IN: Before Step Off
- OUT: During Jumping

ID: 7183

7.184 LL DEPTH JUMP TO DIAG. BOX JUMP: SL LAND. (III)

SUMMARY

The Low-Level Depth Jump to Diagonal Box Jump III is a plyometric exercise, which focuses on developing neural pathways for explosive change of direction during the return & volley, body control & coordination as well as improving skill and speed foundation for complex movements utilizing boxes and agility rings.

PURPOSE

1. Developing neural pathways for explosive change of direction capability (neurological feedback loop) for the **Return & Volley**
2. Improving balance (body control) & coordination
3. Improving skill and speed foundation for complex movements

DESCRIPTION

1. Place boxes onto solid, non-sliding surface
2. Place 2 agility rings in front of box #1; box #2 is diagonal to box #1
3. Step onto the box #1; athlete takes on stance used during his/her service; generally position the feet under the shoulders
4. Step off the box one (1) foot
5. Land with both feet simultaneously into agility rings; **look forward** during ground contact
6. Immediately jump diagonally(1st to the right side then to the left side) with both legs simultaneously, performing a mid-level lateral tuck jump, onto box #2
7. Land on top of box #2 with the **left** leg (right side jumping) and the **right** leg (left side jumping); **look down** during landing

PRE-REQUISITE DRILLS

- Low-Level Depth Jump to Full Extension (II)
- Mid-Level Lateral Tuck Jump (II)
- Low-Level Depths Jump to Long Jump (II)

BREATH IN & OUT

- IN: Before Step Off
- OUT: During Jumping

DEGREE OF DIFFICULTY

3

REQUIRED EQUIPMENT

- Two 6 – 8 Inch Boxes
- 2 Agility Rings

KEY FACTORS

- Focus on perfect movement mechanics and speed (short ground contact)
- Step off box #1 with the leading foot
- Land on both feet simultaneously inside agility rings
- Jump laterally with both feet simultaneously
- Maintain balance; land on top of Box #2 with one leg

COMMON ERRORS

- Athlete lands outside agility rings
- Athlete focuses on maximum height instead of minimizing ground contact time

ID: 7184

7.185 LL DEPTH JUMP TO DIAG. BOX JUMP: SL LAND. (IV)

SUMMARY

The Low-Level Depth Jump to Diagonal Box Jump IV is a plyometric exercise, which focuses on developing neural pathways for explosive change of direction during the return & volley, body control & coordination as well as improving skill and speed foundation for complex movements utilizing boxes and agility rings.

PURPOSE

1. Developing neural pathways for explosive change of direction capability (neurological feedback loop) for the **Return & Volley**
2. Improving balance (body control) & coordination
3. Improving skill and speed foundation for complex movements

DESCRIPTION

1. Place boxes onto solid, non-sliding surface
2. Place 2 agility rings in front of box #1; box #2 is diagonal to box #1
3. Step onto the box #1; athlete takes on stance used during his/her service; generally position the feet under the shoulders
4. Step off the box one (1) foot
5. Land with both feet simultaneously into agility rings; **look forward** during ground contact
6. Immediately jump diagonally(1st to the right side then to the left side) with both legs simultaneously, performing a mid-level lateral tuck jump, onto box #2
7. Land on top of box #2 with the left leg (right side jumping) and the right leg (left side jumping); **look forward** during landing

PRE-REQUISITE DRILLS

- Low-Level Depth Jump to Full Extension (II)
- Mid-Level Lateral Tuck Jump (II)
- Low-Level Depths Jump to Long Jump (II)

DEGREE OF DIFFICULTY

4

BREATH IN & OUT

- IN: Before Step Off
- OUT: During Jumping

REQUIRED EQUIPMENT

- Two 6 – 8 Inch Boxes
- 2 Agility Rings

KEY FACTORS

- Focus on perfect movement mechanics and speed (short ground contact)
- Step off box #1 with the leading foot
- Land on both feet simultaneously inside agility rings
- Jump laterally with both feet simultaneously
- Maintain balance; land on top of Box #2 with one leg

COMMON ERRORS

- Athlete lands outside agility rings
- Athlete focuses on maximum height instead of minimizing ground contact time

ID: 7185

7.186 LOW-LEVEL DEPTH JUMP TO LONG JUMP (I)

SUMMARY

The Low-Level Depth Jump to Long Jump I is a plyometric exercise, which focuses on developing neural pathways for explosive jumping, body control & coordination, flexibility as well as improving skill and speed foundation for complex movements utilizing a box, cones and agility rings.

PURPOSE

1. Developing neural pathways for explosive jumping capability (neurological feedback loop)
2. Improving balance (body control) & coordination
3. Improving skill and speed foundation for complex movements
4. Improving flexibility (Glutes & Hamstrings)

DESCRIPTION

1. Place box onto solid, non-sliding surface
2. Place 2 agility rings in front of the box and 2 cones ~8 feet in front of the box
3. Step onto the box; athlete stands up straight and positions the feet under the shoulders
4. Step off the box with one (1) foot
5. Land with both feet simultaneously into agility rings; **look down** at the ground
6. Immediately jump forward with both legs simultaneously; extend hips and land in squat position
7. **Do not jump past the 2 cones**

BREATH IN & OUT

- IN: Before Step Off
- OUT: During Jumping

DEGREE OF DIFFICULTY

1

REQUIRED EQUIPMENT

- 6 – 8 Inch Box
- 2 Agility Rings
- 2 Cones

KEY FACTORS

- Focus on perfect movement mechanics and speed (short ground contact)
- Step off the box with one (1) foot
- Land on both feet simultaneously inside agility rings
- Jump forward with both feet simultaneously
- Maintain balance during landing

COMMON ERRORS

- Athlete lands outside agility rings
- Athlete focuses on maximum distance instead of minimizing ground contact time

ID: 7186

7.187 LOW-LEVEL DEPTH JUMP TO LONG JUMP (II)

SUMMARY

The Low-Level Depth Jump to Long Jump II is a plyometric exercise, which focuses on developing neural pathways for explosive jumping, body control & coordination, flexibility as well as improving skill and speed foundation for complex movements utilizing a box, cones and agility rings.

PURPOSE

1. Developing neural pathways for explosive jumping capability (neurological feedback loop)
2. Improving balance (body control) & coordination
3. Improving skill and speed foundation for complex movements
4. Improving flexibility (Glutes & Hamstrings)

DESCRIPTION

1. Place box onto solid, non-sliding surface
2. Place 2 agility rings in front of the box and 2 cones ~6 feet in front of the box
3. Step onto the box; athlete stands up straight and positions the feet under the shoulders
4. Step off the box with one (1) foot
5. Land with both feet simultaneously into agility rings; **look forward**
6. Immediately jump forward with both legs simultaneously; extend hips and land in squat position
7. **Do not jump past the 2 cones**

PRE-REQUISITE DRILLS

- Low-Level Depth Jump to Long Jump (I)

BREATH IN & OUT

- IN: Before Step Off
- OUT: During Jumping

DEGREE OF DIFFICULTY

2

REQUIRED EQUIPMENT

- 6 – 8 Inch Box
- 2 Agility Rings
- 2 Cones

KEY FACTORS

- Focus on perfect movement mechanics and speed (short ground contact)
- Step off the box with one (1) foot
- Land on both feet simultaneously inside agility rings
- Jump forward with both feet simultaneously
- Maintain balance during landing

COMMON ERRORS

- Athlete lands outside agility rings
- Athlete focuses on maximum distance instead of minimizing ground contact time

ID: 7187

7.188 LL DEPTH JUMP TO LONG JUMP: SL LANDING (III)

SUMMARY

The Low-Level Depth Jump to Long Jump: Single-Leg Landing III is a plyometric exercise, which focuses on developing neural pathways for explosive jumping, body control & coordination, flexibility as well as improving skill and speed foundation for complex movements utilizing a box, cones and agility rings.

DESCRIPTION

1. Place box onto solid, non-sliding surface
2. Place 2 agility rings in front of the box and 2 cones ~6 feet in front of the box
3. Step onto the box; athlete stands up straight and positions the feet under the shoulders
4. Step off the box with one (1) foot
5. Land with both feet simultaneously into agility rings; **look forward**
6. Immediately jump forward with both legs simultaneously; extend hips and land in single-leg squat position; **look down** during landing
7. Do not jump past the 2 cones

PRE-REQUISITE DRILLS

- Low-Level Depth Jump to Long Jump (II)

BREATH IN & OUT

- IN: Before Step Off
- OUT: During Jumping

PURPOSE

1. Developing neural pathways for explosive jumping capability (neurological feedback loop)
2. Improving balance (body control) & coordination
3. Improving skill and speed foundation for complex movements
4. Improving flexibility (Glutes & Hamstrings)

DEGREE OF DIFFICULTY

3

REQUIRED EQUIPMENT

- 6 – 8 Inch Box
- 2 Agility Rings
- 2 Cones

KEY FACTORS

- Focus on perfect movement mechanics and speed (short ground contact)
- Step off the box with one (1) foot
- Land on both feet simultaneously inside agility rings
- Jump forward with both feet simultaneously
- Maintain balance during landing

COMMON ERRORS

- Athlete lands outside agility rings
- Athlete focuses on maximum distance instead of minimizing ground contact time

ID: 7188

7.189 LL DEPTH JUMP TO LONG JUMP: SL LANDING (IV)

SUMMARY

The Low-Level Depth Jump to Long Jump: Single-Leg Landing IV is a plyometric exercise, which focuses on developing neural pathways for explosive jumping, body control & coordination, flexibility as well as improving skill and speed foundation for complex movements utilizing a box.

PURPOSE

1. Developing neural pathways for explosive jumping capability (neurological feedback loop)
2. Improving balance (body control) & coordination
3. Improving skill and speed foundation for complex movements
4. Improving flexibility (Glutes & Hamstrings)

DESCRIPTION

1. Place box onto solid, non-sliding surface
2. Step onto the box; athlete stands up straight and positions the feet under the shoulders
3. Step off the box with one (1) foot
4. Land with both feet simultaneously on the ground; **look forward**
5. Immediately jump forward with both legs simultaneously; extend hips and land in single-leg squat position; **look forward** during landing

PRE-REQUISITE DRILLS

- Low-Level Depth Jump to Long Jump: Single-Leg Landing (III)

BREATH IN & OUT

- IN: Before Step Off
- OUT: During Jumping

DEGREE OF DIFFICULTY

4

REQUIRED EQUIPMENT

- 6 – 8 Inch Box

KEY FACTORS

- Focus on perfect movement mechanics and speed (short ground contact)
- Step off the box with one (1) foot
- Land on both feet simultaneously on the ground
- Jump forward with both feet simultaneously
- Maintain balance during landing

COMMON ERRORS

- Athlete focuses on maximum distance instead of minimizing ground contact time

ID: 7189

7.190 LOW-LEVEL BOX JUMP REBOUNDS (I)

SUMMARY

The Low-Level Box Jump Rebounds I is a plyometric exercise, which focuses on developing neural pathways for explosive jumping, reaction time, body control & coordination as well as improving skill and speed foundation for complex movements utilizing a box and agility rings.

PURPOSE

1. Developing neural pathways for explosive jumping capability (neurological feedback loop)
2. Improving reaction time for lower extremities (legs)
3. Improving balance (body control) & coordination
4. Improving skill and speed foundation for complex movements

DESCRIPTION

1. Place box onto solid, non-sliding surface
2. Place 4 agility rings shoulder-width apart on the ground; 2 in front and 2 behind the box
3. Step into agility rings in front of the box
4. Jump on top of the box with both legs **simultaneously**, use arm swing to generate force
5. Land with both feet **simultaneously**
6. Immediately jump off the box with both legs **simultaneously** while **looking down** at the ground
7. Immediately jump backwards on top of the box with both legs **simultaneously** while **looking down**
8. Land
9. Jump off landing inside the **agility rings**

BREATH IN & OUT

- IN: Before Step Off
- OUT: During Jumping

DEGREE OF DIFFICULTY

1

REQUIRED EQUIPMENT

- 2 – 6 Inch Box
- 4 Agility Rings

KEY FACTORS

- Focus on perfect movement mechanics and speed (short ground contact)
- Step off the box with one (1) foot
- Land on both feet simultaneously inside agility rings
- Jump forward/backward with both feet simultaneously
- Maintain balance; land in same location inside agility rings and on top of the boxes

COMMON ERRORS

- Athlete lands outside agility rings
- Athlete focuses on maximum height instead of minimizing ground contact time

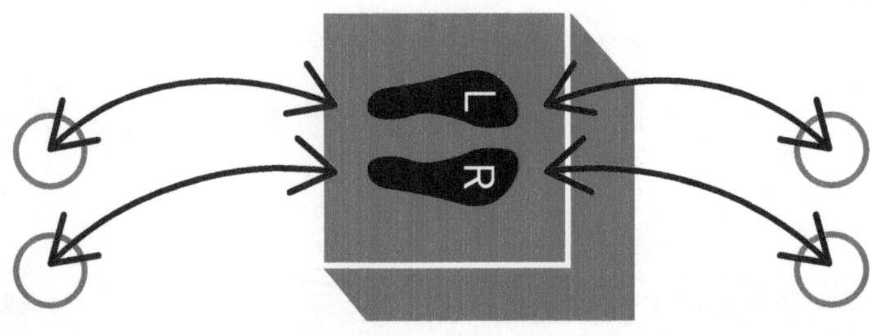

ID: 7190

7.191 LOW-LEVEL BOX JUMP REBOUNDS (II)

SUMMARY

The Low-Level Box Jump Rebounds II is a plyometric exercise, which focuses on developing neural pathways for explosive jumping, reaction time, body control & coordination as well as improving skill and speed foundation for complex movements utilizing a box and agility rings.

PURPOSE

1. Developing neural pathways for explosive jumping capability (neurological feedback loop)
2. Improving reaction time for lower extremities (legs)
3. Improving balance (body control) & coordination
4. Improving skill and speed foundation for complex movements

DESCRIPTION

1. Place box onto solid, non-sliding surface
2. Place 4 agility rings shoulder-width apart on the ground; 2 in front and 2 behind the box
3. Step into agility rings in front of the box
4. Jump on top of the box with both legs simultaneously, use arm swing to generate force
5. Land with both feet simultaneously
6. Immediately jump off the box with both legs simultaneously while **looking forward**
7. Immediately jump backwards on top of the box with both legs simultaneously while **looking forward**
8. Land
9. Jump off landing inside the agility rings

PRE-REQUISITE DRILLS

- Low-Level Depth Jump Rebounds (I)

BREATH IN & OUT

- IN: Before Step Off
- OUT: During Jumping

DEGREE OF DIFFICULTY

2

REQUIRED EQUIPMENT

- 2 – 6 Inch Box
- 4 Agility Rings

KEY FACTORS

- Focus on perfect movement mechanics and speed (short ground contact)
- Step off the box with one (1) foot
- Land on both feet simultaneously inside agility rings
- Jump forward/backward with both feet simultaneously
- Maintain balance; land in same location inside agility rings and on top of the boxes

COMMON ERRORS

- Athlete lands outside agility rings
- Athlete focuses on maximum height instead of minimizing ground contact time

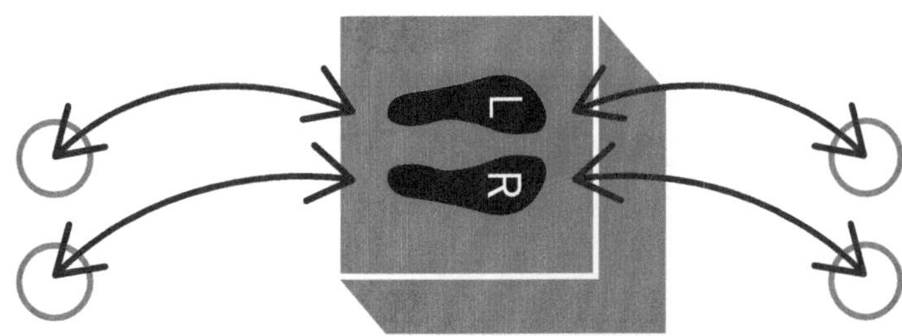

ID: 7191

7.192 LOW-LEVEL BOX JUMP SINGLE LEG REBOUNDS (III)

SUMMARY

The Low-Level Box Jump Single-Leg Rebounds III is a plyometric exercise, which focuses on developing neural pathways for explosive jumping, reaction time, body control & coordination as well as improving skill and speed foundation for complex movements utilizing a box and agility rings.

PURPOSE

1. Developing neural pathways for explosive jumping capability (neurological feedback loop)
2. Improving reaction time for lower extremities (legs)
3. Improving balance (body control) & coordination
4. Improving skill and speed foundation for complex movements

DESCRIPTION

1. Place box onto solid, non-sliding surface ~2 feet apart
2. Place 2 agility rings on the ground; 1 in front and 1 behind the box
3. Step into agility ring with one (1) leg **facing** the box
4. Jump on top of the box with one leg; use arm swing to generate force
5. Land with one (1) foot
6. Immediately jump off the box with one (1) leg while **looking down** at the ground
7. Immediately jump backwards on top of the box with one leg while **looking down**
8. Land
9. Jump off landing inside the agility ring
10. Switch leg

PRE-REQUISITE DRILLS

- Low-Level Depth Jump Rebound (II)

BREATH IN & OUT

- IN: Before Step Off
- OUT: During Jumping

DEGREE OF DIFFICULTY

3

REQUIRED EQUIPMENT

- 2 – 6 Inch Box
- 2 Agility Rings

KEY FACTORS

- Focus on perfect movement mechanics and speed (short ground contact)
- Step off the box with one (1) foot
- Land on one foot inside agility ring
- Jump forward/backward with one foot
- Maintain balance; land in same location inside agility ring and on top of the box

COMMON ERRORS

- Athlete lands outside agility ring
- Athlete focuses on maximum height instead of minimizing ground contact time

ID: 7192

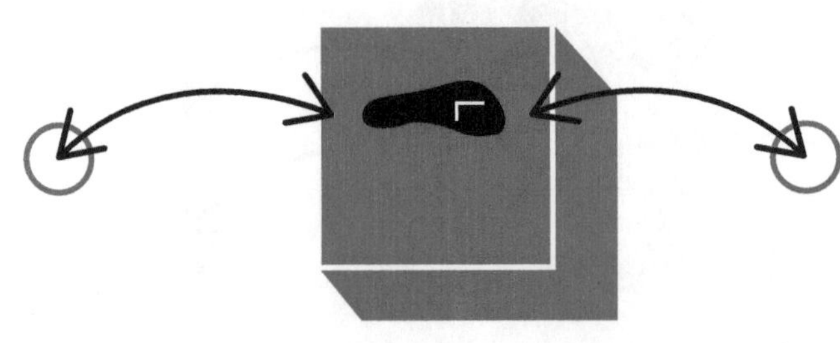

7.193 LOW-LEVEL BOX JUMP SINGLE LEG REBOUNDS (IV)

SUMMARY

The Low-Level Box Jump Single-Leg Rebounds IV is a plyometric exercise, which focuses on developing neural pathways for explosive jumping, reaction time, body control & coordination as well as improving skill and speed foundation for complex movements utilizing a box and agility rings.

PURPOSE

1. Developing neural pathways for explosive jumping capability (neurological feedback loop)
2. Improving reaction time for lower extremities (legs)
3. Improving balance (body control) & coordination
4. Improving skill and speed foundation for complex movements

DESCRIPTION

1. Place box onto solid, non-sliding surface ~2 feet apart
2. Place 2 agility rings on the ground; 1 in front and 1 behind the box
3. Step into agility ring with one (1) leg **facing** the box
4. Jump on top of the box with one leg; use arm swing to generate force
5. Land with one (1) foot
6. Immediately jump off the box with one (1) leg while **looking forward**
7. Immediately jump backwards on top of the box with one leg while **looking forward**
8. Land
9. Jump off landing inside the agility ring
10. Switch leg

PRE-REQUISITE DRILLS

- Low-Level Depth Jump Single-Leg Rebounds (III)

BREATH IN & OUT

- IN: Before Step Off
- OUT: During Jumping

DEGREE OF DIFFICULTY

4

REQUIRED EQUIPMENT

- 2 – 6 Inch Box
- 2 Agility Rings

KEY FACTORS

- Focus on perfect movement mechanics and speed (short ground contact)
- Step off the box with one (1) foot
- Land on one foot inside agility ring
- Jump forward/backward with one foot
- Maintain balance; land in same location inside agility ring and on top of the box

COMMON ERRORS

- Athlete lands outside agility ring
- Athlete focuses on maximum height instead of minimizing ground contact time

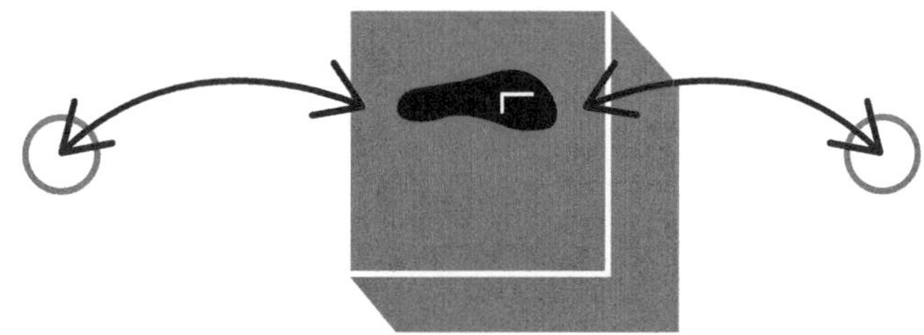

ID: 7193

7.194 LL BOX JUMP SL REBOUNDS (V): 30-60-90

SUMMARY

The Low-Level Box Jump Single-Leg Rebounds V is a plyometric exercise, which focuses on improving anaerobic endurance for competition, developing neural pathways for explosive jumping, reaction time, body control & coordination as well as improving skill and speed foundation for complex movements utilizing a box and agility rings.

PURPOSE

1. Improving anaerobic endurance for competition
2. Developing neural pathways for explosive jumping capability (neurological feedback loop)
3. Improving reaction time for lower extremities (legs)
4. Improving balance (body control) & coordination
5. Improving skill and speed foundation for complex movements

DESCRIPTION

1. Place box onto solid, non-sliding surface ~2 feet apart
2. Place 2 agility rings on the ground; 1 in front and 1 behind the box
3. Step into agility ring with one (1) leg **facing** the box
4. Jump on top of the box with one leg; use arm swing to generate force
5. Land with one (1) foot
6. Immediately jump off the box with one (1) leg while **looking forward**
7. Immediately jump backwards on top of the box with one leg while **looking forward**
8. Land
9. Jump off landing inside the agility ring

- Jump for 30 seconds; record # of repetitions
- Rest for 30 seconds
- Jump for 30 seconds; try to repeat # of repetitions
- Rest for 3 minutes
- Repeat drill with the other leg

PRE-REQUISITE DRILLS

- Low-Level Depth Jump Single-Leg Rebounds (III)

BREATH IN & OUT

- IN: Before Step Off
- OUT: During Jumping

DEGREE OF DIFFICULTY

5

REQUIRED EQUIPMENT

- 2 Inch Box
- 2 Agility Rings

KEY FACTORS

- Focus on perfect movement mechanics and speed (short ground contact)
- Step off the box with one (1) foot
- Land on one foot inside agility ring
- Jump forward/backward with one foot
- Maintain balance; land in same location inside agility ring and on top of the box

COMMON ERRORS

- Athlete lands outside agility ring
- Athlete focuses on maximum height instead of minimizing ground contact time

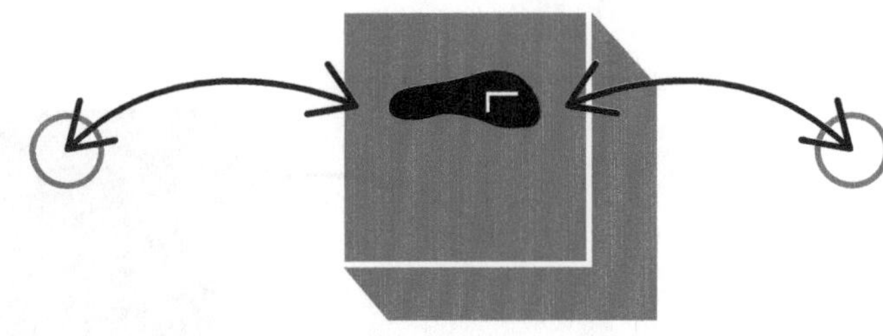

ID: 7194

7.195 LOW-LEVEL LATERAL BOX JUMP REBOUNDS (I)

SUMMARY

The Low-Level Lateral Box Jump Rebounds I is a plyometric exercise, which focuses on developing neural pathways for explosive jumping, body control & coordination as well as improving skill and speed foundation for complex movements utilizing a box and agility rings.

PURPOSE

1. Developing neural pathways for explosive jumping capability (neurological feedback loop)
2. Improving balance (body control) & coordination
3. Improving skill and speed foundation for complex movements

DESCRIPTION

1. Place box onto solid, non-sliding surface ~2 feet apart
2. Place 4 agility rings laterally (sideways) shoulder-width apart on the ground; 2 in front and 2 behind the box
3. Step into agility rings in front of the box
4. Jump on top of the box with both legs **simultaneously**, use arm swing to generate force
5. Land with both feet **simultaneously**; **look down** during landing
6. Immediately jump off the box with both legs **simultaneously** while **looking down** at the ground
7. Immediately jump back on top of the box with both legs **simultaneously** while looking down
8. Land
9. Jump off landing inside the agility rings

BREATH IN & OUT

- IN: Before Step Off
- OUT: During Jumping

DEGREE OF DIFFICULTY

1

REQUIRED EQUIPMENT

- 2 – 6 Inch Boxes
- 4 Agility Rings

KEY FACTORS

- Focus on perfect movement mechanics and speed (short ground contact)
- Step off the box with one (1) foot
- Land on both feet simultaneously inside agility rings
- Jump laterally with both feet simultaneously
- Maintain balance; land in same location inside agility rings and on top of the boxes

COMMON ERRORS

- Athlete lands outside agility rings
- Athlete focuses on maximum height instead of minimizing ground contact time

ID: 7195

7.196 LOW-LEVEL LATERAL BOX JUMP REBOUNDS (II)

SUMMARY

The Low-Level Lateral Box Jump Rebounds II is a plyometric exercise, which focuses on developing neural pathways for explosive jumping, body control & coordination as well as improving skill and speed foundation for complex movements utilizing a box and agility rings.

PURPOSE

1. Developing neural pathways for explosive jumping capability (neurological feedback loop)
2. Improving balance (body control) & coordination
3. Improving skill and speed foundation for complex movements

DESCRIPTION

1. Place box onto solid, non-sliding surface ~2 feet apart
2. Place 4 agility rings laterally (sideways) shoulder-width apart on the ground; 2 in front and 2 behind the box
3. Step into agility rings in front of the box
4. Jump on top of the box with both legs simultaneously, use arm swing to generate force
5. Land with both feet simultaneously; **look forward** during landing
6. Immediately jump off the box with both legs simultaneously while **looking forward**
7. Immediately jump back on top of the box with both legs simultaneously while **looking forward**
8. Land
9. Jump off landing inside the agility rings

PRE-REQUISITE DRILLS

- Low-Level Lateral Box Jump Rebounds (I)

BREATH IN & OUT

- IN: Before Step Off
- OUT: During Jumping

DEGREE OF DIFFICULTY

2

REQUIRED EQUIPMENT

- 2 – 6 Inch Boxes
- 4 Agility Rings

KEY FACTORS

- Focus on perfect movement mechanics and speed (short ground contact)
- Step off the box with one (1) foot
- Land on both feet simultaneously inside agility rings
- Jump laterally with both feet simultaneously
- Maintain balance; land in same location inside agility rings and on top of the box

COMMON ERRORS

- Athlete lands outside agility rings
- Athlete focuses on maximum height instead of minimizing ground contact time

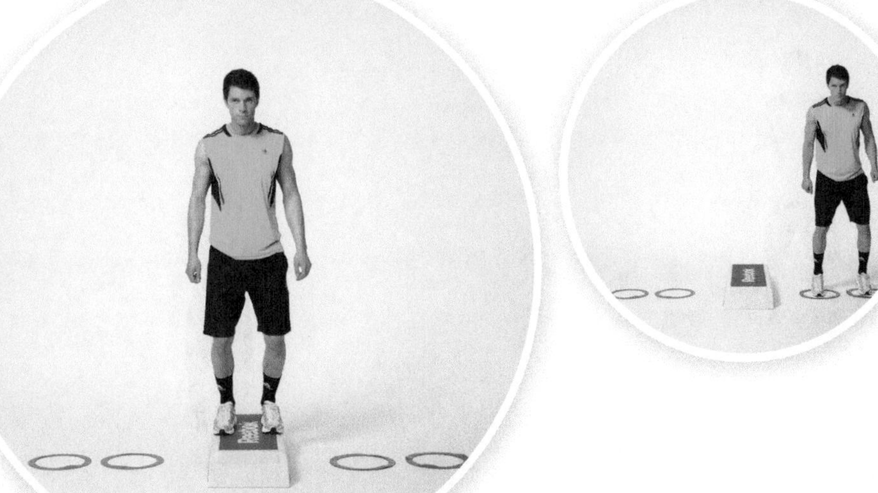

ID: 7196

7.197 LL SINGLE-LEG LATERAL BOX JUMP REBOUNDS (III)

SUMMARY

The Low-Level Single-Leg Lateral Box Jump Rebounds III is a plyometric exercise, which focuses on developing neural pathways for explosive jumping, body control & coordination as well as improving skill and speed foundation for complex movements utilizing a box and agility rings.

PURPOSE

1. Developing neural pathways for explosive jumping capability (neurological feedback loop)
2. Improving balance (body control) & coordination
3. Improving skill and speed foundation for complex movements

DESCRIPTION

1. Place box onto solid, non-sliding surface ~2 feet apart
2. Place 2 agility rings laterally (sideways); 1 in front and 1 behind the box
3. Step into agility ring in front of the box with one (1) leg
4. Jump on top of the box with one leg; use arm swing to generate force
5. Land on the same foot; **look down** during landing
6. Immediately jump off the box with one (1) leg while **looking down**
7. Immediately jump back on top of the box with one leg while **looking down**
8. Land
9. Jump off landing inside the agility ring

PRE-REQUISITE DRILLS

- Low-Level Lateral Box Jump Rebounds (II)

BREATH IN & OUT

- IN: Before Step Off
- OUT: During Jumping

DEGREE OF DIFFICULTY

3

REQUIRED EQUIPMENT

- 2 – 6 Inch Boxes
- 2 Agility Rings

KEY FACTORS

- Focus on perfect movement mechanics and speed (short ground contact)
- Step off the box with one (1) foot
- Land on one foot inside agility ring
- Jump laterally with one foot
- Maintain balance; land in same location inside agility ring and on top of the box

COMMON ERRORS

- Athlete lands outside agility rings
- Athlete focuses on maximum height instead of minimizing ground contact time

ID: 7197

7.198 LL SINGLE-LEG LATERAL BOX JUMP REBOUNDS (IV)

SUMMARY

The Low-Level Lateral Box Jump Rebounds IV is a plyometric exercise, which focuses on developing neural pathways for explosive jumping, body control & coordination as well as improving skill and speed foundation for complex movements utilizing a box and agility rings.

PURPOSE

1. Developing neural pathways for explosive jumping capability (neurological feedback loop)
2. Improving balance (body control) & coordination
3. Improving skill and speed foundation for complex movements

DESCRIPTION

1. Place box onto solid, non-sliding surface ~2 feet apart
2. Place 2 agility rings laterally (sideways); 1 in front and 1 behind the box
3. Step into agility ring in front of the box with one (1) leg
4. Jump on top of the box with one leg; use arm swing to generate force
5. Land on the same foot; **look forward** during landing
6. Immediately jump off the box with one (1) leg while **looking forward**
7. Immediately jump back on top of the box with one leg while **looking forward**
8. Land
9. Jump off landing inside the agility ring

PRE-REQUISITE DRILLS

- Low-Level Single-Leg Lateral Box Jump Rebounds (III)

BREATH IN & OUT

- IN: Before Step Off
- OUT: During Jumping

DEGREE OF DIFFICULTY

4

REQUIRED EQUIPMENT

- 2 – 6 Inch Boxes
- 2 Agility Rings

KEY FACTORS

- Focus on perfect movement mechanics and speed (short ground contact)
- Step off the box with one (1) foot
- Land on one foot inside agility ring
- Jump laterally with one foot
- Maintain balance; land in same location inside agility ring and on top of the box

COMMON ERRORS

- Athlete lands outside agility rings
- Athlete focuses on maximum height instead of minimizing ground contact time

ID: 7198

7.199 LOW-LEVEL ABDUCTOR BOX JUMP REBOUNDS (I)

SUMMARY

The Low-Level Abductor Box Jump Rebounds I is a plyometric exercise, which focuses on developing neural pathways for explosive lateral change of direction capability, reaction time, body control & coordination as well as improving skill and speed foundation for complex movements utilizing a box and agility rings.

PURPOSE

1. Developing neural pathways for explosive lateral change of direction capability (neurological feedback loop)
2. Improving reaction time for lower extremities (legs)
3. Improving balance (body control) & coordination
4. Improving skill and speed foundation for complex movement

DESCRIPTION

1. Place box onto solid, non-sliding surface
2. Place 2 agility rings shoulder-width apart on the ground; 1 to the left side and 1 to the right side of the box
3. Step on top of the box; feet are close together
4. Jump off the box with both legs **simultaneously**
5. Land with both feet **simultaneously** inside agility rings; **look down** to the ground during landing
6. Immediately jump on top of the box with both legs **simultaneously** while **looking down** at the box
7. Repeat

BREATH IN & OUT

- IN: Before Step Off
- OUT: During Jumping

DEGREE OF DIFFICULTY

1

REQUIRED EQUIPMENT

- 2 – 6 Inch Box (width smaller than shoulder-width)
- 2 Agility Rings

KEY FACTORS

- Focus on perfect movement mechanics and speed (short ground contact)
- Step off the box with both feet
- Land on both feet simultaneously inside agility rings
- Jump upwards with both feet simultaneously
- Maintain balance; land in same location inside agility rings and on top of the box

COMMON ERRORS

- Athlete lands outside agility rings
- Athlete focuses on maximum height instead of minimizing ground contact time

ID: 7199

7.200 LOW-LEVEL ABDUCTOR BOX JUMP REBOUNDS (II)

SUMMARY

The Low-Level Abductor Box Jump Rebounds II is a plyometric exercise, which focuses on developing neural pathways for explosive lateral change of direction capability, reaction time, body control & coordination as well as improving skill and speed foundation for complex movements utilizing a box and agility rings.

PURPOSE

1. Developing neural pathways for explosive lateral change of direction capability (neurological feedback loop)
2. Improving reaction time for lower extremities (legs)
3. Improving balance (body control) & coordination
4. Improving skill and speed foundation for complex movements

DESCRIPTION

1. Place box onto solid, non-sliding surface
2. Place 2 agility rings shoulder-width apart on the ground; 1 to the left side and 1 to the right side of the box
3. Step on top of the box; feet are close together
4. Jump off the box with both legs simultaneously
5. Land with both feet simultaneously inside agility rings; **look forward** during landing
6. Immediately jump on top of the box with both legs simultaneously while **looking forward** during lan-ding
7. Repeat

PRE-REQUISITE DRILLS

- Low-Level Abductor Box Jump Rebounds (I)

BREATH IN & OUT

- IN: Before Step Off
- OUT: During Jumping

DEGREE OF DIFFICULTY

2

REQUIRED EQUIPMENT

- 2 – 6 Inch Box (width smaller than shoulder-width)
- 2 Agility Rings

KEY FACTORS

- Focus on perfect movement mechanics and speed (short ground contact)
- Step off the box with both feet
- Land on both feet simultaneously inside agility rings
- Jump upwards with both feet simultaneously
- Maintain balance; land in same location inside agility rings and on top of the box

COMMON ERRORS

- Athlete lands outside agility rings
- Athlete focuses on maximum height instead of minimizing ground contact time

ID: 7200

7.201 LL ABDUCTOR BOX JUMP REB.: SL LANDING (III)

SUMMARY

The Low-Level Abductor Box Jump Rebound: Single-Leg Landing III is a plyometric exercise, which focuses on developing neural pathways for explosive lateral change of direction capability, reaction time, body control & coordination as well as improving skill and speed foundation for complex movements utilizing a box and agility rings.

PURPOSE

1. Developing neural pathways for explosive lateral change of direction capability (neurological feedback loop)
2. Improving reaction time for lower extremities (legs)
3. Improving balance (body control) & coordination
4. Improving skill and speed foundation for complex movements

DESCRIPTION

1. Place box onto solid, non-sliding surface
2. Place 2 agility rings shoulder-width apart on the ground; 1 to the left side and 1 to the right side of the box
3. Step on top of the box; feet are close together
4. Jump off the box with both legs simultaneously
5. Land with both feet simultaneously inside agility rings; **look forward** during landing
6. Immediately jump on top of the box landing on the right leg; **look down** during landing
7. Repeat; also perform drill landing on **left** leg

PRE-REQUISITE DRILLS

- Single-Leg Squat
- Low-Level Abductor Box Jump Rebounds (II)

BREATH IN & OUT

- IN: Before Step Off
- OUT: During Jumping

DEGREE OF DIFFICULTY

3

REQUIRED EQUIPMENT

- 2 – 6 Inch Box (width smaller than shoulder-width)
- 2 Agility Rings

KEY FACTORS

- Focus on perfect movement mechanics and speed (short ground contact)
- Step off the box with both feet
- Land on both feet simultaneously inside agility rings
- Jump upwards with both feet simultaneously
- Maintain balance; land in same location inside agility rings and on top of the box (single-leg stance)

COMMON ERRORS

- Athlete lands outside agility rings
- Athlete focuses on maximum height instead of minimizing ground contact time

ID: 7201

7.202 LL ABDUCTOR BOX JUMP REB.: SL LANDING (IV)

SUMMARY

The Low-Level Abductor Box Jump Rebounds: Single-Leg Landing IV is a plyometric exercise, which focuses on developing neural pathways for explosive lateral change of direction capability, reaction time, body control & coordination as well as improving skill and speed foundation for complex movements utilizing a box and agility rings.

PURPOSE

1. Developing neural pathways for explosive lateral change of direction capability (neurological feedback loop)
2. Improving reaction time for lower extremities (legs)
3. Improving balance (body control) & coordination
4. Improving skill and speed foundation for complex movements

DESCRIPTION

1. Place box onto solid, non-sliding surface
2. Place 2 agility rings shoulder-width apart on the ground; 1 to the left side and 1 to the right side of the box
3. Step on top of the box; feet are close together
4. Jump off the box with both legs simultaneously
5. Land with both feet simultaneously inside agility rings; **look forward** during landing
6. Immediately jump on top of the box landing on the right leg; **look forward** during landing
7. Repeat; also perform drill landing on **left** leg

PRE-REQUISITE DRILLS

- Single-Leg Squat
- Low-Level Abductor Box Jump Rebounds (III)

BREATH IN & OUT

- IN: Before Step Off
- OUT: During Jumping

DEGREE OF DIFFICULTY

4

REQUIRED EQUIPMENT

- 2 – 6 Inch Box (width smaller than shoulder-width)
- 2 Agility Rings

KEY FACTORS

- Focus on perfect movement mechanics and speed (short ground contact)
- Step off the box with both feet
- Land on both feet simultaneously inside agility rings
- Jump upwards with both feet simultaneously
- Maintain balance; land in same location inside agility rings and on top of the box (single-leg stance)

COMMON ERRORS

- Athlete lands outside agility rings
- Athlete focuses on maximum height instead of minimizing ground contact time

ID: 7202

7.203 LL ABDUCTOR BOX JUMP REB: ALTERN. SL LAND. (V)

SUMMARY

The Low-Level Abductor Box Jump Rebounds: Single-Leg Alternate Landing V is a plyometric exercise, which focuses on developing neural pathways for explosive lateral change of direction capability, reaction time, body control & coordination as well as improving skill and speed foundation for complex movements utilizing a box and agility rings.

PURPOSE

1. Developing neural pathways for explosive lateral change of direction capability (neurological feedback loop)
2. Improving reaction time for lower extremities (legs)
3. Improving balance (body control) & coordination
4. Improving skill and speed foundation for complex movements

DESCRIPTION

1. Place box onto solid, non-sliding surface
2. Place 2 agility rings shoulder-width apart on the ground; 1 to the left side and 1 to the right side of the box
3. Step on top of the box; feet are close together
4. Jump off the box with both legs simultaneously
5. Land with both feet simultaneously inside agility rings; **look forward** during landing
6. Immediately jump on top of the box landing on the **right** leg; **look forward** during landing
7. Jump off the box, land, and jump on the box landing on **left** leg

PRE-REQUISITE DRILLS

- Single-Leg Squat
- Low-Level Abductor Box Jump Rebounds (IV)

BREATH IN & OUT

- IN: Before Step Off
- OUT: During Jumping

DEGREE OF DIFFICULTY

5

REQUIRED EQUIPMENT

- 2 – 6 Inch Box (width smaller than shoulder-width)
- 2 Agility Rings

KEY FACTORS

- Focus on perfect movement mechanics and speed (short ground contact)
- Step off the box with both feet
- Land on both feet simultaneously inside agility rings
- Jump upwards with both feet simultaneously
- Maintain balance; land in same location inside agility rings and on top of the box (single-leg stance)

COMMON ERRORS

- Athlete lands outside agility rings
- Athlete focuses on maximum height instead of minimizing ground contact time

ID: 7203

7.204 LOW-LEVEL TUCK JUMP I

SUMMARY

The Low-Level Tuck Jump I is a plyometric exercise, which focuses on improving quick start sequence, body control & coordination as well as improving foot speed utilizing agility rings.

PURPOSE

1. Improving quick start sequence (split-step to 1st step)
2. Improving body control & coordination
3. Improving foot speed (neurological feedback loop)
4. Improving skill and speed foundation for complex movements

DESCRIPTION

Athlete stands up straight and needs to:

1. Position the feet under the shoulders
2. Place 2 agility rings in front of feet
3. Step into agility rings
4. Jump up with both legs simultaneously while **looking down** at the feet; flex knees below hip level
5. Land inside the **agility rings**

DEGREE OF DIFFICULTY

1

COMMON ERRORS

- Athlete moves back and forth inside agility rings during jumps
- Athlete jumps at sub-maximal speed
- Athlete lands outside agility rings

KEY FACTORS

- Focus on perfect movement mechanics and speed
- Jump with both feet simultaneously
- Keep knees below hip level
- Maintain balance – land in same location inside agility rings

REQUIRED EQUIPMENT

- 2 Agility Rings

BREATH IN & OUT

- IN: When landing
- OUT: During Jumping

ID: 7204

7.205 LOW-LEVEL TUCK JUMP II

SUMMARY

The Low-Level Tuck Jump II is a plyometric exercise, which focuses on improving quick start sequence, body control & coordination as well as improving foot speed utilizing agility rings.

PURPOSE

1. Improving quick start sequence (split-step to 1st step)
2. Improving body control & coordination
3. Improving foot speed (neurological feedback loop)
4. Improving skill and speed foundation for complex movements

DESCRIPTION

Athlete stands up straight and needs to:

1. Position the feet under the shoulders
2. Place 2 agility rings in front of feet
3. Step into agility rings
4. Jump up with both legs simultaneously while **looking forward**; flex knees below hip level
5. Land inside the agility rings

PRE-REQUISITE DRILLS

- Low-Level Tuck Jump I

BREATH IN & OUT

- IN: When landing
- OUT: During Jumping

DEGREE OF DIFFICULTY

2

REQUIRED EQUIPMENT

- 2 Agility Rings

KEY FACTORS

- Focus on perfect movement mechanics and speed
- Jump with both feet simultaneously
- Keep knees below hip level
- Maintain balance – land in same location inside agility rings

COMMON ERRORS

- Athlete looks down towards feet
- Athlete moves back and forth inside agility rings during jumps
- Athlete jumps at sub-maximal speed
- Athlete lands outside agility rings

ID: 7205

7.206 LOW-LEVEL TUCK JUMP III

SUMMARY

The Low-Level Tuck Jump III is a plyometric exercise, which focuses on improving quick start sequence, body control & coordination as well as improving foot speed utilizing a tennis ball.

PURPOSE

1. Improving quick start sequence (split-step to 1st step)
2. Improving body control & coordination
3. Improving foot speed (neurological feedback loop)

DESCRIPTION

Coach throws tennis ball at athlete during jumps.

Athlete stands up straight and needs to:

1. Position the feet under the shoulders
2. Jump up with both legs simultaneously while **looking forward**; flex knees below hip level
3. **Catch and return tennis ball**

PRE-REQUISITE DRILLS

- Low-Level Tuck Jump II

BREATH IN & OUT

- IN: When landing
- OUT: During Jumping

DEGREE OF DIFFICULTY

3

REQUIRED EQUIPMENT

- Tennis Ball

KEY FACTORS

- Focus on perfect movement mechanics and speed
- Jump with both feet simultaneously
- Keep knees below hip level
- Maintain balance – land in same location

COMMON ERRORS

- Athlete looks down towards feet
- Athlete moves back and forth during jumps
- Athlete jumps at sub-maximal speed
- Athlete can't catch tennis ball

ID: 7206

7.207 MID-LEVEL TUCK JUMP I

SUMMARY

The Mid-Level Tuck Jump I is a plyometric exercise, which focuses on improving hip flexor speed, body control & coordination as well as improving foot speed utilizing agility rings.

PURPOSE

1. Improving sprinting and jumping capability (hip-flexor speed)
2. Improving body control & coordination
3. Improving foot speed (neurological feedback loop)
4. Improving skill and speed foundation for complex movement.

DESCRIPTION

Athlete stands up straight and needs to:

1. Position the feet under the shoulders
2. Place 2 agility rings in front of feet
3. Step into agility rings
4. Jump up with both legs simultaneously while **looking down** at the feet; flex knees **at hip level**
5. Land inside the agility rings

PRE-REQUISITE DRILLS

- Low-Level Tuck Jump (I-III)

BREATH IN & OUT

- IN: When landing
- OUT: During Jumping

DEGREE OF DIFFICULTY

1

REQUIRED EQUIPMENT

- 2 Agility Rings

KEY FACTORS

- Focus on perfect movement mechanics and speed
- Jump with both feet simultaneously
- Keep knees at hip level
- Maintain balance – land in same location inside agility rings

COMMON ERRORS

- Athlete remains knees below hip level during jumping
- Athlete moves back and forth inside agility rings during jumps
- Athlete jumps at sub-maximal speed
- Athlete lands outside agility rings

ID: 7207

7.208 MID-LEVEL TUCK JUMP II

SUMMARY

The Mid-Level Tuck Jump II is a plyometric exercise, which focuses on improving body control & coordination as well as improving foot speed utilizing agility rings.

PURPOSE

1. Improving sprinting and jumping capability (hip-flexor speed)
2. Improving body control & coordination
3. Improving foot speed (neurological feedback loop)
4. Improving skill and speed foundation for complex movements

DESCRIPTION

Athlete stands up straight and needs to:

1. Position the feet under the shoulders
2. Place 2 agility rings in front of feet
3. Step into agility rings
4. Jump up with both legs simultaneously while **looking forward**; flex knees **at hip level**
5. Land inside the agility rings

PRE-REQUISITE DRILLS

- Mid-Level Tuck Jump I

BREATH IN & OUT

- IN: When landing
- OUT: During Jumping

COMMON ERRORS

- Athlete looks down towards feet
- Athlete moves back and forth inside agility rings during jumps
- Athlete jumps at sub-maximal speed
- Athlete lands outside agility rings

DEGREE OF DIFFICULTY

2

REQUIRED EQUIPMENT

- 2 Agility Rings

KEY FACTORS

- Focus on perfect movement mechanics and speed
- Jump with both feet simultaneously
- Keep knees at hip level
- Maintain balance – land in same location inside agility rings

ID: 7208

7.209 MID-LEVEL TUCK JUMP III

SUMMARY

The Mid-Level Tuck Jump III is a plyometric exercise, which focuses on improving body control & coordination as well as improving foot speed utilizing a tennis ball.

PURPOSE

1. Improving sprinting and jumping capability (hip-flexor speed)
2. Improving body control & coordination
3. Improving foot speed (neurological feedback loop)

DESCRIPTION

Coach throws tennis ball at athlete during jumps.

Athlete stands up straight and needs to:

1. Position the feet under the shoulders
2. Jump up with both legs simultaneously while **looking forward**; flex knees **at hip level**
3. **Catch and return tennis ball**

PRE-REQUISITE DRILLS

- Low-Level Tuck Jump II

BREATH IN & OUT

- IN: When landing
- OUT: During Jumping

DEGREE OF DIFFICULTY

3

REQUIRED EQUIPMENT

- Tennis Ball

KEY FACTORS

- Focus on perfect movement mechanics and speed
- Jump with both feet simultaneously
- Keep knees at hip level
- Maintain balance – land in same location

COMMON ERRORS

- Athlete looks down towards feet
- Athlete moves back and forth during jumps
- Athlete jumps at sub-maximal speed
- Athlete can't catch tennis ball

ID: 7209

7.210 HIGH-LEVEL TUCK JUMP I

SUMMARY

The High-Level Tuck Jump I is a plyometric exercise, which focuses on improving hip flexor speed, body control & coordination, flexibility as well as improving foot speed utilizing agility rings.

PURPOSE

1. Improving sprinting and jumping capability (hip-flexor speed)
2. Improving body control & coordination
3. Improving foot speed (neurological feedback loop)
4. Improving flexibility (Glutes & Hamstrings)
5. Improving skill and speed foundation for complex movements

DESCRIPTION

Athlete stands up straight and needs to:

1. Position the feet under the shoulders
2. Place 2 agility rings in front of feet
3. Step into agility rings
4. Jump up with both legs simultaneously while **loo-king down** at the feet; flex knees **above hip level** (chest); don't go for maximum height but speed
5. Land inside the **agility rings**

PRE-REQUISITE DRILLS

- Loaded High-Level Tuck Jump (I)

BREATH IN & OUT

- IN: When landing
- OUT: During Jumping

COMMON ERRORS

- Athlete looks down towards feet
- Athlete moves back and forth during jumps
- Athlete jumps at sub-maximal speed
- Athlete can't catch tennis ball

DEGREE OF DIFFICULTY

1

REQUIRED EQUIPMENT

- 2 Agility Rings

KEY FACTORS

- Focus on perfect movement mechanics and speed
- Jump with both feet simultaneously
- Keep knees above hip level
- Maintain balance – land in same location inside agility rings

ID: 7210

7.211 HIGH-LEVEL TUCK JUMP II

SUMMARY

The High-Level Tuck Jump II is a plyometric exercise, which focuses on improving hip flexor speed, body control & coordination, flexibility as well as improving foot speed utilizing agility rings.

PURPOSE

1. Improving sprinting and jumping capability (hip-flexor speed)
2. Improving body control & coordination
3. Improving foot speed (neurological feedback loop)
4. Improving flexibility (Glutes & Hamstrings)
5. Improving skill and speed foundation for complex movements

DESCRIPTION

Athlete stands up straight and needs to:

1. Position the feet under the shoulders
2. Place 2 agility rings in front of feet
3. Step into agility rings
4. Jump up with both legs simultaneously while **looking forward**; flex knees **above hip level** (chest); don't go for maximum height but speed
5. Land inside the agility rings

PRE-REQUISITE DRILLS

- Loaded High-Level Tuck Jumps (I)
- Loaded High-Level Tuck Jumps (II)

DEGREE OF DIFFICULTY

2

REQUIRED EQUIPMENT

- 2 Agility Rings

KEY FACTORS

- Focus on perfect movement mechanics and speed
- Jump with both feet simultaneously
- Keep knees above hip level
- Maintain balance – land in same location inside agility rings

COMMON ERRORS

- Athlete remains knees below – or at hip level during jumping
- Athlete moves back and forth inside agility rings during jumps
- Athlete jumps at sub-maximal speed
- Athlete lands outside agility rings

BREATH IN & OUT

- IN: When landing
- OUT: During Jumping

ID: 7211

7.212 HIGH-LEVEL TUCK JUMP III

SUMMARY

The High-Level Tuck Jump III is a plyometric exercise, which focuses on im3n, flexibility as well as improving foot speed utilizing a tennis ball.

PURPOSE

1. Improving sprinting and jumping capability (hip-flexor speed)
2. Improving body control & coordination
3. Improving foot speed (neurological feedback loop)
4. Improving flexibility (Glutes & Hamstrings)

DESCRIPTION

Coach throws tennis ball at athlete during jumps.

Athlete stands up straight and needs to:

1. Position the feet under the shoulders
2. Jump up with both legs simultaneously while **looking forward**; flex knees **above hip level** (chest); don't go for maximum height but speed
3. **Catch and return tennis ball**

PRE-REQUISITE DRILLS

- Loaded High-Level Tuck Jumps (I)
- Loaded High-Level Tuck Jumps (II)
- Loaded High-Level Tuck Jumps (III)

BREATH IN & OUT

- IN: When landing
- OUT: During Jumping

DEGREE OF DIFFICULTY

3

REQUIRED EQUIPMENT

- 1 Tennis Ball

KEY FACTORS

- Focus on perfect movement mechanics and speed
- Jump with both feet simultaneously
- Keep knees above hip level
- Maintain balance – land in same location

COMMON ERRORS

- Athlete remains knees below – or at hip level during jumping
- Athlete moves back and forth during jumps
- Athlete jumps at sub-maximal speed

ID: 7212

7.213 SINGLE-LEG LOW-LEVEL TUCK JUMP I

SUMMARY

The Single-Leg Low-Level Tuck Jump I is a plyometric exercise, which focuses on improving quick start sequence, body control & coordination as well as improving foot speed for low-height jumps utilizing an agility ring.

PURPOSE

1. Improving quick start sequence (split-step to 1st step)
2. Improving body control & coordination
3. Improving foot speed for low-height jumps (neurological feedback loop)
4. Improving skill and speed foundation for complex movements

DESCRIPTION

Athlete stands up straight and needs to:

1. Place 1 agility ring on the ground (flat surface)
2. Step into agility rings with one leg; other leg is off the ground
3. Jump up on 1 leg while **looking down** at the ground; flex knee **below hip level**
4. Land inside the agility ring
5. Switch leg and repeat

PRE-REQUISITE DRILLS

- Low-Level Tuck Jump (I)

REQUIRED EQUIPMENT

- 1 Agility Ring

DEGREE OF DIFFICULTY

1

KEY FACTORS

- Focus on perfect movement mechanics and speed
- Keep knees below hip level
- Maintain balance – land in same location inside agility rings

COMMON ERRORS

- Athlete moves back and forth inside agility ring during jumps
- Athlete jumps at sub-maximal speed
- Athlete lands outside agility ring

BREATH IN & OUT

- IN: When landing
- OUT: During Jumping

ID: 7213

7.214 SINGLE-LEG LOW-LEVEL TUCK JUMP II

SUMMARY

The Single-Leg Low-Level Tuck Jump II is a plyometric exercise, which focuses on improving quick start sequence, body control & coordination as well as improving foot speed for low-height jumps utilizing an agility ring.

PURPOSE

1. Improving quick start sequence (split-step to 1st step)
2. Improving body control & coordination
3. Improving foot speed for low-height jumps(neurological feedback loop)
4. Improving skill and speed foundation for complex movements

DESCRIPTION

Athlete stands up straight and needs to:

1. Place 1 agility ring on the ground (flat surface)
2. Step into agility rings with left leg; right leg is off the ground
3. Start with the leg closest to the cone
4. Jump up on 1 leg while **looking forward**; flex knee **below hip level**
5. Land inside the agility ring
6. Switch leg and repeat

PRE-REQUISITE DRILLS

- Low-Level Tuck Jump (II)

BREATH IN & OUT

- IN: When landing
- OUT: During Jumping

DEGREE OF DIFFICULTY

2

REQUIRED EQUIPMENT

- 1 Agility Ring

KEY FACTORS

- Focus on perfect movement mechanics and speed
- Keep knees below hip level
- Maintain balance – land in same location inside agility ring

COMMON ERRORS

- Athlete moves back and forth inside agility ring during jumps
- Athlete jumps at sub-maximal speed
- Athlete lands outside agility ring

ID: 7214

7.215 SINGLE-LEG LOW-LEVEL TUCK JUMP III

SUMMARY

The Single-Leg Mid-Level Tuck Jump III is a plyometric exercise, which focuses on improving hip flexor speed, body control & coordination as well as improving foot speed utilizing a tennis ball.

PURPOSE

1. Improving quick start sequence (split-step to 1st step)
2. Improving body control & coordination
3. Improving foot speed for low-height jumps (neurological feedback loop)

DESCRIPTION

Coach throws tennis ball at athlete during jumps.

Athlete stands up straight and needs to:

1. Start with the leg closest to the cone
2. Jump up on 1 leg while **looking forward**; flex knee **below hip level**
3. **Catch tennis ball and return**
4. Switch leg and repeat

PRE-REQUISITE DRILLS

- Low-Level Tuck Jump (III)

BREATH IN & OUT

- IN: When landing
- OUT: During Jumping

DEGREE OF DIFFICULTY

3

REQUIRED EQUIPMENT

- 1 Tennis Ball

KEY FACTORS

- Focus on perfect movement mechanics and speed
- Keep knees below hip level
- Maintain balance – land in same location

COMMON ERRORS

- Athlete moves back and forth during jumps
- Athlete jumps at sub-maximal speed

ID: 7215

7.216 SINGLE-LEG MID-LEVEL TUCK JUMP I

SUMMARY

The Single-Leg Mid-Level Tuck Jump I is a plyometric exercise, which focuses on improving hip flexor speed, body control & coordination as well as improving foot speed utilizing an agility ring.

PURPOSE

1. Improving quick start sequence (split-step to 1st step)
2. Improving body control & coordination
3. Improving foot speed for sub-maximal jumps (neurological feedback loop)
4. Improving skill and speed foundation for complex movements

DESCRIPTION

Athlete stands up straight and needs to:

1. Place 1 agility ring on the ground (flat surface)
2. Step into agility ring with left leg; right leg is off the ground
3. Jump up on 1 leg while **looking down** at the ground; flex knee **at hip level**
4. Land inside the **agility ring**
5. Switch leg and repeat

PRE-REQUISITE DRILLS

- Mid-Level Tuck Jumps (I)

COMMON ERRORS

- Athlete remains knees below hip level during jumping
- Athlete moves back and forth inside agility ring during jumps
- Athlete jumps at sub-maximal speed
- Athlete lands outside agility ring

DEGREE OF DIFFICULTY

1

REQUIRED EQUIPMENT

- 1 Agility Ring

KEY FACTORS

- Focus on perfect movement mechanics and speed
- Keep knees at hip level
- Maintain balance – land in same location inside agility ring

BREATH IN & OUT

- IN: When landing
- OUT: During Jumping

ID: 7216

7.217 SINGLE-LEG MID-LEVEL TUCK JUMP II

SUMMARY

The Single-Leg Mid-Level Tuck Jump II is a plyometric exercise, which focuses on improving hip flexor speed, body control & coordination as well as improving foot speed utilizing an agility ring.

PURPOSE

1. Improving quick start sequence (split-step to 1st step)
2. Improving body control & coordination
3. Improving foot speed for sub-maximal jumps (neurological feedback loop)
4. Improving skill and speed foundation for complex movements

DESCRIPTION

Athlete stands up straight and needs to:

1. Place 1 agility ring on the ground (flat surface)
2. Step into agility ring with left leg; right leg is off the ground
3. Start with the leg closest to the cone
4. Jump up on 1 leg while **looking forward**; flex knee **at hip level**
5. Land inside the agility ring
6. Switch leg and repeat

PRE-REQUISITE DRILLS

- Mid-Level Tuck Jump (II)

DEGREE OF DIFFICULTY

2

REQUIRED EQUIPMENT

- 1 Agility Ring

KEY FACTORS

- Focus on perfect movement mechanics and speed
- Keep knees at hip level
- Maintain balance – land in same location inside agility rings

COMMON ERRORS

- Athlete remains knees below hip level during jumping
- Athlete moves back and forth inside agility ring during jumps
- Athlete jumps at sub-maximal speed
- Athlete lands outside agility ring

BREATH IN & OUT

- IN: When landing
- OUT: During Jumping

ID: 7217

7.218 SINGLE-LEG MID-LEVEL TUCK JUMP III

SUMMARY

The Single-Leg Mid-Level Tuck Jump III is a plyometric exercise, which focuses on improving hip flexor speed, body control & coordination as well as improving foot speed utilizing a tennis ball.

PURPOSE

1. Improving quick start sequence (split-step to 1st step)
2. Improving body control & coordination
3. Improving foot speed for sub-maximal jumps (neurological feedback loop)

DESCRIPTION

Coach throws tennis ball at athlete during jumps.

Athlete stands up straight and needs to:

1. Start with the leg closest to the cone
2. Jump up on 1 leg while **looking forward**; flex knee **at hip level**
3. **Catch tennis ball and return**
4. Switch leg and repeat

PRE-REQUISITE DRILLS

- Low-Level Tuck Jump (III)

BREATH IN & OUT

- IN: When landing
- OUT: During Jumping

DEGREE OF DIFFICULTY

3

REQUIRED EQUIPMENT

- 1 Tennis Ball

KEY FACTORS

- Focus on perfect movement mechanics and speed
- Keep knees at hip level
- Maintain balance – land in same location

COMMON ERRORS

- Athlete remains knees below hip level during jumping
- Athlete moves back and forth during jumps
- Athlete jumps at sub-maximal speed

ID: 7218

7.219 SINGLE-LEG HIGH-LEVEL TUCK JUMP I

SUMMARY

The Single-Leg High-Level Tuck Jump I is a plyometric exercise, which focuses on improving hip flexor speed, body control & coordination, flexibility as well as improving foot speed utilizing an agility ring.

PURPOSE

1. Improving hip-flexor speed
2. Improving body control & coordination
3. Improving foot speed (neurological feedback loop)
4. Improving flexibility (Glutes & Hamstrings)
5. Improving skill and speed foundation for complex movement

DESCRIPTION

Athlete stands up straight and needs to:

1. Place 1 agility ring on the ground (flat surface)
2. Step into agility ring with left leg; right leg is off the ground
3. Start with the leg closest to the cone
4. Jump up on 1 leg while **looking down** at the ground; flex knee **above hip level** (chest)
5. Land inside the **agility ring**
6. Switch leg and repeat

PRE-REQUISITE DRILLS

- High-Level Tuck Jump (I)

BREATH IN & OUT

- IN: When landing
- OUT: During Jumping

DEGREE OF DIFFICULTY

1

REQUIRED EQUIPMENT

- 1 Agility Ring

KEY FACTORS

- Focus on perfect movement mechanics and speed
- Keep knee above hip level
- Maintain balance – land in same location inside agility ring

COMMON ERRORS

- Athlete remains knees below – or at hip level during jumping
- Athlete jumps at sub-maximal speed
- Athlete lands outside agility ring

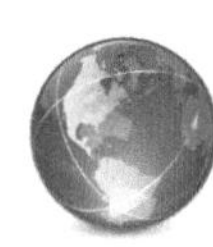

ID: 7219

7.220 SINGLE-LEG HIGH-LEVEL TUCK JUMP II

SUMMARY

The Single-Leg High-Level Tuck Jump II is a plyometric exercise, which focuses on improving hip flexor speed, body control & coordination, flexibility as well as improving foot speed utilizing an agility ring.

PURPOSE

1. Improving hip-flexor speed
2. Improving body control & coordination
3. Improving foot speed (neurological feedback loop)
4. Improving flexibility (Glutes & Hamstrings)
5. Improving skill and speed foundation for complex movements

DESCRIPTION

Athlete stands up straight and needs to:

1. Place 1 agility ring on the ground (flat surface)
2. Step into agility ring with left leg; right leg is off the ground
3. Start with the leg closest to the cone
4. Jump up on 1 leg while **looking forward**; flex knee **above hip level** (chest)
5. Land inside the agility ring
6. Switch leg and repeat

DEGREE OF DIFFICULTY

2

REQUIRED EQUIPMENT

- 1 Agility Ring

KEY FACTORS

- Focus on perfect movement mechanics and speed
- Keep knees above hip level
- Maintain balance – land in same location inside agility ring

COMMON ERRORS

- Athlete remains knees below – or at hip level during jumping
- Athlete jumps at sub-maximal speed
- Athlete lands outside agility ring

PRE-REQUISITE DRILLS

- High-Level Tuck Jump (II)

BREATH IN & OUT

- IN: When landing
- OUT: During Jumping

ID: 7220

7.221 SINGLE-LEG HIGH-LEVEL TUCK JUMP III

SUMMARY

The Single-Leg High-Level Tuck Jump III is a plyometric exercise, which focuses on improving hip flexor speed, body control & coordination, flexibility as well as improving foot speed utilizing a tennis ball.

PURPOSE

1. Improving hip-flexor speed
2. Improving body control & coordination
3. Improving foot speed (neurological feedback loop)
4. Improving flexibility (Glutes & Hamstrings)

DESCRIPTION

Coach throws tennis ball at athlete during jumps.
Athlete stands up straight and needs to:

1. Start with the leg closest to the cone
2. Jump up on 1 leg while **looking forward**; flex knee **above hip level**
3. **Catch tennis ball and return**
4. Switch leg and repeat

PRE-REQUISITE DRILLS

- Mid-Level Tuck Jump (III)

DEGREE OF DIFFICULTY

3

REQUIRED EQUIPMENT

- 1 Tennis Ball

KEY FACTORS

- Focus on perfect movement mechanics and speed
- Keep knees above hip level
- Maintain balance – land in same location

COMMON ERRORS

- Athlete remains knees below – or at hip level during jumping
- Athlete moves back and forth during jumps
- Athlete jumps at sub-maximal speed

BREATH IN & OUT

- IN: When landing
- OUT: During Jumping

ID: 7221

7.222 LOW-LEVEL LATERAL TUCK JUMP I

SUMMARY

The Low-Level Lateral Tuck Jump I is a plyometric exercise, which focuses on improving quick start sequence along the baseline, body control & coordination as well as improving foot speed utilizing a cone and agility rings.

PURPOSE

1. Improving quick start sequence (split-step to 1st side-step)
2. Improving body control & coordination
3. Improving foot speed (neurological feedback loop)
4. Improving skill and speed foundation for complex movements

DESCRIPTION

Athlete stands up straight and needs to:

1. Place 2 agility rings on the ground two shoulder-widths apart and put a cone in between the 2 rings
2. Place the outside foot inside the agility ring
3. Position the feet under the shoulders
4. Jump back and forth over the cone with both legs **simultaneously** while **looking down** at the feet; flex knees **below hip level**
5. Outside foot lands inside the **agility rings**

KEY FACTORS

- Focus on perfect movement mechanics and speed; raise knees to go over the cone
- Maintain upper body over the cone during jumps
- Jump with both feet simultaneously
- Keep knees below hip level
- Maintain balance – land in same location inside agility rings

COMMON ERRORS

- Athlete moves heels towards buttocks instead of raising the knees when jumping over the cone
- Feet are too close together during jumps
- Athlete moves outside agility rings during jumps
- Athlete jumps at sub-maximal speed

PRE-REQUISITE DRILLS

- Low-Level Tuck Jump (I)

REQUIRED EQUIPMENT

- 2 Agility Rings
- One 2 Inch Cone

BREATH IN & OUT

- IN: When landing
- OUT: During Jumping

DEGREE OF DIFFICULTY

1

ID: 7222

7.223 LOW-LEVEL LATERAL TUCK JUMP II

SUMMARY

The Low-Level Lateral Tuck Jump II is a plyometric exercise, which focuses on improving quick start sequence along the baseline, body control & coordination as well as improving foot speed utilizing a cone and agility rings.

PURPOSE

1. Improving quick start sequence (split-step to 1st side-step)
2. Improving body control & coordination
3. Improving foot speed (neurological feedback loop)
4. Improving skill and speed foundation for complex movement

DESCRIPTION

Athlete stands up straight and needs to:

1. Place 2 agility rings on the ground two shoulder-widths apart and put a cone in between the 2 rings
2. Place the outside foot inside the agility ring
3. Position the feet under the shoulders
4. Jump back and forth over the cone with both legs **simultaneously** while **looking forward**; flex knees **below hip level**
5. Outside foot lands inside the agility rings

PRE-REQUISITE DRILLS

- Low-Level Tuck Jump (II)

BREATH IN & OUT

- IN: When landing
- OUT: During Jumping

DEGREE OF DIFFICULTY

2

REQUIRED EQUIPMENT

- 2 Agility Rings
- One 2 Inch Cone

KEY FACTORS

- Focus on perfect movement mechanics and speed; raise knees to go over the cone
- Maintain upper body over the cone during jumps
- Jump with both feet simultaneously
- Keep knees below hip level
- Maintain balance – land in same location inside agility rings

COMMON ERRORS

- Athlete moves heels towards buttocks instead of raising the knees when jumping over the cone
- Feet are too close together during jumps
- Athlete moves outside agility rings during jumps
- Athlete jumps at sub-maximal speed

ID: 7223

7.224 LOW-LEVEL LATERAL TUCK JUMP III

SUMMARY

The Low-Level Lateral Tuck Jump III is a plyometric exercise, which focuses on improving quick start sequence along the baseline, body control & coordination as well as improving foot speed utilizing a cone and tennis ball.

PURPOSE

1. mproving quick start sequence (split-step to 1st side-step)
2. Improving body control & coordination
3. Improving foot speed (neurological feedback loop)

DESCRIPTION

Coach throws tennis ball at athlete during jumps.
Athlete stands up straight and needs to:

1. Place a cone on the ground
2. Stand next to the cone
3. Position the feet under the shoulders
4. Jump back and forth over the cone with both legs **simultaneously** while **looking forward**; flex knees **below hip level**
5. **Catch and return tennis ball**

DEGREE OF DIFFICULTY

3

REQUIRED EQUIPMENT

- 1 Tennis Ball
- One 2 Inch Cone

KEY FACTORS

- Focus on perfect movement mechanics and speed; raise knees to go over the cone
- Maintain upper body over the cone during jumps
- Jump with both feet simultaneously
- Keep knees below hip level
- Maintain balance – land in line with cones

COMMON ERRORS

- Athlete moves heels towards buttocks instead of raising the knees when jumping over the cone
- Feet are too close together during jumps
- Athlete doesn't land in same spot during jumps
- Athlete jumps at sub-maximal speed

PRE-REQUISITE DRILLS

- Low-Level Tuck Jump (II)

BREATH IN & OUT

- IN: When landing
- OUT: During Jumping

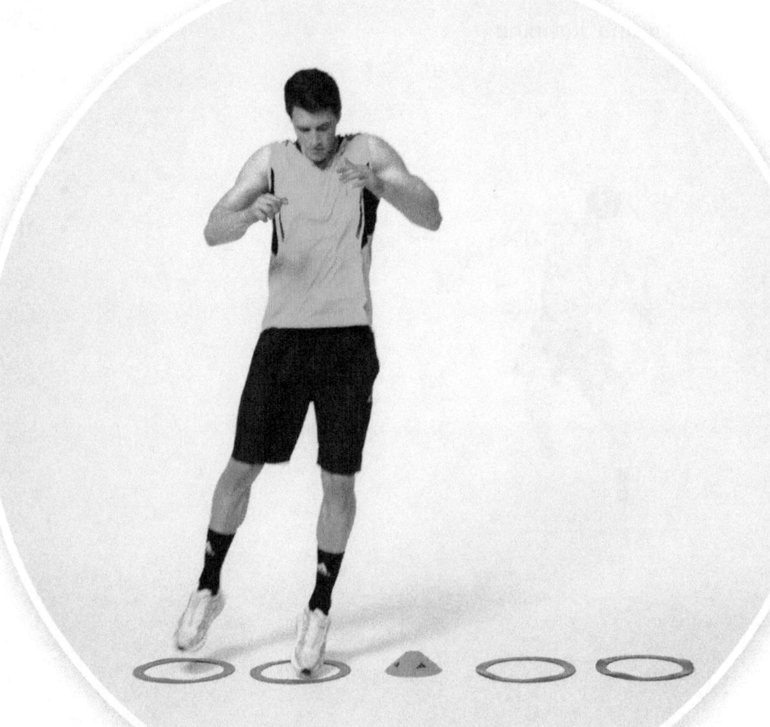

ID: 7224

7.225 MID-LEVEL LATERAL TUCK JUMP I

SUMMARY

The Mid-Level Lateral Tuck Jump I is a plyometric exercise, which focuses on improving quick start sequence along the baseline, body control & coordination as well as improving foot speed utilizing a cone and agility rings.

PURPOSE

1. Improving quick start sequence (split-step to 1st side-step)
2. Improving body control & coordination
3. Improving foot speed (neurological feedback loop)
4. Improving skill and speed foundation for complex movements

DESCRIPTION

Athlete stands up straight and needs to:

1. Place 2 agility rings on the ground two shoulder-widths apart and put a cone in between the 2 rings
2. Place the outside foot inside the agility ring
3. Position the feet under the shoulders
4. Jump back and forth over the cone with both legs **simultaneously** while **looking down** at the feet; flex knees **at hip level**
5. Outside foot lands inside the agility rings

DEGREE OF DIFFICULTY

1

KEY FACTORS

- Focus on perfect movement mechanics and speed; raise knees to go over the cone
- Maintain upper body over the cone during jumps
- Jump with both feet simultaneously
- Keep knees at hip level
- Maintain balance – land in same location inside agility rings

PRE-REQUISITE DRILLS

- Mid-Level Tuck Jumps (I)

COMMON ERRORS

- Athlete moves heels towards buttocks instead of raising the knees when jumping over the cone
- Feet are too close together during jumps
- Athlete moves outside agility rings during jumps
- Athlete jumps at sub-maximal speed

BREATH IN & OUT

- IN: When landing
- OUT: During Jumping

REQUIRED EQUIPMENT

- 2 Agility Rings
- One 4 Inch Cone

ID: 7225

7.226 MID-LEVEL LATERAL TUCK JUMP II

SUMMARY

The Mid-Level Lateral Tuck Jump II is a plyometric exercise, which focuses on improving quick start sequence along the baseline, body control & coordination as well as improving foot speed utilizing a cone and agility rings

PURPOSE

1. Improving quick start sequence (split-step to 1st side-step)
2. Improving body control & coordination
3. Improving foot speed (neurological feedback loop)
4. Improving skill and speed foundation for complex movement

DESCRIPTION

Athlete stands up straight and needs to:

1. Place 2 agility rings on the ground two shoulder-widths apart and put a cone in between the 2 rings
2. Place the outside foot inside the agility ring
3. Position the feet under the shoulders
4. Jump back and forth over the cone with both legs **simultaneously** while **looking forward**; flex knees **at hip level**
5. Outside foot lands inside the agility rings

PRE-REQUISITE DRILLS

- Mid-Level Tuck Jump (II)

BREATH IN & OUT

- IN: When landing
- OUT: During Jumping

DEGREE OF DIFFICULTY

2

REQUIRED EQUIPMENT

- 2 Agility Rings
- One 4 Inch Cone

KEY FACTORS

- Focus on perfect movement mechanics and speed; raise knees to go over the cone
- Maintain upper body over the cone during jumps
- Jump with both feet simultaneously
- Keep knees at hip level
- Maintain balance – land in same location inside agility rings

COMMON ERRORS

- Athlete moves heels towards buttocks instead of raising the knees when jumping over the cone
- Feet are too close together during jumps
- Athlete moves outside agility rings during jumps
- Athlete jumps at sub-maximal speed

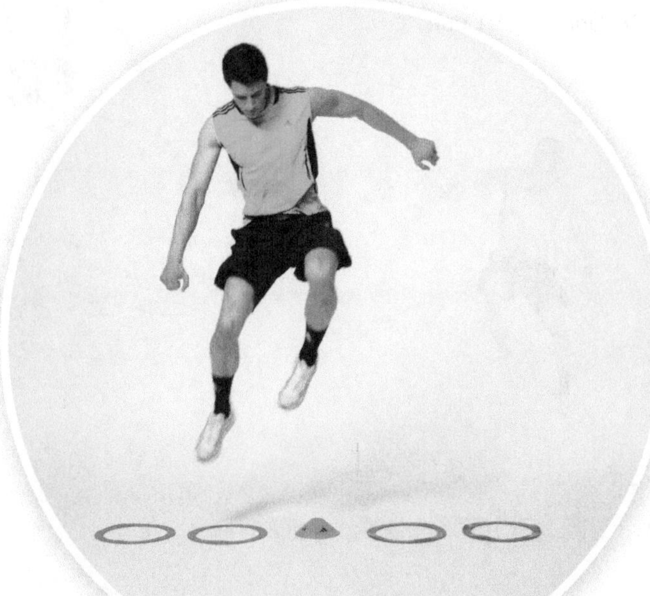

ID: 7226

7.227 MID-LEVEL LATERAL TUCK JUMP III

SUMMARY

The Mid-Level Lateral Tuck Jump III is a plyometric exercise, which focuses on improving quick start sequence along the baseline, body control & coordination as well as improving foot speed utilizing a cone and tennis ball.

PURPOSE

1. Improving quick start sequence (split-step to 1st side-step)
2. Improving body control & coordination
3. Improving foot speed (neurological feedback loop)

DESCRIPTION

Coach throws tennis ball at athlete during jumps.

Athlete stands up straight and needs to:

1. Place a cone on the ground
2. Stand next to the cone
3. Position the feet under the shoulders
4. Jump back and forth over the cone with both legs **simultaneously** while **looking forward**; flex knees **at hip level**
5. **Catch and return tennis ball**

PRE-REQUISITE DRILLS

- Mid-Level Tuck Jump (III)

BREATH IN & OUT

- IN: When landing
- OUT: During Jumping

DEGREE OF DIFFICULTY

3

REQUIRED EQUIPMENT

- 1 Tennis Ball
- One 4 Inch Cone

KEY FACTORS

- Focus on perfect movement mechanics and speed; raise knees to go over the cone
- Maintain upper body over the cone during jumps
- Jump with both feet simultaneously
- Keep knees at hip level
- Maintain balance – land in line with cones

COMMON ERRORS

- Athlete moves heels towards buttocks instead of raising the knees when jumping over the cone
- Feet are too close together during jumps
- Athlete doesn't land in same spot during jumps
- Athlete jumps at sub-maximal speed

ID: 7227

7.228 HIGH-LEVEL LATERAL TUCK JUMP I

SUMMARY

The High-Level Lateral Tuck Jump I is a plyometric exercise, which focuses on improving quick start sequence along the baseline, body control & coordination as well as improving foot speed utilizing a cone and agility rings.

PURPOSE

1. Improving quick start sequence (split-step to 1st side-step)
2. Improving body control & coordination
3. Improving foot speed (neurological feedback loop)
4. Improving skill and speed foundation for complex movements

DESCRIPTION

Athlete stands up straight and needs to:

1. Place 2 agility rings on the ground two shoulder-widths apart and put a cone in between the 2 rings
2. Place the outside foot inside the agility ring
3. Position the feet under the shoulders
4. Jump back and forth over the cone with both legs **simultaneously** while **looking down** at the feet; flex knees **above hip level**
5. Outside foot lands inside the **agility rings**

PRE-REQUISITE DRILLS

- High-Level Tuck Jump (I)

BREATH IN & OUT

- IN: When landing
- OUT: During Jumping

DEGREE OF DIFFICULTY

1

REQUIRED EQUIPMENT

- 2 Agility Rings
- One 6 Inch Cone

KEY FACTORS

- Focus on perfect movement mechanics and speed; raise knees to go over the cone
- Maintain upper body over the cone during jumps
- Jump with both feet simultaneously
- Keep knees above hip level
- Maintain balance – land in same location inside agility rings

COMMON ERRORS

- Athlete moves heels towards buttocks instead of raising the knees when jumping over the cone
- Feet are too close together during jumps
- Athlete moves outside agility rings during jumps
- Athlete jumps at sub-maximal speed

ID: 7228

7.229 HIGH-LEVEL LATERAL TUCK JUMP II

SUMMARY

The High-Level Lateral Tuck Jump II is a plyometric exercise, which focuses on improving quick start sequence along the baseline, body control & coordination as well as improving foot speed utilizing a cone and agility rings.

PURPOSE

1. Improving quick start sequence (split-step to 1st side-step)
2. Improving body control & coordination
3. Improving foot speed (neurological feedback loop)
4. Improving skill and speed foundation for complex movements

DESCRIPTION

Athlete stands up straight and needs to:

1. Place 2 agility rings on the ground two shoulder-widths apart and put a cone in between the 2 rings
2. Place the outside foot inside the agility ring
3. Position the feet under the shoulders
4. Jump back and forth over the cone with both legs **simultaneously** while **looking down** at the feet; flex knees **above hip level**
5. Outside foot lands inside the agility rings

PRE-REQUISITE DRILLS

- High-Level Tuck Jump (II)

BREATH IN & OUT

- IN: When landing
- OUT: During Jumping

DEGREE OF DIFFICULTY

2

REQUIRED EQUIPMENT

- 2 Agility Rings
- One 6 Inch Cone

KEY FACTORS

- Focus on perfect movement mechanics and speed; raise knees to go over the cone
- Maintain upper body over the cone during jumps
- Jump with both feet simultaneously
- Keep knees above hip level
- Maintain balance – land in same location inside agility rings

COMMON ERRORS

- Athlete moves heels towards buttocks instead of raising the knees when jumping over the cone
- Feet are too close together during jumps
- Athlete moves outside agility rings during jumps
- Athlete jumps at sub-maximal speed

ID: 7229

7.230 HIGH-LEVEL LATERAL TUCK JUMP III

SUMMARY

The High-Level Lateral Tuck Jump III is a plyometric exercise, which focuses on improving quick start sequence along the baseline, body control & coordination as well as improving foot speed utilizing a cone and tennis ball.

PURPOSE

1. Improving quick start sequence (split-step to 1st side-step)
2. Improving body control & coordination
3. Improving foot speed (neurological feedback loop)

DESCRIPTION

Coach throws tennis ball at athlete during jumps.

Athlete stands up straight and needs to:

1. Place a cone on the ground
2. Stand next to the cone
3. Position the feet under the shoulders
4. Jump back and forth over the cone with both legs **simultaneously** while **looking forward**; flex knees **above hip level**
5. **Catch and return tennis ball**

PRE-REQUISITE DRILLS

- High-Level Tuck Jump (III)

BREATH IN & OUT

- IN: When landing
- OUT: During Jumping

DEGREE OF DIFFICULTY

3

REQUIRED EQUIPMENT

- 1 Tennis Ball
- One 6 Inch Cone

KEY FACTORS

- Focus on perfect movement mechanics and speed; raise knees to go over the cone
- Maintain upper body over the cone during jumps
- Jump with both feet simultaneously
- Keep knees above hip level
- Maintain balance – land in same location

COMMON ERRORS

- Athlete moves heels towards buttocks instead of raising the knees when jumping over the cone
- Feet are too close together during jumps
- Athlete doesn't land in same spot during jumps
- Athlete jumps at sub-maximal speed

ID: 7230

7.231 SINGLE-LEG LOW-LEVEL LATERAL TUCK JUMP I

SUMMARY

The Single-Leg Low-Level Lateral Tuck Jump I is a plyometric exercise, which focuses on improving quick start sequence, body control & coordination as well as improving foot speed for low-height jumps utilizing a cone and agility rings.

PURPOSE

1. Improving quick start sequence (split-step to 1st side-step)
2. Improving body control & coordination
3. Improving foot speed (neurological feedback loop)
4. Improving skill and speed foundation for complex movements

DESCRIPTION

Athlete stands up straight and needs to:

1. Place 2 agility rings on the ground 2 shoulder-widths apart and put a cone in between the 2 rings
2. Stand on one leg (the leg closest to the cone) and place it inside the agility ring
3. Jump back and forth over the cone while **looking down** at the feet; flex knees **below hip level**

Note: Also perform exercise by jumping with the leg farthest away from the cone.

PRE-REQUISITE DRILLS

- Low-Level Tuck Jump (I)

BREATH IN & OUT

- IN: When landing
- OUT: During Jumping

DEGREE OF DIFFICULTY

1

REQUIRED EQUIPMENT

- 2 Agility Rings
- One 2 Inch Cone

KEY FACTORS

- Focus on perfect movement mechanics and speed; raise knees to go over the cone
- Maintain upper body over the cone during jumps
- Keep knees below hip level
- Maintain balance – land inside agility ring

COMMON ERRORS

- Athlete moves heels towards buttocks instead of raising the knees when jumping over the cone
- Athlete moves outside agility rings during jumps
- Athlete jumps at sub-maximal speed

ID: 7231

7.232 SINGLE-LEG LOW-LEVEL LATERAL TUCK JUMP II

SUMMARY

The Single-Leg Low-Level Lateral Tuck Jump II is a plyometric exercise, which focuses on improving quick start sequence, body control & coordination as well as improving foot speed for low-height jumps utilizing a cone and agility rings.

PURPOSE

1. Improving quick start sequence (split-step to 1st side-step)
2. Improving body control & coordination
3. Improving foot speed (neurological feedback loop)
4. Improving skill and speed foundation for complex movements

DESCRIPTION

Athlete stands up straight and needs to:

1. Place 2 agility rings on the ground 2 shoulder-widths apart and put a cone in between the 2 rings
2. Stand on one leg (the leg closest to the cone) and place it inside the agility ring
3. Jump back and forth over the cone while **looking forward**; flex knees **below hip level**

Note: Also perform exercise by jumping with the leg farthest away from the cone.

PRE-REQUISITE DRILLS

- Low-Level Tuck Jump (II)

BREATH IN & OUT

- IN: When landing
- OUT: During Jumping

DEGREE OF DIFFICULTY

2

REQUIRED EQUIPMENT

- 2 Agility Rings
- One 2 Inch Cone

KEY FACTORS

- Focus on perfect movement mechanics and speed; raise knees to go over the cone
- Maintain upper body over the cone during jumps
- Keep knees below hip level
- Maintain balance – land inside agility ring

COMMON ERRORS

- Athlete moves heels towards buttocks instead of raising the knees when jumping over the cone
- Athlete moves outside agility rings during jumps
- Athlete jumps at sub-maximal speed

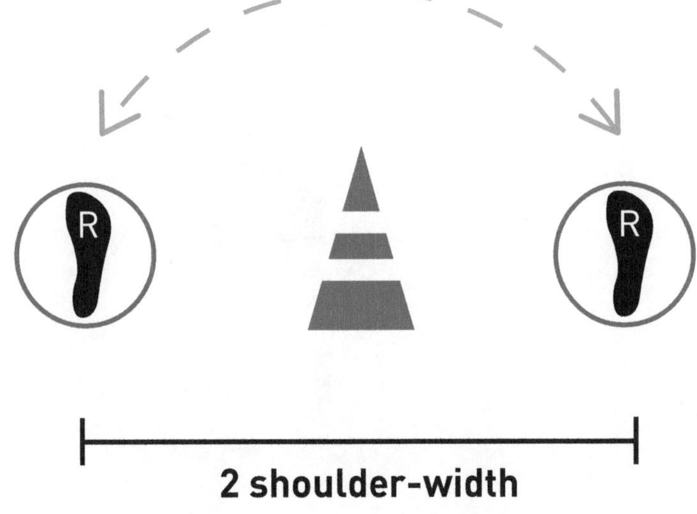

ID: 7232

7.233 SINGLE-LEG LOW-LEVEL LATERAL TUCK JUMP III

SUMMARY

The Single-Leg Low-Level Lateral Tuck Jump III is a plyometric exercise, which focuses on improving quick start sequence, body control & coordination as well as improving foot speed for low-height jumps utilizing a cone.

PURPOSE

1. Improving quick start sequence (split-step to 1st side-step)
2. Improving body control & coordination
3. Improving foot speed (neurological feedback loop)

DESCRIPTION

Coach throws tennis ball at athlete during jumps.

Athlete stands up straight and needs to:

1. Place a cone on the ground
2. Stand on one leg (the leg closest to the cone)
3. Jump back and forth over the cone while **looking forward**; flex knees **below hip level**
4. **Catch and return tennis ball**

Note: Also perform exercise by jumping with the leg farthest away from the cone.

PRE-REQUISITE DRILLS

- Low-Level Tuck Jump (III)

BREATH IN & OUT

- IN: When landing
- OUT: During Jumping

DEGREE OF DIFFICULTY

3

REQUIRED EQUIPMENT

- One 2 Inch Cone

KEY FACTORS

- Focus on perfect movement mechanics and speed; raise knees to go over the cone
- Maintain upper body over the cone during jumps
- Keep knees below hip level
- Maintain balance – land in the same location

COMMON ERRORS

- Athlete moves heels towards buttocks instead of raising the knees when jumping over the cone
- Athlete doesn't land in same spot during jumps
- Athlete jumps at sub-maximal speed

ID: 7233

7

7.234 SINGLE-LEG MID-LEVEL LATERAL TUCK JUMP I

SUMMARY

The Single-Leg Mid-Level Lateral Tuck Jump I is a plyometric exercise, which focuses on improving body control & coordination as well as improving foot speed for low-height jumps utilizing a cone and agility rings.

PURPOSE

1. Improving body control & coordination
2. Improving foot speed (neurological feedback loop)
3. Improving skill and speed foundation for complex movements

DESCRIPTION

Athlete stands up straight and needs to:

1. Place 2 agility rings on the ground 2 shoulder-widths apart and put a cone in between the 2 rings
2. Stand on one leg (the leg closest to the cone) and place it inside the agility ring
3. Jump back and forth over the cone while **looking down** at the feet; flex knees **at hip level**

Note: Also perform exercise by jumping with the leg farthest away from the cone.

PRE-REQUISITE DRILLS

- Mid-Level Tuck Jump (I)

BREATH IN & OUT

- IN: When landing
- OUT: During Jumping

DEGREE OF DIFFICULTY

1

REQUIRED EQUIPMENT

- 2 Agility Rings
- One 4 Inch Cone

KEY FACTORS

- Focus on perfect movement mechanics and speed; raise knees to go over the cone
- Maintain upper body over the cone during jumps
- Keep knees at hip level
- Maintain balance – land inside agility ring

COMMON ERRORS

- Athlete moves heels towards buttocks instead of raising the knees when jumping over the cone
- Athlete moves outside agility rings during jumps
- Athlete jumps at sub-maximal speed

ID: 7234

7.235 SINGLE-LEG MID-LEVEL LATERAL TUCK JUMP II

SUMMARY

The Single-Leg Mid-Level Lateral Tuck Jump II is a plyometric exercise, which focuses on improving body control & coordination as well as improving foot speed for low-height jumps utilizing a cone and agility rings.

PURPOSE

1. Improving body control & coordination
2. Improving foot speed (neurological feedback loop)
3. Improving skill and speed foundation for complex movements

DESCRIPTION

Athlete stands up straight and needs to:

1. Place 2 agility rings on the ground 2 shoulder-widths apart and put a cone in between the 2 rings
2. Stand on one leg (the leg closest to the cone) and place it inside the agility ring
3. Jump back and forth over the cone while **looking forward**; flex knees **at hip level**

Note: Also perform exercise by jumping with the leg farthest away from the cone.

PRE-REQUISITE DRILLS

- Mid-Level Tuck Jump (II)

BREATH IN & OUT

- IN: When landing
- OUT: During Jumping

DEGREE OF DIFFICULTY

2

REQUIRED EQUIPMENT

- 2 Agility Rings
- One 4 Inch Cone

KEY FACTORS

- Focus on perfect movement mechanics and speed; raise knees to go over the cone
- Maintain upper body over the cone during jumps
- Keep knees at hip level
- Maintain balance – land inside agility ring

COMMON ERRORS

- Athlete moves heels towards buttocks instead of raising the knees when jumping over the cone
- Athlete moves outside agility rings during jumps
- Athlete jumps at sub-maximal speed

ID: 7235

7.236 SINGLE-LEG MID-LEVEL LATERAL TUCK JUMP III

SUMMARY

The Single-Leg Mid-Level Lateral Tuck Jump III is a plyometric exercise, which focuses on improving body control & coordination as well as improving foot speed for low-height jumps utilizing a cone.

PURPOSE

1. Improving body control & coordination
2. Improving foot speed (neurological feedback loop)

DESCRIPTION

Coach throws tennis ball at athlete during jumps.
Athlete stands up straight and needs to:

1. Place a cone on the ground
2. Stand on one leg (the leg closest to the cone)
3. Jump back and forth over the cone while **looking forward**; flex knees **at hip level**
4. **Catch and return tennis ball**

Note: Also perform exercise by jumping with the leg farthest away from the cone.

PRE-REQUISITE DRILLS

- Mid-Level Tuck Jump (III)

BREATH IN & OUT

- IN: When landing
- OUT: During Jumping

DEGREE OF DIFFICULTY

3

REQUIRED EQUIPMENT

- One 4 Inch Cone

KEY FACTORS

- Focus on perfect movement mechanics and speed; raise knees to go over the cone
- Maintain upper body over the cone during jumps
- Keep knees at hip level
- Maintain balance – land in same location

COMMON ERRORS

- Athlete moves heels towards buttocks instead of raising the knees when jumping over the cone
- Athlete doesn't land in same spot during jumps
- Athlete jumps at sub-maximal speed

ID: 7236

7.237 SINGLE-LEG HIGH-LEVEL LATERAL TUCK JUMP I

SUMMARY

The Single-Leg High-Level Lateral Tuck Jump I is a plyometric exercise, which focuses on improving body control & coordination as well as improving foot speed for low-height jumps utilizing a cone and agility rings.

PURPOSE

1. Improving body control & coordination
2. Improving foot speed (neurological feedback loop)
3. Improving skill and speed foundation for complex movements

DESCRIPTION

Athlete stands up straight and needs to:

1. Place 2 agility rings on the ground 2 shoulder-widths apart and put a cone in between the 2 rings
2. Stand on one leg (the leg closest to the cone) and place it inside the agility ring
3. Jump back and forth over the cone while **looking down** at the feet; flex knees **above hip level** (chest)

Note: Also perform exercise by jumping with the leg farthest away from the cone.

PRE-REQUISITE DRILLS

- High-Level Tuck Jump (I)

BREATH IN & OUT

- IN: When landing
- OUT: During Jumping

DEGREE OF DIFFICULTY

1

REQUIRED EQUIPMENT

- 2 Agility Rings
- One 6 Inch Cone

KEY FACTORS

- Focus on perfect movement mechanics and speed; raise knees to go over the cone
- Maintain upper body over the cone during jumps
- Keep knees above hip level (chest)
- Maintain balance – land inside agility ring

COMMON ERRORS

- Athlete moves heels towards buttocks instead of raising the knees when jumping over the cone
- Athlete moves outside agility rings during jumps
- Athlete jumps at sub-maximal speed

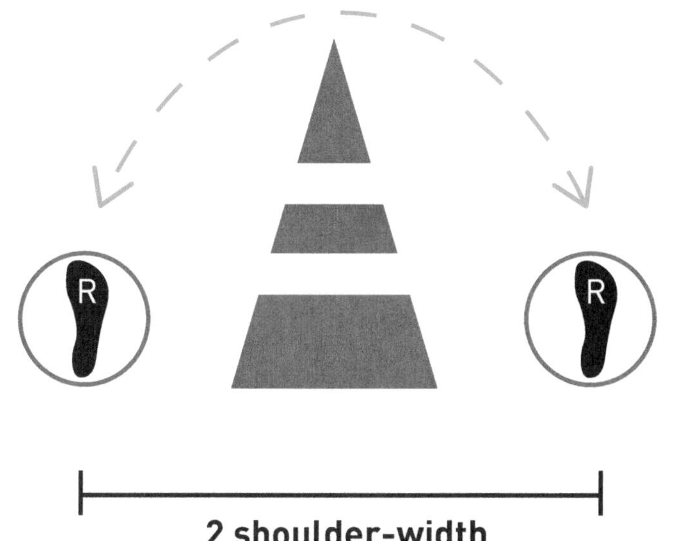

ID: 7237

7.238 SINGLE-LEG HIGH-LEVEL LATERAL TUCK JUMP II

SUMMARY

The Single-Leg High-Level Lateral Tuck Jump II is a plyometric exercise, which focuses on improving body control & coordination as well as improving foot speed for low-height jumps utilizing a cone and agility rings.

PURPOSE

1. Improving body control & coordination
2. Improving foot speed (neurological feedback loop)
3. Improving skill and speed foundation for complex movements

DESCRIPTION

Athlete stands up straight and needs to:

1. Place 2 agility rings on the ground 2 shoulder-widths apart and put a cone in between the 2 rings
2. Stand on one leg (the leg closest to the cone) and place it inside the agility ring
3. Jump back and forth over the cone while **looking forward**; flex knees **above hip level**

Note: Also perform exercise by jumping with the leg farthest away from the cone.

PRE-REQUISITE DRILLS

- High-Level Tuck Jump (II)

BREATH IN & OUT

- IN: When landing
- OUT: During Jumping

DEGREE OF DIFFICULTY

2

REQUIRED EQUIPMENT

- 2 Agility Rings
- One 6 Inch Cone

KEY FACTORS

- Focus on perfect movement mechanics and speed; raise knees to go over the cone
- Maintain upper body over the cone during jumps
- Keep knees above hip level
- Maintain balance – land inside agility ring

COMMON ERRORS

- Athlete moves heels towards buttocks instead of raising the knees when jumping over the cone
- Athlete moves outside agility rings during jumps
- Athlete jumps at sub-maximal speed

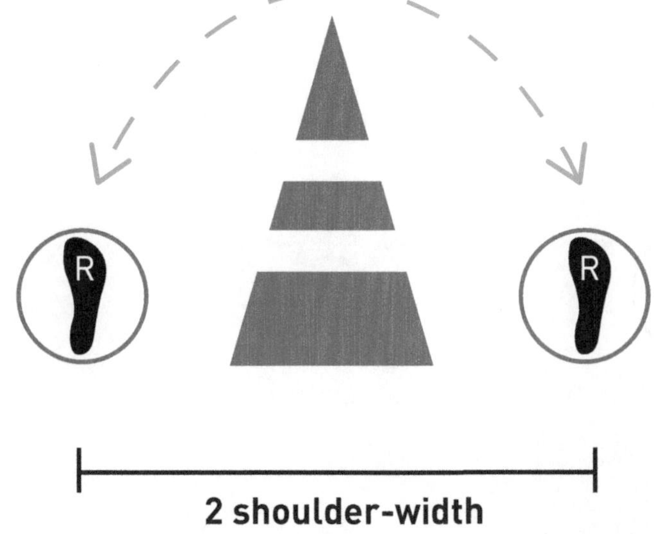

ID: 7238

7.239 SINGLE-LEG HIGH-LEVEL LATERAL TUCK JUMP III

SUMMARY

The Single-Leg High-Level Lateral Tuck Jump III is a plyometric exercise, which focuses on improving body control & coordination as well as improving foot speed for low-height jumps utilizing a cone.

PURPOSE

1. Improving body control & coordination
2. Improving foot speed (neurological feedback loop)

DESCRIPTION

Coach throws tennis ball at athlete during jumps.
Athlete stands up straight and needs to:

1. Place a cone on the ground
2. Stand on one leg (the leg closest to the cone)
3. Jump back and forth over the cone while **looking forward**; flex knees **above hip level**
4. **Catch and return tennis ball**

Note: Also perform exercise by jumping with the leg farthest away from the cone.

PRE-REQUISITE DRILLS

- High-Level Tuck Jump (III)

BREATH IN & OUT

- IN: When landing
- OUT: During Jumping

DEGREE OF DIFFICULTY

3

REQUIRED EQUIPMENT

- 1 Tennis Ball
- One 6 Inch Cone

KEY FACTORS

- Focus on perfect movement mechanics and speed; raise knees to go over the cone
- Maintain upper body over the cone during jumps
- Keep knees above hip level
- Maintain balance – land in the same location

COMMON ERRORS

- Athlete moves heels towards buttocks instead of raising the knees when jumping over the cone
- Athlete doesn't land in same spot during jumps
- Athlete jumps at sub-maximal speed

ID: 7239

7.240 MB TRUNK TWIST PASS (I)

SUMMARY

The Medicine Ball (MB) Trunk Twist Pass (I) is a plyometric exercise, which focuses on improving energy transfer for more powerful stroke production, body control, balance & coordination, explosiveness of the trunk, as well as improving skill & strength foundation for complex movements utilizing a medicine ball and agility rings.

This exercise can also be performed with a partner instead of the wall.

PURPOSE

1. Improving energy transfer for more powerful stroke production (e.g. groundstrokes)
2. Improving body control (balance) & coordination
3. Improving explosiveness of the trunk by enhancing synergy of lower extremities and the trunk (neurological feedback loop); rotational power training for transverse movement (trunk rotation during groundstrokes)
4. Improving skill and strength foundation for complex movements

DESCRIPTION

1. Place 2 agility rings parallel and ~8 feet away from the concrete wall; rings should be shoulder-width apart
2. Step inside agility rings
3. Hold a medicine ball (MB) naturally in both hands in front of the trunk
4. Take on **athletic stance** position; knees and hips are slightly flexed; upper-body is straight
5. Rotate the trunk outwardly until shoulders are perpendicular to the wall (or as far as possible); maintain neutral head position; keep **looking forward**
6. Initiate the pass with the **hips** and **trunk**, not the arms
7. Extend the hips until standing on the balls of the feet, **lean forward** with the upper-body, and **simultaneously** rotate trunk inwardly until shoulders are nearly parallel to the wall
8. Explosively release MB at hip-level and throw MB towards the wall/partner; maintain neutral head position; keep **looking forward**
9. Catch the rebound and quickly repeat

PRE-REQUISITE DRILLS

- MB Trunk Rotation I
- MB Trunk Twist Throw I

DEGREE OF DIFFICULTY

1

KEY FACTORS

- Focus on perfect movement mechanics and explosiveness (maximum speed)
- Maintain neutral head position; keep looking forward
- Extend hips and rotate trunk to initiate outward rotation and ball pass
- Release MB at hip level
- Maintain balance: stay inside agility rings during throw

COMMON ERRORS

- Athlete initiates pass via arms
- Athlete loses balance
- Athlete releases MB early

BREATH IN & OUT

- IN: Before Rotation
- OUT: During MB release

REQUIRED EQUIPMENT

- Concrete Wall/Partner
- 1 Medicine Ball (2lb – 8lb)
- 2 Agility Rings

ID: 7240

7.241 MB TRUNK TWIST PASS (II): DIAGONAL LUNGE

SUMMARY

The Medicine Ball (MB) Trunk Twist Pass (II) is a plyometric exercise, which focuses on improving energy transfer for more powerful stroke production, body control, balance & coordination, explosiveness of the trunk, as well as improving skill & strength foundation for complex movements utilizing a medicine ball and agility rings.

This exercise can also be performed with a partner instead of the wall.

PURPOSE

1. Improving energy transfer for more powerful stroke production (e.g. groundstrokes)
2. Improving body control (balance) & coordination
3. Improving explosiveness of the trunk by enhancing synergy of lower extremities and the trunk (neurological feedback loop); rotational power training for transverse movement (trunk rotation during groundstrokes)
4. Improving skill and strength foundation for complex movements

DESCRIPTION

1. Hold a medicine ball (MB) naturally in both hands in front of the trunk
2. Take on **diagonal lunge position**; distribute weight through the heel (flat footed); knees and hips are flexed at 90°; back remains straight; maintain neutral head position; keep **looking forward**
3. Rotate the trunk outwardly until shoulders are perpendicular to the wall/partner (or as far as possible); maintain neutral head position; keep **looking forward**
4. Initiate the pass with the **hips** and **trunk**, not the arms
5. Rotate trunk inwardly until shoulders are nearly parallel to the wall
6. **Lean forward** with the upper-body and explosively release MB at hip-level and throw MB towards the wall/partner; maintain neutral head position; keep **looking forward**
7. Catch the rebound and quickly repeat

PRE-REQUISITE DRILLS

- MB Trunk Rotation II
- MB Trunk Twist Throw II

REQUIRED EQUIPMENT

- Concrete Wall/Partner
- 1 Medicine Ball (2lb – 8lb)

BREATH IN & OUT

- IN: Before Rotation
- OUT: During MB release

DEGREE OF DIFFICULTY

2

KEY FACTORS

- Focus on perfect movement mechanics and explosiveness (maximum speed)
- Distribute weight through the heel of the front foot
- Rotate trunk to initiate pass
- Maintain neutral head position; keep looking forward
- Lean forward during pass
- Release MB at hip level
- Maintain balance

COMMON ERRORS

- Athlete initiates pass via arms
- Athlete distributes weight through the ball of the foot (toes)
- Athlete releases MB early
- Athlete loses balance (upper-body leans backwards)

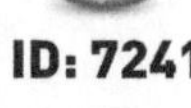

7.242 MB TRUNK TWIST PASS (III): SINGLE-LEG

SUMMARY

The Medicine Ball (MB) Trunk Twist Pass (III) is a plyometric exercise, which focuses on improving energy transfer for more powerful stroke production, body control, balance & coordination, explosiveness of the trunk, as well as improving skill & strength foundation for complex movements utilizing a medicine ball

This exercise can also be performed with a partner instead of the wall.

PURPOSE

1. Improving energy transfer for more powerful stroke production (e.g. groundstrokes)
2. Improving body control (balance) & coordination
3. Improving explosiveness of the trunk by enhancing synergy of lower extremities and the trunk (neurological feedback loop); rotational power training for transverse movement (trunk rotation during groundstrokes)
4. Improving skill and strength foundation for complex movement

DESCRIPTION

1. Hold a medicine ball (MB) naturally in both hands in front of the trunk
2. Take on **diagonal single-leg stance** position; knee and hip are slightly flexed; non-weight bearing knee is flexed at 90°; back remains straight
3. Rotate the trunk outwardly until shoulders are perpendicular to the wall/partner (or as far as possible); maintain neutral head position; keep **looking forward**
4. Initiate the pass with the **hips** and **trunk**, not the arms
5. Rotate trunk inwardly until shoulders are nearly parallel to the wall
6. **Lean forward** with the upper-body and explosively release MB at hip-level and throw MB towards the wall/partner; maintain neutral head position; keep **looking forward**
7. Catch the rebound and quickly repeat
8. Maintain stability after the throw

DEGREE OF DIFFICULTY

3

KEY FACTORS

- Focus on perfect movement mechanics and explosiveness (maximum speed)
- Rotate trunk to initiate pass
- Maintain neutral head position; keep looking forward
- Lean forward during pass
- Release MB at hip level
- Maintain balance

COMMON ERRORS

- Athlete initiates pass via arms
- Athlete releases MB early
- Athlete loses balance (e.g. upper-body leans backwards)

PRE-REQUISITE DRILLS

- MB Trunk Rotation III
- MB Trunk Twist Throw III

REQUIRED EQUIPMENT

- Concrete Wall/Partner
- 1 Medicine Ball (2lb – 8lb)

BREATH IN & OUT

- IN: Before Rotation
- OUT: During MB release

ID: 7242

7.243 MB TRUNK TWIST PASS (IV): ALTERN. DIAG. LUNGE

SUMMARY

The Medicine Ball (MB) Trunk Twist Pass (IV) is a plyometric exercise, which focuses on improving energy transfer for more powerful stroke production, body control, balance & coordination, explosiveness of the trunk, as well as improving skill & strength foundation for complex movements utilizing a medicine ball.

This exercise can also be performed with a partner instead of the wall.

PURPOSE

1. Improving energy transfer for more powerful stroke production (e.g. groundstrokes)
2. Improving body control (stability) & coordination
3. Improving explosiveness of the trunk by enhancing synergy of lower extremities and the trunk (neurological feedback loop); rotational power training for transverse movement (trunk rotation during groundstrokes)
4. Improving skill and strength foundation for complex movements

DESCRIPTION

1. Hold a medicine ball (MB) naturally in both hands in front of the trunk
2. Side-Step to the **left**
3. Step into a **diagonal lunge position** with the **right** foot; distribute weight through the heel (flat footed); knees and hips are flexed at 90°; back remains straight
4. Rotate the trunk outwardly until shoulders are perpendicular to the wall/partner (or as far as possible); maintain neutral head position; keep **looking forward**
5. Initiate the pass with the hips and trunk, not the arms
6. Rotate trunk inwardly until shoulders are nearly parallel to the wall
7. **Lean forward** with the upper-body, explosively release MB at hip-level, rotate non-weight bearing hip forward, land on the **left** foot, and throw MB against the wall; maintain neutral head position; keep **looking forward**
8. Catch the rebound and **side-step** to the other side
9. Step into diagonal lunge with the **left** foot and repeat

PRE-REQUISITE DRILLS

- MB Trunk Rotation IV
- MB Trunk Twist Throw IV

DEGREE OF DIFFICULTY

4

REQUIRED EQUIPMENT

- Concrete Wall/Partner
- 1 Medicine Ball (2lb – 8lb)

KEY FACTORS

- Focus on perfect movement mechanics and explosiveness (maximum speed)
- Distribute weight through the heel of the front foot
- Rotate trunk to initiate pass
- Maintain neutral head position; keep looking forward
- Lean forward during pass
- Release MB at hip level
- Rotate non-weight bearing hip forward
- Maintain stability

COMMON ERRORS

- Athlete initiates pass via arms
- Athlete distributes weight through the ball of the foot (toes)
- Athlete releases MB early
- Athlete loses stability (e.g. upper-body leans backwards)

BREATH IN & OUT

- IN: Before Rotation
- OUT: During MB release

ID: 7243

7.244 MB TRUNK TWIST PASS (V): ALTERNATE SL

SUMMARY

The Medicine Ball (MB) Trunk Twist Pass (V) is a plyometric exercise, which focuses on improving energy transfer for more powerful stroke production, body control, balance & coordination, and explosiveness of the trunk utilizing a medicine ball.

This exercise can also be performed with a partner instead of the wall.

PURPOSE

1. Improving energy transfer for more powerful stroke production (e.g. groundstrokes)
2. Improving body control (stability) & coordination
3. Improving explosiveness of the trunk by enhancing synergy of lower extremities and the trunk (neurological feedback loop); rotational power training for transverse movement (trunk rotation during groundstrokes)

DESCRIPTION

1. Hold a medicine ball (MB) naturally in both hands in front of the trunk
2. Side-Step to the **left**
3. Step into a **diagonal single-leg stance** position with the **right** foot; knee and hip are slightly flexed; non-weight bearing knee is flexed at 90°; back remains straight
4. Rotate the trunk outwardly until shoulders are perpendicular to the wall/partner (or as far as possible); maintain neutral head position; keep **looking forward**
5. Initiate the pass with the **hips** and **trunk**, not the arms
6. Rotate trunk inwardly until shoulders are nearly parallel to the wall
7. **Lean forward** with the upper-body and explosively release MB at hip-level and throw MB towards the wall/partner; maintain neutral head position; keep **looking forward**
8. Rotate non-weight bearing hip forward and land on the other leg
9. Catch the rebound and **side-step** to the other side
10. Step into **diagonal single-leg stance** position with the **left** foot and repeat

KEY FACTORS

- Focus on perfect movement mechanics and explosiveness (maximum speed)
- Rotate trunk to initiate pass
- Maintain neutral head position; keep looking forward
- Lean forward during pass
- Release MB at hip level
- Rotate non-weight bearing hip forward
- Maintain stability

COMMON ERRORS

- Athlete initiates pass via arms
- Athlete releases MB early
- Athlete loses stability (e.g. upper-body leans backwards)

BREATH IN & OUT

- IN: Before Rotation
- OUT: During MB release

PRE-REQUISITE DRILLS

- MB Trunk Rotation V
- MB Trunk Twist Throw V

REQUIRED EQUIPMENT

- Concrete Wall/Partner
- 1 Medicine Ball (2lb – 8lb)

DEGREE OF DIFFICULTY

5

ID: 7244

7.245 OVERHEAD MB PASS (I)

SUMMARY

The Overhead Medicine Ball (MB) Pass (I) is a plyometric exercise, which focuses on improving energy transfer for more powerful stroke production, body control, balance & coordination, explosiveness of the trunk, as well as improving skill & strength foundation for complex movements.

Note: This exercise can also be performed with a partner instead of the wall.

PURPOSE

1. Improving energy transfer for more powerful stroke production (e.g. the serve)
2. Improving body control (balance) & coordination
3. Improving explosiveness of the trunk by enhancing synergy of upper extremities and the trunk (neurological feedback loop); hip flexion and elbow extension speed and strength for sagittal movement (hip flexion and elbow extension during serve)
4. Improving skill and strength foundation for complex movements

DESCRIPTION

1. Hold a medicine ball (MB) in both hands behind the head; remain 6-8 feet away from the wall/partner
2. Take on **athletic stance** position; knees and hips are slightly flexed; upper-body remains straight; face the wall/partner; maintain neutral head position; keep **looking forward**
3. Extend the hips forward, flex the hips and explosively throw the MB **forward** towards the wall/partner
4. Catch the rebound and quickly repeat

DEGREE OF DIFFICULTY

1

REQUIRED EQUIPMENT

- Concrete Wall/Partner
- 1 Medicine Ball (2lb – 8lb)

KEY FACTORS

- Focus on perfect movement mechanics and explosiveness (maximum speed)
- Maintain neutral head position
- Extend hips
- Release MB over the head
- Maintain balance

PRE-REQUISITE DRILLS

- Overhead MB Pull-Over I
- Overhead MB Throw I

BREATH IN & OUT

- IN: When extending hips
- OUT: During Throw

COMMON ERRORS

- Overhead MB Pull-Over I
- Overhead MB Throw I

ID: 7245

7.246 OVERHEAD MB PASS (II): LUNGE POSITION

SUMMARY

The Overhead Medicine Ball (MB) Pass (II) is a plyometric exercise, which focuses on improving energy transfer for more powerful stroke production, body control, balance & coordination, explosiveness of the trunk, as well as improving skill & strength foundation for complex movements.

Note: This exercise can also be performed with a partner instead of the wall.

PURPOSE

1. Improving energy transfer for more powerful stroke production (e.g. the serve)
2. Improving body control (balance) & coordination
3. Improving explosiveness of the trunk by enhancing synergy of upper extremities and the trunk (neurological feedback loop); hip flexion and elbow extension speed and strength for sagittal movement (hip flexion and elbow extension during serve)
4. Improving skill and strength foundation for complex movements

DESCRIPTION

1. Hold a medicine ball (MB) in both hands behind the head; remain 6-8 feet away from the wall/partner
2. Take on a **forward lunge position** with the **right** foot; distribute weight through the heel (flat footed); knees and hips are flexed at 90°; back remains straight; face the wall/partner; maintain neutral head position; keep **looking forward**
3. Extend the hips forward, flex the hips and explosively pass the MB **forward** towards the wall/partner
4. Catch the rebound and quickly repeat
5. Switch legs

PRE-REQUISITE DRILLS

- Overhead MB Pull-Over II
- Overhead MB Throw II

REQUIRED EQUIPMENT

- Concrete Wall/Partner
- 1 Medicine Ball (2lb – 8lb)

DEGREE OF DIFFICULTY

2

KEY FACTORS

- Focus on perfect movement mechanics and explosiveness (maximum speed)
- Distribute weight through the heel of the front foot
- Maintain neutral head position
- Extend hips
- Release MB over the head
- Maintain balance

COMMON ERRORS

- Athlete passes MB without prior hip extension
- Athlete distributes weight through the ball of the foot (toes)
- Athlete loses balance
- Athlete releases MB early

BREATH IN & OUT

- IN: When extending hips
- OUT: During Throw

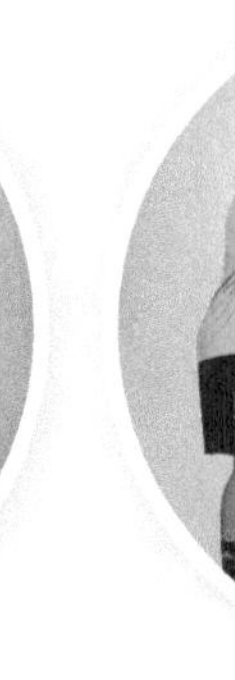

ID: 7246

7.247 OVERHEAD MB PASS (III): SINGLE-LEG

SUMMARY

The Overhead Medicine Ball (MB) Pass (III) is a plyometric exercise, which focuses on improving energy transfer for more powerful stroke production, body control, balance & coordination, explosiveness of the trunk, as well as improving skill & strength foundation for complex movements.

Note: This exercise can also be performed with a partner instead of the wall.

PURPOSE

1. Improving energy transfer for more powerful stroke production (e.g. the serve)
2. Improving body control (balance) & coordination
3. Improving explosiveness of the trunk by enhancing synergy of upper extremities and the trunk (neurological feedback loop); hip flexion and elbow extension speed and strength for sagittal movement (hip flexion and elbow extension during serve)
4. Improving skill and strength foundation for complex movements

DESCRIPTION

1. Hold a medicine ball (MB) in both hands behind the head; remain 6-8 feet away from the wall/partner
2. Take on **single-leg stance** position; knee and hip are slightly flexed; non-weight bearing knee is flexed at 90°; back remains straight; face the wall/partner; maintain neutral head position; keep **looking forward**
3. Extend the hip forward, flex the hip and explosively pass the MB **forward** towards the wall/partner
4. Catch the rebound and quickly repeat
5. Switch legs

PRE-REQUISITE DRILLS

- Overhead MB Pull-Over III
- Overhead MB Throw III

BREATH IN & OUT

- IN: When extending hips
- OUT: During Throw

DEGREE OF DIFFICULTY

3

REQUIRED EQUIPMENT

- Concrete Wall/Partner
- 1 Medicine Ball (2lb – 8lb)

KEY FACTORS

- Focus on perfect movement mechanics and explosiveness (maximum speed)
- Maintain neutral head position
- Extend hip
- Release MB over the head
- Maintain balance

COMMON ERRORS

- Athlete loses balance
- Athlete releases MB early

ID: 7247

7.248 OH MB PASS (IV): ALTERNATE LUNGE POSITION

SUMMARY

The Overhead Medicine Ball (MB) Pass (IV) is a plyometric exercise, which focuses on improving energy transfer for more powerful stroke production, body control, balance & coordination, explosiveness of the trunk, as well as improving skill & strength foundation for complex movements.

Note: This exercise can also be performed with a partner instead of the wall.

PURPOSE

1. Improving energy transfer for more powerful stroke production (e.g. the serve)
2. Improving body control (stability) & coordination
3. Improving explosiveness of the trunk by enhancing synergy of upper extremities and the trunk (neurological feedback loop); hip flexion and elbow extension speed and strength for sagittal movement (hip flexion and elbow extension during serve)
4. Improving skill and strength foundation for complex movements

DESCRIPTION

1. Hold a medicine ball (MB) in both hands behind the head; remain 6-8 feet away from the wall/partner
2. Side-Step to the **left**
3. Step into a **forward lunge position** with the **right** foot; distribute weight through the heel (flat footed); knees and hips are flexed at 90°; back remains straight; face the wall/partner; maintain neutral head position; keep **looking forward**
4. Extend the hips forward, flex the hips, rotate non-weight bearing hip forward, explosively pass the MB **forward** towards the wall/partner, and land on the **left** foot
5. Catch the rebound
6. Side-step to the **right**
7. Step into forward lunge position with **left** foot and repeat

DEGREE OF DIFFICULTY

4

KEY FACTORS

- Focus on perfect movement mechanics and explosiveness (maximum distance)
- Distribute weight through the heel of the front foot
- Maintain neutral head position
- Extend hips
- Release MB over the head
- Rotate non-weight bearing hip forward
- Maintain stability

PRE-REQUISITE DRILLS

- Overhead MB Pull-Over IV
- Overhead MB Throw IV

COMMON ERRORS

- Athlete loses stability
- Athlete distributes weight through the ball of the foot (toes)
- Athlete releases MB early

BREATH IN & OUT

- IN: When extending hips
- OUT: During Throw

REQUIRED EQUIPMENT

- Concrete Wall/Partner
- 1 Medicine Ball (2lb – 8lb)

7.249 OVERHEAD MB PASS (V): ALTERNATE SINGLE-LEG

SUMMARY

The Overhead Medicine Ball (MB) Pass (V) is a plyometric exercise, which focuses on improving energy transfer for more powerful stroke production, body control, balance & coordination, and explosiveness of the trunk.

Note: This exercise can also be performed with a partner instead of the wall.

PURPOSE

1. Improving energy transfer for more powerful stroke production (e.g. the serve)
2. Improving body control (stability) & coordination
3. Improving explosiveness of the trunk by enhancing synergy of upper extremities and the trunk (neurological feedback loop); hip flexion and elbow extension speed and strength for sagittal movement (hip flexion and elbow extension during serve)

DESCRIPTION

1. Hold a medicine ball (MB) in both hands behind the head; remain 6-8 feet away from the wall/partner
2. Side-Step to the **left**
3. Step into **single-leg stance** position with the right foot; knee and hip are slightly flexed; non-weight bearing knee is flexed at 90°; back remains straight; face the wall/partner; maintain neutral head position; keep **looking forward**
4. Extend the hip forward, flex the hip, rotate non-weight bearing hip forward, explosively pass the MB **forward** towards the wall/partner, and land on the **left** foot
5. Catch the rebound
6. Side-step to the **right**
7. Step into **single-leg stance position** with the **left** foot and repeat

PRE-REQUISITE DRILLS

- Overhead MB Pull-Over IV
- Overhead MB Throw IV

BREATH IN & OUT

- IN: When extending hips
- OUT: During Throw

DEGREE OF DIFFICULTY

5

REQUIRED EQUIPMENT

- Concrete Wall/Partner
- 1 Medicine Ball (2lb – 8lb)

KEY FACTORS

- Focus on perfect movement mechanics and explosiveness (maximum speed)
- Maintain neutral head position
- Extend hip
- Release MB over the head
- Rotate non-weight bearing hip forward
- Maintain stability

COMMON ERRORS

- Athlete loses stability
- Athlete releases MB early

ID: 7249

7.250 7 AD DRILL (I)

SUMMARY

The 7 Ad Drill I is an introductory agility exercise, which focuses on improving footwork for groundstrokes, improving footwork for transition game, and improving balance & coordination.

PURPOSE

1. Improving footwork for groundstrokes
2. Improving footwork for transition game
3. Improving balance & coordination

DESCRIPTION

No balls are being fed by the coach. Athlete needs to:

1. Start at the center of baseline facing the net
2. Move rapidly via **side-step** towards rubber ring in ad-court until left foot hits center of the ring
3. Push off with left foot and move quickly via **side-step** towards ring in deuce-court until right foot hits center of the ring
4. Push off with right foot and **sprint** diagonally towards rubber ring in ad-court service box
5. Lunge-slide with right foot pointing forward towards rubber ring (Clay Court) or place right foot in center of rubber ring (Hard Court)

REQUIRED EQUIPMENT

- 3 Agility Rings

KEY FACTORS

- Stay on balls of the feet (toes) when moving laterally (side-step)
- Hit the center of the rings
- Stick the landing on single leg only: step in, push out
- Maintain balance during change of direction and lunge-slide

PRE-REQUISITE DRILLS

- Lateral Fast Feet I

COMMON ERRORS

- Athlete fails to hit center of rubber rings
- Athlete pushes off with the wrong foot (foot outside rubber rings)
- Athlete changes movement pattern after change of direction
- Athletes slides with toes pointing towards sideline

DEGREE OF DIFFICULTY

1

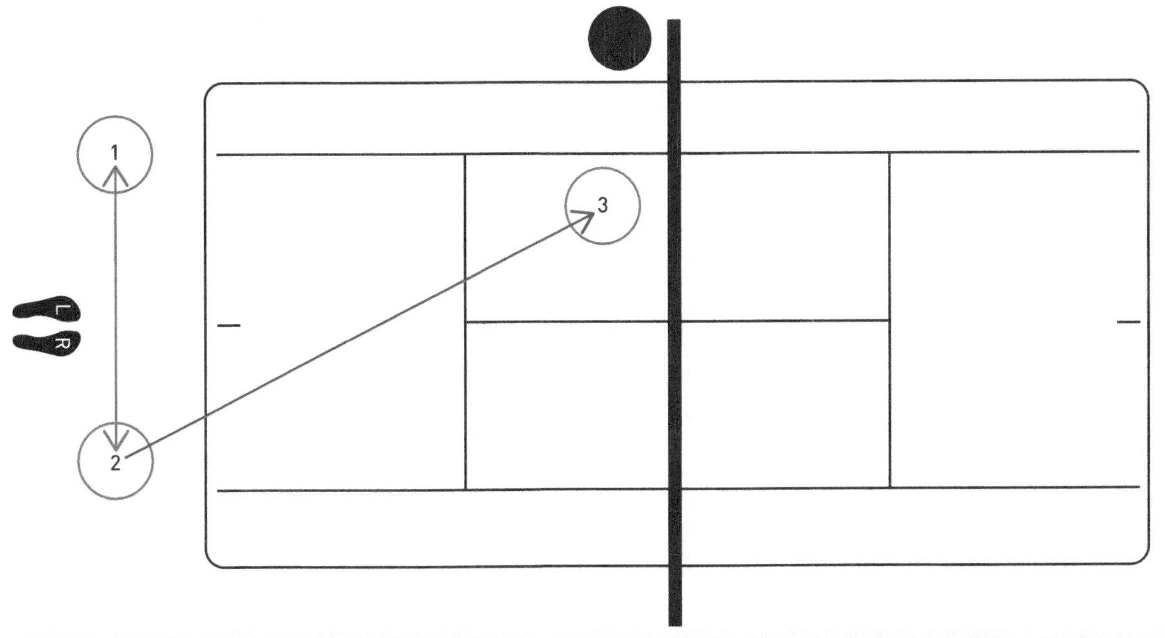

ID: 7250

7.251 7 AD DRILL (II)

SUMMARY

The 7 Ad Drill II is an introductory agility exercise, which focuses on improving footwork for groundstrokes, improving footwork for transition game, and improving balance & coordination.

PURPOSE

1. Improving footwork for groundstrokes
2. Improving footwork for transition game
3. Improving balance & coordination

DESCRIPTION

No balls are being fed by the coach. Athlete is **holding a racquet** and needs to:

1. Start at the center of baseline facing the net
2. Move rapidly via **side-step** towards rubber ring in ad-court until left foot hits center of the ring
3. Push off with **left** foot and move quickly via **side-step** towards ring in ad-court until right foot hits center of the ring
4. Push off with **right** foot and **sprint** diagonally towards rubber ring in ad-court service box
5. Lunge-slide with **right** foot pointing forward towards rubber ring (Clay Court) or place right foot in center of rubber ring (Hard Court)

DEGREE OF DIFFICULTY

2

REQUIRED EQUIPMENT

- 3 Agility Rings
- 1 Racquet

KEY FACTORS

- Stay on balls of the feet (toes) when moving laterally (side-step)
- Hit the center of the rings
- Stick the landing on single leg only: step in, push out
- Maintain balance during change of direction and lunge-slide

PRE-REQUISITE DRILLS

- 7 Ad Drill I
- Lateral Fast Feet II

BREATH IN & OUT

- IN: When extending hips
- OUT: During Throw

COMMON ERRORS

- Athlete fails to hit center of rubber rings
- Athlete pushes off with the wrong foot (foot outside rubber rings)
- Athlete changes movement pattern after change of direction
- Athletes slides with toes pointing towards sideline

ID: 7251

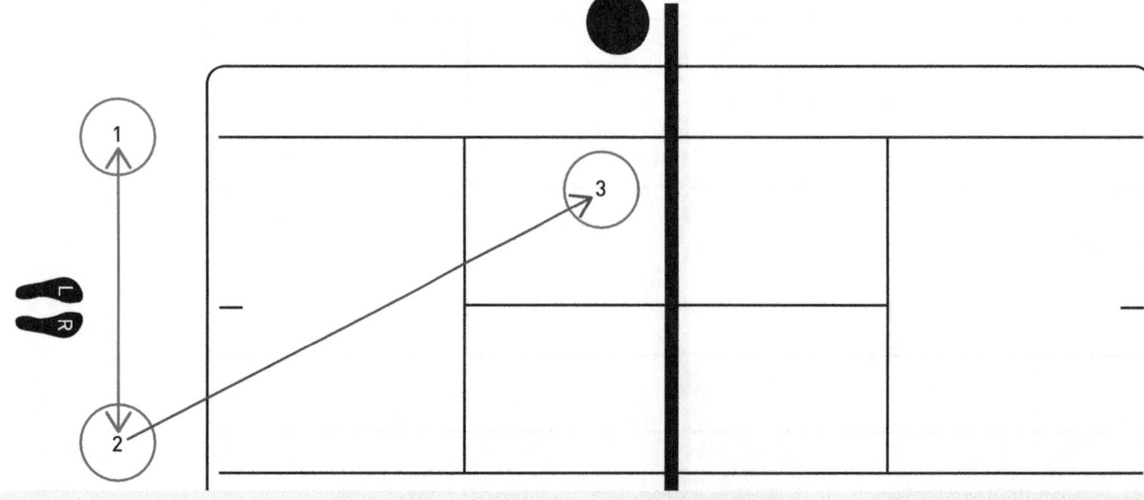

7.252 7 AD DRILL (III)

SUMMARY

The 7 Ad Drill III is an advanced integrated transition exercise, which focuses on improving footwork for groundstrokes, footwork for transition game, balance & coordination, and defense against drop-shots.

PURPOSE

1. Improving footwork for groundstrokes
2. Improving footwork for transition game
3. Improving balance & coordination
4. Improving the counter drop-shot

DESCRIPTION

1 ball is being fed by the coach towards rubber ring in service box. Athlete is **holding a racquet** and needs to:

1. Start at the center of baseline facing the net
2. Move rapidly via **side-step** towards rubber ring in ad-court until **left** foot hits center of the ring
3. Push off with **left** foot and move quickly via **side-step** towards ring in deuce-court until **right** foot hits center of the ring
4. Push off with **right** foot and **sprint** diagonally towards rubber ring in ad-court service box
5. Lunge-slide with **right** foot towards rubber ring (Clay Court) or place left foot in center of rubber ring (Hard Court)
6. **Hit a counter drop-shot**

DEGREE OF DIFFICULTY

3

REQUIRED EQUIPMENT

- 3 Agility Rings
- Tennis Balls
- 1 Racquet

KEY FACTORS

- Stay on balls of the feet (toes) when moving laterally (side-step)
- Hit the center of the rings
- Stick the landing on single leg only: step in, push out
- Maintain balance during change of direction and lunge-slide

PRE-REQUISITE DRILLS

- 7 Ad Drill II
- Lateral Fast Feet III

COMMON ERRORS

- Athlete fails to hit center of rubber rings
- Athlete pushes off with the wrong foot (foot outside rubber rings)

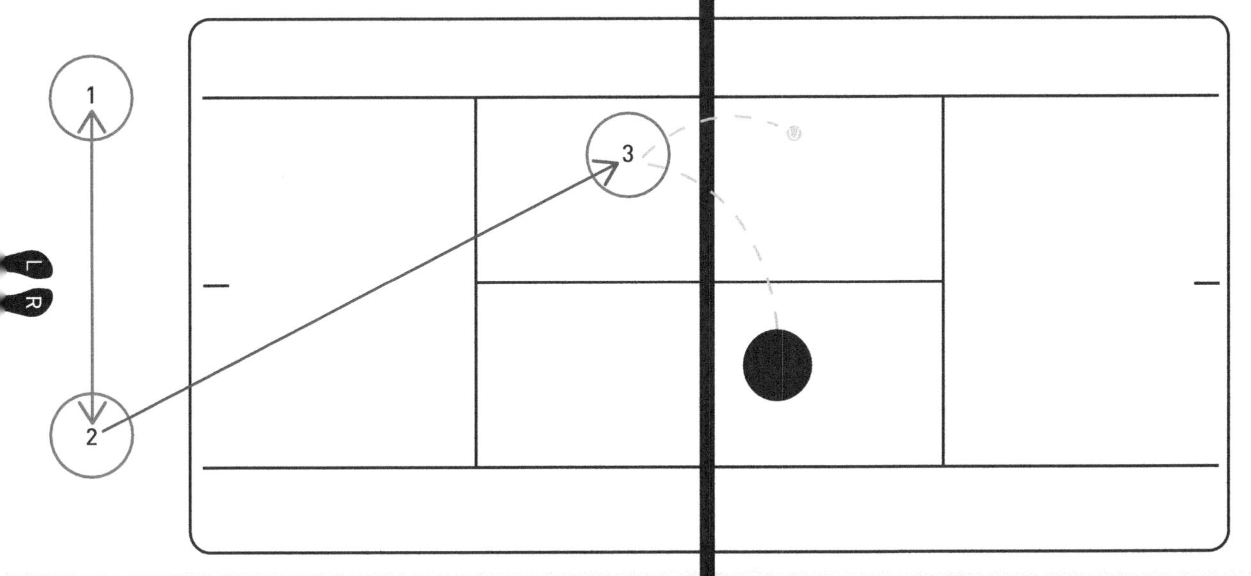

ID: 7252

7

7.253 7 AD DRILL (IV): TARGET

SUMMARY

The 7 Ad Drill IV is a professional integrated transition exercise, which focuses on improving footwork for groundstrokes, footwork for transition game, balance & coordination, accuracy, and defense against drop-shots.

PURPOSE

1. Improving footwork for groundstrokes
2. Improving footwork for transition game
3. Improving balance & coordination
4. Improving the counter drop-shot
5. Improving accuracy

DESCRIPTION

1 ball is being fed by the coach towards rubber ring in service box. Athlete is **holding a racquet** and needs to:

1. Start at the center of baseline facing the net
2. Move rapidly via side-step towards rubber ring in ad-court until left foot hits center of the ring
3. Push off with left foot and move quickly via side-step towards ring in deuce-court until right foot hits center of the ring
4. Push off with right foot and sprint diagonally towards rubber ring in ad-court service box
5. Lunge-slide with right foot towards rubber ring (Clay Court) or place left foot in center of rubber ring (Hard Court)
6. Hit a counter drop-shot into the **target area** (4 cones)

KEY FACTORS

- Stay on balls of the feet (toes) when moving laterally (side-step)
- Hit the center of the rings
- Stick the landing on single leg only: step in, push out
- Maintain balance during change of direction and lunge-slide
- 30% of shots (or more) need to hit target area
- Drop-shot must bounce 3x before passing service-line

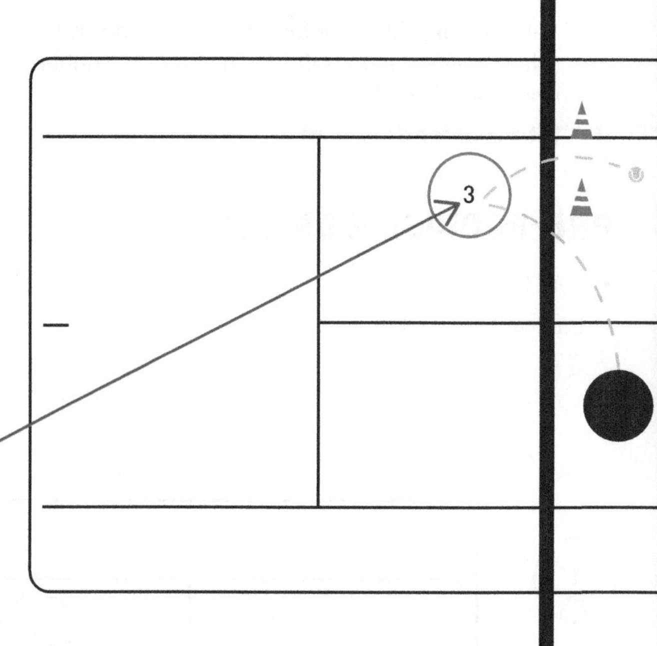

PRE-REQUISITE DRILLS

- 7 Ad Drill III
- Lateral Fast Feet IV

COMMON ERRORS

- Athlete fails to hit center of rubber rings
- Athlete pushes off with the wrong foot (foot outside rubber rings)

DEGREE OF DIFFICULTY

4

ID: 7253

REQUIRED EQUIPMENT

- 3 Agility Rings
- Tennis Balls
- 1 Racquet
- 4 Cones

NOTE

- Use target area location based on training needs
- Use appropriate location for ball feeding

7.254 7 DEUCE DRILL (I)

SUMMARY

The 7 Deuce Drill I is an introductory agility exercise, which focuses on improving footwork for groundstrokes, improving footwork for transition game, and improving balance & coordination.

PURPOSE

1. Improving footwork for groundstrokes
2. Improving footwork for transition game
3. Improving balance & coordination

DESCRIPTION

No balls are being fed by the coach. Athlete needs to:

1. Start at the center of baseline facing the net
2. Move rapidly via **side-step** towards rubber ring in deuce-court until **right** foot hits center of the ring
3. Push off with **right** foot and move quickly via **side-step** towards ring in ad-court until **left** foot hits center of the ring
4. Push off with **left** foot and **sprint** diagonally towards rubber ring in deuce-court service box
5. Lunge-slide with **left** foot pointing forward towards rubber ring (Clay Court) or place left foot in center of rubber ring (Hard Court)

COMMON ERRORS

- Athlete fails to hit center of rubber rings
- Athlete pushes off with the wrong foot (foot outside rubber rings)
- Athlete changes movement pattern after change of direction
- Athletes slides with toes pointing towards

DEGREE OF DIFFICULTY

1

REQUIRED EQUIPMENT

- 3 Agility Rings

KEY FACTORS

- Stay on balls of the feet (toes) when moving laterally (side-step)
- Hit the center of the rings
- Stick the landing on single leg only: step in, push out
- Maintain balance during change of direction and lunge-slide

PRE-REQUISITE DRILLS

- Lateral Fast Feet I

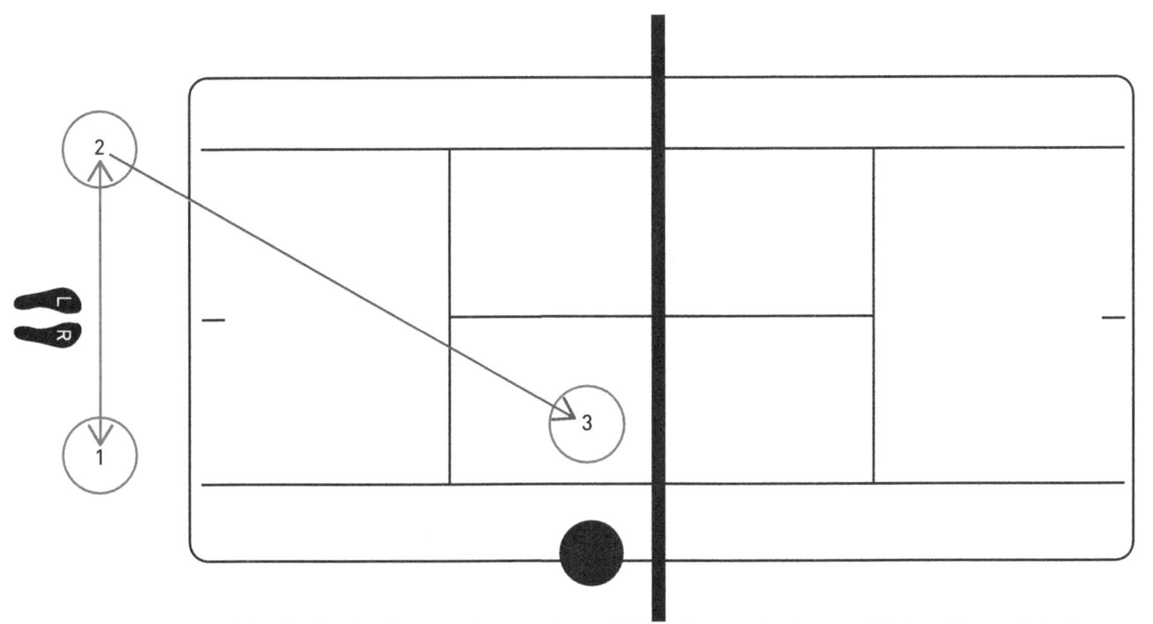

ID: 7254

7.255 7 DEUCE DRILL (II)

SUMMARY

The 7 Deuce Drill II is an intermediate agility exercise, which focuses on improving footwork for groundstrokes, improving footwork for transition game, and improving balance & coordination.

PURPOSE

1. Improving footwork for groundstrokes
2. Improving footwork for transition game
3. Improving balance & coordination

DESCRIPTION

No balls are being fed by the coach. Athlete is **holding a racquet** and needs to:

1. Start at the center of baseline facing the net
2. Move rapidly via side-step towards rubber ring in deuce-court until right foot hits center of the ring
3. Push off with right foot and move quickly via side-step towards ring in ad-court until left foot hits center of the ring
4. Push off with left foot and sprint diagonally towards rubber ring in deuce-court service box
5. Lunge-slide with left foot pointing forward towards rubber ring (Clay Court) or place left foot in center of rubber ring (Hard Court)

PRE-REQUISITE DRILLS

- 7 Deuce Drill I
- Lateral Fast Feet II

DEGREE OF DIFFICULTY

2

REQUIRED EQUIPMENT

- 3 Agility Rings
- 1 Racquet

KEY FACTORS

- Stay on balls of the feet (toes) when moving laterally (side-step)
- Hit the center of the rings
- Stick the landing on single leg only: step in, push out
- Maintain balance during change of direction and lunge-slide

COMMON ERRORS

- Athlete fails to hit center of rubber rings
- Athlete pushes off with the wrong foot (foot outside rubber rings)
- Athlete changes movement pattern after change of direction
- Athletes slides with toes pointing towards sideline

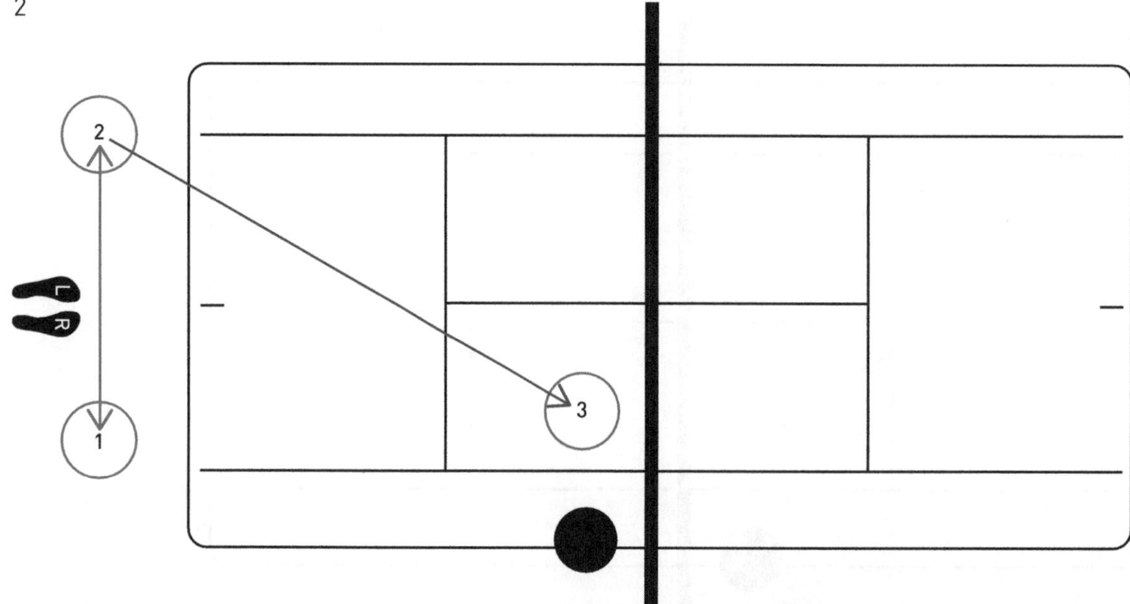

ID: 7255

7.256 7 DEUCE DRILL (III)

SUMMARY

The 7 Deuce Drill III is an advanced integrated transition exercise, which focuses on improving footwork for groundstrokes, footwork for transition game, balance & coordination, and defense against drop-shots.

PURPOSE

1. Improving footwork for groundstrokes
2. Improving footwork for transition game
3. Improving balance & coordination
4. Improving counter drop-shot

DESCRIPTION

1 ball is being fed by the coach towards rubber ring in service box. Athlete is **holding a racquet** and needs to:

1. Start at the center of baseline facing the net
2. Move rapidly via side-step towards rubber ring in deuce-court until right foot hits center of the ring
3. Push off with right foot and move quickly via side-step towards ring in ad-court until left foot hits center of the ring
4. Push off with left foot and sprint diagonally towards rubber ring in deuce-court service box
5. Lunge-slide with left foot towards rubber ring (Clay Court) or place left foot in center of rubber ring (Hard Court)
6. **Hit a counter drop-shot**

PRE-REQUISITE DRILLS

- 7 Deuce Drill II
- Lateral Fast Feet III

REQUIRED EQUIPMENT

- 3 Agility Rings
- Tennis Balls
- 1 Racquet

KEY FACTORS

- Stay on balls of the feet (toes) when moving laterally (side-step)
- Hit the center of the rings
- Stick the landing on single leg only: step in, push out
- Maintain balance during change of direction and lunge-slide

COMMON ERRORS

- Athlete fails to hit center of rubber rings
- Athlete pushes off with the wrong foot (foot outside rubber rings)

DEGREE OF DIFFICULTY

3

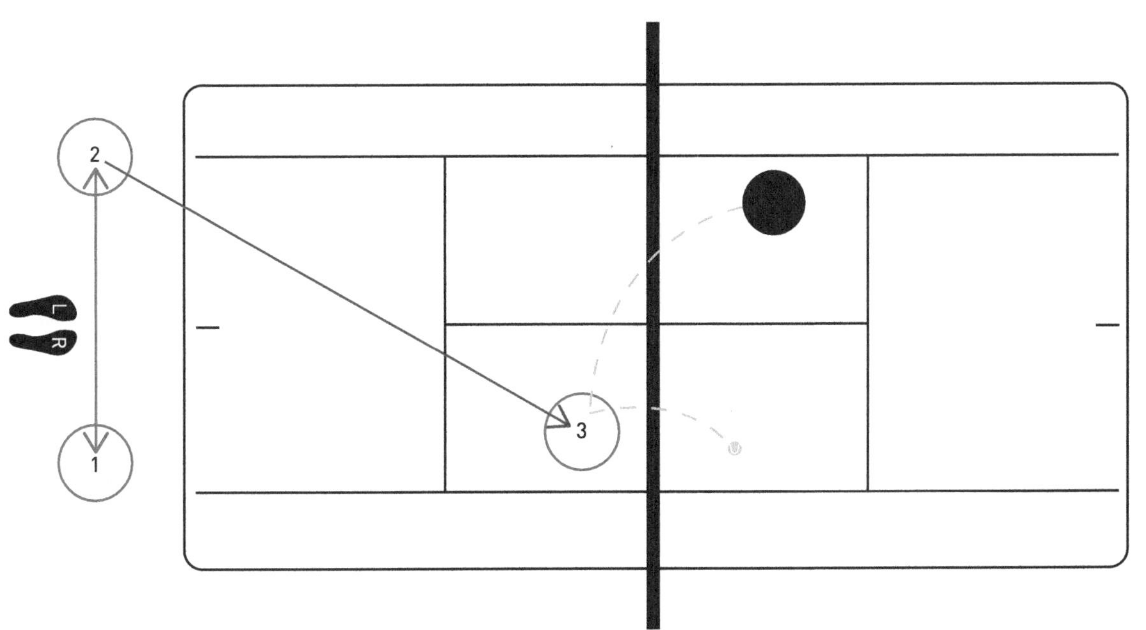

ID: 7256

7

7.257 7 DEUCE DRILL (IV): TARGET

SUMMARY

The 7 Deuce Drill IV is a professional integrated transition exercise, which focuses on improving footwork for groundstrokes, footwork for transition game, balance & coordination, defense against drop-shots, and accuracy.

PURPOSE

1. Improving footwork for groundstrokes
2. Improving footwork for transition game
3. Improving balance & coordination
4. Improving counter drop-shot
5. Improving accuracy

DESCRIPTION

1 ball is being fed by the coach towards rubber ring in service box. Athlete is **holding a racquet** and needs to:

1. Start at the center of baseline facing the net
2. Move rapidly via side-step towards rubber ring in deuce-court until right foot hits center of the ring
3. Push off with right foot and move quickly via side-step towards ring in ad-court until left foot hits center of the ring
4. Push off with left foot and sprint diagonally towards rubber ring in deuce-court service box
5. Lunge-slide with left foot towards rubber ring (Clay Court) or place left foot in center of rubber ring (Hard Court)
6. Hit a counter drop-drop shot into **target area**

DEGREE OF DIFFICULTY

4

REQUIRED EQUIPMENT

- 3 Agility Rings
- 1 Racquet
- Tennis Balls
- 2-4 Cones

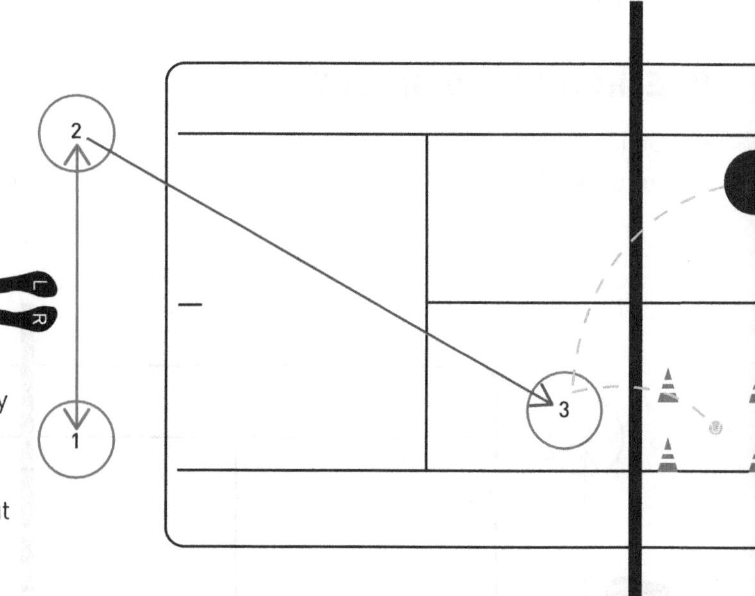

PRE-REQUISITE DRILLS

- 7 Deuce Drill III
- Lateral Fast Feet IV

KEY FACTORS

- Stay on balls of the feet (toes) when moving laterally (side-step)
- Hit the center of the rings
- Stick the landing on single leg only: step in, push out
- Maintain balance during change of direction and lunge-slide
- 30% of shots (or more) need to hit target area
- Drop-shot must bounce 3x before passing service-line

ID: 7257

COMMON ERRORS

- Athlete fails to hit center of rubber rings
- Athlete pushes off with the wrong foot (foot outside rubber rings)

NOTE

- Use target area location based on training needs
- Use appropriate location for ball feeding

7.258 L-DEUCE DRILL (I)

SUMMARY

The L-DEUCE-Drill I is an introductory agility exercise, which focuses on improving footwork for groundstrokes, improving footwork for transition game, improving footwork for forehand slam/slice approach, and improving balance & coordination.

PURPOSE

1. Improving footwork for groundstrokes
2. Improving footwork for transition game
3. Improving footwork for **forehand slam/slice** approach
4. Improving balance & coordination

DESCRIPTION

No balls are being fed by the coach. Athlete needs to:

1. Start at the center of baseline facing the net
2. Move rapidly via **side-step** towards rubber ring in ad-court (1) until **left** foot hits center of the ring
3. Stick the landing (1/4 squat), push off with **left** foot and move quickly via **side-step** towards ring in deuce-court (2) until **right** foot hits center of the ring
4. Stick the landing (1/4 squat), push off forward with **right** foot and **sprint** forward towards rubber ring near deuce-court service box
5. Jump inside the ring with the **left** foot, stick the landing, push-off and **backpedal** past baseline (ring 2)

DEGREE OF DIFFICULTY

1

REQUIRED EQUIPMENT

- 3 Agility Rings

KEY FACTORS

- Stay on balls of the feet (toes) when moving laterally (side-step)
- Hit the center of the rings
- Stick the landing on single leg only: step in, push out
- Maintain balance during change of direction

PRE-REQUISITE DRILLS

- Lateral Fast Feet I

COMMON ERRORS

- Athlete fails to hit center of rubber rings
- Athlete pushes off with the wrong foot (foot outside rubber rings)

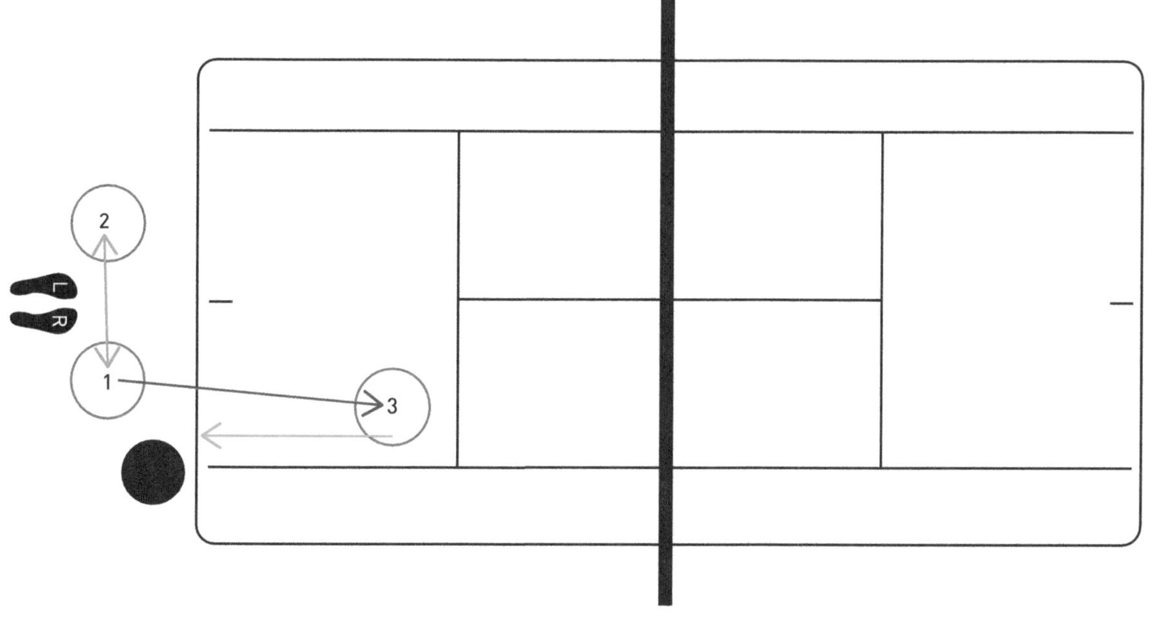

ID: 7258

7.259 L-DEUCE DRILL (II)

SUMMARY

The L-DEUCE-Drill II is an intermediate agility exercise, which focuses on improving footwork for groundstrokes, improving footwork for transition game, improving footwork for forehand slam/slice approach, and improving balance & coordination.

PURPOSE

1. Improving footwork for groundstrokes
2. Improving footwork for transition game
3. Improving footwork for **forehand slam/slice** approach
4. Improving balance & coordination

DESCRIPTION

No balls are being fed by the coach. Athlete is **holding a racquet** and needs to:

1. Start at the center of baseline facing the net
2. Move rapidly via **side-step** towards rubber ring in ad-court (1) until **left** foot hits center of the ring
3. Stick the landing (1/4 squat), push off with **left** foot and move quickly via **side-step** towards ring in deuce-court (2) until **right** foot hits center of the ring
4. Stick the landing (1/4 squat), push off forward with **right** foot and **sprint** forward towards rubber ring near deuce-court service box
5. Jump inside the ring with the **left** foot, stick the landing, push-off and **backpedal** past baseline (ring 2)

PRE-REQUISITE DRILLS

- Lateral Fast Feet II
- L-Deuce Drill I

DEGREE OF DIFFICULTY

2

REQUIRED EQUIPMENT

- 3 Agility Rings
- 1 Racquet

KEY FACTORS

- Stay on balls of the feet (toes) when moving laterally (side-step)
- Hit the center of the rings
- Stick the landing on single leg only: step in, push out
- Maintain balance during change of direction

COMMON ERRORS

- Athlete fails to hit center of rubber rings
- Athlete pushes off with the wrong foot (foot outside rubber rings)

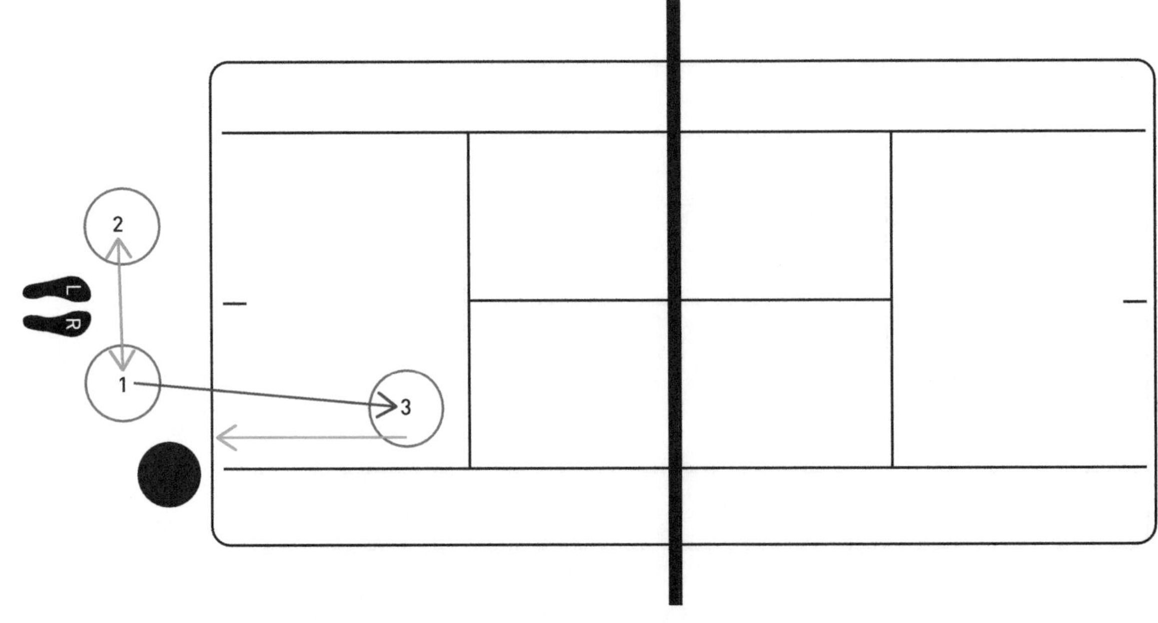

ID: 7259

7.260 L-DEUCE DRILL (III)

SUMMARY

The L-DEUCE-Drill III is an advanced agility exercise, which focuses on improving footwork for groundstrokes, improving footwork for transition game, improving footwork for forehand slam/slice approach, and improving balance & coordination.

PURPOSE

1. Improving footwork for groundstrokes
2. Improving footwork for transition game
3. Improve footwork for **forehand slam/slice** approach
4. Improving balance & coordination

DESCRIPTION

1 ball is being fed by the coach. Athlete is **holding a racquet** and needs to:

1. Start at the center of baseline facing the net
2. Move rapidly via side-step towards rubber ring in ad-court (1) until left foot hits center of the ring
3. Stick the landing (1/4 squat), push off with left foot and move quickly via side-step towards ring in deuce-court (2) until right foot hits center of the ring
4. Stick the landing (1/4 squat), push off forward with right foot and sprint forward towards rubber ring near deuce-court service box
5. **Hit a forehand** slam/slice shot, push-off and back-pedal past baseline (ring 2)

PRE-REQUISITE DRILLS

- Lateral Fast Feet III
- L-DEUCE Drill II

DEGREE OF DIFFICULTY

3

REQUIRED EQUIPMENT

- 3 Agility Rings
- 1 Racquet
- Tennis Balls

KEY FACTORS

- Stay on balls of the feet (toes) when moving laterally (side-step)
- Hit the center of the rings
- Stick the landing on single leg only: step in, push out
- Maintain balance during change of direction

COMMON ERRORS

- Athlete fails to hit center of rubber rings
- Athlete pushes off with the wrong foot (foot outside rubber rings)

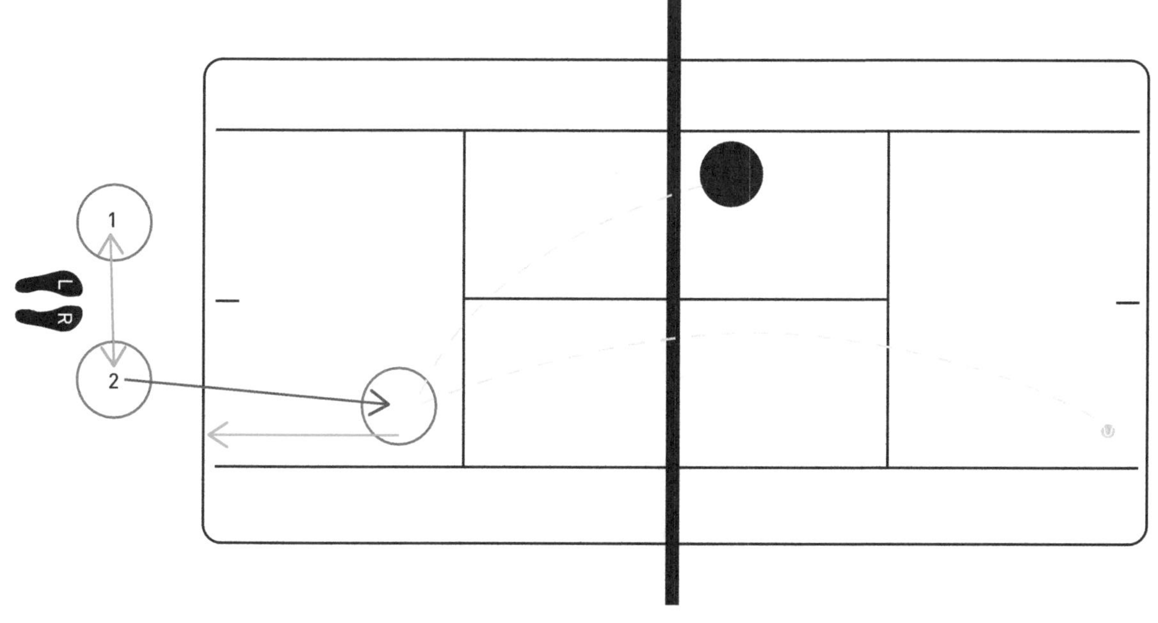

ID: 7260

7.261 L-DEUCE DRILL (IV): TARGET

SUMMARY

The L-DEUCE Drill IV is a professional agility exercise, which focuses on improving footwork for groundstrokes, improving footwork for transition game, improving footwork for forehand slam/slice approach, and improving balance & coordination.

PURPOSE

1. Improving footwork for groundstrokes
2. Improving footwork for transition game
3. Improve footwork for **forehand slam/slice** approach
4. Improving balance & coordination

DESCRIPTION

1 ball is being fed by the coach. Athlete is **holding a racquet** and needs to:

1. Start at the center of baseline facing the net
2. Move rapidly via side-step towards rubber ring in ad-court (1) until left foot hits center of the ring
3. Stick the landing (1/4 squat), push off with left foot and move quickly via side-step towards ring in deuce-court (2) until right foot hits center of the ring
4. Stick the landing (1/4 squat), push off forward with right foot and sprint forward towards rubber ring near deuce-court service box
5. **Hit a forehand** slam/slice shot into a **target area,** push-off and backpedal past baseline (ring 2)

PRE-REQUISITE DRILLS

- Lateral Fast Feet IV
- L-DEUCE Drill III

NOTE

- Use target area location based on training needs
- Use appropriate location for ball feeding

DEGREE OF DIFFICULTY

4

REQUIRED EQUIPMENT

- 3 Agility Rings
- 1 Racquet
- Tennis Balls
- 4 Cones

KEY FACTORS

- Stay on balls of the feet (toes) when moving laterally (side-step)
- Hit the center of the rings
- Stick the landing on single leg only: step in, push out
- Maintain balance during change of direction and lunge-slide
- 30% of shots (or more) need to hit target area

COMMON ERRORS

- Athlete fails to hit center of rubber rings
- Athlete pushes off with the wrong foot (foot outside rubber rings

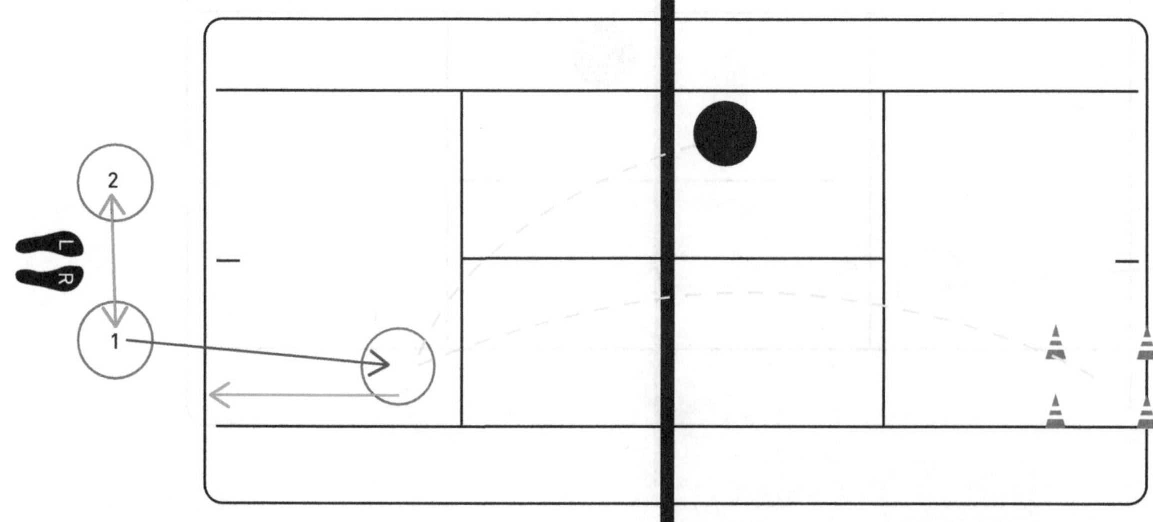

ID: 7261

7.262 L-AD DRILL (I)

SUMMARY

The L-AD-Drill I is an introductory agility exercise, which focuses on improving footwork for groundstrokes, improving footwork for transition game, improving footwork for backhand slam/slice approach, and improving balance & coordination.

PURPOSE

1. Improving footwork for groundstrokes
2. Improving footwork for transition game
3. Improve footwork for **backhand slam/slice** approach
4. Improving balance & coordination

DESCRIPTION

No balls are being fed by the coach. Athlete needs to:

1. Start at the center of baseline facing the net
2. Move rapidly via **side-step** towards rubber ring in deuce-court (1) until **right** foot hits center of the ring
3. Stick the landing (1/4 squat), push off with **right** foot and move quickly via **side-step** towards ring in ad-court (2) until **left** foot hits center of the ring
4. Stick the landing (1/4 squat), push off forward with **left** foot and **sprint** forward towards rubber ring near ad-court service box
5. Jump inside the ring with the **right** foot, stick the landing, push-off and **backpedal** past baseline (ring 2)

PRE-REQUISITE DRILLS

- Lateral Fast Feet I

DEGREE OF DIFFICULTY

1

REQUIRED EQUIPMENT

- 3 Agility Rings

KEY FACTORS

- Stay on balls of the feet (toes) when moving laterally (side-step)
- Hit the center of the rings
- Stick the landing on single leg only: step in, push out
- Maintain balance during change of direction

COMMON ERRORS

- Athlete fails to hit center of rubber rings
- Athlete pushes off with the wrong foot (foot outside rubber rings)

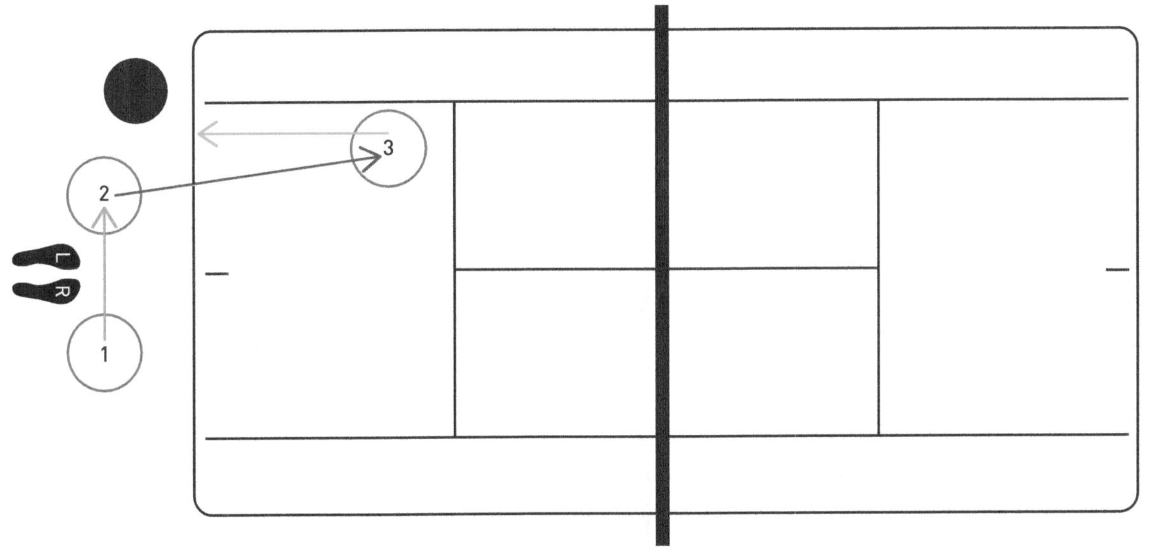

ID: 7262

7.263 L-AD DRILL (II)

SUMMARY

The L-AD-Drill II is an intermediate agility exercise, which focuses on improving footwork for groundstrokes, improving footwork for transition game, improving footwork for backhand slam/slice approach, and improving balance & coordination.

PURPOSE

1. Improving footwork for groundstrokes
2. Improving footwork for transition game
3. Improve footwork for **backhand slam/slice** approach
4. Improving balance & coordination

DESCRIPTION

No balls are being fed by the coach. Athlete **holds a rcquet** and needs to:

1. Start at the center of baseline facing the net
2. Move rapidly via side-step towards rubber ring in deuce-court (1) until right foot hits center of the ring
3. Stick the landing (1/4 squat), push off with right foot and move quickly via side-step towards ring in ad-court (2) until left foot hits center of the ring
4. Stick the landing (1/4 squat), push off forward with left foot and sprint forward towards rubber ring near ad-court service box
5. Jump inside the ring with the right foot, stick the landing, push-off and backpedal past baseline (ring 2)

PRE-REQUISITE DRILLS

- Lateral Fast Feet II
- L-AD Drill I

DEGREE OF DIFFICULTY

2

REQUIRED EQUIPMENT

- 3 Agility Rings
- 1 Racquet

KEY FACTORS

- Stay on balls of the feet (toes) when moving laterally (side-step)
- Hit the center of the rings
- Stick the landing on single leg only: step in, push out
- Maintain balance during change of direction

COMMON ERRORS

- Athlete fails to hit center of rubber rings
- Athlete pushes off with the wrong foot (foot outside rubber rings)

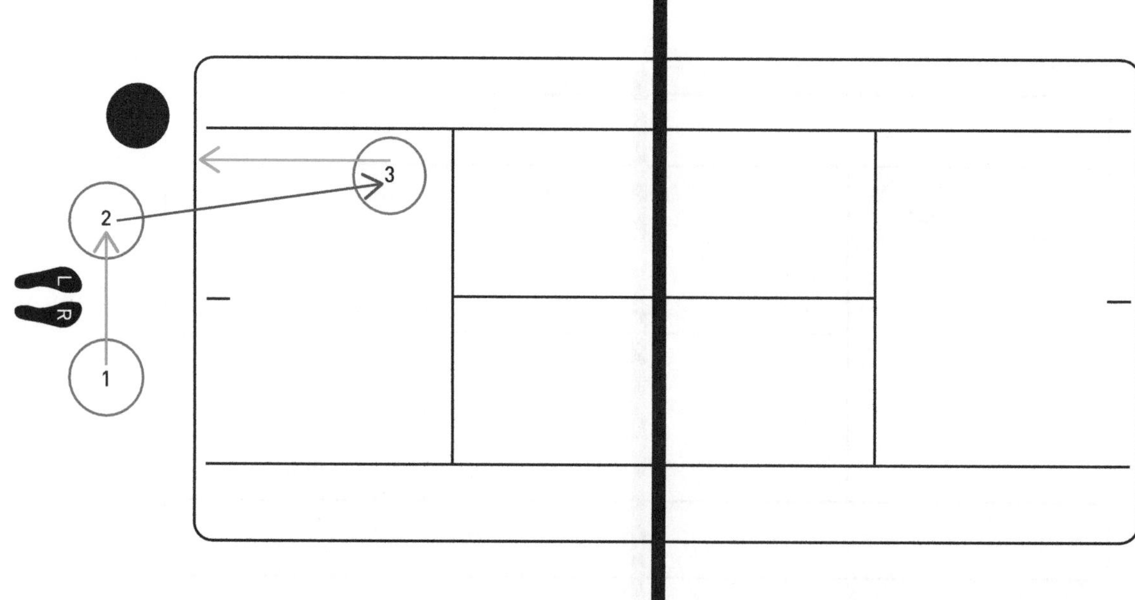

ID: 7263

7.264 L-AD DRILL (III)

SUMMARY

The L-AD-Drill III is an advanced integrated agility exercise, which focuses on improving footwork for groundstrokes, improving footwork for transition game, improving footwork for backhand slam/slice approach, and improving balance & coordination.

PURPOSE

1. Improving footwork for groundstrokes
2. Improving footwork for transition game
3. Improve footwork for **backhand slam/slice** approach
4. Improving balance & coordination

DESCRIPTION

1 ball is being fed by the coach. Athlete **holds a racquet** and needs to:

1. Start at the center of baseline facing the net
2. Move rapidly via side-step towards rubber ring in deuce-court (1) until right foot hits center of the ring
3. Stick the landing (1/4 squat), push off with right foot and move quickly via side-step towards ring in ad-court (2) until left foot hits center of the ring
4. Stick the landing (1/4 squat), push off forward with left foot and sprint forward towards rubber ring near ad-court service box
5. **Hit a backhand** slam/slice shot, push-off and back-pedal past baseline (ring 2)

PRE-REQUISITE DRILLS

- Lateral Fast Feet III

DEGREE OF DIFFICULTY

3

REQUIRED EQUIPMENT

- 3 Agility Rings
- 1 Racquet
- Tennis Balls

KEY FACTORS

- Stay on balls of the feet (toes) when moving laterally (side-step)
- Hit the center of the rings
- Stick the landing on single leg only: step in, push out
- Maintain balance during change of direction

COMMON ERRORS

- Athlete fails to hit center of rubber rings
- Athlete pushes off with the wrong foot (foot outside rubber rings)

ID: 7264

7.265 L-AD DRILL (IV): TARGET

SUMMARY

The L-AD-Drill VI is a professional integrated agility exercise, which focuses on improving footwork for groundstrokes, improving footwork for transition game, improving footwork for backhand slam/slice approach, improving balance & coordination, and backhand accuracy.

PURPOSE

1. Improving footwork for groundstrokes
2. Improving footwork for transition game
3. Improve footwork for **backhand slam/slice** approach
4. Improving balance & coordination
5. Improve backhand accuracy

DESCRIPTION

1 ball is being fed by the coach. Athlete **holds a racquet** and needs to:

1. Start at the center of baseline facing the net
2. Move rapidly via side-step towards rubber ring in deuce-court (1) until right foot hits center of the ring
3. Stick the landing (1/4 squat), push off with right foot and move quickly via side-step towards ring in ad-court (2) until left foot hits center of the ring
4. Stick the landing (1/4 squat), push off forward with left foot and sprint forward towards rubber ring near ad-court service box
5. **Hit a backhand** slam/slice shot into **target area**, push-off and backpedal past baseline (ring 2)

DEGREE OF DIFFICULTY

4

REQUIRED EQUIPMENT

- 3 Agility Rings
- 1 Racquet
- Tennis Balls
- 4 Cones

KEY FACTORS

- Stay on balls of the feet (toes) when moving laterally (side-step)
- Hit the center of the rings
- Stick the landing on single leg only: step in, push out
- Maintain balance during change of direction
- 30% of shots (or more) need to hit target area

PRE-REQUISITE DRILLS

- Lateral Fast Feet IV

NOTE

- Use target area location based on training needs
- Use appropriate location for ball feeding

COMMON ERRORS

- Athlete fails to hit center of rubber rings
- Athlete pushes off with the wrong foot (foot outside rubber rings)

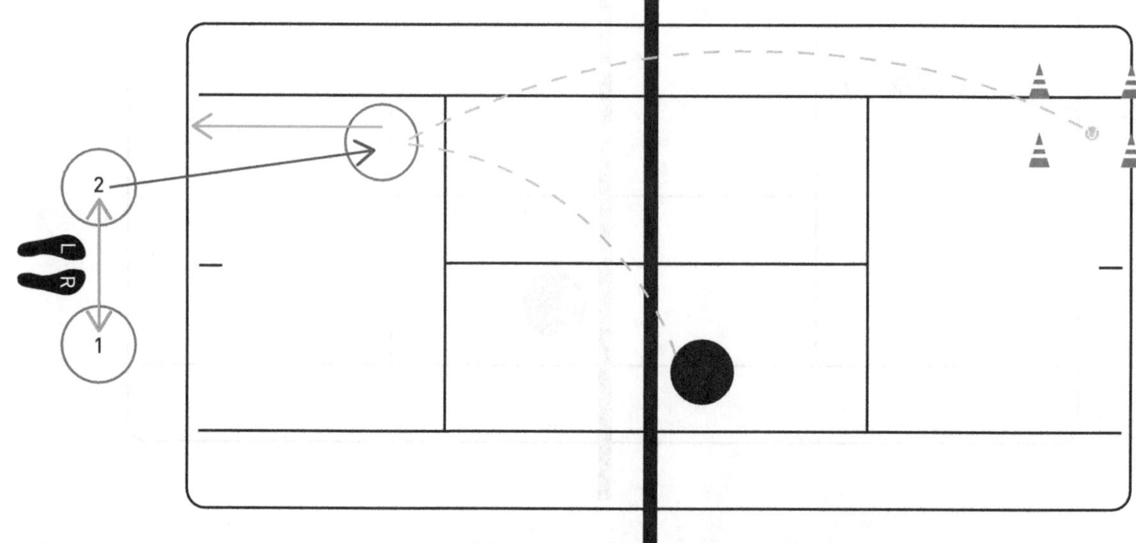

ID: 7265

7.266 RECTANGLE RUN (I)

SUMMARY

The Rectangle Run I is an introductory agility exercise, which focuses on improving footwork for ground strokes, footwork for transition game and improving stability & coordination.

Note: Other combinations of calisthenics may be used as applicable (e.g. carioca).

PURPOSE

1. Improving foot work for ground strokes
2. Improving footwork for transition game
3. Improving stability & coordination

DESCRIPTION

Athlete faces the net and needs to:

1. Start next to cone #1 behind the baseline of the doubles alley facing the net
2. **Sprint** rapidly forward towards rubber ring of cone #2, **look down** to the ground, hit the center of the ring with the **right** foot and stick the landing
3. Push off with **right** foot and move quickly via **side-step** towards rubber ring of cone #3, **look down** to the ground, hit center of the ring with the **left** foot and stick the landing
4. Push off with **left** foot, **lean forward** and **back-pedal** towards rubber ring of cone #4, look down to the ground, hit center of the ring with the **left** foot and stick the landing
5. Push off with **left** foot and move quickly via **side-step** towards rubber ring of cone #1, **look down** to the ground, hit center of the ring with the **left** foot and stick the landing

DEGREE OF DIFFICULTY

1

REQUIRED EQUIPMENT

- 4 Agility Rings
- 4 Cones

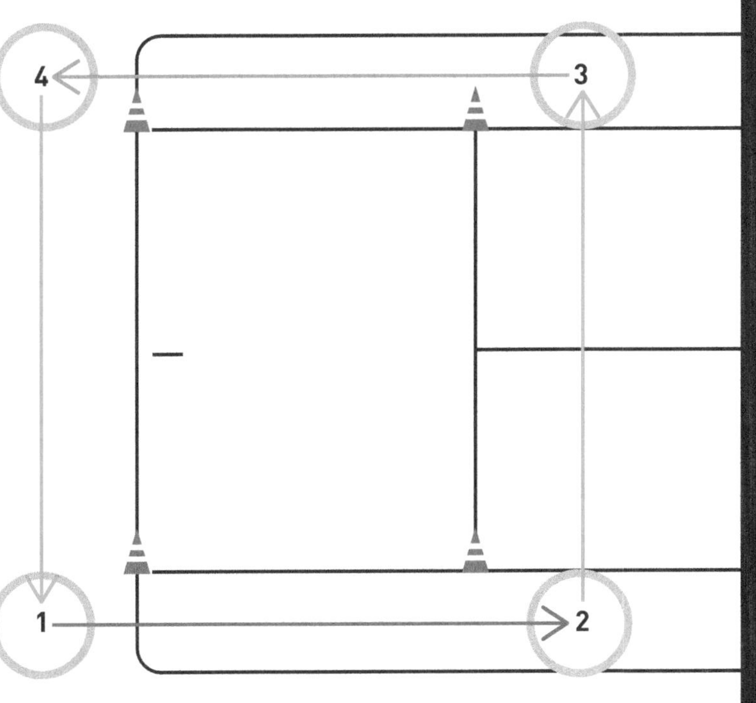

PRE-REQUISITE DRILLS

- Fast Feet I
- Lateral Fast Feet I

COMMON ERRORS

- Athlete fails to hit center of rubber rings
- Athlete pushes off with the wrong foot (foot outside rubber rings)
- Athlete changes movement pattern after change of direction

KEY FACTORS

- Stay on balls of the feet (toes) when moving laterally (side-step)
- Hit the center of the rings
- Stick the landing on single leg only: step in, push out
- Maintain stability during change of direction

ID: 7266

7.267 RECTANGLE RUN (II)

SUMMARY

The Rectangle Run II is an intermediate agility exercise, which focuses on improving footwork for ground strokes, footwork for transition game and improving stability & coordination.

Note: Other combinations of calisthenics may be used as applicable (e.g. carioca).

PURPOSE

1. Improving foot work for ground strokes
2. Improving footwork for transition game
3. Improving stability & coordination

DESCRIPTION

Athlete **holds a racquet**, faces the net and needs to:

1. Start next to cone #1 behind the baseline of the doubles alley facing the net
2. **Sprint** rapidly forward towards rubber ring of cone #2, **look down** to the ground, hit the center of the ring with the **right** foot and stick the landing
3. Push off with **right** foot and move quickly via **side-step** towards rubber ring of cone #3, **look down** to the ground, hit center of the ring with the **left** foot and stick the landing
4. Push off with **left** foot, **lean forward** and **back-pedal** towards rubber ring of cone #4, **look down** to the ground, hit center of the ring with the **left** foot and stick the landing
5. Push off with **left** foot and move quickly via **side-step** towards rubber ring of cone #1, **look down** to the ground, hit center of the ring with the **left** foot and stick the landing
6. Record time

REQUIRED EQUIPMENT

- 1 Stop Watch
- 4 Agility Rings
- 4 Cones
- 1 Racquet

DEGREE OF DIFFICULTY

2

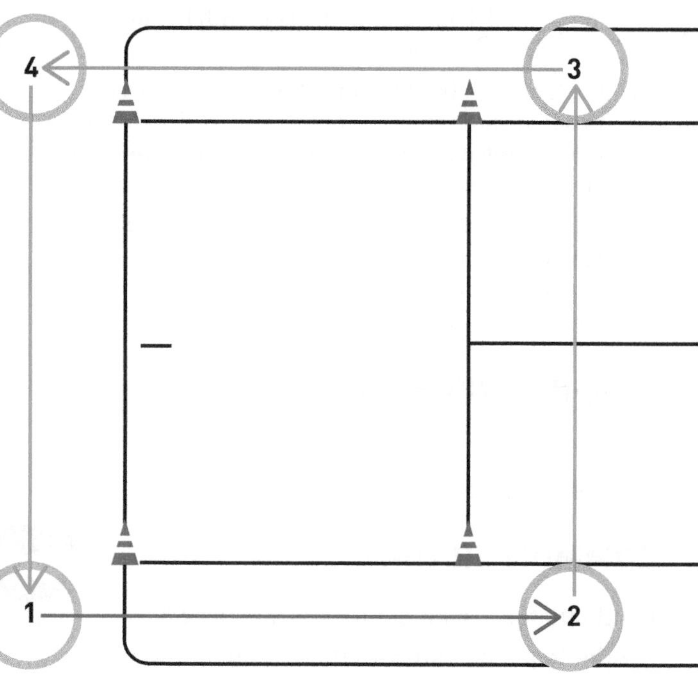

KEY FACTORS

- Stay on balls of the feet (toes) when moving laterally (side-step)
- Hit the center of the rings
- Stick the landing on single leg only: Step in, push out
- Maintain stability during change of direction

ID: 7267

COMMON ERRORS

- Athlete fails to hit center of rubber rings
- Athlete pushes off with the wrong foot (foot outside rubber rings)
- Athlete changes movement pattern after change of direction

PRE-REQUISITE DRILLS

- Fast Feet II
- Lateral Fast Feet II
- Rectangle Run I

7.268 RECTANGLE RUN (III)

SUMMARY

The Rectangle Run III is an advanced agility exercise, which focuses on improving footwork for ground strokes, footwork for transition game and improving stability & coordination.

Note: Other combinations of calisthenics may be used as applicable (e.g. carioca).

PURPOSE

1. Improving foot work for ground strokes
2. Improving footwork for transition game
3. Improving stability & coordination

DESCRIPTION

Athlete **holds a racquet**, faces the net and needs to:

1. Start next to cone #1 behind the baseline of the doubles alley facing the net
2. Sprint rapidly forward towards rubber ring of cone #2, **look forward**, hit the center of the ring with the right foot and stick the landing
3. Push off with right foot and move quickly via side-step towards rubber ring of cone #3, **look forward**, hit center of the ring with the left foot and stick the landing
4. Push off with left foot, lean forward and back-pedal towards rubber ring of cone #4, **look forward**, hit center of the ring with the left foot and stick the landing
5. Push off with left foot and move quickly via side-step towards rubber ring of cone #1, **look forward**, hit center of the ring with the left foot and stick the landing
6. Record time

REQUIRED EQUIPMENT

- 1 Stop Watch
- 4 Agility Rings
- 4 Cones
- 1 Racquet

DEGREE OF DIFFICULTY

3

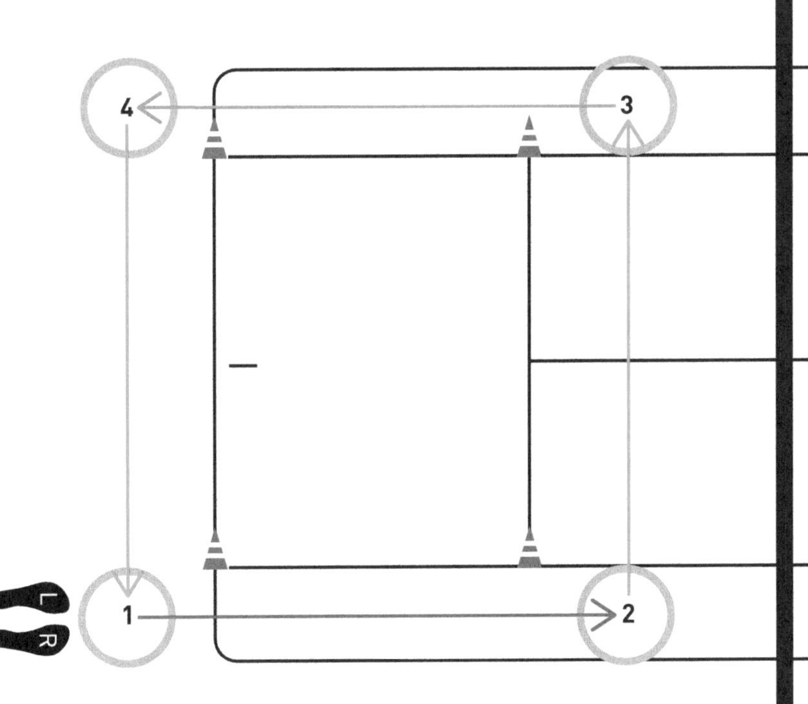

KEY FACTORS

- Stay on balls of the feet (toes) when moving laterally (side-step)
- Hit the center of the rings
- Stick the landing on single leg only: Step in, push out
- Maintain stability and look forward during change of direction

COMMON ERRORS

- Athlete fails to hit center of rubber rings
- Athlete pushes off with the wrong foot (foot outside rubber rings)
- Athlete changes movement pattern after change of direction

PRE-REQUISITE DRILLS

- Fast Feet III
- Lateral Fast Feet III
- Rectangle Run II

ID: 7268

7.269 RECTANGLE RUN (IV)

SUMMARY

The Rectangle Run IV is a professional agility exercise, which focuses on improving footwork for ground strokes, footwork for transition game, reaction time and improving stability & coordination.

Note: Other combinations of calisthenics may be used as applicable (e.g. carioca).

PURPOSE

1. Improving foot work for ground strokes
2. Improving footwork for transition game
3. Improving stability & coordination
4. Improves reaction time

DESCRIPTION

A coach/partner provides an **audible cue** and **randomly** calls out the cone #. Athlete holds a **racquet**, faces the net and needs to move with perfect form and appropriate movement calisthenics (sprint, side-step, back-pedal, carioca, etc.) as fast as possible.

DEGREE OF DIFFICULTY

4

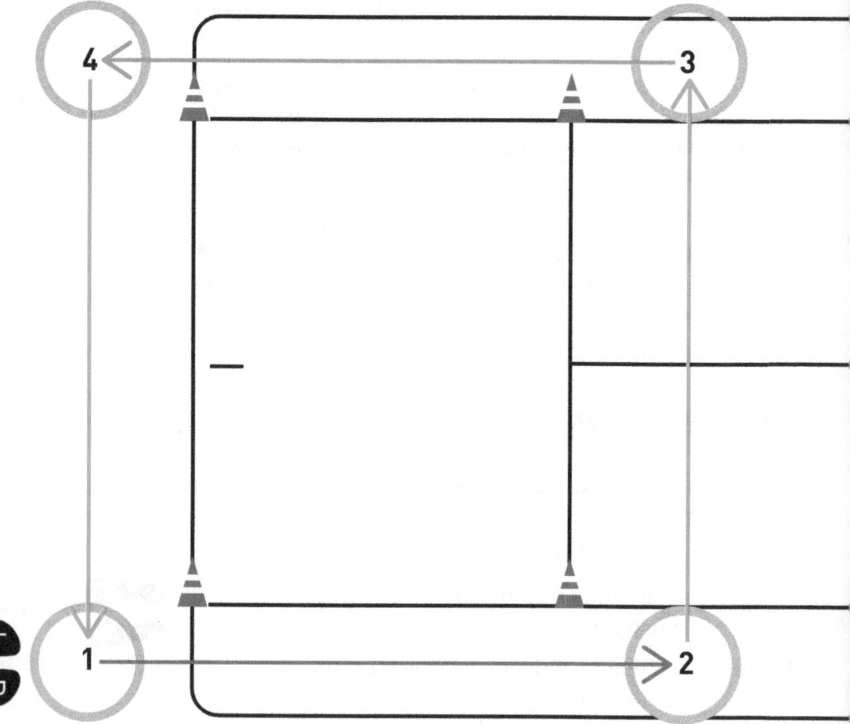

PRE-REQUISITE DRILLS

- Fast Feet IV
- Lateral Fast Feet IV
- Rectangle Run III

REQUIRED EQUIPMENT

- 4 Cones
- 1 Racquet

ID: 7269

COMMON ERRORS

- Athlete pushes off with the wrong foot (foot outside rubber rings)
- Athlete changes movement pattern after change of direction

KEY FACTORS

- Stay on balls of the feet (toes) when moving laterally (side-step)
- Stick the landing on single leg only: step in, push out
- Maintain stability and look forward during change of direction

7.270 8 WAY RING DRILL (I)

SUMMARY

The 8 Way Ring Drill I is an introductory agility exercise, which focuses on improving footwork for ground strokes, footwork for transition game and improving stability & coordination.

Note: Other combinations of calisthenics may be used as applicable (e.g. carioca).

PURPOSE

1. Improving foot work for ground strokes
2. Improving footwork for transition game
3. Improving stability & coordination

DESCRIPTION

Athlete starts at the service T, faces the net and needs to:

1. Split-step, lean forward, rapidly **back-pedal** towards ring #1, **look down** to the ground, hit the center of the ring with one foot and stick the landing
2. Push off with **same** foot, **sprint** forward towards service-T, **look down** to the ground, and split-step
3. Push off with **right** foot, **side-step** towards ring #2, **look down** to the ground, hit center of the ring with the left foot and stick the landing
4. Push off with **left** foot, return quickly via **carioca** towards service-T, **look down** to the ground and split-step
5. Push off with **both** feet, **sprint** forward towards ring #3, **look down** to the ground, hit center of the ring with the right foot,and stick the landing
6. Push-off with the **right** foot, lean forward, rapidly **backpedal** towards service-T, **look down** to the ground and split-step
7. Push off with **left** foot, **side-step** towards ring #4, **look down** to the ground, hit center of the ring with the right foot and stick the landing
8. Push off with **right** foot, return quickly via **carioca** towards service-T, **look down** to the ground and split-step

DEGREE OF DIFFICULTY

1

PRE-REQUISITE DRILLS

- Fast Feet I
- Lateral Fast Feet I
- Carioca

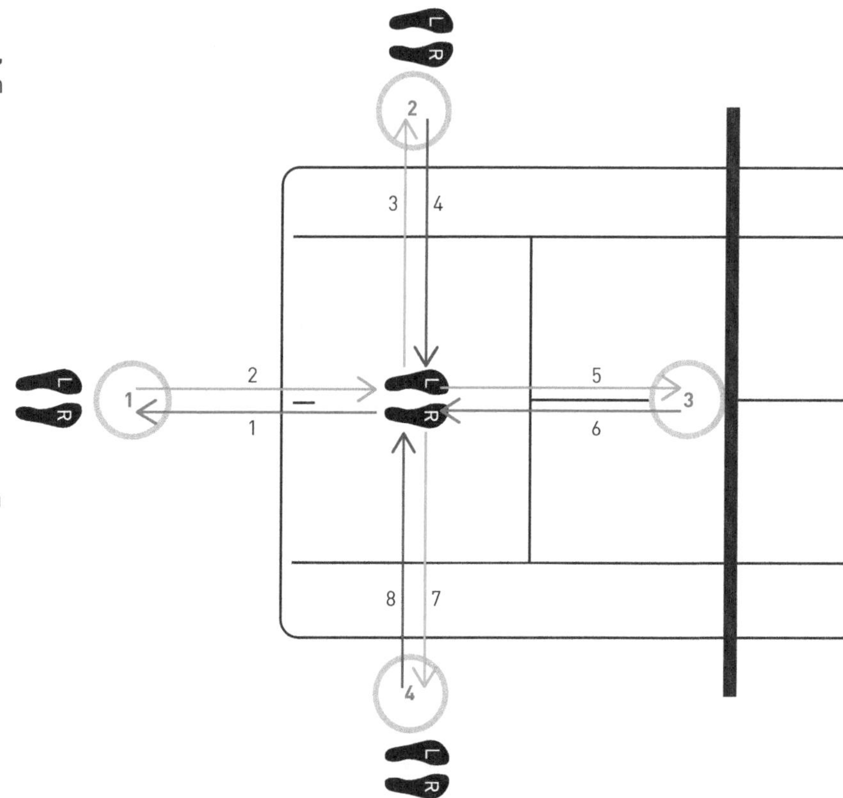

REQUIRED EQUIPMENT

- 4 Agility Rings

COMMON ERRORS

- Athlete fails to hit center of rubber rings
- Athlete pushes off with the wrong foot (foot outside rubber rings)
- Athlete changes movement pattern after change of direction

KEY FACTORS

- Stay on balls of the feet (toes) when moving laterally (side-step)
- Hit the center of the rings
- Stick the landing on single leg only: step in, push out
- Maintain stability during change of direction
- Split-step before change of direction

ID: 7270

7.271 8 WAY RING DRILL (II)

SUMMARY

The 8 Way Ring Drill I is an intermediate agility exercise, which focuses on improving footwork for ground strokes, footwork for transition game and improving stability & coordination.

Note: Other combinations of calisthenics may be used as applicable (e.g. carioca).

PURPOSE

1. Improving foot work for ground strokes
2. Improving footwork for transition game
3. Improving stability & coordination

DESCRIPTION

Athlete starts at the service T, faces the net, **holds a racquet**, and needs to:

1. Split-step, lean forward, rapidly **back-pedal** towards ring #1, **look down** to the ground, hit the center of the ring with one foot and stick the landing
2. Push off with same foot, **sprint** forward towards service-T, **look down** to the ground and split-step
3. Push off with right foot, **side-step** towards ring #2, **look down** to the ground, hit center of the ring with the left foot and stick the landing
4. Push off with left foot, return quickly via **carioca** towards service-T, **look down** to the ground and split-step
5. Push off with both feet, **sprint** forward towards ring #3, **look down** to the ground, hit center of the ring with the right foot,and stick the landing
6. Push-off with the right foot, lean forward, rapidly **back-pedal** towards service-T, **look down** to the ground and split-step
7. Push off with left foot, **side-step** towards ring #4, **look down** to the ground, hit center of the ring with the right foot, and stick the landing
8. Push off with right foot, return quickly via **carioca** towards service-T, **look down** to the ground and split-step
9. Record time

REQUIRED EQUIPMENT

- 1 Stop Watch
- 4 Agility Rings
- 1 Racquet

KEY FACTORS

- Stay on balls of the feet (toes) when moving laterally (side-step)
- Hit the center of the rings
- Stick the landing on single leg only: step in, push out
- Maintain stability during change of direction
- Split-step before change of direction

COMMON ERRORS

- Athlete fails to hit center of rubber rings
- Athlete pushes off with the wrong foot (foot outside rubber rings)
- Athlete changes movement pattern after change of direction

PRE-REQUISITE DRILLS

- Fast Feet II
- Lateral Fast Feet II
- Carioca II
- 8 Way Ring Drill (I)

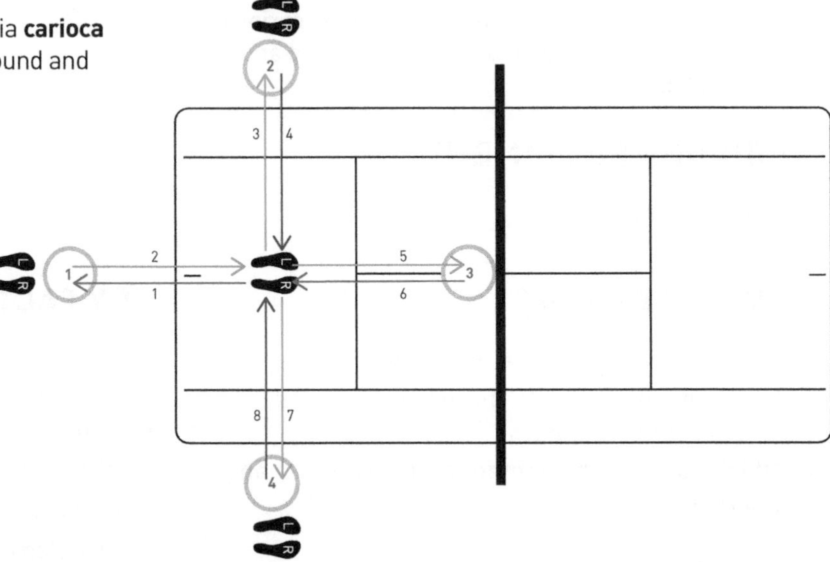

ID: 7271

DEGREE OF DIFFICULTY

2

7.272 8 WAY RING DRILL (III)

SUMMARY

The 8 Way Ring Drill III is an advanced agility exercise, which focuses on improving footwork for ground strokes, footwork for transition game and improving stability & coordination.

Note: Other combinations of calisthenics may be used as applicable (e.g. carioca).

PURPOSE

1. Improving foot work for ground strokes
2. Improving footwork for transition game
3. Improving stability & coordination

DESCRIPTION

Athlete starts at the service T, faces the net, **holds a racquet**, and needs to:

1. Split-step, lean forward, rapidly back-pedal towards ring #1, look forward, hit the center of the ring with one foot, and stick the landing
2. Push off with same foot, sprint forward towards service-T, **look forward**, and split-step
3. Push off with right foot, side-step towards ring #2, **look forward**, hit center of the ring with the left foot and stick the landing
4. Push off with left foot, return quickly via carioca towards service-T, **look forward** and split-step
5. Push off with both feet, sprint forward towards ring #3, **look forward**, hit center of the ring with the right foot and stick the landing
6. Push-off with the right foot, lean forward, rapidly back-pedal towards service-T, **look forward** and split-step
7. Push off with left foot, side-step towards ring #4, **look forward**, hit center of the ring with the right foot and stick the landing
8. Push off with right foot, return quickly via carioca towards service-T, **look forward** and split-step
9. Record time

REQUIRED EQUIPMENT

- 1 Stop Watch
- 4 Agility Rings
- 1 Racquet

KEY FACTORS

- Stay on balls of the feet (toes) when moving laterally (side-step)
- Hit the center of the rings
- Stick the landing on single leg only: step in, push out
- Maintain stability during change of direction
- Split-step before change of direction

COMMON ERRORS

- Athlete fails to hit center of rubber rings
- Athlete pushes off with the wrong foot (foot outside rubber rings)
- Athlete changes movement pattern after change of direction

PRE-REQUISITE DRILLS

- Fast Feet III
- Lateral Fast Feet III
- Carioca III
- 8 Way Ring Drill (II)

DEGREE OF DIFFICULTY

3

ID: 7272

7

7.273 8 WAY RING DRILL (IV)

SUMMARY

The 8 Way Ring Drill IV is a professional agility exercise, which focuses on improving footwork for ground strokes, footwork for transition game, reaction time and improving stability & coordination.

Note: Other combinations of calisthenics may be used as applicable (e.g. carioca).

PURPOSE

1. Improving foot work for ground strokes
2. Improving footwork for transition game
3. Improving stability & coordination
4. Improving reaction time

DESCRIPTION

A coach/partner provides an **audible cue** and **randomly** calls out the cone #. Athlete starts at the service T, **holds a racquet**, faces the net and needs to move with perfect form and appropriate movement calisthenics (sprint, side-step, back-pedal, carioca, etc.) as fast as possible.

PRE-REQUISITE DRILLS

- Fast Feet IV
- Lateral Fast Feet IV
- Carioca IV
- 8 Way Ring Drill (III)

DEGREE OF DIFFICULTY

4

REQUIRED EQUIPMENT

- 4 Agility Rings
- 1 Racquet

KEY FACTORS

- Stay on balls of the feet (toes) when moving laterally (side-step)
- Hit the center of the rings
- Stick the landing on single leg only: step in, push out
- Maintain stability during change of direction
- Split-step before change of direction

COMMON ERRORS

- Athlete fails to hit center of rubber rings
- Athlete pushes off with the wrong foot (foot outside rubber rings)
- Athlete changes movement pattern after change of direction

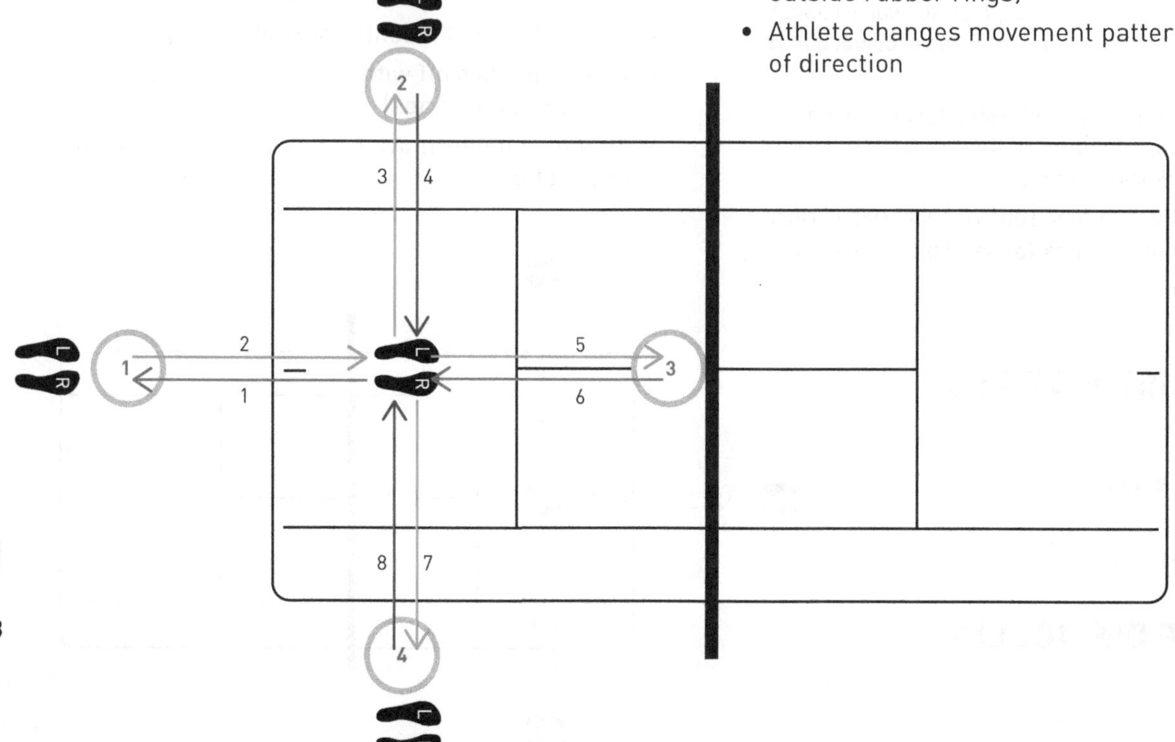

ID: 7273

CHAPTER 8:

“The Science of Sports Nutrition”

THE SCIENCE OF SPORTS NUTRITION

To become conscious of your diet is as important as working in the gym or on the court because without proper foods the body cannot perform at its best but the question remains, how to decide what foods to eat and where to look for advice? Since there is a lot of information available we will introduce the profession of "Sports Nutrition", help distinguish between myths and facts and explain why sports nutrition is important.

UNDER THE MICROSCOPE

CRUNCH FITNESS: PERSONAL TRAINER KILLS CLIENT

In 1999, Crunch Fitness was sued by Anne Marie Capati, a 37 year old woman who was suffering from high blood pressure (hypertension). A Crunch personal trainer "prescribed" the herbal weight loss supplement Thermadrene, which contained:

- 20 mg of active ephedra (basically works like an amphetamine; it removes norepinephrine from the transmitting nerves → makes adrenaline/epinephrine more potent)
- 150 mg Guarana seed (which is basically caffeine)
- 80 mg caffeine (caffeine causes the epinephrine/adrenaline to stay longer in the synapse, so it makes it more powerful)
- 75 mg purple willow bark (it's Aspirin©; Aspirin© makes you more sensitive to caffeine)
- 60 mg cayenne pepper
- 40 mg ginger root

When Mrs. Capati took the "prescribed" supplement based on the recommendation by her personal trainer, she suffered a fatal brain hemorrhage, which resulted in a $320 million lawsuit against the personal trainer and the Crunch Fitness company.

Proper nutrition is important in many ways to an athlete and being knowledgeable about principles of nutrition is a must for every aspiring professional tennis player. Every player should receive proper advice from a **licensed individual** (Registered Dietitian; RD) that specializes in sports nutrition and understands the particular demands of a tennis player because sports nutrition requires the thorough understanding of exercise physiology and nutrition principles in conjunction with the effective application of both to maximize athletic performance. The sports nutritionist (Registered Dietitian; RD) applies exercise physiology and nutrition principles in order to help you:

1. Have more available fuel for physical activity
2. Enhance the repairing and rebuilding process of muscle tissue that follows physical work
3. Optimize athletic performance for competition
4. Feel healthier overall

Because sport nutrition requires the thorough understanding of exercise physiology and nutrition principles, employing the expertise of a Sports Nutritionist/Registered Dietitian (RD), who can prescribe individualized nutritional programs, is highly recommended.

To find an RD, contact the American Dietetic Association (ADA; www.EatRight.org). If you are wondering why a registered dietitian is needed instead of just your coach, the answer is simple: Contrary to popular belief, **only a RD has the legal authority to prescribe nutrition!**

UNDER THE MICROSCOPE

RD LICENSURE REQUIREMENTS

- In most states (46 and Puerto Rico) nutrition professionals must obtain a license to practice nutrition counseling and education
- License requires proof of RD credential in good standing with the ADA (American Dietetic Association; www.EatRight.org)
- License is regulated by state law and individuals who practice restricted nutrition practices can be prosecuted

For more information on licensing requirements and why hiring a RD makes sense see **"Under the Microscope – RD Licensure Requirements"** and **"Under the Microscope – Crunch Fitness: Personal Trainer Kills Client".**

What, then, should a coach do? He should refrain from giving personal, subjective recommendations or advice or authorization to use a certain substance. Instead, the coach should use objective language that's based on an accredited/acceptable higher authority (e.g. FDA or American College of Sports Medicine; ACSM) when giving advice. It is permissible to say something like "according to general guidelines…". For more information take a look at **"Under the Microscope – What Coaches Can Say".**

SPORTS NUTRITION – THE PROFESSION

The world of nutrition changes rapidly as new insights are gained from continuing scientific experiments. Many contradicting claims can be observed in the mainstream media and the consumer is bombarded daily with false information through commercials or ads.

UNDER THE MICROSCOPE

WHAT COACHES CAN SAY

ACCEPTABLE

- „According to general guidelines…"
- Orange juice is a good source of vitamin C
- Wild salmon has more Omega 3 acids than farm-raised salmon
- A caloric deficit of 500 kcal/day is necessary for 1lb of fat loss/week

UNACCEPTABLE

- „You need to drink more orange juice" OR „You need to take 1000 mg of vitamin C"
- „Take an Omega 3 acid supplement"
- „This supplement will help reduce your appetite"

Another interesting fact is that nobody receives proper education about the principles of nutrition, regardless of one's level of education. Neither in high school nor in graduate school are people being exposed to nutritional information. Unless people take it upon themselves to take an elective class in nutrition or to buy literature at the local bookstore (or online), they are kept uninformed about the benefits of proper nutrition. Even most NCAA Division I college athletes are uneducated with regards to nutrition because, for the most part, they receive 5 different answers to one single question, depending on who they ask. The sources student athletes consult for nutrition advice are often inadequate.

A recent study found that NCAA Division I athletes get most of their nutritional advice from:

1. Strength & Conditioning Coaches or Athletic Trainers
2. Personal Trainers
3. Commercials

Even though most NCAA Division I schools have a registered dietitian (RD) on staff and available to the athletes, most of the athletes are not aware of it. A study conducted by Burns et al. called Student Athlete Use of Nutritional Supplements and the Role of Athletic Trainers and Dietitians in Nutrition Counseling found that:

- 27% of respondents in the study did not realize that a RD was available for the athletes
- ~ 41% of athletes received information from their Strength Coach or an Athletic Trainer
- 88% of respondents used some form of nutritional supplement
- Most common supplements were vitamins/minerals and the athletes believed they improved performance

So, how can anyone rely on the information received from mainstream media outlets, including the internet? Generally speaking, you cannot rely on any of the information because **the source of the information is compromised** for one reason or another (e.g. sponsoring). For example, some scientists believe athletes need to take in water every 15 minutes when exercising (general recommendation: if an athlete lost 3 pounds of body weight he/she will need to consume 6 cups of water). Other scientists claim that those scientists are sponsored by Gatorade (ACSM; Gatorade is the official sponsor of the American College of Sports Medicine) and that all this drinking is being pushed on us by the industry. In reality, no animal on this planet needs to be told when to drink, so why do humans need to know in advance how much to drink?

This observation leads some scientists to argue that people should only drink when dictated by thirst. Studies show that athletes following that regime perform just as well if not better. Also, many supplement companies will claim that their findings are based on independent laboratories, which are most often located in their basements. This just goes to show how important the source of your information really is. One good source is the International Society of Sports Nutritionists (ISSN; http://www.sportsnutritionsociety.org. For more info on the ISSN see "Under the Microscope: International Society of Sports Nutritionists". A source for more general information is the Institute of Medicine (http://www.iom.edu/).

Generally, you can follow the 60-30-10 formula when it comes to mainstream media information about nutrition:

- 60% of the information is completely false
- 30% has a little bit of truth to it
- 10% is actually the truth

Take for example Don L. He introduces himself as the "#1 Online Nutritionist". He claims on his website that his supplement, a proprietary blend, contains 36 different amino aids.

First of all, what significance does the statement "I'm the #1 Online Nutritionist" have? None whatsoever; it doesn't reveal any significant competency. Another problem is that as of today only 20 amino acids have been identified and named. So, unless he has discovered 16 new amino acids that other leading scientists are unaware off, one can assume that his claim is unreliable.

UNDER THE MICROSCOPE

INTERNATIONAL SOCIETY OF SPORTS NUTRITIONISTS

One of the better sources for nutritional information is the International Society of Sports Nutrition (ISSN). The ISSN employs real sports nutritionists (that also have PhDs in Exercise Physiology) as well as a panel of experts consisting of 20-30 doctors, who have great knowledge. They take a pool of data compiled by PhDs as the basis for their guidelines for athletes. For more information visit their website at http://www.sportsnutritionsociety.org/.

SUPPLEMENTS

Many athletes use supplements to improve performance and these substances (e.g. creatine) are referred to as **ergogenic aids**. It is important to point out that almost none of the supplements sold at stores such as GNC or The Vitamin Shop are FDA approved - or even evaluated by the FDA. Therefore, a product manufacture's claims regarding product benefits and the purity of the ingredients have not been verified by the FDA. This doesn't mean that all supplements are bad and using them should be avoided. What it means is that you are taking them at your own risk and that you need to do your homework with respect to choosing a brand containing the desired ingredients (ergogenic aids).

Also keep in mind supplements are not meal replacers! Supplements should be used in conjunction with regular foods and not in place of breakfast, lunch, or dinner.

UNIVERSITY OF MIAMI (UM) – STEROIDS STUDY

An interesting phenomenon is illustrated by in recent study by the University of Miami (UM). In that study, researchers focused on steroid use and leg-press (exercise) strength in college students. It was easy to find volunteers for the experiment. The researchers put up flyers to find participants for the study saying that they were going to test the use and effectiveness of steroids to increase leg-press strength. Unsurprisingly, they received a huge response. Participants were told from the beginning that they were either receiving a **placebo** (a substance causing nothing; e.g. water pill) or real steroids; the research team then assessed how much stronger the participants got by testing them on a leg press.

During the course of the semester, leg-press tests were performed and the group that was on the steroids increased leg press capabilities by ~33%. The members of the groups were asked/told to take the steroids or the placebo, respectively, every day – the group taking the neutral pills were told that their pills would have no effect while the other group was convinced it was taking steroids. The "placebo" group, not surprisingly, thought that they hadn´t gotten stronger over the semester.

Now, what was interesting about the study is that what both groups actually took were water pills (placebos) but the group that thought they were taking steroids got significantly stronger. This shows how significant the placebo effect can be but there is another thing to consider!

Imagine you are the owner of a supplement company. Wouldn't the information from the study be valuable to you and your company? The only thing you need to do is to go out there and convince people that your supplement works and it will work!

MYTH OR FACT?

In the following section we will present certain situations or statements that you might have experienced in the past in order to illustrate that the source of any information is most important and that working with a RD consequently makes real sense.

Many teenage female tennis players are concerned with their body weight and overall shape. It is not unheard of for coaches to weigh their players regularly to ensure that they don't become overweight. Sometimes a player will approach a coach to ask for advice about losing weight. Take a look at the following statement: "My coach told me to take hydroxycut and pyruvate 2x/day to lose weight". What's wrong with that statement?

First of all, the coach has no legal authority to prescribe hydrocycut. Second, hydrocycut is a popular weight loss supplement that contains, amongst other ingredients, **caffeine**, **hydroxyl citrate**, and **pyruvate**.

Caffeine increases lipolysis (fat breakdown) and facilitates the release of triglycerides (free fatty acids) into the blood stream but that doesn't mean that those free fatty acids are being absorbed and used by the body. Instead, they are released into the blood and then stored again as fat if there is no need for them; remember that the body prefers carbohydrates as fuel. Therefore, if the body has enough carbohydrates available, it will not use the free fatty acids for fuel.

Hydroxyl citrate is known to inhibit the production of the enzyme citric lyase, which is responsible for fat (fatty acids) synthesis (making of fat).

Pyruvate has been shown in clinical studies to facilitate weight loss but:

A. the individuals taking part in the study were extremely obese and
B. the reduction in weight was insignificant.

Group A (taking pyruvate) lost on average 28 lb, whereas the control group (taking placebo) lost 27 lb. Also, the amount of pyruvate used in the study was 10x higher than the pills sold at your local drug store and the pills are very expensive. Pyruvate actually provides energy (comes from a 6-carbon sugar glucose split in half into small units of pyruvate at the end of glycolysis) and if hydrogen is added to it, it becomes lactate, which is waiting to be metabolized.

Why would a coach recommend that an athlete take in more energy (pyruvate) if weight loss is accomplished through the creation of an energy deficit? The real problem, however, is that a coach has no legal authority to prescribe for nutrition in any case! That role is reserved for a registered dietitian (RD).

A coach could, for example, say, "I have heard that pyruvate facilitates weight loss in clinical studies" or "hydroxycut contains certain substances that suppress appetite". In general, coaches can give advice based on general guidelines but they cannot tell someone to buy and take a supplement – that's illegal!

Another possible scenario would be: "The coach told me to take B vitamins for energy ". Again, the coach has no legal authority to prescribe for nutrition. B vitamins are water-soluble and many people believe that when they take large amounts of B vitamins, like those found in energy drinks, the vitamins will just go through their system because they are water-soluble. Unfortunately that's not completely accurate but what is certain is that they make your urine really expensive. Generally, B vitamins are involved in protein synthesis and aid in the release of energy: NAD {niacin is a B vitamin] & FAD [riboflavin]) during aerobic metabolism via the Krebs Cycle. This does not mean that extra amounts of B vitamins will give you more energy.

In mainstream news or commercials you will see something like: "This specifically formulated weight loss formula/supplement targets fat between the thighs". This statement is absolute nonsense because there is no spot reduction of fat; the body decides where it stores or removes fat.

THE IMPORTANCE OF SPORTS NUTRITION

The importance of optimal sports nutrition can be seen in elite athletes like Duane Wade, a member of the Miami Heat NBA basketball team. Duane Wade used to brag about his poor eating habits, saying he ate lots of fries and burgers. Early in his career one could observe that he suffered from many injuries and over the years it was reported that he changed his eating habits. He has been injury free and retuned ever since, becoming an outstanding athlete again. How much of this can be attributed to proper nutrition is unclear but it appears plausible that nutrition contributes to enhanced performance.

Remember that the nutritional goals are:

1. Having more available fuel for physical activity
2. Enhancing the repairing and rebuilding process of muscle tissue that follows physical work
3. Optimizing athletic performance for tournaments
4. Feeling healthier overall

FUEL FOR PHYSICAL ACTIVITY

Most athletes take in fewer calories than they need, which affects their performance. Losing weight throughout a tennis season is one thing that should never happen. When you lose weight, you are also losing glycogen stores along with fat free mass (muscle mass). Carbohydrates are the main fuel underpinning performance and if you don't have enough carbohydrates available to fuel physical activities, you will begin to use muscle protein (branch chain amino acids) to replenish glycogen stores and fuel the physical activity. An elite athlete like Roger Federer, at ~80 kg body weight, consumes 480 g – 640 g of carbohydrates daily, which is the equivalent of 1,920 kcal – 2,560 kcal just coming from carbohydrates – we haven't accounted for the fat and protein needs yet!

There is a linear relationship between your glycogen levels and your rate of perceived exertion (RPE; a scale of how difficult the work feels/is; **see page 712**). As muscle glycogen stores get lower, blood glucose levels decrease and the RPE goes up. During a marathon (26.2 miles), the first 20 miles are ok but the last 6.2 miles represent the real challenge because that is when the glycogen stores are near depletion and RPE increases dramatically ("hitting the wall").

REPAIR AND REBUILDING PROCESS FOLLOWING PHYSICAL WORK

It's very important to take in carbohydrates and proteins within 30 minutes of finishing physical activity. This aids in the repairing and building process of (muscle) tissue. After a workout (endurance, cardio or weight lifting), muscle glycogen and liver glycogen stores are low. Muscle glycogen stores will be the first to deplete followed by the liver, which releases as much glucose as it has. Once the liver runs out of glucose reserves, the body will choose muscle protein breakdown instead of allowing blood glucose levels to drop too low because we need blood glucose to survive – the brain relies on glucose for fuel. If the body cannot find an alternative fuel source, glucose would eventually be unavailable and we would experience a coma. So, if you drink some CHO/protein drink after a workout, you will prevent some muscle loss and muscles will feel less sore the next day. Imbibing CHO/protein drink actually reduces DOMS (delayed onset of muscle soreness) because you reduce the amount of protein degradation and hence there will be less muscle pain after the workout.

OPTIMIZING ATHLETIC PERFORMANCE FOR TOURNAMENTS

Sometimes matches can last 2-3 hours or longer and nutrition can play a decisive role in your performance. Take the recent Wimbledon match (2010) between John Isner (USA) and Nicolas Mahut (FRA), which lasted over 11 hours. Wouldn't you think that during a match that long proper nutrition would have played a decisive role?

In the general population, the relationship between body-fat-% (BF%) and the amount of calories consumed is linear (BF% up the more calories consumed) but with elite athletes that relationship is the opposite – the more calories they took in, the less body fat they had and the less calories they took in, the more body fat they had!

This can occur because when they don't consume enough calories their muscles are wasting in between bouts of exercise, which results in their %BF to increase (because they are loosing lean mass). So, it wasn't that the athletes were gaining fat – they were loosing muscle. Those athletes that took in more calories were able to preserve their muscles (lean mass) and had less BF%. How many calories you will need will be discussed in the "Applying Sports Nutrition" section.

FEELING HEALTHIER OVERALL

Immune cells use protein for fuel because they proliferate – they adapt to the immune system – in response to infection and increase production of immune cells. So, without adequate protein stores immune cells cannot function efficiently.

When you see how many athletes get injured and/or sick (colds) it becomes obvious that proper nutrition plays a crucial role in injury & disease prevention during intense training and competition.

Also, because of the fact that many people believe in the notion that "more is better" when it comes to training, **overtraining** which results in a decline in performance and a susceptibility to sickness and/or injury becomes an issue. There is no clear-cut measurement to determine whether one has overtrained or not but major markers for overtraining are lack of energy, weight loss, muscle pain/injury and recurring sickness. If you experience some of the aforementioned symptoms, training volume and intensity should be adjusted accordingly.

NUTRITIONAL GOALS DURING TRAINING & MATCHES

Knowing what to eat and drink during practice and competition is essential and will be discussed in more detail in the next section "Applying Sports Nutrition"on **page 717**. Here we give a quick analysis of the role nutrition plays during training and competition.

UNDER THE MICROSCOPE

OVERTRAINING

Major makers for overtraining are:

- Lack of Energy
- Weight Loss
- Muscle Pain/Injury
- Sickness

REHEARSAL OF COMPETITION STRATEGY

This is an important concept with the goal of getting a player accustomed to eating and drinking the same foods during training that he will consume on match day. For example, if you are used to drinking Gatorade during practice, you should not change to drinking PowerRade during competition. If you are not accustomed to Gatorade and you use it for the first time during competition, all kinds of problems can arise, including gastrointestinal (GI) distress (stomach pains). In tournaments, nutrition makes a huge difference because you need to recover between matches. Any abrupt changes in nutrition can negatively impact your performance level.

ENHANCING ENERGY SUPPLY

Enhancing energy supply to prolong the onset of fatigue is also important, especially during a long match. For example, during a long 3 set match in humid or hot conditions, you try to prevent "hitting the wall", which means that you have to slow down tremendously because you become hypoglycemic (low blood sugar). Since you can't burn (metabolize) fat in the mitochondria of the cells by itself (it needs to be in combination with a primer – CHO), the body needs to break down protein to make more glucose available so that fat can be used for fuel again. Therefore, you have to slow down in order to use fat/protein as a fuel source. Most athletes can last ~ 90 minutes before "hitting the wall" but there are carbo-loading strategies and pre-exercise drinks that can be used effectively to prolong the availability of CHO for fuel, which we will discuss in more detail in the "Applying Sports Nutrition" section.

MINIMIZING DEHYDRATION

There is no definite answer on how to prevent dehydration. As previously mentioned, some scientists believe athletes need to take in water every 15 minutes of exercise (general recommendation: if athletes lose 3 pounds of body weight, they need to consume 6 cups of water). Other scientists claim that those scientists are sponsored by Gatorade (ACSM; Gatorade is the official sponsor of the American College of Sports Medicine, by the way) and argue that all these drinks are pushed on us by the industry. In reality, no animal on this planet needs to be told when to drink, so why do humans need to know in advance what to drink?

That school of thought argues that people should only drink when responding to the dictates of thirst. Studies show that athletes following this regime perform just as well if not better than the regulated group. We recommend that you come to your own conclusion as to which strategy works best for you.

MINIMIZING HYPONATREMIA

Hyponatremia refers to low blood sodium levels. You can reduce sodium (salt) levels in the blood by overdrinking water. When that occurs, you can get a really bad headache; if it gets worse a seizure can result and if it gets even worse death can occur. Nearly 40% of all women that finished the Iron Man Marathon in 2007 had hyponatremia (mild levels of it) because many endurance athletes overhydrate. When the blood sodium levels decrease, the brain will take out some of the water and this is what causes a severe headache.

INTRODUCTION TO NUTRITION

Many chemical reactions occur inside the body every second you are alive. These chemical reactions are referred to as **metabolism**. Metabolism includes chemical reactions that make molecules (synthesis; anabolic reactions) and break down molecules (catabolic reactions). In order for anything to occur, energy is required and the same holds true for each and every tiny cell in the body – they need energy to function properly. Energy is never lost, it can only be converted into different forms of energy. Since cells require energy they must be capable of converting foodstuff (nutrients) into a biological form of energy and this process is referred to as bioenergetics.

In order for you to practice on the court, lift weights or run for hours, the body needs to convert energy from foods into energy that muscle cells can use to power the action. If the body cannot supply muscle cells with energy fast enough, muscles are no longer able to work properly and cramping occurs, which can ultimately force you to stop playing altogether.

Proper nutrition is necessary for competitive training, optimal performance and adequate recovery and being knowledgeable about nutrition principles is a must for every professional tennis player. The proper amounts of nutrients in a diet keep you healthy and optimize your performance on the court.

THE NUTRIENTS

All food products contain two categories of nutrients, macronutrients and micronutrients. **Macronutrients** provide caloric energy and are found in various forms of carbohydrates, fats, and proteins. They are called macronutrients because the body requires them in large quantities. **Micronutrients** include vitamins and minerals, which provide no caloric energy, but regulate the function of all bodily systems and cells. They are called micronutrients because the body needs them in small amounts.

The body breaks down the energy-yielding nutrients to provide fuel for its activities. This process is called metabolism!

The function of nutrients is to:

- Repair body tissue (e.g. muscle tissue)
- Maintain bodily functions
- Help the body to grow

In order to enjoy all these benefits you need to follow a well-balanced diet that provides ample amounts of all nutrients.

Let's begin by taking a closer look at the energy-yielding macronutrients.

UNDER THE MICROSCOPE

HOW TO CONVERT KCALORIES TO KJOULE

Energy requirements/values are expressed in different units, depending on your location (e.g. Europe or USA). In the US kilocalorie (kcal) is used but the internationally accepted unit is the kilo joule (kJ).

Kcal is a measure of heat energy; it is the amount of energy required to raise the temperature of 1 kilogram (kg) of water by 1°C

kJ is a measure of work energy (work = [force x distance] / time); the amount of energy needed to move 1 kilogram (kg) 1 meter (m) with a force of 1 newton (N).

To convert kcal into kJ, multiply kcal by 4.2

UNDER THE MICROSCOPE

LACTOSE INTOLERANCE

Lactose intolerance occurs when the intestinal cells do not produce enough of the enzyme lactase to ensure that the disaccharide lactose is digested and absorbed efficiently. Lactase production declines with age. Only about 30% of the world's population will retain an adequate amount of lactase production throughout their lifetime.

The symptoms of lactose intolerance are:

- Bloating
- Abdominal discomfort
- Diarrhea

Total elimination of milk products is not necessary, since the body can take in about 6 g of lactose (1/2 cup milk) without any symptoms. One strategy to deal with lactose intolerance is:

- To gradually increase the amount of milk products that are consumed
- To take milk products with other foods
- To spread their intake over the day. This will change the bacteria in the GI tract allowing the change in bacteria to help digest & absorb more lactose; there is no reappearance of the missing enzyme lactase

ENERGY-YIELDING MACRONUTRIENTS

Macronutrients include carbohydrates (CHO), fats, and proteins). As previously mentioned, they are called macronutrients because your body requires them in large quantities, i.e. several grams daily (several grams per day).

In order to maintain your body well, you need to eat foods that supply it with enough energy and nutrients so that you have the capacity to do work, which is the definition of **energy**.

More precisely, the energy released by carbohydrates, lipids (fat) and proteins is measured in kcal (1kcal = 1000 calories). The amount of energy released from food depends on the amount of carbohydrates, lipids and proteins in the food.

Fat has the highest **energy density**, the most calories per gram, but your body prefers to run on CHO. Protein's energy contribution is rather minimal (up to 5%).

Generally speaking, foods with low energy density are desirable if you want to lose weight. On the other hand, to gain weight foods with a high energy density should be eaten.

There are acceptable macronutrient contributions (see Table) that have been established by the Food & Nutrition Board, Institute of the National Academies. These recommendations, called **Dietary Reference Intakes (DRI)**, are for healthy people only and might not be applicable to people suffering from disease. The different percentage ranges depend on age, gender, height, weight and activity levels.

Macronutrient	% Contribution
Carbohydrates	45 – 65%
Protein	10 – 35%
Fat	20 – 35%

CARBOHYDRATES

Ingested carbohydrates are the key source of energy for any muscular contraction. There are different types of carbohydrates that all provide 4 kcal per gram. Most sources are broken down into two categories: simple or complex carbohydrates.

Simple carbohydrates include **glucose** (main source used by the body – all other types are broken down into glucose), fructose (in fruits), galactose, lactose (in milk), maltose, and sucrose (table sugar). Simple carbohydrates primary provide quick energy with much lower nutrient value. They should be avoided during a match because they cause a rapid increase in blood glucose levels (blood sugar) as well as a subsequent rapid decline, which impairs performance.

Conversely, complex carbohydrates include **starches** and **fiber**, which should comprise the majority of carbohydrates consumed as they provide key nutrients and energy (starches). Starches are glucose in storage form in plants; fibers have little or no energy but can lower blood glucose levels (blood sugar). Fibers are complex carbohydrates but their bonds cannot be broken by human enzymes, meaning they don't contribute any energy to the body because they can't be broken down into glucose.

Glycogen is glucose in storage form inside the body in the liver and muscle cells and it provides ½ of all energy used by muscles. The other ½ of the body's energy is provided mostly by fat. Glucose or glycogen is not eaten directly; energy from foods that is not used by the body will be stored as glycogen or fat. Excess glucose that couldn't be stored in the form of glycogen will be broken into smaller compounds in the liver. The liver breaks down glucose in smaller molecules and puts them together (synthesizes) in the form of **fat**. The fat is then transported from the liver and stored in fatty tissues in the body.

Dietary Reference Intake	
Estimated Average Requirements (EAR)	Amount needed to stay ok for ½ of population
Recommended Daily Allowance (RDA)	Amount recommended for everybody to stay healthy
Adequate Intakes (AI)	Average amount consumed by healthy people; similar to RDA but without sufficient research evidence to come up with a recommendation
Tolerable Upper Intake Levels (UL)	Limit before the quantity of a substances become toxic

Athletes generally should follow a high-carbohydrate diet because glycogen stores are relatively small and can be depleted within a few hours due to vigorous training or matches. Since glycogen replenishment is an ongoing process, a high-carbohydrate diet ensures that the body can replenish glycogen stores efficiently.

FIBERS

On average, Americans get about 12 – 15 g of fiber daily from their diet, which is approximately 50% of what is needed in order to experience the benefits that are associated with a high fiber diet. There are other countries in the world where you can find an abundance of fiber in the average diet. One such place is China, where the average Chinese citizen consumes approximately 77 g of fiber daily!

If you take a look at the restaurants most Americans frequent, such as fast food chains like McDonalds, where can you find fiber? Maybe the pre-packaged apple slices you can buy have some fiber in them? The point is that you won't find any foods at, for instance, McDonalds that are high in fiber. This is unfortunate since most Americans eat in such places because the food is very cheap, their advertising is unbiquitous and they are conveniently located.

Fiber consumption and death rates are correlated. In all studies of High-Fat-Low-Fiber diets, the incidence of heart disease and cancer is high. You will soon find out what the lack of fiber in your diet means with respect to disease prevention but having too much fiber will prevent the proper absorption rate of fat-soluble vitamins (Vitamin A, D, E, and K). So why does fiber have such an impact on your health?

BENEFITS OF FIBER

Fiber plays such an important role in maintaining overall health because it can prevent diseases such as heart & vascular disease, obesity, diabetes and cancer. Fiber accomplishes this via different mechanisms but most importantly fiber:

- Lowers cholesterol
- Lowers the glycemic index
- Increases thermo effects of foods
- Reduces exposure to carcinogens
- Increases intestinal health

Fiber lowers **cholesterol** by binding intestinal lipids, hence preventing the absorption of fat (cholesterol). The mechanism consists of soluble fibers binding to intestinal lipids thereby preventing the absorption of fat. Having too much fiber in your diet prevents the proper absorption rate of fat-soluble vitamins (Vitamin A, D, E, and K). This does not mean that when you eat fiber you will be able to eliminate getting certain diseases (e.g. heart disease, cancer). What it means is that one can observe an association between lack of fiber in the diet and the risk of getting certain diseases. In other words, the likelihood/risk of developing cancer or heart disease, for instance, is higher when one consumes inadequate amounts of fiber in the diet. The daily adequate intake (AI) of fiber, which is the average amount consumed by a healthy person, is 38 g for men and 25 g for women.

The **Glycemic Index (GI)** indicates how quickly food is being absorbed in order to provide energy and hence raise blood glucose levels. Whenever you eat fiber together with carbohydrates, the insulin response will be lowered naturally because fiber slows down the gastric emptying process, decreases the absorption of glucose and reduces insulin spikes. Because of the aforementioned benefits, fiber has a positive effect regarding the incidence of diseases such as diabetes, obesity, heart disease and cancer.

When you eat foods rich in fiber, the body will try to digest it, which it cannot do. This causes the muscles in the gastrointestinal (GS) tract to have to work hard at trying to break down the fiber. Because smooth muscle cells are found in the lining of the GI tract, (that also have actin & myosin, just like other muscle cells) a lot of calories will be burned in the process of digestion (energy; heat), hence creating the thermic effect of food. Because of the increased digestive muscle activity, the thermic effect of food is relevant in the fight against obesity.

Carcinogens are cancer-causing agents and fiber has the ability to dilute them by adding bulk (increases fetal bulk) to digestion. By doing so it really reduces the synergies of carcinogens and hence lowers the risk of cancer.

Fiber forms short-chain fatty acids in the intestine (butyrate), which has been shown in research studies to elicit cancer cell death and reduce GI tract inflammation hence improving intestinal health.

SOURCES OF FIBER

As far as (water) soluble fiber goes, beans, oats and nuts (BON) lower cholesterol. Insoluble fiber (e.g. vegetable, fruit) help increase the thermic effect of food, reduce the exposure to carcinogens (these are certain cancer-causing agents) and increase interstitial health.

Generally speaking, stay away from processed foods and buy more agricultural foods. Various supplements and pills may offer a cost-effective and convenient alternative.

UNDER THE MICROSCOPE

Don't you wonder why you store fat even though you consume foods that are fat free (e.g. jelly beans)? So how can jelly beans, for instance, increase fat storage? The answer is simple: Excess carbohydrates in your diet are stored as fat. Excess carbohydrates (glucose) that couldn't be stored in the form of glycogen will be broken into smaller compounds in the liver. The liver breaks down glucose into smaller molecules and puts them together in the form of fat. Then the fat is transported from the liver and stored in fatty tissues in the body.

The Role of Insulin

A complex carbohydrate (starches & fiber) will travel through your entire gastrointestinal tract (GI; 15 feet) before it is fully absorbed but the simple carbohydrates (sugars) will be absorbed very early on (within the 1st foot). So, simple sugars (e.g. white bread) will be absorbed quickly in the small intestine, whereas whole grains (complex carbohydrates) will take about 15 feet worth of travelling in the GI before they are fully absorbed and digested into the blood stream. Therefore, the simple sugars will cause a rapid increase in blood insulin levels causing elevated blood glucose levels.

Insulin is released by BETA-cells in the pancreas in response to high blood glucose levels. Insulin actually moves glucose from the blood into tissue/cells (also into fat cells), thereby replenishing glycogen stores and reducing blood glucose levels. In other words, glucose going into muscles is a good thing, helping restore muscle energy levels (glycogen) for muscular contraction.

(Continues on page 697)

According to dietary guidelines (American College of Sports Medicine; ACSM), the following foods represent good sources of fiber:

- Bread, Cereal, Pasta, Rice
  - Use 100% Whole Wheat Bread, pumpernickel, or rye bread
  - Use cereal with a minimum fiber content of 5g (e.g. 100% bran cereal)
  - Eat oatmeal or grits regularly
  - Brown rice
- Meat
  - Choose lean cuts ("loin" and/or "round")
  - Trim visible fat
  - Choose wild (living) over farm-raised products (e.g. fish)
  - Eat meat in moderation (e.g. couple times/week)
  - Try soy alternatives
- Fruits
  - Start day with glass of orange juice or grapefruit juice (not concentrate)
  - Use fresh or dried fruits as between-meal snacks (apple, banana, kiwi, peach, nectarine, orange)
  - Choose variety of fruits; different colors
- Vegetables
  - Eat a variety of different veggies (potatoes, corn, lettuce, etc.)
  - When eating out, order (steamed) veggies on the side (e.g. broccoli)
  - Try drinking vegetable juices instead of sodas
  - Eat large salads (beware of dressing; no Taco salads!) instead of a burger, etc.
- Vegetables (Part II)
  - Try mixing up veggies by taste and color (broccoli, cabbage, carrots, corn, green peas, beans, spinach, potatoes)
  - Add veggies whenever possible (e.g. veggie pizza)
- Dairy
  - Use skim milk or 1% fat milk
  - Use more reduced-fat cheese than regular cheese
  - Use low-fat or fat-free products (e.g. ice cream)

RECOMMENDED FIBER INTAKE

According to dietary guidelines, based on a 2,000 kcal diet one should consume 900 – 1,300 kcal of carbohydrates (225 – 325g), depending on the carbohydrate range used (45 – 65% of nutrients should come in form of carbs). This amount of fiber is adequate, surpassing the RDA (Recommended Daily Allowance) of 130 g/day, which is based on how much glucose the brain uses at a minimum to function properly.

The DRI (Dietary Reference Intakes) recommends consuming 14g/1,000 kcal/day of fiber, whereas the American Dietetic Association suggests 20 – 35g (80 – 140 kcal) of dietary fiber daily, which is more than twice the amount of fiber consumed by most Americans!

In more detail, the DRI recommends:

- For Men:
  - 19 – 50 years old → 38 g/day
  - 51+ → 30 g/day
- For Women:
  - 19 – 50 years old → 25 g/day
  - 51+ → 21 g/day

But glucose uptake into fat cells also occurs due to insulin. When glucose enters fat cells, it can be turned into glycerol or fatty acids, which is why glucose is associated with high triglyceride (glycerol + 3 fatty acids) levels. Once glucose turns into fat it cannot be converted into glucose again – it is going to stay fat until it is metabolized because of the one-way enzyme pyruvate dehydrogenase (PDH)!

The other affect insulin has is that it lowers fat utilization because insulin will prevent the oxidation of fatty acids by blocking fats from entering the mitochondria. Therefore, insulin has the direct ability to prevent you from using fat for fuel. This is where exercise comes into play. During exercise, insulin levels decrease so that you have the ability to use fat (deliver fat to mitochondria and "burn it" in the carbohydrate flame [aerobic glycolysis]) for fuel. That's the reason why insulin is suppressed during exercise! Chronic elevated insulin levels decrease cellular sensitivity/responsiveness and increase the risk of diabetes.

Recommended IntakesStarches & Fibers	
RDA for CHO	>130 g/day
Daily Value CHO	300 g (based on 60% of 2000 kcal diet)
Daily Value Fiber	14 g/1000 kcal
UL Fiber	40 g/day

When sugar enters fat cells it starts as a 6-carbon sugar but there are different enzymes along the way (e.g. hexocanase, pfk, aldolase, etc.) that split it into a glycerol-3-phosphate. So, a fat cell can make glycerol and add 3 fatty acids and form a triglyceride or it can take pyruvate (enzyme that removes a hydrogen from pyruvate; pyruvatedehydrogenase [PDH]), remove a hydrogen from it, and get acetyl CoA (2-carbon; acetyl groups added on to each other become acidic acids, which are fatty acids). Therefore, the body can turn sugar into fat directly!

The thing about the enzyme pyruvatedehydrogenase (PDH) is that insulin will activate it and increase it (one way enzyme). Hence, once sugar turns into fat this process cannot be reversed to produce the glucose (sugar) again. So, once sugar is turned into fat it will remain fat until it is metabolized by the body. Insulin also promotes another enzyme, FAS (fatty-acid synthase), which has the affect of promoting fat storage. The body can either make (in the liver) glycerol or fatty acids from a triglyceride but not glucose.

This is the same principle the Atkins diet employs – by lowering simple carbohydrate intake, individuals also lower blood triglyceride levels by lowering insulin levels, thereby decreasing fat storage. When you take a closer look at pre-diabetics, they have elevated insulin levels (hyperinsulania) that promote more fat storage and this then spirals out of control. For this reason people suffering from metabolic disease (e.g. pre-diabetics) or hyperinsulania will benefit by following the Atkins diet.

FYI – For Your Information: Consuming 1 soda (not diet soda) per day translates into consuming 32.5 lb of sugar annually!

FATS (LIPIDS)

Fats belong to the group of nutrients called lipids. They provide the most calories per gram (9 kcal/g) and are the body's most preferable storage form of energy. The lipid family includes three categories:

- Triglycerides
- Phospholipids
- Sterols

UNDER THE MICROSCOPE

HEALTH BENEFITS FROM MONO-UNSATURATED FATS & POLYUNSATURATED FATS

Replacing both saturated fats and trans-fats with monounsaturated fats & polyunsaturated fats is the most effective dietary strategy in preventing heart disease; they lower blood cholesterol levels (LDL).

Vegetable oils are a good source of monounsaturated & polyunsaturated fats.

Benefits of Omega-3 Fats

Omega-3 polyunsaturated fatty acids have shown to decrease the risk of heart disease by:

- Preventing blood clots
- Protecting against irregular heart beats
- Lowering blood pressure, especially in people with hypertension & atherosclerosis!

Excessive amounts of cholesterol in the blood can cloG the arteries, a disease called atherosclerosis (athero = "porridge or soft"; scleros = "hard"; osis = "condition") that causes heart attacks and strokes!

HYDROGENATION PROLONGS SHELF-LIFE

In order to protect fat-containing products against rancidity, companies saturate some or all of the points of unsaturation by adding hydrogen molecules, known as hydrogenation.

Hydrogenation has 2 advantages:

- Prolonging shelf-life (hydrogenation prevents oxidation by making unsaturated fats more saturated)
- Altering texture of fats/oils

TRIGLYCERIDES

Triglycerides (fats and oils) compose 95% of all lipids in food and 99% of all lipids inside the body (lipids also include fat-soluble vitamins). All triglycerides consist of 1 glycerol ("ol" = alcohol) molecule and 3 fatty acids, they also contain carbon and are therefore organic.

FATTY ACIDS

Fatty acids are the primary fat fuel source used by muscles and are composed of 4 – 24 (even numbers) carbon atoms:

- 18-carbon fatty acids are most common in foods
- 12 – 24 carbon fatty acids are most common in meat, fish, and vegetable oils
- 6 – 10 and <6 carbon fatty acids can be found in diary products

A **saturated fatty acid** has all hydrogen atoms and only one (1) single-bonded carbon atom! If a fatty acid has two (2) hydrogen atoms missing, it must have one (1) double-bond between two carbon atoms, which is referred to as the **point of unsaturation** and the acid is called an **unsaturated fatty acid**. More precisely, it is referred to as **monounsaturated fatty acid** because it only has one double-bounded carbon atom. If the acid has two or more double-bonded carbon atoms, it is called a **polyunsaturated fatty acid** (= it has 4 or more hydrogen atoms missing).

Athletes should consume unsaturated fats. For the health benefits of mono – and polyunsaturated fats take a look at Under the Microscope – Health Benefits from Monounsaturated Fats & Polyunsaturated Fats.

The level of unsaturation, monounsaturated or polyunsaturated, influences the characteristics of the food and impacts your health. All fats become rancid when exposed to oxygen. In particular, the degree of unsaturation influences:

- Firmness of the fats and oil (the shorter the carbon chain the softer the fat/oil)
- Stability (the fewer double-bonds, the more resistant fats become to turning rancid); saturated fats are most resistant to oxidation and hence least likely to become rancid

HEALTH RISK OF SATURATED FATS & TRANS-FATS

Saturated fats in the diet, not food cholesterol, will raise blood cholesterol dramatically by raising Low-Density Lipoproteins (LDL) levels, which are cholesterol transporters! Cholesterol accumulates in the arteries, restricting blood flow and increasing blood pressure. The higher blood cholesterol levels are, the higher the risk of getting a heart attack or stroke.

Trans-fats (trans-fatty acids) alter blood cholesterol levels the same way saturated fats do, by raising Low-Density Lipoproteins (LDL) cholesterol levels. Major sources of trans-fats are:

- Deep fried foods
- Cakes, cookies, doughnuts, pastry, crackers
- Chips
- Margarine
- Meat & dairy products

CHOLESTEROL: GOOD VS. BAD

The reason why Low-Density Lipoproteins (LDL) are associated with "bad" cholesterol is because they transport cholesterol towards the cells, whereas High-Density Lipoproteins (HDL) transport the cholesterol back to the liver for recycling or disposal, therefore getting rid of cholesterol. The cholesterol in LDL and HDL is the same but the proportions and types of lipids and proteins within them are different!

The more **lipids** the lipoproteins have, the **lower the density.**

The more **proteins** they have, the **higher the density.**

Food companies modify the level of unsaturation in many products you consume. Read Under the Microscope – Hydrogenation Prolongs Shelf-Life.

A DESIRABLE BLOOD-LIPID PROFILE IS:

- Total cholesterol < 200 mg/dull
- LDL cholesterol < 100 mg/dull
- HDL cholesterol >= 60 mg/dull
- Triglycerides < 150 mg/dL

PHOSPHOLIPIDS

Phospholipids are not used as a source of energy by muscles during exercise. The best-known phospholipid is lecithin. Lecithin and other phospholipids are part of cell membranes; they help fats move in and out of cells membranes because phospholipids are water and fat-soluble. Phospholipids allow fat-soluble substances like hormones and vitamins to pass easily in and out of cells. The food industry uses phospholipids as **emulsifiers** (substance that allows mixing of water and oil) to mix fats with water.

STEROLS

Sterols have a 4-ring structure, like steroids. Sterols are alcohol derivates with a steroid ring structure. The most famous sterol is **cholesterol**. Foods derived from plants and animals contain sterols but only those sterols derived from animals contain cholesterol! Among other functions, the body uses cholesterol to produce the sex hormones estrogen, progesterone, and testosterone.

"Good" cholesterol does not refer to a type of cholesterol found in foods. "Good" cholesterol refers to how the body transports cholesterol in the blood! Cholesterol is not some bad ingredient of food. See **Under the Microscope – Cholesterol: Good vs. Bad.**

Instead, it is a compound made by the body (the liver) from carbohydrates, fats, and protein sources and used by the body (cholesterol made by the body is called **endogenous**; "endo" = within; "gen" = arising). The liver actually produces its own cholesterol (800 – 1500 mg/day) and the daily recommended value of cholesterol coming from foods is 300 mg/day (cholesterol coming from foods is referred to as **exogenous**; "exo" = outside the body). In other words, the liver produces 3/4 of daily cholesterol needs itself!

High blood cholesterol levels are a major risk for cardiovascular disease; blood cholesterol levels are used to predict the likelihood/risk of having a heart attack or stroke. For more information on which substances raise cholesterol levels take a look at **Under the Microscope – Health Risk of Saturated Fats & Trans-Fats.**

PROTEINS

Most people associate protein with strength and meat with protein. As a result, they eat steaks to gain muscle mass and get bigger but that's not very efficient. Meat is one good source of protein but so are eggs, milk, grains & vegetables. Proteins are important but they are only one of the nutrients needed to maintain the body.

AMINO ACIDS

Amino means "nitrogen containing". **Amino acids** are the building blocks of proteins. There are a total of 20 amino acids; 9 are **essential** (body can't synthesize them) amino acids and the remaining 11 amino acids are **non-essential** (body can synthesize them).

9 Essential Amino Acids	11 Non-Essential Amino Acids
Histidine	Alanine
Isoleucine	Arginine
Leucine	Asparagine
Lysine	Aspartic Acid
Methionine	Cysteine
Phenylalanine	Glutamic Acid
Threonine	Glutamine
Tryptophan	Glycine
Valine	Proline
	Serine
	Tyrosine

Amino acids are connected to each other via condensation reactions, forming peptide bonds. When numerous amino acids join together, they form a **polypeptide**, which essentially is called a **protein**.

When one eats foods that contain protein, the body doesn't store that food protein directly but breaks it down into amino acids from which the body then can make its own protein.

Proteins are partially broken down in the stomach via the enzyme **pepsin** before they move into the small intestine, where they are further broken down and digested. The amino acids can be used to provide energy (remember, only 5% of energy comes from proteins) or to make other needed compounds. All amino acids that are not immediately being used are transported to the liver via capillaries.

Because of the fact that the body produces its own enzymes, it doesn't make any sense when someone recommends that you "eat enzyme A because it will help digest your food faster". Enzymes in food will themselves be digested instead of influencing any reaction.

PROTEIN QUALITY

The quality of protein is based on two factors:

1. Digestibility
2. Amino Acid Composition

In order to provide the amino acids for protein synthesis, the body breaks down the protein from food sources into amino acids. The food serving as the source of a protein influences its digestibility and hence rate of availability. In general, animal proteins (90 – 99%) have a higher digestibility than plant proteins (70 – 90%), soy protein (>90%) being the exception.

Amino acid composition is important because the body needs to have all the amino acids that are needed available at once to make protein. Since the liver can produce any non-essential amino acids, the diet has to supply the essential amino acids; otherwise the body breaks down its own protein (e.g. muscle protein) to obtain them. In other words, the more essential amino acids the protein provides, the higher its quality. Apart from soy protein, plant protein from vegetables, nuts, seeds, grains, and legumes are lower in quality because they lack one or more of the essential amino acids. Consuming a combination of the aforementioned vegetable proteins enhances the quality of proteins but it is not very convenient.

UNDER THE MICROSCOPE

EVALUATION OF PROTEIN QUALITY

- Determine food protein's amino acid composition (mg of product / g of protein)
- Compare food protein's amino acid composition with the reference protein
- Pick food amino acid with biggest discrepancy and assign score
- Multiply the amino acid score by the food protein's digestibility % to determine PDCAAS
- Multiply a standard serving of the protein (e.g. soy) in g by the PDCAAS
- Divide value by the recommended standard for protein

EVALUATION OF PROTEIN QUALITY

The Committee on Dietary Reference Intakes has created a system that evaluates the quality of protein – the **Protein Digestibility-Corrected Amino Acid Score (PDCAAS)**. The protein's amino acid composition is compared to the amino acid requirements of pre-school aged children. The amino acid with the lowest ratio is the limiting amino acid!

First, the protein's amino acid composition is determined, which shows the quantities of each amino acid present in the protein. Second, those values are compared with the amino acid requirements of pre-school aged children. Third, the amino acid value with the biggest discrepancy, the one that falls short of the reference values the most, is selected - the most limiting amino acid.

If the food protein's limiting amino acid is only 80% of the amount required by the reference protein, it receives a score of 80 (Amino Acid Score).

HIGH-PROTEIN DIETS - ELEVATED RISK FOR DEHYDRATION

Weather for losing body weight or gaining muscle mass, athletes will go on a high-protein diet for different reasons. What they don't realize is that they need to adjust their water consumption as well when following a high-protein diet to avoid decreases in performance. Otherwise, the new diet will be more harmful than beneficial!

Protein consists of carbon, hydrogen, oxygen and nitrogen. If one increases the amount of protein in the diet, the amount of urea (ammonia & carbon dioxide), a waste product the body produces, will increase as well because urea is used by the body to get rid of excess nitrogen.

In order to get rid of the urea via urine, the body uses water. Because the body needs the extra water to excrete the urea via urine, insufficient water reserves in the body will cause dehydration, which impairs the body's metabolism and hence decreases performance.

There are some athletes that use high-protein diets to lose weight, which is counterproductive because:

- They increase the risk for dehydration, which impairs performance
- Losing weight (water weight) doesn't mean losing FAT. Once they return to their "normal" diet they will regain the water weight that is associated with carbohydrate storage

Lastly, multiply the amino acid score by the food protein's digestibility % to determine PDCAAS.

PDACC = protein digestibility x amino acid score

The food protein's digestibility % is based on values determined from rat studies and the PDCAAS is used to determine the "% Daily Value" on food labels. All food labels must state the quantity (in g) of protein but not its quality (% Daily Value")! The "% Daily Value" is required only when the food makes a protein claim/health claim. The PDCAAS method is used to determine the quality of the protein. Therefore, the "% Daily Value" is reflective of the quantity & quality!

For a summary of all steps see Under the Microscope – Evaluation of Protein Quality

Food Sources for High-Quality Protein are:

Meat	Cheese
Fish	Eggs
Poultry	Yogurt
Soy Products	Milk

Generally speaking, tennis players should avoid high-protein diets due to the elevated risk of dehydration. We recommend working with a Registered Dietitian before making any significant changes to your diet. This ensures that you use dietary compounds effectively to increase your performance. For more information read Under the Microscope - High-Protein Diets: Elevated Risk for Dehydration

VITAMINS

Vitamins are organic by virtue of containing carbon but they don't provide any energy! Instead, they **support the release of energy** from carbohydrates, fat, and protein. There are 13 different vitamins, some are **water-soluble** (9) and others are **fat-soluble** (4).

WATER-SOLUBLE VITAMINS – VITAMIN B & C

There are eight (8) B vitamins as well as vitamin C that are water-soluble. All of them help with the release of energy and have other various responsibilities. Following are the respective responsibilities in more detail.

Vitamin C

Vitamin C acts as an **antioxidant**, which means that it spares a compound from oxidation and is oxidized in its place. It aids in the synthesis of collagen and carnitine and enhances iron absorption and availability. Another function occurs during chemical reactions, where vitamin C contributes as a cofactor in hydroxylation reactions (i.e. dopamine to norepinephrine).

The B Vitamins (8)

Thiamin (B1) facilitates the conversion of pyruvate to acetyl Co-enzyme A (CoA) in carbohydrate breakdown. It also participates in membrane and nerve conduction, sugar synthesis and oxidation of amino acids.

Riboflavin (B2) is responsible for hydrogen transfer during mitochondrial (aerobic) metabolism.

Niacin facilitates hydrogen electron transfer during glycolysis and mitochondrial (aerobic) metabolism (promotes energy burning). It also plays a role in fat and glycogen synthesis (in liver & muscle cells) as well as tryptophan conversion to niacin; excess niacin suppresses fatty acid mobilization, increasing glucose utilization; toxic levels cause nerve damage.

Piroxidine (B6) is used in protein synthesis and glycogen metabolism (promotes energy burning) and as a coenzyme in the transamination (break down of amino acids in the liver) reaction. It forms a precursor for heme in hemoglobin and is a coenzyme for phosphorylase, facilitating glycogen release from the liver.

Vitamin B12 acts as a coenzyme in nucleic acid metabolism. It also influences protein synthesis and serves as a mediator in gastrointestinal (absorption & transport), bone and nervous tissue function.

Folic Acid (Folate) is a coenzyme in amino acid metabolism and nucleic acid synthesis. It is essential for the formation of red/white blood cells and protects against neural tube defects.

Pantothenic Acid is a component of the aerobic metabolism intermediate acetyl CoA and is used during synthesis (making) of cholesterol, phospholipids, hemoglobin, and steroid hormones.

Biotin plays an essential role in CHO, lipid, and protein metabolism. It is also used as a carboxyl unit transport and during gluconeogenesis and fatty acid synthesis and oxidation.

Vitamin	Responsibility
Vitamin C	Antioxidant
	Synthesis of collagen and carnitine
	Enhances iron absorption and heat acclimation
	Facilitates iron availability
	Cofactor in hydroxylation reactions (I.e. dopamine to noradrenaline)
Thiamin (B1)	Facilitates the conversion of pyruvate to acetyl CoA in carbohydrate breakdown
	Participates in membrane - and nerve conduction
	Participates in sugar synthesis
	Participates in oxidation of amino acids
Riboflavin (B2)	Responsible for hydrogen transfer during mitochondrial metabolism
Niacin	Responsible for hydrogen electron transfer during glycolysis and mitochondrial metabolism (promotes energy burning)
	Role in fat and glycogen synthesis (in liver & muscle cells), tryptophan conversion to niacin; excess niacin suppresses fatty acid mobilization increasing glucose utilization;
	Toxic levels cause nerve damage
Piroxidine (B6)	Used in protein synthesis and glycogen metabolism (promotes energy burning)
	Coenzyme in transamination (break down of amino acids in the liver) reaction
	Forms precursor for heme in hemoglobin
	Coenzyme for phosphorylase → facilitates glycogen release from the liver
Vitamin B12	Coenzyme in nucleic acid metabolism
	Influences protein synthesis
	Serves as a mediator in gastrointestinal absorption & transport and bone and nervous tissue function
Folic Acid (Folate)	Coenzyme in amino acid metabolism, nucleic acid synthesis
	Essential for formation of red/white blood cells
	Protects against neural tube defects
Pantothenic Acid	Component of the intermediate acetyl CoA
	Synthesis of cholesterol, phospholipids, hemoglobin and steroid hormones
Biotin	Essential role in CHO, lipid, protein metabolism
	Carboxyl unit transport
	Gluconeogenesis
	Fatty acid synthesis and oxidation

FAT-SOLUBLE VITAMINS

There are four (4) fat-soluble vitamins (**ADEK**); vitamin A, vitamin D, vitamin E, and vitamin K.

Vitamin A functions as a visual pigment (retinol) and plays a role in the maintenance of epithelial tissues. It is also used during carbohydrate synthesis (saccharide synthesis; CHO).

Vitamin D promotes growth and mineralization of bones and increases absorption of calcium.

Vitamin E functions as an antioxidant to prevent cell damage.

Vitamin K is important for blood clotting.

Fat-Soluble Vitamin	Responsibility
Vitamin A	(retinol) visual pigment, maintenance of epithelial tissues, role in saccharide synthesis (CHO)
Vitamin D	Promotes growth and mineralization of bones, increases absorption of calcium
Vitamin E	Functions as an anti-oxidant to prevent cell damage
Vitamin K	Important for blood clot-ting

MINERALS & ENZYMES

Minerals are basic chemical elements. They do not yield any energy and are used by the body only in small amounts (micronutrients). They are, however, essential for muscular contraction and hence need to be readily available in order to maintain force production and power output.

CALCIUM

For muscular contraction to occur, actin must bind with calcium ions (+ charged). While you exercise hydrogen ions (- charged) build up. Hydrogen and calcium compete for **troponin C**, which is the binding site for calcium. So, if hydrogen ions accumulate while calcium ion availability decreases, you have less cross-bridge binding, which means power production capabilities decrease and the muscle is weaker.

MAGNESIUM

ATP provides energy because of it's adenosine, which is ribose + adenamine dinucleotide plus three (3) phosphates. That's why it's called adenosine **tri**-phosphate (ATP). These phosphates will stabilize with magnesium, which is why magnesium plays a role in energy production; it is a cofactor (coenzyme) for energy production. As the body splits ATP, hydrogen ions build up but there is an elevation of magnesium, too. So, as the work rate increases you get higher levels of magnesium, which also interferes with calcium binding to troponin C and hence fatigue sets in. It is always proton build-up, not lactate build-up, inside the cells that causes fatigue!

POTASSIUM

Potassium plays an important role in the working of muscles. When muscle cells are active (polarized), sodium goes inside the cell while potassium goes outside the cell (Sodium-Potassium pump). During high work rates the sodium-potassium pumps work harder and potassium levels built up inside the cell, causing fatigue.

ENZYMES

Contrary to popular believe, enzymes do not yield any energy whatsoever; enzymes only regulate the release of energy! In other words, consuming lots of enzymes will not give you extra energy. Enzymes' efficiency as an energy regulator depends on two factors:

- Temperature
- pH levels

When you start playing tennis the body temperature increases and enzymatic activity is enhanced but if you push yourself too far (e.g. lifting heavy weights with no rest intervals), the body's pH levels shift from "normal" to "red" and enzymatic activity stops, thereby decreasing energy availability and you have to stop exercising.

During a match or practice you sweat and hence lose minerals (e.g. calcium, sodium) that are important for muscular contractions. Electrolyte drinks like Gatorade or PowerRade replenish minerals during activity thereby prolonging effective physical activity.

When making food choices it is important to distinguish between the general population and athletes. "Under the Microscope – Why High Sodium Levels Usually Do Not Increase Blood Pressure" shows why.

INTRODUCTION TO EXERCISE PHYSIOLOGY

As previously mentioned, sports nutrition requires the thorough understanding of exercise physiology and nutrition principles in conjunction with the effective application of both to maximize athletic performance. Previously we introduced you to the nutrition principles and now we present exercise physiology principles. Even though you are most likely not a registered dietitian (RD), understanding the information presented here will be invaluable to you because it will help you making informed decisions regarding your career.

PHYSIOLOGICAL ANALYSIS

A specific physiological analysis of tennis is very difficult because of various parameters that constantly change (e.g. gender and age of player, humidity, court surface, duration of play, etc.). Therefore, we focus on a universal physiological analysis and assume that the other variables can be taken into account.

This analysis is based on a male professional tennis player that prefers a baseline style of play; he will be playing on a hard-court surface and playing best-of-three sets in a mild climate (80 F).

MOVEMENT CONSIDERATIONS

In a match you move in multiple directions during rallies. On the baseline you mainly move side-to-side, when approaching the net you run forward, and when hitting an overhead you backpedal. On occasion you might even be sliding. You perform all of these movements at, or near, maximal speed for ~15 seconds with 20 second rest intervals in between points and 60 seconds intervals during change-overs for a match duration of 45 – 150 minutes. In other words, tennis is a mixture of endurance, power, and agility.

WHY HIGH SODIUM LEVELS USUALLY DO NOT INCREASE BLOOD PRESSURE

Why High Sodium Levels Usually Do Not Increase Blood Pressure

You probably have heard before that sodium increases blood pressure and that you should therefore avoid consuming foods with high sodium content. That statement by itself is false! It should read: "If you have kidney problems, high sodium intake will lead to an increase in blood pressure".

High sodium levels can only increase blood pressure if your kidneys are not working properly. In other words, if you are a healthy individual (kidneys are ok), lowering your sodium intake will have no effect on your blood pressure. In fact, if you have perfectly functioning kidneys, you can consume lots of sodium and it will not increase blood pressure. But someone who has elevated blood pressure can lower their blood pressure if they consume less than 2,100 mg of sodium a day.

So why is sodium associated with causing high blood pressure?

Anywhere sodium goes in the body, water follows because sodium & water are attracted to each other like a magnet. When the sodium content in your blood goes down, blood volume and blood pressure decrease as well. When that happens, baroreceptors (sense pressure) and osmoreceptors (sense fluid levels) in your kidneys and brain will sense lower blood pressure and the body reacts to it by activating mechanisms that will increase blood pressure. That is the reason sodium is associated with high blood pressure.

What has not been established yet is if high sodium diets will decrease sensitivity to sodium.

Accordingly, multiple energy systems are predominantly in use during different times of a match, including the immediate energy system (ATP-CP), anaerobic energy system (anaerobic glycolysis; no oxygen), and the aerobic energy system (aerobic glycolysis; with oxygen).

Therefore, we provide a brief introduction for each energy system as it relates to nutrition; nutrition provides the fuel the energy systems use. It is important to understand that all the energy systems work together all the time but one of them will be dominant at any particular time.

ENERGY PRODUCTION

Imagine you go to the gym and go on the treadmill at 5 mph for a while. Then you increase the running speed to 10 mph and now you choose to run at 10 mph with a 10% (grade) incline. So, now you a running a 5-6 minute/mile but you are basically running up a mountain. How long do you think you will last on the treadmill before you have to a decline in running speed and need get off? Maybe 10 seconds! This scenario is similar to performing an all out sprint. How long can you maintain an all out sprint before you have to slow down? Maybe 5-10 seconds, after that you are gradually slowing down. If you maintain that high work rate for about 10 seconds, regardless of how well trained you are, the work output is going to decline. This happens because the major source of energy you use is the energy that is already immediately available inside your muscles, adenosine tri-phosphate (ATP) and creatine phosphate.

IMMEDIATE ENERGY SYSTEM: ATP-CP

Muscle cells have an Adenosine Triphosphate (ATP) and creatine deposit and when the ATP deposit is depleted, new ATP can be made (synthesized) with the help of creatine. Creatine and an inorganic phosphate (Pi) form creatinephosphate (CP).

Then the enzyme creatine kinase splits the creatinephosphate, thereby releasing energy which is added to form ATP (the split phosphate is added, called re-phosphorylated, to Adenosine Diphosphate
{Di = 2}, forming Adenosine Triphosphate {tri = 3}).

NUTRITIONAL STRATEGIES TO IMPROVE ATP-CP SYSTEM

There are two (2) supplements that have been used to improve the performance of the immediate energy system: **creatine** and **ribose**. How both supplements are beneficial in increasing power output and serving as an aid during recovery will be discussed next.

CREATINE

One of the mechanisms of fatigue involves creatine. Interestingly enough, when a muscle cell is at optimal length and all the cross-bridges are available to bind for force production, fatigue occurs to a greater extend. That indicates that a metabolic property is missing there. ATP and creatine phosphate are the missing substances (creatinephosphate), which is the immediate reservoir for replacing ATP (Adenosine TriphosPhate).

ATP = ADP + Pi + hydrogen ion

What happens is that the enzyme **creatine kinase**, which is the most abundant enzyme in all muscle cells, will take creatine phosphate as well as the hydrogen ions that accumulate during exercise and it will re-synthesize ATP almost at the rate it was used! That's the reason why you can maintain your power output. The enzyme creatine kinase has the ability to accept hydrogen ions hence also acting as a buffer. So, in order to remake (resynthesize) ATP the body utilizes creatine, phosphate, and hydrogen ions. If there were no creatine kinase reaction, you would experience a drop in pH even sooner, which would ultimately stop energy production. Instead, creatine stabilizes pH and replenished ATP quickly because it's only one enzyme hence it only requires one reaction. That's why you can maintain high power output for ~10 seconds. For example, the weight you can lift for 1 second you can also lift for 10 seconds but you cannot maintain it for 30 seconds. So when you take creatine supplement, you will be able to increase creatine phosphate stores and might be able to push high power output to 12 seconds instead of 10.

Creatine also aids in the recovery process. After a heavy set of squatting you will be breathing harder because of the oxygen debt, which is the reason for the increased aerobic energy production. The body is re-synthesizing creatine phosphate and hence is replenishing the creatine phosphate stores. That's how creatine helps with the recovery transfer; you have more creatine available and you can make more creatine phosphate stores a lot faster.

RIBOSE

Ribose is a supplement used for the immediate energy system and the boosting of its performance. Especially when playing on fast surfaces (e.g. grass court; hard court), the use of ribose as a supplement can be beneficial. The goal is to maintain ATP stores. Remember that Adenosine Triphosphate = Adenosine Diphosphate + inorganic phosphate (ATP = ADP + Pi). Adenosine is adenine plus ribose. In other words, ribose is part of ATP. So, the belief is that by taking ribose, ATP stores can be produced and stored much faster inside muscle cells. That's the belief but there are only a few studies that show this and there haven't been any significant studies to ensure that the belief actually is correct.

The theory is that because ribose is made of sugar (it's a special sugar; it's not 6 carbon like glucose; it's 5 carbon and therefore takes a different transporter) and doesn't travel with glucose in the blood, it stays ribose. That's why researchers think it is bio-available because it's a different type of sugar.

ANAEROBIC METABOLISM: ANAEROBIC GLYCOLYSIS

During anaerobic energy production (no oxygen available), the body uses sugar (glucose), which is a carbohydrogen and oxygen (glucose is 6 carbons long, 12 hydrogen, 6 oxygen). Unlike aerobic energy production (explained shortly), ATP is not produced in the mitochondria but in the sarcoplasm. During anaerobic ATP production carbon dioxide is a byproduct (the body still takes the carbons off and still rips the hydrogen off) via dehydrogenation. Hydrogen ions build up but the body can't make water due to the lack of oxygen (which is available in the aerobic metabolism). So during anaerobic metabolism hydrogen ions accumulate, which lowers pH, and a change in pH decreases energy production. In order to continue with the energy production the body takes pyruvate (a byproduct of anaerobic metabolism) and fortunately makes lactate out of it to get rid of the hydrogen ions. The lactate acts as a buffer; it helps the body remove hydrogen ions, hence prolonging energy production. In short, anaerobic metabolism uses a six-carbon glucose and turns it into lactate to continue with energy production. More specifically, the body turns it into lactate by ripping off hydrogen and hooking them onto pyruvate. Therefore, lactate is nothing but a reduced form of pyruvate!

FATIGUE: CAUSED BY PROTONS, NOT LACTATE

The pain you feel when you fatigue is due to protons (e.g. magnesium, potassium, calcium). Protons (+) are particles that have a positive charge, similar to electrons (-) but they are negatively charged. Protons stimulate pain receptors (open nerve endings) (e.g. when you put salt in an open wound) which respond due to an accumulation of protons (e.g. hydrogen; potassium, magnesium, calcium). For a more detailed analysis of the protons calcium, magnesium and potassium and how they relate to energy metabolism read "Under the Microscope: The Role of Protons in Energy Metabolism".

When ATP is used for fuel the body goes through a process called hydrolysis (splitting of hydrogen). Therefore, the by-product of ATP reproduction is not just ADP + Pi (inorganic phosphate) but also hydrogen! As a result, every time the body splits ATP (ATP = ADP + iP + H), hydrogen ions build up (are produced). So, as your work rate goes up, hydrogen accumulation increases and pain sensation occurs. Thus, lactate is not causing the pain; the body uses lactate to remove hydrogen out of the system and continue with energy production. This phenomenon can be observed in people suffering from McCardle's syndrome". See "Under the Microscope: McCardle's Syndrome".

Also, lactate is not responsible for muscle soreness the day following a hard workout; it is caused by swelling and inflammation. During activity protons (e.g. built up of magnesium, potassium, calcium, hydrogen ions; for more info read "Under the Microscope: Fatigue - The Role of Protons") cause fatigue but feeling fatigue the next day is caused by inflammation (swelling & inflammation) and immune cells that are infiltrating the inflamed area (like parasites and macrophages). Basically how it works is that you damage your muscles through training and the new additions of immune cells show up at scene of the swelling. For more info take a closer look at "Under the Microscope: Don't Workout a Sore Muscle".

The swelling is red blood cells and the swelling and edema (water accumulation) that is being created presses against receptors in the muscle cells that send out pain signals. It's similar to wrapping a rope around your finger until it starts to swell - after a while it starts to hurt because of the swelling. Whenever you have swelling and an increase in osmotic pressure (fluid retention in an area) the swelling presses on sensory receptors that give you a sensation.

When you hear people say: "Get a massage tomorrow to get the lactate out of the system" this is completely false and total nonsense! This doesn't mean that a massage is bad for you after a workout. In fact, massage helps with increasing blood flow, which brings more nutrients to the muscle and hence helps with recovery but it's not going to get rid of lactate (or lactic acid).

UNDER THE MICROSCOPE

MCCARDLE'S SYNDROME

McCardle's syndrome patients cannot use glycogen (storage form of glucose) for fuel. They lack the enzyme myofasforlase and hence can't use glycogen. Instead they have to use available glucose. Since they can't use glycogen at the beginning of exercise, they are not producing any lactate. Therefore, they should not feel any pain but in realty they feel major pain at the beginning of exercise (more than an average person would) and if they would infuse lactate the pain sensation would cease! So, lactate is in fact a buffer but is often found guilty by association. When you are fatiguing due to higher work rates, lactate accumulation increases as well.

DON'T WORKOUT A SORE MUSCLE

When you feel pain after working out it is not recommended to hit the same muscle group again the next day because you want the muscle to recover. Pain is a sign that you have the immune cells coming in, which help to get rid off the damaged muscle proteins. The immune cells (phagocytes) make room for "new" proteins to come in and repair the muscle tissue. When you keep pounding the muscle while it is trying to repair itself, you will not see a gradual improvement. As a joke: Monday is international bench press day. So what happens if you bench press Monday through Thursday? You are not going to see any improvement (strength or size) because you constantly keep damaging the muscle tissue. Therefore, you never want to work out a sore muscle hard but some research suggest that working out a sore muscle moderately/lightly will be beneficial by increasing blood flow and hence creating more nourishment for the damaged muscle tissue. The obvious thing would be complete rest for the muscle group.

THE ROLE OF PROTONS IN ENERGY METABOLISM

CALCIUM

For muscular contraction actin binds with calcium ions (+ charged). Hydrogen is negatively charged. Hydrogen and calcium compete for troponin C, which is the binding site for calcium. So, if hydrogen ions are around, you have less cross-bridges binding, which means power production capabilities decrease and the muscle is weaker. In other words, due to elevated proton levels a decrease in pH occurs, causing actin & myosin binding sites to be weaker because fewer actin & myosin filaments attach because hydrogen and calcium are in competition for the same binding site.

MAGNESIUM

ATP gives us energy because it is adenosine, which is ribose + adenamine dinucleotide and 3 phosphates. That's why it's called adenosine triphosphate (ATP). These phosphates will stabilize with magnesium, which is why magnesium is a cofactor (coenzyme) for energy production. As the body splits ATP, hydrogen ions build up but also elevations of magnesium occur. So, as work rate increases, levels of magnesium increase, which also interferes with calcium binding to troponin C and hence causes fatigue.

POTASSIUM

When cells are polarized during activity, sodium goes inside the cell while potassium goes outside the cell (Sodium-Potassium pump). During high work rates, sodium-potassium pumps work harder and potassium levels build up inside the cell, causing fatigue.

LACTIC ACID THRESHOLD & VO2MAX

We have now established that lactate (lactic acid) does not cause fatigue. The **lactic acid threshold** determines how long you can perform well in sports (e.g. in running it's very important). The lactic acid threshold is the point where lactate starts to accumulate rapidly in your blood. Again, it doesn't mean that lactate is causing the fatigue, just that it is getting into the blood at that point and hence can be used as a marker of anaerobic metabolism. So, if you took the same athlete before and after training, and lets say before training, when they ran 10 km/hour, that's when they reached their lactate threshold. Well, after training (because they can rely more on aerobic energy and fat for fuel) their lactate threshold now occurs at higher speeds of 12 km/hour (now they can run at e.g. 12 km/hour before hitting their lactate threshold).

Lactate threshold determines performance potential better than VO2max (maximum oxygen volume); lactate threshold is more indicative of who really is the better athlete even if there are two athletes with the same VO2max. For example, Athlete A and athlete B have the same VO2max but athlete A has a lactate threshold of 70% of his/her VO2max and athlete B has his/her lactate threshold at 65% of his/her VO2max. That means that athlete A will be able to maintain a higher pace before hitting the anaerobic threshold (before they begin relying on anaerobic energy as fuel) at, let's say, ~8 km/hour. Athlete B however, even if his/her VO2max is the same, is going to hit the anaerobic threshold at ~6.9 km/hour, which means he/she is only going to be able to run at this slower pace before relying on anaerobic energy for fuel. Therefore, the lactate threshold really determines performance potential better than VO2max. Athletes with the same VO2max can have different speeds at which they reach their respective lactate thresholds. Even though lactate doesn't cause fatigue, as a blood marker it tells you when you start to rely more on anaerobic glycolysis (energy production) and less on aerobic metabolism.

NUTRITIONAL STRATEGIES TO IMPROVE ANAEROBIC METABOLISM

Minerals like calcium, potassium and magnesium play a role during muscle contractions especially when muscles have been widely used. Some of you remember when American Michael Chang beat Ivan Lendl in the fourth round of the 1989 French Open. It was a long hard-fought match where Chang suffered from severe cramping and he started eating bananas during changeovers.

Since that time, the intake of minerals has been used by tennis players during matches to enhance or prolong their performance. We are going to introduce four (4) other supplements to you that have been shown to improve performance.

SODIUM BICARBONATE

Sodium bicarbonate, basically baking soda, is an acid buffer that is beneficial during anaerobic metabolism and strength training. It is therefore somewhat surprising that sodium bicarbonate or similar buffers are omitted in most supplements. Sodium bicarbonate gets into your blood and increases your blood pH. That increase in blood pH draws acids out of the cells faster, thereby maintaining normal pH levels inside the cell, so the cells can continue to work at the homeostasis (maintaining equilibrium; normal levels) level. So, during activity hydrogen ions and lactate are exiting from the cell quickly, which is advantageous because that means you are able to buffer hydrogen ions faster and hence are able to continue at higher work rates. So, one thing that is shown without a doubt, study after study, is that sodium bicarbonate ingestion will improve any performance that lasts from 45 to 90 seconds.

When cramping occurs "**alka-serzer**" intake (sodium bicarbonate) will help by removing hydrogen ions thereby increasing pH levels and getting pH levels back within the normal range. Sodium bi-carbonate acts as a buffer but not without side effects. The side effect from taking sodium bi-carbonate, especially when taken before exhausting activity, is alkalosis (opposite of acidosis), which can kill you. Death never occurred during any studies but if you have elevated blood acid levels, breathing will accelerate because you have to get rid off all the carbondioxide, which ultimately causes hyperventilation – increased breathing to get rid of increased acid blood pH accumulation. It could be deadly!

Sodium bicarbonate does not necessarily help buffer lactate but it does help remove hydrogen ions and lactate out of muscle cells to facilitate homeostasis inside the cells (returning to normal pH levels).

BETA ALANINE

Beta Alanine is an intracellular buffer that helps produce **carnosine**, which the cells produce automatically. It helps with the removal of hydrogen ions, not lactate, but it works kind of like lactate! The more you train at high intensities in the anaerobic system, the more carnosine you will put inside the cell.

Beta alanine is now being used by supplement companies to boost carnosine levels and it has been shown to work.

When you take beta alanine supplements you will get a tingling sensation in your whole body and you won't know if that's a good thing or not. This plush feeling throughout your whole body results from the fact that beta alanine is also a precursor of histamine and you get a temporary short-lived reaction to it. It is supposedly not dangerous! Histamine causes the constriction of blood vessels (vasodialation) in your capillaries and this is what causes that sudden flush which makes you feel very hot and tingly all over for a few minutes.

Beta Alanine with niacin produces histamine and a high dose of niacin causes a similar flush for the same reason; because it, too, produces histamine.

RYCALS

Rycals is actually a drug sold by pharmaceutical companies. It can improve performance significantly. Rycals accomplishes this by lowering proton concentration (preventing calcium leakage) in cells, thereby prolonging energy production. The pharmaceutical company that developed rycals did it for people suffering from severe muscle weakness and muscle wasting. The target population is the the elderly and people who need to resist fatigue. It is usually not used for sports performance enhancement.

SODIUM PHOSPHATE

Another drug sold by pharmaceutical companies is sodium phosphate, which also improves performance significantly.

AEROBIC METABOLISM: AEROBIC GLYCOLYSIS

Aerobic metabolism uses carbon fuel (carbohydrogen, oxygen, acidic acid or carbohydrate). The body sends it into the mitochondria (power plant of the muscle cell) and the body then produces H2O because it rips off the hydrogen (H) and combines it with oxygen (O) to make water (H2O). In that process the body gets rid of carbon as CO2, which you exhale (which we buffer), and then the body uses the energy, the attraction between hydrogen and oxygen, to make ATP.

A byproduct of this ATP production is heat, which is why for example a chair you are sitting in is warmer than an "empty" chair. If you are sitting down reading this right now, you are turning oxygen into carbon dioxide in the mitochondria of your cells aerobically and you are producing heat and ATP. That's why a calorie is a measurement of how much ATP you are producing. So, you can measure calories, which tells you how much ATP you are producing, which in turn tells you how much oxygen you are consuming. Therefore kcalories is a measurement of oxygen consumption as well!

The aerobic energy systems mainly fuel endurance activities. Therefore, if you are playing three (3) sets, the aerobic energy system gradually starts taking over energy supply. If you go on a treadmill, set the speed at 5 mph, which is the speed where you switch from walking to running. How long would you be able to run before fatiguing? This obviously depends on your training status but generally the average person would last ~ 90 minutes because certain factors will come into into play that will contribute to fatigue. We will examine these next.

PERFORMANCE LIMITING FACTORS

There are four (4) factors that can have a negative impact on your performance on the court. First we will introduce each of these factors before we offer nutritional strategies to offset any negative impact.

CENTRAL FATIGUE

Central fatigue refers to fatigue of the central nervous system, which consists of the brain and spinal cord. The nervous system in our body is used to perceive and respond to events that occur inside (internal environment) and outside (external environment) of the body. We have receptors all over the body that can detect or sense changes in our internal and/or external environment such as touch, pain, temperature change and chemical stimuli. Information that the central nervous system (CNS) receives from our sensory organs is referred to as **sensory information** and information received from the internal environment via chemical messengers is called **visceral information** (visceral = internal organs, especially the ones located in the chest).

The nervous system responds to events/stimuli either by voluntary movement or it changes the rate of release (or quantity) of chemical messengers (neurotransmitters) from the endocrine system, which is involuntary.

The nervous system fulfills the following functions:

1. It controls the internal environment (in connection with the endocrine system)
2. It controls voluntary muscular movement
3. It controls involuntary movements (programs spinal cord reflexes)
4. It is responsible for assimilating the experiences that are being stored in our memory, which help us to learn.

One example that demonstrates that central fatigue is a factor in sports is running on a treadmill while looking at the time. If you run on a treadmill watching each second go by you will want to get off after 30 minutes. That's why most people cover it up with a towel – they don't want to see the time because they think it never goes by fast enough. Same thing can happen on the tennis court, especially during an intense match or practice. When you fatigue, you feel it mentally and physically; your legs are sore and you feel drained or "empty".

TEMPERATURE OR HUMIDITY

The general rule of thumb when considering hydration factors related to performance or thermoregulation is: if temperature or humidity goes over 70 degrees or 70%, respectively, you will feel dehydrated after working for 90 minutes. If after 10 minutes you ask yourself how you feel based on the rate of perceived exertion scale **(see „Borg Rating of Perceived Exertion Scale" on page 712)**, your answer will be that it is "light" exertion **(RPE 2)**. If you ask again after 30 minutes you would say that it is getting tougher **(RPE 3)** and after 45 minutes, even though the speed hasn't changed, you would say it's pretty tough **(RPE 5)**. After 90 minutes you will feel like you have to get off the treadmill **(RPE 9)**. The depleted glycogen levels are what make the exercise more and more difficult even though the speed has remained the same. In short, glucose availability. When you practice hard for 90 - 120 minutes, the limiting factors with respect to sports nutrition is glycogen availability, hydration and central fatigue. Psychologically you can manipulate neurotransmitters by making branch chain amino acids more available. So the central fatigue, the nervous system part, can be influenced by ingredients in your diet.

GLUCOSE AVAILABILITY

Glycogen is stored in the liver and muscle cells. Therefore, blood glucose/liver glycogen stores is one unit and muscle glycogen stores is the other unit. So they are the two compartments you have to rely on for energy. When you are taking glucose gels/pills during exercise, it increases the availability of blood glucose only, not the storage of glucose (glycogen). In other words, glucose gels/pills can spare muscle glycogen stores a little bit but they don't increase muscle glycogen. Interestingly enough, glucose pills actually increase insulin levels, lower cortisol (stress hormone), and decrease the rate of perceived exertion (RPE).

Remember that using carbohydrates as an energy source during exercise is more efficient than using fat. Generally, after ~90 minutes, glycogen levels are depleted and you start "hitting the wall" because the conversion process from fat to energy is not as efficient. There are a couple of ways/strategies that can help you fight the "hitting the wall" syndrome (becoming hypoglycemic). We will introduce those shortly in "Nutritional Strategies".

THERMOREGULATION

During exercise in climates of >70° F it is recommended that you consume 1 cup of water every 15 minutes to maintain thermoregulation. Sports drinks (e.g. Gatorade, Powerade) are actually better than water. Researchers from the University of California, Berkley have shown in studies that, as a rule of thumb, marathon runners will add 1 minute to their usual final time for each degree fahrenheit that their body goes over 59° F. That's how important thermoregulation is when it comes to performance. When you constantly train in a hot/humid environment (e.g. Florida), the body makes adjustments such as sweating more (which is ironic – people living in south Florida wil start sweating earlier and produce more volume than someone from the north), which is an efficient way of cooling. Plasma (blood) volume increases (e.g. Floridians have a higher proportion of liquids in their blood), which allows them to sweat more and cool more efficiently. So, the acclimation process involves having more liquid available in your blood, which then allows you to sweat more! What people refer to as "the blood thinning" is really just a way of saying that the liquid levels increase and hence the "density" decreases; the blood becomes more deluded.

OXIDATIVE STRESS

Oxidative stress plays a role in limiting performance, in particular via the formation of **free radicals**. During aerobic metabolism, for every aerobic cycle (Krebs Cycle), oxygen, water and heat are produced and 2-5% of this production produces free radicals. So, every time you consume oxygen and use it, free radicals are produced with it, which causes cellular damage thereby causing a decrease in energy production.

One place that is very vulnerable to free radicals is the calcium releasing organelle in muscle cells which is called the sarcoplasmic reticulum (calcium is needed for muscular contractions). This is a key component in explaining why some players fatigue more during long training sessions or long matches. The generation of free radicals is making muscles weaker because the muscle cannot release as much calcium as is needed intracellularly. This results in decreased muscle contraction capabilities due to a decrease in actin-myosin binding sites and hence less force production.

BORG RATING OF PERCEIVED EXERTION

0	NO EXERTION
1	VERY LIGHT
2	LIGHT
3	MODERATE
4	SORT OF HARD
5	HARD
6	MODERATELY HARD
7	REALLY HARD
8	VERY HARD
9	EXTREMELY HARD
10	MAXIMUM EXERTION

Another possibility is that the body´s handling of calcium itself can be affected. We will next explore what supplements are helpful in preventing the oxidative stress that negatively affects performance.

TREATMENT OPTIONS FOR PERFORMANCE LIMITING FACTORS

OXIDATIVE STRESS

There is one particular ingredient that you can use which significantly helps you to play more consistently during practice or competition. You will be able to last longer before fatigue sets in, namely, **caffeine**! This doesn't mean you should be drinking gallons of coffee or soft drinks. 80 mg, or two cups of coffee, are already sufficient for improved performance. Caffeine acts directly on the release channels of the sacroplasmic reticulum, causing a greater permeability/release of calcium.

GLUCOSE AVAILABILITY

You can use glucose sparing agents so that glycogen stores will not be depleted or used as quickly. You have to take them regularly (e.g. every 30 min) to maintain effective blood glucose levels because, in reality, you are still using muscle glycogen but the blood glucose comes in and replaces the "lost" glycogen stores.

Glucose sparing agents are supplements like glucose pills and glucose-electrolyte solutions (6% glucose & sodium concentration {Gatorade}; 8% Powerade). If you mix/add caffeine to your intake of glucose pills or electrolyte drinks, your muscle cells will use the glucose sooner because glucose will be oxidized more quickly. If you use a sugar mix drink containing glucose, fructose, and maltose (e.g. Gatorade), glucose will oxidize more quickly and glucose will become available more quickly. That's why Gatorade is the ideal mixture. The sugar-mix has been optimized focusing on glucose oxidation rates and hence the rate of glucose availability. The key, however, is that you need to be used to whatever drink or pills you use so that you can digest and use the nutrients efficiently! Whatever you use during training you have to use during competition. World Class marathon runners & tri-athletes are even using Coca Cola these days.

Another strategy is to try to get the muscle to become more efficient at using/converting fat for fuel, thereby allowing the glycogen stores to last longer. A well-trained tennis player will have more **intracellular fat stores** than an unfit player that he/she can rely on, thereby sparing glycogen. An untrained individual won't have as much fat available and hence will have to use more glycogen. In terms of diet, you can increase fat oxidation by using more **caffeine**. Caffeine increases the release of epinephrine (hormone) and fatty acids from fat. In untrained individuals caffeine does not increase the use of fat for fuel but in trained individuals (e.g. Roger Federer) caffeine does increase the ability to use fat for fuel. Also, trained individuals have larger mitochondria (power plant of muscle cells) than untrained people. Therefore, trained individuals have a larger potential to use fat for fuel – they have a bigger engine or battery. In an untrained individual, the extra available fat doesn't make a difference because the mitochondria are not big enough to use the fatty acids. So, instead of hitting the wall in ~90minutes, trained individuals might hit it in ~120 minutes.

Instead of trying to spare glycogen stores, there is also the option of increasing glycogen stores via two (2) carbo-loading techniques: the classic method and the new method.

CARBO-LOADING: THE CLASSIC METHOD

In the past (1970's/1980's), athletes would carbo-load by starting 6 days before a tournament. The first 3 days you basically just eat fat and protein (Atkins diet) while training like crazy, thereby completely depleting your glycogen stores. All the liver glycogen and muscle glycogen is gone, which leads to dramatic loses in body weight due to fluid loss (an average person [175 lbs] might loose 6-7 pounds.

How it works is that the enzyme glycogensynthase (makes) synthesizes glycogen in your muscles and liver. Its level, meaning how well it works, is directly related to how depleted your glycogen levels are. Therefore, as you deplete your glycogen stores, levels of glycogensynthase increases adversely proportionally – it is ready to store as much glycogen as possible. So, on the 4th day, when you start eating a high carbohydrate diet your body starts making/storing a lot of glycogen (up to 250% increase from normal levels). You can measure that yourself by weighing yourself (after eating high carbs on day 4, 5, and 6) and comparing it with your weight after completion of day 3.

You will see that your body weight increased drastically. Most likely, you will regain the 6-7 lb you lost plus an additional 4-5 lbs. The extra 4-5 lb are not fat but ready-to-be used glycogen! It's going to provide you with more energy and hence you can last longer – this process is called **super-compensation**.

SIDE EFFECTS

Apart from the aforementioned weight loss you will feel horrible, very sluggish and cranky, and your risk of injury increases. Your motivation goes down and you don't even want to think about competition. Stability of your joints and muscles is also impaired because you are using more protein for fuel. Muscle soreness is going to occur and your immune system suffers, making you more prone to illness. This all occurs while being on an Atkins diet and training hard.

CARBO-LOADING: THE NEW METHOD

Nowadays, you eliminate the depletion-phase of the classic method because of all the side effects that we previously mentioned. You don't want to have a higher risk of injury the week before competition! Most athletes, though, prefer the classic method.

The first 3 days you taper your training down and even eat a normal diet (8 g of carbohydrates per kg of body weight). Your glycogen levels come down a little bit and then the last 3 days you don't do any exercise but eat a lot of carbohydrates, eating every 2 hours at a rate of 10 g of carbohydrates per kg (2.2 lbs) of body weight. By doing this, you can load the same amount of glycogen that the classic method achieves.

BATTLING CENTRAL FATIGUE

One thing that you can do nutrition-wise, which helps to combat central fatigue is using branch chain amino acids (BCAA's) supplements. The focal point of this approach is the neurotransmitter **tryptophan**, which is associated with higher serotonin levels, more fatigue and less motivation. For example, when you eat foods with high serotonin levels (turkey, or cheddar cheese), you will become really sleepy. Tryptophan and branch chain amino acids compete for absorption across the blood brain barrier, so the branch chain amino acids that we get from the muscle cells as we fatigue compete with tryptophan for transporters across the blood brain barrier.

So, as you use more branch chain amino acids, because your glycogen stores are depleted, tryptophan will succeed in moving across the blood brain barrier because you have used your branch chain amino acids to supply energy – branch chain amino acids are being used to replenish glycogen stores. So, tryptophan easily finds its way into the blood brain barrier, where it is easily converted (5-hydroxytryptamine is serotonin) into serotonin and serotonin is associated with lower levels of arousal, which is what you need to push through training, fighting fatigue.

Whey protein supplements have branch chain amino acids. When consuming a 3:1/4:1 carbo -protein mix, time to exhaustion can be extended – you can last longer before you get exhausted.

Rhodiola rosea, also called the arctic root, can also be used to battle central fatigue. It was found in Siberia and it is actually an anti-depressant. It was given to people living in Siberia to deal with the cold and the depressing weather, helping with mood swings. When athletes take it they experience lower levels of RPE during practice or competition.

NUTRIENT INGESTION

Making decisions in regards to nutrition is as important as working out in the gym or practicing on the tennis court. Since you need to eat and drink before, during and after practice or competition, supplements are effective and convenient. Most tennis players have to eat 2,500 – 4,000 kcal in the form of carbohydrates alone. There is no way that you are going to get that many carbohydrates from your regular diet. The following recommendations are based on recent research findings and will help you to achieve optimal health and performance goals.

PRE-TRAINING/MATCH RECOMMENDATIONS

The first thing is to improve (endogenous) glycogen stores, which will be a limiting factor for any exercise (match/practice) lasting 90 – 180 minutes long. That can be seen in the previous treadmill example where during the time one is running at 5 mph even at a low intensity it becomes more and more difficult. As glycogen stores diminish, intensity, pace and work output decrease (e.g. hitting the wall) and there is the possibility of immune system dysfunction (e.g. muscle soreness, injury, infections). The biochemistry behind this is that work output decreases because you have to rely on protein and fat for energy, and immune dysfunction occurs because you are using more proteins and the immune cells have to rely on protein. The immune cells use glutamine to proliferate and provide protection. Therefore, immune response is hindered.

Maximal (endogenous) glycogen stores are attainable via a high glycemic, high carbohydrate diet on a regular basis in conjunction with the help of supplements such as **carbohydrates**, **amino acids**, **protein** and **creatine**. This can be accomplished by adding creatine to Gatorade/Powerade and using whey protein drinks/shakes or various energy bars. Whey protein powders are excellent because you can mix them to your liking.

In terms of competition (tournament) you should eat 4 hours before an event, 1.5 g/kg (body weight) of carbohydrates and ~0.2 g/kg (body weight) of protein. Here is an easy trick for remembering this: If it's 3-4 hours before an event, you take the 3 and divide it by 2 (3/2=1.5) equaling 1.5 for CHO, then you take the 4 (hours) and divide it by 2 (4/2=2) equaling 2 for protein. Since CHO intake must be higher than protein intake, it is not 2 g of protein but 0.2 g of protein. So, it's 0.2 g/kg of protein and 1.5 g/kg of CHO. The best source of protein is whey protein because of its high digestibility and absorption rate and you get whey protein from diary products. So, if you had a cereal before the event you would be right in line with the recommendations. A Peanut Butter & Jelly sandwich would also work 3-4 hours before the event even though there is some fat in there, but 4 hours before would be better. Again, this is for competition, not training. During training there is no anxiety and if you eat 4 hours before going to the gym, for example, you will be starving while lifting weights, which is less than ideal.

So, if you have a match at 10 am, you need to eat between 6-7 am. If competition starts too early (e.g. 7 am), you should eat a carbohydrate/protein mixture ~30 minutes before the match so you have something in your system.

The reason for this is the 4 hour digestion window; before competition, there is always a bit of anxiety/nervousness (even for Roger Feder) and anxiety inhibits digestion. So, if you have some food 1-2 hours before competition and you are anxious and nervous, whatever you had is going to be in your stomach during the match.

This phenomenon can be seen at marathon events. Before the event, most runners have to use the restroom with digestive problems (reflexes, diarrhea) and the bathroom lines are long and disgusting. Many are using the portable toilets and are sticking their heads out asking for toilet paper. Most of them have an upset stomach because they probably ate breakfast one hour before, are nervous about the race and the food is sitting in their belly right now. If you eat something within 3 hours before the event, the chances are that a lot of the food is going to be left over in the stomach and will not be digested effectively because the natural reflex of the gut whereby stress inhibits digestion. Massive contractions that will try to empty your stomach can also occur and you don't want to have anything sitting in your GI tract during an event. You have to get rid of it and that's basically accomplished by diarrhea. So, to avoid having an upset stomach you should eat 3-4 hours before the event.

PRE-MATCH RECOMMENDATIONS

So if you are hungry 2 hours before the match what can you eat? Previous recommendation would have been not to eat anything 30-45 minutes before an event because your glucose is going up, insulin surge is going to follow, and by the time the event starts you have rebound hypoglycemia (low blood sugar) and it's going to affect your performance negatively. Recent studies have shown that the rebound hypoglycemia to which some people are subject doesn't impair performance at all. It has nothing to do with insulin sensitivity (the belief was that people are insulin sensitive), so it must be something else. The bottom line is if you are hungry before the event, a carbohydrate/protein mixture (Gatorade with some Whey Protein), same as what you would consume **during** the event, would be appropriate. Even if you are affected by the rebound effect, it shouldn't have an adverse effect on your performance. Also, because it is Gatorade and whey protein, it shouldn't really cause any gastrointestinal (GI) problems either. If you can drink it during the match then you definitely can drink it before the match without any GI discomfort. Don't eat an apple or banana 30 minutes before an event, something that has fiber in it, because it will start undergoing digestion by the time you are on the court and the body doesn't digest fiber well. Fiber can cause GI distress. Eating a high fiber cereal is generally really good for you but before a match it can cause problems and hence should be avoided because the fiber cannot be absorbed and will stay in your intestine. Generally, you should eat foods that you can handle without any problems and whatever you consume during competition should also be used during training so that the body is used to it. The problem with having foods in your GI tract during competition is that the smooth muscles in your GI tract are breaking down the food are using blood flow, oxygen, ATP and are wasting energy. They can also cause cramping due to all the muscular activity, taking blood from other areas. The smooth muscles in your GI tract are battling skeletal muscles for oxygen and you want to avoid that. The skeletal muscles need all the energy they can get so you can perform effectively.

Generally, **chocolate milk** is great but it might be problematic for some people because it has casein in it, which causes a slower protein absorption in the GI. For **recovery**, however, chocolate milk is excellent, likely even better than most supplement recovery drinks.

UNDER THE MICROSCOPE

SUMMARY OF PRE-TRAINING/ MATCH NUTRIENT RECOMMENDATIONS

- Endogenous glycogen stores only last 90 – 180 minutes depending on exercise intensity
- Maximal endogenous glycogen stores can be achieved by following a high glycemic, high carbohydrate diet (~8-10 g/kg of body weight)
- Pre-Match: Four (4) hours before competition consume 1.5 g/kg (body weight) of carbohydrates and ~0.2 g/kg (body weight) of protein
- Pre-Exercise: Drink a carbohydrate & protein mixture; consume 1.5 g/kg (body weight) of carbohydrates and ~0.2 g/kg (body weight) of protein

PRE-RESISTANCE TRAINING RECOMMENDATIONS

Ingesting carbohydrate & protein mixture promotes higher levels of protein synthesis. So, protein with carbohydrates, like in milk or Gatorade together with whey protein, actually induces a higher level of protein synthesis, which is a good thing if you want to increase muscle mass and increase strength. Carbohydrate & protein is better than carbohydrates alone or protein alone in terms of body composition (body fat vs. muscle).

CARBO-LOADING RECOMMENDATIONS

Maximal endogenous glycogen stores are attainable via a high glycemic, high carbohydrate diet on a regular basis; 8-10 g/kg of body weight per day are appropriate, which is a lot of CHO! So, if an athlete weighs 100 kg, he/she needs to consume (100 x 10 g = 1,000 g; 1,000 g x 4kcal = 4,000 kcal) 4,000 kcal just from carbohydrates! Where can an athlete get 4,000 kcal of carbohydrates per day? That's where supplements come into play! You have to get something before, during and right after activity. There is no way you get that from your diet – you cannot eat 4,000 kcal of pasta! You have to find good sources of supplements.

IN-TRAINING/MATCH RECOMMENDATIONS

Remember that you should be using the same drinks and foods during a match that you use during training. So, if you drink Gatorade during practice, you shouldn't drink Powerade during the match.

Maximizing muscle glycogen stores before a tournament (carbo-loading), and before practice, is a must so you can perform at your best. The frequent replenishment of carbohydrates during the match and hence availability of carbohydrates is important so you can continue playing well the entire match. Also, regular carbohydrate ingestion increases muscle glycogen stores, which steadily decline from match to match. Therefore, regular carbohydrate ingestion becomes even more important the longer you stay in the tournament because the carbo-loading effects cease and your endogenous glycogen stores before each match will decline. This phenomenon is analogous to a battery's lifespan. If you use and recharge a battery over and over again, the amount of available energy after each recharge slowly but surely declines.

Using different sources and forms of carbohydrates will positively affect your performance. For instance, if you had some high glycemic food to eat before the match then Gatorade/Powerade and a power bar during the match will ensure optimal performance from an energy standpoint. Be aware that consuming drinks and foods high in fructose can cause digestive problems, which you want to avoid during a match.

THE APPLICATION OF SPORTS NUTRITION

Good nutrition is necessary for competitive training, optimal performance and adequate recovery. As previously mentioned, all food products contain macronutrients and micronutrients. Macronutrients provide caloric energy and are found in various forms of carbohydrates, fats and protein. Micronutrients include vitamins and minerals, which provide no caloric energy, but regulate the function of all bodily systems and cells. The proper amounts of micronutrients and macronutrients in a diet keeps an athlete healthy and on the court. Next we take a closer look at how to calculate your macronutrient needs.

CARBOHYDRATES

Ingested carbohydrates are the key source of energy for any muscular contraction. There are different types of carbohydrates that all provide 4 kcalories per gram (4 kcal/g). The Recommended Daily Allowance (RDA) of carbohydrates for an average individual ranges from 45% - 65% of the diet depending on age, gender, height, weight and activity level. The main sources should come from whole grains, fruits and vegetables. It is best to obtain less than 10% of daily carbohydrates from simple sugar or processed sources. It should also be noted that simple carbohydrates cause a quick spike in blood sugar levels – usually resulting in a rush of quick energy followed by a feeling of sluggishness. Complex carbohydrates provide a steady stream of energy for longer periods of time.

AVOID "EMPTY CALORIES"

Calories are not just calories. For instance, compare the nutrient value of a can of cola versus a class of milk. Soda provides a lot of calories in the form of simple sugars but they are "empty calories" because you are getting no protein, vitamins or minerals (e.g. calcium, iron) when you drink sodas. If you choose a glass of milk instead of the soda, you will receive a similar amount of calories but you also get protein, vitamins and minerals with those calories. Therefore, you are getting more important nutrients that your body can use (immune function, proper nervous system activity, release of energy, protein synthesis etc.) for the same amount of calories. That's why it is advisable to stay away from "empty calories". In other words, you can be in a caloric surplus but in a nutrient deficit at the same time. Choose foods with high density!

FATS (LIPIDS)

Fats provide 9 kcalories per gram (9 kcal/g), making it the densest form of energy available. They are the storage form of energy in the body, with excess storage referred to as adipose tissue.

Ingestible fats are known as triglycerides and are comprised of fatty acids. Fatty acids are divided into saturated and unsaturated categories. There are **mono**, **poly**, and **trans unsaturated fats**. Mono and polyunsaturated fatty acids are the healthiest sources of fat that can be found in plant and fish sources. Some Omega-3 unsaturated fatty acids are shown to reduce cholesterol, which makes them cardio-protective. **Trans-fat** can be found in processed foods and pastries and is known to greatly increase the risk of heart disease. This occurs because of its ability to increase Low Density Lipoprotein (LDL) levels - which propagate plaque filled blood vessels - and decrease High Density Lipoproteins (HDL) levels – which help to 'clean' excess cholesterol/fat accumulation in blood vessels. Trans-fats are so dangerous to overall health that they have been banned in many states. Saturated fats are primarily found in animal meat sources. **Saturated fat** is not considered heart-healthy, as it is also known to raise LDL levels in the blood.

Less than 35% of the diet should come from fats. A diet with greater than 35% of calories coming from fats greatly increases the risk of obesity and other health disparities. Less than 10% of fat in the diet should come from saturated fats, while total avoidance of trans-fat is recommended. As a tennis player you may want to reduce your total fat intake and increase your protein intake compared to the general population. Some athletes may need all the calories they can get and/or may need ample fats - it all depends on the situation.

PROTEINS

Proteins provide 4 kcalories per gram (4 kcal/g). Their main role is to build and repair bodily tissues. Amino acids are the basic structural units of proteins. There are essential and non-essential amino acids. The 11 non-essential amino acids are produced by the body, but the 9 essential amino acids must be ingested in the diet.

Complete proteins such as meat and dairy products contain essential amino acids, while incomplete proteins in many vegetable sources like beans do not. There are exceptions to this rule, for instance, soybeans.

The RDA for protein lies in the range of 10% - 35% of the diet. For athletes, this range should be towards the higher end to accommodate the extra activity. 20% - 25% may be more appropriate for optimal tissue recovery. One must make prudent protein choices as many times protein sources are complemented with saturated fat. For an easy way to calculate protein requirement based on body weight use the following equation: 1.4 g - 1.6 g x kg of body weight (1 kg = 2.2 lb). Most of the research points toward this range as an optimal amount for high intensity athletics and weightlifting.

SUMMARY OF ACCEPTABLE MACRONUTRIENT CONTRIBUTIONS

These recommended values have been established by the Food & Nutrition Board, Institute of the National Academies.

These recommendations, called Dietary Reference Intakes (DRI), are for healthy people only and might not be applicable for people suffering from disease. The different % ranges depend on anthropometric values (age, gender, weight, height) and one's activity level.

Macronutrient	% Contribution
Carbohydrates	45 – 65%
Protein	10 – 35%
Fat	20 – 35%

Calculating Available Energy from Foods

Macronutrients	Energy/g	Example
Carbohydrates (CHO)	4 kcal/g	7g of CHO x 4kcal/g = 28 kcal
Protein	4 kcal/g	10g of Protein x 4 kcal/g = 40 kcal
Fat	9 kcal/g	8g of fat x 9 kcal/g = 72 kcal
		Total kcal = 140 kcal
To determine the % of calories that each macronutrient contributes:		(Macronutrient kcal / Total kcal) x 100
		Example (fat): (72 kcal / 140 kcal) x 100 = 51.4%

RMR Multipliers

Lifestyle	Men	Women	Description
Sedentary	1.0	1.0	Normal independent living
Low Active	1.4	1.3	Some physical activity (1 – 3 days)
Active	1.65	1.55	Strenuous physical activity most days (3-5 days)
Very Active	1.9	1.7	Daily strenuous physical activity
Pre-Competition	2.15	1.95	Carbo-loading 5-7 days prior to competition

CALCULATING ENERGY FROM FOODS

The energy released by carbohydrates, lipids and proteins is measured in kcalories. The amount of energy released from food depends on how many carbohydrates, lipids and proteins are in the food. Fat has the highest energy density (the most calories per gram), 9 kcal/g, followed by protein and carbohydrates, which yield 4 kcal/g each. Generally speaking, foods with a low energy density are desirable if you want to lose weight. To gain weight you want to choose foods with a high energy density.

Let's assume you eat something that contains 7 g of carbohydrates, 10 g of protein, and 8 g of fat. In order to find out how many kcalories you are consuming as a whole and/or for each component you have to do the following:

Since carbohydrates yield 4 kcal/g you have to multiply 7 g times 4 kcal/g, yielding 28 kcal (7 g x 4 kcal/g = 28 kcal). Similarly, you would multiply 10 g of protein by 4 kcal/g yielding 40 kcal (10 g x 4 kcal/g = 40 kcal) and 8 g of fat by 9 kcal/g yielding 72 kcal (8 g x 9 kcal/g = 72 kcal), respectively. Therefore, you consume 28 kcal of carbohydrates, 40 kcal of protein, and 72 kcal of fat totaling 140 kcal (28 kcal + 40 kcal + 72 kcal = 140 kcal).

If you want to determine the % of kcalories that each macronutrient contributes just take the respective macronutrient kcal and divide them by total kcalories and multiply by 100 ({Macronutrient kcal / Total kcal} x 100). To see the calculations in more detail take a look at "Under the Microscope – Calculating Available Energy from Foods".

HOW TO CALCULATE YOUR ESTIMATED ENERGY REQUIREMENTS (EER)

The question is how many calories do you need to stay on top of your game? The first thing to do is to find out what your basal [resting] metabolic rate (BMR or RMR) is. This entails the base amount of calories a person needs without considering any activity: your metabolism at rest. There are many equations for establishing a basal caloric need. We will present two (2) alternatives to you. One involves a body composition test (Harris-Benedict Formula; non gender-appropriate) to calculate your RMR and the other alternative, using the Convenience Formula (Harris-Benedict Formula; gender-appropriate), does not.

HARRIS-BENEDICT FORMULA

The following equation can be used to find basal caloric need and has an elevated degree of validity when compared to others.

(Lean Mass {kg} x 21.6) + 370 = RMR

You will need to undergo a body composition test first to find out your level of body fat (see Fitness Assessments Chapter for details). Once body fat percentage is established, you can perform the following calculations to obtain values for the BMR equation.

1. Body Fat % x Total Body Weight (lbs) = Body Fat in lb
2. Total Body Weight (lbs) – Fat Mass (lbs) = Lean Mass (lbs)
3. Lean Mass (lbs) / 2.2 = Lean Mass (kg)

Once the RMR value is found, the caloric need for your activity level needs to be calculated. This is best done using the Harris-Benedict Formula. There are different multipliers for different levels of daily activity; for a description of each, see ("Under the Microscope – RMR Multipliers"). There are 4 lifestyle categories: sedentary, low active, active and very active. The respective RMR multipliers (Male/Female) are: sedentary (1.0/1.0), low active (1.4/1.3), active (1.65/1.55) and very active (1.9/1.7). You must decide to which category you belong and calculate the best estimate of total daily calories needed. Simply take the RMR value and multiply it by the value specified for the applicable activity level. Remember that this value will be an estimate and does not have to reflect an exact value in the diet.

CALCULATING EER – GENDER-APPROPRIATE HARRIS BENEDICT FORMULA

A 30 year old male wants to calculate his ERR. He is 5 feet 11 inches tall and weighs 178 lb. He works out hard in the gym and on the court 4 days per week; his lifestyle is "active".	
Height: (5 ft x 30.48) + (11 inches x 2.54)	= 180.34 cm
Weight: (178 lbs / 2.2)	= 80.91 kg
Age:	= 30 years
The RMR calculates how many kcalories need to be consumed daily to maintain current weight.	
RMR Male: 66 + (5 x ht) + (13.8 x wt) - (6.8 x age)	
66 + (5 x 180.34) + (13.8 x 80.91) – (6.8 x 30)	= 1880.258 kcal/day
RMR Female: 655 + (1.8 x ht) + (9.6 x wt) - (4.7 x age)	= ______________ kcal/day
EER calculates how many kcalories should be consumed daily to meet energy demands.	
EER = RMR x Lifestyle Multiplier	
= 1880.258 x 1.65	= 3,102.42 kcal/day
Conclusion: He needs to take in ~3,100 kcal per day to meet his caloric needs and maintain his current weight.	

CALCULATE YOUR EER

Height: (______ft x 30.48) + (______inches x 2.54)	= ________ cm
Weight: (__________lbs / 2.2)	= ________ kg
Age:	= ________ years
The RMR calculates how many kcalories need to be consumed daily to maintain current weight.	
RMR Male: 66 + (5 x ht) + (13.8 x wt) - (6.8 x age)	= ______________ kcal/day
RMR Female: 655 + (1.8 x ht) + (9.6 x wt) - (4.7 x age)	= ______________ kcal/day
EER calculates how many kcalories should be consumed daily to meet energy demands.	
EER = RMR x Lifestyle Multiplier	= ______________ kcal/day

HARRIS-BENEDICT CONVENIENCE FORMULA

When using the convenience formula, a body composition test is not required.

First, you convert your body weight and height into metric units, meters (m) and kilogram (kg), respectively.

Then you choose and apply the gender-appropriate Harris Benedict formula via resting metabolic rate (RMR) to calculate your caloric intake requirements.

Finally, you use your RMR and choose the appropriate lifestyle multiplier.

RMR Male: 66 + (5 x ht) + (13.8 x wt) - (6.8 x age)

RMR Female: 655 + (1.8 x ht) + (9.6 x wt) - (4.7 x age)

As an example let's say you are a 30-year old male, 5 ft 11 inches, 178 lb and you have an "active" lifestyle.

1. Height: (5 ft x 30.48) + (11 inches x 2.54) = 180.34 cm
2. Weight: (178 lbs / 2.2) = 80.91 kg
3. Age: 30 years
4. RMR Male: 66 + (5 x ht) + (13.8 x wt) - (6.8 x age)

   66 + (5 x 180.34) + (13.8 x 80.91) – (6.8 x 30) = 1,880 kcal/day

5. EER = RMR x Lifestyle Multiplier

   = 1880.258 x 1.65

   = 3,102 kcal/day

According to the calculations, the man in our example would need to consume ~3,100 kcal per day. For an example with detailed calculations see "Under the Microscope – Calculating EER: Gender-Appropriate Harris Benedict Formula" To calculate your own EER use "Under the Microscope – Calculate Your EER".

Now you know how many kcalories you need per day but how many should come from each of the macronutrients carbohydrates, proteins and fats? Next you will learn how to calculate just that.

CALCULATING DAILY NUTRIENT CONTRIBUTIONS

After calculating the daily estimated energy requirement (EER), it is helpful to determine the respective nutrient contributions so that you know how many calories to consume from each nutrient class.

To calculate your daily nutrient contributions in kcal and grams (g) and multiply your ERR by the respective lifestyle category.

In our previous example, the total daily estimated energy requirement (EER) for the athlete is ~3,100 kcal. His lifestyle category is "active".

Accordingly, we multiply 3,100 kcal times 0.6 to get carbohydrate contribution of 1,860 kcal (3,100 kcal x 0.6 = 1,860 kcal), 3,100 kcal times 0.2 to get protein contribution of 620 kcal (3,100 kcal x 0.2 = 620 kcal), and 3,100 kcal times 0.2 to get fat contribution of 620 kcal (3,100 kcal x 0.2 = 620 kcal).

Therefore, according to his lifestyle, the athlete should consume approximately 1,900 kcal in the form of carbohydrates and 600 kcal from protein and fat sources, respectively. If you want to find out how many grams (g) you need to consume of each macronutrient then divide 1,860 kcal by 4 kcal/g (1,860 kcal / 4 kcal/g = 465 g of carbohydrates) to get 465 g of carbohydrates, 620 kcal by 4 kcal/g (620 kcal / 4 kcal/g = 155 g of protein) to get 155 g of protein, and 620 kcal by 9 kcal/g (620 kcal / 9 kcal/g = ~69 g of fat) to get ~69 g of fat (See EXAMPLE table).

Daily Nutrient Contributions				
Lifestyle (%CHO; %Prot; %Fat)	**EER**	**Calories from CHO**	**Calories from Protein**	**Calories from Fat**
Sedentary (50; 20; 30)		EER x 0.5	EER x 0.2	EER x 0.3
Low Active (55; 20; 25)		EER x 0.55	EER x 0.2	EER x 0.25
Active (60; 20; 20)		EER x 0.6	EER x 0.2	EER x 0.2
Very Active (65; 15; 20		EER x 0.65	EER x 0.15	EER x 0.2
Pre-Competition (70; 15; 15)		EER x 0.70	EER x 0.15	EER x 0.15

Lifestyle (%CHO; %Prot; %Fat)	EER	CHO in g	Protein in g	Fat in g
Sedentary (50; 20; 30)		EER/4	EER/4	EER/9
Low Active (55; 20; 25)		EER/4	EER/4	EER/9
Active (60; 20; 20)		EER/4	EER/4	EER/9
Very Active (65; 15; 20		EER/4	EER/4	EER/9
Pre-Competition (70; 15; 15)		EER/4	EER/4	EER/9

Example				
Lifestyle (%CHO; %Prot; %Fat)	**EER**	**Calories from CHO**	**Calories from Protein**	**Calories from Fat**
Sedentary (50; 20; 30)				
Low Active (55; 20; 25)				
Active (60; 20; 20)	**3,100 kcal**	**1,860 kcal**	**620 kcal**	**620 kcal**
Very Active (65; 15; 20				
Pre-Competition (70; 15; 15)				

In our example, the total daily estimated energy requirement for the athlete is ~**3,100 kcal**. Therefore, according to his lifestyle, the athlete should consume approximately **1,900 kcal** in the form of **carbohydrates** and **600 kcal** from **protein** and **fat sources**, respectively.

Lifestyle (%CHO; %Prot; %Fat)	EER	CHO in g	Protein in g	Fat in g
Sedentary (50; 20; 30)				
Low Active (55; 20; 25)				
Active (60; 20; 20)	**3,100 kcal**	**465 g**	**155 g**	**69 g**
Very Active (65; 15; 20				
Pre-Competition (70; 15; 15)				

GLOSSARY

SYMBOLE

A

B

C

Q

R

S

T

U

V

W

Z

REFERENCE LIST

American College of Sports Medicine. Position stand: Progression models in resistance training for healthy adults. Medicine and Science in Sports and Exercise. 34(2):364-380. 2002.

Anderson, K.G., and D.G. Behm. Maintenance of EMG activity and loss of force output with instability. Journal of Strength and Conditioning Research. 18(3): 637-640. 2004.

Baechle, T.R., R.W. Earle, and D. Wathen. (2000). Resistance Training. In: Essentials of Strength Training and Conditioning (2nd Ed.). T.R. Baechle, and R.W. Earle, Eds. Champaign, IL: Human Kinetics.

Behm, D.G., Anderson, K., and R.S. Curnew. Muscle force and activation under stable and unstable conditions. The Journal of Strength and Conditioning Research. 16 (3): 416-422 . 2002.

Behm, D.G., A.M. Leonard, W.B. Young, W.A.C. Bonsey, and S.N. MacKinnon. Trunk muscle electromyographic activity with unstable and unilateral exercises. The Journal of Strength and Conditioning Research. 19 (1): 193-201. 2005.

Behm, D.G., M.J. Wahl, D.C. Button, K.E. Power, and K.G. Anderson. Relationship between hockey skating speed and selected performance measures. 19 (2): 326-331. 2005.

Biagioli, B. (2007). Advanced Concepts of Personal Training. Miami, FL: National Council on Strength & Fitness.

Boyle, M. (2004). Functional Training for Sports. Champaign, IL: Human Kinetics.

Brown, L.E. and Ferrigno, V.A. (2005). Training for Speed, Agility, and Quickness. Champaign, IL: Human Kinetics.

Buell, J.L., Calland, D., Hanks, F., Johnston, B., Pester, B., Sweeney, R., and Thorne, R. (2008). Presence of Metabolic Syndrome in Football Linemen. Journal of Athletic Training, 43(6), 608-616. National Athletic Trainer's Association

Campbell, B., Kreider, R.B., Ziegenfuss, T., La Bounty, P., Roberts, M., Burke, D.,...and Antonio, J. (2007). International Society of Sports Nutrition position stand: protein and exercise. Journal of the International Society of Sports Nutrition , 4:8. doi:10.1186/1550-2783-4-8

Caraffa, A., G. Cerulli, M. Projetti, G. Aisa, and A. Rizzu. Prevention of anterior cruciate ligament injuries in soccer: A prospective controlled study of proprioceptive training. Knee Surg. Sports Traumatol. Arthrosc. 4: 19-21. 1996.

Chek, P. Swiss ball exercises for swimming, soccer & basketball. Sports Coach. 21 (4): 12-13. Summer 1999.

Christ, E. R., Zehnder, M., Boesch, C., Trepp, R., Mullis, P.E., Diem, P., and De´combaz, J. (2006). The effect of increased lipid intake on hormonal responses during aerobic exercise in endurance-trained men. European Journal of Endocrinology, 154, 397–403. DOI: 10.1530/eje.1.02106

Christopher S.D. Almond, M.D., M.P.H., Andrew Y. Shin, M.D., Elizabeth B. Fortescue, M.D., Rebekah C. Mannix, M.D., David Wypij, Ph.D., Bryce A. Binstadt, M.D., Ph.D.,...David S. Greenes, M.D. (2005). Hyponatremia among Runners in the Boston Marathon. British Journal of Sports Medicine, 352:1550-6. Retrieved from www.nejm.org

Cook, C.M., and Haub, M.D. (2007). Low-carbohydrate Diets and Performance. Current Sports Medicine Reports, 6, 225-229. Current Medicine Croup LLC

Cosio-Lima L.M., K.L. Reynolds, C. Winter, V. Paolone, and M.T. Jones. Effects of physioball and conventional floor exercise on early phase adaptations in back and abdominal core stability and balance in women. Journal of Strength and Conditioning Research. 17 (4): 721-725. 2003.

Esposito, K., Marfella, R., and Ciotola, M. (2004). Effect of a Mediterranean-Style Diet on Endothelial Dysfunction and Markers of Vascular Inflammation in the Metabolic Syndrome: A Randomized Trial. JAMA, 292(12), 1440-1446. doi:10.1001/jama.292.12.1440

Fitzgerald G.K., M.J. Ake, and L. Snyder-Mackler. The efficacy of perturbation training in nonoperative anterior cruciate ligament rehabilitation programs for physically active individuals. Physical Therapy. 80 (2):128-140. 2000.

Floyd, R.T. (2007). Manual of Structural Kinesiology 16th Ed. New York, NY: McGraw Hill

Gambetta, V. (2006). Athletic Development: The Art & Science of Functional Sports Conditioning 1st Edition. Champaign, IL: Human Kinetics

Gambetta, V. Let's get physio. For swim-specific weight training, get on the ball. It's easy with our simple but effective physioball routine. Rodale's Fitness Swimmer. 8 (3): 30-33. May/June 1999. Hot Topics: Unstable Resistance Exercises www.nsca-lift.org

Garhammer, J. Free weight equipment for the development of athletic strength and power. National Strength and Conditioning Association Journal. 3: 24-26. 1981.

Harris, W.S., Reid, K.J., Sands, S.A., and Spertus, J.A.(2007). Blood Omega-3 and Trans Fatty Acids in Middle-Aged Acute Coronary Syndrome Patients. American Journal of Cardiology, 99, 154–158. doi:10.1016/j.amjcard.2006.08.013

Hodges, P.W., and C.A. Richardson. Feed forward contraction of transversus abdominis is not influenced by the direction of arm movement. Experimental Brain Research. 114: 362-370. 1997.

Hoffman, J., Ratamess, N., Kang, J., Mangine, G., Faigenbaum, A., and Stout, J. (2006). Effect of Creatine and ß-Alanine Supplementation on Performance and Endocrine Responses in Strength/ Power Athletes. International Journal of Sport Nutrition and Exercise Metabolism, 16, 430-446. Champaign, IL: Human Kinetics

Houglum, P.A. (2005). Therapeutic Exercise for Musculoskeletal Injuries 2nd Ed. Champaign, IL: Human Kinetics.

Jentjens, R.L.P.G, and Jeukendrup, A.E. (2002). Prevalence of Hypoglycemia Following Pre-exercise Carbohydrate Ingestion Is Not Accompanied By High Insulin Sensitivity. International Journal of Sport Nutrition and Exercise Metabolism, 12, 398-413. Champaign, IL: Human Kinetics

Kerksick, C., Harvey, T., Stout, J., Campbell, B., Wilborn, C., Kreider, R.,...and Antonio, J. (2008). International Society of Sports Nutrition position stand: Nutrient timing. Journal of the International Society of Sports Nutrition, 5:17. doi:10.1186/1550-2783-5-17

Kolt, S.K. (2003). Physical Therapies in Sport and Science. Philadelphia, Pennsylvania: Churchill Livingston.

Lambert, E.V., Goedecke, J.H., van Zyl, C., Murphy, K., Hawley, J.A., Dennis, S.C., and Noakes, T.D. (2001). High-Fat Diet Versus Habitual Diet Prior Carbohydrate Loading: Effects on Exercise Metabolism and Cycling Performance. International Journal of Sports Medicine and Exercise Metabolism, 11, 209-225. Champaign, IL: Human Kinetics

Lambert, C.P., Frank, L.L., and Evans, W.J. (2004). Macronutrient Considerations for the Sport of Bodybuilding. Sports Med, 34 , (5), 317-327. Adis Data Information BV

Lopez-Garcia, E., van Dam, R.M., Li, T.Y., Rodriguez-Artalejo, F., and Hu, F.B. (2008). The Relationship of Coffee Consumption with Mortality. Annals of Internal Medicine, 148, 904-914. Retrieved from www.annals.org

McCurdy, K.W., G.A. Langford, M.W. Doscher, L.P. Wiley, and K.G. Mallard. The effects of short-term unilateral and bilateral lower-body resistance training on measures of strength and power. Journal of Strength and Conditioning Research. 19(1): 9-15. 2005.

Murray, B. (2007). Manufactured arguments: turning consensus into controversy does not advance science. British Journal of Sports Medicine, 41, 106-107. doi:10.1136/bjsm.2006.030106

Myer, G.D., K.R. Ford, and T.E. Hewett. Methodological approaches for training to prevent anterior cruciate ligament injuries in female athletes. Scandinavian Journal of Medicine and Science in Sports. 14: 275-285. 2004.

Myer, G.D., K.R. Ford, J.P. Palumbo, and T.E. Hewett. Neuromuscular training improves performance and lower-extremity biomechanics in female athletes. 19 (1): 51-60. 2005

Neumann, D.A. (2010). Kinesiology of the Musculoskeletal System: Foundations for Rehabilitation 2nd ed. St. Louis, Missouri: Mosby.

Noakes, T. D. (2003). Overconsumption of fluids by athletes. BMJ, 327, 113-114. doi:10.1136/bmj.327.7407.113

Noakes, T. D., & Speedy, D. B. (2006). Case proven: exercise associated hyponatraemia is due to overdrinking. So why did it take 20 years before the original evidence was accepted?. British Journal of Sports Medicine, 40, 567-572. doi:10.1136/bjsm.2005.020354

Noakes, T. D., & Speedy, D. (2007). The aetiology of exercise: Associated hyponatraemia is established and is not "mythical". British Journal of Sports Medicine, 41, 111-113. Retrieved from http://bjsm.bmj.com/cgi/content/full/41/2/111-a

Noakes, T. D., & Speedy, D. B. (2007). Time for the American College of Sports Medicine to acknowledge that humans, like all other earthly creatures, do not need to be told how much to drink during exercise. British Journal of Sports Medicine, 41, 109-111. Retrieved from http://bjsm.bmj.com/cgi/content/full/41/2/109-a

Nordin, M. and Frankel (1989), V.H. Basic Biomechanics of the Musculoskeletal System 2nd Ed. Philadelphia, Pennsylvania: Lea & Febiger

Marieb, E.N., Mallat, J., and Wilhelm, P.B. Human Anatomy 5th ed. San Francisco, CA: Pearson

Mena, M.P., Sacanella, E., Vazquez-Agell, M., Morales, M., Fito´, M., Escoda, R.,...and Estruch, R. (2009). Inhibition of circulating immune cell activation: a molecular antiinflammatory effect of the Mediterranean diet. American Society for Nutrition, 89, 248–56. doi: 10.3945/ajcn.2008.26094.

Poortmans, J.R., and Dellalieux, O. (2000). Do Regular High Protein Diets Have Potential Health Risks on Kidney Function in Athletes?. International Journal of Sport Nutrition and Exercise Metabolism, 10, 28-38. Champaign, IL: Human Kinetics

Powers, S.K. and Howley, E.T. (2007). Exercise Physiology: Theory and Application to Fitness and Performance 6th ed. New York, NY: McGraw Hill

Roetert, P. and Ellenbecker, T. (2007). Complete Conditioning for Tennis 1st Edition. Champaign, IL: Human Kinetics

Roetert, P., and Kovacs, M. (2011). Tennis Anatomy. Champaign, IL: Human Kinetics

Sale, D., and D. MacDougall. Specificity in strength training: a review for the coach and athlete. Canadian Journal of Applied Sport Sciences. 6 (2): 87-92. June 1981.

Santana, J.C. Hamstrings of steel: Preventing the pull. Part II- training the "triple threat". Strength and Conditioning Journal. 23 (1): 18-20. February 2001.

Stanton, R., P.R. Reaburn, and B. Humphries. The effect of short-term Swiss ball training on core stability and running economy. Journal of Strength and Conditioning Research. 18 (3): 522-528. 2004.

Utter, A.C., Kang, J., Nieman, D.C., Williams, F., Robertson, R.J., Henson, D.A.,...Butterworth, D.E. (1999). Effects of carbohydrate ingestion and hormonal response on ratings of perceived exertion during prolonged cycling and running. European Journal of Applied Physiology, 80, 92-99. Berlin, Germany: Springer-Verlag

Utter, A.C., Kang, J., Nieman, D.C., Dumke, C.L., McAnulty, S.R., Vinci, D.M., and McAnulty, L.S. (2004). Carbohydrate Supplementation and Perceived Exertion during Prolonged Running. Medicine & Science in Sports & Exercise, Jun;36(6):1036-41. WN: 0415701727017. New York, NY: H.W. Wilson Company

Vera-Garcia, F.J., S.G. Grenier, and S.M. McGill. Abdominal muscle response during curlups on both stable and labile surfaces. Physical Therapy. 80: 564-569. 2000.

Verstegen, M., and P. Williams. Core Performance. New York, NY: Rodale, Inc., 2004.

Vrijens, D. M. J., & Rehrer, N. J. (1999). Sodium-free fluid ingestion decreases plasma sodium during exercise in the heat. Journal of Applied Physiology, 86, 1847-1851. Retrieved from http://www.jap.physiology.org

Whitney, E.N. and Rolfes, S.R. (2005). Understanding Nutrition10th ed. Belmont, CA: Thomson/Wadsworth Publishing Co.

Willardson, J.M. The effectiveness of resistance exercises performed on unstable equipment. Strength and Conditioning Journal. 26 (3): 70-74. 2004.

Woolf, K., Bidwell, W. K., & Carlson, A. G. (2008). The Effect of Caffeine as an Ergogenic Aid in Anaerobic Exercise. International Journal of Sport Nutrition and Exercise Metabolism, 18, 412-429. Champaign, IL: Human Kinetics

Yessis, M. Using free weights for stability training. Fitness Management, November 2003: 26-28.

Zatsiorsky, V.M. and Kraemer, W. J. (2006). Science and Practice of Strength Training 2nd ed. Champaign, IL: Human Kinetics.

CPSIA information can be obtained at www.ICGtesting.com
Printed in the USA
LVOW01*1133030314

375771LV00005BB/6/P

9 783981 539202